THE COMPLETE BOOK OF RÉSUMÉS

Simple Steps for Writing a Powerful Résumé

KAREN SCHAFFER

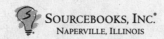

SOURCEBOOKS, INC.
NAPERVILLE, ILLINOIS

Published by Sourcebooks, Inc.
P.O. Box 4410, Naperville, Illinois 60567–4410
(630) 961–3900
Fax: (630) 961–2168
www.sourcebooks.com

Library of Congress Cataloging-in-Publication Data

Schaffer, Karen.
    The complete book of résumés: simple steps for writing a powerful résumé / Karen Schaffer.
        p. cm.
    Includes index.
    ISBN-13: 978-1-4022-0601-6
    ISBN-10: 1-4022-0601-1
    1. Résumés (Employment) I. Title.

HF5383.S32 2005
650.14'2—dc22

                                                    2005025010

Printed and bound in the United States of America.
HS 10 9 8 7 6 5 4 3 2 1

DEDICATION

This book is dedicated to Bruce Powell and Randy Quarin—who have looked at hundreds of résumés with me and taught me everything they know about the subtleties of marketing oneself in a résumé—and, as icing on the cake, are fun to work with too.

CONTENTS

ACKNOWLEDGMENTS

Thanks to:

- Bethany Brown and her very brave copyediting team at Sourcebooks, Inc. Shout outs to Bethany, Rachel Jay, Dawn Pope, Ewurama Ewusi-Mensah, Terri Hudoba, and everyone else who gave their time to pull this huge project together.
- Shelley MacDonald—for her active and supportive dedication *especially* at crunch time (the first AND the second time).
- Wendy Kwong—for being there in a pinch.
- Everyone at IQ Partners who helped answer all those "question of the moment" moments with their valued expertise.
- Mark Swartz—for being my favorite go-to online expert.
- Erin Reel of the Erin Reel Literary Agency for making this possible for me to write.
- Tony Saad for helping me create www.karenschaffer.com with such ease.
- Mark Rutherford—because you rock. Thanks for all the grilled cheese.

There were lots and lots and lots of people who helped assemble résumés and I will not be able to name you all. Just know you go with my gratitude. Some of you are:

- Kelly Ann Cowan, Karen Hood Caddy, Kaila Kukla, and Laurence Follows (the gang of four who remind me about life-work-spirit balance).
- The Career Centers and Participating Students of: St. Mary's University, Mount St. Vincent University, and Dalhousie University.
- IQ Partners
- RGA Recruiting, particularly Jessica Goldfarb who came through in such short time.
- Kathleen Smale Casby and The D-Coders
- Judy Sheridan
- AV Jobs.com
- Havergal College Old Girl's Community (especially online)
- My present and former clients, friends, friends of friends, and lovely strangers who responded to my contact calls and donated résumés to the cause.
- All the people who contributed résumés and stories for chapters in this book or who took the time to talk to me about their experiences.
- Thecla Sweeney (and family: Chris, Chev, and Neil), Karina Miller (and fellow thespians), the ever patient Martha McGrath.
- Jack Ponte, Carmen Jefferies, Melissa Woodley, Sandra Kovacs, Hugh Munro, Jack Bond, Shannon Moon, Michelle Domet, Bruce Sellery, Carrie Walpole and friends, Chuck Le Boutellier, Jody Bishop, Don Hutchinson (the brainstorm king), Kathy Murphy (always Pashby to me), Guy Beaudin and Joseph, Cris Matheson, Christine Barton, Stephanie Palazzi, Quintin Siemer, Julie Kivlichan, Jennifer Hazen, Michael Welch, Dennis Garnham.
- The HR staff, hiring managers, and recruiters who generously and authentically gave me their feedback on what they look for in a résumé.

PART I

Introduction—It's All about You

No one likes writing their résumé.

Ever notice how you can offer brilliant advice to someone else who is writing a résumé but blank out the moment you sit down to write your own? That's because writing a résumé is a collective crazy-making exercise. It's the one thing we have to produce in our working life that challenges how we see ourselves. It catalogs what we've done, how well we've done it, and what the result was of our doing it.

Imagine yourself sitting down to write a résumé: seated in your chair, hands on the keyboard, and facing off against the blank page. You type your name, then your address and your phone number. You decide which email address you're going to use. You list your last few places of employment. Then…what? The rest of the résumé stretches out before you, a vast, wide, empty page.

The Fear Factors

There are several factors that can cause writer's block when starting a résumé.

1: The Intimidation Factor. In a job search the future seems to hinge on what you're about to write on this piece of paper. Contemplating the Work Experience section, your mind does cartwheels. What kind of impression will I make? Do I have anything good to say? Will I measure up?

2: The Small Details Factor. Sweat drips off your forehead. Because after surmounting The Intimidation Factor, and actually writing something worthwhile, comes The Small Details Factor. Yes, all those teeny, tiny minutiae of the résumé—periods, capital letters, bullet points, and computer skills—that make up the myriad of decisions you have to make before you send out the final product. Where to start? How to arrange everything after you've typed your name? What font to choose? A subtle or bold use of underline?

3: The Endless Tweak Factor. Just when you think you're done with the work, you show your résumé to other people. Then rears the ugly Medusa's head of what I like to call The Tweak Factor, also known as "Everyone Else's Opinion." Implement feedback from one person, and the very next person will give you a whole different set of pointers, some that may contradict what came before. Résumés are like parenthood and relationships—every person you talk to will have their own "tried and true" opinion on what works.

4: The Submission Factor. Finally, when all is said and done, you have a product you're proud of. And then you get to a website submission and discover that you can't submit your résumé in Word. Or the person on the other end can't open your PDF document. Or you suddenly realize there's something about keywords you need to know, but you don't remember what it is or where to look for it.

The New Standard, or How Did We Not Know There Was One?

The résumé has definitely evolved over the last two decades. Both minor and radical changes have crept into résumé protocol, some of which have been written about by career experts but have not necessarily penetrated the mass market yet.

Why don't you know some of these important shifts? Well, think about who you normally go to when you want to write a résumé.

You probably either:

- Update your old résumé—it worked for you the last time.
- Ask a friend who seems to be good at that kind of thing—it worked for him or her the last time.
- Learn about résumé writing from one of the billion "experts" out there who come in the form of seminar leaders, recruiters, high school teachers, career counselors, outplacement firms, Internet sites, other books and resources, and that guy who helped your friend do his résumé.

Consider the source. No matter how professional sounding the information you've received, make sure you know where it ultimately came from. Most of the advice that gets thrown around about the résumé is somebody's subjective opinion. It's a misinformation jungle out there.

Trends hit résumés just like they hit everything else. For instance, for the last few years it has been out of fashion to include the sentence "References available upon request" at the end of your résumé. Not because it isn't true or a reasonable line, but just because employers know that already and therefore most feel it is a wasted addition. Another time-honored leadoff, the "Objective," has been taking a beating from modern résumé experts for some time.

Some essential stylistic changes effect the form of the résumé, such as getting off the old standard of starting with Education, Special Accomplishments, Work History, and so on, that you learned in high school.

Other changes have to do with content, for example, how to state accomplishments rather than merely list responsibilities and when to give context to companies you've worked for. But it's in understanding the whole *purpose* of the résumé—and what that means for the content of your CV (curriculum vitae)—that the most radical changes have taken place.

At first glance, the new standard of résumés looks pretty similar to the old. Your name is still written and the top, it still includes your work experience and your education and perhaps some personal interests. The biggest change is the purpose of the résumé itself.

It's a Future-Forward Document

A traditional view of résumés is as a collection or recitation of your **history**—a record of your work history and responsibilities. It is a document that highlights what you've done.

The new standard is a résumé that speaks to your **future**—a document that is actively marketing you for *what you want to be doing*, not what you've done. Further, you will be writing a document that sells not only your applicable qualifications for a role, but also the WIIFT factor—what's in it for them?

Not a lot of people have gotten that shift so far. Quite a few are using Microsoft templates or the template they learned in high school. As a result, you have a unique opportunity to create an exceptional résumé that pops out of the pile. In terms of speaking to your reading audience, the new standard résumé is *more vital, more effective, and more readable.*

It's a Business Document

A résumé is a professional document primarily used in a business transaction—a hire. Therefore, like all business documents, it needs an executive summary, a sentence or paragraph that:

- Tells them what you're going to tell them in the rest of the résumé.
- Highlights key points and takeaways from your experience.

Basically, if the executive summary—or the profile—is all they read of your résumé, they should still walk away with a good understanding of who you are.

The résumé is also a business document in the sense that it should be legible, credible, and professional. Most résumés are now submitted, processed, and stored electronically. The strategy of mailing a copy of your résumé might not work because no one knows where to put it. This is especially true for employers and recruiters who see high volumes—instead of paper files they have huge databases instead.

While you still may want to think about the paper your résumé is on for a face-to-face meeting, paper choice as a whole has become increasingly unimportant for résumés in the new millennium. What's most important is to have a résumé that is professional and targeted to your industry.

It's a Marketing Document

An executive summary or a profile is not just a professional examination of who you are. As career experts increasingly focus on teaching clients to "sell" themselves, the résumé naturally follows suit. Your profile should inspire the reader—tease them, get them involved and engaged and wanting to meet you—the same way a commercial tries to excite the viewer into thinking or talking about their product. In this vein, you want to talk not only about your experience and accomplishments but also detail your potential and WIIFT.

It's a Brand

I'll call this the "association" someone has with your name. In a résumé, your name at the top of the page is your brand. Your goal in résumé writing is to create a strong association between your name and your message (your envisioned role, qualifications, personality, accomplishments, and unique benefits).

My goal in this book is to help you hijack the reader's thought process right off the top and define yourself before they define you. This is your brand.

It's an Authentic and Powerful Representation of the Author

Most of all, I want this résumé to be a true and high impact presentation of you. The more real and human you are, in your language and approach, the more the reader responds.

So there you have it. Your résumé is not just going to be a historical document chronicling places you worked and things you did. It is going to be a fresh, compelling, marketable document that, in the first few lines, tells the reader who you are in such a way that they will know immediately whether they want to speak to you or not.

It's All about You

You are going to get into shipshape résumé condition. You're going to master the marketing message and sift through your work experience for great accomplishments. You're going to pick fonts and create white spaces to deliver your message beautifully.

Feel free to visit my website at www.karenschaffer.com to contact me or find additional resources.

But that all said, the key message to you is this: your résumé starts and ends with you. It is only one tool in your job search kit, and it's the one you tackle after you figure out who you are and what you want to do. The résumé is important. But **you** are the most essential element.

The core of my résumé philosophy is that you are not a one- or two-page person. You are an interesting, talented human being who will shine in the right job in the right setting. Your résumé is just one route to getting there; at the end of the job search process it will be you who earns the confidence of the employer who hires you.

There is something special about writing a résumé. Once you get past the aggravation—the writer's block, the endless fussing over word choice and font size, the well-meaning contradictory comments from friends, family, and perfect strangers—a transformation happens. When you really let yourself dive into this process and find the words, phrases, and description that reflect who you are in your career and then see those accomplishments impressively presented in concert with your personality, you can (and will!) experience a deep satisfaction and confidence in yourself that will carry positively into your job search and your next job.

CHAPTER 1:

Overcoming Writer's Block and Getting Started

Sitting down to write a résumé is similar to the torture of Sunday nights when you finally had to stop all the weekend fun and do your homework. Only worse, because you feel that as a grownup you should be better by now at sitting down and doing things you don't like.

Many people start the process of résumé writing—more specifically, they turn on the computer and open up a Word document—but then things slow down to a painful halt. It's writer's block! That painful but familiar state happens all the time in the résumé writing process. This chapter will help you talk yourself past the biggest blocks and then show you the first three easy steps for getting the writing underway.

I Really, Really Don't Want to Write My Résumé...

This is the whine of the inner teenager, the one who has to write a paper on the Spanish Armada for that really hateful history teacher by tomorrow at 10:30 a.m. It's the cry of dismay at the start of any meaningful endeavor that might be painful, boring, or worse. You may find yourself with an unexpected or irresistible urge to start six loads of laundry, sort scarves in the front hall closet, or rearrange your spice rack. You might note that tonight is a very special night of Must See TV reruns or that it's the one night your Aunt Martha is available for that important, once-a-year check-in. These are just symptoms of Inner Teenager Syndrome and should be ignored.

Take yourself away from all distractions. Turn on the computer. Go to the "Getting Started" section (p. 14) in this chapter and work through Steps 1 and 2. Do not stop until you have brainstormed a list of your recent roles and responsibilities. That is a very good place to start, and will motivate your inner adult into realizing you can in fact write your résumé, even if you really, really don't want to.

I Don't Feel I Succeeded at My Last Job

Another writer's block moment may come if you are feeling particularly uncomfortable or disappointed with your prior (or current) job. If you've been burned in your most recent situation—maybe it wasn't what you expected, or you didn't achieve what you wanted to achieve when you first took the job even if it wasn't your fault, or it ended badly due to a downsizing—you can feel pretty lackluster, even fearful about writing it up in a résumé.

This block is often one related to *resolution*. Resolution is when you come to terms with disappointments and missed expectations. Perhaps it was a decent job that turned ugly toward the end. Perhaps you deserved a promotion and didn't get it. Perhaps you never met the measures your employer set out for you to meet. Perhaps it was just one of those jobs that you knew in the first week was a big mistake. Whatever it was, you need to take a little time to get in touch with that disappointment, and then let it go.

For the purposes of writing a résumé to get another job, you sometimes don't have time to really dig into the hurt and then let it go. However, sorting out your feelings about a past job disappointment will help you be more confident in a future job interview situation.

So, for job disappointments, you have to ask yourself a few questions.

How Long Was I There?

If this was a one-week to four-month mistake job, you may be better off not mentioning it all together. If you were really off track, and you don't want to talk about the job, better not to have it right at the top of your résumé. You may still have to account for a gap, but you may be able to do so by mentioning a "contract" job without saying much more about it.

Are There Other Things I Achieved?

Often, the things people are hired to achieve actually aren't the things they accomplished while they were there. Rather than feeling bad about the missed goals, take heart that the reader of your résumé has no idea why you were hired. You get to tell them what you contributed. For instance, you may not have generated as much business as you were supposed to, but you mentored others who did. Or perhaps you didn't sell as much product, but you got good PR for the company. Look for other measures to evaluate your performance that weren't necessarily the ones you were trying to achieve.

Can I Forgive Myself and Do a Functional Résumé?

If the last job was truly a flop, and yet too long to be ignored, it may be better to do a functional résumé that talks about Skills and related Accomplishments before getting to Work History. This format allows you to rely on earlier jobs and point out direct strengths that may not have been tapped in your last job.

Overall, the best thing to do is stop beating yourself up and look for the best things that happened in the job. If you're still having trouble doing that, I recommend talking to someone who can be objective about it for you, like a career coach or counselor or a good friend who can help you write that section.

I Haven't Done Anything Good Enough to Write on My Résumé

Okay so you're feeling like you haven't done *anything* good. So much so, that trying to come up with examples of accomplishments leaves you feeling blank. There are a few reasons for this feeling.

You Were in the Wrong Job or Career

Most of the time, when I work with someone on their résumé by digging through their previous jobs, I find more than one accomplishment per job. When I don't find accomplishments, it gets me to thinking. For instance, I worked with a young guy who didn't seem to do *anything* special at his customer service jobs. I couldn't find one out-of-the-ordinary thing he did. Meanwhile, he was practically catatonic, answering my questions in a strangely disgruntled yet monotone voice. The session was like pulling teeth. By midway, I felt as depressed as he sounded. That's when I got suspicious.

I asked, "Did you even like your job?" He thought about it and then said, "No." Then I asked, "Have you liked any job you've had?" Again, a "No." We talked about it further, and it turned out he *hated* customer service. That is why he had no good examples or accomplishments to include.

It's important to know what you want when you're writing a résumé. Because if you hate customer service, which comprises the basis of your experience, then doing a standard résumé is only going to get you more jobs doing what you hate.

If you're struggling to come up with accomplishments or energy around previous jobs, you may have to reevaluate the path you're on, or the message you want to send out to employers. First and foremost, think about what you like doing. Then create a functional résumé or one that puts less emphasis on the things you don't like doing and don't feel good about and focuses more on the activities and roles you do want to do more of.

You Are a Perfectionist

Would you say that it's easier for you to see what's missing in a situation rather than what's going right? Do you notice that you often have high expectations for yourself? Do you think that you should be further into your career by now? Perhaps that means you are a perfectionist, or even a perfectionist-ish type person, who remembers the past by what hasn't been accomplish rather than by what has.

Our society creates high achievers. We like to reward people who have done extraordinary things, or have made lots of money, or who have won awards. We're not always good at recognizing the little things that people do every day that make a good team member, a good manager, or a deadline delivery person whom a company can count on. If you are evaluating yourself based on the fact that you were senior account manager but think you should have been promoted to vice president by now, maybe you have unrealistic expectations of yourself and of the marketplace.

Combining a high-achieving personality with the natural human inclination to play down what has been accomplished and play up what is missing gives you a ripe set of circumstances for feeling "not good enough" when it comes to writing your résumé.

Patience is the most important thing for perfectionists who want to get over writer's block. When you hear yourself saying, "It wasn't good enough," it may be because you've conveniently dismissed some of your most important accomplishments. If you can move through what didn't happen, you can begin to think about what did.

Working through your jobs with someone else will help you to see your accomplishments through their eyes. A close coworker, friend, or spouse will probably remember your best days better than you do. Or you can talk to someone like a career coach who will dig into your experiences, ask you lots of questions, and then help you to put it all together.

You Had a Difficult Year or Job Situation for Other Reasons
and Didn't Perform to Expectations

We can't all choose what happens in life. Maybe you didn't do what you set out to do at your last job for reasons beyond your control—in your personal life or at the job. Common personal experiences include having a sick parent, spouse, or child; moving, death, divorce, or other stress-inducing events. At work it could be having a toxic boss, a difficult workplace or corporate culture, or being hired to do something that the management wasn't truly committed to implementing. Many companies have "sick" cultures that create conditions that are impossible to overcome, like unrealistic sales targets or deadlines so that you (and all your coworkers) are always failing.

Rather than beating yourself up further for circumstances beyond your control, admit that the work suffered and let it go. It will take some finessing, both in detailing the job on your résumé, and in thinking through your answers about the job in an interview situation, but recovering from a toxic job or a difficult personal life is possible. Most people come up against this problem at least once in their career.

Focus less on your last job, and work on marketing yourself to a company that's a better fit. Think of it as starting over. It's not as if you won't mention this job, but you won't give it prominence. In work-related issues, there are ways to show accomplishments *despite* problems, which demonstrates your perseverance in tough situations.

For personal matters, prepare a thoughtful, direct, short statement for your interview. "Despite some achievements, I would have liked to have done more. Unfortunately, my father was very ill in April and died in August, and it effected my ability to do my job at peak performance. Thankfully, he is at peace, and I am fully ready and focused to do the good work I am capable of." This is *not* to be explained on a résumé. The only exception would be to explain why you took a sabbatical.

There is always a way to spin everything. Remember that no one knows why you were hired when they read your résumé, so tell them the best version of the story. Lean on earlier jobs for more laudable accomplishments and experience. Remember, you only have to clear this hurdle once—you only need one new job for this one to fade quietly on your résumé.

You Didn't Meet Expected Measures for the Jobs You've Had Thus Far Even Though You Tried

Feeling like you haven't been doing anything good might mean you aren't hitting your core competencies in the roles you've been choosing. Still, you may not outright hate your job—in fact, you may really like it, but you still find that you're having a hard time achieving great results.

This might be a good time to stop and evaluate your previous roles and how you feel about your level of success so far. Maybe you are okay with not being the best, or not working for the top companies if it means doing what you like to do. Maybe there are elements of the job that you're good at, just not the whole thing. Perhaps if you could focus more on them, it might make a difference. Play up those skills in your résumé. Or maybe it's time to evaluate your choice of career path to see whether the roles you've been taking truly fit you.

I Don't Want to Brag

Sometimes what holds us back from writing a super-spectacular résumé isn't that we haven't got good things to say, it's just that we have been taught, or believe, that it is not proper or modest to say them.

Not wanting to brag is a value, often a cultural belief, or one modeled for us by our family. Some clients I work with hold this value sacred, as a way to define themselves as different from all those manipulative sharks out there who lie and blow themselves out of proportion to get work. My clients don't want to be like "those people," so when they come to me they play down their abilities because in their world that makes them "nicer." "Being nice" is a deeply cherished belief for lots of people. And sometimes this belief is so deeply ingrained as a way of operating in the world that someone holding it has difficulty writing down their true and complete accomplishments and results.

Being nice is a worthy value to hold. Humility and modesty are excellent traits. However, they can definitely get in the way of you getting the job you want—an outcome that would encourage the proliferation of nice people in the workplace.

Think of it this way: you got a job, and you went out and did things in the special and unique way you have of doing them. Now you might not think they were special, because you would have done them that way whether or not anyone was watching. And you wouldn't want anyone to think you thought they were special. *But they are special because they comprise the results of you being you every day.* They are just results. They aren't bragging. They are just so.

If you approach your résumé as if you were trying to communicate the kind of person you are naturally every day, and the results of being that kind of person, you will do exactly what you need to write a great résumé. And every time you feel tempted to play something down, ask yourself, Did I do this? Was this regarded by someone—a client, a boss, a coworker—as helpful or useful? Were others glad I did it? Was I rewarded in some way for it? If the answer is yes, put it in.

If you know yourself well enough to know that, without encouragement, you will still avoid putting in your awards and accomplishments, get someone to be your objective source. It has to be someone who *doesn't* have this issue. Find someone who will encourage you to talk about the things you are good at and who will ensure that you are putting your best (and truthful!) self forward in your résumé.

I Don't Have Enough/Any Experience

Sometimes you can feel that you have no experience at all, especially when you are just starting out, or when changing careers. Start working on the first few steps at the end of this chapter, and then flip to your particular section for special advice.

Recent Grads

Being a recent grad is the most vulnerable time to enter the workforce. It's hard to know what you want to do when you haven't experienced anything. It's also hard to prove that you want to do something that you've done at most a couple of summers or in an internship position. However, you can organize your experience into something powerful for an employer to read. Turn to chapter 6 and Part II to see some great examples.

Career Transition

Deciding to take your career in a new direction is a courageous choice. However, that decision doesn't always feel so courageous when you're trying to figure out how to write a résumé to convince someone to let you do something you've never really done. Check out Chapters 6 and 7 for the very specific guidance you'll need.

I'm Not a Good Writer

If writing isn't your strong suit—which is true of many people, by the way—remind yourself that you do not have to be a creative genius to write a résumé. Simple, clear language and the truth tend to work wonders. Your first attempt doesn't have to be perfect. Write as awkwardly as you need to get it out of your head. Simplifying and cleaning up are later steps, even for good writers.

For the parts of the résumé that require a little extra finessing, like the profile or Personal Interests, you may need a little help. Call a friend or mentor and ask for help with the trickier wording.

Don't ask them to write the whole thing. That takes away the experience and the ownership from you. You know what you did the best. You are the expert on your experience. Give them the sense of what you think you might want to say, and have them help you get it together in words.

Remember to send a thank-you note to anyone you've asked for help, or take them for lunch.

I've Done So Many Different Things I Can't Think How to Organize It All

If you are someone who has not taken a traditional career path, or does multiple contracts and work that has overlapped in time, starting a résumé the traditional way can cause a writer's block. What do you put first? How do you explain the business you had that led to a year's contract which led back to the business and four other contracts that were smaller and not full-time all at once?

Don't worry about how to organize your résumé until you've had a good look at the raw material. List all of the different things you've done without worrying about order and dates. Once you look at the whole picture, you may find certain themes will emerge and that you can group whole pieces of experience under, for instance, "Web Development Experience," followed by "Project Management Experience."

Or you may need to "name" yourself as a company—"Your Name and Associates" is a good fallback—where all the contracts were directed to and handled. This is something you can do for résumé clarity, regardless if you've registered yourself as a business.

You also may be able to use style and indents to indicate several jobs or contracts under one major umbrella.

I Get Really Anxious When I Write a Résumé

The feeling of anxiety, however it might manifest, is a real obstacle to writing. Whether it's a racing heart or sweaty palms, you can easily get caught up in the symptoms and move away from the steps to take that will produce a résumé.

The source of the anxiety isn't important—it could be something mentioned above, or it could be another source all together. The key is to neutralize the anxiety so that you can focus on the task at hand.

- **It helps to take things slowly.** Break your résumé building into many parts. Start with one step at a time (see below), and take lots of breaks between steps.
- **Breathe deeply.** Deep breathing helps calm a racing mind, which is usually the source of the physical symptoms of anxiety. Start right now. Breathe through your nose evenly and slowly, filling your lungs to the top. Hold for just a moment and then gently exhale, keeping your breath as even as possible. Try to make your exhalation longer than your inhalation. Do that three times and feel your body relax as you do so. Repeat any time you can feel yourself revving up too far again.
- **Create a calming environment.** A writing space that feels warm and welcoming may help you feel supported and encouraged. For instance, put on soothing music to write to—something without words, but that is warm and familiar and gives you a positive feeling. Clear your desk of other papers and projects. Put something in your sightline that makes you happy, like a joke, or a photo of a loved one, or a picture of a scene that makes you feel calm.
- **Build activities around your résumé writing that decrease anxiety.** Take a bath or go for a walk as a break between résumé writing bouts. Staring at your credit card bills or yelling at your neighbor will only renew your anxiety.
- **Ask for encouragement.** A kind word or a warm hug helps reduce anxiety. Before you go write your résumé, talk to someone you trust who is a positive and calming person. Make sure you choose someone who leaves you in a calm state of mind.

Your anxiety might not go away completely, but one or more of these ideas may mitigate its effects and help you to get going on your résumé.

Getting Started

Follow each of these steps in order to create a rough draft outline of your résumé.

Step 1: Find or Write out a Specific Role or Job That You Are Targeting in Your Job Search

Those of you who *know* and can *clearly articulate* the role you're applying for—be it "plumber," "speech pathologist," "VP finance," or "usability specialist"—can move ahead to Step 2.

It is absolutely essential that you have a particular role in mind when writing a résumé. Though you have a ton of skills that makes you versatile and able to apply for more than one job, people may have a hard time getting a sense of who you are and what you want. And as frustrating as it can be to have to earmark yourself for one role, it is a necessary step to marketing yourself—even if you are marketing slightly different stories to different people.

> Pick a job ad that has some meaty information. Look for a list of qualifications with a mix of personality traits, core skills, and experiences. Take a few moments to review the ad and underline the parts that particularly appeal to you or apply to you.

If you feel vague or uncommitted to a direction when writing your résumé, the résumé will inevitably come across as vague or uncommitted as well. Most people *start* their job search with their résumé. While your résumé is an important document that will help you present yourself to potential employers and opportunities, it is *not* the first place to start. The first place to start is you.

The key to an efficient and timely job search is to have a clear sense of what you want to do, and then *communicate that clearly to others*. Sending a strong, consistent message out to your networks and to employers will help you connect with a targeted job.

> One of the biggest complaints heard from recruiters is that potential candidates try to keep their options wide and general—they aren't specific about the role they want.

When recruiters or employers find an unfocused résumé in an inbox, or meet with an uncertain person, they can tell pretty quickly and will tend to shut you down. When you know what you want, there are more options to steer you where you want to go.

Ask yourself what you learned at your last job, what you think you want to do, and what steps you want to take to get there. When you can clearly and absolutely answer the question, "What am I looking for?" come back to your résumé. I guarantee writing will become a heck of a lot easier. Otherwise you will be pulling your hair within about a half an hour.

If you know you want to target more than one role or job area, and you can clearly define each of those roles, then you will want to create separate résumés that focus on each of those roles. While most of the content will be similar, the profile will be different, the Key Qualifications will emphasize different things, and even the order of the contents of your work experience may be different.

For the sake of getting the first résumé done, pick one—ONE—role and stick with it during the writing process. Once your final draft is done, you can create a second, and perhaps a third résumé to more specifically target other roles.

Step 2: Make a Great Big List of Everything You've Done (Recently)

Before trying to think of a marketing message, the specific wording of your personality and qualifications, or experimenting with Georgia font, *the very first thing to do is to list everything you've done that you can think of*. This is the raw material for your résumé.

One of the hardest things about starting a résumé is that you don't examine or record what you do in your day-to-day working life—you just do it. So when you're asked to come up with enough information for a résumé, it can be like reaching back into a black hole to remember certain things that happened five years ago, a year ago, or even six months ago.

One of my clients experienced his biggest successes over seven years earlier when the company he worked for was at its peak. We had to dig for a while before he remembered what it was like when he was running four events and managing two publications, rather than the later years when parts of the company were being sold off.

As you begin to write things down, see if you can expand each item on your list with detailed descriptions.

Responsibilities for Office Management
Accounting
- Payables/receivables
- Monthly reports
- Meetings with top managers to deliver monthly reports
- Special meeting with president and vice president for my input on retooling reports
- Learning new report format

Then take one of the items from that list and break it down further, if possible.
Monthly Reports
- Office expenses report
- Payroll report
- Income report
- Outstanding invoices report
- Once a year totals report, 4 short quarterlies

You won't be mentioning every single "report" in your résumé. The aim of this exercise is to jog your memory and create a master list so that when you begin to narrow down your experience and results, you will be able to pick those that are most applicable to your targeted role or specific job application.

When you're done with this list, sit back for a minute. Look out the window or get up and walk around. Then look at the list again and dig into your memory for three more things to add. Take another break and come back to the list a few more times to ensure that you've thought of everything.

Now you've got an excellent list of raw material that you can begin to organize into a résumé.

Step 3: Deciding on Shape, Form, and Structure

Choose a résumé style that appeals to you—one that suits your experience and your job search objectives. Review these questions and activities to make a selection.

Do you have a straightforward career?

Do you have a pretty straightforward career, or has your last five years been a mix of roles, contracts, and overlapping jobs? If you have a straightforward career, a straightforward résumé is best. If you are in a career transition, you may need a different format. You can learn about that in more detail in Chapter 7.

If your last few years have been a little more topsy-turvy, you will need to do a little bit more work to organize your résumé in such a way that the reader can digest what you've been doing and when. Look at the themes. Think about your target job. Perhaps that means putting jobs under descriptors like "Project Management Experience," or "Branding Experience."

If you are having trouble sorting it out all right now, focus on picking a résumé structure and play with the readability once you have a draft to work with.

Decide on a structure: chronological, functional, or other

Next, decide what kind of résumé you are going to do—chronological or functional.

The rule of thumb is, if you are looking for a similar job in a similar industry, chronological résumés are the best. Overall, recruiters and hirers tend to prefer the chronological resume for its simplicity and ease of style. Usually, they want to skim your résumé to see where you were and when—and functional résumés often leave readers scrambling to figure that out.

Functional résumés focus on drawing out skills and accomplishments that are needed in the job, and work well for someone who is doing a career transition. A functional résumé helps to get the reader thinking about the skills, not the job title.

Other résumés may be a blend of these two styles or a more creative style depending on the job being targeted. Computer and tech-related résumés often have project and programming skills lists rather than job descriptions.

Get an idea of the different résumé styles

Some of you will want to get started on your résumé and fiddle with the style later. But others may find that to figure out what to do next, it helps to picture the look you're aiming for. Take a moment to look through the many résumés in Part II of this book for some ideas. See which ones attract your attention. Don't feel obligated to use the résumé format suggested by the person who was closest to you in the industry. After double-checking your own industry standard, you may find your perfect format in another section.

As a note of caution, avoid using Microsoft templates and others easily available online. Their creators mean well, but template résumés are easily recognizable with their standardized monotony. You could start with a form if that makes you comfortable, but be sure to adapt it to your particular experience and needs, as well as change obvious layouts and Times New Roman font.

Pick one that seems to work for your situation as a "get started" model, take a stab at it and see if it works!

You've been résumé browsing—now there's nothing to do but try it on. Start to organize some of your list information inside of the form you've picked out. You're off!

A Helpful List to Jog Your Memory

- Places you've worked
- Roles you've had
- Responsibilities in each role
- Accomplishments in each role
- Best accomplishment of each role
- Tasks you've loved
- Results of the tasks you've loved
- Extra initiatives you've started at a job
- Extra responsibilities you took on at a job
- Things the boss asked you to do specially
- The best day you had on the job
- Unusual circumstances on the job
- Teams you've worked with
- Meetings you've chaired
- On-the-job groups you've created or supported
- Education level you've achieved
- Diplomas you've received
- Training you've received
- Extra training you've received
- Conferences you've attended
- Clubs you belong(ed) to
- Associations you belong(ed) to
- Awards you've received
- If appropriate—Client names
- If appropriate—Computer programs you know

CHAPTER 2:

The Dos and Don'ts of the Résumé

Like any project or undertaking, while there is a lot of scope for imagination, there are also some definite dos and don'ts to writing a résumé. Talk to any plugged-in HR person, recruiter, or regular hirer (and I did)—all readers hope to see certain things when they open your résumé file. And some other things are just plain bad news that will affect the reader's ability to take you seriously.

While I will address the step-by-step construction of a résumé in a later chapter, consider this chapter as the overview of what should be in your résumé and what absolutely should not.

The Dos

After you've finished putting your first mangled, tangled draft together, sit down and consider exactly what you're aiming for in your résumé. Each of the following items is considered a "must have"—that is, they need to be and should be present in any and every résumé, regardless of the format or the industry.

Don't worry about achieving all of these at once.

Think about the Reader

Because a résumé is about the person writing it, most writers' focus is on themselves asking, "What do I want people to know about me?" But the focus should be on the reader, or more specifically asking, "What does the *reader* want to know about me?"

The experience of résumé readers is a little bit the same and a little bit different for everyone. In my observation and interviews of those who read and hire from résumés, certain elements often remain consistent.

Here are some of the questions that occur for readers as they first set eyes on your résumé.

- Is this one going to be difficult to read?
- What does this person want to do? Which job are they applying for?
- What companies have they worked for, and do I recognize them?
- Does this person have the skills and qualifications that I'm looking for?
- Is there any proof that this person was good at what they say they've been doing?
- Is there anything here that makes me wary of this person?
- Am I excited or interested in phoning or meeting this person?
- Who is this person and should I take a gamble on meeting them?

Then there are differences in opinion. Because people are human and are guided by their own logic in both the grand concepts and small details of the résumé, there will of course be differences of opinion of what makes them happy. Some readers will have certain résumé pet peeves, for example, those who will search your résumé for bad grammar, and others won't care two hoots about grammar as long as you have listed every computer program you've ever looked at.

The reaction to your résumé says almost as much about the person reading it as it does about the person who wrote it. A logical, give-it-to-me-in-black-and-white-type person will want the résumé information stated cleanly and clearly, and will moan at receiving a functional résumé, even if that style puts your skills and accomplishments at the forefront. These people make their decisions by looking at the chronological flow of your work experience, and when you make accessing that flow more difficult, they have a harder time understanding you.

On the other hand, creative or nonlinear people are deadly bored with clichés and will look for something that is more vibrant. Nonvisual people can't stand seeing extra graphics, whereas visual people will reject a résumé with no style. Some people will warm to the fact that you've described yourself as entrepreneurial and others will take it as a red flag that you're too independent for their tastes. The subtle interactions that readers have with the messages you're sending are unpredictable for the most part, and completely unavoidable.

Does this ultimately affect how they see you if your experience is good enough? Yes and no. If you are a borderline candidate, or applying when a lot of people are submitting résumés, readers' pet peeves might make them hesitate. However, as long as they can easily find, read, and digest the most important information, they will be compelled to call or meet with you if you match their qualifications.

If you follow some golden résumé must-have rules, it will endear you to the most hardened of readers. Over and above that, you make your choices and take your chances. If you think that overall a functional résumé suits your experience and job search goals the best, then prepare that kind of résumé and prepare it well so that if it lands on our black-and-white résumé reader's desk, they might moan a little, but will still consider you.

Overall Readability

The first thing a reader wants to see in a résumé is that it is easy to read and understand—everything important can be located in a quick scan. Overall, you are aiming for a résumé that is clear, concise, informative, and appealing. At a glance, a reader should easily find:

- Who you are
- What you've done
- When and where you did it
- How you succeeded at it

The most important parts of the résumé should POP and nothing in style or content should hinder the reader from seeing that salient information.

Overall Style

Style is a little more specific than overall readability in that it is more about formatting.

- Is the text easy to read?
- Is it consistent?
- Is there enough white space and no dense blocks of text?
- Is the chosen style appropriate for the role (that is, a creative style for a creative job, a professional style for a professional job)?

Clear Marketing Message

Aim for an appropriate message, clearly stated, near the beginning of the résumé. The unique skills and abilities of your pitch must be optimal for the targeted position. The rest of the résumé will back up that message with examples and accomplishments. Résumé readers might call it a marketing message—or they might call it a professional objective (though they don't mean the more traditional notion of objective), an executive summary, or a profile. Some might not even think about it at all. But they love it when they see it, because it answers some of their most pressing questions without wasting more of their time.

Style Consistency

Whatever style you choose should be echoed throughout the résumé. If you choose to do something a specific way, be sure to keep it the same throughout. For instance, if you decide to put a period at the end of a point, do so with every point. Headings, line breaks, and other titles should also be consistent.

Industry Appropriate

If there is a particular standard within the industry you are targeting, adhere to the standard (though often you may find that you can wiggle in a touch of personality and marketing message). Your résumé should be appropriate to the targeted industry. For instance, creative profession résumés should have a good sense of design about them, technical résumés should have much more detail about computer skills and programs, while banking résumés should be professional and emphasize team accomplishments.

A Touch of Personality

Your voice should come through in your résumé, even if only in one or two places. Your résumé should be a reflection of you. The glimpse of personality should be light, and should not overwhelm the professionalism of the résumé. A touch of personality can appear especially when the writer goes to some lengths not to spit out obvious clichés ("I work well on a team and also as an individual") and tries some new phrases or word choices ("Loves team interplay and brainstorming, but can be counted on to get her work done on time").

Proof of a Job Well Done

Be sure to present your accomplishments along with responsibilities and state specific measurable results for major projects and initiatives. The word "success" should not be substituted for an actual result (compare "Successfully opened Broadway show" to "Opened Broadway show to rave reviews and standing ovations").

When you provide a result or accomplishment, the reader can easily link it to a specific job. And to stay in tune with the marketing message, your accomplishments should support the main message provided at the beginning of your résumé (a fashion professional has his accomplishments in running fashion events, not in bookkeeping).

Remember the Basics

You also need to consider the most basic elements of the résumé that affect how a reader interacts with it.

Spelling/grammar/clarity

- No spelling errors should be found in your résumé.
- Your sentences should be clear, readable, and grammatically correct.

These two elements are so essential that you should ask someone else to read over your résumé before sending it out to double-check for small details you might have missed. Spelling and grammar speak to your intelligence, your diligence, and your comfort and fluency with language. This is even more important if English is not your native tongue.

Length

The length should be consistent with experience at two pages maximum—unless the industry demands three pages. This is the only basic element with exceptions. Certain individuals, such as computer programmers, PMPs, and academics, have much longer standard résumés as a way to communicate the length and depth of their responsibilities, programs, projects, publications, and so forth.

Most readers, however, address the majority of their attention to the first page, and that focus diminishes with every page. If your résumé is too long for your industry—or your age and stage—your reader will give out on you before the end.

Printing the document

When your résumé is printed straight from the electronic document, it should print within margins and with no lines dropped to an extra wasted page.

Sometimes you send something and think that it is perfect within the page. But computers are fickle and something that you think fits perfectly ends up with weird page breaks or drops one important line at the end. You may want to check that it transmits correctly by sending it to a friend to see if it looks right on their end. If you change the margins to get more on a page, make sure that nothing moves or goes missing when it prints out.

White space

Keep enough white (open) space around different sections to be able to read the résumé without strain or confusion.

This became a golden rule way back at the beginning of my working life as a résumé coach when I first understood the importance of white space in allowing the reader to easily read the content. Think of arranging your content on the page like laying out a publication—not as an exercise in cramming as many characters as you can onto a page.

The Don'ts

Now armed with the big picture information of what you want to do in your résumé, let's take a brief pause and consider what doesn't work. Readers might dislike some elements, but they won't penalize you for including them. However, some mistakes—bad formatting, using an objective, and providing *too much* information—can sabotage you from the beginning.

Style is just deciding on fonts, bolds, lines, italics, bullets, and various combinations of white space and text. But combined, those things can make reading beautiful or they can create the worst kind of monster—an indecipherable format that turns the reader off before they have read one word. Hiring people hate having to read poorly formatted text.

So like it or not, it's important to realize that style is slightly more important than substance if only because it gets you read. Good presentation means that people are nicer to your résumé—they'll give it a chance. Without style, your substance will go either un-read or unappreciated.

The Biggest Readability Killers

What readers want most is to be able to read your résumé quickly and easily, so it's important to know what style mistakes can get in the way of your overall readability—that is, your message and the impact of your résumé on the reader. The five style points that follow describe the most common complaints.

Dense text

Writing a long paragraph or putting all of your points one after another without any sort of white space or break—that's dense text. Dense text is deadly because it's very difficult to read. It's not that you can't read it; it's that you don't want to. It feels like it will take too much effort. In a résumé you need to make your points, but simply and clearly, with natural breaks in the text.

Over bold

While using the bold function is important in a résumé to highlight words, phrases, and titles of importance, using too much bold can also overwhelm your reader. Bold is meant as a highlight. Too much bold has the eye not knowing where to look. Allowing for both highlighted and nonhighlighted text guides the reader to notice different sections and scan for importance.

Wild and crazy

If you think that over bold is hard on the eye, watch what happens when you add every style function all at once: **the bold**, *the italic*, <u>*and* the underline</u>. It's too much. Throw in the **shadow effect** and you're squinting at a graphic design nightmare. No one wants to squint at a résumé. Too many stylistic flourishes overwhelm the reader and makes the text unreadable. Keep it simple and consistent. And if you attempt some stylistic leaps, make sure it's part of your job description (that is, creative director, graphic designer, brand consultant, and so forth).

Too junior

A few style no-nos can make a résumé seem like a first draft. One example is an oversimplified résumé (that is, no marketing statement and just a list of jobs and responsibilities using dashes) in Times New Roman. If you're going to use Times New Roman, you should also plan on using some unique formatting. If you have short form points, don't use a dash or hyphen (-) because it looks like you just jotted some notes and never thought about them again. Use a bullet (•), an asterisk (*), or a cross (†). There are lots of interesting yet clean-looking alternatives in place of dashes. After you've written your content, take time to center some things, bold others, and take your résumé to the next level. It means being fussy and it takes time, but it's worth it.

Inconsistent style

The last thing to look out for is inconsistency in your style. If you start to format your résumé one way, keep it going throughout. If you decide to box the heading W o r k E x p e r i e n c e, then every heading should look the same. If you put a period at the end of your points, every point should have a period. If you don't put in the periods, don't start halfway through. Think the three Cs: clean, clear, and compelling.

Using an Objective Weakens Your Pitch

A long time ago in résuméland, somebody somewhere came up with the idea of an "Objective"—stating right at the top of the résumé what job you're looking for. It was a good idea—in the nineties.

It has since evolved into one of the most useless parts of the résumé, a lingering, cliché-ridden section that doesn't tell employers anything more than they would have known already.

More often than not, résumé writers use an objective, or *what they want for themselves* from the position. At first read-through, *hiring managers don't really care what you want.* They want to know if you fit what they need, and if they see an Objective with no meat, they know they will now have to comb through your résumé and make some assumptions on their own. Therefore the "Objective" gambit, rather than firing up readers, has the opposite effect by essentially dousing their interest immediately by changing the reading focus to a fishing expedition.

Meanwhile you—the writer, for whom this objective holds such importance—lose a prime opening to sell yourself right off the top to attain the very objective you wrote.

Here are some actual objectives I've seen on résumés as part of a job application. Perhaps you've written or read some that sound like one of these.

For fun, try to identify the jobs or roles the person is targeting with these objectives.

Objective: A position that utilizes my communication and personal skills with a dynamic company.

Objective: A job that will challenge me and let me grow into an entrepreneurial type position.

Objective: To find a marketing/advertising position for the successful achievement of business development objectives.

Objective: To further diversify my skills in print design as well as web design/marketing.

Objective: Seeking a position with your company.

Sound familiar?

Do they add anything to the reader's understanding of the applicant as a qualified candidate?

Though readers may skip over these statements, it doesn't mean that they don't care about your professional career objectives. They will care about them later when they've qualified you and you're further into the process, like in at the interview stage.

There IS Such a Thing as Too Much Information

Putting in too much information will most likely ruin your chances for a callback—it leaves a strange aftertaste for the reader that mars their perception of you, or even causes them to fear contacting you. So how and why do people go too far?

1: **They're new to the résumé process, or they're from another culture, or are nonnative English speakers.** This "Don't" is often perpetrated by people who are not used to job hunting in the field they're applying for, or are new to applying for jobs. Sometimes weird or awkward résumés can result from a translation issue or arise from cultural differences when the writer is from another country, particularly if they are writing a second language.

2: **They want to stand out from the crowd.** This "Don't" can occur from a sense of frustration at being ignored in the job search process or wanting to make an impression or to stand out from the pile, which may go too far.

3: **They're trying to be truthful and end up sharing too much.** Sometimes people think that they have to confess everything up front or they will somehow be lying, which leads to the résumé as a confessional, rather than a professional, document.

If you're new to the résumé process, or are from another culture, or are a nonnative English speaker

Everyone had to go through this learning curve at some point, so you're not alone. It's important to ask for help from others to make sure you are speaking to the right audience and in an appropriate tone.

Different countries have different styles—in one country, your pitch may be far too casual, while in another country with the same pitch you might come across as too stiff. That's why it's essential to check with people here who are in the know.

For instance, often people from England and other parts of Europe have much longer résumés that list more personal information, such as social security numbers and birth dates. In the United States and Canada it's illegal to ask for that sort of information, so it's inappropriate to put it on a résumé. Because discrimination policies are very strict, it has also become the norm not to include photos, so readers may find it disturbing if you do add one.

Whether you're new to the résumé or new to the country the solution is threefold.

1: Research. Get as much information as you can on industry-specific résumés. There are many sources and specific places and ways to get help. For example, take retail. Go into a few stores and ask to speak to a manager. Ask about what they look for in a résumé. They may even ask you to bring yours back to show them. Look online for websites and industry-specific message boards where you can get information and ask your own questions. Taking some time at the beginning to learn a bit about what people expect will save time later on and will help you break through the pile.

2: Get Help. If you are new to the country or are writing your first résumé, contact your local employment center or community center to see whether they offer special résumé classes. College students and recent grads should have access to their campus career center, where counselors and workshops designed to help you prepare a résumé may be available.

3: Get Feedback. Every résumé writer requires some feedback, but newbies most of all. If English is not your native tongue, look for somebody who does speak and write English fluently to review what you've written and ensure that the grammar is correct. It's also a good idea to seek out second and third opinions in this case.

If you want to stand out from the crowd

Wanting to stand out from the crowd is perfectly understandable, especially when you're heading for a career transition. Just remember that doing something daring is risky and takes certain finesse. Sometimes the experiment works, and sometimes it doesn't.

Here's an example of when it does work. The president of a toy company received a résumé that was constructed like a game board. The creator had made a game out of his skills and work experience, and further, he'd actually made it like a game where the reader could move around a "board" and learn about his skills. The president picked up the phone, called the guy who wrote it, and invited him in for an interview. The story ended on a happy note, as the creative writer was hired and was still working for the company when the story was told to me. Taking a creative and playful gambit in a résumé for an industry that relies on these traits and sending it to a person who had the authority to do something about it was a good move.

However, other gambits don't work half as well. Other people try to play fast and loose with traditional formats but fall short of the mark. Here's one that left the recruiter who received it reeling in astonishment.

This message, embedded in the email, goes on. The real sell happens if the reader makes it to the last of the questions (Why should you hire Raleigh?).

```
I am:

RALEIGH TUTLIES

(Raw-lee Toot-lee)

Who?...keep reading

Who is Raleigh Tutlies and why is he contacting me?

Raleigh is interested in applying for the Project Manager position at
PeopleRecruiters; and is looking for an opportunity to interview. He
currently works in the film and television production industry as a
Production Coordinator and Production Manager; and at times as a
Freelance Writer, daily Set Dresser, and Buyer. The film industry tends
to lean towards seasonal work and government tax credit cycles trends,
which therefore prevents freelance workers to have consistently steady
work.

How can I contact Raleigh Tutlies?

55 Bailey Rd, Nashville, TN, 37211
Phone (615)555-1212, Cell: (615)555-1313   E-mail rtutlies@yourname.com

Where has Raleigh Tutlies received his education?

Raleigh Tutlies attended Happy View High School for five years. He
graduated in 1996. Directly after high school, Raleigh pursued a career
in aviation at a Nashville flight center. He acquired the Private Pilot
and Night Rating Licenses in late 1998. Raleigh decided to get a
University education at Tech University with a strong interest in Film
and Television Production; Graduating in 2000 with a BFA (Film Option).
```

Now this was a good idea in some respects. Raleigh handled one problem—a strange and probably often mispronounced name—with humor and aplomb. Had he thought about what the reader really wanted to know and ordered the questions differently to be more marketable, he might have inspired interest instead of bewilderment.

This tactic presents several problems. First, the writer sent it to the wrong audience. Recruiters are looking for a specific set of qualifications and requirements regardless of how the résumé looks. They are not really your target audience; they are the hurdle between you and your target audience.

Another downfall of Raleigh's tactic was the actual delivery. Though it made an   interesting start (ask a question and get the reader to keep reading), in too many other places the idea fell flat in the execution. After about two sentences, the "pitch" became too much (Why is this guy giving me all this information?).

For instance, we don't need to know why he is available especially before we know why *we care* about him being available. Or for that matter, why do we care that he has a pilot's license? He's applying to be a project manager, not to fly cargo to the Congo.

So if you want to send something more interesting or innovative to get attention, you need to remember three rules:

1: Know your audience and speak to it.

2: Always balance your creative splashes with professionalism and specific measurable results.

3: Once you've found your style, realize that you're taking a risk—you need to be okay with readers who think it's too much or weird. If you've gauged it right, only the companies who truly like your style will contact you.

If you are tempted to share too much

In the case of really sharing too much, here's a good example of a squirmy addition to the end of a résumé:

<u>**Objective:**</u> **"I am determined to earn more than my ex-husband and establish myself in an executive position within a reputed organization."**

This statement carries too many hints that this person is competitive, angry, bitter, and/or strange. Though it may not actually be true, saying you want to make more than your ex-husband is a pretty strong statement. That may be the driving force for you, but it reads as "psycho" on the other side. Keep these kinds of personal motivations to yourself.

I've seen résumés with statements such as "looking for a team that is full of integrity and does not work to bring others down." Now, this résumé writer could have been deeply hurt by in-fighting or ambitious coworkers. But I also read it like "Yuck, this is a person waiting to be betrayed by the world," and that's a potential disaster for a prospective employer. Even in the best-case scenario—she is a virtuous person brought down by a toxic workplace—it reads as though she has yet to get over the hurt, pain, and shock. That's too personal for a résumé. If you've had a toxic workplace experience that is affecting your ability to sell yourself as a confident person, get career coaching help. It's not your new employer's problem.

Your résumé is not the time to make side comments on what you want to do, or in this case, what you don't want to do:

EDUCATION

Casual part-time readings begun in **health science and education** at University of Pittsburg (**N.B.** *No professional interest in health services or in any area of the health care business.*)

Part-time coursework in **commerce**, McGill University, Montreal (**N.B.** *No career interest in the areas of finance, accounting, insurance, etc.*)

Little notes to the reader like these only cause them to think, So what DO you have an interest in? Focus on what you want to do. Let the other parts of your résumé do the talking. If you are worried about what people are going to assume from your extracurricular interests, put this last, or leave it out all together.

And finally, in the category of Way, Way, Way Too Much Information, here is this résumé's Work History:

Austin, TX
June 1998–March 1999
Temporary work in daily newspaper publishing technology (administrative) and insurance (EA and office manager in small business office). (*Relocated from Naples owing to criminal mischief.*)

Naples, FL
April 1996–May 1998
Temporary admin work, including secretarial and assistant duties through personnel agencies, plus telemarketing support. (*Relocated from Orlando owing to criminal mischief.*)

Orlando, FL
August 1993–May 1995
Contract work in the Operations department reporting to the Vice President of Operations. Implemented the transfer of securities for safekeeping at home office to the appointed guardian. (*Relocated from Miami owing to major crime.*)

And that was just the beginning.

For future reference, though I might talk about adding "personality," what I mean is a turn-of-phrase, a new way of saying something, or a unique element that adds a hint of the real you. Not your deepest fears and vulnerabilities, not why you took the degree you did, not your hopes for your children or the religion you believe in, not why you think nobody likes you or why you haven't been hired yet—but a positive, promising, interesting thought, or a purposely humorous phrase that reflects *well* on you.

If you can read what you write and think *This is my best foot forward; I sound like a confident, self-assured person I'd be happy to meet*, great. If you aren't sure, then it's probably a borderline statement that you may want to revise. And if your friends and family get an odd look on their face when they read it—dump it.

So now you know all your major Dos and Don'ts. Your résumé is going to be readable, clear, and stylish, with a strong opening message and touch of personality—without scaring the pants off the reader!

CHAPTER 3:

Marketing Yourself in the Profile or Executive Summary

The first quarter of the first page of your résumé is the most important and powerful space in the document. If you were to think about the spaces in your résumé in terms of advertising dollars, the top quarter would cost the most. If you were a journalist, the top quarter would correspond to getting not only a front page story, but the story at the top of the front page. If you were a photographer or a supermodel, the first quarter of the page would be like the front cover of a magazine.

This is the place that receives the reader's initial eye contact, and the most focus. As the reader begins to move down the first page and on to the next page, their eyes actually move faster and begin to skim, stopping only if something specific catches their attention. Thus, this first quarter is the place to take a stand, create a brand, and leave a lasting impression. And this chapter's going to teach you how to do that.

Baby, Remember My Name

Your name is your brand. It's what you what people to remember about you. Think of how people pass names along like treasures. "Ask for Tammy at the salon, she's the best." "Have you heard of Rajit Khan? He's amazing with these sorts of programs." "I've got the name of the best obstetrician in the city." Making your name the most visible part of your résumé has a purpose—to link your name with all the accomplishments and benefits that follow.

Your Name and Contact Info

It may seem sort of nonsensical at first to start with what seems like an obvious no-brainer: your name and contact information. Isn't that the part that everyone should ace?

Unfortunately, most people are unaware of the message they send to the reader from the very first choice of how they present their name. That's why we're starting from the very beginning.

Who Are You? Presenting Your Name

Your name and contact information orients the reader to who you are, where you're located, and how to contact you. Because your name is the first statement you make, make a great impression.

Your name is important. And, if you apportion the same font size to your name as you do to your address, the impression left is that you equate yourself with your street number. Now this doesn't mean you have to make your name size 72 bold with shadow effect—in fact I don't recommend it—but your name should be at least a little bigger than the rest of the contact information. It shows confidence.

Some résumé writers helpfully add the words "Résumé" or "Curriculum Vitae" in type larger than their name at the top of the page before launching into the rest of the contact information. Given the instantly recognizable outline of a résumé, the reader will probably know they are looking at a résumé without you having to waste precious first-page space.

Get Off to a Good Start with the Three S's

Style, Space, and Simplicity: your name is the priority, followed by how to reach you. But none of your contact information should be more than one-eighth of the whole page.

Ineffective

Resume

Joe Not Very Bold
123 3rd Street
Suite 1288
Los Angeles, CA 90211
646-555-6868
Jnotverybold@companyABC.com

Kaila Kufferfluffer

123 Helffunker Street West, Birmingham, AB 35201 Telephone 205-555-1234
Email kufferfluffer@indecipherable.com

Effective

Joe Personality

123 3rd Street, Suite 1288 Los Angeles, CA 90211
jpersonality@abccompany.com 646-555-6868

Where Do You Live? Giving Your Address

Though employers are unlikely to mail you anything in this wired day and age, it is still important to include your address. It gives the reader a geographical sense of where you live.

Do employers judge you by where you live? They might, most likely in evaluating whether you are going to have problems getting to work because you're on the other side of town or in another city. If you are in another geographical location, you will need to address your intention and ability to relocate at the beginning of your email or cover letter, to answer that question first for the reader.

Take responsibility for where you are located and how you will handle an interview or a job in a different location. Trying to hide your current address by not including it tends to raise question marks. If you intend to move closer to the job location, regardless of whether you get this particular job, you can signal this by putting "Interim address" on your contact information or mention it in your email or cover letter.

Some people will not consider you for a job or want to meet with you until they are sure you are living where the job is located, so as soon as you get a local address, local phone number, and even a locally recognized email address, put it onto your résumé.

You can include a general email address, and perhaps a local cell phone number, just to get them to call you back. However, your true address will come out sooner or later—it's just whether you want it to be now or later. If you think there's an advantage to this approach, try it and see. Sometimes the smallest changes can breed responses to résumés.

Some people use post office boxes for various reasons. If your reason is a good one, like a need for security or privacy, leave it be. Otherwise; if you can, give an actual street or house address.

Regardless of these nuances, your location information is the least important of the contact information, so don't use up a lot of space displaying it. Using three lines to type out your complete address in the traditional letter format is a waste. It should be one or two lines, and in a smaller font. There are many visually pleasing ways to present this.

Oscar W. Tiplady

25 Sweeney St., Atlanta, GA 30301 ♦ Phone 770.555.1222 ♦ oscarwt@hotmail.com

---

Mark Rougeforte

2694 Rocky Rd.   **Res: 920-555-9999**
Green Bay, WI 54308   **Email: markrougeforte@email.com**

---

123 3rd St. Toronto, ON M2J 1L6   416.555.5245   mclear@canada.com

M a r y
C l e a r

How Can I Reach You? Offering Your Contact Information

Can an employer get in touch with you immediately? Your contact information is essential so that you can be contacted quickly and easily.

This may seem obvious, but you wouldn't believe a recruiter's frustration or an HR person's dismissal when they can't locate someone they want to contact about a position. Recruiting or hiring for positions often has an initial burst of speed at the outset of a search; once there is a slate of good candidates and the interview stage begins, the process slows down. While the deal is never done until the offer letter has been signed, not being available or not responding quickly in that initial stage may shut down your best opportunity to be considered. Be sure to double check that the numbers and email address that you leave are correct and up-to-date.

If you are sending your information from your current place of employment, and you know that you will leave your job eventually, cover yourself. If you are sending your résumé to a recruiter, or to a hiring manager or HR person in a large company, know that they will likely hold it in their database for future reference. You want to be sure to give an alternate email or phone from your current workplace so that they can find you no matter where you land. In fact, it's probably the best practice to have alternate contact information from your current employment regardless, unless you are absolutely certain that you can maintain confidentiality, or your that employer knows you are searching.

Check the phone number. If it's a home number, make sure everyone at home knows how to answer the phone politely and to get you without yelling.

Prep Your Home Team

Ask the people in your life—be they family, spouse, or roommates—not only to be ready to take a message for you, but to ask what you need to know. If a call comes in that sounds like it could be job search-related, ask them to write down the following:

- The name of the person calling (and ask for the spelling if it sounds difficult so you can write it and pronounce it properly).
- Their return phone number.
- The name of the company they are calling from. This will allow you to prepare for the return call because you will know which employer or recruiter responded.
- A good time to call back.

And then, as soon as the caller hangs up, have your family member or roommate try to reach you as soon as possible so that you can get back to the caller quickly.

The Facts on Fax Numbers

Employers are unlikely to ever fax you, so giving them a fax number isn't really necessary. On occasion, a recruiter might use a fax to send you postings, but more and more recruiters are doing their business via the Net, so unless there's a specific reason or request for it, they don't need your fax number. The only time you might want to provide a fax number is when the job requires work from home or passing other documents back and forth—so showing that you have access to a fax is an asset.

Use Hyphens in Phone and Fax Numbers

Because electronic documents may not always have the same line breaks at the receiving end of an electronic message, use hyphens to separate the elements of phone and fax numbers. Hyphens denote that the elements clearly go together and that the element is not yet complete. A period usually indicates the end of an element so may be more confusing. Example: 208-555-6224, not 208.555.6224

HuggyBear2 Is Not Considered Professional

Sometimes your email address is so much a part of you that you don't think about the fact that you're sending employers contact information that requests them to get back to KingoftheWorld26@hotmail.com or SexyLady277@yahoo.com or just even the weird stuff that our friends think is funny, like the obscure laughladyfromthemoonpie@hotmail.com or MetalRocks4EverinMy Mouth@yahoo.com
You get the picture.
Most email servers give you more than one email name option. Or you can create one especially for your search. The best email "handle" to go with is some variation of your full name.

Please, if you are a mature person (that is, out of college) living at home and you are applying for more senior jobs, try to get a separate phone line with a separate voice mail. There's nothing more awkward or annoying than encountering a mama who's trying to weasel information for her "baby," or a young sibling screaming out "It's for you!!" at the top of their lungs. It's hard to imagine you as an authority in your field. Also, make sure the home voice mail is professional though homey sounding—no cutesy messages or long musical numbers while you're job searching.

If you provide a work number, make sure that it is your phone and voice mail alone that it goes to. It's better if your number is direct so that they can't misdial or reach the receptionist. Make sure that you have a place to go where you can shut the door and have a free conversation with a potential employer or recruiter. Have a backup plan, like reserving a meeting room or taking your cell phone outside.

The best choice in terms of "reach-ability" is a cell phone number. It's yours, you can have it with you at all times, and you're the only one who will answer it. However, remember that cell phones conversations can sometimes be hard to hear on the other end, particularly if you've answered it while walking down the street on a windy day or in a noisy restaurant or the subway. So, before automatically answering the phone, think about where you are and whether you can quickly get to somewhere quiet and sheltered. You can always answer the phone and suggest that they call back in ten minutes when you're better situated.

You may want to get yourself a cell phone, phone number, or email address dedicated to your job search that you'll keep through many jobs. That way there is never any obstacle to finding you when that dream job shows up. And don't forget to check voice mail and email boxes regularly!

Your Profile

After dispensing with your name and contact information, you want to market yourself. This is the hardest section of the résumé because it's like writing a product summary. It needs to be short, tight, and yet illuminating.

The ultimate goal of this section, however, is simple. You want to take charge of how the person who reads your résumé thinks of you—to define yourself before they define you. You want to sell the unique benefits of hiring you while simultaneously reassuring them that you have all the requisite qualifications.

The Profile section is the place in the résumé where you can sell yourself most effectively.

What do I mean by "take charge" of how the reader reads your résumé? When someone reads your résumé, they really only scan it for about ten seconds the first time they go through it. They

Did You Know?

A person will spend ten to twenty seconds tops reading your résumé through for the first time to decide whether it's a "yes," a "maybe," or a "no."

are looking to determine who you are and what pile to put you in—Yes, Maybe, or No. These are the most vital questions a hiring manager considers:

- Do I know what position this person is applying for or sees themselves as?
- Is this person qualified for that position?
- Are they interesting?
- Should I call them?

You want that reader to think, "Yes, yes, yes, yes!" to all of the questions above. That's what getting in the Yes pile is all about. Unfortunately, many résumé writers leave the reader to skim the whole résumé looking for answers to those questions. If you want to be a Yes pile person, the key is to learn how to write a killer profile.

> **YOU Are Your Brand**
>
> Hijack the reader's thought process and deliver a clear message right off the top. What's your point of difference? Why would hiring you benefit them?

Writing a Profile

What the heck is a profile?

A profile is a summary of you with an eye toward marketing yourself to the reader and making yourself visible—a standout in a vast sea of similar résumés. It presents the distinctive and unique part of you, while also covering what a hiring manager is looking for in an applicant. The profile is also known as an Executive Summary, and occasionally a Professional Objective, though often that is put in a future tense, while the profile is a present tense construction.

Résumé writers can use the profile section to hijack the readers' thought process—to convey what you want the readers to think as they read the rest of your experience. You can get them to feel confident about you before they even get past the first quarter of your résumé. And then you can add some personality that creates a spark of interest.

> **A Dictionary Definition of Profile:**
>
> 1: Degree of exposure to public notice; visibility
> 2: A biographical essay presenting the subject's most noteworthy characteristics and achievements
> 3: A formal summary or analysis of data, representing distinctive features or characteristic

Easier said than done? Actually only three basic steps will help you create a solid profile:

1: State Who You Are
2: State the Unique Benefit(s) of Hiring You
3: Add Key Qualifications (specific to the position, industry, or job ad)

> **The Résumé is a Marketing Document**
>
> Résumés are designed to generate a response, so be sure to define your audience and speak directly to them. Make it easy for the reader to decide who you are.

The profile will be your unique statement, both in style and content, that tells the reader everything they need to know about you in the first quarter of your résumé. Once you've created a powerful profile, the reader spends the rest of the résumé reading through and absorbing your experience from the point of view that you have just created. Thus *you* are in charge of the reading experience, not the hirer.

Thanks for Asking: State Who You Are

The very first thing you want to think about is *the job title, position, or type of work* you are targeting.

Are you a customer service rep? A marketing expert? A B2B product developer? A junior account manager? A business consultant?

There are different ways of looking at naming your desired role. If you are submitting your résumé to recruiters, or letting friends and colleagues know what you're looking for, you'll want to stick mainly with the one role that you are interested in.

This isn't meant to limit your capabilities or box you into a corner. People often worry that picking something specific may limit the positions the recruiter will consider them for. Here's a secret about recruiters: they're pretty good at looking at experience and knowing where to fit people, but they are also short on résumé reading time.

The more clearly and specifically you state who you are and what role you see yourself in, the more quickly and powerfully they'll think of you when the role appears. It's about being committed to the position you want so that people think of you when that position appears. Try to be all things to all people, and no one will remember you.

There are often degrees of difference in a job that would fit you well. If there are some clear variations in what you can do and you are truly passionate about each of those alternatives, you may want to have two or three different résumés highlighting the different roles to directly apply for those positions, or use a title that can speak to some variations, such as using "Director, Media and Communications" to encompass all possible director-level jobs. This is especially true if what you do has different titles in different companies, or if you are an entrepreneur or consultant who has held many different roles.

Declare Who You Are!

Use that first quarter space on your résumé to declare who you are **right now!** Not what you want to be someday, but who you think you are today. Even if your previous job title didn't say it exactly, if you did some part of a role you can use it to name yourself. This is part of taking charge of how people will read the rest of your experience.

However, if you submit your résumé to a recruiter, you need to pick one title and be it. Your primary goal is to meet with a recruiter so they know you and think of you when a position that's a good fit for you appears. The same goes for a hiring manager. Trust their intelligence in reading a résumé—they are more interested in finding where you fit than in shoving you into a box and keeping you there. You can always mention interest in slightly different roles in your email or cover letter—or better yet, in your interview after you've already connected with them.

Put this declaration in the present tense. Say who you are now and whether you have a job. A writer doesn't stop being a writer if they aren't writing; a lawyer is still a lawyer even when they aren't at trial, so why would you stop being who you are when you're between jobs? Say it specifically, and say it with confidence.

I've had clients ask me if getting too specific rules them out. In fact, getting specific makes people take notice, because you're talking right to them. For example, I had a young woman named Darby in my office who had worked at only one company for her adult career and was looking to make a change. We narrowed her role to this:

Project Manager with a Passion for Product Development

Looking for a sophisticated, business-to-business, constantly-evolving product to launch, manage, and/or support.

- Strong analytical, problem solving, and project management skills, exemplified over the six-year period at ABC Co.
- Excellent interpersonal and communication skills; equally comfortable with scientists, marketing team, and senior management
- An innovative self-starter, requiring little supervision

Darby worried that the first two lines would limit her search. They had the opposite effect. In fact, a recruiter in my office took one look at her opening three lines and asked her to come in for an interview. He was hiring for a B2B project manager role, and her résumé had excited him because she was speaking right to his need.

A good recruiter shouldn't treat you like cattle by farming you out to what's available. Good recruiters are looking to make great matches. Great matches happen when both sides know what they want and recognize it in each other. Clearly and specifically stated goals make it easier for the person reading your résumé to place you in a great match.

When you're networking with colleagues, leave them with a strong impression of what you are looking for. The more people know what you want, the better prepared they are to remember you if they hear about something interesting. Twenty people with their ears to the ground for a specific role has a more powerful effect than just you yourself could.

So unless you are adapting your résumé for a particular job or job ad, you need to have a primary job role target that leads off your résumé.

Here's How I Can Help: State the Unique Benefit(s) of Hiring You

Next, you want to distinguish what makes you different from every other business analyst or creative director or content specialist out there. What are the unique benefits of hiring you?

Is it your years in the business? The fact that you are creative with a technology bent? The fact that you speak four languages and worked in Germany? That you have exceeded your quota on every job? That you've managed huge budgets? That your PR ability includes experience with branding strategy? Think about all the "extras" the hiring company gets when they get you.

> Everyone uniquely contributes to every single job or situation in life. Themes and patterns of who we are can be found in all of our experiences. Figure out your unique contribution and articulate it in your profile.

Stop and think about the last time you washed dishes. How did you do it? Rinse every plate carefully? Have a special scrub brush? Spray generously with the hose? Researchers once discerned that there are 250 ways to wash dishes. Now, that's a lot of ways to get food residue off a plate. If there are that many ways to accomplish a simple household task, how many ways do you think there are for creating an advertisement, finishing a report, building a computer program, or leading a team? The permutations are endless.

Finding the unique benefit of hiring you means taking your skills one step further. It's not just that you listen so well, it's that your listening to customers results in sales. It's not just that you are great to work with, the benefit is that you tend to harmonize work environments and make teams more productive. A skill is being able to write—the benefit of writing well is that the department issues useful and clear memos enabling positive communication with staff.

> ## Know Your Skills and Find the Benefit to the Employer
> **Overall Skill:** good communicator
> **Specific and Detailed Skills:** listening to customers; responding positively to problems
> **Benefit to Employer:** increased sales; minimize customer upset; happy, satisfied customers; good word-of-mouth
>
> **Overall Skill:** works well individually
> **Specific and Detailed Skills:** understands assignments; asks good questions or asks for guidance when stuck; comfortable meeting timelines with little supervision
> **Benefit to Employer:** manages herself so you don't have to; will ask for help to keep projects moving forward swiftly

The unique benefit answers the questions, Why is this important? or What result do I get from this skills that you have?

So as you are composing your unique benefits, start with the overall skill. Then get a little more specific about that skill by describing it in more detail. Finally, ask yourself, Why is this skill important to the employer? or What are the results of employing that skill? The answers are the key message to incorporate.

Look at the flip side

Another way to get a sense of your unique benefits or to know what to highlight is to take a look at the job ad you picked as your job role example.

Reread the ad you chose. What words and phrases jump out at you? If it is a sales role, the ad may ask for someone "visual." Do you consider yourself a visual person? How is that a benefit? Why does the company running the ad think that is a benefit? Pick out the other main elements that fit you. They are likely clues to your unique benefits.

After thinking about some unique benefits, as well as about what the employer might be looking for, compile a list what you've discovered so far. If you had to say which one was the most outstanding, which one would it be? If you could name only three top benefits you'd bring to the company, which three would you choose? Which would other competitors for the job be most unlikely to have? Zero in on the key message about who you are that you want to send to employers.

What's your tag line?

After thinking about who you are and how to describe what you do, you'll want to figure out which ideas and phrases you'll actually use. Once people get going on this process, they often end up with more words or concepts than they need.

You don't want to be a page of fabulous things—not that you aren't that fabulous, of course—but you want the reader to focus on one message, not twenty. At this point, you are like a stick of gum (or at least a marketer of a stick of gum). Are you going to sell yourself as "minty fresh," "sugarless," or "breath-saving"? Which will be the most important to the buyer?

Decide on the most important message to get across in your résumé and focus on delivering that message to your buyer—the person who is hiring. How could you express your uniqueness simply and memorably? Sometimes I ask people to think of some phrase or tagline that encapsulates the main idea, kind of the way a movie poster creates a one-line summary of the movie.

See whether you can place these movie taglines from their posters and ads:

- With the right song and dance, you can get away with murder.
- Love is wonderful. Until it happens to your only daughter.
- She brought a small town to its feet and a huge corporation to its knees.
- Even the smallest person can change the course of the future.

If you said *Chicago, Father of the Bride, Erin Brockovich,* and *The Lord of the Rings…*you're right. And how you guessed that (other than apparently spending a little too much time in the lobby of your local movie theater) was that the tagline perfectly summarized a big idea in a short phrase.

The tagline idea in a résumé is meant to give a little punch to a more professional idea and should be used only if you are comfortable with it and have a good one. The most important thing to understand from the tagline metaphor is that your goal is to make the profile be a summary of you, encapsulating everything the reader really needs to know in a few short lines.

Standing out from the pile just means saying something specifically and powerfully and that inspires people to want to meet you.

Leading people Leading projects Leading change

I am a **Project Manager** with 3 years experience in new media. I specialize in developing new media products and projects from conception to launch, managing transition, and transforming dysfunctional or suboptimal departments into productive, empowered teams. My main areas of expertise are vertical industry portals, online education, medical new media publishing, and broadcasting for radio and the Internet.

Here's an example of how a tagline might look:

Let me be clear about this—your résumé doesn't have to have a tagline. But if you find one that you like and that feels right to you, it may be a way to quickly grab the reader's attention and summarize who you are.

Hot Tips for Good Writing

Writing isn't everyone's forte, so let's take a moment to think about ways of taking your résumé writing to the next level even though you aren't Hemingway. Some simple techniques and tricks can make your material sound fresh and interesting.

Tip #1: Get Interesting by Getting Specific

Details ring true. The clues to the real person are found in the details.

Getting more specific helps show employers that this résumé represents an actual person—not an automaton spewing out expected words and phrases.

Your job in the profile or résumé—or even your cover letter if you send one—is to give the reader a sense of who you are and how you perform. How do you go about your tasks—with knowledge, skills, training, experience and nuances, understanding of the industry—to make the desired outcome happen?

What are your strengths? What are the benefits of those strengths? Do you have a specific story that happened at your work that brings that strength to light immediately?

For instance, many people state that they have "exceptional communication skills." What does that mean? What kind of communication skills are you particularly good at? It could be that you're good at any of these:

- Listening to customers and getting them to talk about themselves. Thus, you make above-quota sales effortlessly as you are able to anticipate customer needs. For example, you know that one of your big customers loves to golf, so you sold him extra computer software that automated many bookkeeping functions allowing him to get out on the course more often.
- Being the lead communicator in the department so that your department is connected and supported within the rest of the company. You thereby helped raise the profile of one of the new product launches in your department because you created buy in with other departments.
- Working one-on-one with team members, creating an emotionally supportive atmosphere. For example, you helped a coworker understand why she hated working with another coworker by demonstrating how they were miscommunicating. After that she was able to lead presentations with him.
- Writing memos that everyone always reads, because everyone loves that little bit of extra humor and insight you put in your written communication. Even your boss said she learned something from reading your memos—and she asked for them to be written!

Your examples or stories need to be tight and focused. However, when you trust in the power of a narrative, the story aspect of a specific example illuminates you in the mind of the reader—they can actually picture you in action. That creates both interest and confidence in you.

Writing Tip #2: Avoid Clichés and Overused Phrases

It is easy to write a résumé in "professional" language using comfort phrases that résumé writers head back to again and again and again. Phrases like these seem to flow so easily: "excellent communications skills," "dynamic individual," "exceptional visionary," and the old favorite "I work well alone and also as part of a team." Just to prove the point, all of these examples came up when I opened the door to my office and asked the three recruiters sitting outside at their desks. It took less than thirty seconds for each of them to come up with an answer. And you could probably add others to the list if you thought about it for as long.

Those words flow so easily because they have been used before. They are clichés—expected and overused phrases that hundreds upon thousands of people have used in their job search materials. They were good words once—long ago when the first few thousand job searchers used them. But now they're overused and make the reader skip ahead, rather than make an impression.

Imagine these different possibilities for "Can work independently and also with a team":

> A *cliché* is by definition a "trite or overused expression or idea." It also means "a person or character whose behavior is predictable or superficial." By using résumé clichés you consign yourself to providing only predictable, superficial information that doesn't help the reader get to know you. Step out of overly professional language, even for just a sentence. It makes the reader pause (often with relief at seeing something different) and say, "Wow, I've got to meet this person."

- Creates a sense of community without losing individuality
- Thrives in a collaborative environment in which everyone freely and actively participates
- Enhances the performance of the orchestra by being both an integral member of the ensemble as well as a strong soloist
- Olympic-level team player

Creative writing may not be your strength. That's okay. Getting past a cliché is about sitting with the phrase you want to say, and taking an extra few minutes to think about saying it a slightly different way. You may not get every single one different, but that's okay because you don't want to come off as an author masquerading as an IT developer.

The extra bonus of a mighty writing effort is worthwhile, because in addition to smoothing out the way your résumé reads, the extra work prepares you to give good, thoughtful interviews when employers ask these questions in person.

And yes, sometimes keywords need to be used either to echo the job description or jump out in a scanned résumé. But you can use some of those keywords and still make your résumé interesting for the person who actually has to read it. Trust me. They're bored.

Writing Tip #3: Look at Some Examples for Inspiration

Let's look at some examples of how stating who you are and stating unique benefits in a fresh, interesting way might look like. Note the different style and wording of each profile, even though they are all accomplishing the same thing. The variations in style, tone, and word choice are what make each profile authentic, powerful, and unique—and therefore readable.

Ritta Chang: Visual Designer
My main goal as your employee is to provide clients with maximum quality, features, and service, while remaining affordable and accessible to all levels of the community.

Copywriter / Content Strategist

creative and bright, I develop content that appeals to your market

strategic focus on developing voice and brand

skilled strategist with strong eCRM and online content background

expert researcher, editor, and project driver

organized, efficient, and always deadline ready

enthusiastic, entrepreneurial, and ready to take on an exciting new project

---

Customer Service and Sales Professional Summary

Passionate sales/service professional with proven intelligence and leadership abilities. Known for high integrity & patience in motivating and educating clients and consumers.

Key Service Motto:

To help individuals make informed buying decisions based on accurate information. To make every client a loyal client.

Key Service Skills:

Emotional and Practical Intelligence, Integrity, Value-Added Service

---

These profiles would all be fine on their own, followed immediately by Work Experience. However, sometimes it is beneficial to add one more section that speaks directly to a job ad or specific requirements and qualifications needed for a job. This allows you to keep your benefits in your profile, while still responding directly to what the recruiter or hiring person is looking for.

Key Qualifications That Are Specific to the Position, Industry, or Job Ad

You may choose to include two to four points that highlight qualifications required for the job in either your profile or in a separate list. The purpose is to provide a scannable list of your key qualifications as they relate to the job you're applying for.

Start by reading the job description you are interested in. Make notes on what you think the key qualifications are. Is it the number of years of experience, a specific skill set, or previous management experience? Don't just focus on the soft skills, but also on the "deal-breaker" elements they want for the position.

Create some key qualifications in your profile, either as part of the profile or as a bulleted list underneath it.

Return to the job description, find the key qualifications, and then decide which of them most closely resemble your strongest competencies. If you could only put forward one or two, what are the absolute, hands-down, best skills or qualifications that you would want remembered?

If you choose to add a qualifications summary section, use it to speak directly to the needs of the job. If they want three years of retail experience, start with the first point of "4 years retail experience on floor and at cash." If they mention trade shows as part of the job description, and that's one of the things you did a lot of, put it up in the key qualifications— "Extensive traveling with high-end trade shows over the last three years."

What Is a Deal Breaker?

A deal breaker is a qualification or element of experience that is essential for the job. While some things are nice to get, or the employer hopes to get, deal breakers are the things that must be present.

Brand Manager

The successful candidate will be responsible for developing and implementing the long-term strategic vision, business plans, and objectives. You will manage multiple projects including advertising, development, and implementation of new products; launching of new products and product innovations; handling public relation and, category development; managing brand profit and loss; identifying strategic opportunities for brand; developing brand positioning strategy; developing and building cohesive teams with supply chain, marketing, sales, finance, and advertising agencies. You must thrive in a busy environment; be an energetic, strong team player; and have exceptional leadership skills. You will be able to use your strong analytical skills to solve problems, and you will influence people with your ability to build and retain relationships at all levels. You are creator with innovative ideas. The suitable candidate will have 5–8 years of expertise in the consumer packaged goods industry with Tier 1 training.

Though this ad is trying to get a lot of qualifications and elements from a candidate in terms of responsibilities and personality traits, the deal breaker is in the last line. Up to that point, there was likely no end of possible candidates. But this is the cutoff. Candidates need a certain number of years of experience and need "Tier 1" training. That means you need to have worked with a top-drawer, big-name corporation with a reputation for brand training, such as Procter and Gamble. If you have this background, you would definitely highlight it in your key qualifications so that you'll fall in a Yes pile faster.

Sometimes the deal-breaker elements of the ad are subtler, so you will need reread the ad carefully to make an educated guess about which elements you think are the most important requirements for the role.

Here are some examples of how the Qualifications Summary might look:

Sample #1

QUALIFICATIONS SUMMARY

• Results-oriented Internet professional with a 5-year history of success building online brand experiences and communities to acquire and retain customers.
• Balanced skill set with proficiency in client relations, business analysis, project management, and site analysis and reporting.
• Customer service focus resulting from agency experience and 8 years of technical support, help-desk management, and software training experience.
• Resourceful, creative thinker with a strong technical aptitude suited to bringing marketing ideas together with technology solutions.

Sample #2

Key Jewelry Store Qualifications

• **4 years in retail sales (cash, floor, stock)**
• **3 years working with jewelry and accessories**
• **Accomplished Artisan: have worked with many different materials (gold, silver, platinum) and can communicate that knowledge to the customer**
• **Lifelong love of jewelry**

Sample #3

COMPUTER SKILLS:

Operating Systems:
Windows 95, 98, 2000, NT; Apple Macintosh; knowledge and brief experience with UNIX

General Applications:
MS Office, MS Word, PowerPoint, Excel

Page Layout, Graphic, and Video/Audio Design Applications:
8 years working with QuarkXpress and Adobe Acrobat Distiller.
7 years working with Adobe Photoshop and Illustrator.
5 years working with Adobe Premiere and After Effects.
7 years working with QuickTime, SoundEdit, and RealPlayer.
School experience of working with form•Z, Electric Image, Softimage, and Maya.
7 years experience in photo scanning and retouching.

Web Design and Internet Applications:
5 years working with Macromedia Director, Dreamweaver, Flash, Fireworks, and Adobe ImageReady.
7 years working with Internet Explorer, Netscape Navigator, and AOL.
4 years of reading and writing HTML, JavaScript, and CSS.
Knowledge and experience with CGI scripts, XML, DHTML, XHTML, ASP, and SQL.

Putting It All Together

After collecting all of the information about yourself, you then need to put it into a form that speaks to your audience and represents who you are. To do so, you need to know your audience. Both your content and your style should reflect what the job is and the type of company you're "speaking" to. For example, creative flourishes in your resume may be appreciated in places with a flair for innovation—it speaks to them more than a traditional, buttoned-down resume would. But in a buttoned-down company your fancy graphics or funny lines may not read so funny.

Here are some sample résumé openers:

Crispin Fraser

Interactive Director • Seattle, WA • 206-555-2255 (cell)
crispy@mediamedia.com

Senior Executive and award-winning Creative Director with 10+ years of blue chip ad agency experience in traditional advertising, plus heavy online and interactive media involvement since 1997:

• Founded, managed, and developed interactive team that Globe ranked 13th in the world (2003).
• Personally won dozens of top awards, including: Top to Watch, Berlin, International Design.
• Attracted major new agency clients, including Big Co., TV Co. and Film Co.

Amita DeSouza

PROFESSIONAL PROFILE

Cosmetics professional with 7 years of diverse experience in the industry. Results-driven account executive that optimized sales through skillful execution of presentations and attentive management of client relationships. Self-motivated individual with demonstrated ability to develop creative solutions that direct and improve corporate initiatives and opportunities.

Key Strengths:
• Honed skill-set in progressively senior positions, including Account Management, Product Development, Marketing, Merchandising, and Operations.
• Extensive knowledge of market trends, style direction, and textile development.
• Confident communicating throughout all levels of an organization.

Editing Checklist

Your Name and Contact Information

- I spelled my name right
- My name is prominently displayed, with a larger font than my other contact information or other information on my résumé
- My contact information is up-to-date, and there is somewhere that a recruiter or hirer could reach me once I leave my current job
- I can be reached by phone and I answer this phone regularly
- If I am not available, the phone number they call has a professional sounding message or people who are prepared to take a message for me
- I can be reached by email
- This email address is professional sounding
- I check this email regularly
- My contact information only takes up at most one or two lines
- I've accounted for my geographical location elsewhere if I am out of the city, province, or country

Your Profile

- I have a profile—a marketing statement or executive summary of myself at the beginning of my résumé
- My profile is not about what I want from a company, rather it's about what I can bring to a company

Inside the Profile

- I have declared who I am or the role I see for myself in the first line
- I have written a tight, professional sounding summary of who I am in that role
- I have highlighted approximately three main points about my experience and personality traits
- I have stated some of the benefits of my traits and skills *or* I have stated some specific results as success measures (awards, honors, and so forth)
- If it works with my marketing statement, I have included some key qualifications as they pertain to the job I'm applying for
- I've tried to avoid obvious clichés and dug a little deeper to say something specific
- I've thought about and researched my industry, my targeted role, and the company I am applying to and I am sure that I am speaking to that audience
- If someone read my profile, they would agree that it was me

CHAPTER 4:

Creating Work Experience That Works

You've typed your name and your contact information in a pleasing fashion (or if this is still the rough draft no fashion at all). You've tackled a profile statement, which is also perhaps in a rough draft state, and maybe stated some key qualifications, a sweet aperitif, if you will, to tease the appetite of the reader.

Now comes the meat and potatoes, the stick-to-your-ribs stuff—or in the metaphoric world of a wheat-avoiding vegetarian, the quinoa and kale casserole of your résumé.

Your Work Experience

Your work experience has to fulfill the expectations of the profile. On a first pass, a reader is unlikely to read everything about each job in depth, but will skim for keywords, phrases, names, and numbers that will help them decide what level of responsibility you currently have, how your career has progressed, the kind of results you've achieved, and with whom and where you've been working.

It's amazing how fast a seasoned recruiter can look through a jumble of work histories and come up with a rapid-fire picture of the writer. In fact, it's amazing how fast a recruiter can come up with the potential problem areas of a résumé on a first pass. Their livelihood rests on finding and meeting presentable candidates while avoiding dead ends and misleading ones. It behooves them to scan for the holes and the issues before reading the details.

So one of the goals of this chapter is to teach you how to handle your holes—which sounds rather rude, but is vitally important. While nothing can change pure fact, you can emphasize that you've been somewhat of a job hopper with a year's gap in your résumé and an unclear education, or you can minimize that impression by tackling the problem head-on with confidence.

Another essential part of the work experience process is the difference between responsibilities (what you were hired to do) and your accomplishments (the results of carrying out those responsibilities with acuity). It's surprising how many professional workers who have been in the corporate world for years have still not quite grasped the distinction, and thus lose a vital opportunity to highlight their achievements differently from what they were hired to do. Therefore, when looking at the substance of the work experience, I will also talk about how to best present specific and measurable results of your time at a job.

Let's begin with the simple act of writing down your title, your company, and the time you worked for them.

Ordering Your Work Experience

Some ways of listing your experience provide more clarity to the reader and strengthen their impression of you. Others will divert the reader and interfere with the reading experience. You don't want to distract the reader from your most important point—how well you did at your job. The *date* is one place your message delivery can get off track.

Recruiters and hiring managers say that in the first line of your work experience, you want to put the company or the position first and put the date last.

Always.

EFFECTIVE

Project Manager, DataSystems	**June 2002–present**
DataSystems – Project Manager	**June 2002 to present**

DISTRACTING

June 2002 – Present	**Project Manager, DataSystems**
June 2002 to the Present **Project Manager, DataSystems**	

Why? If you put June 2002 first, you risk distracting the reader with calculations of your time spent at the job versus the first punch of the company and title. This is especially true if your dates are at all complex.

People who speak English read from left to right, and thus give the most weight and authority to what they read first. By putting your job title or company first, you place more weight and significance to those words rather than to the dates. If you are trying to decide whether to place the title before the company, ask yourself what you want to emphasize—a well-known company or a good job title. Then use that style consistently throughout your résumé. And, in any case, the best counsel is to keep the dates you worked to the right of the page.

Some résumés have beautiful layouts that indent the main text with the date floating on the left. However, dates can take up far too much space. White space is good. Too much white space can move some of your best accomplishments to the second page. Just another reason to put the date to the right side.

Be Clear about Where You Were When

Recruiters and hiring managers scan the dates on their second pass of your résumé to calculate where you were when. If you took a year off or did something different for a period of time, be sure to include that so that there isn't a huge time gap. People who read a lot of résumés notice gaps—they become proficient at it—and they will wonder about what happened if the gap question isn't answered.

The Big "Gap" Question: What Are You Trying to Hide?

Taking charge of the gap with a one-line descriptor puts you in charge of how the reader responds. For example:

Sabbatical 2001—*Stayed with ill mother and organized charitable run. Traveled for last two months (New Zealand, Australia).*

If you are nervous about a period of unemployment, think about other things you did during that time. Most people get involved in something, even if only for a day or two. Did you organize something, work on a small contract, or take a course? If you helped a friend with their business by having coffee and brainstorming ideas, consider saying you were "consulting" on a business.

Even if they aren't full-time pursuits, listing something will show that you have been developing yourself and your skills during those months. I suggest putting in something to handle the gap if you've been out of work longer than four or five months. Look to add in a contract, a sabbatical, or something along those lines.

If you took the time to try something different—such as a new career direction or to start your own business—and you're worried that it will look confusing on a specifically directed résumé, keep that new direction to one or two lines. The recruiter or HR person will notice the gap, and if they interview you they will ask you about it anyway. The sooner you deal with it, the better.

You aren't necessarily fooling the reader—let's agree that they know as well as anyone how long it can take to connect to the right job—but you are reassuring the reader that you have been an active participant in your life despite the circumstances.

Consultant - Jack Chin and Associates   2003-2005

Successfully sold a longstanding business, taking a well-deserved hiatus before launching myself as a consultant to offer independent advice to small- and medium-sized firms. Projects include:

- Consulting for a Floridian high-end women's fashion brand wanting to expand in a market captivated by low-quality, high-ticket import labels.

- Developing a New Media strategy for a well-established ad agency magazine.

- Creating a blueprint for a manufacturing firm to expand through the U.S. using partnership programs in lieu of complex franchise agreements that automatically trigger costly bureaucratic federal and state licensing requirements.

HELPING HANDS OF DOWNTOWN CHICAGO, Treasurer – Finance (Volunteer)   Jan–May 2002

- Reviewed the historical accounting records of the organization and, with the Executive Director, made the required adjustments to improve the quality of financial information maintained by the organization.
- Designed and implemented improved accounting and internal control procedures to provide the organization with more accurate and timely financial information.
- Developed and implemented a training program for new staff members to execute the daily accounting procedures for the organization.

Be Clear about What the Company Does

A short explanation of the company you worked for isn't always necessary and isn't a deal breaker, but some recruiters like to know what the company is about—especially if the company isn't from their industry of specialty or isn't easily recognizable, such as IBM or Deloitte and Touché. If it's a smaller company, an overseas company, or even your own company when you were self-employed, it is a good idea to include a one-line statement about it right under your title line.

Sometimes people put this information in italics to separate it from the rest of the content, which can also be beneficial. It doesn't need to be bolded, as it is not crucial information.

ABC Consulting Company   **1996–1997**
My own consulting firm specializing in health care initiatives; had two full-time employees.

HR Consultant, Happy Company, USA   **Sept 2002 to date**
A management consulting firm employing 20 on staff, with business interests in training and development, leadership development, and management consulting.

General Manager, United Co., United Arab Emirates	December 1995 to May 2000

A $250 million organization, employing 1,500 on staff, with business interests in insurance, retail, distribution, engineering, and chemicals.

The Contents of Your Work Experience

While the first sections of your résumé convey style and message, the actual content is the substance of your résumé. It's where you say not only what you've done, but how it all turned out.

Often résumé writers find this section difficult because they don't generally sit around discussing past work accomplishments with other people. Often this is the "pulling teeth" section—the part you really have to strive to remember, particularly if you've been at a job a long time.

I had a client, Abby, who was in a panic because she needed to get a new job after having the same one for fifteen years. In the last three years the company had shuttered several of its departments and business arms. Where once she had been responsible for a variety of marketing initiatives, her last few years had been spent helping the company stay afloat and move to different offices. She'd blanked out on all her previous accomplishments and could only remember the bare-bones responsibilities she currently had.

It took us two hours of discussion, with me asking probing questions and repeating over and over "What else did you do?" before she remembered what her early years at the company had been like when she'd been a multitasking, highly visible employee. Despite being an advanced species, humans all seem to have short-term memories so remembering all the various components and outcomes of a job takes time and focus.

Once you have the framework for displaying your work history, you then have to decide what to say about what you did at each job. This is where concise descriptions of your work experience need to be professional and comprehensible, and reinforce the profile statement you created.

You know that standard phrase "I was responsible for _____"? It's one of the typical phrases in the résumé handbook—so expected it has become a résumé cliché. But though it gives a sense of your level of expertise or authority, it actually doesn't tell the reader everything they need to know.

"Responsible for" tasks are what you were hired to do. You were obligated to do those tasks or else the employer would have fired you. It is important to know what you were responsible for at your job because that helps the reader understand the scope and depth of your position. Still, nobody's going to pin a medal on you for doing the tasks that were part of your job description when you started.

Demonstrating successes or *accomplishments* offers proof that you did the job well.

Present your work experience in two ways:

1: What you were responsible for—the tasks, jobs, projects, and so forth you did within your overall work
2: What you accomplished—the areas where you were successful at the work you did

See if you can figure out which of these is the accomplishment:
- Successfully developed business objectives and strategies
- Determined profitability and expense budgets
- Consistently exceeded targets by 20%
- New partner relationship development and negotiation
- Identified and leveraged opportunities between partners, internal and external business units
- Development of customer value methodology used to develop successful marketing strategies

If you picked the third statement, you're right. The other statements are responsibilities —big responsibilities to be sure, but nothing a recruiter can be 100 percent sure was done well. Even the ability to exceed targets is muffled because we're not sure which targets are being exceeded.

Also, myriads of résumé writers try to signal that they were successful by using the word itself.
- Successfully completed pet food project
- Took website to successful launch
- I was highly successful in leveraging my customer relationship skills, innovative ideas, technical background, and the engineering resources of the company into long-term volume business

The problem with using the word "successful" is that it is often substituted for the proof of that success. Don't let the reader wonder *how* you were successful. Let them know what that favorable outcome *is*.

How do you do that? Well, for each job you list, particularly the most recent and most applicable to the position you are applying for, you want to think about what the specific measurable results were of your being there.

Some examples of specific measurable results are these:
- Sold $250,000, 15 percent above quota
- Positive customer feedback has resulted in continued attendance of 300+ at company-sponsored conferences

Lots of people hate doing this part, usually because they don't actually think they make a difference, or they assume that the same result would have happened anyway, or that they are bragging if they say a big number. That's just not true. You made an impact at that job because there is no one else in the world like you. Therefore whatever the imprint, it was yours alone. Your job is to figure out what that imprint was, and then speak of it as an accomplishment. Speak the truth—but if you can't remember exactly, say something that you would feel comfortable defending in an interview or confirming with a reference from that company. Your figures may not be exact, but instinctively you know about where the number should be.

Creating the Contents of Your Work Experience

So the first thing to think about is, What did I do? Think back over your time at the job, be it six months or six years. One of the best ways to think about this question is to think about how the job was when you started and then think about how it is now. For instance, when you came on board things might have been a mess, and since then things have straightened out. Did you have anything to do with that? What was the problem you were hired to solve? And how did you solve it?

Think about what you accomplished within the job description, and also think about what you established outside of it. That's where many people have added their true value. They were able to fulfill on their obligations *and* create a whole new filing system. You may be competent at your job, but your real bonus is that you created diversity workshops that are still being held.

Once you begin thinking down this path, the accomplishments usually start popping up. It's a matter of seeing your job with a different eye.

Regional Office Logistics and Development Coordinator, 2001–2003
The Los Angeles Foundation - Media Project

- Coordinated operational logistics in the production of videotaped interviews of historical testimonies.
- Developed computerized tracking system for tracking thousands of videotaped interviews shipped to Los Angeles.
- Utilized computer skills for database maintenance; streamlined office space procedures.

Check out this example. When Motek came in for a session, his résumé was lengthy but didn't offer much depth in terms of success.

Motek had done this particular job a while ago, so I started where I typically start: "What did you do every day?" As he began to explain the job and his role, his memory started working overtime and he began animatedly describing how he was inspired to   create a whole new filing system.

I asked if he had been asked to create a filing system. No, he'd just created it on his own because he realized there was a more efficient way. Did it work? Well, yes, it did and it helped him streamline the office administration because now people put requests for help in a specific place instead of interrupting him all the time.

That led to a discussion of how the office was when he arrived, and what the company's goals were: fifty interviews a week. Were they accomplishing that goal when he arrived? No. Did they meet their goal of completing fifty interviews a week after he got there? Yes, they did. Surprise, surprise (or maybe not, if you listen to how much he liked to organize).

So now we had something to work with.

Regional Office Logistics and Development Coordinator, 2001–2003
The Los Angeles Foundation - Media Project

• Originally hired to coordinate regional interview collection and office administration in the production of videotaped testimonies.
• When hired, the office had goal of 50 interviews a week, but was stuck at about 20.
• Took initiative to organize entire office system from chaos to order by innovating and implementing consistent and key organizational structures.

Accomplishments

• After my arrival and systems implementation, the office began to hit their target of 50 interviews a week, which held over my time at the job.
• I took the initiative to develop a computerized tracking system for tracking thousands of videotaped interviews shipped to Los Angeles; *I never lost a single tape* and my records were better than UPS.
• I utilized computer skills for database maintenance and streamlined office space procedures.
• My innovations were praised by the company President's "right-hand man," who was sent to check on regional office procedures.

Notice the description begins by saying how it was when Motek arrived. This is a way for readers to understand how things changed as a result of you being there. It's like a ministry inside of your content. It doesn't always work, but is a good technique for delivering your work experience.

Notice that we stylistically broke up Motek's responsibilities and accomplishments—for several reasons. It emphasizes the accomplishments, and when applied to several jobs, gives the overall impression of someone who was proficient in many jobs. It also helps the reader to clearly differentiate between the responsibilities and accomplishments. And finally, it helps avoid using a long list of bullets.

Another way to present your work experience is to talk specifically about a main project you worked on and incorporate a sense of what the project was like at the beginning, what you did to change it, and what the results were. Or if you just had one job over a long period, instead of feeling like there's too much white space, dig down further to give a deeper picture of what you did. In the next example, notice how Violetta did just that.

Violetta Pamchenko
Services Coordinator and Events Director

ABC Company   **1998–March 2003**

ABC Co. is a nonprofit organization that matches federal grants with charities and runs several fundraising events throughout the year.

Project Management

[Charity Database]

Responsible for the collection of large database of over 2,000 volunteer questionnaires for research requirements:

- Present process and objectives for approval to senior management team
- Create incentive program for volunteers
- Convince 200 people to participate in forums and complete the questionnaire
- Catalogue and organize data, deliver completed database

Result: The database I created out of this project continues to support ABC executives in determining where money goes more efficiently and has been used as a model to other organizations looking to create something similar.

[Additional Projects]

- Forecast and maintain annual event budget ($250,000.00). Responsible for coordination of logistics, design, and speakers

- Assist in creating new company image (re-brand 1999) new corporate name, repositioning of services and company, updated mission statement, new marketing strategies

- Participate on the core team in defining and implementing service strategies, product branding, and positioning by incorporating specifications, design, distribution, promotion, and channel strategies

Communication

- Participate on cross-functional teams, engineering, sales, investor relations, and marketing departments, often working as liaison between executive charities and marketing

- Research and present new charities and organizations to the executive decision makers

- Write articles for nonprofit magazines and newsletters

- Created and produced content for website, corporate messages, and presentations

Initiation/Leadership
- Initiate enhancement recommendations of existing services to improve usability (website, database, phone response time)

- Identify and rebuild the floundering relationships with some charity reps:

  - Introduced a monthly newsletter
  - Produced support material CD
  - Set up "Let Us Know What You're Thinking" workshops/breakouts at ABC Foundation events to allow for face-to-face contact

- Recruit and manage a Marketing Coordinator

Notice how Violetta had just one job (her first out of school). But by grouping the different aspects of her job, she can expand and draw out more details and successes. Another way to do this is to focus on each job you had within the overall organization.

Finally, you can always write a tight summary of the job experience that puts everything together, leading with your strongest achievement.

Brand Manager – ABC Company   **1999–2003**

Joined a brand under siege from all sides—inferior product, noncompetitive pricing, and poor copy. Gained management alignment to new, revitalized brand vision and led cross-functional team to determine strategies to deliver on this vision.
New product/line extension launches agreed; team reenergized to go out and win.
Recently promoted in position to Brand Manager, and added the Commercial Services Product assignment, doubling total volume and product responsibility.

This likely wasn't the only "win" for the Brand Manager in this example, but it was the most important and influential. We know the status of the project when he started, his successful solutions, his sense of teamwork, and his promotion—which is a specific result that demonstrates his success in the eyes of his company.

Sales accomplishments demonstrate the need to clarify specific measurable results with good context. Always measure your sales against what was expected of you. Although $2 million is an impressive number, it isn't if you were hired to sell a minimum of $4 million. On the other hand, if you were expected to bring in $500,000 in new sales and you brought in $2 million, a recruiter will want to meet with you.

APPETEL TECH WORLDWIDE INC.   *1997–2001*

Account Manager, Northeast Region

Industry-leading vendor of specialized high-end software applications for the film, television, and Internet production industries.

- Integral part of sales team that grew annual revenue from $12M to $20M and increased the customer base from 800 to over 2,250 installed systems.
- Managed hundreds of indirect accounts through a national reseller channel.
- Initiated several successful domestic sales promotions that were critical in achieving regional sales targets and growing the prospect database from 6,000 to 18,000 leads.

WorldTakeover Copiers (1999–2005):

Reporting to the Director of North American Sales in Rochester, NY; started the dealer division for WorldTakeoverCopiers in NJ. The primary objectives were to recruit dealers and develop support programs for the mutual success of WC and its partners. Performance was measured by the number of new clients/dealers recruited and revenues.
Results
- 2000 - 425% of recruitment plan (no revenue plan for 1999)
- 2001 - 250% of recruitment and 132% of revenue plans
- 2002 - 150% of recruitment and 172% of revenue plans
- 2003 - 168% of recruitment and 123% of revenue plans
- 2004 - 158% of recruitment and 102% of revenue plans

Account Management	• Delivered formal presentations, including accompanying visuals, to present customized image solutions to senior-level corporate and hotel executives, resulting in a 95% sell-through rate. • Traveled internationally to consult with clients, prospect new business, and install high-end uniform programs for USD$1.5M/yr portfolio of accounts. • Provided exceptional product knowledge; educated clients on all aspects of product, from latest developments to integral details of manufacture and care. • Managed national and independent accounts through attentive customer service, effective communication, and adept anticipation of future client needs, resulting in every client managed buying additional services from the company.

What to Highlight and What to Leave Out

Here are a few things to consider as you think back over your time at each job and decide what you are going to bring to the attention of the reader.

What Job Am I Going For?

As you create some deeper content for your work experience, you may find yourself with a bigger list than you need. Don't overwhelm the reader with every single thing you've done. Get smart. Use your list to craft a specific résumé for a specific job application, highlighting the things you did that apply to the current posting.

For instance, if you are talking about being an information architect or about human computer interaction, but the job title and description refer to usability—use the word "usability." I once was involved in a recruitment situation where words were everything. IQ Partners had a great candidate for a usability job that crossed our desk. The problem was we didn't know it.

Sasha's most recent job title was "Quality Assurance" and the word "usability" never appeared in her résumé. Her résumé sat in a "maybe" pile until luckily one of us read between the lines and invited her in for an interview. It turns out that she had deep experience as a usability specialist, but her old company didn't call it by that term. We sent her as one of only two people to the client for an interview (after she sent us a new version of her résumé). Sasha got a lucky break that time. But if she had coordinated her wording with ours from the beginning, she would have guaranteed that she wouldn't be missed.

How Long Ago Did I Do It?

If your work experience has for the most part been sequential—that is, you've moved up the responsibility ladder over your last few jobs—the longest content should be found in those first few jobs.

As you get to the back (end) of your résumé and experience, a reader will assume that you were in more junior roles, and therefore you don't need to include every last thing you did. In fact, in those early roles, you might just mention the role and company. In other cases, if you pulled off some really juicy accomplishment, include only one or two lines about that accomplishment. Often the meat of what you do is echoed in your last few jobs. It gets repetitive to see it in every single job description. After covering it in your first one, two or three jobs, let the rest stand in history.

Occasionally, a job you had several years back was the one you loved and wish you could have again. In that case, you may want to reorganize your résumé to a functional first page that emphasizes skills and accomplishments, with a second page showing a chronological outline. Or you can minimize the space the first few jobs take by focusing solely on accomplishments and get that job you loved on page one.

Remember to highlight the aspects of your previous job that fit with the job you're applying for. This may mean rewording it slightly (not lying—just using the terminology that the job description uses) or changing the order of your responsibilities and accomplishments to emphasize the most applicable ones.

Thus, a typical résumé would list your first one to three jobs with some meaty responsibilities and accomplishments, with earlier jobs fading in significance and having one or two lines, or perhaps none at all if they are further back unless something really interesting or compelling happened in one of those jobs.

Is What I Did Something I Like to Do?

Don't emphasize that you did accounting if you hated it. Honestly, even if it's a huge accomplishment and makes you look professional, you are guaranteed that the attention you get will be for the thing you hated. People will just gravitate to your ability to do that part of the job and will want to hire you for it. If you must mention it, don't list it first, second, or even third. Make it a passing mention or you'll keep snagging jobs you never want to do again.

For instance, I had another client who couldn't understand why he kept ending up doing back-end tech support when what he really liked to do was to be out in front in creative development and client relationships. Companies always ended up throwing him a lot of administration and accounting work. In going through his résumé, it seemed that a lot of his early experience was in administration and bookkeeping and he'd referenced it throughout his résumé.

The rule of thumb is *Don't tell them if you don't want to do it again.* Serve your reader a good solid meal by presenting your responsibilities and accomplishments in a clear, digestible style.

Next you'll learn how to flavor that meal with your other accomplishments and skills, with the flourish of personal interests for dessert.

Editing Checklist for Your Work Experience

Presenting Your Work Experience
- o I have organized my work experience with the title or company first and the date to the far right
- o I have decided whether to put title or company first, and I kept it consistent throughout the résumé
- o I haven't used bold, underline, and italic in the same two-line space
- o I have accounted for any gaps in my résumé
- o I have kept my presentation style consistent throughout the résumé
- o I have given a short description of what the company does if I don't think the reader will know of it (and then kept this format consistent for each job)

The Content of Your Work Experience
- o The contents are broken up into eye-pleasing sections
- o There is a balance of responsibilities and accomplishments (the ideal target is three of each), but accomplishments are emphasized
- o Accomplishments include specific measurable results (proof that I did the job successfully)
- o Key phrases and descriptions related to the job I'm applying for are emphasized
- o The parts of jobs I had that were my favorite are also emphasized
- o My most hated aspects of jobs I had are minimized or not present
- o Content descriptions read clearly and coherently
- o I have edited out or minimized discussing work experience that I did long ago, or that is not applicable to the work I'm doing now
- o My work experience does not exceed two pages especially if I am still in the first fifteen years of my working life

CHAPTER 5:

Adding Character and Personality

The final sections of your résumé are where you can further demonstrate character and add a little bit of personality to the process.

These sections can show your versatility, well-roundedness, your smarts, your go-get-it-ness, and your breadth of experience. While your primary aim is to show your expertise, knowledge, and level of involvement in communities and activities that support your learning, growth, and development, you can also mention a few activities that don't directly apply to your current industry or role to show your diversity and adaptability.

A lot of the decisions about what you put in this space will be decided by a few questions.

- **How much room do you have?** If you are creating a one page résumé, or have already gone long on your work experience, now is not the time to tell the reader everything you do. Instead, a few well-chosen items will be best.

- **How many extracurricular activities are you involved in?** Obviously, if you aren't involved in a lot of extras, you don't want to leave lots of room at the end of the résumé for the reader to notice the gap. In that case, keep it short and tight, and emphasize education and some engaging personal interests.

- **What have you already talked about?** If you have already mentioned your languages, computer skills, or published articles earlier in your résumé, don't repeat yourself—unless it is an award, or some other important item or event and you were unable to explain the whole thing or give context to earlier.

- **What does the industry like to see?** Some industries, like computer programming for example, aren't really interested in anything outside of your computer programming knowledge and expertise, whereas industries having interdependent roles, such as marketing or PR or business development, require people who are "out there" and networking in other social circles.

- **What stage of career are you at?** If you are just starting out in the work force, extracurricular activities can boost the experience portion of your résumé and demonstrate that you are active, interested, and engaged in life, which can bode well for a new hire. If you are at a midlevel position and plan to work your way up, mentioning memberships on committees and boards, speaking engagements, and participation on panels will highlight your growing expertise and respect within the community. At senior executive levels, it becomes less important to impress readers— they expect you to be devoting a large portion of your time to your firm, although being on the boards of other organizations speaks highly of your respected position within the community.

- **How far back does your extra experience date?** Most of the time, you want to stay fresh. Anything that ended more than a few years ago isn't crucial or necessary, unless it is an experience that relates specifically to a specific job or company.

Once you've decided how much room you have for this section, you want to think about how to best use your skills, knowledge, and experience to continue to paint a picture of the kind of person you are, and why you are unique and valuable employee. Subtle messages about what you've been doing can emphasize such things as your growing status as an expert, the respect of colleagues, your knowledge of what's happening in your industry, your ability to contribute to others and do good works, and your ability to continue learning out of school.

This section is all about balance, and by weighing all factors, you will find the right balance to suit you.

Getting Started

Here's how to create a thoughtful back section of your résumé.

List Everything You Can Think Of
- Education—degrees, mid degrees, diplomas after high school (unless high school is your most recent experience)
- Conferences you've attended
- Extra training or certifications
- Extra courses you've taken that weren't diploma-oriented
- Awards you've won
- Panels or boards you've sat on or chaired
- Associations you belong to
- Articles you've written or been interviewed for
- Computer programs you know well
- Languages you can speak or read
- Volunteer work you have done (be it for a day or a year)
- Anything else that you've done in your extracurricular life that relates to your career or personal self-development

This write-down-everything approach is important because you'll have to jog your memory to remember all the different things you've done over the years. Writing down one thing will remind you of something else, which will remind you of something else—and before you know it you'll have a much bigger list than you probably need.

Begin Whittling
- Place a star next to the activities and training that most apply to the job you're going for. Those are "must haves" on the list.
- Place a check mark next to the ones that are the most recent, or are your favorites, or show you off as smart or well-rounded. Those are probable ones to add if you have room and you want to emphasize them.
- Cross out anything older than five to seven years ago, unless it is crucial to the upcoming job or is unique or shows you in such an incredible light that you cannot pass it up.

The Back Section

Creating your "Back Section" is like creating the perfect potpourri or assembling the perfect car. You think about what each part says about the whole and you aim to make a statement, establish ability, breadth, and interest without taking up too much room. It's a delicate job, but done right, it should support your initial marketing message on the first page and create a sense of interest about you.

There are times you don't need much of anything in terms of extras, excepting education. Usually this is when your experience is directly related to the role you're applying for, or if you're trying to keep the résumé tight (one page), or the place or role you're applying for is pretty cut and dry and only interested in the work experience.

Build Your Section Headings

You may only have one or two (Education, Personal Interests) or you may have four or five, depending on how much room you have and what you want to highlight. Create clear and definitive sections instead of cramming skills, accomplishments, and courses all under the same heading with a long bulleted list, which loses the impact of diversity.

Education

Education, especially if it's essential to the job, should have its very own section and should appear either right after your work experience or as the last thing before your Personal Interests. Thus the first rule of education is to give it a place of status rather than cram it in with everything else.

The key factors of your education should always appear—the name of the degree or diploma, the place you earned it, and the dates. You also want to add any honors (magna cum laude, dean's list). Depending on the role and its requirements, you may also mention minors, dissertations, and other courses you took—but only as they apply, and without using more than one or two extra lines.

There is no need to put your high school name and diploma on your résumé, unless this is the last and only education that you received, and it is required for the position. College degrees should be offset from other kinds of training. The rule of thumb is that if it took you three or four years to complete, it's important and gets its own section.

If you choose to put other diplomas and certifications under the education heading, make the college degree a little different. People usually do this because their job target is something different from what they studied, as below.

> ### Starting from the Top
>
> In most cases, education should not appear first on your résumé because it makes your résumé look like that of a recent grad. The recent grad tends to put their degree first because it is typically their most applicable experience or best qualification.
>
> The exceptions are if your education *is* your most applicable experience, or if your education is an MBA or other designation that give you an advantage over others applying for the same role.
>
> If it is your most applicable experience (say you are a recent grad or someone making a transition), put only the applicable piece of education at the front. Other training and schooling can be at the end.
>
> One way around having a whole education section take up the top of your résumé is to put abbreviations for your academic degrees beside your name (particularly for MBAs and PhDs) or refer to education in your list of qualifications (for example, "university-educated"). People who read a lot of résumés tend to look automatically to the end of the résumé to find out about your schooling and expect to find it there. So use the beginning of your résumé for the marketing message.

> EDUCATION
> - Professional Financial Planning Course (P.F.P.C)
> - Conducts and Practices Handbook (C.P.H.)
> - Series 7 Securities Course
> - Villanova University, Honors BA: Double Major: Political Science, Social & Cultural Anthropology

Although this person is trying to emphasize their financial training, the organization suggests that a four-year degree is equal to one course. A university degree is important to emphasize if you've got one. Redo to this:

EDUCATION
Villanova University, Honors B.A. 1995
Double Major Political Science, Social & Cultural Anthropology

ADDITIONAL FINANCIAL TRAINING AND CERTIFICATION
• Professional Financial Planning Course, **(P.F.P.C)**
• Conducts and Practices Handbook, **(C.P.H.)**
• Series 7 Course

In the second example, the university degree gets its proper place with the weight on the degree, not on the subject—though employers who want to hire diverse and well-rounded employees will probably appreciate your chosen subject matter. The eye is then drawn separately to the financial training and certification that enhances the message of being a financial person.

Of course, if space is limited you may not be able to create separate headings.

EDUCATION, FINANCIAL TRAINING, AND CERTIFICATION
Villanova University, Honors B.A. 1995
Double Major Political Science, Social & Cultural Anthropology

• Professional Financial Planning Course, **(P.F.P.C)**
• Conducts and Practices Handbook, **(C.P.H.)**
• Series 7 Course

If your education—a particular degree or diploma—is incomplete, you have a few choices. Do you intend to complete it? When? Under education, list with a sense of how much is completed (such as two-thirds complete or 80 percent of coursework completed) and include an expected graduation date.

Education & Professional Development

MScIT, Duke University – approximately 75%, completing Dec 2006
• Novell Certified NetWare Engineer (Novell - 1996)
• Diploma in Digital Electronics Engineering (National Radio Institute, Washington U.S.)
• Radio and TV Electronics Diploma (National Technical Schools, California U.S.)

If you did not complete your schooling, and have no intention of going back, you will have to consider whether to mention that on your résumé. A good recruiter or hiring manager will question you if there is no date of completion, or if the number of years are off, or if something is incomplete about the way you presented the information. If you completed two years of a three-year degree, or you are one credit shy of completion, you may want to say so. Just be prepared to answer questions in your interview about why you didn't complete it. If you were hired before you went to school, or switched majors, or feel you got the full training in your subsequent real-life experience, say so confidently without going into extra detail.

If you only did some of the degree work and the topic or major has little to do with your current job, it might be better not to mention it at all.

If you were educated in another country at a school that may not be familiar to U.S. employers, you may want to give context to your college or university, such as noting that it is one of the top five in its country, or well-known for specializing in your particular discipline. If the school accepts only a small percentage of applicants each year, or if you won some award, be sure to clearly state this. It helps bring the prestige of your background to the reader's attention.

However, you should also try to take some kind of training or certification in the United States. You don't need to be in school for a long time, or full time. But doing so helps dispel the notion that you aren't familiar with U.S. culture and assures the reader you can succeed at a recognizable institution. It may not seem fair (and it isn't, especially when you've spent time and money and hard work to earn your degree(s) already). But it is the way of the world...people value what they know best and speaking to that value is a good way to ease your transition.

Here is a very BAD example of putting *way* too much emphasis on education (yes, this is a real-life example):

Education Is Important

If your schooling is incomplete, consider picking up some sort of diploma or additional certification in the area of work you're interested in. Completing some form of education is a good way of moving past earlier education choices that didn't work out for whatever reason.

However, if you are just not a school person, tighten up your résumé so that the other information is compelling and speaks to your accomplishments. Don't leave a lot of space at the end of the résumé where someone will notice the missing education section. Get the reader interested at the top so that when they get to the end and notice no formal education, it isn't a big deal.

Objective	To gain employment as an Assistant Project Manager.
Education	January 2004 – Small Town USA University • **Working toward the 3-year Bachelor of Management degree** October 2003 – Training America • **Successfully completed a 3-day Humantech training course in ergonomics** October 2003 – Training America • **Successfully completed Six Sigma Green Belt Training** • **Completed a greenbelt/continuous improvement project worth over $250,000.00** June 2003 – Small Town USA Fire Service • **Successfully completed First Aid and C.P.R. training** May 2003 – Small Town USA Program • **Successfully completed Ontario Health and Safety Certification** February 2003 – Small Town USA Program • **CNC Connections 3 day Makino Operation** January 2003 – Small Town USA Program • **Attended ISO/TS 16949:2002 Awareness Training** October 2002 – Small Town USA • **Received W.H.M.I.S. Certification** November 2001 – Attended the U.S. Emergency Preparedness College in ST, USA • **Received Certification for Emergency Public Communication**

June 2001 – Attended the U.S. Emergency Preparedness College in ST, USA
- **Received Certification for Emergency Site Management**

November 2000 – Attended Emergency Measures in Big City, USA
- **Received Certification in Emergency Preparedness and Response**

November 2000 – Small T Fire College
- **Successfully completed Component One of the Firefighter General Level Curriculum**
- **Currently working thru Small Town Fire Service to complete the Curriculum**

May 1997 – Attended the University of CityTown
- **Completed a course in Intermediate Refrigeration Level 2**
- **Successfully completed an apprenticeship for my Operating Engineer Class B Refrigeration from the Technical Standards and Safety Authority of State**

May 1995 – Attended the University of CityTown
- **Completed a course in Basic Refrigeration Level 1**

1991 – Graduated Carter High School in Smalltown, USA
- **Received Secondary School Diploma**

Phew! An exhausting list, no? And what did all that have to do with being a project manager? A subtle skill of résumé writing is in knowing how to edit. Most potential employers don't need to know that a project manager has CPR skills and knows how to fix a refrigerator—unless the project is refrigeration-related. And they certainly don't need to know the amount of detail that fills up the whole first page of the résumé. Even if education was this fireman's only direct experience, it still needs to be tighter and more succinctly written to begin with. Then a case could be made for project management in some of his other roles.

Let's look at a good example that appeared at the end of a professional résumé.

Education/Qualifications

Technical University of Nova Scotia   Halifax, NS, 1990
- Completed two Electrical Engineering Post Graduate courses in machinery control and rotating machinery

Royal Naval Engineering College   Plymouth, UK, 1989
- Applications Course Certificate, with Honors

University of Michigan   Ann Arbor, MI, 1988
- B.Sc., Mechanical Engineering

Also, remember to include in the education section any advanced degrees, such as master's level and above, or schooling you took to receive high-end special designations, such as a CA (Chartered Accountant) designation. If you have more of these, consider creating a separate Special Designations or Other Certifications section.

Other Certifications

Though your formal education may have ended when you left college, you may have otten other kinds of certifications, upgrades, and diplomas since then. Certifications or diplomas affirm your achievements through a recognized and formalized process—you were likely tested, passed the tests, and received the additional training endorsement.

Certifications are important as they can show an ongoing commitment to keeping your skills up-to-date, and bring your training and education in alignment with your current job roles. Therefore, they require a separate section where the reader can clearly absorb your level of training.

If your training is irrelevant to the current role (such as the refrigeration firefighter above), you might want to consider leaving it out. If the extra certification shows an interesting diversity and quietly balances your actual qualifications, including it may provide insight into your multilayered personality or may lead to comfortable chitchat in an interview.

There is subtlety in every choice you make in a résumé—sometimes half the battle is in knowing what to leave out.

Training and Conferences

A few HR people despise the company training and conference lists that most résumé writers include. One such person stated that if the course wasn't actually certified (offering a bona fide diploma or certificate at the end), how could she know what you really got out of it? If you were forced to attend the course, or attended to get a break from work, how could she evaluate its value to your present knowledge?

Often people will load up their résumé with every single course, training day, conference, and event they've ever attended. In this case I agree with our HR representatives—this is overkill.

Think about your training and conference attendance in relation to the position that you are targeting. Also think about how and why you ended up doing these activities. If management asked you personally to attend sessions as a way to grow in your position, mention that. If you were sent to a conference as the company representative, mention that. Give these extras some context that gives them weight. Otherwise, edit the list to a few key items that show you willingly participate in your own continuing learning.

Professional Development

Extensive leadership, technology, project, people, and change management training.
Personal Mastery Executive Management 3 Year Program
- Organizational Development Resources (ODR) Change Management
- Tooling the Partnership – Harvard Business Group
- Quality Assurance Institute – Standards Development Program

---

TRAINING

BellSouth Corporation: Prime Integrator training, Project Management/Management training, Doors training, ABT Workbench training.

EDS: Change Management Training/Problem Management training.

Tulsa Community College: 21 credit hours of Computer Science courses. Major: Mainframe programming languages and operating system.

Prioritize and present your training and conference descriptions in a way that best suits you, your skills and accomplishments, and the position you're going for. Refer to things that apply to the job at hand, for instance, you might have attended a three-day conference on insurance that wasn't crucial but might be nice to add if you are going for a position that requires understanding that industry.

Skills

Another section that can cause some confusion is Skills. "Skills" is a catch-all word that can be applied many different ways, often leaving this section rather vague. If you've created a really good marketable profile—and even without the addition of a Key Qualifications section—you may be able to keep this section short and sweet or leave it off all together.

Skills sections can be defined very differently by different people. It may be helpful to think of skills in one of three ways: personality, knowledge, and functional skills. Personality skills are *how* you do things ("cheerful," "hard-working"). Knowledge skills are things you *know* or have to learn ("Microsoft Word," "French"). Functional skills are things you *do* ("program networks," "rewire a house," "lead a campaign"). You may not need to list personality skills, especially if you've written some personality into your profile, but you may want to think of the knowledge and functional skills needed for the role and how you might represent them in this section.

Don't let your skills section become a dumping ground for all the miscellaneous things that you can do so that it becomes impossible for the reader to distinguish your computer skills from your languages and your ability to rope a steer. If you find that your skills list is getting too long and diverse for one section, consider splitting them into their own sections (Applicable Skills, Additional Skills, Computer Skills, Relevant Skills, and so forth).

Computer programs or computer skills section

Because more and more jobs these days require some modicum of comfort and familiarity with computers, most résumés make some sort of reference to computers.

Most employers assume that you will have some knowledge of computers. Thus, you really don't need to say on your résumé that you are concerned about your basic computer skills or that you are computer competent. This is particularly true for roles that do not mention computer skills, or where the computer is just another aspect or tool of the job, not its focus.

Excel, Adobe Acrobat, and PowerPoint are slightly more complex programs that have basic and sophisticated users. If you are a sophisticated user of one of these programs, let potential employers know that as it might be a bonus. But, if it is not specifically required by the job, and you're only a basic user, don't mention it.

At the next level computer programs become even more complex, entailing development in different directions, such as knowledge of database programs or visual programs like Photoshop. Usually, a job description will state whether this is a necessary qualification. In this case, mention your familiarity with these types of programs to demonstrate your skill set.

If you can program computers, it's worth mentioning—even if that is not what the job is about. Your computer knowledge and ability can become something that makes you unique—you can market the product *and* communicate with the tech people in their own language.

Here is one employer pet peeve regarding computer skills on résumés: if you can program Java, and you put that skill under the same category as knowing how to use Microsoft Outlook, it just diminishes one and makes the other look silly. Separate them into different categories—or even better, trust that readers will make the leap that a Java programmer can probably send an email.

Finally, if your computer skills are essential to the job, you may want to put them in Key Qualifications on the first page. If you are in the technology world, your computer skills are your ticket to the job. Tech recruiters tend to read your list of computer skills first. They'll look at your breadth and depth of skills (as well as how up-to-date they are) and the number of years you've had the skills, and will use this information to determine where to place you in the ever-growing spectrum of technology roles. Therefore listing your computer skills in a clearly, detailed, and organized manner on the first page is essential.

Computer Phobic?

If you are one of those people who avoid computers because you missed the whole computer revolution, or fear that if you ever use a computer you will press a button that blows the thing up or erases everything it doesn't have to be that way. There are many ways to get basic training without spending any serious dough.

- Check your local library or look for community education classes—often they offer free or low-cost tutorials
- Some computers or server companies offer free online tutorials (some are stored in your own computer as part of the set-up package)
- Ask a friend who knows about computers and is patient enough to walk through the basics with you

COMPUTER SKILLS
Languages: JavaScript, VBScript, CGI, ASP, HTML, Visual BASIC, Pascal, COBOL, JCL, UNIX, PL/I, SQL, Ada, XML, XSL.
Software Tools: Doors (Requirement Management Tool), PARTS, MS FrontPage, Visual InterDev, Access, Project 98, Microsoft Office 2000, SAS, SABRE, Object Manager, Adobe PhotoShop, TSO, Visio, ORACLE E-business Suite 11i, Microsoft Site Server.
Operating Systems: OS390, Windows, UNIX, VMS, TPX, CICS, DOS.

CERTIFICATION
Project Management Professional (PMP), Project Management Institute (PMI), July 2001; Certified Internet Webmaster (CIW).

or

SKILLS: **DFA Manage; HTML; CorelDraw; Photo Paint; Internet; Interactive Research Tools**

or

Highlights
• 12 years clerical experience, type 50 w.p.m.
• Proficiency in the use of various software programs including, but not limited to: Quicken, Excel, FrontPage, Adobe PhotoShop, PaintshopPro, Lotus 1-2-3, MS Office, and a general tendency to learn to use new software very quickly
• Patience and a propensity for training others

Languages

Having a firm grasp of an extra language or two is a way of both demonstrating intelligence and having a unique additional qualification. Few job opportunities will be won or lost on whether or not you can speak Mandarin Chinese, but there are others in which it might become a vital factor in the hiring decision, such as if your target company does work with China.

If you are comfortable in a second language, it is an excellent idea to target jobs that either absolutely require that language or those where it gives you an edge, since it narrows the market of available hires. Think about where and with whom you will have an advantage. For instance, target global companies or those who work with specific countries or trade with wholesalers who speak your language.

If English is not your native language, you need to be careful about how you present your language capabilities. People who speak English and who also know a few other languages usually don't mention their knowledge of English on their résumé. That's assumed. Therefore, hiring managers are quick to pick up on people who put "Languages: English, French, Chinese" or "Languages: English (fluent), Korean (fluent)" on their résumés because it tips them off that the other language is likely the native language.

Unfortunately, the tip-off of your native language may create a bias or raise a concern in the mind of a potential employer, as a big issue is whether new hires can communicate well. If you were educated in another country, and your name is difficult for English speakers to say, it may be important to include other hints that you are comfortable in English, such as including your English name (Sivasankar "Joseph" Ramachandran), or training received in the United States. Highlighting your fluency in another language may actually work against you here.

Volunteer Work

Listing some of your volunteer work is a nice way of demonstrating your interest in your community, and a balance to your work life. You might help coach children, be a Big Brother or Sister, run or walk a marathon for breast cancer, or any number of other things.

If you do specific work for the community that relates to your career, such as providing free accounting services to a community center when you're a CA, this becomes a great lead off.

If you volunteer a lot, or are involved in multiple activities, you may want to edit your list—not that your contributions aren't valuable or important, but it always seems a little strange when the volunteer section seems deeper and longer than the work experience. Aim for about three lines of volunteer work, and see if you can combine some of them, such as heading charity marathons, and give a few examples instead of listing all twelve.

When volunteer work is your work experience

Occasionally, recent grads or people in career transition find that their applicable experience for the role is volunteer experience. For instance, you may have designed and programmed a website for someone for free, or you may have worked a cash register at your local charity's bazaar, and that's what kind of role you hoped to apply for. Everyone tells you to get volunteer experience when you want to make a change, but how does that work on a résumé?

Surprisingly well, actually. The first thing is to value your volunteer experience as work experience. It is work experience—the only thing missing is the paycheck. Label your work experience as "Relevant Work Experience," and you can include your volunteer experience off the top. Don't relegate your best stuff to the end where one usually finds volunteer experience! Treat it like work experience, while noting its volunteer capacity. Remember to include results and accomplishments to lend weight to your experience. You can also gain references from these volunteer experiences.

Here's an example from someone who is looking to become a physical educator. This was on her first page, right after her one earlier paid teaching experience:

Relevant School-Related Teaching and Learning Experiences:

Volunteer Program:
State University, New York   Spring 2002–2003
Volunteered in preparing informational booklets for the Help Hot Zone.
Participated and observed new teaching strategies and concepts, along with creative ideas for physical education.

Internship:
 New York – Easy Street Middle School   2003–Present
• Participant and observer for 25 hours in a secondary physical education setting.
• Progressed from taking attendance and leading warm-up activities to teaching the class.

Service Elementary – Third grade math tutor   Summer 2000
• Worked with students one-on-one who were having difficulty in specific math areas.
• Accumulated 30 hours of tutoring; two hours daily.

Observations:
• Visited several schools, including the Jingleschmidt School in Anytown, New York to observe autistic, learning disabled, and handicapped students in a physical setting and in the classroom.
• Observed several other schools and analyzed classroom dynamics, motivational techniques, diversity, classroom management, student feedback, etc.

City of Anytown Department of Public Safety: Violence Protection Program Spring 2001
• Volunteer tutored troubled students in Philadelphia.
• Worked with students in a drug-infested area coping with problems concerning school related & non-school related issues.

Committees, associations, boards, and other memberships

Other excellent additions to your volunteer activities are memberships and participation in associations relevant to your discipline and industry. Even if you only attend an occasional event or meeting, being a member shows your interest in learning and mingling within your community, and hints to the employer that you might come with a full-fledge network of potential contacts and resources. At the very least, it demonstrates a long-term commitment to the path you've chosen.

That sense of commitment becomes stronger as you become more involved. If you belong on a committee in one of these associations or groups, or better yet have demonstrated leadership by chairing a committee, this furthers the notion that you are someone who is interested in leading and changing your industry. Or you may sit on a board. A board is something you are invited to join, and speaks to the community's respect for your experience, input, and wisdom.

While it is good to have some of these positions on your résumé, employers will become suspicious if your list of memberships, associations, and committees takes over the second half of your résumé. They want to know you will have the time and energy to focus on their job and their company, not be flitting about with too many other responsibilities elsewhere. Therefore be sure to present only the most essential and applicable memberships and positions.

Teaching Classes, Speaking, or Publications

You may do other activities that further demonstrate your expertise in your field. Teaching classes, speaking to groups, or publishing papers are all ways that establish comfort, familiarity, and respect for your ability. While they are unlikely to win you the job, noting them on your résumé will help to underscore your learning about, commitment to, and development of your subject matter.

Again, if teaching, speaking, and writing aren't your primary job responsibilities (that is, you're not an academic) don't overload your résumé with all the titles of your papers or the name of every conference you've spoken at. Pick the most lauded or the most applicable to the job you're applying for and mention them "among others."

Awards

It never fails to amaze me how often people panic during their résumé writing process and forget to mention in their accomplishments the special awards they've won. This is particularly true of sales people, call center people, and those who tend to achieve their quotas regularly and forget all the recognition they've received for doing this.

Have you ever been Employee of the Month? Have you ever been specially recognized by your peers? Have you worked a job where quotas were measured in weekly, monthly, or yearly awards? Have you been singled out in some other way by your manager or employer?

You may have also won awards outside of work, perhaps at an industry function or during your school years. Awards are always relevant, as they are a concrete way of establishing the impression that you're "top of the pack."

Remember to give awards their proper context so that the reader understands the significance. Saying you won the company "High Merit Award" is nice, but it is better if you can say "High Merit Award—yearly award given to three out of three hundred employees judged by management to have contributed the most to company morale and reputation."

Early Work History or Additional Accomplishments

There are almost as many permutations of what you might have accomplished in life as there are résumés. Remember to evaluate all your accomplishments, skills, and abilities and then pick the most significant and specific job-related ones for your résumé. If you are unsure of how to best categorize an accomplishment, you can create a small section called Additional Accomplishments.

As for Early Work History, create this category if you want to demonstrate or cover your early work history but you don't want to make it part of the more formal work experience.

Previous Work Experience at a Glance

Sales and Marketing – 1980–1986
Various positions held with ABC Communications, Mail Corporation, the Touring Travel Group, Anytown Board of Education.

Education and Travel – 1973–1980
Working traveler for two years in Australia and New Zealand.
High school teacher and coach for Anytown and NearAnytown Boards of Education.

Personal Interests

Nobody gives much thought to the "Personal Interests" section. We just get there and if there's room at the very end—before we stick that old tired saw "References on Request"—we throw in a line or two about our hobbies, usually a laundry list of activities. It starts to sound a little bit like a personal ad: "Loves walks, running, reading, golf, rowing . . . sunset on the beach, walks in the rain." It's strange, but our most personal and passionate activities fall into boring recitations on the typical résumé. Our life becomes a cliché.

Hobbies: Running, golf, tennis, reading, movies, sports
Personal Interests: Outdoor activities, reading, movies, friends
Extracurricular: Folding laundry, watching paint dry, making me sound boring

---

This section is where a lot of résumés could become invigorated, by adding a last final touch of personality and humanistic connection before the reader decides who you are and whether or not to call you. This section could even be the difference between the reader simply assessing your résumé and qualifications or warming to you as a fellow human being. This shift is very simply done. Once again, it's about digging a bit deeper and saying something more specific so that it sounds real and authentic instead of like you tossed it off just before you hit send on your computer.

Bookend Your Résumé with Personality

Use your personal interests section to continue the theme of "being real." Don't end with "References on Request" but with something of curiosity, interest, or playfulness.

This section shouldn't be longer than a line or two. With some forethought, you can make your Personal Interests more interesting to read. Is your golf score good enough to mention? What kind of books do you read? Do you do something fun or exciting regularly or travel somewhere on a yearly basis?

Use specific statements to give insight into who you are as a person (Interests: Read an average of two books a week, 500 hundred books a year, especially Stephen King). Another angle is to think about what you are in the process of doing ("Taking piano lessons") or would like to accomplish this year ("Have just volunteered as a Big Brother").

Here are some examples of a few of the ways that people have shared their personal interests and free time activities:

Interests and Activities
• Sundance Film Festival Devotee—25 films a year (and about the same number of lattes)
• Long Distance Running—London (England) Marathon, Buffalo (USA) Marathon, four half-marathons
• Improvisational Workshops

> **Adventures:**
> Former member of The HappyFeats – the highest grossing club band in Anytown two years running (1990, 1991).
> Attended dozens of toy expositions including the granddaddy of them all—The New York Toy Fair—researching potential in-packs for cereal promotions.
> Burnt the soles of my feet walking inside an active volcano in Saint Lucia, bettered shortly thereafter by going deep-sea fishing and catching a prize-winning…sunburn.

Activities	
Organizations	• Member of: AIMX, Chamber of Commerce
Recreation	• Sports: Running, Golf, Camping, Kung Fu
Hobbies	• All things design

Sometimes the trick is to keep it simple, with just one point of interest.

> **PASSIONS**
> My dog Friday, digging in the garden, reading anything from *Paris 1919* to cookbooks

People just love the thought of a dog named Friday. Don't ask me why, but this person gets asked about her dog in almost every interview. And she loves her dog, so when she gets asked about him, her face lights up and she gets comfortable with the interviewer. Sometimes personal interests helps you feel comfortable or excited in a conversation as much as it helps the interviewer catch a glimpse of you.

> **EXTRACURRICULAR:**
> Before having children – golf, squash, hiking, skiing, watching videos once
> After having children – building forts, fake karate, drawing stick people, watching the same Disney video 35 times.

That example never fails to win a smile, or in the case of other parents, a full on laugh. And that makes you human, likeable, and someone they just have to meet.

So don't write off your personal interests—you never know when someone else will have run the same marathon or seen the same movie twenty times. Let your humanity make you a "must-meet" person.

Putting It All Together

Making sure you've got the "best of the rest" at the end of your résumé is as much about judging how much space you have and weighing that against what you want to say. You've done many amazing things in your jobs, but maybe it's best to whet the appetite with some solid winners and back them up with a strong, well-rounded learning and active life. Or maybe you'd rather keep the focus on your work, and keep the extracurricular activities to the bare minimum.

Remember—there is no magic formula for these sections, there is only what feels right to you in relation to the role you're aiming for.

Editing Checklist

Education and Other Extracurricular Accomplishments

o I have thought of every single thing I've done outside of work for the last ten years

o I have starred my favorites or the accomplishments I am most proud of

o I have thought through each one, assessing its applicability to the current position

o I have given education and training a special section or place of status

o I have balanced elements that apply to the job and those that show breadth

o I haven't included every little thing, but have thought about why each one is there

o I haven't let my accomplishments and extras create extra résumé pages—I've worked with the space I have

Personal Interests and Activities

o I feel comfortable adding something personal to my résumé

o I said something more specific about my interests, goals, and activities that makes this section feel a little more human

o I ran the "funny bits" past a friend or two for their reaction and edited what didn't work

o My Personal Interests section does not dominate my résumé and takes no more than four lines

o The interests I've mentioned are truthful, and show me in a good light

CHAPTER 6:

Targeted Job Searches

Now that you have a good version of your résumé together, you need to think about how to use your résumé to assist you in a targeted search—that is, a search for a specific role.

If you've been in one role for a significant period of time, or have been building on a role to make a linear progression and you intend to target a similar role, creating that kind of résumé—if you follow the guidelines of earlier chapters—is pretty straightforward.

But what do you do if:

- You want a particular job very badly and will do anything that puts you ahead of the pack?
- You are targeting a new job, one that differs in a minor to major way from any previous work experience?

That's when you need to think about creating a targeted résumé or a career transition résumé.

A *targeted résumé* is one that is particularly designed to "speak" to a specific role, résumé reader, or company. For the sake of clarification, consider that all résumés in this chapter are targeted résumés aimed toward a particular job or role. The role may be different from what the person is currently doing, but is supported by what they currently do. In Chapter 7 I will look at career transition résumés for more dramatic career changes.

Going the Extra Distance—Targeted Job Approach

The targeted search goes the extra distance to speak to a specific employer. I'm going to get right into providing some examples.

Going the Extra Distance—Preity's Story

The first story is about an applicant who was already pretty qualified for the job, but who went the extra distance in the interview to nail the offer and put herself in front as the lead candidate. It is an excellent example of a specific, targeted search that allowed a determined person in one career stream to leap into a smaller, warmer atmosphere where she felt she could make a lasting impression.

Preity spent most of her working life in a university setting. She originally enjoyed the atmosphere, and was glad to have had the opportunity to cut her "real working world teeth" there. But for the last year, she had begun to find the job less meaningful. Preity went back to the campus because it was familiar and because she'd been offered a good role, but something was missing. What she really wanted was something with similar responsibilities but in a different environment. The university was so big and sprawling, and the politics so convoluted that she longed to be somewhere that she could make a difference daily.

The job she targeted was at an elite private girls' school. Here's an abbreviated job description.

Position: Associate Director, Advancement Services

Reports to: Director of Advancement

Scope/Accountability:
The Associate Director, Advancement Services is accountable for the quality of Lord Edward's Advancement's database and the Office's ability to track and extract fundraising and friend-raising information. The Associate Director, Advancement Services plays a key role in the overall success of the school's Advancement program.

Purpose:
The Associate Director, Advancement Services
• Manages the service operations of the Advancement Office
• Directs and manages the electronic and hard-copy information support services necessary for successful fundraising, friend-raising, and communications programs at Lord Edward's Hall. The incumbent is responsible for understanding and meeting the information needs of Advancement colleagues, senior administration, and key volunteers through the maintenance and effective manipulation of a well-integrated database.
• Participates in a variety of broad Advancement initiatives including market research and records retention management.
• Performs duties in accordance with the mission and values of the school and works in a manner that will enhance the activities of the entire Advancement function.

Key areas of responsibility:
• Assumes primary responsibility for the management and upkeep of Lord Edward Hall's in-house Advancement database—The Raiser's Edge—maintaining security and field definition; creating new campaign, fund, and appeal codes; data entry and manipulation; report generation and the establishment of key business rules.
• Supervises the client service operations of the Advancement Office including, but not limited to, payment of bills, budget reports, office policies and procedures, storage of files and materials, reception.

Education and Experience:
• University Degree or College Degree relating to Information Management, Library Science, or Systems Analysis
• Working knowledge of Raiser's Edge software
• Proven database management skills
• Demonstrated ability and experience in office management
• Proven experience in managing and maintaining a relational database
• Demonstrated understanding of institutional advancement
• Proven experience managing staff

Relevant Skills and Attributes:
• Excellent computer and communication skills
• Understanding of the processes of fund development
• Strong attention to detail
• Strong interpersonal skills and service orientation
• Ability to organize and prioritize work, deal with interruptions, and manage several tasks simultaneously
• Resourcefulness
• Tact, diplomacy, and discretion
• Ability to successfully work in a team environment

As you can see, the description contains a lot of job elements, and applicants need to read it closely several times (on top of which, this is a shorter version). Preity created her résumé to suit the application, and highlighted her comfort with databases and managing multiple projects.

PREITY ZINTA

2300 Dublin Road, Unit 210 Boston, MA 10101 (617) 555-1212 priety@email.com

PROFILE

A dedicated professional who excels at developing and implementing business strategies, displays entrepreneurial and leadership skills in project management, demonstrates initiative in effectively managing human resources for multiple projects, and is proficient in program assessment and development.

CAREER EXPERIENCE

Project Manager – Records & Database Management   **2003 to 2004**
Division of University Advancement, University of Anytown

Accountabilities
• Develop project charter, scope for records and database (SAP) projects, assemble a project team, assign and track tasks while adhering to the critical path
Achievements
• Identified database processes that would have a negative effect on revenue generation (fundraising capacity) and implemented a solution

Project Manager – Retail Division   **2001 to 2003**
Super Display Inc.

Accountabilities
• Manage budget for retail division – over $3 million annually
• Manage nationwide programs for major retailers including *The Box, Big Store and Sports Inc*
Achievements
• Doubled sales in retail division in first year
• Successfully implemented expansion project to the Southern United States

Assistant Manager, Alumni and Gift Records   **2000 to 2001**
Advancement Services, Development and University Relations, University of Anytown

Accountabilities
• Oversaw integrity of all financial data in the donor database (SAP), production of receipts and acknowledgement letters, monitor all outstanding pledges
• Create user and business specifications to enhance database modules and features
• Define and re-engineer business processes to improve office efficiency
• Manage full-time staff of twelve and part-time call center
Achievements
• Implemented custom database modules for donor recognition and pledge management
• Established policies, standards, and procedures related to finance and customer service

Donor Services Coordinator   **1999 to 2000**
Development and University Relations, University of Anytown

Accountabilities
• Determine the parameters and priorities needed for developing donor services plans and support systems. Identify optimum results; develop ways and means to achieve targets
• Manage projects in donor recognition, such as *The National Report*
• Supervise 3 staff members
Achievements
• Created and managed a department dedicated to serving donor needs
• Implemented database modifications and upgrades to provide better service to the donor

PREITY ZINTA – PAGE 2

ADDITIONAL EXPERIENCE

Donor Services Representative
Development and University Relations, University of Anytown

Donations Management Clerk
Development and University Relations, University of Anytown

EDUCATION

Bachelor of Arts – Administrative and Commercial Studies
The University of State, Anytown, USA
• Recipient of the Merit Scholar Award

PROFESSIONAL DEVELOPMENT

Descartes University – Continuing Education Division
• Fundamentals of Project Management

University of Anytown - Derrida School of Management Executive Development Programs
• Project Management

Council for Advancement and Support of Education (CASE)
• Summer Institute in Advancement Services

University of Anytown Staff Development
• Leadership for Managers and Supervisors
• Great Customer Service
• Advancing into Management (AIM)

RELEVANT SKILLS

Computer
• Strong command of Development/Fundraising Databases, SAP Finance (FI), and Development
        Information Systems (DIS)
• Microsoft Word, Excel, PowerPoint, Outlook, Microsoft Project, Visio

Languages
• Fluent in English and French (verbal and written)

The résumé helped her get an interview. However, where most people stop preparing anything other than answers to questions, Preity went a step further. She created a special document that she took with her to the interview.

In this document Preity took apart their job description, looked for the key elements—the deal breakers—and slotted her experience under the different headings she'd created. She wanted to make it really easy for them to see how qualified she was. The document not only did that, but also demonstrated her deep interest in and commitment to getting the job.

Preity did another thing to show her preparedness for this particular job. The one major strike against her was that she had never used the database specified in the job description. Rather than hope it wouldn't matter, she took the extra step of getting a friend at another private school to help her out. He set her up with the person in an equivalent position at his school where they used the same database. This contact spent two hours with Preity talking about the job and showing her the database.

In the interview, Preity mentioned her research as well as offered the expanded résumé pitch she'd prepared. The school representatives were very impressed. It was further proof that this candidate was the one they were looking for. Preity practically received a job offer during the interview—the best kind of feedback.

The only problem? Taking the job would be a major pay cut. Though Preity had learned the importance of doing things that make herself happy, the cut was too big. But luckily, as the far-and-away lead candidate, Preity had lots of room to negotiate. School representatives raised the salary figure up $10,000 more than their original offer, which Preity knew was very difficult for them to do. But this action showed her how committed they were to her needs. Preity also got an extra two weeks vacation and a nice title. She took the job.

Now she's in a work environment that is committed to her success and where she can command certain authority and respect she didn't have before. And on top of it all, she enjoys her work! Taking extra steps to target your search and show your commitment can pay off.

The Recent Grad Becomes Desirable—Mary Jane's Story

Perhaps you're a recent grad who is trying to figure out how to be taken seriously in the real world after having only jobs that helped pay school bills rather than advance careers.

Trying to get that first full-time job that will potentially lead somewhere you want to go can be confusing and frustrating. One of the first steps you can take is to narrow your ideas of where you want to be to a specific industry or role. That way you can create a targeted résumé and also pursue extra classes, courses, and extracurricular activities to support that direction.

Let's take the case of Mary Jane. She came to me in that year after graduation when she was trying to make the leap from the jobs she'd done as medical receptionist (mostly for her dad) to a job that would have more potential future career opportunities.

Mary Jane brought me a résumé containing the usual list of various disconnected jobs that almost everyone has around at age twenty-four and asked how she could improve it for her dream job as a pharmaceutical sales rep.

Pharmaceutical sales is an attractive option after college—it has great compensation, decent training, you can start right out of school, and it's a great way to get experience in sales. However, these great reasons are exactly why available roles are highly sought after—and not just anybody gets them.

I asked her what she knew about pharmaceutical sales and was surprised to hear her say, "Quite a bit, actually." Having been the point of first contact for many of such people since first working as a medical receptionist, Mary Jane was well versed in what a pharmaceutical salesperson does and knew firsthand what the best approaches are for getting a busy receptionist to convince a busier doctor to find time to hear a pitch.

So that's what we worked on with her résumé—drawing out the idea that she was the perfect pharmaceutical sales candidate because she knew from the other side what worked best.

On top of that, I encouraged her to put in a little humor and personality—not only would this be a valuable characteristic in a salesperson, it's a great technique for recent graduates who need to get a recruiter's attention to get that coveted first break. We also minimized jobs that didn't apply to the role she was targeting, focusing instead on giving one specific accomplishment that happened while she was there.

MARY JANE SULLIVAN

*123 Lake St. * Cleveland, OH * (216) 555-1212* MJS@email.com*

> **The Perfect Pharmaceutical Salesperson**
> I've worked medical reception since the age of thirteen and have an intimate knowledge of doctors, pharmaceutical products, and all the tricks for getting past reception.
> I am also very comfortable with product promotion, customer service selling, and I am highly motivated to succeed.

PERSONAL CHARACTERISTICS

- University-educated and results-oriented
- Pleasant, friendly, and professional appearance
- Well-organized and hardworking
- Have worked with over 15 doctors in past 10 years

EDUCATION

University of Any State West B.A.   2003

WORK EXPERIENCE

Dr. Alan Almos and Partners   Sept. 2003–Present
Receptionist/Office Manager   Mount Holly, NJ

Walk in everyday with phones ringing off the hook and ill, annoyed patients wanting to see the doctor. Day consists of putting patients in rooms, weighing babies, testing urine, booking specialists, handling insurance companies, lawyers and pharmacies, OHIP billing, ordering, and deflecting pharmaceutical salespeople.

All handled with excellent multitasking and communications skills, big coffee, and a smile. Known as "The Lollipop Lady" by all the children and their mothers.

Anytown District School Board   May 2003–Sept. 2003
Accounting Assistant   Laurel Springs, NJ

Reported directly to the Manager of Accounting. Maintenance of the general ledger and preparation of accounting statements. Took initiative on special projects and learned new tax filing system before anyone else in the office.

Livingston Hunt & Country Club   Jul. 2002–Oct. 2002
Tennis Program Coordinator   Livingston, NJ

Coordinated tennis tournaments and games for club members, and tennis pro shop sales.
Arranged various special events for club members, such as the "Country Club Triathlon" a full day event of tennis, golf, and skeet shooting.

The Day's End   Nov 2001–April 2003
Server   Laurel Springs, NJ

Manager would regularly create incentive contests to get rid of a particular stock
and whoever sold the most won. I won these contests on many occasions.
Invited to be on promotions teams.

The Donaugh Hotel   May 2001 – August 2001
Bar & Restaurant Assistant   Dublin, Ireland
Family Physicians Walk In Clinic   Dec. 2000 – May
2001 *Receptionist*   Laurel Springs, NJ

Various Doctor's Office (intermittent and as summer job) 1993 - 2000
Receptionist   Mount Holly, NJ

OTHER SKILLS

- Fast and accurate typing skills, 60+ wpm.
- Received Smart Serve Certification.
- Proficient in many software applications including, but not limited to: Windows 95, 2000 &
  XP, Microsoft Office Programs including Word, Excel, PowerPoint, Access, Outlook,
  various SAP based database systems, and miscellaneous fax and scanning software.

ACTIVITIES

- Member of Pi Beta Phi Sorority at the University of Any State West
- Assisted with the organization of the 2002 New Member Recruitment for the sorority
  system at the University of Any State West.

INTERESTS

Love reading good narrative fiction, history, and current events. Don't like running on the treadmill
but do it anyway. Enjoy my friends and family and mother my four younger siblings.

The best part about this résumé is that after Mary Jane did the hard work of putting it together, she had a great résumé that got her interviews and she was well prepared to answer questions at those interviews. Preparing a good targeted résumé will ensure that you can answers questions like, "Why do you want to be in pharmaceutical sales?" and "What makes you think you'll succeed?" with ease and aplomb.

And in what will be a recurring theme throughout this chapter, Mary Jane did more than prepare a great résumé. She job shadowed with other pharmaceutical sales reps. She signed up for an exam that someone would usually take after joining a company. And best of all, on her own initiative she created a survey and sent it out to doctors to find out what they liked and didn't like about pharmaceutical sales reps. She brought those results to her interview and discussed how she learned that doctors don't like to be sold as much as informed.

Mary Jane won the position over several other candidates, including one with extensive previous experience and another applying from within the company.

Score another one for a targeted résumé and a targeted search!

Targeting an Interim Job during a Career Transition

There's another thing that happens on our way to an ideal job—we have to get a different job while making our dream job happen. Nora hadn't quite decided on her dream job yet—it was either to open a cheese shop or to start a closet organizing business—but she knew that a career change was going to be part of her future.

The only problem was that after a six-month sabbatical break from her crazy, high-pressure sales jobs, Nora still wasn't quite ready to start a business. It was time to get working again, but at the same time, she didn't want to work in the environments she'd previously been in.

Nora wanted to work with a company that had a product or service she admired. She decided it would be less stressful to be in a call center environment but focus more on the customer service aspect, although it could have a sales element. Nora targeted a job with a locally based television/cable/telephone company that was taking on the larger competitors with excellent service and pricing. Since she'd had a good experience with them as a customer, she felt that she could well represent them as an employee and the role was providing solution-oriented customer service and product sales. This became the job she focused on while writing her résumé.

Nora had two résumés, both two pages long, and each highlighting different accomplishments. When looking at them we decided to bring all the important bits together, and tighten the résumé to one page with strongly positioned accomplishments and an emphasized message of exceptional customer service, while quietly down-playing her early years in administration.

Nora Lee

123 Learning St., Unit 415, Anytown, USA, 10101 Phone: (999) 555-1212, E-mail: noralee@email.com

CUSTOMER SERVICE & SALES REPRESENTIVE

Customer service and sales professional with 7+ years in a call center environment.
An award-winning, go-the-distance employee who puts customer relationship above all else.

PROFESSIONAL EXPERIENCE

Sabbatical   Travel, time with family construction business, contract work   **April 2005–present**

Sales and Marketing Representative, QUIVER ELECTRONICS INC.   **Feb 2001–March 2005**
I provided inbound sales, customer service, billing, & technical support for an electronics distribution company. I sourced electronic components for various large and small manufacturing companies as well as R&D clients. I responded to all customer inquiries through email, fax, and phone for pricing and delivery.

Accomplishments
- Nominated by peers for "Fabled Service" award in 2002 & 2003 and won in 2003
- Awarded Employee of the Month in 2003 (for top sales and on time delivery)
- Achieved Top 10 Performer in 2002 out of 65 Sales Reps
- Finished out 2002 with 110% average (percentage to plan)
- Hit or exceeded monthly targets 44 of 48 months
- Manager sat 15–20 new people with me to show them the ropes

Customer Service Representative, ECOM NET   **1997–2001**
At this Internet service provider I was a customer retention specialist and in charge of improvement in our customer service. Our goal was to reduce turnover during a difficult period of this company's history.

Accomplishments
- Closed $875,000 in new business, upgrades, and renewals in 2000
- Monthly reviews started off well; improved over time as I consistently met or exceeded expectations
- Management sat new people with me on their first training day
- Received extensive training in high-end internet technology; able to "talk" the language
- Favorite Accomplishment: Calmed and supported a customer with no password access to her files. She emailed our company President her praise, who then forwarded it to upper management as an example.

Inside Sales Representative, INTER-STAR COMMUNICATIONS   **1995–1997**
Presented line of Internet based products to prospective clients. Provided customer service to clients. Qualified high-end business customers. Trained staff in new procedures, billing, and Internet technologies.

Accomplishments
- Top sales rep in 1996 and 1997
- Consistently exceeded established sales quotas
- Management asked me to train new staff in sales, billing procedure, and Internet Technology
- Contributed to development of customer service through writing modules for the training manual on how to handle special calls and irate customers
- On liaison committee to our head office and reported to them at weekly virtual meetings

EDUCATION
CAPISTRANO COLLEGE (Stenography), 1991–1992, **STATE COMMUNITY COLLEGE** (Photography), 1987–1988, **STATE UNIVERSITY** (completed three years towards BA Political Science) 1985–1987

TRAINING
Courses: Excelling at Excel, Extensive Customer Service and Sales Training, Administrators at Work

PERSONAL INTERESTS
Making the bride look good as a wedding photographer; Teaching piano to adults and children; Traveling to Massachusetts, Connecticut, New York City, Vermont, Ottawa, Montreal visiting friends (two of whom were former customers)

Tourland and Co.

Dear Mr. Wiseman,

I am sending you my resume for consideration as a Tour Escort. Sy Martinez, a former Tourland Tour Escort, has emailed you as a way of introduction. While my official background has been as a theater director, you will see that my time has been largely spent traveling the world. Sy has spoken often about the rewarding experience he had leading tours with Tourland Holidays and his enthusiasm has rubbed off. Now that I am at a stage in my career where I am seeking diversity and change, combining my love of travel with my leadership skills is a welcomed thought. I see being a Tour Escort as an excellent part-time compliment to my theater life.

I have a broad base of skills that I believe would be applicable at Tourland, specifically:

1. Travel Experience:
- *Independent traveling for years.* My first European adventure was a three-month backpack tour when I was twenty-three. I am currently thirty-six years old. I've been in Europe many times since. I've schooled and worked out west for many years including three wonderful summers at the Mountain School of Fine Arts.
- *Self-guided research trips to exotic locals.* I have traveled as a way of researching and preparing for plays. It's the best way to discover a place and come away with a real sense of the people and history. This I then pass on to the artists involved in realizing the play.
- *Touring a concert series* to over forty cities throughout North America and Asia. From the Kennedy Centre, to Roy Thompson Hall, to the Petronas Towers Concert Hall in Malaysia I have adapted the concert series to each unique venue and symphony organization.

2. Leadership:
- *Directing actors* through my vision of the play is the central undertaking of any production. At the Big Theater Festival, for example, the scale is enormous. It is my responsibility to inspire those about me through joy, laughter, and assured direction.
- *Managing productions.* Alongside the creative development are the responsibilities of budgets that reach into the hundreds of thousands, schedules (there is always an opening night!) and to lead the production without constant supervision. I am given a play and expected to produce a production within clear and strict guidelines.

I look forward to speaking with you regarding the possibility of being a Tour Escort for Tourland Holidays. I am confident about my ability to provide the detailed leadership required. I am excited by the possibility of sharing my love of travel with your trusted members.

Thank you for your consideration. I will follow up with you later this week.

Sincerely,

Michael Romero

Nora had such good, specific, measurable results that it was really unnecessary to spend a lot of time talking about her responsibilities or job tasks. Once the role had been explained, she got right into her accomplishments that demonstrated success on the job. We took a risk in eliminating several earlier years of administration work since often readers like to see the whole length of the career, but when targeting a specific role with such applicable experience, we were confident that there would be enough to bring her in for an interview.

We were right. Nora sent the résumé to her preferred role, and also another company with a similar role. Where previous to this résumé similar applications took longer get a response or not at all, both companies called back within two weeks. She got an offer at not only her targeted role, but at the other as well.

If your experience is direct, and the role you're going for is well clarified, get right to the point in your résumé and demonstrate success through strong accomplishments. Notice how Nora's résumé sends the same consistent message of good customer relationships from the Profile to the Personal Interests.

This résumé is a great example of how to handle experience that doesn't quite match your current goals.

Targeting a Completely Different Job (Without Letting Go of Your Old One)—Michael's Story

Michael had been a theater director during his entire career. His dream of becoming a director had started at a young age and had never wavered through high school, through getting a Fine Arts degree at a university, and through further education as a Master of Fine Arts with a specialty in direction. After winning awards, directing plays at well-known festivals, and being chosen to direct new works as an honor by top playwrights, Michael felt he was doing well in his chosen field.

Still, even for the best theater directing can be a feast-or-famine job. Part of the year involves intensely prepping a play. It opens to, hopefully, standing ovations and thunderous applause. And then the play continues to run, but the director's job is over. And Michael was back to waiting around for the next opportunity. It made for a lot of downtime.

In that downtime, Michael—the man of laser-career focus—began to wonder what else is out there. Was theater always going to be the only thing for him?

So he decided to try something different, something he could do during the "down" periods of directing. He made his mind up to follow another passion—travel—with the idea of becoming a tour guide.

Now how on earth does a director of the lofty stage start leading twenty tourists with cameras and nametags across the great cities of Europe?

Why, he directs them of course.

No, really. Michael loved the idea of becoming a tour guide. After asking around among the people he knew, he found a high-level connection to a travel company that he decided to approach. He prepared a targeted résumé and cover letter that focused on the skills he already had that he felt would be essential to leading a tour.

Notice how Michael's résumé carefully echoes the themes and skills he's focused on in his cover letter. He keeps travel first, since that's a key aspect of the job, but also highlights his leadership experience, because leading a tour is all about keeping a disparate group of people together over a fairly intense period of time, keeping them well organized, and making sure they all get out of the trip what they came for.

When Michael got around to sending his pitch and talking to the man who ran the company, it turned out that Tourland had just started considering the possibility of creating a special theatrical tour that would take in well-known theaters and their history, as well as provide last-minute tickets to the hottest productions in New York and London. Tourland had just been discussing the need for a theater person to lead that tour.

And who better to help them research, create, and—of course—lead that trip than a renown artist and director?

That's right. Michael's pitch was in synergy with Tourland's goals and opportunities. Tourland gave him the job to design tours in four different theater locales and hot spots, and then trained him to lead those tours. Thanks to his targeted approach, Michael now has an alternate form of work to balance his up-and-down artistic life.

MICHAEL ROMERO

7th Ave, Apt 404, NY, NY   212-555-1234
mromero@email.net

TRAVEL EXPERIENCE:

• Tour Director
Six years experience touring an International Concert Series. Duties included onsite tour coordination, leading rehearsals with fifty piece orchestras and running performances in large venues. Tour cities included: Kuala Lumpur, Detroit, Seattle, Washington, Oklahoma City, Long Beach, Ft. Lauderdale, Jacksonville, Minneapolis, Atlanta, Salt Lake City, Denver, Boulder, Phoenix, Charleston, Long Island, Vancouver, Edmonton, Calgary, Winnipeg, Halifax, and Toronto.

• Research Trips
In order to better understand plays that I am directing, I create my own research trips. A few examples: For the premiere production of ITALIA that I directed at the Art Place in Bigtown, I traveled the countryside of Tuscany and Vinci. OF MICE AND MEN (produced at the Colony Theater and Premiere Theater Centre) took me to the Salinas Valley, California. The play CLOSER took me to London, England. For the romantic French play, S.S. TENACITY, I traveled around Northern France and researched Calvados, chocolate, and wine.

• Personal Travel
In 1992 I backpacked through Europe. For three months I journeyed from London to Greece and all the countries in between. I expanded my Kuala Lumpur concert trip to include Thailand and Hong Kong. I recently celebrated a Costa Rica Christmas.

• Freelance Work
I have spent a month or longer directing theater productions in cities across the U.S., from New York to Los Angeles and many places in between.

THEATER EXPERIENCE:

• Theater Director
For the past eight years I have been a Freelance Professional Director working across the U.S. Directing includes the hiring of the actors and design team, formulating a directing concept, and implementing this concept through rehearsals and meetings.

• BigName Festival and the BiggerName Festival
My directing career began as a directing Intern at the BiggerName Festival. I returned there every year for six seasons. I have spent three seasons directing main stage productions at the BigName Festival. One example: THE SCARLET PIMPERNEL, set in Paris and surrounding countryside, was comprised of a cast of thirty and a running crew of twenty for its nightly performances. The production budget was nearly two million dollars. One hundred thousand people saw it. From initiation to execution, this project took a year to realize.

• Group of Six Artist Retreat
In 2002 I created an annual retreat for artists. Six artists are invited for a conference where I lead them through a weekend designed to encourage and regenerate their talents. Participants have shown increased productivity and enthusiasm as a direct relation to their participation in the conference.

EDUCATION:

• Masters of Fine Arts Degree, 1993   State University
• Bachelor of Fine Arts Degree, 1990   FarState University

AWARDS:

• Two-time nominee for Best Direction, **Lucan Award**.
• Awarded a **Silverado Award** for Best Direction of a play.
• Listed in **Who's Who** Annual Publication.

In all of these examples, ensuring that the résumé was targeted to a particular job helped convince hirers that they were looking at the right person. Once you put the effort into creating a targeted résumé, you too will notice the "extra" distance you can go to facilitate landing the job. Focusing on what you want helps bring a kind of synergy to your search. The clearer and more specific you are about what you want, the easier it is for the rest of the world to see you as the perfect, unique candidate.

So take charge of your job search: decide where you want to work, create a targeted résumé and message to speak to that company or role—and then go for it.

CHAPTER 7:

Moving toward a Full Career Transition

Wonderful synergy, as described in the previous chapter, does happen all the time in career and job searches. And yet, for a lot of people, nothing is more difficult in their worklife than a career transition. Every career stage has its challenges. In the beginning, you have no substantial experience; in the growth period, you're looking to increase your responsibilities and salary; and in the later years, you have to come to terms with how far you've gotten and what you need to do next to move into retirement and beyond.

But a career transition—moving from one established career to another completely different one—is often the most difficult of stages. One of the main reasons is that you already need and expect to receive a certain salary and are familiar with a certain level of responsibility and authority. Nobody ever wants to go backwards. It feels impossible to approach a job with the innocence of a recent grad, especially when you know how much time it takes to build respect in a new industry. And yet often in a transition you will be asked, if not to go back to the beginning, at least to pay your dues and prove yourself all over again at something different.

The career transition stage is also the most challenging because it's unknown. You don't have the same networks and contacts, you don't know the ins and outs or culture norms or the language of the industry. You don't have the direct experience to back up your claim that you can do it. There are so many unknowns, the biggest of which are personal: *Can* I do it? Is it *really* possible? Our own self-doubt and lack of focus creates the most problems in a career transition.

Yes, It Is Possible!

Despite the challenges, an effective career transition is possible. Better yet, successful and fruitful career transitions happen all the time. I know a woman who was fifty-eight years old when she decided to go back to law school—she made partner by age sixty-five.

So whether you choose a career transition or it is thrust upon you, take a deep breath—and tell yourself that not only is this transition possible, it will be a very good transition indeed.

In fact, lots of great examples of career transition résumés and the stories behind them prove beyond a doubt that if one is focused, prepared, and patient, a career transition can be easier than you think.

Before I Get to the Résumés

In a truly effective career transition, it is your behavior, not your résumé, that ultimately makes the transition happen. This principle holds true for other job searches, but doubly so for career transitions.

That's because career transitions rely on your knowing what you want, speaking that message clearly to others, and getting out there and meeting people in a position to help you make a transition happen. Your résumé can help reassure the people you meet about your past successes, but only you can convince them that you are up to the challenge of bringing that success into a whole new area.

In the stories and résumés in this chapter, I'll emphasize how the person behind the résumé also actively went out and targeted the new role, and networked to find support and confidence when approaching potential employers. So don't just look at the résumés. Take the time to learn from all of the activities and behaviors of the following examples.

The Career Transition Résumé

One of the biggest stumbling blocks in a career transition is a résumé. In the past, your résumé format started with A, which led to B, which led to C—but now it's going to veer off wildly to Z, or perhaps even to six to the power of nine. Thus your traditional and much beloved chronological résumé will have every reader seeing that your last job was animal hospital receptionist, not marketing specialist.

Some of the worst cases of career transition blues I have diagnosed were rooted in bad résumé planning. In an early example, I found myself on a local cable TV show speaking about careers. This station had a mandate to help the community by providing volunteer roles for people so that they could gain experience in the field to get a job. One such volunteer, a young woman, came up to me after the show and expressed her frustration. She said she'd been volunteering at the station for almost two years but had never been hired properly by another show or station. She smiled bitterly as she handed me her résumé and asked if I could help.

In looking at it, the first thing I saw was "Work Experience—waiter—3 years, admin 2 years" and so forth. I turned over to the second page and noticed a small note under volunteer work about her cable volunteer work.

Relevant Work Experience

Relevant work experience can happen anytime during your life, whether or not it was long-term or you got paid for it. It might have been an internship, a job shadowing, volunteer work, an extra course, or a mock project. The point is that if it connects in some way to what you want to be doing, it needs to be on your résumé in a conspicuous place. Anything that will get the words and concepts of the industry to your front page is good.

And to avoid confusion, use a heading such as "Relevant Work Experience" or even "Relevant Experience." Under it you can list past jobs and volunteer work. And remember, the stronger your front page message is, the better.

I said, "Tell me all the roles you've played here." She described seven different skill sets and roles from teleprompter to b-roll editor. "There's your problem," I said. "Your very best experience is buried on the back page where no one can see it. What you need to do is put all of these things on the first page." Her face lit up, and she got it. She finally had permission to put her volunteer work in the spotlight.

Poorly positioning relevant experience is just one of the ways to hamper a job search. A career transition requires that you be smart, persistent, patient, and active. It also means crafting a résumé that speaks to your targeted new industry as much as possible.

The career transition résumé is entirely different animal from the normal résumé. The normal résumé—particularly a chronological one—assumes that you have make a linear progression through your career. A career transition is nonlinear. Thus, the chronological résumé is not necessarily for you.

The Degrees of Change

I'm going to look at a few career transition searches and accompanying résumés. A smaller degree of change is much easier, because you can pull instances from your current and past experience to create a résumé that echoes the key qualifications required, despite your actual job titles or previous specialties.

Sometimes your transition will be from one side of the work to another—for example, from being the client to servicing the client, or from getting a pitch behind the desk to giving the pitch in front of the desk.

In such instances, you can "speak the language" of your targeted role or industry better than someone coming in from the outside. Using that knowledge of language and required experience can help convince the reader that you deserve a shot at the position.

An entrepreneur's career transition presentation is always a bit tricky. When you've been responsible for everything, you likely have a vast range of experience and qualifications. However, targeting a specific job means narrowing your focus and presenting depth instead of breadth. The good news is that more than one job option is likely available.

Finally, there's the quantum leap of going from one job to another that's so different it makes for a great story in *People* magazine. These changes often take the most courage, but are by far the most fun. Usually when a person decides to make a 180-degree turn, it's because they've decided to follow a new passion or latent dream.

Take a moment to think about your career transition.

- How big a leap are you making? How much of your previous experience will remain relevant?
- What skills do you have that will apply in a new situation?
- What successes do you have under your belt that will demonstrate your ability to be a success in a whole new field?

This reflection will help you to determine how much emphasis your résumé will have, and how much more research you have to do to understand where you're heading. The more you know about the new industry, the better you'll be able to find potential contacts, talk sensibly to them, and feel confident about making the change and doing what you say you can.

Let's start by looking at a few résumés that "speak" the language of the new industry in varying degrees of change.

I Speak the Language of Advertising—Patrick's Story

Patrick came to me as a client because he was very discouraged about his industry. Filmmaking in his city had taken some hard hits due to politics, bad press, and tightened advertising budgets.

Patrick had produced commercials for ad agencies and their clients for several years. He'd worked for some big-name brands and in conjunction with several different agencies over the years. Though he was on the delivery side of the business, Patrick was well aware of what happened on the creative (client) side, having sat in on many meetings.

So when he came to me, he had made a choice. He was tired of trying to make a better product with a smaller budget; he was tired of working with other grumpy filmmakers competing for the same dollar. And he wanted to move into a more traditional career now that he was getting married. It was time to make a change by flipping to the advertising side of the table.

His challenge was, among other things, to get the notoriously hierarchical ad world to see him as an account manager despite his nontraditional beginnings. Now you may be thinking—the guy's worked with clients, he knows the process of client management, he knows how to create and deliver a product, he even understands the brand—why wouldn't they take him seriously? Well, some fields and industries do like people to start at the beginning and work their way up, and the ad agency world is one of them.

Patrick needed a résumé that would echo the language of the ad world and play up his knowledge of these areas, while playing down the words "film" and "producer." His biggest leap was to say that he was an "account manager" in the profile.

His role as a film producer was much like that of an account manager—it just had a different title. Patrick could argue that he had mastered an account manager's responsibilities and the title was semantics. If he could make the case for those skills and responsibilities, he needed say so right up front so there was no distraction from his job target and no mistaking who he was or what he wanted. If you want to use this tactic, you have to be ready and willing to persuasively argue why this title holds true. The title holds so long as people buy into it, given your experience.

Patrick O'Brien

320 Carew St., Anytown, AZ 85009   602.555.7129   pobrien@patrickobrien.com

PROFILE

An **Account Manager** with strong, effective, result-oriented skills and the proven ability to create, plan, develop, and execute complex projects on strategy, on budget, and on time.

A broad and diverse production and advertising background that has produced memorable television commercials, award winning music videos, successful "high end" corporate videos, and lead-generating direct response television advertisements.

CORE SKILLS

• Outstanding client skills effective in developing trust and respect; able to disarm the most difficult of client over strategic conflict and budget issues with a pragmatic, amiable resolve.

• Proactive project manager with strong strategic, execution, and trouble shooting abilities; able to plan ahead and meet unexpected challenges with innate resourcefulness and pragmatic creative solutions.

• Supportive "hands-on" management style that keeps team motivated, focused, and effective.

• Dedicated to creative excellence, going above and beyond to achieve and maintain the creative integrity and strategy of the project.

WORK EXPERIENCE

CREATE INC.   April '03–June '04
ACCOUNT MANAGER/SENIOR CREATIVE PRODUCER
Create Inc. is a fully integrated, multi-disciplined creative house offering marketing, advertising, and business communication services for both corporate and commercial clients.

• Client lead on high-profile accounts for Content Communications, I-Talk, I-Talk Mobility, and Bray-Zdybel Financial.
• Managed projects from developing the creative strategy to execution, to ensure the product effectively delivered to the client's business objective.
• Accountable for managing the client budget, as well as Create's revenue.
• Hired, managed, and negotiated freelance production/post-production crew, talent, and suppliers.

ACCOMPLISHMENTS
• Initiated and secured $125,000 worth of repeated business to the company in 8 months.
• Made profit on top of mark up on each and every job.
• Consistently delivered all projects on strategy, on budget, and with quick turnaround.
• Instrumental key player in Create's re-branding including redesign of logo, identity, and corporate message; creative "retooling" of printed sales packages, demo reels, and company website currently still being used by the company.

FREELANCE PRODUCER/PROD. MANAGER/COORDINATOR May '00–Present
VARIOUS COMPANIES - Television Commercials/Music Videos/Corporate Videos
Project manager, responsible for acting as production company's representative and liaison between director, agency, and client to execute an approved advertising concept.

Produced commercials and projects for Radio Inc, Flag Foods, Toyota, OLGC, Pizza Hut, Bud Light, Optimum Online, Hanes, Quaker Oats, G.E. Financial, EMI Canada, BMG Music, and Universal Records to name a few.

• Manage budgets ranging from $30K to $600K, actualize costs, and reconcile overages
• Actively involved in the creative decisions and logistics regarding editorial, talent, art department, wardrobe, hair, and make up, and post-production elements.
• Ensure all production elements/departments, the director's, agencies', and clients' requests and concerns have been addressed on strategy on schedule and within production budget.
• Hire, manage, and negotiate key production staff position talent and supplier rates.

ACCOMPLISHMENTS
• Consistently delivered projects on time & on budget, 95% made profit above markup.
• Won and nominated several MTV Music Video Awards for music videos I produced.
• Facilitated and managed large productions with U.S. production companies, crews, agencies, clients, and talent.

CALL TO ACTION LTD. Nov. 1998–March 2000
PRODUCER/DIRECTOR/WRITER/HEAD OF PRODUCTION
An Anytown based marketing and production company focusing on direct response television commercials primarily for the American market.

• Produced both long and short form, lead-generating direct response and retail television commercials.
• Involved in creative decisions on all projects; consulted with client over creative matters.
• Wrote and edited copy/scripts/job awarding proposals/treatments.
• Directed testimonials, product shots, and insert (b-roll) footage.
• Responsible for all production and post-production; developing and managing budgets, hiring and negotiating crew supplier and shoot day operations, logistics, and schedules.

EDUCATION

State College, 1992 - Bachelor of Arts Degree – Political Science Major
R.T.T.R., 1995 - Bachelor of Applied Arts Degree – Radio & Television Arts
Institute of Advertising, 2000 - Introduction to Advertising

OTHER ACTIVITIES, INTERESTING FACTS, AND INTERESTS

🖝 Produced two independent Films: ***Clown Therapy*, Dancing Monkey Productions and *Anderson*, Femur Films**: *Clown Therapy* debuted at the Boston Short Film Festival. *Anderson* made its debut on a chilly February night at the Flin Flon Film Festival. Since then, both films have been in other obscure film festivals around the planet.

On my own time, I have been known to read a book, take a picture, catch a flick, rock out, write witty prose, sauté, flambé, and frappe (not necessarily in that order) and, every so often, strand myself on some obscure island on some obscure lake in the middle of State Main Park.

Patrick used this résumé and his good humor and charm to talk to everyone on the advertising side of the business that he knew or had met in his years of film production. He stuck to it and landed a six-month account management contract. That's a great start—a chance to prove himself in a company with a potential for more work. And if it doesn't pan out, he's now got direct account management experience to put on his résumé. The more he builds his actual experience in advertising account management, the more he can minimize his previous work in film on his résumé.

Aiming for the Brand Manager Role—Tiandra's Story

Tiandra liked new challenges. Her work background went from banking to broadcasting to music, most recently in the role of a project manager. She felt it was time to round out her business experience. She wanted to broaden her focus, and she was most interested in becoming a brand manager—a role that encompassed the creative aspects of marketing with finance, strategy, and execution.

Though others thought this might be a difficult career transition, brand manager is a role that most business people envision moving toward in a linear fashion, so Tiandra wasn't worried. She made her target associate or assistant brand manager, figuring the best way to achieve her ultimate goal would be to gain the additional experience needed under someone already in the role.

So rather than starting to apply for roles with her project management-focused résumé, Tiandra began meeting with HR people and, more importantly, brand marketing managers—the position she hoped to eventually have one day. In meeting with marketing managers, she asked for an informational interview, that is, she went in without trying to get a job, and instead asked for feedback on what they were looking for in a candidate. She looked at the feedback from two levels. She wanted to clarify what being a brand manager all about so she would have a clear picture of her goal and move confidently in the right direction. And she asked a lot of questions about what they would be looking for in a candidate.

Tiandra got lots of résumé feedback.

Here is the résumé she ultimately used.

TIANDRA LOPEZ, MBA
57 Sage Gate, Seattle, WA, 98105
(206) 555-9799   tiandra.lopez@email.com

POSITIONING STATEMENT:
To packaged goods companies, Tiandra Lopez is the Assistant Brand Manager that can successfully develop and execute plans in order to achieve business objectives due to her focus, determination, solid communication skills, creativity, and strong leadership.

EDUCATION:

Master of Business Administration, Aristole School of Business, Windfarm University   **Apr 2001**
• Brand Management, Marketing Communications, Consumer Behavior, Direct Marketing, Strategic Management, Finance, Accounting, Economics, Business Law, Arts & Media

Bachelor of Commerce, Fred Hegel School of Business, Nietzsche University   **Jun 1996**
• Marketing and Business courses as above, plus Organizational Behavior, Human Resources Management, Psychology, Sociology, Critical Thinking, Anthropology

KEY ACCOMPLISHMENTS:

Co-Marketing Project Manager (Television)   **June 2002 to Present**
Sing-a-long Entertainment Inc.
• PROMOTIONS & ADVERTISING: Lead cross-functional teams through the execution of co-marketing campaigns for Z *Network*, *OLT, PTV,* and *HORROR*. Manage the production and evaluation of promotional and brand creative, branded content, product placement, and contest management.
• DEVELOPMENT OF PLANS: Apply consumer insights to develop strategies and tactics for aligning clients' brands with network properties. Generated $100,000 in incremental revenue in Fiscal '04.
• INNOVATION: Continue to find unique and exciting ways to break through ad clutter by developing rich product integration initiatives that speak directly to clients' target demographics.

Manager, Content Development & Marketing   **May 2001 to Apr 2002**
Faith Broadcasting Company
• MARKETING RESEARCH: Designed, executed, and analyzed market research to support product development. Provided recommendations to senior staff, resulting in improved product features.
• EVENT/CONTENT PRODUCTION: Managed online events, promotions, and content for the music, film, and sports categories, including concept development, coordination of digital video shoots (on-location and in-studio), copywriting, artist contract negotiations, and client management.

Assistant to the President   **May 1998 to Aug 1999**
Big Bad Music Canada
• EFFICIENCY: Developed reports and presentations on behalf of senior executives, streamlined information, and managed the day-to-day effectiveness of the president's office.

Lead Customer Service Officer/Investment Specialist   **Jul 1996 to May 1998**
ET Bank Financial Group
• MANAGING DIRECT REPORTS: Managed 6 Customer Service Officers, including the monitoring of sales objectives, training and development requirements, and handling escalated customer concerns.
• SALES PROMOTION: Developed a promotional campaign targeting Anytown-area students to attract new business and retain current clients, resulting in 112 new accounts, 179 new VISA applications.

Marketing Communications Support   **Summers – 1993 to 1996**
Rutherford-Deans *(formerly Sweeneyhouse Inc.)*
• PERFORMANCE: Received "Making a Difference Award" for contributions to a special project.
• TRADE MARKETING: Created and distributed corporate marketing materials and product literature to support sales initiatives.

COMPUTER SKILLS: Excel, PowerPoint; Adobe Photoshop; SalesLogix

VOLUNTEER/INTERNSHIPS:
• Aristotle School of Business, Arts & Media MBA: Guest Speaker, Mentor   Oct 2002 to Present
• American Breast Cancer Foundation: Organizing Committee, "Run for the Cure"   Jul 2001 to Oct 2002
• Theater "Extravaganza": Marketing Assistant (Internship)   May 2000 to Aug 2000
• Party On Music Conference & Festival: Asst. Volunteer Coordinator/Team Leader   Apr 1998 to Jun 2000

Tiandra's résumé was targeted directly to the people who would hire an assistant brand manager position—and she knew that because she'd spoken with them directly. She needed to take two more steps to prepare for an interview. She began to focus on specific companies, and she spoke to friends who had been in marketing interviews to determine the kinds of questions they'd been asked.

In her research and preparation, Tiandra discovered an online job bank and marketing community website that posted roles specifically for marketing. It wasn't one of the big ones, in fact, it was little known outside the marketing community. But she found a posting there for a job that sounded like exactly what she was looking for.

She sent her résumé in on Sunday, and got a call on Monday. After a short phone interview Tiandra was invited in for a more formal interview. After a few interviews, they offered her the position.

Tiandra told me with some surprise that she got the job "quite easily." Her homework prepared her to answer those interview questions and it showed. When someone has connected and committed to a very specific job path, and has done the proper preparation beforehand, an actual job search can happen quite easily.

Some of the biggest leaps don't have to seem that big if the right approach and attitude are taken. We'll see this in our last two stories of career transition.

A Résumé of Success—Guy's Story

In the previous story, Tiandra dreamed of becoming a brand manager. This story is about a brand manager who wanted to be something completely different. Where Tiandra was extremely excited about getting closer to her goal, Guy felt like one more day as a brand manager was one day closer to being dead. He'd loved it, he'd done it, he was done.

He'd gone through a year-long process of self-discovery, and almost to his surprise, realized he was ready to pursue a long-shelved dream of on-air journalism. With this goal firmly set, Guy took a few more months at his job to plan, and then quit. He intended to spend the summer preparing and researching his new job choice. His goal was to start at an amazing new job in broadcasting within the next three months.

He had wisely decided on specific niche within television journalism—business. By choosing business reporting Guy could lean on his work history, and could also refine the parameters of his search to a narrow focus. Instead of eliminating opportunities, this strategy actually helped him send a powerful message to his friends, community, and others he met, keeping them as focused and clear as he was on his goal.

Coming from the world of packaged goods and a very structured methodology, Guy approached his job search as a "Guy Marketing Campaign"—looking at himself much in the way he would a jar of mustard or a tube of toothpaste. He planned his campaign, he planned his strategy, and then he worked them both to a positive outcome.

Here's a sample of his objectives and strategies midsummer:

Guy Nashman – Career in Broadcast Journalism

Objective	Strategies	Action Plans
Find an amazing new job in broadcasting the next three months. **Focus: Reporting on Business News because of interest and perspective**	1. Understand the industry via networking, informational interviewing, and research.	(1)~~Develop industry networking sheet~~ (2)Develop probe areas for informational interviews (3)Make appointments to talk with people (4)Read industry books (ie. Fresh Air) (5)Go online to check out websites (6)Join Journalists Association
	2. Generate story ideas.	(1)~~Read the major newspapers; business sections~~ (2)~~Watch the news every day~~ (3)~~Sign up for cable~~ (4)Set up time with people to talk ideas and 'focus' (5)Set up broadcasting binder
	3. Improve relevant skills.	(1)~~Read 'Writing for Broadcast News'~~ (2)~~Take Broadcast Performance course~~ (3)~~Take Writing for Broadcast course~~ (4)Do writing tests with feedback
	4. Leverage other life experience.	(1)Think through 'fit' with business type programs (2)Re-presence business skills via review of 'Strategy/Marketing' mags (3)Review basic Macro Economic policies (4)Review "hot advertising"
	5. Create supportive community and buy-in for my goals.	(1)~~Share goals with friends/family~~ (2)Determine structure with career coach (Peter) (3)Develop 'conditions of satisfaction' for job (4)~~Get complete with former job and colleagues~~ (5)~~Get prepped for new financial situation~~

Guy's outline of goals and objectives also had columns for timing and current status so he could track the results of each strategy.

Over that summer he watched a lot of business television shows and made lists of producers' names and shows that interested him. He put the word out that he was looking for anyone who knew anyone connected to television who could help him achieve his goals.

He created a networking grid to support this step.

Networking Grid

Network	Contact	Conduit	Timing	Status
DDN	Tina J.	Rajat	Tues 4pm	Meeting set
DBD	TBD	Sally P.		Call in with Sally
DBD(N)	(Tim Donaugh's producer)	Abby	This week	Abby looking up name and getting back to me
NKB	TBD	Sylvia B.		
Bloomberg	TBD	Salvador G.		
Fox	TBD	TBD		

But before he could officially start his networking process, Guy needed a résumé. We started by talking through the objectives of the résumé. First, he needed to emphasize a background understanding of television where there wasn't much. We spent a lot of time thinking about how to do that and what he might put down from all his experiences.

During our conversation, however, we hit on the real purpose for the résumé. In effect, it would be part of his sales pitch about why he felt he could be a success in television. And the pitch was this: "Here is this successful guy—he's exceeded expectations everywhere he's worked and succeeded at everything he's put his hand to. Now he wants to be in television where he will be just as successful." His résumé needed to be a track record of success, a document that said, "Even with no extensive TV background you want me anyway."

This is what we came up with:

GUY NASHMAN

203 Curson St., Los Angeles 90018   Tel: 323-555-9659   email: GNashman@email.com

BROADCASTING EXPERIENCE:

- **Reporter/Anchor - Studio E - The Einstein's University Television Show**
Four years experience writing, reporting, anchoring, and editing the weekly half hour cable TV show.

- **Voice-over Work - Big Packaged Goods Co.**
Voiced marketing videos and pilot TV advertising.

- **Broadcasting Training - Aristotle's School of Radio and Television Arts**
Workshops in Broadcast Performance and Writing for Radio and Television.

BUSINESS EXPERIENCE - BIG PACKAGED GOODS CO.:

- **Brand Manager - Special Facial Tissue**
Accountable for volume and profit on the business. Developed a new marketing strategy for this ailing brand and led the cross-functional team to deliver it. Managed the training and careers of four direct reports. Met aggressive deadlines and worked well under significant pressure from senior management.

- **Assistant Brand Manager - Tighty White Diapers**
Led the launch of New "Tighty White Night" - from the product concept to the marketing plan. Awarded "Best Initiative" for 1996 at BPGC Canada with shipments up 20% and profit up 40%. Learned to gather data, analyze it quickly, smell out the critical issues, and draw conclusions.

- **Account Executive - Sturge Distributing Account**
Developed productive relationships under adverse conditions and delivered excellent results. Volume at Sturge, the largest independent wholesaler in the province, increased 17% to $17 million in one year under my control.

- **Leader of the design and rollout of Diversity Training**
Developed a solid understanding of controversial workplace issues and found a way to facilitate productive discussions that moved the dialogue forward in a very conservative environment. With the rollout of this program to all 3,000 employees, I oversaw 30 facilitators at 7 sites across the U.S. Scores for the two-day course averaged 4.5/5.0 and were among the highest in U.S. company history.

EDUCATION:

- Einstein's University: Anytown Honors Bachelor of Commerce 1993.
- Institut de Gestion de Rennes: Rennes, France International Exchange Student 1992.

ACTIVITIES AND INTERESTS:

- *Tour Escort* - Led up-market tours all over the world for Sunset Holidays.
- *Personal Travel* - Eastern and Western Europe, Australia, New Zealand, and Central America.
- *Volunteer Work* - Counselor on Peer Support Phone Line; Coach for Leadership Training courses.
- *Long distance running* - Three marathons; five half marathons over the past three years.
- *Sundance Film Festival Devotee* - 25 films in one week every year.
- *Improvisational Workshops - Second City.* Beginning level four of six levels.
- *Live Theater* - Fan of musical theater, the Fringe, and the classics.

Dear Ali,

As background to our conversation this morning, attached is a copy of my resume. You can see from a quick scan that I spent four years writing, reporting, and anchoring at Studio E, the Einstein's University television show. For the next five years I worked in Marketing at Big Packaged Goods Co. (BPGC). I am now looking to combine my Broadcast Journalism experience with my Business experience and return to Television.

I have a broad base of skills that I believe would be applicable at World of News Business, specifically:

1. **Experience thinking through complex business issues.**
   - Retained BPGC responsibility as Brand Manager of a $60 million business.
   - Cut through mountains of consumer and market data to develop actionable strategies at BPGC.
   - Facilitated BPGC's 'Strategic Methods of Communication' course for three years.
   - Achieved academic excellence at one of the best business schools in the country.

2. **Writing that is clear and engaging:**
   - Writing and editing news stories for Studio E.
   - Formal Broadcast Writing training at Ryerson's School of Radio and Television Arts.
   - Researching and writing insightful and succinct business documents for BPGC.

3. **Communicating ideas powerfully:**
   - Reporting/anchoring for Studio E.
   - Leading Sales presentations at BPGC's top customers.
   - Speaking to groups of people on the tours that I led all over the world for Sunset Holidays.

I have an extensive business background. I write well. And I am an effective communicator. I look forward to talking with you further about how I could make use of these fundamentals skills at WNB.

Sincerely,

Guy Nashman

We also created a cover letter that outlined a chosen path to journalism with extensive experience in business.

Here are the results of Guy's preparation. He started with a few names of people in the industry he could contact who were friends or contacts of his friends. One of those people gave him the name of three producers of business television shows. He met with each of them.

One of these producers was preparing to launch a new business show in about three weeks. She was in a bind and needed someone she could count on to make phone calls to find enough guests to make a show. After meeting with Guy at a coffee shop, it didn't take her long to offer him the job.

"You can't do that," said Guy aghast. "I haven't told you anything about my background. You can't offer me the job until I tell you about myself."

"All right, go ahead," she said, rolling her eyes.

Guy then gave a five-minute pitch, based on his résumé: what his best strengths and abilities were, and how his background tied into his potential to be great in business television.

When he was done, she looked at him and said, "Great, *now* will you take the job?"

He did—a month and a week before his targeted date.

But taking the time to pitch his broadcast goals paid off. Because Guy was so adamant in telling the producer about his dreams of being on air, she helped to mentor him to on-air freelance work by introducing him around and helping to prepare his first scripts.

And if you turn on the TV to a station reporting business news, it's likely at some point that you will see him on air.

Serving Coffee to Serving the Community—Russell's Story

Russell's is our final story of career transition. He had done a variety of things in his eventful life, but as our tale opens he was serving coffee in a well-known coffee chain and dreaming of his next step.

Russell was in his late thirties and felt it was time to get paid for doing work he could feel proud of. Having been HIV positive for eighteen years, he knew a thing or two about adversity. He had also contributed greatly to his community through volunteer work, including cycling across Africa to bring attention to AIDS, raising thousands of dollars for research and relief both in Africa and back home, running an Ironman Triathalon, and speaking at community events.

But he'd never been paid for any of those achievements. It seemed to him, as he poured another nonfat soy caramel macchiato, that perhaps he could somehow get paid to do these community things he loved and was passionate about. What if he could *get paid* to raise funds?

Now here was Russell's dilemma. How could he write a résumé for a paid fund-raising role when his current paying job is foaming lattes and sprinkling cinnamon shavings?

Russell needed help. So he went to a friend who is also good at this career help sort of thing. They talked a lot about the skills and abilities he had and about the skills and abilities that nonprofit places were looking for.

Russell Jefferson   123 Dury Lane, Boston, MA 02104
                          (617) 555-1234   rjefferson@yourname.com

---

OBJECTIVE

To expand my experiences as a person living with HIV, health promotion, and fundraising into a professional role that allows me to contribute to the programs and services offered to the HIV/AIDS community.

PROFILE

Five years experience working on HIV/AIDS related issues with adults and youth
- Provided information about HIV/AIDS to secondary school students
- Presenter at corporate sensitivity training workshops
- Promoted the role of healthy living in the management of HIV/AIDS through workshops and presentations
- Raised awareness of HIV/AIDS issues with youth groups, orphanages, and hospitals in southern Africa

Experienced in developing and coordinating volunteer driven programs
- Led a volunteer executive committee to achieve organizational goals
- Developed and presented workshops to train volunteers on effective speaking and presentation skills

Self-starter with a strong sense of initiative and leadership
- Designed and implemented fundraising programs securing over $34,000 in donations for Finnegan House Foundation and the American African Partnership for AIDS (AAP AIDS)
- Motivated and coordinated members of LongRunners to volunteer at community events
- Led employees in a positive environment to ensure service and operational standards were met

Collaborative team player
- Contributed to a positive team environment by developing programs to enhance morale and performance
- Maintained relations with the International Student Travel Confederation - ISIC Association Services (ISTC - IAS) and exchanged information on program development in U.S.

Resourceful, organized with a strong ability to prioritize and multi-task
- Liaised with a variety of service providers to ensure clients' travel needs were met
- Maintained and updated comprehensive client profiles and accounting records
- Supervised the distribution and marketing of 200,000 identity cards annually with sales of $1.2 million

Creative problem solver with the ability to translate concepts into workable solutions
- Represented clients' post-travel concerns to find satisfactory resolutions with suppliers of travel products
- Developed innovative marketing initiatives and campaigns

Dynamic written and verbal skills
- Over 19 years of experience in public speaking and performing in community theater productions
- Maintained online journals for sponsors and organizations chronicling my fundraising efforts
- Designed and produced various marketing materials

Conscientious, reliable, and dependable
- Consistently received above average ratings during performance reviews
- Promoted and/or given additional responsibilities by my employers

Extensive media experience
- Interviewed on issues related to living with HIV-AIDS by various publications (*New York Times*, *Another Magazine*, *Advocates*, *Health Story*)
- Interviewed by Lucia Rutherford on CBC Radio on the HIV/AIDS pandemic in Africa, my own experience with HIV/AIDS, and my fundraising efforts in southern Africa
- Spokesperson for Finnegan House Foundation and AAP AIDS during fundraising efforts

VOLUNTEER AND COMMUNITY BASED EXPERIENCE

AAP AIDS, Ride for Hope (2004)
Completed a 6,000 km bicycle ride across Africa bringing awareness to Americans about the AIDS pandemic on the continent while providing inspiration and hope to Africans living with HIV/AIDS. Contributed to the success of raising $20,000 for AIDS relief in Africa.

IronMan for Finnegan House Foundation (2003)
Spearheaded a fundraising campaign securing over $14,000 in donations for Finnegan House Foundation. Engaged in health promotion activities in the HIV/AIDS community focusing on the role of fitness in the management of HIV/AIDS. Completed a personal achievement by finishing the IronMan Wisconsin Triathlon.

People with AIDS Foundation (1998–1999)
Volunteered as a member of the Speaker's Bureau providing information on HIV and AIDS. Developed and presented workshops and seminars to train other volunteer speakers with effective presentation skills.

LongRunners Boston (2003–2004)
Served as President of the Executive Committee. Coordinated a volunteer Executive committee. Organized and motivated volunteers for various club events.

National Air Cadet Senior Leadership Course (1978)
Provided training at a six-week summer course in effective speaking, instructional techniques, and leadership.

Community Theater (1985–2004)
Nineteen plus years experience performing with various community theater groups in over twenty-five productions.

PROFESSIONAL HISTORY

Shift-Supervisor, Bigbucks Coffee Company (2002–2003)
Supervised and deployed a team of employees and delegated tasks to create and maintain an enjoyable experience for customers.

Travel Coordinator, Tourland Inc. (2000–2001)
Developed programs and policies to foster company-wide and client budget efficiencies. Matched client needs to corporate programs for business travelers using travel agencies and other vendors.

ISIC Marketing and Public Relations Officer, Travel on a Budget (1997–2000)
Developed marketing and promotional materials to grow ISIC within the American market. Provided public relations and communications for all inquiries about the ISIC from retailers and clients. Provided support, service, and training to issuing offices across America.

Senior Travel Consultant, Travel on a Budget (1993–1997)
Provided excellent customer service in the sale of international and domestic airfares and holiday packages.

EDUCATION AND TRAINING

Capistrano College, Boston (2004–2005) Fundraising and Volunteer Management Certificate

Desmond College, Middlesex (1984–1985) Performance Studies

National Air Cadet Senior Leadership Course, Green Bay, WI (1979) Leadership, Effective Presentation, and Instructional Skills

The real joy of this career transition résumé is that what Russell does on a day-to-day job basis doesn't appear until the second half of page two . . . and yet his résumé is a clear, focused, and legitimate application for the role he is targeting. Russell turned his résumé upside down and focused on the nine skills and strengths he felt his target job would require.

As he worked get to this final résumé, Russell asked himself questions like, "What do I think I have achieved?" and "What would I say my mark on life has been thus far?" The answers led him to his truth—that it was not his paid work that had made the mark or made him proud, it was the activities he'd accomplished in the rest of his life. All he had to do was make the rest of his life the focus of the résumé.

You might have noticed that Russell has an objective, clearly stated as a brief summary of individuality and as directed and focused toward a particular role. In this case it works.

The profile works well because unlike a lot of functional résumés, this one reads clearly and easily. Notice how the skill is stated in only takes one line (a lot of people overwrite this part) and is attached to specific accomplishments that can be easily matched with the jobs in the chronological portion of his résumé.

Moving down the page, the nonprofit words and phrases pop out ("fund-raising," "raising awareness," "promoted the role of healthy living") plus, given his objective, so do many specific activities that relate to HIV/AIDS awareness and fund-raising. Russell doesn't distinguish between volunteer and work experience here, and it leaves a good impression.

Flipping to page two, he puts the volunteer activities first, clearly and succinctly. He also notes his air cadet leadership training in from way back, because he is proud of it and it relates to the work he's done.

Finally, he states what he was doing at the time he put the résumé together, and it just doesn't seem to matter after everything else. He doesn't oversell the coffee shop job, nor does he try and hide it. He just highlights the one or two things that might be transferable and moves on.

So if you're pouring coffee, or entering data, or doing a job that is deadening your soul, take heart. Start asking deeper questions about who you are, what you've achieved, and where you want to make an impact, and you can begin to visualize what it will take to get you to a place that is more satisfying, challenging, and soulful.

Targeting Your Career Transition Résumé Works

If the targeted résumé is important, having one for a career transition is even more vital. What all these people had in common and what made their career transition "pretty easy" was they took the time to think through what they wanted and where they wanted to do it, long before they worked on their résumé.

And after presenting their résumé to the public, they didn't stop. They each kept doing what needed to be done to show their commitment and determination. Each person maintained a great attitude, and had faith that with persistence, focus, and preparation they could break through.

Keep your eyes on the prize, and keep your résumé tight and focused. Get help from the people who hire. Don't be shy about following your dreams. Trust yourself. You never know—if you put your mind to it, you could be doing the very job you want to do, or on the pathway there. Take those first steps and create a targeted résumé to suit your career transition goals.

CHAPTER 8:

Submitting Your Résumé!

Well, you've done it. You have a finished résumé. Take a moment to savor the triumph.

Now what do you do with it?

The Chapter That Makes This Book Complete

Since this book is called *The Complete Book of Résumés*, I wanted to give you a truly complete book. One area that other résumé and career books often neglect is how to **submit** this golden gem you've created. And if you don't now how to properly submit a résumé, an employer could miss the gold and end up treating it like a technical error that needs to be deleted.

Only a few years ago, submitting a résumé was not such a big deal. The process often required more logistics and physical exercise, as many résumés would be dropped off in person or into the hands of someone who could "take it in for you." Or perhaps you applied by sending it through mail, or in later years faxing it. All of these scenarios required a hard copy of your résumé.

Among other things, that meant thinking about paper choice. Career coaches and counselors like me talked a lot about paper choice. Office supply stores grew niche businesses in résumé paper—the linen, the matte, the stone grey marble. People expressed themselves with neon pink and rainbows.

Those days are almost gone now. While there are definitely still occasions and job applications that require hard copies—such as service industries like retail and restaurants—most industries, and *certainly* medium and large companies have gone completely electronic. Résumés are stored in databases, not file drawers. Recruiters, hiring managers, companies large enough to have HR departments, or any institution with more than fifty employees will keep résumés on file electronically. And many will have absolutely no idea what to do with a hard copy of a résumé.

In fact, when paper résumés come by mail to the recruiting company, it's a tragic event. The paper will be handed around, usually landing on receptionist's desk in the hope that they would call the résumé writer to ask for an electronic copy. Because the one that was mailed in is going in the garbage. Not to be mean or anything, but where would we put it? How would we remember that we had it?

This is not to say that people seeking to hire someone *only* look at résumés online. Online submission is an effective way to collect, sort, and share résumés. However, when a recruiter goes to a meeting with a client and wants to "present" a set of candidates, they will invariably offer a set of hard-copy résumés of the top candidates printed from their database. And when an HR person sets up an interview, they will likely want to have a hard copy of your résumé to refer to.

So you see the dilemma. On the one hand, you have to be electronically savvy and know how to cut and paste a document into an online ATS (I'll get to that). And on the other hand, when someone on the other end clicks open your résumé to read or share, it should look good and read clearly. The level of sophistication required in today's submission process is mind-boggling.

Here to Help…and with Reinforcements!

That's why, along with the contributions of career and job search specialist Mark Swartz, *The Complete Book of Résumés* is here to help. Mark wrote a book about online submissions called *Get Wired, You're Hired*, which was amazingly useful when all this electronic submission jazz started up in the first place.

I'll talk a little bit about email text versus a cover letter, following up an email, checking submission guidelines carefully, what to do when you have to hand in a hard copy, and other submission details. Then Mark will provide guidance and instructions on electronic submissions. After that, it's up to you!

Targeting Your Submission

Though I've covered most of this material in the last few chapters, I want to review the steps to "customizing" your submission for a particular job application or approach.

1: **Read and reread the job ad or description (and keep a highlighter handy).** Before popping off your résumé, make several passes of the job description. Are you sure you're in the running? Many hiring managers and HR folks get frustrated by large numbers of applicants who are completely inappropriate for the job. Scan the ad for the different job elements required to make sure you have covered as many as possible on the first page of your résumé.

2: **Look for keywords and key ideas as well as the deal-breaker elements.** As you scan, look for the keywords this employer is using and try to determine their company's philosophy and goals in hiring. See if you can pinpoint the deal-breaker elements of the experience, that is, the key qualification must-haves for the ideal candidate.

3: **Make sure your profile statement echoes the role title and incorporates some of the keywords.** Once you've looked at the keywords, revisit your profile statement, and any key qualifications. Rather than including every single keyword, carefully edit and choose those that best describe you and that you feel *most correspond* to what the reader is looking for. If the job ad requires a certain number of years' experience and you have it, make sure your profile shows it. If there is a certain educational qualification required, note that you have it. And if something you have makes you unique for the prospective position (for instance, one requirement is trade show experience and you have lots of that) be sure that is clearly stated.

4: **Make sure the rest of your résumé echoes the key responsibilities of the job.** Once your profile tightly reflects the ad, consider the rest of your experience. If the ad highlights certain responsibilities, make sure they appear first in the pecking order of your work experience.

Emails Versus Cover Letters

This chapter mostly deals with electronic submissions to posted jobs. However, you might approach someone who doesn't necessarily connect to a specific job (a "cold" email if you will). Your approach should be more of an introduction, much in the way you might use a traditional cover letter in a mailing. (See the Appendix on page 580 for more on writing cover letters)

The tricky part about applying or contacting people online is this—the difference between the cover letter and the text of the email you send. Is it better to put your cover letter in the body of an email? Or to attach a cover letter to your résumé with a brief note in the body of the email?

Later in this chapter, Mark Swartz assumes that your email is your cover letter. That's one good approach.

However this approach doesn't work for everyone. It is now acceptable to approach people in a slightly less formal way using email. This relaxing of cultural norms means that you have more room than ever to approach people in a friendly way to create a relationship with them before they've actually met you or heard your voice on the phone. Thus, I suggest that you think about the text of your email as a place to have a warm, friendly message to the reader, taking care not to become overly familiar or use bad grammar or spelling. Here is a good example:

Dear Ms. X,

Thanks for the opportunity to apply to your company. I am so pleased to see that you are hiring as I've had Burnside Designs in mind for quite awhile, because of your amazing products (I particularly love your modern line. I've been buying the "Edge" line for the last three years whenever I can—very sleek and affordable).

I've attached both a cover letter and a résumé for you to get to know me and my background. I feel like I've been training in customer service management and working with furniture lines for the express purpose of helping you streamline furniture operations.

I look forward to hearing from you.

Stephanie

Another difference the email culture has thrust upon us is a culture of brevity. An email is rarely very long, and most people will not read a long email thoroughly unless it is from someone they know and pertains to something of interest. So your email approach must also be brief and to the point. The email is not where you take time to sell yourself; rather it's where you try to whet the appetite of the reader so they will want to look at your attached and/or embedded résumé.

If you have a cover letter that is more than a paragraph or two, you may want to consider attaching it separately (or as part of the résumé document) and create an even shorter and tighter message in the email body. Use that space to begin to create a relationship with the reader.

Here's a way to approach someone for an interview or to obtain a contact name using a "warm" email.

Notice how the email stays brief and to the point without sacrificing key pieces of information. There is a call to action at the end, and a clarification of next step. The résumé is used as an additional information piece that the reader can choose to read or not.

Email can be a powerful tool for making connections and introductions if used correctly.

Dan,

Good morning! You have never met me, but I'm hoping you can help me.

Here's Me in brief: I am a bank contract employee in the Chicago office. While working on databases for the last year, I completed a masters in counseling psychology, as well as some training courses on customer service and skill- building. I also taught small seminars within the local bank environment, and now I am hoping to parlay all of this into a training job with the bank.

Here's You in brief: You are a vice-president of employee relations at Mega Bank who was recommended to me by Lydia Smeaton. She gave me your name as she thought you'd be a stellar resource, especially considering your work with NIT.

Here's my request: I would love ten minutes of your time to get your ideas on how to best approach training departments at banks.

If you agree, please email me your phone number and tell me when would be a good time to call.

Thanks a million,
Connie

P.S. I've attached my résumé for a more detailed look at my background if you need that.

Following Submission Guidelines

Before doing anything at submission time, go back and read the ad one more time for the express purpose of reaffirming the requested submission method. This is an important step because every online job ad has a slightly different way they want you to submit.

Some will absolutely want a cover letter attached with the résumé. Some will not. Some will want you to reference something specific in the subject line and some will want you to name your document in a certain way. Take the time to read these instructions because not following them could get you thrown out of the Inbox pile before you get your shot.

Sometimes the ad will also tell you who the documents are going to, which means you can address your email to the right person.

Subject Lines and Naming Your Document

If there are no instructions about what to put in the subject line of the document, you may still want to think through what might be easy for the person who will receive it. Typically, if you are responding to a recruiting position, the recruiter has more than one assignment going. So using the position you're applying for—and perhaps your name—would be the most helpful subject heading.

Naming your résumé document is also important. It is best to use your name for your résumé and perhaps a code so you know you're attaching the right résumé for this job. You don't want to just name it by the title of the job, as the reader will not be able to distinguish you when flipping through their inbox. Saving your name in their files is easier.

Ultimately, this is a branding exercise because your name is the most important thing you want them to remember.

Unique Approaches and Résumés Saved in Programs Other Than Word

We've had some unique approaches come through email to our recruiting office, usually for jobs that require some creativity, such as an art or creative director or other role that requires a portfolio. One such approach was in Acrobat. It contained a series of shots of a portfolio book on a desk (with the shot of the torso of our interviewee and his coffee mug). Each screen shot had humorously written text at the bottom, and the option to click photos in the portfolio for a closer view. My favorite part was the shot where the coffee mug had turned into a daiquiri with an umbrella. At the end, one could click a page that said résumé to get a summary of the places the résumé writer had worked.

Now that was an interesting approach using both humor and innovative design. It was so enjoyable that everyone in the office had a look at it (the original recruiter sent it around). However, there are a couple of flaws with this approach. If the original person receiving it had not had Acrobat on their computer, our innovative genius would have been out of luck. And once we all had a look at it, some of us saved it as interesting, and some of us didn't. Because of the format, it didn't fit our recruiting database. Mark Swartz recommends always sending a regular résumé in Word format, which this person could have attached along with his "showmanship" document.

> **Every Résumé Database Is Different**
>
> There are many types of résumé databases. Some collect scanned information, some require unique hand entry through an online portal, and some will take your Word document along with other key information.
>
> Before sending a plain text résumé to every database, it may be worth finding out if they can store your spruced up version. If the office is small enough—say a recruiter or a smaller company—call reception and ask what the best format is.

Sometimes we receive résumés in PDF format. Those are always nice from a print point of view (our computers won't mess with lines and format the way they sometimes do in Word) but cause more problems when saving in our database. Again, if you like the design of your PDF, by all means send it—just be sure to send a regularly formatted version as well. Remember, most people have some sort of word processing program, but not everyone has more than that.

I have also seen some really good hard copy approaches through snail mail. Usually the great ones are for design-oriented roles using some great portfolio or résumé brochure. On the rare occasions we get a good one, the recruiter will often show it to me. Once again, we may all admire it, but it goes into the "Good example of a hard copy" file rather than the "Considered for a job" file. If you want to demonstrate your design prowess (if that's appropriate to the role you want) through a hard copy document, be sure to follow up with the person you sent it to, and offer a straightforward electronic document for their files.

When to Have a Hard Copy of Your Résumé

Whenever you go to meet in person with a recruiter, HR person, or any other interviewer, have an extra copy or two of your résumé handy. Interviewers often have the best intention of having your résumé in front of them but may have been stymied by a printer jam or may have lost your email. Or someone else joins the conversation and wants to be brought up-to-date by perusing your résumé.

Carry a professional-looking binder or file. Try not to fold your résumé so you can hand it over wrinkle free.

It might also be a good time to have an extended copy of your résumé. Perhaps in keeping your résumé down to one or two pages you had to knock out a lot of good material. An interview might be the time to pull out something more extensive if the conversation moves to more detailed discussions.

Bringing a copy of your résumé to information interviews and casual meetings is always a good idea. You may not want to pull it out and wave it around every time, but if you need it, it's there.

Should You Post Your Résumé on the Web?

There are two main ways to post résumés on the web. The first is on your own website, and the second is in a job bank or job site like Monster.com or Workopolis.com.

Posting on Your Own Website

Pros:
- You control how you're seen.
- You can offer a straight link.
- You can show computer savvy if that's the type of role you're going for.

Cons:
- If it's not password protected, there are significant privacy issues—anybody can get your information and contact you or take your information, reproduce it as their own, or even turn it around in some subversive way and repost it as authentic.
- Many people don't want to take what they perceive as an extra step to look at a whole website. Typically, there isn't a good reason to post your résumé on your own site, unless you're applying for something techie or design-related. Most recruiters or hirers won't be searching the Web for random hits on résumés, and you don't want to force people to go online just to see your words of wit.

Posting on a Job Site

Pros:
- Somebody that you don't know how to reach may find out about you.

Cons:
- If you want all prospective employers to see your résumé, but not your current company, you have to use a job bank that allows you to block specific companies. Even then, if you live or work in a small community you could be fair game for exposure.
- Most "employers" posting jobs online are actually recruiting firms. So you might get called in for jobs that you didn't apply for or aren't interested in.
- Career companies like Bernard Haldane and insurance companies go trolling for prospects here too. No big deal—just a nuisance.

And Now Introducing Mark Swartz

Mark Swartz, who has master's degrees in both business administration and education, is a leading North American career specialist and a friend of mine. We met when we authored our first books at the same publisher at the same time. He helped me out then with the "tech world" of careers and he's back (thank goodness!) to help me—and you.

He authored the best-selling book *Get Wired, You're Hired*, and writes a career column for one of the largest newspapers in the United States. Mark earned his stripes as a consultant to the world's foremost career management/outplacement firm. Moreover, he was downsized twice when in the corporate world and understands firsthand the necessity of being out on the leading edge in your job hunt. You can visit his website and read his many enlightening articles at http://www.careeractivist.com.

Mark and I decided to have a conversation about what to do about electronic résumés and submissions in this day and age.

Karen and Mark's Q & A: Electronic Résumés

KS: There is a lot of talk about sending your résumé electronically these days. What's going on?

MS: There's been a revolution in the past decade in terms of how job seekers apply for openings, and how employers expect to receive résumés. Frankly, it's amazing. Less than ten years ago, electronic résumés were those sent by fax. Today it means submitting your résumé and cover letter via email, both as an attachment and within the body of the email itself, with keywords included. It also includes uploading or copying and pasting to online forms within job websites.

KS: Is it really important to know how to do this properly?

MS: Actually, Karen, it's more critical than ever to know how and when to use the right techniques, especially now that so many employers nationwide are recruiting online. Sending your material incorrectly could disqualify you right off the bat—for instance, if they've asked for a scannable version and you mistakenly send them one that's improperly formatted.

KS: Why are so many employers embracing electronic résumés?

MS: Basically it's a matter of economics and convenience. A job posting in any major city can attract hundreds of applicants within days. To sort through them manually is a chore most Human Resource specialists find tedious and inefficient. Plus storing all those paper versions becomes a hassle—not to mention that they can't be searched electronically for keywords.

Intuitively, it makes sense that if you automate the process, you'll save time, free up your Human Resource staff to focus on higher-level strategic issues, and generate more consistent results in terms of hiring qualified candidates. So, in their quest to find the perfect candidates, employers have turned to applicant tracking systems (ATS), online résumé repositories such as Monster.com and CareerBuilder.com, and scanning technology.

KS: Applicant tracking, résumé repositories, and scanning. Sounds complicated. Can you explain what each of these terms mean?

MS: Collectively, they're ways of capturing résumés electronically so they can be searched by specific criteria or keywords. For instance, an employer might be looking for a candidate with experience in marketing and sales, who lives reasonably close to the head office, is willing to travel extensively, and has earned at least an undergraduate degree. With the above technology, employers can specify exactly what they're looking for. Then only those résumés matching on all criteria will be made available for their private viewing (for a fee, of course).

Applicant tracking systems (ATS) are software programs that link with an employer's website on the pages where they post their job openings. If you're applying to a company using ATS, you'll be asked to fill out an online form that asks basic questions about your work background, education, and experience. Then they'll request that you upload your résumé.

The ATS puts your résumé into its private database. Then, whenever the employer wants to search for applicants, they need only boot up their computer and input the desired criteria to have instant access to all matching candidates. In fact, the better applicant tracking systems

---

Ask the Expert

Mark, what's with documents that look fine when you create them but look funny when opened on another computer? Do you know what I mean? I hate when things don't fit neatly, but then I realize sometimes it's a Word thing. Is there a way to "lock" the document?

Yes and no. (Randomly generated so that YOU can figure out which answer belongs to the correct question!) In response to your query about the unreliability of formatting when you send your Word document to someone, it's because they may have their page settings different than yours. I recommend keeping your margins at 1 inch all around (it's the default setting anyway). That way you're most likely to match what they have at the other end.

will rank and sort the résumés in terms of those who come closest to being ideal. They may even automatically send out a customized email to every applicant acknowledging receipt of their résumé and indicating next steps, if any.

Résumé repositories are the flip side of all those online job banks out there. Once you've searched for posted positions on Monster.com, CareerBuilder.com, and the like, you can upload your résumé to as many job banks as you'd like to, for free in almost all cases. Your info will be stored in each job bank's respective database (which are actually applicant tracking systems). Employers and recruiters pay a fee to run searches on each database. If your résumé meets the standards, it will be made available for viewing by the people paying for the search.

The other approach, **scanning**, is where you send in a paper version of your résumé (via regular mail or courier, less commonly by fax) when applying for a position. At the employer's end, they take the hard copy of what you've submitted and run it through a special scanner that uses optical character recognition (OCR) programming. It reads your pages electronically and turns your material into a Microsoft Word-compatible file that can be input directly into an ATS for keyword searching. You should respond this way only if the employer has specified it in their job ad. Otherwise your résumé might be ignored or overlooked.

KS: Gee, with all this technology floating around, do you even need to create a paper version of your résumé anymore?

MS: Absolutely. I advise having a nicely formatted traditional résumé available. Visually it is much more impressive than a plain text version, which I'll discuss in detail shortly. You could also use a scannable, all-purpose résumé, also reviewed below.

KS: Before I get into that, what's the best way to respond to a job posting if all you have to go on is the potential employer's email address?

MS: To ensure that employers receive and are able to read your cover letter and résumé fully, copy and paste a plain text version of your cover letter and résumé directly into the body of your email message, and attach a copy of your fully formatted cover letter and résumé to the email, as well.

This duplication will ensure that the employer has easy access to your information in whatever format they prefer.

Note that the drawback of inserting your material into the body of your email is that it loses its fancy formatting. Bold lettering, special fonts, underlines, bullet points—all of these may be converted by default into unadorned Courier type. For this reason, I suggest that you create your own plain text version first, to make sure the layout doesn't get messed up in this type of conversion process.

KS: What is the best way to turn your word processing files into plain text?

MS: To make sure your material appears as you want it to, first convert your word processing cover letter and résumé to plain text (also known as ASCII text) before pasting it into the body of your email. Use the steps as outlined below:

1: Once you're satisfied with your cover letter and résumé, save them together in a single word processing file. Make sure the cover letter is at the beginning, followed by your résumé. Keep this file open.

2: If you are using Microsoft Word, under the File menu click Save As. Look at the bottom of this window where it says Save As Type. Put your cursor on the down-pointing arrow and click Plain Text or Text Only. Click Save. This creates a new file that does not overwrite or affect your fully formatted file in any way.

3: Close the new text only file.

4: Go to the File menu and click Open. Choose the new file you've just saved. It will have a ".txt" ending (your regular file has a ".doc" ending).

5: Once you've opened your plain text file, review it carefully. Make sure that all your text is left aligned and that none of your material has shifted awkwardly. When satisfied, save the file again if you've made any changes. You now have what you need to apply to job ads in the body of your email.

KS: And how do you insert the contents of this file into your email message?

MS: All you have to do is copy and paste, as follows:

1: Once you have your plain text file open, go to the Edit menu and click Select All. This highlights all the text. Under the Edit menu select Copy to pick up and store all the text.

2: Open your email program.

3: Click the New Mail or Compose Message icon (or whatever your   program uses to create a new message).

4: Put your cursor in the uppermost, left-hand corner of the message area. Press the Enter key once to anchor the text, then select Paste from the Edit menu to insert the text from your file into the body of your email message.

5: Make any adjustments needed to customize the layout or wording of your text (for example, personalizing the cover letter to that particular company).

6: Review your document to make sure it is complete, as well as error free.

7: Type in the recipient's email address.

8: Type in the topic of your message in the Subject line. It should be short, and should mention the job you're after (quote the job number if applicable).

9: Remember to attach a fully formatted (.doc) version of your résumé as well.

10: When you're satisfied that everything is okay, click Send.

11: Remember to check your Sent Mail folder to ensure that your email message was, in fact, sent, and check your email inbox later to ensure that your message has not bounced back.

KS: Is it possible to make your plain text résumé stand out, even though you lose all the fancy formatting?

MS: You can try using a couple of techniques to spice things up a bit visually:

- Insert dashes instead of horizontal lines to separate portions of your résumé.
- Substitute capital letters with fancy formatting (for example, bold, underline, or shading).
- Replace bullets with asterisks (*).
- To indent text, use the space bar instead of the tab key. Don't bother trying to center text, as you don't know the width of the page at the other end.
- Include as much white space (using carriage returns) as possible for that "open" look.

KS: What do you do in the case of applying to a job posting directly on an employer's website when they ask you fill out their information form and then upload your résumé?

MS: When you see an online form like this, you can be pretty sure the employer is using an ATS. As mentioned earlier, your résumé will be put into their   private database so that it's searchable by keyword. After you've filled in the form by typing in the required information, you'll be asked to upload your résumé. Unless they specifically request a formatted version, just click the Browse button they provide, and search your computer's hard drive for the plain text version of your résumé. Attach it by simply selecting it. Do the same for your cover letter if they allow you to do so in a separate area. (Don't forget to customize it any way you can before sending it.)

KS: How can you ensure that you have appropriate keywords in your résumé so that you have the best chance of being selected when a database search is conducted?

MS: There are no hard and fast rules about how many keywords to use, where to position them, or which ones to use. A sound tactic is to write your résumé as you normally would, focusing on quantifiable achievements. Then do the following:

- Consider what kinds of keywords the employers you are applying to might use when they're conducting résumé database searches. For instance, if you are applying for a position as a financial manager, you will want to include such words as finance, financial, financing, accounting, profit and loss, P&L, reconciliation, bottom line accountability, forecasting, variance analysis, and so forth.
- Review the job advertisements carefully for clues. What words do the employers use in their position description? And how do they define their ideal candidate (for example, self-starter? outgoing? driven? a leader?) Use the same words and phrases they do, and think up related ones to incorporate into your résumé.
- If you can't fit all the keywords into the body of your résumé as part of your accomplishment statements, you can add a separate "Keywords" section and include the remaining terms you believe are appropriate.

KS: What if you're asked specifically for a scannable résumé? Does it mean you have to have yet another version of your material at the ready? Or that you can submit the plain text one that looks, well…plain?

MS: Possibly. Some folks opt for a scannable version of their résumé to use in situations where appearance *and* scanability are important. What you end up with is a single résumé that you can use or customize for all situations except for online forms, where a plain text résumé is essential. The scannable copy is fundamentally a compromise between your fully formatted edition and the plain stripped-down one.

Here's how you can make a scannable document for yourself:

1: Open your fully formatted (.doc) résumé file.

2: Change the font to one that is easily read by optical processors, such as Arial, Helvetica, Universe, Optima, or Futura.

3: Keep font sizes between 10 and 14 points.

4: Remove the following elements if you've included them:
- Tables or columns
- Round, hollow bullets (replace them with round, filled bullets instead so they won't be read as the letter "o")
- Drawings, photos, or graphics of any kind
- Percent signs (%), ampersands (&), or foreign characters (they may get misread)

5: Retain vertical and horizontal lines and underlining, so long as they do not make contact with your lettering.

6: To deliver the document to the employer, attach it as a .doc file to your email message—if they've given you an email address to respond to. If not, and you want to send it in by regular mail or courier (faxing is only recommended as a last-ditch method as it degrades the resolution of your document, making it harder for the scanner to read), keep the following in mind:

- Don't staple the pages together or else it might confuse the scanner when the staple's removed
- Use light-colored or white nonglossy paper for printing
- Send the document without folding it, preferably between pieces of stiff cardboard (sheets of white construction paper also work nicely)

Here's an example of a typical management résumé with keywords and plain text.

```
Ram Govind

456 Maple Leaf Street
Anytown, USA

Email RamG@email.com, Phone (555) 555-4444

KEYWORD SUMMARY

Results oriented Administrative Manager, 12 years
experience, professional, operations, management experience
with small to mid-sized companies in start-up,
reorganization, expansion, downsizing, growth

Supervise administration, operations, managing staff,
accounting, accounts receivable, accounts payable, payroll,
budgeting, forecasting, collections, facilities management,
employee development, marketing, customer support,
planning, supervisory

COMPUTER LITERATE: Word processing, Word, WordPerfect,
Spreadsheet, Lotus, Excel, Presentations, PowerPoint,
Harvard Graphics

WORK EXPERIENCE

1996 - Present
BRANCH ADMINISTRATOR, Acme Widgets, Somewhere, Michigan
--Largest widget manufacturer with revenues of more than
$32 million, over 350 employees and seven branches in
Ontario.

-Supervise 46 employees in administration; accounts
receivable/payable; sales support; human resources;
employee development; quality control; customer service.

-Direct the daily operations of the branch and increased
profitability by 12% year over year.

-Developed a self-directed management team to implement
progressive changes. Rose to 1st place in customer service,
profitability, overall performance, and realized a 44%
growth.
```

-Decreased the days outstanding in collections for delinquent accounts. Dropped from 49 days to 36 days in 3 months. Branch was no.1 in collections in 1992.

-Wrote a Sales Coordinator Training Manual, after evaluating all of the procedures required for tracking new business from sales to installation. The manual was adopted company-wide.

1988 - 1991
MANAGEMENT CONSULTANT, Jane Doe Consulting - New York area; Dallas, TX; and Portland, OR.
--Provided consulting to companies that were in start-up situations, reorganization or that needed computer and new business development assistance.

-As COO, managed a potentially $2 million company and developed the client tracking process for a start-up career marketing company. Had the business operational in six weeks.

-Reorganized an executive suites company in Dallas, TX, as CENTER MANAGER. Rehired and trained 16 employees, developed the budget, and increased revenues by 45% in the first 5 months of 1990.

-Expanded a major party linen company in Queens, as GENERAL MANAGER. Set up the northern Virginia distribution facility. Hired and trained all personnel, developed the budget and all accounting systems, set up all office procedures and delivery schedules which allowed for the center to be up and running in 20 days, and attained revenues within 2% of goal.

-Created Courthouse Square Association in History, OR, as volunteer DIRECTOR in 1988. Developed goals, directed public relations and fund raising for the square, thereby increasing the public knowledge of the availability of the facility for private functions. Worked with the City Council, Redevelopment Agency, private investors, and venture capitalists.

1983 - 1987
OWNER, GENERAL MANAGER in New York City, of two specialty retail toy stores, and three department stores specializing in seasonal and Christmas items.

-Directed advertising; public relations; accounting and tax compliance; merchandising; inventory control; sales supervision; budgeting and forecasting. Supervised 100 employees.

1977 - 1983
DIRECTOR, Police Administrative Services Bureau, Any Police Department, Middle City, NY.

-Supervised 146 employees; the day-to-day operations; Accounting Division; Property Management; Evidence Management; Building Services Division; $30 million budget; Human Resources.

EDUCATION:

BA Art History - State University

MBA Program - Well-known Business College

ADDITIONAL TRAINING:

Re-engineering the Corporation - 1994 Conflict Management - 1994 Training the Trainer - 1993 Self-Directed Team management by Blanchard - 1993 Managing Negativity in the Work place - 1993 Total Quality Management, TQM, courses - 1993 Criminal Justice System and Civil Service - management courses from 1977 until 1983.

Here is an example of a scannable résumé:

KIM CHAN
2323 Main Street, Apt 12A
Anytown, USA 00000
(000) 555-0000

Objective: A Staff Accountant position with a well established, customer-oriented corporation.

RELATED EXPERIENCE:
A & B CORPORATION, Anytown, USA
Internal Audit Analyst (July 2000 to Present)
Supervisor: Mary Jones, Internal Audit Manager

• Discuss procedures and audit findings with clients.
• Prepare recommendations relating to audit findings.
• Analyze operational and financial compliance of clients.
• Assist in preparing audit programs.
• Has highest positive ratings on "closed" files.

SMITH & COMPANY, Anytown, USA
Staff Accountant (May 1996 to May 2000)
Supervisor: Mark Smith, CPA

• Prepare and examine compilations and reviews.
• Prepare and check various types of tax returns.
• Design custom spreadsheet programs for internal use.
• Prepare quarterly and yearly payroll reports.
• Maintain and reconcile general ledgers for clients' businesses.
• Positive feedback from clients rated high scores on reviews.
• Asked specially to assist in training new employees.

EDUCATION:
State University - Anytown
Graduation: May 1996
Accounting Major

ACTIVITIES:
Delta Omega Fraternity
• Executive Board
• Academics Chair
• Activities Chair
Order of Omega (Greek Honor Fraternity)
Student Accounting Society

Following Up

Once you've submitted your résumé, it's hard to know what to do next. If the recruiter or hirer has a good system, you'll get an email confirming that your submission was received. If not, you have to cross your fingers or follow-up to make sure that it did get received.

While following up is a good idea most of the time, it's not always appropriate. If the job submission instructions specifically say that only potential candidates will be contacted, that's a signal that they don't want to wade through many follow-up phone calls. Some postings deliberately keep names and numbers out of the ad to keep people from following up.

However, if there are clues about who placed this ad and no specific instructions *not* to follow-up, a follow-up is appropriate. The idea is not to sell yourself too hard or talk too long. Focus on ensuring that you've been noticed in the pile and inquire what stage the search is at. If you take this tactic, remember this important point: *Be prepared for an impromptu phone interview.*

When you get someone on the phone to ask about the status of your application, do not let them know that you are annoyed because you haven't heard from anyone yet. No one wants to hire someone who's being self-righteous or putting the employer in the wrong before getting started. Be positive and accommodating, or don't call.

The Conclusion—The Résumé Isn't the Winner—You Are

You've worked hard and, hopefully, you now have a great résumé to show for it. Before concluding, I wanted to make one last pitch to you about where your résumé fits into your overall job search.

Because your résumé is such a tangible element of a job search, it's easy to over-focus on it and forget that the majority of searches are completed successfully because people took active steps to find and research potential companies, introduced themselves to and met with other active and interested people who might help lead them to new opportunities, and made the calls and connections necessary to let others know exactly what they were looking for. These activities are just some of the many that encompass a full and active job search.

So if you have worked your résumé to perfection or have endeavored to get your résumé to comply with everything we've discussed so far, and your résumé is still not getting responses from employers or recruiters, *it's time to step away from the résumé.* Your résumé may not be the problem.

You could tweak your résumé forever—always finding another thing to say or another style that looks and sounds better. But at a certain point, you are just making changes for the sake of making changes.

How do you know if you're there? If your résumé folder has so many iterations you have trouble finding timmysmithversion25.doc, or you have asked more than ten people for their opinion and you change your résumé each time you talk to someone, or you have been working on it steadily over three weeks without doing anything else toward your search—it's time to rein it in. That's when you have to remember that the résumé does not hold all the answers. It's just one tool.

You Are the Most Important Part of the Job Search Equation

The reasons that a résumé may not be working, beyond the résumé itself, may have to do with your personal presentation, your phone conversation, the availability of the job role you're targeting, the current job market, whether people are actually perceiving that you can do what you say, your job search strategy, your reliance on others to market you, or your own personal feelings about your work. There are many, many reasons why a job search can go off the rails.

One of the main instances of job search breakdown occurs when people rely on their résumé to do all the work to get them a job. Unfortunately, even with the greatest résumé, you will still have to do most of the work. You have to network, shake hands, answer questions, and meet people. Your résumé can't do that for you. The résumé is there to help get you an introduction and to give structure to a meeting or interview. It can't be the "closer."

Look back at Chapters 6 and 7 and notice the extra efforts that the people in those chapters took to land what they wanted. Be creative. Think about the job more deeply than anyone else who is applying for it. Consider taking extra steps to understand the job, the company, and the needs of the employer, and find ways to show your determination and commitment. Get active. Be alive! This is a process that lets you learn more about who you are and what you want. Take charge of the experience instead of being at the mercy of it.

It is never too late to get in the game. The key is not to lean on your résumé too hard to help you handle the anxiety of a job search. I'll say it again: **you are not your résumé.** You are not a person who can be fully understood in one or two pages. You are a multidimensional human being with talents, abilities, and interests well beyond what a résumé could ever convey. Therefore, you need to be out there to be recognized.

Remember there is a great job for you out there with a company who will want you for exactly who you are today. Your task is to find it. I've offered some direction and guidance on what constitutes an exceptional résumé, but please don't expect your résumé to do it all. In a recent survey reported, 42 percent of global respondents found their new jobs through connections, in other words, through networking.

Good news! Résumés aren't everything!

Happy writing and best of luck with your search.

PART 2:

The Great Big Index of Résumés

Well folks, don't say I didn't warn you when I called it *The **Complete** Book of Résumés*. I have a ton of résumés for you to peruse. The sheer number and variety should help guide you to create a great résumé that works.

You can use this résumé index in a number of ways:

- To get a sense of how many different types of résumés there are, and thus, to reassure yourself that there is no one perfect format
- To look at a variety of formats and styles in order to choose the one (or a blend!) that works for you
- To look at résumés in your industry or field to gauge where you fit and what you need to emphasize to make an impression
- To look at résumés from your level—be it starting out, somewhere at midlevel moving forward, or more senior and executive résumés—and at how people at your career stage present their experience
- To look at résumés from above your current level to get a sense of what roles and responsibilities you need to start taking on, or what extra learning and development you need to do, to move up
- To see lots of great examples of accomplishments, specific measurable results, profiles, qualifications, training, extracurricular activities, and interests and that give context to jobs, roles, and companies
- To look at some not-so-great résumés so that you can contrast and compare the better ones to see what a difference readability (among other things!) makes

There are lots of uses for this section and you may come back to it again over time for different reasons.

Now, don't get overwhelmed as you go through these résumés. Remember why you're here—to find a style that works for you and to increase your learning about what works. Don't get too hung up on other people's accomplishments and education and so forth. You have your own accomplishments, and they are likely not going to be the same as the people here in the examples because you are a different person, with different strengths and specialties. Your task is to figure out what makes you special, not obsess over someone else's uniqueness.

A Few Words of Caution

I've fictionalized everybody mentioned who graciously gave us their résumé. I have willfully changed school names, companies, associations, course names, and so forth. So, please do not try to create your résumé from this guide word for word. Lying gets you nowhere, particularly when you copy something that in your industry may be nonsensical or an obvious fake. Also, most résumés don't say "references on request" but it is implied. Don't forget that someone is going to check on what you've said you did, so be sure that you did do it.

You may notice some variances in different fields such as fewer accomplishments or things that don't jibe what I've said. Overall, each of these résumés represents a good example of a résumé. I've tried to provide a variety of styles to help you find what you need without getting too bogged down in the details. However, you will also notice how much stronger it is to have accomplishments, a clear declaration of a role, dates on the right, and so forth so that you will be convinced to do the same.

Not all industries are the same, which is why some résumés (like project managers and engineers) are longer and some (like pilots) have fewer accomplishments and more specific information (like flight hours and aircraft). Remember that this collection represents only a tiny sampling from each industry. It would behoove you to double check the standard for the industry you are targeting as it may differ from state to state.

In putting this section together, I learned that often in later stages of career, there are a lot of roles that people don't have résumés for, such as coaches and lawyers. That isn't to say they couldn't write one, it's just that they may not be as likely to need one. And academics' résumés are way too long to have been included, what with all their publications, papers, lectures, and so forth.

While collecting these résumés I learned about career paths and jobs that I couldn't possibly have remembered or even have known existed. If you are looking for your role and it isn't in this book, know that I just couldn't possibly represent the thousands upon thousands of jobs out there, despite the claims of completeness. My aim has been to include jobs and industries that are often recruited for or that a lot of people go into, as well as a few quirky ones to stir your interest in other paths and possibilities. If your role is not included, then use the résumés as examples mingled with some research into your field or industry standard.

Do your research. Pick a target job. Be clear and concise.

You have all the tools to create a great résumé and I know you can do it.

So take your time, flip through the following pages, and allow yourself to be inspired!

CONTENTS

The Great Big Index of Résumés

ACCOUNTING: Recent Grad

John J. Johnston

123 Learning St. Anytown, USA 10101 • (999) 555-1212 • johnj@yourname.com

Accounting and Finance Entry-Level

- Organization experience exhibited through coordination of a 28-team summer softball league.
- Communication skills enhanced by working directly with clients, suppliers, and management.
- Sales experience demonstrated by solely initiating, planning, marketing and ultimately the running of a successful graduation trip to the Caribbean for 82 University students (it went smoothly and feedback was highly positive).
- Leadership experience exhibited through various volunteer commitments including Captain of the varsity Cross Country Running Team.
- Practical financial experience gained through accounting includes: analysis and development of financial statements and the preparation of complex financial ratios and adjusted cost bases.
- Computer expertise in Eviews and OX, Case Ware, Case View, Tax Prep, and HTML.

EDUCATION

STATE UNIVERSITY –   **Sept 2000–Aug 2004**
Honors Bachelor of Economics and Finance (Co-op Option)

- **Entrance Scholarship**, for achieving an average of 83.5% in 6 final year courses (2000)

PROFESSIONAL EXPERIENCE

ANDERSON & ANDERSON – *Student in Accounting (Co-op)*   **Jan 2003–April 2004**

- Completed a large number of tax returns, both personal and corporate, ranging from basic to complex.
- Prepared notice to readers, reviewed engagements and in-house audits for numerous clients.
- Visited clients' places of business on a number of occasions to help perform audits. Clients were widely diversified and representative of multiple economic sectors.
- Developed an excellent working relationship with the firm and continued part time in between co-op terms to assist with the workload in periods of high demand.

HAMMER HEARING INSTRUMENTS - *Training and Development (Co-op)*   **May–Aug 2002**

- Reviewed and revised all of the operational procedures. This reduced downtime and repetition of tasks for employees by clarifying responsibilities and outlining proper procedures.
- Conducted an inventory audit and assisted in the development of a new system to track inventory which reduced inventory costs by 10%.
- Assisted the accounting department with general ledger entries at month end.

LEADERSHIP EXPERIENCE

VARISTY SUMMER BASEBALL – *Convener*   **Sept 2003–Present**

- Organized semi-weekly games, tournaments, a rafting trip, and various social events throughout the summer.
- Increased the scope of the league by opening it up to other sectors. This resulted in an increase from 22 teams in the prior year to 28 teams this year.
- Solicited sponsorship from local area businesses for each of the 28 teams and our 3 tournaments.
- Managed a budget of over $30,000.

VARSITY CROSS COUNTRY RUNNING – *Captain*   **Sept 2002–Dec 2003**

- Acted as a mentor to new and returning runners and conducted recruiting with the coach.

ORIENTATION WEEK – *Icebreaker*   **Sept 2002–April 2004**

- Responsible for a group of 40 first-year students 24 hours a day for a week.

STUDENTS UNION – *Public Relations*   **Sept 2001–April 2003**

- Ran two semi-annual trade shows called "Market Place" for the students. This involved soliciting different businesses to come to the school to show their products and services to the students. On average had 30+ businesses which paid $200 to participate in the event.

PERSONAL INTERESTS: Investment Club; Running Club; Re-watching Favorite DVDs

ACCOUNTING: Clerk

Alice J. Johnston

123 Learning St. Anytown, USA, 10101
999-555-1212 (Cell Phone)   Email: alicej@yourname.com

Accounting Clerk – Results- and detail-oriented with ability to work independently.
Give me a task or your overflowing inbox and I'll take it on & get it completed—fast.

Key Qualifications

- 6+ years in accounting roles
- Hold Accounting diploma as well as BA in Business Admin
- Solid skills in various computerized accounting software, such as **QuickBooks,** Great Plains Dynamics, ACCPAC, and Simply Accounting
- Practical skills in dealing with G/L, A/P, A/R, Bank Reconciliation, Trail Balance, Payroll, Financial Report and year end adjustment
- Ability to prepare and complete personal and business related tax returns (T1, T2 returns), GST/HST, PST returns

Work Experience

Accounting Bookkeeper, Small Business Accounting Inc.   Apr. 2003–Present

- Booking incoming and outgoing data
- Processing data and preparing GST/HST and PST returns
- Preparing financial reports and year end adjustments
- Performing clerical and front desk duties, such as filing and mailing
- Preparing Tax Returns (T1 and T2)
- Recording Capital Cost Allowance Schedule

Accounting Clerk, Dreams Ltd   Feb. 2001–Apr. 2003

- Performed A/P and A/R duties: coding and recording invoices, issuing checks, and making collections.
- Processed daily cash receipts and made bank deposits
- Prepared bank reconciliation
- Responsible for bi-weekly payroll calculations

Accounting R/C Clerk, Evening Wear Ltd   Feb. 1999–Jan. 2001

- Performed A/R and A/P duties, made collections
- Recorded journal entries and prepared bank reconciliations

Administrative Assistant, XYZ Bank   Feb. 1998–Feb. 1999

- Answered phone calls, greeted and directed visitors, and made reservations
- Assisted in preparing bi-weekly business activities reports
- Checked and verified employee expenses reimbursements documents
- Verified payroll amounts for accuracy

Education & Training

Accounting Diploma   *Jan. 2001–Apr. 2003*
State College

Bachelor Degree of Business Administration   *Sept. 1998*
State University, Hong Kong

Interests: Long distance running, karaoke, and meeting new people

ACCOUNTING: Supervisor

111-123 Learning Street, Anycity, Anystate, 10101 * (555) 999-1212 * johnj@yourname.com

John J. Johnston CA CPA

Accountant with experience and interest in IAS and PCA taxation and related fields.

Professional Experience

ProConsult LLP   **Anycity, AS**   **2002–Present**
Tax Manager
• Areas of practice include US personal and corporate income tax compliance and planning, international assignment compliance and planning, inbound and outbound planning as well as US estate planning.
• Member of several internal office committees, including the hiring committee and social committee, and a recognized leader in marketing initiatives.

Numbers Chartered Accountants   **Anycity, AS**   **2000–2002**
Accounts Manager
• Areas of practice included audit, review, and compilation engagement financial statements, personal and corporate taxation, management consulting, and business valuation.
• Responsible for review of personal tax returns, management consulting business plans, and staff senior on audit engagements.
• Responsible for meeting and dealing with clients on a daily basis.

UState Student Union   **Anycity, AS**   **1998–1999**
Vice President, Operations
• Elected position responsible for the operation and management of the UState Student Union Building including all entertainment bookings, staffing, and budgeting; conflict resolution between staff, management, and entertainers.
• Member of several boards within the Student Union including the executive council, student union council, hiring committee & finance committee & advisor for the state presidential search committee.

Education

US Institute of Chartered Accountants In-Depth Tax Course   **Anycity, AS**   **2002–2004**

International Certified Public Accountant Qualification Examination   **Nov 2003**
                    • Obtained Certified Public Accountant designation (Anycity).

Eastern School of Chartered Accountancy **Anycity, AS**   **1999–2001**
                    • Obtained Chartered Accountant designation

University of State (UState)   **Anycity, AS**   **1999**
                    • Bachelor of Business Administration, first class standing

Professional Memberships
• US Institute of Chartered Accountants
• Anycity Board of Examiners
• Institute of Chartered Accountants of Anystate
• Institute of Chartered Accountants of Otherstate

Awards
• Full tuition scholarship to UState; maintained throughout the duration of BBA degree
• **Memorial Award**: Presented to the graduating UState accounting student who best exemplifies the qualities of Norm Crunch, a respected CA and politician in Anystate.
• Memorial Trust Award; Estate Bursary

Volunteer: Sales committee member for the Arthritis Society of Anystate; lead advisor for the Morell chapter of Junior Achievers of Anystate; annual volunteer for the Anycity's Blueberry Festival
Interests: Avid golfer and softball player, traveling; skiing; socializing with family and friends

ACCOUNTING: CMA, Midlevel

123 Learning St.
Anytown, US, 10101
Tel: (999) 555-1212 (home)
Email: alicej@yourname.com

Alice J. Johnston, CMA

Profile   A highly motivated CMA with experience in indirect tax consulting with Big Consulting Firm. Technically competent. An innovative self-starter with strong organizational, interpersonal, and leadership abilities. Fluently bilingual in English and French.

Professional Experience

Senior Consultant, Disbursement, & Indirect Tax
Big Consulting Firm LLC   July 2004–present

- Lead audit role on client engagements, including coordinating and attending high level management meetings with client tax personnel
- Perform recovery audits, including data analysis and on-site audit work
- Provide written and oral presentations to clients on audit progress
- Prepare refund claims and written submissions for tax recoveries to clients and/or government authorities

Indirect Tax Senior Associate
Clinghousen LLP   July 2001–July 2004

- Analyze tax legislation related to client operations for the purpose of minimizing client tax liabilities
- Consult with clients to determine and ultimately provide indirect tax solutions ranging from obtaining registrations (federal and/or provincial taxes), completing tax returns and elections, preparing Notices of Objection and Voluntary Disclosures, and performing indirect tax diagnostics
- Identify, propose, and sell additional services to clients consistent with sales and business development initiatives
- Principal writing role in *Commodity Clips*, a bi-monthly publication on emerging indirect tax issues
- Contribute to peer education initiatives at "Lunch and Learn" technical sessions
- Promote cross Line of Service interaction through direction of client issues to appropriate professionals (i.e. Corporate Tax, Customs, Property Tax)

Auditor-Audit Recruitment Apprenticeship Program
Internal Revenue Service   May 1999–November 2000

- Completed work phases in: Collections, Client Services, and Underground Economy during 18-month program
- Apply Income Tax and Excise Tax Acts
- Verifying tax returns according to the legislation and applying adjustments and/or penalties where applicable
- Negotiating with taxpayers for claim resolution

ACCOUNTING: CMA, Midlevel (cont.)

Human Resources Assistant

Public Service Commission   March–May 1999

- Provided administrative support to District Director and HR Officers for public service recruitment, student employment programs, and employment equity initiatives
- Administered Second Language Evaluation testing process (English and French) for current and prospective federal government employees in addition to other required employee testing
- Maintained and updated computer and telephone systems for the use of staff and the public

Intern, International Centre

Brookdale College   June 1998–February 1999

- Provided direct support to the Executive Director for implementation of internationalization plan
- Planned and organized meeting committees and panels of the International Centre
- Created and developed International Centre website to introduce Brookdale into the international education arena
- Addressed queries of Brookdale's international students and domestic students seeking study abroad

Academic Achievements

Accreditation Graduate, 2001–2003

Strategic Leadership Program

Certified Management Accountant Program

Society of Management Accounts

- Two-year program concentrating on contemporary and emerging strategic management and management accounting practices while developing communication, interpersonal, and leadership skills

Pre-Professional Graduate, 2000–2001

Accelerated Program

Certified Management Accountant Program

The Society of Management Accountants

Diplôme Supérieure d'Études Françaises (French Language and Lit), 1996–1997

L'Université de France, France

Bachelor of Commerce (Accounting and French), 1992–1996

State University

Linguistic Profile

- English and French: fluent in written and spoken skills
- Spanish: basic written and spoken skills

Professional Development

- Team Building
- Project Management
- Time Management

ACCOUNTING: Manager

John Johnston
T. (555) 999-1212 Email johnj@yourname.com
111 – 123 Learning Avenue, Anycity, Anystate, 10101

Accounting and Finance Manager with strong Problem Solving, Analytical, and Logical approach to Accounting/Finance. Deep and varied background in Film Finance.

Employment
Accounting Supervisor, Lender Co. Ltd.   2004–2005

Duties & Responsibilities:
- Managed all day-to-day operations of Accounting/Finance Dept.
- Manage and trained staff of 5
- Member of Senior Management Team
- All reporting requirements: auditors, banks, corporate office & government

Finance Manager, In-house Production/Creative Services   2001–2004
Movie Broadcasting Inc.

Accomplishments:
- Brought in all projects under budget
- Negotiated better terms with vendors
- Development relevant cash-flow reports for management
- Brought in-house all tax credit schedules, formerly outsourced
- Wrote and implemented time/cost saving payroll measures
- Wrote procedures for all Joint Ventures & Managed all Joint Ventures
- Ran internal seminars to educate Technical/Creative Staff

Accounting Manager, Film Productions Incorporated   1999–2001
Duties & Responsibilities:
- Responsible for all General Finance & Accounting supervision of 2 staff members
- Prepared all Cavco & OMDC Tax Credits
- Prepared Telefilm US Co-Production Schedules

Accomplishments:
- Developed IT/Accounting solution that cut waste to NIL
- Worked with all Technical Staff to streamline Production
- Worked closely with clients to quickly eliminate problems
- Negotiated new & discounted terms with vendors
- Negotiated contracts with broadcasters & distributors

Retail Sales Accountant/Finance Manager, Top Hardware   1996–1999
Duties & Responsibilities:
- Supervisor of all staff associated with Retail & Franchisees
- Head of Franchise Operations

Accomplishments:
- Eliminated O/S Account Receivable by 80%
- Completed Variance Analysis for all departments

Accounting Manager, Mental Health Center (Contract)   1995

Education
University of Commerce – Anycity, Anystate – **Bachelor of Commerce** (Graduated 1992)
Certified General Accountant – Completed Program December 2004

Computer Programs: Excel, Access, JD Edwards, Lotus 1-2-3, MYOB, Epicor, Vista, Simply Accounting, FRx, Bpcs, Crystal Writer, Showcase, Hyperion

ACCOUNTING: Audit Manager, Sr. Accounting

John J. Johnston CA
off. 999.555.1212, h. 999.555.1313 johnj@yourname.com

Work Experience:

Audit Manager/Senior Accountant, Nov. 1999 to present, BIG FIRM LLC,

- Performed GAAP/GAAS audits of large and mid-size public corporations in the software, communications, and electronics industries; applied technical accounting and auditing pronouncements relevant to high-tech industries (significant clients: Big Copy People, Big Media, Big Bank Inc., Software Inc., etc.)
- Performed strategic business risk analyses and process analyses in planning of audits; performed process measurement and process auditing; financial reporting process consulting project for a leading media conglomerate
- Supervised and managed audit teams, coordinated engagements
- Interacted closely with client management, executives and Board members
- Performed financial due diligence and transactions services, IPO's and RTO's, compilation engagements for financial statements for major public corporations (significant clients: Big Phone Company, ABC LLC, etc.)
- Presented reports, audit, and controls recommendations to management

Senior Accountant, Oct. 1997 to Nov. 1999, Tim Tonybrook LLP

- Performed UA GAAP audits of major corporations in the consumer products, advertising, media, manufacturing and exploration industries, predominantly subsidiaries of large multinationals (significant clients: AXB, Big Car Company, Snap it, Big Food Company, Software LLC etc)
- Provided accounting assistance to CFO on incomplete records projects at one of the largest tour operators in Northeast (North American Relaxation Group)
- Supervised and managed audit teams
- Received extensive training in risk analysis, process analysis, and process metrics

Staff Auditor, May 1995 to Aug. 1997, Owen & Cosmo Inc.

- Audits of multinational companies in accordance with Italian accounting standards, IAS and U.S. GAAP: utilities, telecommunications, oil and gas, chemicals, manufacturing, banks; exposure to valuations

Academic Preparation and Training:

Chartered Accountant, November 2000, ranked among top Uniform Final Examination scorers within BIG FIRM; wrote the CPA equivalency exam
US GAAP & GAAS/ SEC Matters: Internal 5-day training course
Business Management Processes and Process Auditing: numerous training courses in recent audit methodology
State University, UpState University, OutofState University
- Intermediate and advanced accounting, auditing, and taxation courses

UpState University, B.A. in Business Administration
- Concentration in marketing, advertising, and management studies

ACCOUNTING: Tax Specialist (CPA)

John J. Johnston
123 Learning St., Anytown, USA 10101 Tel: (999) 555-1212 Email: johnj@yourname.com

PROFILE–JUNIOR TAX SPECIALIST
My professional experience includes Project Management and Accounting and I am interested in specializing in taxation. I am therefore actively pursuing my accounting designation. I have recently completed a six-month contract working as a tax specialist for ABCD, which has allowed me to get practical experience in both U.S. and international taxation.

EDUCATION
- Currently pursuing the CGA accounting designation
- CPA Courses–writing the CPA in 2005
- State University Accounting and Finance Courses

EMPLOYMENT HISTORY

TAX SPECIALIST   ABCD Inc.
                                                   May 2004–Present

Duties
- Processing U.S. Tax Returns
- Researching international tax issues
- Writing articles and news bulletins for clients and firm-wide distribution
- Tax research for consulting projects
- Reviewing tax returns; compliance work

Achievements
- Writing research articles for the U.S. Tax Department in areas of international and U.S. taxation
- Contributing to the writing of articles in published tax journals
- Presenting Technical Tax Sessions on various U.S. accounting issues
- Tax consulting project: saved client $250,000 and future projected savings $350,000 due to reapportionment and reallocation of income and reorganization

ANALYST   ABC Inc.
                                                   July 2003–May 2004

Duties
- Process and Logistics; managing the full accounting reporting cycle; process reengineering
- Ad-hoc projects; budgeting, costing, forecasting and financial analysis, and tax planning

Achievements
- Set up and integrated the organization's information systems and have reengineered processes so as to increase efficiency by 15%
- Developed new marketing and distribution channels

Tax Experience
- General corporate taxation work in tax analysis

RETAIL CORPORATE ACCOUNTANT   The Shoppe Inc.
                                                   January 2003–July 2003 (contract)

Duties
- A/R, A/P entry and reconciliation and cash flow management; Budgeting, forecasting and risk analysis
- Auditing and analysis of Balance Sheet items and P&L Statements
- Compliance of corporate policies with Federal and Provincial regulations
- Systems development and management; journal entry and bank reconciliation.

Achievements
- Revamped accounting processes and procedures and consolidated procedures for management of retail outlets; involved in restructuring of corporate entity

Tax Experience
- Involved in the consolidation of four separate entities into one organization

ACCOUNTING: Tax Specialist (CPA) (cont.)

John J. Johnston
123 Learning St., Anytown, USA 10101 Tel: (999) 555-1212 Email: johnj@yourname.com

FINANCIAL ANALYST	Paving Guys Inc.
	January 2001–January 2003

Duties
- Budgeting and forecasting; generating monthly reports and presenting this to the Board of Directors
- Analyzing revenue streams and improving cash flow; analysis of AP & AR and GL
- Capital expenditure analysis; procurement analysis and invoicing; marketing; and ad hoc projects

Achievements
- Resolved U.S. tax issues and researched tax implications of U.S. sales; saved client $40,000 (projected)
- Implemented Performance Management System to increase efficiency and improve delivery of services
- Process reengineering and developed internal compliance procedures

Tax Experience
- General corporate taxation work
- Resolving tax issues; researching sales tax implications of sales
- Involved with setting up of new management company

ACCOUNTANT	Oakley & MacDonald Corp
	September 1998–December 2000

Duties
- Auditing, bookkeeping; preparing WIP and completing audit files; preparation of financial statements
- Consulting; corporate insolvency work
- Preparation and supervision of corporate audits for small clients with a turnover of c. $ 125,000 to large clients with a turnover in excess of $200 million.

Achievements
- Developed new systems and processes to address client needs to promote business efficiency
- Developed processes to simplify reporting on off-shore trusts
- Managed audit and corporate insolvency files

Tax Experience
- Sales Tax issues; completion and filing of Sales Tax returns for the UK and the EU
- Tax Returns—both corporate and personal and European regulatory matters
- Dealing with correspondence from the Government Tax Authority
- Specialized in Double Taxation research and Tax Havens

PROJECT MANAGER	Telescopic Inc.
	January 1996–September 1998

Achievements
- Team Leader, Project Management Best Practice Guidelines Initiative
- Developed Best Practice Guidelines for PM processes and Management of Information Systems
- Built a database in support of the project
- Managed development and integration of 6 projects and the bid writing of several projects

TRAINEE ATTORNEY	Grant & Lee Associates
	May 1995–January 1996

EDUCATION
- State University (1995), LLB (Hons) (Thesis in Double Taxation and Transfer Pricing)
- State University of (1992), BA Political Science

SKILLS
- Certification in Access, database development, and management
- Excel; Microsoft Project; Solution 6; PowerPoint; Sage; Solution 6 Corporation Tax; ACCPAC; Atlas; GoSystems RS

Alice J. Johnston

123 Learning St.
Anytown, USA
10101
Phone: 999-555-1212

Hair: Dark Blonde
Eyes: Grey-Blue
Height: 5'11"
Weight: 150lbs
Age Range: 16–25

Television

Box Talk	Featured Extra	CBO-TV Productions

Theatre

Clementine	Nadia (young cancer patient)	State College
Waiting for Godot	Vladimir	State College
A Doll's House	Torvald	State College
Oedipus Rex	Oedipus	State College
Log-On	Zoey (confused teenager)	Drama Festival
Won't You Be My Neighbor?	Cindy (real-estate agent)	Drama Festival
Changes	Angered Teenager	Public School

Training

Rachael Lynch	Introduction to Drama	State University
Anna Olsen	Script Analysis	State University
Cyril Soderburg	Dramatic Arts	College School
U of S Acting Dept.	Audition Workshop	State University
Caspian Bice	Film and Television	The Drama Workshop
Susie Camper	Improvisation	The Improv House
Drama Workshop	Drama Camp	Drama Workshop
Molly Weld	Monologue Training	Duo Academy

Special Skills and Interests

Snowboarding, Ultimate Frisbee, Soccer, Animals, Photography, Writing, and Children.

ACTING: Midlevel

Alice Johnston   999-555-1212

SAG/AFTRA   Hair: Brunette   Eyes: Blue   Height: 5' 6"   Weight: 115

FILM/TELEVISION

THE PUB	Principle	ZBC Primetime
UNTIL AFTER TOMORROW	Featured	YBC Daytime
MAY FLOWERS	Elevator Girl	PD Media
DON'T TAKE MY DRUGS	Supporting	Crazyman Films
DON'T REHEAT THE MEAT*	Lead	Mini D Productions

   *Premiered Sundance Film Festival

NEW YORK THEATRE

THE ALICE AND JED SHOW	Various	The Hoop Theater
FEMALE THREAT GANG	Tanya/Shelley	Singing Space
HEP TO YOUR HOP	Mattie	Raw Materials
CISCO & THE CRUMMY DAY	Celie/Dorimene	Act Large Theater
UP CLOSE AND PERSONAL	Lisa/Maggie	Raw Materials
JUGGLER'S BLUES	Cinderella	Manhattan Mystery Space
YUMMY SPOONFULS (Reading)	Beth	Connecticut Theatrical
SPUNKY: The Sex Talks	Ensemble	Fascinating Theatre
GIRL'S LESSONS	The Girl	Ensemble of Fools
ZAK'S GOT TEN	Jane	Fembots Festival
TWELFH NIGHT	Fabian	Technion Space
LIES FOR LOVERS	Belinda	The Grand Old Theatre
IN MY BLOOD	Margaux	NY Fringe Festival
STATE OF CHURCH (*The Pulpit* Adapt.)	Bishop's Whore	Ensemble of Fools

THEATRE

CHINA TALKS	Shen Te	The State University
KARINA'S SONG	Amalia	The State University
SING IT AGAIN BUTLER	Young Wife	Local Theatre, Anytown
DEAD AT LAST DORTHY!	Telephone Call	Local Theatre, Anytown
THE COOK IN THE PANTRY	Geraldine	Residential College Theater
ROSENCRANTZ & GUILDENSTERN ARE DEAD	Gertrude/Alfred	Residential College Theater

TRAINING

The State University   **BA Theatre & Linguistics**

Shakespeare	Scene Study	Dan Genius
Improvisation	Dennis Miller Technique	Grant Smart
Voice	Leeann Rimes	

SPECIAL SKILLS

Conversational Japanese, Spanish; Dialects
Stand Up Comic (Caroline's, Stand Up NY, Gotham Comedy Club, etc.)
Circus Skills (Acrobatics, Partner Balancing); Multiple Sports; Flexibility

ACTING: Sr. Level

RISING Talent Inc.

JOHN J. JOHNSTON
6'2.5" 180 lb H: Brown E: Blue Tenor/Baritone SAG/AEA/AFTRA

FILM AND TELEVISION (selected)

Delta, Delta Call Me	Dr. Rock/Principal	Universe, Blane Buckskine
Stained Pants	Gerry Posh/Principal	Stained Pants Prod., Jugs McJuice
God's Own People	Clerk/Principal	Regulate Inc., Leslie Lopez
Trout and Minnow	Freddy/Support	PE Prod., Cindy Who
Principal! (Series Regular)	Mr. Herbert	Funnytimes, various
Alive Asleep	Orange Julius Clerk	Blue Hippo Films, R. Higden
Buckaroo	Pentagon Official	Seawest, Jed Jucavic
Big Celebrity Bomb	Supply Clerk	Rum River, R.L. Stubbards
The Gruesomes Go Hiking	Zombie Family Head	Filmic Fancy, Sarah Partager
Art Freaks	Curator's Assistant	Celebrate, Pasta Parmigiana
Psycho Sheet Walkers	Tony/Support	Celebrate/Fox, P. Parmigiana
The Jellyfish Attack!	Salesman/Principal	Seawater Prod, J. Verne
A Bunch of Mean Guys	Donovan/Principal	Fates Prod., M. Chickenhammer
Just Outside the Cage	Joe/Support	BRISK Int., Candace Cammy
The Moments Before Dinner	Motel Manager	BRISK Int., Sidney Sinksbottom
Cat's Tickler	Attendant/Principal	Fates Prod., Emmet Beasley
Biscuits and Gravy	Scurvy Jed/Principal	MegaMax, Ita Molly Moore
Hearts and Body Parts	Hector/Princ.	Recognize Inc., Marcello Masteroni
Scary Larry and the Gang	Master Raymond/Princ.	Picklodeon, Zak "Crazy" McGee
Biting Wit Gets Nowhere	Harry/Actor	Lulu Mixtner, Charlie Rudolf
Notable Charity Event	Improv	Live to Tape, Whisky Club
Who's Afraid of Traffic?	Harris/Princ.	Makeascene, P.K. Varato
Shapes and Plates	Kagan/Princ.	Ronald Murphy, Bill Kowalski
Grover Cleveland: In Love	Soldier/Principal	Public Service, Sally Sustrain

THEATRE (selected)

Where are you going?	Sly	Poodle Productions, Karen H. Caddy
Anton	Robert Gregory	SOLDAD, Percy Pinsky
Nurse Me Back To Hell	Junior Muskirk	Lake Bannock, Jesse Jakesky
Man of La Mancha	Barber	Lake Bannock, Jesse Jakesky
The Sneeze	Smirnov	Lake Bannock, Percy Pinski
Short Bursts of Funny	Ensemble	Silcon Valley Slickers, Improv
The Owl and the Pussycat	Felix	Lake Bannock, Chris Carterall
The Little Prince	The Pilot	Anytown Prod., Casey Cool
Running in Circles	Ensemble	Mid-city Fringe, Karina Miller
Pericles	Various	Theater Neat, Jesse Jakesky
Walking Around	Man	Play Right Prod., Percy Pinski
Translate Huh?	Marvin	Set the Stage Theater, Jane Enroute
Delicious Organ Lunch	Harry	Play Right Prod., Kelly Ann Cowan

Current & Ongoing MEMBER of 'Hot Seat' Players : Silver medalists, World Improv Tournament, 1994: Gold medalists at International Theatresports Tournament, 1994; Just For Laughs Festival, 1993-2001

VOICE and DUBBING (selected)

Sky Raiders	Council President	Animate, Kevin Kelloway
Kangaroo Town	Various	Happyfun, Lana Fudge
Fennel and Rosemary	Dill the Dullard	Bouncy, Chip McGee
Rolling Thunder	Various	Bouncy, Laurence Seer

123 Learning St. t : (999) 555-1212
Anycity, AS   f: (999) 555-1313
USA 101010   e-mail: rising@name.com

SPECIAL SKILLS
IMPROVISATION, CHARACTER ACTING,
Mime, Clown, Juggling, Acrobatics, Stand-up Comedy
DANCE : Tap, Jazz and Classical Ballet

ADMINISTRATION: Reception, Midlevel

Alice J. Johnston

aliceJ@yourname.com 999-555-1212

Providing incomparable Receptionist and Administrative Support

By understanding the true value of this position, Alice ensures the smooth function of daily company communications and the responsibility of representing the first impression.

How is this demonstrated, you may ask? Through displaying remarkable results at her work. Point blank, Alice...

1. Gives great phone. By understanding the importance of this initial contact, Alice has developed the voice as well as the patience to field all inquires. As such, she...

- **Can think on her toes**. If she doesn't know the answer, she will find the route to the answer and if all else fails will state as such and provide helpful tips and options.
- **Will ensure that manners and common courtesy are always exhibited.** From "please" and "thank you", to "you're welcome" as well as Alice's personal favourite of "*may* I tell the person who is calling?" politeness is essential.
- **Is tough.** As your first line of defence, she is not afraid to tell someone no, if it is appropriate. Supporting and enforcing boundaries is always done graciously.

2. Is tremendously organized. Because of Alice's almost extraordinary abilities with this skill she is able to appropriate her time more efficiently while also providing useful solutions. As a result, she...

- **Can multi-task better than any circus performer**. Being only human, some tasks may have to run at a slower pace but they're always being juggled while continually utilizing a professional demeanour.
- **Is able to locate any item faster than a speeding bullet.** Through the use of logic, she uses her deduction powers for searches, while reason is used for procedures.
- **Does not miss deadlines.** By respecting the need and importance of deadlines, Alice's time is effectively managed so that all projects are on time.

3. Functions marvellously well with computers. Through many years of professional and personal growth aided by computers Alice is confident in working within various programs but also can usually unearth logical sequences associated with their design. Because of this experience, she...

- **Knows thoroughly, has working knowledge of, or can easily figure out the following programs:** Word, Word Perfect, Excel, Lotus, Access, Act, Alpha 5, WinFax, Outlook, Outlook Express, Explorer, Netscape, Adobe Acrobat, PowerPoint, Publisher, Norton Anti Virus, plus numerous scanning, burning, and repair platforms.
- **Is not afraid of getting her hands dirty**. This by nature makes Alice a self-starter, if she needs to do something and is only left to her own devices, she can quite often discover the answer through reasonable calculations.
- **Can type almost as quickly as she thinks.** Although quickest when composing, transcribing makes a strong second showing.

Where has Alice performed these wondrous feats and who will attest to these amazing abilities? **The testimonials will be just as astounding**.

Want to know more about this outstanding individual who provides such top-notch dedication to her employment? Is she as remarkable in person as her superior skills would demonstrate?

Contact Alice and discover just how excellent this deal really is, as you'll make a smart choice in choosing her to be your next employee!

ADMINISTRATION: Admin. Assistant, Midlevel

Alice J. Johnston

123 Learning Street, Anytown, USA 10101
Phone: 999-555-1212   *alicej@yourname.com*

Profile:

An enthusiastic, customer service oriented Administrative Assistant. Skilled in time management with the ability to efficiently handle numerous tasks simultaneously aiming to meet project deadlines. Computer literate, and able to handle complex, multiple responsibilities.

Skills:

- **Software:** Microsoft Office Suite, Microsoft Publisher, Microsoft Outlook Express, Adobe Acrobat v4.0, Visio, Quick Books, ACT Database, Lotus Notes, SAP, Speedx (Expense and time tracking software), Oracle Application (remote time entry), MiraScan v4.02 (card scan), CaptureEze Pro, Web and Audio Conferencing, Roxio (CD and DVD Burner)
- **Graphic Design Software:** Coral Draw, Viewlet Builder 3, 4 (Qarbon)
- **Operating Systems:** Windows NT Server and Workstation 4.0, Windows 95/98/2000/XP, Novell, DOS, UNIX, AS400 Systems (ISIS)
- **Proven Capabilities**: Project Management Skills, Problem Solver, Excellent Technical and Data Manipulation Skills

Experience:

Abc Company – *Executive Assistant to the VP* February 2005–Present (1 month temp. assignment)

- Managing multiple calendars; Travel and appointment coordinating; Preparing reports

Smarts Inc. – ***Administrative Assistant/Office Manager*** March 2003–January 2005

- Provided administrative/office management for 4 companies under one umbrella, Smarts being the parent company
- Administrative Support to the Consultants, Managers (VP of Sales, Engagement Managers), President, and CEO
- Managing Executive Calendars; travel and appointment coordinating
- Maintaining the Employee Directory and Vendor contact information
- Preparation of Reports, financial data and presentation materials using PowerPoint, Word, and Excel completed before deadlines. Documents include company proposals, marketing promotional folders for clients, creating and editing employment ads, correspondences, creating stylish email invites. The use of my background in graphic designing was utilized in the creative use of graphics in presentations where needed.
- Arranging for recognition items to be sent out to employees and business contacts. (This involved researching appropriate items for the occasion and scheduling delivery within the company's budget.)
- Office management (interface and negotiation with vendors, purchase of office supplies, liaison with property management regarding facilities, coordinating, and managing the day to day activities of the office related to facilities)
- Setting up and disabling security access cards; ordering and sometimes designing business cards

HR Department

- Scheduling interviews and meetings to be held at the office as well as coordinating video and teleconferences for management and employees for meetings held after business hours. The different time zones at hand were a significant factor when participants were calling in from different locations such as the UK and Hong Kong. When scheduling videoconferences/meetings for candidates/participants they were provided with a site convenient in location as well as all necessary information for access.
- Scheduling courses/training for consultants and managers to attend
- Formatting and maintaining employee's resumes into the standard company profile format
- Standardizing forms for Recruiting Department; administer technical and functional test for candidates
- Maintaining the U.S. and Canadian employee manuals

PAYROLL Department

- Orienting new employees on the basic working of Speedx, a time and expense tracking database and acting as support for individuals with questions with regard to time and expenses
- Assisting Accounting with outgoing and incoming invoices and employee expense processing
- Tracking that status reports and Speedx time entries are submitted and up-to-date on a weekly basis
- Correcting employees Speedx entries for holiday/illness/vacation accrued
- Generating new timecards for the EntryT system in a format that would allow me to upload them into the company system

Accomplishments

- – Standardized and maintained employee/consultants profiles (These are employee resumes that were formatted to a standard structure and updated after each project.)
- – Recreated the employment ad so that a soft copy was available—can be updated and emailed to the press ready for posting
- – Initiated a project to create a complete database of business contacts in one place for all executives
- – Created viewlets for EYT (EntryT Systems) these viewlets can be used in training sessions to initiate hands-on learning

ADMINISTRATION: Admin. Assistant, Midlevel (cont.)

Other Experience:

Big Car Corp. - January 14, 2002–January 24, 2002 (temp.)
Human Resources-Assistant
- Filing
- Preparation of reports

Fast Courier - December 30, 2002–January 13, 2003 (temp.)
Billing Department- Assistant
- Data Entry
- Applying credit to accounts
- Filing

Hands Inc. - November 22, 2002–December 13, 2002 (temp.)
Receptionist/Administrative Assistant
- Travel and appointment Coordinating
- Reception, greet visitors
- Preparation of reports

Logistics Inc. - July 2002–November 22, 2002 (temp.)
Data Entry Clerk
- Data Entry
- Filing

George Corporation - May 27, 2002 (temp.)
Receptionist
- Reception, Greet Visitors
- Travel and appointment Coordinating

PRI Audio Video - March 2001–April 2002
Office Manager/ Customer Service Rep.
- Customer Service/Sales
- Appointment Scheduler
- Reception
- Preparation of reports

Big Bank - November 1999–February 2000 (temp.)
Bank Agent
- Data Entry

P.A Enterprises - June, 1996–December, 1998
Office Manager/Customer Service Rep./Graphic Designer
- Assistant to Owner
- Desktop Graphic Designer
- Reception
- Customer Service/Sales
- Office Manager

Education:
- State College-Network Technician Diploma-1999–2000
- Hill Senior Comprehensive-Business Diploma-1995–1997

Personal Interests:
- Reading a good book; wine tasting seminars; horseback riding; swimming lengths
- Volunteer: Big Sister Organization – Big Sister for 3 years

ADMINISTRATION: Trademark

ALICE J. JOHNSTON

123 Learning Street, Anytown, USA 10101
Home Tel: 999-555-1212   Email: alicej@yourname.com

Trademark Searcher with specialized education and experience in trademark searches and applications. Highly-detail oriented and leaves no room for doubts. High comfort level with Intellectual Property database software.

Professional Experience

AB & Associates April 2002–present
Intermediate Trademark Searcher

Responsible for all duties within the firm's Trademark Department, including: verifying for similar or confusing trademark names, printing and reviewing the weekly Trade-marks Journal, internet research; verifying all the filing particulars of applications and advertisements.

Additional responsibilities include the firm's advertising and promotions. Duties include updating and revising current ads, ensuring deadlines are met, contacting prospective advertisers.

Anytown International Film Festival June–Oct 2001
Raiser's Edge Database Administrator/ Finance Assistant

Responsible for maintaining and updating the database with all contacts and gifts, proofread and verify all sponsor information to be published in Festival Program, liaison with the Development division to ensure payment of major gifts and donations, invoicing, various administrative duties.

Cina-meida Productions (State College mentorship) May 2001
Research Assistant

Ministry of Municipal Affairs and Housing Feb–Aug 2000
Administrative Assistant- Communications Division

Responsible for updating database of ministerial correspondence and contacts, assisting in formatting memos for Senator's office, media clippings distribution, reception, various administrative duties.

Anytown Museum April–Nov 1999
Contract Administrative Assistant—Media Relations

Education
- **State College** 2000/01—Post-graduate Certificate in New Media
- **State University** 1993—B.A Major Anthropology

Professional Conferences and Symposia

Law School Professional Development course—October 2002
Topics included: Section 45 proceedings, trademark confusion/similarity

INTA (International Trademark Association—2003 Roundtable on Trademark Searching

ADMINISTRATION: Secretary, Sr. Level

Alice J. Johnston

123 Learning St., Anytown, USA 10101
Tel: (999) 555-1212 Mobile: (999) 555-1313 alicej@yourname.com

SECRETARY AND OFFICE MANAGER, OVER 10 YEARS EXPERIENCE

Highlights

• 12 years clerical experience, type 50 w.p.m.

• Proficiency in the use of various software programs including, but not limited to: Quicken, Excel, Front Page, Adobe PhotoShop, PaintshopPro, Lotus 1-2-3, MS Office and a general tendency to learn to use new software very quickly

• Patience and a propensity for training others

MOST RELEVANT OFFICE MANAGER EXPERIENCE

Diagnostic Institute   **1992–2002**
Office Manager
Responsibilities: Managed the day-to-day administration and operation of a professional medical practice comprised of 5 locations in the state. Acted as first point of contact for new patients, explaining and promoting services available. Answered phoned-in questions for all 5 locations for new patients, described all medical services and fees. (Different incoming lines, patients calling from throughout, and outside the state.)

Administration & Accounting

• Scheduled and booked appointments for the physicians and other health workers using "Medic" software for UNIX

• Administered accounting, billing, and insurance claims. Ensured health professionals were paid, posted all checks (including non-payroll) to Quicken, and prepared yearly reports for accountants

• Created new forms as needed: patient questionnaires for each medical program (Weight Loss, Sexual Dysfunction, etc.)

• Called patients with past due balances to arrange payment

• Mediated/resolved disputes over bills when/if insurance would not pay for services. Explained to patients which services were covered and which were not

• Answered email questions with regards to the clinic's radio show and general questions. Filled prescriptions under medical supervision

Training

• Trained office staff in administrative procedures; packaging and shipping of medications to staff physicians' specifications and to comply with current labeling regulations

Marketing & Promotion

• Implemented promotional initiatives through correspondence with all physicians in the area describing the services of the clinic, phone-in radio shows and monthly articles for Local Times

• Represented company at health shows

• Created website and brochures

RECENT EXPERIENCE

Green Party of Anytown, U.S.   5/3/2004–6/16/2004
Telephone Outreach Workers Group Supervisor
Promoted to this role after a few months when manager recognized my organizational and "keep everybody calm" skills. The role included the Telephone Outreach Worker's tasks plus:

• Prepare focused lists for other Telephone Outreach workers to call

• Invoice hours for the group

• Check in frequently with Membership Director for further instructions and keep group apprised of changes, new calling goals, etc. Keep Membership Director apprised of calling statistics

• Answer any questions that Telephone Outreach workers have, and help whenever necessary

Green Party of Anytown, U.S.   03/22/2004–05/03/2004
Telephone Outreach Worker
• Call current members and former members of the Green Party and request donations, membership renewals, and referrals. Answer any questions members and former members have regarding the current platform

• Call people on focused lists and discuss their concerns: "What is your most important issue in the upcoming election? What are your concerns with regards to the environment?" Try to illicit some interest in the Green Party in a conversational manner, leading up to an invitation to join the Green Party and/or make a contribution

Unclaimed Luggage & Goods Store   2002–2003
Sales Manager
In this role I was responsible for all day-to-day operations of the business and acted as primary front counter salesperson

• Hired, trained, & paid part-time employees (use of cash register, general sales techniques, etc)

• Responsible for advertising and accounting

OTHER SECRETARIAL EXPERIENCE

Psychosomatic Institute   1989–1992
Secretary/Receptionist
• Responsible for the day-to-day administration and operation of a professional medical office

• Acted as first point of contact of new patients explaining and promoting services available

• Undertook promotional initiatives through correspondence with all physicians in the area describing the services of the clinic

EDUCATION
State University Major in Economics
• French course at ABC College, June 2004

ADMINISTRATION: Sr. Administration & HTML

#111, 123 Learning Road
Anycity, Anystate 10101
Telephone: 555-999-1212
Email: alicej@yourname.com

ALICE J. JOHNSTON

Profile

- Corporate administration support with data entry and HTML experience. Fourteen years corporate experience supporting senior executives in highly respected companies.

Summary of Qualifications

- Over 10 years of customer service (inbound sales and technical support)
- Ability to communicate professionally with personnel at all levels
- Self starter, flexible, independent, organized, and punctual
- Multi tasker with excellent organizational skills
- Experienced Online Calendar manager
- Flexible, highly motivated, trustworthy, confident, and hard-working
- Proficient in HTML

Work Experience

Fulltime Contract: July 2002 to present

Position:	**Currently placed at ABC Computers through Recruiter Services Inc.**
Responsibilities:	Provide executive administrative support to one Director and five Senior Managers. Daily tasks include managing schedules, arranging travel, scheduling meetings, handling client inquiries, and coordinating conference calls. Handle sensitive and confidential matters relating to personnel. Coordinate special projects as required.

Position:	**Project Administrator**
Responsibilities:	Assist project manager in coordinating objectives including assembling team, projecting budget estimates, etc. Position included attending client meetings, recruiting suppliers, and managing project schedule.

Position:	**Website Content Manager**
Responsibilities:	Update content on an entertainment website using HTML, Basic PHP, and Photoshop technology. Provide support by email. Answer fan emails.

Fulltime Permanent: 1982–2002

Financial Consultants Inc. - July 1990 to June 2002

Position:	Administrative Assistant
Responsibilities:	General administrative duties including providing help desk support to 300+ tax professionals USA. Provided training over the phone using Net meeting and PowerPoint technology; calendar management, arranging travel and events. Responsibilities also included managing content on the Internet and Intranet using HTML and in Lotus Notes database; updated process documents, training manuals, and tax calculators in an excel spreadsheet.

Education

- State College Continuing Education
- Various IT Certificates

ADMINISTRATION: Executive Administration Specialist

Alice J. Johnston

123 Learning St., Anytown, USA 10101, Home (999) 555-1212, alicej@yourname.com

PROFILE
An **Executive Administrative Specialist** with editorial and project-based experience.

KEY QUALIFICATIONS
- ✓ Ten (10) years as an administrator with strong knowledge of membership development; volunteer management and event coordination
- ✓ A team player, often approached by colleagues and superiors alike due to demonstrated professionalism, resourcefulness, and insightful contributions
- ✓ Excellent organizer and communicator, known for bringing life new and/or developing projects
- ✓ Take great satisfaction and pride in seeing results and positive impact on the customer/client

EMPLOYMENT

Health Sciences LLC

Senior Executive Assistant to the President and CEO, May 2001 to Present
This position has the same duties as Executive Assistant with the addition of the following responsibilities:
- Lead a team of 18 administrative support staff to champion common issues, set administrative policies and procedures, share/implement best practices, ensure continuous quality improvement (CQI), foster team spirit, and organize the orientation process for new administrative support staff

Executive Assistant to the President and CEO, April 1999 to Present
- Organize and attend Board of Governors and Committee meetings
- Plan/organize the Annual General Meeting of corporate members, which includes a keynote address lunch/reception for members and invited guests
- Editor and production coordinator of a quarterly staff newsletter
- Proofread and edit as required by various departments, including continuing education and marketing
- Secretary to the Scholarships and Bursaries Committee, which includes coordinating and attending meetings, preparing all communications for the committee, developing promotional material, coordinating an annual awards ceremony, administering all scholarships and bursaries, and liaising with award recipients and sponsors
- Maintain organization's Policies and Procedures manual
- Maintain all relevant information on organization's Internet and Intranet sites
- Oversee production, review, and regular updates of editorial style manual
- Member of internal committees, including Continuous Quality Improvement (CQI) and Intranet Committee
- Prepare and manage annual budget for the president's office

American Anaesthesiologists' Society (AAS)

Coordinator, Administrative Services/Executive Assistant, September 1994 to April 1999
- Developed promotional material for membership recruitment and retention, and charitable donations
- Liaised regularly with volunteers, members, and organizations affiliated with AAS
- Organized several components of the annual conference, including the annual business meeting, awards ceremony, board and committee meetings, and other affiliated meetings
- Served as staff liaison to four volunteer committees, which included Memberships and Awards, Research Advisory, and Bylaws
- Administered the Research Awards program, which included regular communication with award recipients, industry sponsors, and Chair of the Research Advisory Committee
- Prepared and monitored the budget for membership, officers, and Board of Directors
- Served as secretary to the Board of Trustees for Society's charitable organization
- Conducted regular staff performance reviews and prioritizing sessions

ADMINISTRATION: Executive Administration Specialist (cont.)

Membership Coordinator, July 1993 to September 1994
- Maintained membership database, including the generation of invoices/renewal notices, processing of payments and response to subscriber questions and concerns
- Generated monthly and annual statistical reports

Journal Assistant, August 1992 to July 1993
- Maintained data base for subscribers to the *Journal of Anaesthesiology* including the generation of invoices/renewal notices, processing of payments, and response to subscriber questions and concerns
- Generated monthly and annual statistical reports

Specific Accomplishments

Project Management
- Planned and implemented a successful membership drive with a limited budget, which generated more than the targeted number of new membership accounts
- Organized two revisions of the AAS Constitution and Bylaws, which were necessary to incorporate new policies and procedures; liaised regularly with legal counsel during the process
- Assisted with the development and implementation of a new governance structure, which included the development of a new orientation manual for members, and independently organizing the first meeting of the newly structured Board of Directors

Organization
- Organized and served as a staff resource for four working groups and one task force all struck to review and/or develop new policies relative to remuneration, constitutional bylaws, allied health professionals, standards of practice, physician resources and the structure of volunteer committees
- Successfully organized five annual business meetings and five awards ceremonies
- Assisted with, and acted as liaison during the development of bylaws for the organization's charitable organization

Support
- Created membership reports that were used to prepare annual budgets and quarterly statistical analysis
- Provided ongoing support and resource information for new members of the Board of Directors

Management and training
- Effectively co-managed an office of five for two months in the absence of the Executive Director
- Interviewed and hired four AAS staff members
- Trained employees in committee organization, membership, subscription fulfilment, and general administration

EDUCATION

American Society of Association Executives
1995–1997, Association Management Education Program
Courses include leadership, change, strategy and structure, membership services, operations, and developments.

State University Faculty of Arts
1985–1989, Bachelor of Arts in English Literature

CONTINUING EDUCATION COURSES

National Quality Institute, **Framework for Excellence, Continuous Quality Improvement**, 2003
Editors' Association of America **Copyediting I**, February 2000
ASAE, **Communicating and Marketing Intangible Membership Benefits**, October 1998
State College Continuing Education Center, **Leadership and Supervisory Skills**, October 1998
Effective Business Writing Skills for Executives and Managers, February 1998

ADVERTISING: Account Director

123 LEARNING STREET, ANYTOWN, USA 10101
PHONE 999-555-1212• CELL 999-555-1313 • EMAIL johnj@yourname.com

JOHN J. JOHNSTON

ACCOUNT DIRECTOR - Proven manager, able to lead direct reports and focus extended teams on business objectives. Consistently forges deep working relationships with clients, third party stakeholders, and co-workers based on respect, trust and understanding. Polished presentation and communication abilities.

Core Skills

Strategic and creatively oriented - lives and breathes pop-culture, media and advertising in the pursuit of developing work and programs that move businesses forward.

Leadership and employee mentoring, training, advancement, and evaluation.

Budget development and administration, with a track record of turning unprofitable accounts into money-makers.

Key Accomplishments

Managed the repositioning of Vodka Inc. with an integrated campaign that has invigorated the brand's leadership position in USA, with a number of its television spots now airing internationally. Leveraged local and global learning to move "Big Russian Brand" to category leadership, redefining the cooler segment.

Championed the development of original creative on Big Cereal after 10 years of running adapted global spots. After achieving record brand growth in USA the campaign has rolled out to Canada and England where two spots have now run. Similarly, built a case to re-introduce Raisin Cereal advertising after a six-year hiatus that has resulted in substantial top-line growth for Big Cereal's largest brand.

Represented as a speaker at industry workshops and conferences—Thinkers Magazine 2002 Effective Market Conference (presented Vodka Case Study), 2001 NAMA Town Hall.

Launched the GHF University and Business Kinetics training programs with a focus on career pathing for junior and intermediate employees. Also developed and selected a number of third party training programs designed to grow the core skills of GHF staff.

Transformed Bigstar account to high client satisfaction and profitability, while increasing overall revenue, two years running.

Promoted from Supervisor to Account Director at GHF.

ADVERTISING: Account Director (cont.)

Experience

Account Director, GHF - Sept 2002 to present

Responsible for the management of accounts, representing USA on international teams. Lead all financial and strategic initiatives for managing 3 junior reports on 5 brands. Involved in managing integrated programs consisting of promotional activity, direct marketing and digital.

Account Supervisor, GHF - July 1999 to Sept 2002

Primary responsibilities included managing the strategic and creative development of consumer communication for clients, reporting to VP Group Account Directors.

Senior Media Planner, MacDonald MacLane - Dec 1998 to July 1999

Managed the development, presentation, and execution of communications plans for clients including Big Breweries and Bigstar Sports and Entertainment (Car Race).

Media Planner/Buyer, GHF - Oct 1997 to Dec 1998

Planned media expenditures for large brand name clients. In addition to typical media responsibilities, developed integrated promotional campaigns that ranged from sampling opportunities to major contests. Promoted from Jr. Media buyer.

Media Assistant, Canyon Advertising & Marketing - Mar 1997 to Sept 1997

Responsibilities included buying print and broadcast in North American markets, as well as general campaign maintenance for major entertainment industry clients.

Education

State University, 1991–1995,

Bachelor of Arts, Honors Political Science

Interests

A belief that "to be interesting you must be interested" has resulted in a diverse and varied pursuit of things athletic, artistic, and topical. Ex-rugby player; current hockey player and snowboarder; aspiring golfer.

ADVERTISING: Marketing Manager

Alice J. Johnston

555-999-1212; alicej@yourname.com

Professional Profile

A creative marketing and advertising professional with eight years of experience within various industries including retail, telco, and e-commerce. Proven track record in developing and launching successful traditional and web marketing campaigns on time and within budget. Exceptional at managing multiple projects from conception to completion. A team player that is highly organized and demonstrates self-motivation, creativity, and initiative to achieve corporate goals.

- ◆ Start-up e-commerce experience
- ◆ Brand Equity Experience
- ◆ Key Account Management
- ◆ Loyalty Program Management

- ◆ 8 years of marketing experience
- ◆ Promotions & Events
- ◆ Advertising/Media Planning
- ◆ P&L Management

Employment History

E3COMMERCE.COM, Anycity, Anystate   June 2000 to present
Marketing & Vendor Relations Manager
E3COMMERCE.COM is the world's first Internet company to combine the virtual and physical presence of e-commerce via staffed delivery depots where E3COMMERCE customers shop online and pick up their purchases at their convenience.

► Responsible for the development, execution, and evaluation of B2C marketing campaigns encompassing offline and online strategies.
► Outstanding success in integrating and managing twelve key accounts such as Bookstore.com, Food.com, and Clothes.com.

Accomplishments:
► 50% conversion from registered to purchaser; 30% multi-purchasers; 31% first time online shoppers.
► Successfully developed and managed new member acquisition programs resulting in increases from +27% to +40% in new registrations.
► Launched cross promotion with PizzaPieZone®. Results include a 7% redemption rate for free pizza coupons and a +56% increase on E3COMMERCE.com page views.
► Developed and managed online Xmas promotion that increased sales +32% above targets.

MEDIA INTERACTIVE, Anycity, Anystate   December 1998 to June 2000
Regional Marketing Manager
Media Interactive is North America's leading interactive voice response software developer with annual sales of $100 million.
► Primary responsibilities included acquisition of new members and retention of existing members (member servicing and added value); business planning and analysis.
► Responsible for developing and managing all advertising, brand management, direct marketing programs, promotions, and customer service relations. Worked closely with advertising agency on the development of quarterly media plans.
► Responsible for the Central USA region which generated a total revenue of $25 million.

Accomplishments:
► Increased the Anycity marketplace revenue by +49% and profitability by +58% in FY99 vs FY98.
► Increased revenue in Central region by 3% in FY99 vs FY98. New member acquisition rose by 13% vs budget in Q4 FY99.
► Oversaw major marketing initiative programs that focused on retention resulting in an increase of 5% in sales across twenty-five markets in the USA.
► Joined organization as a Marketing Manager and promoted to above position in October 1999.

ADVERTISING: Marketing Manager (cont.)

Alice J. Johnston   Page 2

LUXURY CLOTHING INC., Anycity, Anystate   September 1996 to December 1998
Marketing Manager
Head office of a luxury international retailer with annual sales of $30 million.

▶ Developed and managed media sponsorships, special events, advertising, and direct marketing campaigns. Conceived creative concepts for in-store POP and promotions.
▶ Point of contact for advertising agency (based in Anycity, Anystate).
▶ Responsible for writing and editing press releases and other promotional materials.
▶ Business planning and budget development.
▶ Fragrance buyer for national stores.
Accomplishments:
▶ Increased overall exposure of the Luxury brand in print and television by effectively building relationships with media representatives.
▶ Created direct marketing campaign that contributed to a 55% sell through at full-price.
▶ Saved over $10,000 in two seasons by assuming the design and production of national newspaper ads.
▶ *Factory Outlet Boutiques*: Initiated creation of brochure for tourist kiosks—increased sales by 2%. Implemented Outlet Privilege Card which increased sales by a minimum of +10%.
▶ *Special Events*: Organized fragrance launch at Fancy Street boutique. Oversaw the coordination of the fashion show for the Anycity Fashion Show Committee in October 1998 in support of women's cancer care and the Local Hospital. Oversaw opening gala of flagship boutique on Fancy Street. Each event received extensive print and television coverage.

EFFECTIVE COMMUNICATIONS, Anycity, Anystate   February 1996 to September 1996
Sales & Marketing Coordinator
Effective is the publisher of "Strategic Magazine" and "Music Magazine".

NATIONAL ADVERTISING, Anycity, Anystate   July 1994 to February 1996
Production and Graphic Artist
National is North America's largest recruitment advertising firm based in Anycity, Anystate with offices across the U.S.

POSTAL CORPORATION, Anycity, Anystate   March 1993 to October 1993 (contract)
Design Assistant within Retail Operations dept.

EDUCATION

Internet Business & Technology Diploma, University of Anycity   1999–2001
▶ E-commerce courses with a focus on brand equity & marketing (1 year university program)

Bachelor of Arts, Anycity University   1988–1992

Other: Various professional courses in Marketing, PR, and art direction.

ADDITIONAL SKILLS

Computer literate in word processing and desktop publishing programs including
Excel, Visio, FrontPage, PowerPoint, QuarkXPress, and PageMaker.

INTERESTS

Fine arts, watching and playing sports, traveling to new spots around the world, World Vision Sponsor

ADVERTISING: Senior Account Executive

Alice J. Johnston
123 Learning Street, Anytown, USA 10101
999-555-1313 (M) 999-555-1212 (H)
Email address: alicej@yourname.com

PROFILE

An **Advertising Executive** with emphasis placed on packaged goods across a broad range of categories. Extensive experience in managing North American relationships, strategic analysis, long term planning, qualitative and quantitative research, in-market monitoring, competitive creative analysis, and original creative development. An enthusiastic individual possessing strong communication & leadership skills with a commitment to excellence & superior business results.

CAREER HISTORY

TierOne Agency
Senior Account Executive—Big Chew Co.   **August '03–June '05**

Key Accomplishments:
- Hired onto account and moved after one month onto flagship brands.
- Played integral role in development of new brand platform, which is being used to restage brand in U.S. market; currently leading creative development.
- Launched integrated '02 TV, print & radio campaign for GoodGum resulting in significant increases in both consumer measures & brand sales since campaign launch in Jan '05.
  - *After 3 months, on-air directional results indicated +10% build in volume sales.*
  - *Campaign selected as AdReview.com's hot spot of the week.*
- Instrumental in development and implementation of new corporate budget system for TierOne.
- Supervised Account Executive and Account Coordinator in daily account management.
  - *Turned around an unmotivated team by ensuring appropriate day-to-day training and fostering a friendly working environment.*

Supra Agency
Account Supervisor—SuperSoftener   **June '02–August '03**

Key Accomplishments:
- Instrumental in the development of a new brand vision to establish a unique place for SuperSoftener in the fabric care category.
  - *New Brand Vision embraced and used against all Brand initiatives.*
- Launched new SuperSoftener into the U.S. marketplace with TV, print, and outdoor.
  - *Initiated use of new research technique (Internet Nielsen test) allowing for accelerated test results.*
- Developed SuperSoftener OtherBrand Defense plan to defend against launch of OtherBrand.
  - *Recommendation resulted in media heavy up.*
- Supervised Assistant Account Manager in daily account management.

ADVERTISING: Senior Account Executive (cont.)

Belly & Best Ad Agency
Account Manager   BodyandHand Cream/YummyMustard   **May '99–June '02**

BodyandHand Cream:
Key Accomplishments:
- Management of 9 brands within the BodyandHand Cream portfolio (Soapy/Dishy/Fragrant/Liquid/ManderinLake/GelCream etc)
  - *Promoted January '98 to Account Manager.*
- Initiated qualitative research to determine whether Southwestern strategy was appropriate for BodyandHand in the northern coastal market.
  - Resulted in leading the development of a coastal specific creative.
  - *BodyandHandCream (Liquid) grew +39% Northern Coastal Market (4 weeks ending Feb 27 '99)—campaign began January '99.*
- Played integral role in strategic/creative development for launch of Squirt and Spray in U.S. in response to a new competitive glass cleaner entry.
  - *Supervised North American creative initiative with senior management.*
  - *Grew total Squirt and Spray by 8 share points; achieved advertising awareness of 46% within 4 months.*
- Led effort to incorporate high-end furniture manufacturer endorsement into Wiper campaign to help reinforce key brand strategic equity of "Best On Your Best Car".
  - *Launch of campaign helped reverse consecutive trend of declines and was adopted globally.*

Condiment Foods:
- Played integral role in attaining the Condiment Foods account for our agency; researched and produced initial presentation deck that secured solid client/agency partnership.
- Spearheaded the strategic/creative development for the launch of YummyMustard.

OTHER ACCOMPLISHMENTS
H&M/FCB Social Committee   **September '99–June '02**
- Appointed by the president to ensure company morale stays high through continued social events; led organization of Christmas party, which received 90% attendance.

Alpha Pi Sorority   **1995–1997**
- Rush Committee Chairperson; co-organized numerous social events.

EDUCATION
Postgraduate
International Marketing—Latin American Profile
State College, 1998

Undergraduate
Bachelor of Arts—Political Science/Philosophy
State University, 1993–1997

SKILLS & INTERESTS
- Working knowledge of Spanish
- Athletic activities with emphasis on tennis, rock climbing, and sailing

AIRLINE: Corporate Flight Attendant

Alice J. Johnson
123 Learning Ave., Anytown, U.S.A.
Phone Number: 999-555-1212
Email: alicej@yourname.com

CORPORATE FLIGHT ATTENDANT

Objective: Seeking a position as a corporate flight attendant or contract with an executive jet company allowing me to utilize my extensive knowledge of the aviation industry, first-class service, and customer service.

Education:

Beyond The Best Corporate Flight Attendant Training - September 2004
Emergency training taught at Flyright Aviation Center, Othertown, State (part 142 qualified facility) by a part 142 trainer and follows part 91, 125, and 135 guidelines.

Cooking Institute of Otherstate - September 2003
Certificate in Food Prep

American Heart Association - January 2004
Certified in First Aid, CPR, and AED

California College - September 1995

Employment History:

Flight Attendant, BIG CARRIER Airways   January 1996–Present

Provide the highest level of comfort, customer service, and safety for both domestic and international air travel. Facilitate flight attendant coordination, in-cabin service, and all aspects of cabin safety as senior flight attendant. Received in-flight excellence awards. Trained flight attendants in new in-flight programs.

Customer Service Agent, OTHER CARRIER Air   November 1994–January 1996

Provided the highest level of customer service in both domestic and international ticketing, worked arrival flights and baggage service department. Completed four weeks of domestic ticketing, two weeks of international ticketing, and one week training in Frankfurt, Germany with British Airways for international inaugural flight to Europe.

International Passenger Service Agent, Super Sky Group   Dec 1990–June 1994
Provided all aspects of passenger and airport services for charter, international, and domestic airlines; ticketing, boarding, worked arrival flights, departing flights, international documentation, security procedures, and screening.

Aircraft/Simulator Training: Certified on the following aircrafts:
A319, A320, A321, A330, B727, B737, B757, B767, MD-80, DC-9, F-28,
F-100, Gulfstream, Challenger, BBJ, Falcon

CPR/Defib Training: First Aid, CPR, and AED certified by the American Heart Association January 2004

Miscellaneous:

Fluent in Spanish

* Current Valid Passport * Ready to Fly!

*Highly motivated *Detailed oriented *Dedicated *Personable *Dependable *Reliable *Strong communication and interpersonal skills *Team player *Creative *Cabin protocol and culinary training * Attention to detail

AIRLINE: Aviation Manager

JOHN J. JOHNSTON

123 Learning St., Anytown, USA 10101 (h) 999-555-1212 **johnj@yourname.com**

Management - Aviation

EDUCATION:

Recognized University, Anytown, ST
Bachelor of Science in **Aviation Technology**
Graduation Date: May 2003
Cumulative GPA: 3.30/4.00 (May 2003)

RELEVANT COURSEWORK:

Aviation Human Factors, Air Traffic Control, Boeing 727 & ERJ systems, Crew Resource Management, Airline Indoctrination, Business Writing, Technical Speech & Communications

EXPERIENCE:

Easy Airlines d/b/a Northwest Flights   Spring 2004–present
City Manager—Northwest Station
- Oversaw day-to-day flight operations & station functions
- Established and maintained company & FAA documents and files
- Completed requisite reports & audits for the company and airport
- Provided guidance, mentoring, and training to station personnel
- Oversaw Easy Operations in our Anytown (AYT) contract station

Easy Airlines d/b/a Northwest Flights   Summer 2003–2004
Customer Service Representative—Othertown Station
- Conducted ticketing and check-in at ticket counter & jet gates
- Performed ramp and operations duties during flight operations
- Traveled to other Easy stations for temporary duty when needed
- Assisted station manager with office work & record keeping

Recognizable University Human Factors   Winter 2001–2003
Applied Research Projects
Together Airlines—BIG Airport Safety Team project member
- Performed time and motion studies at BIG
- Assisted team of several members in creating work process map
- Implemented Safety Metrics Program

ABC Corporate Flight project member
- Audited ABC's International flight department in Paris, France

Recognizable's Union Catering & Events   Summer 2001–2003
Banquet Server
- Prepared facility for scheduled events
- Directed employees in the daily activities of our facility
- Trained new personnel
- Represented our company on off-premises functions

ACTIVITIES:

Secretary, Aviation Technology Student Council
Freshman Orientation Airport & Facilities Tour Guide

INTERESTS/ HOBBIES:

Ice hockey & outdoor activities, international travel, music & piano, attending college football bowl games

John J. Johnston
123 Learning St., Anytown, USA 10101
RES. (999) 555-1212   BUS. (999) 555-1313

A multi-faceted Airline Marketing Executive with 10 years of progressive experience delivering results in getting people places by air.

BUSINESS EXPERIENCE

BIG AIRLINES, Manager, Marketing Communications   **1995–Present**

Responsible for the planning, development and implementation of integrated marketing and communications plans to achieve specific marketing and corporate objectives. Scope includes strategic planning, brand management, advertising, promotions, direct mail, online marketing, and sales support/collateral development.

- Team leader on the oneworld alliance (an alliance of seven major airlines) Marketing and External Communications working group. Jointly managed the global launch of oneworld through a combination of advertising, collateral, direct mail, and online communications.

- Directed the efforts of cross-functional teams in the design and implementation of national consumer promotions including "You Want to Win" (1998), "Fly! Fly Free" (1997) and "YAPP" (1996) promotions. The "YAPP" promotion delivered the largest market share gains in the history of the airline in both the eastern and western shuttle markets. The "Fly! Fly Free" promotion exceeded forecasted returns by over 100%.

- Led the development and execution of an integrated marketing and communications plan to support the launch of the "Shuttle" brand and product. In only one month, the campaign achieved highest recorded top of mind brand awareness nationally and in shuttle markets.

- Directed the design of a highly responsive retail pricing ("seat sale") process that gives Americans the ability to both lead initiatives and react to competitive actions within a 24-hour period. The revised process has generated millions of dollars in incremental revenue by capitalizing on "first mover" advantage and by minimizing the impact of competitor led initiatives.

- Managed the development and execution of the first multi-language, pan-Asian advertising campaign to support the launch of the Club Fantastic (Business Class) product and brand in Asia (1996). The campaign was successfully rolled out across Asia generating incremental high yield revenue and achieving record awareness and approval ratings in the key Hong Kong market.

AIRLINE: Airline Marketing Exec.. (cont.)

Murphy J Jones, Project Manager/Consultant   1994–1995

Project leader for several complex and time sensitive marketing projects for clients including ABC Air Lines, XYZ Airways, and China Airlines. The projects were diverse in scope and included customer segmentation analysis, direct marketing and promotions. The ability to build cohesive teams and alliances of diverse stakeholders was effectively applied to implement the different projects on time and on budget.

- XYZ Airways: directed the development of a customer segmentation and retention program for the Frequent Traveler Program based on an analysis of sales transaction and demographic data. In tandem with the customer segmentation project, designed a direct marketing pre- and post-promotion measurement template using statistical methods to predict and validate incremental response and revenue results.

- ABC Air Lines: designed, developed, and implemented five separate promotions direct marketed to over three million qualified targets. The promotions involved multiple offers targeting different customer segments pulled from several internal and external databases.

CAT AIRLINES, Manager, Passenger Marketing   1991–1994

- Initiated and led a weekly cross-departmental team focused on identifying specific route and system revenue opportunities, establishing revenue and market share objectives and developing plans to achieve them. The "Pacific Revenue Team" model was later used as the template for separate Atlantic and Domestic teams.

- Project leader on the national launch of the ZAG Airlines worldwide alliance. The launch consisted of a joint retail pricing promotion and "Passport to Europe" travel product launch. The launch was communicated through national advertising, direct mail, sales support collateral, and trade communications.

BIG FLYER, Marketing Analyst   1988–1991

- Directed the development and implementation of first direct mail campaign in the United Kingdom. The promotion targeted Big Plastic Card Inc. cardholders in the UK with demonstrated spending history in the U.S. and achieved over a 2.5% response.

- Acted as the primary liaison with alliance partner SAS (Swiss Airline System) and coordinated all joint marketing efforts to support the cooperative service between New York, Copenhagen, and Stockholm.

EDUCATION

HBA (Business Administration), 1988 - Focus: Marketing
School of Business Administration - State University

MCS (Communications Studies), candidate for 2001
Focus: Marketing and Organizational Communications
Part-time student, entering year four of a five-year program

INTERESTS: Skiing (Alpine, Nordic, and Telemark), Running, Mountain Biking, Hiking/Backpacking, Swimming, Rollerblading, and Writing.

AIRLINE: Pilot

John J. Johnston

123 Learning Place A-1, Anycity, Anystate 10101
Primary Phone: 555-999-1212 Alternate Phone: 555-999-1414
Email Address: johnj@yourname.com

Primary Objective: Pilot

Total Flight Time: 900

Pilot in Command	864	Second in Command	3
Turbojet	5	MEL/Turboprop	150
Single-engine	710		

FAA second Class Medical: January 30, 2005

Awards and Honors
First in class from flight school (Airline Transport Professionals). Graduated ahead of schedule (May 2002).
Meritorious promotions in the USMC (E2, E3, E4).

Experience
Aviation Services - Anycity, Anystate   Jan 24, 2005–Present
Flight Instructor, Pilot, maintained duty records, pilot and aircraft logbooks. Handled sale of used aircraft, including purchase of training aircraft. Assisted in airport construction projects and improvement plans.

Local County Airport - Flight Instructor   2002–2005
Independent Contractor/Instructor: private/commercial students

USMC   1995–2003
Led Marines on a platoon level in various construction and humanitarian projects. Served in Guatemala, Jamaica, and The United States. Served as interpreter (English/Spanish).

Additional Skills
Fluent in Spanish and speak conversational German.

Education
Wind Valley State College (online)   Jan 08, 2004–Present
Major: Aviation

Southern State University, Anycity   Aug 24, 1997–Dec 22, 2001

Military Service
United States Marine Corps   Sep 1995–Sep 2003

AIRLINE: Pilot (Captain)

John J. Johnston

123 Learning Street
Anytown, USA 10101
Primary Phone: 999 555 1212 Alternate Phone: 999 555 1313
Email Address: johnj@yourname.com

Primary Objective: Pilot

A&P Mechanic, EMT/CPR Certified, Chief pilot background, International Experience, RVSM trained, Typed DA-50, 900 Differences trained, DA-20

Total Flight Time: 10300

Pilot in Command	6800
Turbojet	2800
MEL/Turboprop	2500
Single-engine	1500
Second in Command	3500
Civilian Aircraft G.W. less than 75,000 lbs.	3500

Certifications
- ATP Certification
- FAA Physical Class: 1   Aug 21, 2004

Experience

Executive Air Inc. -   Oct 15, 2004–Present
Captain Falcon 900. Part 135 Passenger transport worldwide.

Self Employed - Anytown USA   Dec 15, 2003–Oct 15, 2004
Contract Pilot-Part 91 Falcon 20, Falcon 50, and Falcon 900.

Big Telecommunications Inc Flight Operations -   Apr 01, 1997–Dec 20, 2003
Captain Falcon 20. Part 91 Passenger transport. Department Safety Officer.

Shore Aviation -   Jun 01, 1995–Apr 01, 1997
Captain BE-90 Part 91 Passenger transport within the state.

Princess Airlines -   Sep 01, 1993–Dec 01, 1995
First Officer F-27. Part 121 Federal Express feeder.

Awestruck Airlines -   Jun 01, 1993–Sep 01, 1993
First Officer DHC-6. Part 135 Passenger transport.

Big Dessert Airways -   Jun 01, 1991–Jun 01, 1993
Captain CE-402. Part 135 Passenger transport.

Education

State Aeronautical University   Aug 01, 1981–Dec 01, 1989
Degree: B.S.
Major: Professional Aeronautics

Military Service

ARMY   Sep, 1985–Jun, 1988

AIRLINE: Airline Manager

John J. Johnston   123 Learning Isle, Anycity, AS 10101

johnj@yourname.com • Cellular 555-999-1212 • Home 555-999-1414

Aviation Manager with extensive production management experience.

Summary
Aviation Management professional with a background that spans over 25 years in the Airline industry. Leadership experience includes excellent team building, organizational, written, and oral communication skills. Recognized for cost reduction, increased productivity, and customer service. Earned top recognition and awards for developing a repair scheme for cargo decompression panels on the A300 fleet which realized a yearly savings of 2 million dollars for Flight Airlines. Attained 1997 Employee of the Year Honors in Line Maintenance. Currently department Lead Environmental Coordinator, manager in charge of FAA Audits, and Aircraft Recovery Team Member.

Experience

Flight Airlines, Anycity, Anystate   1998 to Present
Manager of Production
Leads a night shift team of 120 mechanics, 8 Crew Chiefs, and 7 Supervisors. Responsible for the timely and safe completion of the overnight workload consisting of 30 aircraft and 8 international departures.
- Reduced overtime expense 2% by forming a work rules review team which redefined roles resulting in increased productivity.
- Established new lines of communication by instituting a monthly business review meeting with the TWU leadership.
- Increased MEL removal rate 26% on A300 aircraft resulting in #1 rating in the system.
- Skilled in internal customer relations, problem solving, and creating a more supportive team environment.
- Managed development and implementation of Aircraft Taxi/Movement plan used by the Anycity Hub.

Flight Airlines, Airport Anystate   1990 to 1998
Avionics Supervisor
Administered and Supervised the Avionics Department. Responsible for the timely completion of the overnight Avionics workload. Scheduled required and recurrent training. Supported department tooling and calibration requirements.

- 1997 Line Maintenance Employee of the Year.
- A300/757 Product Team representative for Airport Anystate.
- Established A300, 757 B check tooling and parts requirements. Initiated checks at station.

Flight Airlines, Airport Anystate   1989 to 1990
Line Maintenance Mechanic
Line Maintenance experience includes: 727, 747, 757, 767, A300, MD80, DC10, MD11.
- Performed in a relief Crew Chief capacity.

Local Airlines, Anycity, AS, Airport Anystate   1979 to 1989
Line Maintenance Mechanic
Line Maintenance experience includes: L1011, A300-B4K, DC9, 727.
- Overhaul Sheet metal mechanic in Anycity 1979–1981.

Education
Academy of Aeronautics, Airport Anystate   1976
A.A., Occupational Studies

ANALYST: Business Analyst MBA

John J. Johnston MBA

BUSINESS SYSTEMS ANALYST

- President's Award at Stream Corp. in 1999 for outstanding contribution.
- Excellent verbal, written, and interpersonal skills as revealed through facilitation of joint requirement planning sessions, client presentations, and proposal writing.
- Strong customer passion and customer focused attitude.
- Creative problem solver and idea generator.
- Team skills and entrepreneurial spirit.
- Bilingual (Spanish and English).

Stream Corporation - January 1998 to Present

Role: Business Systems Analyst - January 2003 to Present
Responsibilities:
- Conducting interviews with key stakeholders to develop requirements;
- Researching and proposing the best-suited web content management solution that matches the requirements gathered; and
- Completing help documentation.

Achievements:
- Exceeded client expectations with solution provided;
- Secured further work for the organization; and
- Presented account information to the account management team at the end of the project.

Role: Functional Analyst - December 2001 to December 2002
Responsibilities:
- Modeling the current and future business processes;
- Reviewing business and technical specifications; and facilitating requirement-gathering sessions.

Achievements:
- Secured client signoff for system development;
- Developed all training materials; and mapped client requirements for a complicated business process.

Role: Bid Member - September 2001 to November 2001
Responsibilities:
- Working directly with the Account Management team, VP of Business Development, the Proposal Management team, Senior Architects, and Support Managers for proposal preparation;
- Establishing relationships with third-party representatives, forming teaming agreements and Service Level Agreements (SLAs).

Achievements:
- Submitted a proposal that earned Allstream a $1.5 Million contract to work with the Office of the Superintendent of Bankruptcy on phase 1 of its multi-phase e-filing project.

MBA for Science and Technology - State University -
Leave of absence - May 2000 to August 2001

John J. Johnston
Phone 1: 999-555-1212
Phone 2: 999-555-1313

123 Learning Street, Anytown, USA 10101
Fax: 999-555-1414
Email: Johnj@yourname.com

Stream Corp. - Voice Services Business Office -
Role: Manager - April 1999 to April 2000
Responsibilities:

- Managing a successful team of thirty (30) staff members who participated in the following business processes: billing operations, sales commissions, customer care, and financial reporting;
- Allocating staff resources according to project priorities and work loads; and
- Supporting senior management in weekly executive operations meetings by identifying key metric deviations and providing solutions to any of the issues identified.

Achievements:

- Reduced business office backlogs from 3 weeks to 48 hrs, which decreased lag times for customer implementations, the payment of sales staff commissions, and the realization of revenues;
- Designed and implemented web-based operational reports to ensure ubiquitous access to company statistics and reports for senior management; and
- Increased monthly revenue base through revenue assurance projects initiated in conjunction with finance, sales, project management, and billing operations.

Stream Corp. - Performance Management Team -
Role: Financial Analyst - June 1998 to March 1999
Responsibilities:

- Reviewing potentially large sales contracts against financial hurdles such as ROI and NPV calculations;
- Conducting audits on the sales commission and regional order implementation processes and presented a report to senior management with conclusions and recommendations, many of which were adopted for both processes; and
- Working with business unit managers of ailing departments as an internal consultant to generate working documents that would provide for process success within their department.

Achievements:

- Reorganized the Care Business office to better align it with the operational needs of the customer; and
- Developed and implemented a strategy to decrease productivity issues in the Calgary Customer Care Office with the support from the Senior Vice-President of Operations.

EDUCATION

State University MBA for Science and Technology   2001
The University's MBA is the top ranked MBA program in America.

State University B.Sc. Environmental Economics   1997

John J. Johnston
Phone 1: 999-555-1212
Phone 2: 999-555-1313

123 Learning Street, Anytown, USA 10101
Fax: 999-555-1414
Email: Johnj@yourname.com

ANALYST: Investment Analyst

JOHN J. JOHNSTON, CFA	123 Learning St., Anytown, USA 10101 Phone: 999.555.1212 Email: johnj@yourname.com

INVESTMENT ANALYST ▣ FINANCIAL ANALYST

Highly competent, challenge and results driven professional with a passion for conducting detailed financial analyses, designing financial models, and compiling effective reports. Self motivated, analytical and methodical in approach, multi-tasker, works efficiently and effectively to meet deadlines. Articulate, friendly, builds profitable rapport with all persons, internally and externally; proactive negotiator, recognized for addressing issues expeditiously and amicably. Reliable, effective team player; provides direction and support for peers to succeed and deliver.

Core competencies include:

▪ Corporate Valuations	▪ M&A Advisory
▪ Financial Analysis & Modeling	▪ Financial Negotiations
▪ Equities Research	▪ Client Relations
▪ Interactive & Compelling Presentations	▪ Marketing & Business Development

EDUCATION

Institute of Chartered Business Valuators **2004**
Completed the **American Society of Appraisers** study program

CFA Institute, **CHARTERED FINANCIAL ANALYST** **1998**

University of Italy, **MASTER OF SCIENCE – Economics** **1994**

PROFESSIONAL EXPERIENCE

Johnston Family, **HOUSE HUSBAND** **2002–present**
- Charged with caring for daughter aged 4, allowing spouse to pursue her career goals.
- Conduct research and study towards the American Society of Appraisers accreditation.

ABC Ltd., Indonesia, **PRINCIPAL RESEARCH ANALYST** **1998–2002**
- Selected by the Chief Executive Officer due to reputation and work ethic to assist with ABC's corporate finance mandates, which included large corporate debt restructurings, a merger, private equity transactions, sales of businesses, and independent expert valuations.
- Acted as representative at various corporate finance meetings; supported and guided senior client management through complex corporate transition periods.
- Conceived and produced operating and financial forecasts for companies in a large number of industries.
- Performed a key role during bilateral and multilateral negotiations with financial institutions from three continents: North America, Asia, and Europe.
- Assignments included companies from the following industries: property development, manufacturing, agriculture, chemical manufacturing, infrastructure, and retail.

Accomplishments
- Shared knowledge with companies after gaining a reputation as an expert valuator; developed a hedge mechanism, working off purchasing power parity for a debt restructuring of a US$230 M debt.
- Played a key leadership role in a multicultural environment in partnering with industry experts, tax consultants, lawyers, and actuaries tasked with transitioning a large business group through a process equivalent to a Chapter 11 debt reorganization.
- Developed a presentation providing financial education to Indonesia's stock market regulator for purposes of the first merger between listed companies in Indonesia.

XYZ Securities Ltd., Indonesia, **HEAD OF RESEARCH & BANKING ANALYST**   1997–1998
- Recruited to the lead research position with only 3 years experience after developing a reputation for impressive work.
- Regarded in companies' global offices as the Indonesia expert; frequently asked to provide opinions on the Indonesian market and economy.
- Provided research coverage of Indonesian bank stocks, economics, and investment strategy.
- Marketed to institutional client base, including an extensive marketing trip to the United States.
- Trained, coached, and supported junior analysts.

Consultants Inc. Indonesian affiliate, Indonesia, **EQUITIES ANALYST & ECONOMIST**   1995–1997
- Facilitated a marketing trip to Singapore to meet with Fund Managers.
- Researched, compiled, and distributed reports on bank stocks, representing 12% of stock market capitalization, and the Indonesian economy.
- Interacted with diverse professionals across the private and public sectors to obtain information.

Big Brand Company, Indonesia, **INTERN**   1994–1995
- Chosen to participate in a process reengineering assignment for a large viscose manufacturer.
- Supervised computerization of the inventory system.
- Assigned to complete various consulting projects in the corporate finance and business services department.

Software Inc. Germany   1993–1994
ACCOUNTANT (part-time)

Institute for Research in Innovation Management at the University of Italy   1990–1992
STUDENT ASSISTANT

VOLUNTEER WORK

Local Committee of RIGHTS at the University   1990–1993
TREASURER & VICE PRESIDENT

ANALYST: Sr. Systems Analyst Designer

JOHN JOHNSTON

123 Learning St.
Anytown, USA
10101

Res: (999) 555-1212
Mobile: (999) 555-1313
johnj@yourname.com

PROFESSIONAL SUMMARY

Eleven years of experience in various capacities including **Senior Analyst** and **Project Lead** with strong analytical and team management skills. Experienced in gathering business requirements, assessing the impact on business, and preparing development plans. Excellent user interface and negotiation skills. Ability to act as a liaison between the business and IT side of the organization. Experienced in providing technical solutions for a large client community spread over 14 states. ***Currently enrolled in an MBA program.***

BUSINESS EXPERIENCE

XZY Consulting, **Team Lead**   Anytown, USA   **2001–2003**

- As Team Lead, created and reviewed project plans, and followed through to implementation and post-implementation activities
- Identified opportunities for cost savings by identifying redundant processes that were no longer demanded by the core business
- Undergone training on .NET migration tools and played a key role in setting up the environment at the Atlantic Development Center (ADC) for offshore migration projects
- Worked on the APM team with a large financial client and provided technical support to clients in a Legacy environment as well as developed new processes from time to time
- Attended ***Macroscope Methodology*** trainings and familiar with processes involved in maintenance and delivery

Accomplishments:
- Promoted to Level C4 (Team Lead/System Architect) from Level C3 (Senior Analyst) as of May 2002
- Played a key role in the data and process recovery for a client who was affected by September 11th incidents
- Instrumental in developing a strong office culture and organized several events including the MS bike tour, a presentation on India, office lunches, and events

ABC Communications, Lead Engineer   Anytown, USA   **1999–2001**

- Team Lead for on going major projects including introduction of one invoicing system for the Internet and Print customers for Yellow Pages and porting of the entire application to a different mainframe machine
- Fully conversant with the working of the entire Accounts Receivable system and developed programs around the GEAC delivered package to customize reporting and data processing
- Analyzed and completed incoming requests for reports and new functionality
- Maintained contact with users, gathered requirements, and analyzed new requests

Accomplishments:
- As Project Leader for the MVS Applications Porting project, played a major role in completing the project three weeks ahead of schedule
- Improved communications with clients (users) and provided training on most effective use on functionality of the AR system, which resulted in over 50% reduction of daily requests
- Established a production monitoring log and provided permanent solutions to frequent problems, resulting in a saving of over $200,000 per year
- Reviewed and streamlined the daily operations of Accounts Receivable and Payables team and eliminated two contract positions, creating a saving of over $125,000 per year.

BUSINESS EXPERIENCE (CONT'D)

Compu Corporation, Anothertown, USA   1998–1999

Consultant - Programmer/Analyst   1998–1999
- Worked with a major telecommunication company on the Data Harvesting Redesign project to replace existing system with a new code to improve efficiency and add new business rules to the data
- Analyzed existing code and created redesign document underlining new methods of look-ups for VSAM files and thereby decreasing the IO time and increase efficiency
- Developed, tested, prepared documentation, and implemented new code as per redesign requirement
- Developed a set of Jobs and Procedures to address the new method of data processing for the code

Accomplishment:
- Assumed the role of Career Leader and provided career counseling and feedback to junior Consultants

Consultant - Programmer/Analyst   1998
- Worked with a major telecommunication company on a New Interest Rate Project making changes to the batch and online programs with a different interest rate for student loans
- Analyzed and developed code changes to online programs to prevent abends, while working with the Tech Initiatives Team

Accomplishment:
- With a deadline just three months away, over 100 modules were changed and tested successfully.

ABC Corporation   1996–1997

Consultant - Programmer/Analyst, Anytown, USA
- Coordinated with Programmers to analyze programs, performed modification, conducted unit and system tests, and implement latest version of program
- Worked on Alpha-15 project; implemented changes to both batch and on-line programs in order to process telephone numbers up to 15 digits
- Worked on Year-2000 project; analyzed all date routines existing in the CLASS system consisting of 600 odd programs; changed, tested, prepared specification for and implemented Year 2000 compliance
- Developed new date routine, unit tested, and implemented of same

Accomplishment:
- Acted as the central point of contact for several Programmers working on the Y2K conversion and assisted the Project Manager in assigning modules of work

Programmer/Analyst, HCL Consulting, Madras, India (IT consulting)   1996

- Offshore team member, prepared specifications received from on-site counterpart, coded new programs (root modules and sub programs) according to specifications, conducted unit and integration testing, and code and test reviews

Engineer, Rama Ahshoka, Hosur, India (Automobile Manufacturer)   1993–1995

- Supervised 60 employees at the Axle assembly unit and obtained training in the Systems department and gained exposure to IT within a manufacturing unit as well as in purchasing and production control

---

EDUCATION

State University, MBA (Part-time) Big   **In Progress, Graduating Spring 2006**

College of Engineering, Bachelor of Technology (Mechanical Engineering) Trivandrum, India   1993

PROFESSIONAL DEVELOPMENT/SKILLS/MEMBERSHIPS AND PERSONAL INTERESTS

- Completed **Strategic HR management** and **Marketing** management courses offered by State University.
- Completed training on **VB.NET** (offered by Microsoft), sound technical knowledge of **Legacy** environment.
- Training at GEAC facility for E-Series Accounts Receivable Implementation and Processing
- Member **Information Society** (IS); **Toastmasters** International
- President of the **South India Cultural Association** (SICA) in Anytown, a non-profit organization. Responsible for organizing monthly events, budget management, and introducing new activities.
- Volunteer with **MS Society**, participant in the annual MS Bike tour, and fundraiser for the cause.

ANALYST: Sr. Business Analyst

ALICE J. JOHNSTON _____ *123 LEARNING STREET*
Anytown USA 10101
Bus: 999-555-1212 Res: 999-555-1313
Email: alicej@yourname.com

Senior Business Analyst

Helping management find & implement innovative technological business solutions

A results-driven IT professional with extensive experience in Project Management & Application Development. Best known for effective communication skills at all levels...creative problem-solving...and a willingness to 'go the extra mile'.

ABC INC.   **May 99–present**
Senior Consultant

- Developed & implemented the Corporate Website and our 'web presence', as well as a Corporate Intranet to better address the needs of internal staff.
- Conducted in-depth assessments on the potential, limitations, and feasibility of Extranet applications for our corporate customers.
- Designed project management standards, templates, and job descriptions for our Professional Services Teams.
- Developed our corporate advertising, plus a wide range of collateral marketing materials.
- Managed a number of technically-complex Corporate Seminars for over 100 customers, business partners, and business alliance members.

People's Gas   **1993–1999**
Senior Project Manager, Interactive Marketing   (May 97–May 99)

- Project management responsibility for developing and implementing the corporate website. Responsibilities extended from concept & creation...through to full implementation of the original People's Gas' website...as well as the additional rebranded website.
- Worked closely with the Corporation's Rebranding Committee on the name change conversion from Big Gas to People's and was responsible for assuring the new corporate vision was well-represented on the new website.
- Coordinated internal clients and outside advertising firms to ensure all on-going marketing initiatives were well represented on our website.
- Identified business and marketing opportunities that needed to be installed into our website for our corporate clients.
- Tested and monitored the effectiveness of the new website through web reporting systems and customer surveys.
- Pioneered and piloted the effectiveness of corporate advertising on the website.
- Identified and integrated innovative technologies so customers could talk with customer service representatives directly through our website.
- Established change control systems for all future changes and revisions.
- Developed service level agreements for ongoing website maintenance and support.

ALICE J.JOHNSTON

PEOPLE'S continued...

Senior Business Analyst, Customer Care (Jan. 93–May 97)

"The Call Center Consolidation Project" – My mandate was to put together a 'Virtual Call Center' by consolidating 7 call centers into 3…introducing and implementing the necessary telephony hardware/software technology…and ultimately assuming Project Management responsibilities for evaluation and acquisition for all new call center technology.

- Found and implemented a networked CTI (Computer Telephony Integration) solution.
- Found an IVR (Interactive Voice Response) unit to offload repetitive non-revenue generating calls from the Call Center.
- Project managed external developers on the design and development of numerous IVR applications.
- Implemented NetForce version of TeleCenter System's (TCS) workforce planner.
- Implemented outbound dialing applications using the Davox platform.
- Implemented the QA monitoring system.
- Provided on-going support on Nortel's Meridian line of call center products including ACD, NACD, and CCR.

SOFTWARE

Excel … Access … PowerPoint … Ms Project … Lotus SmartSuite
ccMail… HomeSuite… WebTrends
Visio … FrontPage …Cobol … Basic … Fortran … Mark IV … JCL

ON-GOING EDUCATION (SPECIAL COURSES)

Websites That Work … Nortel's Meridian Max … Networked ACD … Nortels' Customer Controlled Routing … TeleCenter Systems Workforce Planning … Effective Communications … Managing Organizational Change … Business as Unusual… Team Building & Outcomes

CONFERENCES

CTI Work '96 … Energy Marketing & Customer Service '97 … Incoming Call Center Management '97 & '98 … TeleCenter Systems User Forum '97 … Internet World '98 & '99 DEES Universe User Forum '97 … International SL1 User Association '97, '98, '99 Effective Call Center Management '96

EXTRA-CURRICULAR INTERESTS

Mission Coordinator, Hometown Anglican Church … Responsible for organizing all missions:

- Mexico - team of 25 … home construction for a homeless family
- Guatemala - team of 36 … home construction … working with children
- Mexico - team of 18 … orphanage renovations and working with children

REFERENCES

Available on request

ANALYST: Excellent Analyst, Midlevel

John J. Johnston

johnj@yourname.com   123 Learning St., Anytown, USA 10101 999-555-1212

Profile – Technical team leader excellent at designing and developing secure e-commerce systems or integrating enterprise systems by using the UML, J2EE, and PKI.

Skills

Design Tools:	UML: Use Cases; Class, Collaboration, Sequence Diagrams; Data Flow Diagrams, Flowcharts, Java Patterns
Architectures:	J2EE, PKI
Application Servers:	NetDynamics
Languages:	Java 2, XML, C++, C, Visual C++, Visual Basic, HTML 4.0, Smalltalk, Lisp, Scheme, ML, Prologue, AWK, Perl, Bourne shell scripting, SQL
Development Tools:	Borland JBuilder 3, MS Visual Studio, NetDynamics, Solaris, and Irix C++ compilers
Operating Systems:	UNIX (Solaris and Irix), Linux, NT 4.0, Windows 95.
Databases:	Oracle 8i (SQLPlus, JDBC), DB2, SQL, MS Access
Specialized Software:	SPSS-X, MATLAB, AutoCAD, FormZ, FrameMaker
Inter-personal:	Friendly, intelligent and dependable; enjoy teamwork; a leader.

Employment Experience

March 2000 - Present, Senior Systems Analyst, Service Management, Big Telephone Inc.
BTI provides voice and data services to commercial customers.

Technical Lead – 11 Months:
I was responsible for assembling, forming, and documenting technical opinion on XML, Portal, Web Self-Care, Security System, DSL Provisioning, Order Management, and Data Availability projects. Participant in Business Process Intelligence product selection project. I worked closely with project managers on 7-figure projects. I reported to the director or a senior manager of Service Management.

I evaluated the role of **XML** as inter-process communication tool in influential system-interface report. I developed a **Document Type Definition** for messaging. I articulated the problem of maintaining n^2 system interfaces.

I evaluated and depicted the **Order Management** system architecture using **UML** and **DFD**s. I helped introduce a **Model-View-Control, n-tier** architecture to open and extend the existing system. I provided a desired architecture for a system involving **Oracle**, **MQSeries**, and **NetDynamics**. I developed **Java** classes for use under the **NetDynamics** application server.

I worked with Marketing and Systems staff to formulate customer **Portal** and **Internet Security** requirements. I used **UML** to describe problems of integrating Security System, Portal, and Portal Applications. I organized, managed, and conducted evaluations of Viador, SilverStream, Epicentric, Hummingbird, and NEON portal products, among others.

I worked with Customer Care staff to formulate **Web Self-Care** and **Customer Care** application requirements, using **DFD**s. I carefully evaluated **Customer Relationship Management** products offered by PeopleSoft, Siebel, and Clarify for fit and openness.

I led top Technical staff in defining **data availability** problems raised by the Portal project. I articulated the need for **business objects**, defined them, and specified gaps between existing and needed service levels by business object. I identified the need for a message broker and demonstrated the **correctness** of concurrent message processing in a given treatment.

I led Technical staff in defining enterprise **Security** needs and evaluating web security products. I am intimately familiar with technical aspects of delegated administration, resource and user profile management, single sign-on, authorization, authentication, and non-repudiation as they relate to e-commerce and a complex systems environment. I conducted thorough examinations of Netegrity, Securant, and enTrust/enCommerce products with top technical, vendor staff. I am familiar with Access360 products, eScotia, JAWS, Bill C-6 and its IT ramifications, and modern network topologies.

I worked with Corporate Security in formulating arguments for a centralized **Security** system and implementing a **PKI** to manage digital certificates. I worked with enterprise Architects in examining **X.509** and **LDAP** directory products.

I worked closely with EDS, Interactive Biz, and Cook & Associates in various projects. I worked with top Technical staff in formulating business and technical requirements of **Business Process Intelligence** software.

May 1999–March 2000, Java Developer, Big Health Inc.
BHI provides real-time electronic claims processing for the insurance industry.
Java Servlet Design and Development - 9 months: I specified, planned, and implemented 2 Java servlets used to test insurance claim adjudication system program and business rule correctness for dental and pharmaceutical insurance claims. I used **Java 2**, **JWS 1.X**, **JDK 1.2**, **HTML 4.0**, **Oracle 8i**, **SQLPlus** and **JDBC**. I modeled data, created Oracle tables, and used JDBC to manage data in and out of the database. I created thread-safe Java servlets in JBuilder 3 to manage interactions between the browser, database, and adjudication engine. I wrote the interface in HTML 4.0 following the **MVC** development model with Java classes.

May 1994–Dec 1998, Application Developer, Blurred Vision Inc.
VDI made a C++, Java, and VB 3-D interactive data visualization class library. I designed, developed, and deployed 3D interactive applications using the C++ and Java versions of the library.

Project Management - 2 of 4 years: I estimated, planned, organized, and delivered projects for the large Corporations. I was responsible for information gathering, software specification, design, development, and meeting software delivery dates.

Software Development - 3 of 4 years: I designed and developed applications in Java, C++ and another proprietary OO language using the class library in conjunction with MFC, AWT, Swing, and X Windows tools. I manipulated data with AWK, Perl, and C. I modeled client data as relational database tables. I developed reusable classes and portable application frameworks using MVC design ideas.

Interface Design - 4 of 4 years: I designed 3-D interactive interfaces with financial, military, pharmaceutical, and manufacturing clients.

Pre-Sales Support - 2 of 4 years: I conducted hundreds of product demonstrations at trade shows and with sales people throughout North America. I spoke to large groups about 3-D data visualization and VDI products.

Oct 1991 - Aug 1992, Event Coordinator, Big Advertising Company,
Responsible for Big Car Dealer Marketing Association executive support, dealer network newsletter development & execution, nat'l conference planning & support, Dealer database & dealer contact.

Education
    B.Sc., Computer Science, with **Distinction**, May 1999. State University

    Computer Science Courses: The Design of Human-User Interfaces, Object-Oriented Analysis and Design, Databases, summer 1994, State College

    B.E.S. (Pre-Architecture), Sept 1992–Apr 1994. State University
    Dean's Honor List student, 2 of 3 years completed. I left B.E.S. studies for a software career.

    Hon. B. Arts Sc. And Psychology (Combined) April 1990, State University

Other Notables
    User Interface Design: First Place, Interface Design Competition, State University, 1999

    Leadership: President, student residence; **Author**, Quality of Residence Life report
    Campaign Manager, successful Students' Union President candidate

    Performance: Cast Member, singing and dancing in Singing Along musical group on international tour, 1987–88

ANALYST: BAD—Business Analyst

John J. Johnston
11- 123 Learning Blvd.
Some City, USA 10101
Tel. # (555) 999-1111
e-mail : johnj@yourname.com

CAREER OBJECTIVE

To secure a challenging position within an organization that will effectively utilize my professional experience and background to result in mutual growth and success.

PROFESSIONAL SKILLS

A result oriented self-starter, able to multitask and train simultaneously, an extremely quick learner possessing strong qualities in exercising decisions, well experienced in supervisory roles, decision making, customer relationship and product/systems analysis and testing.

EMPLOYMENT EXPERIENCE

ABC Securities

(April 2001 – July 2002)

BUSINESS ANALYST – GLOBAL TECHNOLOGY
Reporting to the Manager, Applications & E-commerce
Responsibilities include:

- Participating in Work Flow analysis
- Code table definition and setup
- Transaction mapping
- Analyzing and documenting the General Ledger and reporting requirements
- Designing specifications for reports and interface requirements
- Creating test scripts/cases to test functional requirements
- Acting as liaison between the Business Units and Vendor to implement soft[w...]
- Ensuring that staff are completing tasks as assigned
- Providing updates to Project Manager
- Communicates critical issues to Project Management
- Writing/updating the procedure manual
- Developing the Conversion Plan
- Participating in the conversion process
- Participating in the parallel process

Profitable Financial Services
(June 2000 – April 2001)

CORPORATE FINANCE – APPROVAL OFFICER
Reporting to the Manager, Operations
Responsibilities included:

- Processing of manufacturer request for floor plan funding
- Interacting directly with manufacturers and distributors in finalizing approva[l...]
- Answering client inquiries pertaining to the various aspects of floor plan fu[...]

What's Wrong?

- Too many bullet points
- Lackluster objective/profile or lack thereof
- No declared job role
- No accomplishments or specific and measurable results

AUTOMOTIVE: Automotive Management

Alice J. Johnston, B.Eng.
123 Learning St, Anytown, USA, 10101

Phone: 999-555-1212   Email: alicej@yourname.com

CAREER SUMMARY

Throughout my career I have held leadership positions ranging in scope from shop floor operations to business management. My diverse experiences have provided me with a solid foundation of skills in the management of safety, people, quality, productivity, and costs.

One common theme in my career has been my ability to act as an agent of change, transforming to varying degrees every organization I have been a part of. I now seek a new challenge where I can play a leadership role in an organization that is in the pursuit of continuous improvement and other change initiatives to achieve increased productivity and profitability.

CAREER HISTORY

Big Car Manufacturer LLC   2000–present

I have held a series of positions in Big Car, touching most areas including first line supervision, business plan deployment, engineering, and quality.

Brand Quality Manager - American Headquarters

- Interact with vehicle platform executives in Mexico, the U.S. and Canada and report emerging quality issues on 10 different front wheel drive truck and W car brands
- Member of the Current Product Improvement Team (CPIT), designed to assess current and future programs in terms of quality issues and metrics
- Analyze product concerns, warranty data, and parts sales to identify emerging product issues for report out and determination of next steps at CPIT meetings

BCM Facilitator - Smallertown Truck Assembly Centre

- Member of the Executive Steering Committee for Global Manufacturing Systems (BCM); plant champion for Visual Management and Value Stream Mapping
- As a 'GO FAST' coach, facilitated departmental workshops to identify opportunities for improved competitiveness including implementation plans and performance measurement frameworks
- Lead implementation of plant-wide lean manufacturing initiatives
- Conducted internal assessments to evaluate the plant's rate of completion for BCM implementation including the development of countermeasures with department staff and Executive Steering Committee to reach the goal of 90% complete

Business Manager - Truck Assembly Center

- Responsible for deployment of a strategic business plan and the resulting departmental performance of final assembly (approx 400 production operators, 15 supervisors and 4 superintendents)
- Managed the department budget, decreasing departmental operating cost from $15.4/vehicle to $10.8/vehicle exceeding the stretch target set for the department
- Lead implementation of lean manufacturing initiatives, exceeded department metrics in hours per vehicle. Plant was recognized by Critical Trucks Consultants as the leader in productivity for the full size truck segment for four consecutive years
- Coordinated the 2003 mid-cycle enhancement model change which impacted over 60% of the workstations in final assembly with no deterioration in quality and no interruption in production
- Directed activities supporting maintenance of ISO 9002 and 14001 certification, zero non-conformances during department internal and external audits
- Resolved employee safety concerns with the AAW union, plant was recognized for 1 million hours without a lost time injury
- Redeveloped employee suggestion implementation process resulting in a 28% increase in employee participation, with employee suggestions saving over $250,000 and a process that was adopted across the plant

AUTOMOTIVE: Automotive Management (cont.)

Alice J. Johnston, B.Eng

Production Supervisor - Paint Shop and Final Assembly

- Responsible for managing a group of approximately 50 production operators and achieving group scorecard metrics daily
- Filtered and analyzed the production data, utilizing statistical process control to identify emerging quality concerns within our process, implemented immediate containment, performed root cause analysis, and implemented corrective action
- Awarded the Corporation's North American team award for "Quality People, Quality Product" for most improved quality as a member of the Smallertown Truck Fit Zone Team

Cosmetics Inc., Brand   **1999–2000**

Pilot Group Leader

Responsible for working with all functional areas to determine the best manufacturing procedure for various emulsions, powders, and lipsticks utilizing the pilot facility, the engineers, and technicians in the pilot group.

- Supervised a team of nine technicians and an engineer in scaling up pressed and loose powders, emulsions, and hot pour products from concept formula to full scale production in accordance with GMP (Good Manufacturing Practices)
- Responsible for process design from compounding of the batch to filling and packaging of the final product
- Compiled a release to production knowledge folder for each new product and conducted release to production batches and training in the Manufacturing facilities in Belgium, the U.S. and Canada
- Successfully released over 40 products to production with no missed deadlines

Big Energy LLC   **1996–1999**

Facility Supervisor

The sole supervisor, responsible for a radioactive medical isotope facility which produces over 90% of the world's supply of Molybdenum -99.

- Supervised a group of twelve unionized operators and technicians
- Coordinated production schedule with shipping and transport to ensure product was delivered to MDS Nordion with the required amount of nuclear decay
- Responsible for preventative maintenance and coordinating skilled trades for the facility, successfully completed a project for the removal and replacement of the hot cell window

Armed Forces   **1991–1996**

Aerospace Engineer

Served in the Air Force beginning as an Officer Cadet and reaching the rank of Lieutenant.

- Completed work term placements in several countries around the globe.
- Supervise maintenance personnel and provide technical support to the Tactical Helicopter Squadron.

EDUCATION/PROFESSIONAL DEVELOPMENT

Military College

Bachelor of Engineering (Chemical and Materials Engineering), 1995

- Global Manufacturing Systems Training, Big Car Manufacturer University (2004)
- GoFast Coach for productivity and cost reduction workshops, (2003)
- Internal auditor ISO 14000 and ISO 9000, (2001)
- Reducing Your Organizations Cycle Time, State University (1999)
- Strategic Planning, Career Management Specialists (1998)
- Volunteer for Junior Achievement administering the Economics of Staying in School Program
- Organize the Take Our Kids to Work day at company headquarters

AUTOMOTIVE: Auto Racing Sales & Publishing

123 Learning St.
Anytown, USA 10101

T: (999) 555 1212
E1: johnj@yourname.com

John J. Johnston

Profile:

Results driven, commercially minded, sports media professional with seven years of proven experience in sponsorship, sports marketing, publishing, and digital-interactive media environments.

Excels in prospecting and establishing relationships, negotiating, and closing business initiatives at manager, director, and 'C' levels that generate maximum revenues and provide b2b-networking opportunities. Surpassed forecasted revenue targets and yields for largest private owned media & publishing company in the U.S. Global contacts in business, sport, media owners, and agencies.

Professional Experience:

Super Fast LLC - Interactive Media

Commercial Manager - BOB . Com   2002–2003

- Responsible for advertising sales/sponsorship target budgets of $1.5 million plus additional content sales and development budget of $2 million +.

- Increased rich media revenue by 32%, site inventory increases of 12%, and secured record level of sponsorship revenue from Vodafone and other blue chip global clients.

- Managed accounts for B.A.T. & Formula 1 sponsorship campaigns.

- Proposed promotional platforms to optimise revenue, lead sourcing, site usage, activity, and demographics resulting in increase of agency/client account wins and media firsts.

- Measured performance data/research (Ned Stat, Engage, Hit Wise, ABCe monthly reports) for agency campaigns/client presentations, pitches, and specific marketing briefs.

Fast Cars Publishing - F1 Magazine   London, UK

Commercial Manager - Advertising and Sponsorships   Jan. 2001–Mar. 2002

- Executed new launch of *Formula 1 Magazine* which secured record revenues in sphere of publishing.

- Attended F1 race weekends to negotiate commercial/advertising opportunities at decision-making levels within Formula 1 community through account/sponsorship management.

- Generated high revenues & yield rates by managing B2B, B2C, FMCG, OE clients, corporate sponsors, and manufacturer accounts. Some being – **Client:** Big Bank Inc., Hoity Toity Clothing Inc., SAP, Big Oil Company, **Agency:** Mindmeld, VMG - PMD-Europe, Towerstone - Mediatrix, MediaDot, Ad & Ad Brand, Plakara.

Super Fast Publications

Advertising Manager – ZOOM SPORT MAGAZINE   1999–Jan. 2001

- Responsible for ad sales targets of $4.5 million on a market leading motor sport weekly.

- Increased revenues and exceeded budget projections by 20% in 2000/01. Achieved highest rates for sponsorship (ZOOM Awards and within Super Fast Special Projects).

- Utilized MMS, TGI, and NRS market research data to win client/agency pitches.

1

AUTOMOTIVE: Auto Racing Sales & Publishing (cont.)

Breaking Ranks Design

<u>Managing Partner</u>   1996–1999

- Directed computer design consultancy for 3-D animation & creative solutions.

- Increased client portfolio by 38%, and developed new business accounts using proactive methods: direct marketing, trade advertising, conferences, shows, and PR.

Education & Development: 1990–1993 & 95   State University

- 4 years - International Studies Minor: electives in B.Comm & Mrkt.

- Super Fast Career Development Program I & II - Sales & Marketing (1999) & Management Training (2000)

Computer Proficiency: XP 2000 Professional, MS Office, Access - database, Media research data & tracking (Digital: Engage Ad Manager, NedStat, Hitwise - Print: MMS, NRS, ABC, BPA - TV: BARB, ACN-MMS).

Interests & Details: Design & technology, motorsport, basketball, volleyball, hockey, golf, rock climbing, martial arts, hiking, mountain biking, sailing, and music.

AUTOMOTIVE: Sales Trainer

John J. Johnston

123 Learning St., Anytown, USA, 10101   Phone: 999-555-1212   Email: johnj@yourname.com

Automotive Sales Trainer for a multi-location dealer group.
With over 26 years experience I am highly qualified to prepare others for the automotive industry. There are literally hundreds of individuals who hold jobs in the automotive field from Salesperson to General Manager who credit me for having trained them for success.

EXPERIENCE:

Online Automotive, Inc., President   May 2005–Present
I am the majority stockholder in this pre-owned automotive dealership. My son is the operator, buying and selling pre-owned vehicles mostly on-line and on eBay. I advise him in all aspects of the operation.

Kempt's Subaru, Inc., President/General Manager   March 1996–May 2005
I was majority stockholder and day-to-day operator of this Subaru franchised dealership. The dealership averaged 350 new Subaru sales per year, 1000 used vehicles per year, and a bottom-line net profit of $625,000 per year. I was responsible for all aspects of this operation.

During this time I mentored or coached on average 30–40 employees and potential employees a year, both within my dealership and elsewhere. My replacement was someone who was mentored by me and who has continued to lead the dealership in both sales and good management.

Big Boys Ford, General Manager/Minority Stock Holder   Jan 1993–March 1996
Dealership operator with sole-responsibility for the day-to-day operations. Prior to my taking the position, the dealership sold less than 100 total units per month and lost over $500,000 in one year. During my tenure the dealership averaged over 350 total unit sales per month and averaged a net bottom-line profit of over $2,500,000 per year. The dealership won sales and customer satisfaction awards year after year.

Corsen Mitsubishi, General Manager/Minority Stock Holder   Dec 1989–Jan 1993
Dealership operator with sole-responsibility for the day-to-day operations. Prior to my taking the position, the dealership sold less than 90 total units per month and lost over $200,000 in one year. During my tenure the dealership averaged 250 total unit sales per month and averaged a net bottom-line profit of over $1,000,000 per year. The dealership won sales and customer satisfaction awards year after year.

King Ford, General Sales Manager   Dec 1983–Dec 1986
Responsible for all aspects of the sales department. Trained all sales managers and sales people. Dealership went from last in sales in the district to first during my tenure.

EDUCATION:
Western State University
Attended 2 Years General Studies 1973–74

PERSONAL:
Member and past President of Granite Oceans Golf and Country Club
Mentoring young people on their future careers
Enjoying time with family and friends

BANKING: Banking Manager

123 LEARNING ST • ANYTOWN, USA • 10101•
PHONE 999-555-1212(H) OR 999-555-1313(C)

EMAIL: alicej@yourname.com

ALICE J.JOHNSTON

PROFILE

A dedicated and enthusiastic Banking Manager with 20 years sales and management experience who has developed strong working relationships and provided consistent results. Has a proven history in sales, supervision, and time management. A professional who has been described as a strong motivator & mentor of team members.

Special skills include: exceptional negotiating skills, excellent telephone etiquette, and strong problem solving techniques.

AWARDS

- Awarded a partnership award for flexibility, supportiveness, and strong contributions to Branch Managers & Community Office Leaders in this Community.

- Awarded satisfactory ratings from both the State Compliance Officer and the Internal Audit in the area of Mutual Fund Compliance.

- Awarded the highest rating on the Mutual Fund Regulatory Managers team due to excellence in Time Management, Client Relations, and Organization.

- Awarded a Quarterly Achievers award for Excellence in People Management. This nomination was submitted by all branch staff & supported by Community Office.

- Awarded a Service Excellence award for Excellence in Sales. This nomination was to recognize the highest sales volumes for car loans in the branch.

WORK EXPERIENCE

State Bank of Commerce: 2002–2003 Mutual Fund Regulatory Manager

Identified and escalated regulatory risk issues and took immediate action to minimize potential financial loss and maintain the reputation of SB and SB Securities Inc.

- Completed daily and monthly compliance of mutual fund transactions and conducted report verification in 14 daily branches and 7 monthly branches.

- Provided 200 mutual fund reps and their leaders (branch managers, community managers, segment leaders) with coaching, workshops, and on-going feedback on a daily and monthly basis.

- Consulted and provided support to 30 mutual fund compliance administrators in the handling and resolution of client complaints, mutual fund rep. non-compliance incidents, training of new reps, etc.

- Successfully managed an area 3 times the size of my colleagues across America, while still maintaining the highest levels of efficiency.

State Bank: 1998–2002: Branch Manager

- Managed the effective implementation & marketing of bank initiatives, strategic direction.
- Identified opportunities for increasing sales penetration through coaching and facilitating of up to 15 sales individuals.
- Ensured that investment and credit portfolios were managed effectively to achieving sales targets.
- Reviewed and adjudicated sales representative lending applications to ensure adherence to bank polices as well as to uncover additional sales opportunities.
- Completed performance appraisals for up to 15 direct reports providing both constructive feedback and opportunities for growth.
- Achieved over 135% of branch sales target and 75% of referral targets for 2000, exceeding region targets and results. Dramatically increased branch results from last to first place in community of 13 branches.

State Bank: 1993–1998: Personal Banking Manager

- Developed ability to examine client base and identified potential for further business.
- Successfully supported the transition and referral of over $1 million dollars in retail banking business to the Imperial Service (high value) segment by utilizing value-based questions to ascertain the clients' inherent goals.
- Sold and marketed various SB products to clients, such as mortgages, personal loans, personal lines of credit, credit cards, bank accounts, mutual funds, etc. This includes the adjudication of lending products within prescribed limits.
- Effectively managed and facilitated training sessions to all branch personnel (up to 15 individuals at once) to increase operational capabilities and client satisfaction ratings.
- Effectively and successfully managed the most successful 401K campaign for the department in the flagship branch of the bank.
- Completed performance appraisals for all Personal Banking staff to ensure appropriate career plans were in place with necessary actions to support.

Well Known Bank: 1990-1993 Assistant Manager Personal Banking

- Achieved the highest sales results in mortgages, car loans, and 401Ks at the flagship branch. These results were achieved in the same fiscal year.

INTERNATIONAL EXPERIENCE

Big Bank- England 1989 Unit Trust Liaison

PROFESSIONAL DEVELOPMENT

Branch Compliance (Manager) Course (SB): - Completed Jan 2002

Foundations of Leadership (SB): - Completed May 1996

Personal Financial Management Course (ICB): - Completed August 1994

Personal Banking Retail Curriculum (SB): - Completed October 1993

Professional Selling (SB): - Completed September 1990

Mutual Funds (SB): - Completed September 1989

BANKING: Program Manager, IT Bank

JOHN J. JOHNSTON

123 LEARNING ST.
ANYTOWN, USA 10101

999-555-1212
JOHNJ@YOURNAME.COM

Senior Manager, Banking and Cable

During my 15 years of professional experience, I have over 7 years in technology management. My strengths include the ability to manage operational tasks including budgeting, financial modelling, risk management, and personnel issues. Drawing on both a broad technical background and an accomplished business insight, I have been successful at integrating organizational goals with customer needs to provide effective results.

PROGRAM MANAGER, *Big Bank Financial Group* 2004–Present

- Developed and managed the Scientific Research & Experimental Development Tax Credit Program Initiative within all business units and subsidiaries of BB BFG, leading to over $7 million in tax credits.
- Extensively involved in the negotiation of consulting contract ($2 million).
- Systematically increased exposure and buy-in of the program enterprise-wide from Senior Executives to project managers.
- Defined and instituted real-time processes to capture and detail eligible projects, leading to a significant decrease in time and cost to prepare claim.
- Enabled the program to be permanently integrated into the PMO and established a program team.
- Presented the program at the BB PM World Conference.

SENIOR MANAGER, *Big Guys Consulting* 1999–2002

Clients: Big Tele, Digivision LLC, Readers RUS.

- Led RFP responses, projects and strategy at key clients with budgets up to $15 million; consistently expanded client presence, sales, and revenue.
- Built and managed large team of consultants.
- Wrote and presented White Paper on Enterprise Application Integration

Digivision LLC

- Acting director (in consultancy role) of an e-commerce site for the largest cable provider in the Tri-State area. Upgraded rudimentary website to a mission critical system by providing the following: complete retooling of website functionality, implementation of a scalable backend and deployment of extensive custom internal order entry as well as fulfillment modules.
  - Facilitated negotiation meetings with individual sponsors and their departments to define strategies, budgets, and new procedures: Marketing, Sales, Shipping, Finance, and IT.
  - Managed the on-going site maintenance, enhancement, and cross-site integration, including real-time XML interfaces with multiple legacy systems.
  - Technologies: Vignette Story Server 5.0, Oracle 8i, Sun 420, VeriSign, WebTrends, DoubleClick, XML, UPS WorldShip, eBarz, Loadrunner, CableData, MS Project, Visio, UMLTools, and Rational Rose.
- Managed a team of 15 client staff to implement an internal 24x7 e-commerce hosting facility encapsulated within an existing network. Also managed a third party development team to build and deploy the first e-commerce site in this new facility, ensuring both proper implementation of functional specification and quality assurance through extensive scalability testing. My institution of comprehensive project management and quality control processes satisfied severe time constraints and ensured on-time delivery of these projects.
  - Technologies: Sun 480s (clustered x 4, Raid 5), WebSphere Enterprise Application Server, Java, Oracle 8i, VeriSign, WebTrends, LoadRunner, MS Project, Visio, UMLTools, and Rational Rose.

Big Tel, Telecommunications

- Senior Technical Lead on an Enterprise Application Integration (middleware) product selection, a $30 million project.
- Defined customer engagement process strategy for evaluation and selection of current and future projects across the enterprise; led teams in evaluating and recommending the project selections.
- Identified and completed initial electronic bill presentment initiative, worth $2.5 million.
- Technologies: Vitria, Tibco, IBM (MQSeries, Integrator), Neon, XML, MS Project, Visio, and UML.

CONSULTING PROJECT MANAGER, *XYZ LLC.*   1996–1999

- Instituted project management methodology that enabled accurate project and resource scheduling, ensuring delivery within time and budget constraints.
- Responsible for SOWs, SLAs, project budgets and billing.
- Consistently identified and closed new sales opportunities.

State Insurance Inc.

- Managed client and consultant teams to design, develop, and deploy Sales Force Automation (SFA) project connecting 2500 brokers' laptops to multiple company systems; first successful implementation of an internet-based SFA in the insurance industry.
- Main contact for project sponsors: Executive Committee, CIO, marketing, sales, and IT.
- Negotiated for the enhancement of administrative and deployment applications, including a custom XML multi-application installer, significantly reducing overhead.
- Technologies: IIS 4, Visual Basic, SQLServer, Win95+Active Desktop, Contact Partner, AIS 400, and MS Project.

Big Credit Inc.

- Installed the Facilities Department's network.
- Identified, designed, and implemented an application to track the power flows at a multi-building complex; lead to an estimated 4x increase in response time.
- Directed team that developed custom document management and messaging application pilot.
- Technologies: NT 3.51, Win95, SQLServer, Access, Visual Basic, and PrintServer.

DEVELOPER/CONSULTANT, *XYZ Management Inc.*   1995–1996

- Identified, designed, built, and deployed multiple internal resources and staffing applications.
- Implemented UNIX and qad's MFG/Pro (ERP) for various clients.
- Technologies: Progress, Informix, Sybase, qad, Access, and Visual Basic.

Technical Experience and Continuing Education

- **Middleware and Data tools**: Vitria, Tibco, Neon, MQ Series Integrator, Active, Constellar, Vality, Trillium, Acxiom, XML.
- **Web**: IIS, ASP, Vignette, WebSphere, WebLogic, WebTrends, VeriSign, XMLSolutions.
- **Databases**: SQL, Informix, Progress, Sybase, Oracle.
- **Operating Systems and tools**: NT, XP, UNIX, Solaris, Tivoli.
- **ERP/CRM**: Siebel (API Integration), SAP (iDocs), qad (MFG/Pro).
- **Other**: Visual Basic, Visual C++, C, C++, Java, SourceSafe, Exchange, Project, PowerPoint, Word, Excel, Access, Visio, UML tools, Rational Rose.
- **Certifications:** Project Management Professional (2004), Microsoft Certified Solution Developer (1996), Microsoft Certified Systems Engineer (1998).
- Enterprise Application Integration specialist.
- Multiple Project Management and Executive training programs.

(Honors) Diploma in Computer Programming and Systems Analysis   1995

Bachelor of Arts in Economics, State University   1990–1994

Travel Sabbatical (Africa, Europe, Southern U.S.)   2002–2003

BANKING: Relationship Bank Manager & CA

ALICE J. JOHNSTON CA

123 Learning Avenue, 1A • Anycity, Anystate • 10101 (home) 555.999.1212 • alicej@yourname.com

> **Background:** Seasoned finance, consulting, and e-commerce professional with broad-based skill set in many industries, geographies.
> **Motivation:** Driven by creative problem solving, challenging situations and entrepreneurial environments. "Formulating and developing ideas that are financially and strategically sound to conquer the digital domain."

AMERICA MARKETSITE (AMERICA BANK E-MARKETPLACE), Anycity   2000–present
Manager, Affiliates (Business Development Solutions)
- Responsible for developing and implementing strategy for business services in e-marketplace.
- Investigating potential investments in e-marketplace and other internet-enabling businesses.
- Investigating customers' needs, mapping the technical capabilities of our marketplace solutions, and evaluating a host of service providers from all service sectors. Proposing and implementing relevant e-business services to increase customer liquidity and increase revenues at high ROIs. Examples include logistics, e-enablers, information services, various ASP solutions, RFP platforms, and others.
- This business development role involves working with finance, operations, sales, communications, and sometimes other bank groups to ensure services meet the objectives of the strategy I developed.
- Several business models for e-commerce success in U.S. and globally evaluated.

ACHIEVEMENTS:
- Launched first services after expedited negotiations following my hire to meet launch date.
- Developed unique value propositions with service providers from all parts of online and off-line businesses. Developed solutions for different customer segments and stakeholders.

ABC BANK USA, Anycity   1997–2000
Relationship Manager, Corporate Finance
- Responsible for client relationship management, M&A, valuation, new client proposals, comprehensive financial and business analysis and negotiation for debt raising, lending, treasury.
- Industries: technology, communication, manufacturing, financial services, other.

ACHIEVEMENTS:
- Provided comprehensive acquisition/valuation advice focusing on business modeling and analysis.
- Completed advisory mandates and credit approvals under tight credit environment.
- Developed and implemented financial solutions for U.S. and international clients.
- Managed special strategic projects for bank president and head office.

CREDIT FIRST, Anycity   1996–1997
Relationship Manager, Corporate and Investment Banking
- Responsible for managing portfolio of $350 M with restructuring and other business proposals.
- Financial analysis and client proposals on major corporate finance advisory opportunities.
- Position eliminated in restructuring.

ACHIEVEMENTS:
- Promoted to manager after four months.
- Consulting and monitoring of client financing activities and legal negotiations, market intelligence.
- Analyzed financial statements and client operations for lending, investment banking, and project finance opportunities. Prepared, defended, implemented marketing and credit proposals.

ALICE J. JOHNSTON CA

Ford ASSOCIATES, Anycity   1994–1996
Senior Consultant
- Responsible for developing, researching, analyzing, and presenting corporate, pricing, and marketing strategies for U.S. blue chip and medium-sized companies.
- Main project issues included merger implementation, new product introduction, market share erosion, pricing change sensitivity and opportunities, and change in strategic direction.

ACHIEVEMENTS:
- Successfully managed projects from proposal, research, industry, and customer analysis through to written strategic reports and presentations to senior management.
- Project management of professional team. Client consultation and implementation support.
- Industries: financial services, publishing, communications, IT, manufacturing, consumer.

INDEPENDENT CONSULTANT (Included MBA studies below)   1991–1994
- Responsible for strategic and operations projects in mutual fund management, forensic accounting, cash flow analysis, business development/investment finance sourcing, valuations and accounting.
- Clients mutual funds, Electronics Int'l, Forensic Accountants, resource companies.

ABC FINANCE, Anycity   1989–1991
Manager, Forensic Accounting
- Responsible for case project management and report writing in the areas of financial analysis, cash flow compilation and projection, valuation, due diligence, transaction analysis, funds tracing, civil, insurance, and fraud loss valuation. Completed CA designation requirements.
- Worked with and led professional project teams, reporting to partners and client.
- Selected industries included real estate, transportation, manufacturing, oil products, finance, consumer products, food processing.

TOM ROSS AND COMPANY, Anycity   1986–1988
Staff Accountant (Auditor)
- Responsible for auditing and tax consulting to a broad range of clients in manufacturing, publishing, communications, financial services, and other services. Initiated CA study program.

EDUCATION, INTERESTS

E-Commerce Course, Serenity College, enrolled 2000
Series 7, 1997
MBA, Business University, 1992–1993
Top business school in U.S. Integrated strategy program, focusing on international business. Thesis project with Electronics International, finance focus. Graduated top quartile.
Chartered Accountant, 1989 - Passed final exam in first attempt.
B. Comm. Honours, State University, 1982–1986   Macleod Scholarship

Reading: *Business 2.0, Line 56, Industry Standard, Red Herring, ZDNet, Wired*, E-commerce texts.
Interests: Squash, sailing, skiing, historic books, and novels.
Computer skills: Proficient in all Windows-based programs and e-commerce platforms.
Traveled extensively through Europe and Asia between above assignments.

BANKING: Product Dev. Bank, Director Level

John J. Johnston
123 Learning St., Anytown, USA
999-555-1212 (cell), 999-555-1313 (home)
Email: johnj@yourname.com

Profile

A senior management professional with a broad range of international experience in IT, Project Management, Business Analysis and Performance Improvement for companies in the financial services, management consulting, consumer products, communications, healthcare, and energy industries.

- Exceptional ability to quickly learn new concepts (business, process, technology, etc.) and define practical strategies and tactics leading to business success.
- Applies a wealth of cross-industry experience and knowledge and develops creative solutions to a variety of traditional & new business problems.
- Possesses holistic hands-on understanding of running a business.
- Creates highly effective teams and leads them to success.
- A committed and ethical team player, who partners well with other business leaders to deliver effective business solutions.

Work Experience

Big Bank Inc. - IIS Value Added Services   2001–Present
Director of Systems & Product Development Office

- Reporting to the Vice President - Value Added Services, leads a large, cross-functional team of business analysts, developers, production support and product support, staff.
- Responsible for supporting two global product lines (***Assets Optimization*** - Securities Lending and Triparty, and ***Benchmark*** - Investment Performance Measurement, Analytics, Attribution, VaR Analysis, and Compliance Monitoring) in the areas of systems strategy, business analysis, business & systems architecture, production support, project management, and training management.
- Successfully managed the development and launch of an in-house Performance Measurement, Analytics and Attribution platform. Established functional scope control and testing process and procedures that significantly improved communication between multiple project teams.
- Ensured on-schedule and high-quality delivery of multiple major releases of several key products/components: Risk Metrics VaR calculation engine, Charles River system for post-trade compliance monitoring, derivatives performance measurement, Global Industry Classification (GICS) based reporting.
- Led the technical and architecture efforts in acquiring and implementing a third-party online trading platform for Securities Lending. Working under tight time constraint (3 months for acquisition/requirements/design), ensured optimal integration of the acquired system into legacy infrastructure and sufficient understanding by the business unit of the potential implications of specific integration options to the strategic business requirements within the 2–5 year horizon.
- Recognized the need for and introduced several HR initiatives throughout the department. These initiatives clarified the department's role and responsibilities vis-à-vis other business partners, brought better understanding of job expectations to the team members and improved team productivity and cohesiveness.

XZY Company Inc.   2000–2001
Manager (Financial Services Practice - CRM Strategy)

- Managed a competitive assessment of lending software market for a major North American bank. Responsible for defining the analysis framework, conducting primary and secondary research, summarizing and analyzing collected data, and presenting final analysis and recommendations to the client.
- Managed multiple aspects of a program to operationalize new customer segmentation strategy for a major American bank. Responsible for cross-channel "premium" client identification requirements, framework and tool kit for measuring progress and performance of new "premium" campaigns and relationship-level profitability reporting.
- Assisted a major North American bank with strategic initiatives prioritization. Responsible for development and setup of the prioritization process, resulting data analysis, and presentation.

John J. Johnston

ABC Group   1998–2000
Senior Management Consultant (Business Transformation Services)

- Developed business architecture for an online store of a major American retailer. Ensured consistent holistic view of the whole operation by the business sponsors, highlited critical areas requiring business decisions, provided comprehensive structure for engagement planning and control.
- Developed an emergency command center as an "umbrella" for a number of risk mitigation strategies and business continuity plans for an American insurance company.
- Developed shared services IT strategy for a major American newspaper as part of a major acquisition effort. The strategy encompassed short and long term plans for integrating applications, IT & IS complement, and technology of several newly acquired regional newspapers into a single common infrastructure with the head company.

Consultants Management LLC   1997–1998
Manager (Business Process Reengineering)

- Conducted a benchmarking study for the best practices in the Performance Measurement and Executive Information Systems for a major American retail company. This study served as a starting point for a major Performance Measurement System Development initiative.
- Managed a costing project for ABC Home Oxygen. Responsible for identification of costs involved in development of survey, surveying, benchmarking for best practices, analysis, and preparation of the final reasonableness assessment and recommendations.
- Redesigned operations of the Finance & Accounting function of a major accounting firm's office in Europe.
- Conducted a benchmarking study for the best practices in the software development industry. Findings presented in the final report allowed client to better position itself within its competitive environment.
- Assisted a middle-size software development company in assessment of testing component of their comprehensive software development and implementation methodology.

A& B Consulting LLC   1992–1997
Senior Consultant (Financial Services Practice - BPR)
- Managed the "definition of internal consulting role" initiative for an Operations Development group of a major European bank. Identified stakeholders and their needs, determined critical dimensions of service delivery and their influence on internal consulting processes, skills, tools, and deployment.
- Managed development and deployment of an MS Access based IT reporting database for a U.S. branch of a major European bank. Responsible for business requirements, database design, systems documentation, and deployment of the tool sets.
- Planned, designed, developed, and implemented a project management planning, structuring, reporting, and control tool kit for a U.S. branch of a major European bank.

Supervisor (Management Consulting Practice)
- Managed implementation of a management information system for the finance and order processing areas of an affiliate of a major Swedish packaging company. Reduced the load of manual operations, optimised information flows, and increased analytical capabilities of management.
- Managed the development of an information systems strategy and architecture for a major oil & gas producing company. This project allowed the company to receive EBRD financing and to build an effective cost analysis system.
- Assisted several global companies with their organizational restructuring initiatives. Achieved significant cost savings due to cross-functional synergies, optimized structure and processes, and increased efficiencies.

Education & Training

MBA in Foreign Trade & Accounting, cooperative institute.
Courses in: American Securities, Project Management, Selling Skills, BPI, Facilitated Sessions, Systems Implementation and Package Enabled Reengineering.

Other Interests

Taking photos of my kids; showing photos of my kids; letting my kids teach me how to snowboard; ripping it up on the slopes once they leave me alone; alone time with my wife; social gatherings which hopefully include a BBQ.

BANKING: Executive Finance Bank

JOHN J. JOHNSTON

123 Learning Avenue   T 999 555-1212
Anytown, ST   F 999 555-1313
USA   johnj@yourname.com

PROFILE

Experienced Investment and Finance Professional

Focusing on privately held service and hi-tech companies with $5 to $30 million revenue. 1996 Chartered Accountant with extensive experience building and managing the financial operations of high-growth companies. A results-driven financial leader with expertise in private financings, acquisitions, start-ups, and turn-around situations.

PROFESSIONAL EXPERIENCE

BIG NAME BANK   1998–2005

Senior Manager, BNB E-business Group, 2003–2004

Business leader of cross-enterprise teams evaluating financial and business viability of evolving technology-driven businesses and products.

- Forecasted financial models and prepared business plans for next-generation financial technologies including contactless payments and electronic marketplace payment infrastructure
- Advised business executives on portfolio management, restructuring investments, and financial reporting

Chief Financial Officer, SupplyTrade (a BNB investment), 2000–2002

CFO of internet-based B2B marketplace and supply chain management company. Venture exited by BNB.

- Established state office and grew customer base to 450 business customers over 18 months
  - Created financial operations including treasury, tax, forecasting, HR, privacy, and legal
  - Hired and managed sales, marketing, operations, and technology staff (total 15)
  - Successfully negotiated technology and partnership agreements with North American partners
  - Developed business and financial strategy in consultation with shareholder representatives
  - Delivered investment presentations to targeted corporations
  - Led financial reporting and investor relations for North American corporate shareholders

- Represented BNB's US$10M investment in SupplyTrade, a state-based JV
  - Partnered with SupplyTrade executives to launch to North American customers after only four months
  - Increased investment by negotiating USD $6M warrant in BigX stock in restructuring

Senior Financial Advisor, BNB Capital Inc., 1998–2000

Virtual CFO of four venture capital funds providing capital and management to early stage technology ventures

- Senior Advisor to fund CEOs on Corporate Finance, Investment Analysis, Negotiation and Financing issues
  - Worked with funds to analyze and negotiate investments in technology firms
  - Led corporate finance role in the due diligence, valuation, and management of investments
  - Managed external legal and technical teams to evaluate and close investments up to $5M
  - Designed financial models to plan and present investment opportunities internally and externally

- Business Advisor and Relationship Manager to fund managers and their portfolio companies
  - Advised executives on pricing, costing, and U.S. market strategy for electronics middleware company
  - Advised fund managers on risk management, compensation, and HR

John J. Johnston   Page 2

BIOTECH TELL ALL INC.   Anycity, AS 1997–1998
Chief Financial Officer
CFO of venture capital firm—and its portfolio companies—raising equity capital and providing corporate management for early stage companies in the biotechnology therapeutics sector.

- Prepared business plans and offering documents to raise private equity capital from $1 to $5M
  - Performed due diligence on potential investments to evaluate viability and financing opportunities
  - Presented investments to and negotiated term sheets with VC syndication partners

- Responsible for the company's financial planning, strategies, and policies
  - Evaluated and structured investment strategies including IPO, RTO, merger and divestiture
  - Managed annual audit and designed financial reporting for management, board, shareholders
  - Negotiated contracts with U.S., UK, and Canadian suppliers to outsource R&D projects
  - Managed compliance filings for securities exchanges and taxation

TOMPKINS & MAY LLP   Anycity, AS 1994–1997
Analyst, Corporate Advisory Services
- Prepared business valuations, financial models, and litigation support for use in M&A and legal situations
- Assisted in preparing business plans for software companies to raise private equity capital
- Developed a database and targeted companies in state's biotechnology industry
- Member of High Technology, Software, and Biotechnology industry teams

Senior Staff Accountant, Assurance Services
- Planned and supervised financial and due diligence audits of public and private companies
- Specialist with clients in electronics manufacturing, natural gas transmission, engineering services.

BOARD EXPERIENCE

Softdisk Enterprises   Anycity, AS 2000–Present
Independent director on board of private, Anytown-based software firm, $10 million revenue, 80 staff operating in 6 countries including Australia.

- Advising President & CEO on strategic financial matters including discussions with venture capitalists, debt financing, performance measurement, and compensation
- Counseling Chairman on corporate finance issues such as exit strategy, executive succession planning, and stock purchase plans

PROFESSIONAL ACTIVITIES

Guest Lecturer, Tandy's School of Business (MBA), Entrepreneurial Finance, 1999–Present
Ongoing Professional Development: Purchase and Sale of Private Businesses, Valuation of Private Businesses, and Financing Alternatives for High Technology Companies

EDUCATION & ACHIEVEMENTS

Chartered Accountant, Anystate 1996 and AnotherState 1998
- 2nd Place, state taxation exam 1994
Bachelor of Science, State University, 1993
Gold Medalist, State Rowing Regatta, 2000

BANKING: BAD—Mutual Funds

Alice J. Johnston
123 Learning St, Anytown, USA 010101   (999) 555 1212

OBJECTIVE

Administrative position where my speed, strong knowledge of mutual fund products coupled with excellent interpersonal, communication and mathematics skills, can be most effectively utilized.

SUMMARY

Eight years of management accomplishment in such areas as sales management, customer service, and inventory control system in the manufacturing, retailing and exporting industries.

RELEVANT WORK EXPERIENCE

Big Money Inc.   Dec. 99 - Present
Mutual Fund Administrator

- Process trades, customer services, input daily prices, transmit files and reconcile the daily trade blotters.
- Settle the trades, adjust the accounts' error and monitor/fix trade rejections on FundSERV and ISM.
- Communicate with the Reps to resolve problems regarding the trade transactions.
- Maintain trade surveillance to meet corporate trade policy and compliance guidelines.
- Review "Know Your Client Rule" (KYC) to comply with legislation and compliance regulation.

Your Funds Inc.   Dec. 98 – Dec. 99
Registered Products Administrator

- Processed fund purchase/transfer/switch/redemption accounts in an accurate and timely manner.
- Coached administrators with respect to policies, procedures of securities and taxation legislation.
- Communicated and explained any correction/rejection to th processed the client transactions.
- Investigated and resolved errors and problems with applica determining solutions in compliance with taxation and poli

State Bank   Oct. 96 – Dec. 98
Customer Services Rep

- Performed Automatic Banking Machine deposits and paym
- Resolved customer inquiries by referencing computer recor differences.

St. Andrews' Hospital for the Sick Children   Aug. 96 – Oct. 9
Data Entry Operator

- Administered and maintained the computer system.

What's Wrong?

- Dense text—I'm too bored to read this all.
- Too much information about out-of-date or inapplicable jobs
- Lackluster objective/profile or lack thereof
- Uninspiring and boring
- Name is too small or address is too large or both

BRAND: Brand, Beginner

John J. Johnston

123 Learning St., Anytown, USA 10101- 999.555.1212 johnj@yourname.com

PROFILE: STRATEGY AND BRAND

- Marketing expertise – Implemented full-scale marketing program, Talentturkey.com
- Strategic thinker – Researched and prepared creative briefs, RM&P Advertising
- Entrepreneurial mindset – Successful personal business venture
- Proven Adaptability – International Academic Exchange, Greece

EXPERIENCE

Careersandsoforth.com, *Brand Manager: Profiler Site,* Sept–Jan 2001
- Responsible for independent business unit producing $700K+ in annual revenues
- Developed unique and effective marketing strategies to attract both jobseekers and employers to 15 independent and dynamic private label Profiler Sites
- Designed advertisements for placement in national publications (portfolio available)
- Negotiated large sales contracts with important clientele
- Developed and implemented 4 separate Profiler Site launch plans

Munny, May & Partners Advertising, *Strategic Planning Coordinator,* Jan–May 2001
- Conducted primary and secondary research to identify consumer trends and insights for client accounts and new business pitches
- Performed the function of strategic planner for various pro-bono accounts
- Prepared creative briefs based on consumer insights and research findings
- Formulated and coordinated promotions and public relations stunts for clients

Routers Inc, *Associate Buyer/Reports Specialist*, May–Sept 2000
- Created, implemented, and fine tuned a myriad of purchasing related reports
- Provided primary direction in guiding team to decrease de-expedites and cancellations resulting in an inventory reduction in excess of $4 million
- Designed spreadsheets in Excel to streamline purchasing and expediting processes
- Member of 4 person focus team, formed to develop an Oracle based data-warehouse for global usage

Fire Flames, power boat licensing program, *Entrepreneur*, May 1999–Present
- Prepare and teach lessons to children and adults for up to 40 students per course
- Coordinate all business functions including accounting, advertising, and marketing

Big Island Sailing School, *Head Instructor/Race Coach,* Summers 1995–1999
- Devised and implemented new policies and improvements
- Supervised and directed 8 staff instructors and assisted in hiring
- Responsible for overall performance of the school with over 50 students
- Promoted after first two years as an instructor

VOLUNTEER EXPERIENCE
Coach, **Students for Literacy**, 2000–2001

EDUCATION
Honors Bachelor of Business Administration (Co-Op) – History Minor, **State U,** 2002
International Exchange – Greek University of Economic Sciences, Jan–May 2002

SCHOLARSHIPS AND AWARDS
Award in Entrepreneurship, $1000 for entrepreneurial excellence
State University Entrance Scholarship, $1000
State Scholarship, for achieving an average of 87%

Other
- Enjoy playing hockey, snowboarding, squash, and mountain biking on a recreational basis
- Interested in construction related projects, especially working with my dad at the cottage

BRAND: Associate Brand Manager

John J. Johnston

123 Learning St. • Anytown, USA • 10101 • johnj@yourname.com • (999) 555-1212

Brand Manager-level professional with full product management experience. Excels at analyzing data for best targets and providing innovative builds on previous campaigns to sustain and grow brands.

Associate Brand Manager (New Product Focus), Solutions®   8/02–10/03

- With minimal direction from Brand Manager, fully managed new product development from consumer insight ideation to product development with R&D. Created and advanced (with Global R&D) two new product ideas that produced a concept that strongly exceeded testing benchmarks. Led the development of test product for in-home usage test (Bases II). Product set to launch in 2005.
- Developed both the U.S. and global carpet care advertising briefs that resulted in above norm copy results in both Europe and U.S.
- Managed the development of Solutions Steam advertising strategy development that led to highest scoring creative on the history of the brand.

Accomplishments

- Managed the repositioning of Elevate's #1 sub-brand strategy with a new concept that drove purchase interest +16% versus control and an advertising strategy that consumers favorably responded to.
- Created and executed Elevate's 2003 defense plan in order to protect brand against increased competitive activity with results that closed a $6M dollar sales gap in the 1st half of 2003.
- Developed forecasting model that allowed the brand team to better understand retail inventories shifts and growth requirements from various classes of trade at both the consumption and factory sales levels.

BBB CONSUMER CARE,   11/99–07/02
Associate Brand Manager, Elevate®

- Served as acting Brand Manager for Elevate for three months (ending 01/15/02), including managing team of two assistant brand managers.
- Successfully utilized market research data, including IRI, Neilsen HH panel, MMA analysis, ASI testing, Firstep, Mediscope, concept optimization, prime prospect analysis, consumer perception studies, and Brand Fitness to make numerous business building recommendations.
- Managed the development of advertising concepts that led to three successful advertising executions.

Accomplishments

- Managed Elevate's television and radio advertising that delivered break-through advertising and increased brand sales +30% (since 11/99).
- Drove $5M in incremental sales by providing the new product idea, positioning, and launch of Elevate's new product in 2001 (Elevate Easy Open Lid).
- Drove an increase of 20% in physician recommendations through innovative and efficient medical marketing initiatives aimed at hospital and a physician base.
- Managed Elevate's cross-functional marketing team in developing Elevate's $80M marketing brand plan.
- Attained 8% increase in trade merchandising efficiency in 2001 by leading the assessment and analysis of the brand's trade promotion that led to numerous recommendations including a major shift in the brand's bonus pack strategy.

Assistant Brand Manager, Formula®   08/98–10/99

- Researched and recommended the second and third generation Formula Specialized Blends line extensions. Managed all aspects of product development, from idea conception to sales launch strategy for the two new SKU's (Bedtime & Rest, Joint Health).

Accomplishments

- Developed new consumer promotions programs such as internal and external cross-coupon initiatives that drove trial +7%.
- Thoroughly analyzed brand and competitive activity to provide key business insights, implications, and recommendations to senior management through monthly and annual brand status reports.
- Developed and maintained a category and brand forecasting model that became an integral tool for managing revenue expectations and brand spending.
- Worked on major multi-level marketing research project that included numerous versions of qualitative and quantitative research aimed at identifying and creating the optimal world that the Formula brand lives within.

ABC Company,   1997
Brand Management Intern, Blerb®
Accomplishments

- Researched and developed an Internet strategy for all products under the $450M Blerb brand name.
- Worked on product line extensions into the Canadian market in an effort to increase sales by 4%.
- Evaluated regional Hispanic marketing campaigns on various Blerb products and made recommendations for future advertising and promotional programs.
- Prepared a competitive analysis of household cleaning products category for key trade accounts.

HEALTH CARE Inc.,   1991–1995
Pharmaceutical Sales Representative, Corkize®

- Managed hospital based territories of approximately $4 M in sales. Marketed products to physicians and hospitals in the fields of Cardiology, Diabetes, Gastroenterology, and Smoking Cessation.
- Identified opportunities through market share and territory data analysis. Utilized information to prioritize issues and create focused strategies that consistently provided outstanding results.
- Monitored and gauged prescription data through pharmacies to target growth areas.
- Worked in a team setting, as a member of the Regional Marketing Committee, to develop solutions for regional marketing issues. First sales representative to initiate and lead a regional marketing plan.
- Established new approaches for coordinating Continuing Medical Education seminars for hospitals, all day medical workshops, and hospital education rounds in a way that met evolving educational needs.

Accomplishments

- The top performance over quota in the nation in 1992 and was in the top 10% in 1993, 1994, and 1995.
- 1993 National Junior Representative of the Year.

INFORMATION GROUP,   1989–1991
Sales Representative - Advertising and Marketing Services

- Sold marketing services and print advertising to national automotive and industrial accounts.
- Increased sales 20%, through value added products such as direct mail, product information return cards, trade-show space, creative services, and telemarketing services.
- Increased the new client base by 25%.
- Developed new revenue generating ideas, which accounted for 12% of total sales.

EDUCATION

SCHOOL OF BUSINESS ADMINISTRATION
State University
Master of Business Administration, June 1998
President, Marketing Association
Concentration: Marketing
Scholarship Recipient

STATE UNIVERSITY,
Bachelor of Arts in Economics, June 1989

INTERNATIONAL EXPERIENCE   1996
Traveled to Australia, Asia, South America, and Europe. Himalayas and an extensive stay with a native family in the rain forest of Indonesia.

BRAND: Brand Management

John J. Johnston

123 Learning St., Anytown, USA 10101 999.555.1212 johnj@yourname.com

VP Marketing / Brand Management Executive, in both traditional advertising and digital marketing arenas.

PROFILE

- 19 years experience in traditional advertising, integrated marketing, live events, and digital marketing solutions environments.
- Experience operating & leveraging resources within global advertising & retail networks.
- Comprehensive vertical experience includes retail, travel, financial services, telecommunications, package goods, and high-tech industries.
- Unique combination of business, strategic planning, management, and creative skills.
- Award winning print, TV, and digital portfolio.

EXPERIENCE AND ACCOMPLISHMENTS

EXPERIENCED BUSINESS MANAGER

- P&L and operations management experience at Reily, Interactive Inc., and Brandlett, with demonstrated excellence in leadership across business unit, client, and discipline management.
- Mgt experience of mid/large size teams (40+) and projects in multiple locations and countries.
- Proven track record of attracting and retaining top quality talent in multiple disciplines at senior and intermediate levels.
- Experience in transition management during reduction in force market conditions at both Interactive Inc and Brandlett.

PROVEN STRATEGIC PLANNING ABILITIES

- Developed online strategy that positioned Cheapies Store as a new online category between vendor and boutique while maximizing gift card presence and simplifying checkout process. Results included improved conversion of searchers into browsers, and browsers into buyers.
- Market segmentation development work for Delivery Co. formed basis for relevant marketing strategies and tactics for small/medium business audiences. Result was exponential market penetration in key markets.
- Strategic development work for P-Service helped the telecommunications company reposition itself from "Old-P" to more nimble, 21st century customer service organization.
- Development of groundbreaking communications solutions for Older Bank pension products in a newly deregulated financial market. Results enabled Older Bank to become the first UK bank to successfully market non-traditional financial products.

SEASONED BUSINESS DEVELOPMENT LEADER

- Strong conceptual selling and leadership skills. Successfully spearheaded focused business development efforts with multi-functional teams.
- Identified online needs and opportunities for Sky Air, pitched and won multi-million dollar digital business. Subsequent "Dream Team" participation with worldwide agencies for all digital initiatives and strategies.
- Pitched and won Cheapies Store.com business; developed Cheapies Store.com, subsequently winning awards.
- Successful new business pitches for a number of financial institutions, including BNB, ABB.

PROVEN BRAND DEVELOPMENT EXPERTISE

- Comprehensive brand development work for Sky Air. Integral member of Sky Air's "dream team"—an integrated, interdisciplinary group that repositioned the airline and developed the "defy" expectations /comparison global, integrated on and off-line marketing & ad campaign.
- Online brand development for the highly visible Cheapies Store brand. Completed brand alignment with Cheapies Store's overall brand strategy and enhanced the online relationship consumers are accustomed to with the Cheapies Store off-line brand.

AWARD WINNING CREATIVE PORTFOLIO

- Portfolio breadth encompasses TV, print, radio, live events, on-line ads, and web dev't.
- Recent awards for Cheapies Store.com include Com Arts Show Interactive.

EMPLOYMENT HISTORY

2001–Present   **BRANDLETT Inc.**   *President & Chief Creative Officer*
Brandlett development, extension, auditing & consulting across broad spectrum of Fortune 500 clients including: Big Airline, Big Retail Store.

1999–2000   **REILY**
Worldwide Engagement Director & Executive Creative Director
Serving dual role of North American Engagement Director & Executive Creative Director with responsibility for project P&L and office management, as well as overall responsibility for marketing, design, information architecture, editorial, and production.

1998–99   **INTERACTIVE Inc.**
Creative Director
Responsible for Interactive Inc.'s marketing initiatives, strategic implementation of digital and e-commerce solutions, creative, and an in-house team of 40 programmers, designers, writers and producers.

1993–98   **COMMUNICATIONS & ENTERTAINMENT Corp.**
Creative Director
Responsibility for creative direction, strategy, and shared client management across a broad spectrum of Fortune 500 companies, including Big Airlines, Big Bank, International Couriers.

1989–93   **AAADC**
Account Director / Planner
Strategic direction and P&L management for several Fortune 500 companies, including Big Phone Company, Big Food Disc.

1986–89   **BOWER Inc.**
Account Planner
Strategic development for several blue-chip, British companies, including Big Bank, House of Stores, and Cloud Television.

1980–86   **LUXURY CAR COMPANY**
Marketing Executive
Fielded to Public Relations, Product Marketing, Advertising, and Distribution departments before being promoted to Marketing Executive.

EDUCATION

State University: Creativity and Innovation program.
Polytechnic, University: Advanced black & white photography.
State College: Major in English & Art.

BRAND: Brand or Product Dev. Manager

Alice J. Johnston
123 Learning Street, Anytown, USA 10101
Home (999) 555-1212, Work (999) 555-1313
Email: alicej@yourname.com

Career Objective: Position in Brand Management and/or Product Development for Health and Nutrition-Related Products

Professional Profile

- **Marketing Professional with ten years experience,** specializing in the areas of Brand Management and Product Development of consumer products.
- **Strategic thinker,** skilled in analyzing and problem solving.
- **Creative & resourceful,** proven ability to plan, initiate, and execute projects on tight deadlines.
- **Success oriented with high energy and a positive attitude.**

Professional Experience

Brand Manager, Pharmaceutical Inc.   Dec 2002–Sept 2004

Responsibilities:

- Developed and implemented strategic marketing programs for a line of functional foods, skin care, and vitamin & herbal products.
- Prepared and presented annual marketing plan and sales forecasts.
- Gathered continuous intelligence on brand performance, customer and dealer attitudes, etc.
- Initiated product improvements to meet changing market needs.
- Worked closely with advertising and merchandising agencies to develop media campaigns and promotional programs to increase brand awareness.
- Trained and supervised three Marketing Assistants to work as Nutritional Consultants; promoting assigned brands during a six month feasibility test in one of America's largest mass merchandisers.

Accomplishments:

- Exceeded sales expectations during feasibility test, resulting in the National Rollout of 11 products with two American mass merchandisers.
- Developed new strategic direction for one of assigned brands and successfully won support of senior management to implement the brand's repositioning.
- Executed successful "Back to School" promotion, resulting in a 400% sales increase.
- Negotiated with suppliers to deliver merchandise at a competitive price within critical time frames, resulting in lower costs of goods sold.

Product Manager/Developer, Games Limited   Nov 1999–Sept 2002

Responsibilities:

- Led the development of a variety of licensed children's products from conception, packaging, product design, and cost of goods sold, through to launch.
- Developed product strategies, monitored results & made recommendations for corrective action.
- Liaised with inventors, licensors, designers, purchasing, quality control, and Health Safety USA to ensure adherence to design specifications and legal requirements.
- Negotiated with suppliers to deliver merchandise at a competitive price within critical time frames.

Accomplishments:

- Spearheaded start-up of girls' toy division; and administered key organizational systems required to smoothly move the company through this venture.
- Successfully developed and launched the popular children's toy Talking Teddy, which ranked 2nd in the soft doll category, at Big Toys in 2000.

- Introduced research methods such as focus group testing and surveys as a means of assessing new products' acceptance and potential in the marketplace.

Senior Product Developer, Toys Limited   March 1998–Nov 1999
Responsibilities:
- Spearheaded the development of 400 designs for the "Rainbow Collection" plush toy and gift line.
- Created soft doll characters for popular entertainment licenses.
- Corresponded with vendors in Asia on pricing, manufacturing, scheduling, and quality control issues.
- Prepared and presented product development plan, forecast, budget, and cost of goods sold analysis.

Accomplishments:
- Organized two buying trips to Asia, which resulted in improved communications with overseas vendors, securing of new vendors, and greater understanding of the toy manufacturing process.
- Aided the company through a difficult transition by assuming additional responsibilities, when the Product Development Manager left the company during a crucial time of the year.

Product Manager   January 1997–March 1998
Assistant Product Manager   May 1996–Jan 1997
Toys Limited
- Assisted Product Development Manager in the development and launch of new products.
- Designed line extensions, POP materials, and sales promotions for assigned product lines.
- Negotiated pricing and determined cost of goods sold.
- Maintained inventory levels relative to sales and monitored production & shipping schedules.
- Coordinated the editorial, photography, layout, and graphic art for catalogues featuring 500 products.
- Stimulated interest in and support of products among the sales force and distributors.

Education
Registered Nutritional Consultant (Part-time studies), 2001–present
Graduate Diploma in Management, State University, 1989
Bachelor of Arts-Major: Communications; Minor: Marketing, State University, 1994

Special Skills
Computer Knowledge – Microsoft Office Word, Excel, Lotus Notes, and PowerPoint
Languages – Fluent in English and Spanish

Community Involvement
- Cancer Research Fund - Chairperson, Annual Fall Bash '01 - Planned and executed the event, supervised 60 volunteers, and solicited donations from corporations. Proceeds raised exceeded $33K.
- Cancer Research Young Professionals Association 1991–1998 - member.
- "Run for the Cure"'1997–1999 - participant 10K Run.

Personal Interests
Running for exercise and pleasure, learning to cook as well as my mother, investment club.

BRAND: BAD—Brand Events

Alice J. Johnston

123 Learning Street
Anytown, USA, 10101
(999)555-1212
alicej@yourname.com

QUALIFICATIONS

Post Diploma in Sports Administration (Deans Honor List). Degree in Kinesiology with a focus in sports administration and a minor in history. Two plus years of special events/sponsorship experience. One year of brand management experience.

COMMUNICATION SKILLS

- effective management skills developed through special event planning
- leadership skills developed through captaincies and sport experiences
- organizational skills refined through management experiences
- ability to interact with people on an outgoing and upbeat basis through sales and teaching experience
- marketing skills gained through brand management experience
- effective verbal communication skills gained through teaching and sales
- effective written communication skills developed through public/media relations and sponsorship proposal writing
- computer experience using WordPerfect, Microsoft Excel, Word, Power Point, E-mail, the Internet, Simply Accounting and other Windows based applications

EXPERIENCE

January 1999- Present	Special Events Coordinator/Brand Manager The Poster Group - produced P & L analysis' of special events - determined fit between brand and event - generated strategic plans for growth of brands - developed and implemented advertising and public relations opportunities - executed sponsorships according to contractual obligations - budgeted for marketing and special event dollars - communicated special events/sponsorships with sales force so that they could effectively leverage our involvement
January 1998- January 1999	Marketing Coordinator Sports Management, Inc., assisted Director of Marketing and President with the development of new business, client management and client servicing - supervised activities of Administrative Assistant - liased with suppliers and vendors on the creation of materials for various projects - wrote and created sponsorship proposals, media kits, media releases and promotional materials on behalf of clients - involved in the development of merchandise programs
September 1996- September 1997	Sales Representative/ Office Administrator Biscuitt Sales, - responsible for sales of a variety of premium products to major grocery chains

Alice J. Johnston

- maintained product base and listings through regular call cycle
- developed new accounts through cold calls
- coordinated information distribution throughout office
- designed commission tracking system

November 1996-
April 1997

Ski Professional
Black Hills Ski Resort
- taught skiing to an assortment of skill levels
- developed excellent verbal communication skills
- easily interacted with different age groups and personalities

April 1996-
September 1996

Sales/Merchandising Representative
The Poster Group
- responsible for sales and merchandising of Poster products in the convenience channel
- managed the territory of Anytown and surrounding areas
- blossomed under independent working conditions
- established rapport with customers, supervisors and reps
- increased distribution of existing products and introduced new premium products to the stores

EDUCATION

1997-1998

Post Diploma Sports Administration
State College

Studied the business aspects of sport including entrepreneurship, management, computer applications, financial, and event planning.

1992-1996

Bachelor of Kinesiology, History minor
State University.

Studied the physical, biological, sociological and humanities' aspects of physical education and health. Also included were practical and laboratory components.

VOLUNTEER

- 1997 Special Olympics World Winter Games, Volunteer Services
- 1999-2000 – Assistant Coach, Minor Midget AA Hockey Team

EXTRA CURRICULAR

- State University Alpine Ski Team, 1992-1996, Manager and Captain 199
- active member of Physical Education Society, 1994-1996
- take pleasure in sporting activities of all types, team and individual
- enjoy reading books of any nature and various genres

What's Wrong?

- Too many bullet points
- Lackluster objective/profile or lack thereof
- Too much wasted space
- No declared job role
- No accomplishments or specific and measurable results
- Too many unnecessary extras and/or irrelevant information and/or repetition
- Sends a mixed message
- Leaves a strange or weird impression or doesn't suit the industry

BUSINESS DEVELOPMENT: Incentive Marketing

Alice J. Johnston
123 Learning Ave. Apt 123, Anycity, AS
Cell: 555-999-1212
Email: alicej@yourname.com

Personal Profile:
As **Manager of Incentives**, I have demonstrated my passion and ownership for the product. By creating multiple growth channels and corporate retention initiatives, I have grown card sales from $60 million (LY) to $85 million (YTD) and reduced credit customer churn by 20% using the core skills of leadership, innovative twists on current products, and good old-fashioned hard work.

Professional Experience

Manager, Sales Incentives (Sales Inc.), Oct 2002-Present
- Created B2B direct mail campaigns targeting past customers and grew existing accounts by $1.3 million in sales.
- Creative positioning, pricing strategy & copy approval for all sales incentives direct mail pieces.
- Measured response rates for B2B direct mail campaigns, average response of 2.5%.
- Managed the financial plan and a marketing budget of $8 million.
- Created and managed a field sales team to solicit the Sales Gift Card to corporations which accounted for 50% of the current B2B sales.

Accomplishments:
- Built the annual marketing plan (with all internal and external initiatives), which grew Sales Gift Card sales from $60 million (LY) to $85 million (YTD).
- Devised a re-loadable spending card CRM program which increased Sales credit card customer spend by 6 times and store visits by 2 times.
- Initiated the use of the gift card in the Sales credit card acquisition which decreased churn of new credit card holders by 20%.
- Established cross marketing B2B opportunities with external corporations (ex: RentAMovie, Gateway, Post Services), resulting in $8 M of sales in the B2B channel.

Marketing Manager, SalesConnect (Sales Telecom Co), Oct 2000–Oct 2002
- Decreased acquisition cost by 60% for the long distance business.
- Managed a marketing budget of $4 million.
- Implemented mass media as a complementary tool for the direct mail campaigns.
- Developed and launched SalesConnect internet service (partnered with Compucell), and paging service (partnered with Telenet) which added $2 million in revenue.

Accomplishments:
- Created the marketing plan for all acquisition channels which grew the long distance subscribers to 250,000 customers (largest switchless long distance reseller in U.S.) and sales of $33 M.
- Developed marketing channels for all SalesConnect products which included statement messaging, preprint, outbound call center & direct mail averaging a response rate of 4%.
- Recommended and implemented a creative strategy which focuses on a consistent communication and sales "trust" in all customer collateral.
- Built & launched the SalesConnect wireless service which added $1.2 M in revenue per year.

Associate Marketing Manager, Rich Oil Ltd., June 1998–Oct 2000
Accomplishments:
- Planned and executed the customer communication strategy for the Rich loyalty program, which increased sales volume by 15%.
- Managed and analyzed retail promotion; gaining a market growth of 25%.
- Determined the "value equation" of gas consumers, which provided the foundation for a customer loyalty program.
- Initiated a car wash direct marketing program, resulting in a 4% increase in sales.

Analyst, Partners for a Better Future for Anycity, summer 1997
Accomplishments:
- Created and implemented the first performance evaluation for homeless shelters in U.S., which measured success in its operations.

Education: Honors Business Administration, Prestige School of Business 1998
Languages: Fluent in English, French, and Cantonese
Interests: Trying surfing for the first time; sun, sand and ocean; reading a good business book

BUSINESS DEVELOPMENT: Business Development Manager

John J. Johnston
123 Learning St., Anytown, USA 10101
999.555.1212 johnj@yourname.com

PROFILE: Sr. Business Development, Marking, and Strategic Planning Professional

Energetic, team player with over 10 years of sales and marketing experience ready to apply strong analytic, market strategy, interpersonal and communication skills to Tier One and Two clients.

EMPLOYMENT HISTORY

Software Inc.   2002–2005
   Director of Business Development
   Software Inc. is a software firm setting up new operations Anytown. Provide enterprise wide stakeholder experience management solutions for FP 100 firms.

   Responsibilities included: set up operations, local market analysis, market strategy development, execute prospecting campaign, profiling and networking, qualify leads, manage sales cycle.
   - Established Anytown operations.
   - Negotiated 2 marketing partnerships.
   - Successfully generated leads and sales process with Big Bank, Big Life Insurance Comp, Big American Bank, Big Retail Store, Big Phone Company.
   - Achieved each year targets set with VP to grow operations resulting in a **150% growth** for this new location of Software Inc. over the last 2 years.

ABC Media   1999–2002
   Account Executive   2000–2002
   ABC, part of XZY Media, is an 800 person e-business strategy and services company providing multi-channel marketing solutions. Service offerings include Internet development, integration, and hosting as well as 'convergence bundles' with Moon Publishing and National Paper print services.

   Responsibilities in this position included: develop annual sales plan, generate and qualify leads, manage sales cycle, manage sales support team, negotiate and finalize sale, co-ordinate implementation with project manager, maintain on-going relationship, generate forecast.
   - Achieved **110% of sales quota** 2001.
   - Achieved **120% of sales quota** in 2000.
   - Managed up to 5 direct reports.
   - Developed account strategy, implemented account plan, and organized sales support team to win major multi-year contracts.
   - Negotiated multi-year services delivery **partnership with Big Phone Company.** Supported the 15-member e-business account team and services delivery within ABC.

   Inside Sales Representative   1999–2000
   Held this position with Interactive Inc., was purchased, in January 2000, as part of the creation of ABC Media. Interactive was a 'boutique' Internet strategy development and implementation firm, providing e-business solutions to national and international organizations. Responsibilities at Interactive included: develop and execute prospecting campaign, qualify leads, comanage sales process.
   - Achieved **120% of annual sales quota.**

BUSINESS DEVELOPMENT: Business Development Manager (cont.)

John J. Johnston
999.555.1212
- 2 -

ZAP INC.   1995–1998

Product Manager
ZAP is a global leader in semiconductor design, producing CCDs (light-sensitive integrated circuits) for OEM sales in factory automation and document scanning.

Hired to analyze global CCD technology market and industry for growth opportunities. After one year, responsibilities expanded to include new product development and new product launch campaigns.

- Defined **10 new product development technical requirements** for chip and camera electronics.
- Developed and executed **3 new product launch plans**; involving magazine ads, trade shows, mailers, data sheets, brochures, channel communications, demonstrations, and beta plans.
- Managed annual **new product development planning** for 50 scientists and engineers.
- Generated **competitor analysis and market strategy** reports **contributing to 45% annual growth**.

COMMUNITY INVOLVEMENT

Anytown Board of Trade, Up-and-Coming Professionals   1999–2003
- **Vice President Corporate Development 2003**: mandated to liaise with Anytown's corporate community to improve profile and expand membership.
- **Chair Challenging Fix-Up 2002**: organized and managed a 30 person event to re-paint a residence for developmentally challenged children.
- **Vice-President 2000–2001**: responsible for executive leadership of 5 community and social events including Kid Build, a 75 person event to construct a building at a Children's camp.

State School of Business Alumni Association   2002–2003
- Member Alumni Sponsorship Committee for Local Alumni Association.

Anytown Central Sport and Social Club   1999–2003
- Participant on Soccer, Ultimate Frisbee, Floor Hockey and Curling teams.

EDUCATION
- American Professional Sales Association's "Skills for Sales Success" certificate   2003
- IBM Certified for e-business, Solution Advisor   2002
- IBM Signature Sales Methodology certificate   2001
- State University, Continuing Education, Project Management for Sales Executives   2001
- IBM e-Business Products and Solution Selling   2000

Master of Business Administration   1993–1995
STATE SCHOOL OF BUSINESS, State University
- Top quartile standing (1993–94)

Bachelor of Landscape Architecture and **Bachelor of Arts**   1985–1990
STATE UNIVERSITY

LANGUAGES
English - Excellent;   German - Excellent;   Spanish - Fair

BUSINESS DEVELOPMENT: Bus. Dev. and Strategy Executive

JOHN J. JOHNSTON, B.COM, LLB

123 Learning Avenue ♦ Anycity, AS ♦ 10101 ♦ Tel: (555) 999-1212 ♦ *johnj@yourname.com*

Experienced Director-level professional in Business Development and Corporate Strategy for leading high-tech and consulting organizations.

- Proven experience in identifying key business issues and developing proactive market strategies.
- A record of introducing and implementing effective process and operational improvements across a wide spectrum of industries, including financial services, utilities, and transportation.
- Skilled at coaching and developing effective multi-disciplinary teams, and partnering with client organizations to reach bottom-line objectives.

CAREER OVERVIEW

DEEP TECHNOLOGY CORPORATION   2000–2002

Initiated and developed alliance relationships with large and intermediate sized systems integrators, consulting organizations and partners to achieve integrated offerings and business growth.

Director, Strategic Alliances

➢ Developed worldwide partner relationships with ABC Consulting, Finance Consult Corp, and several smaller consulting companies, and sales relationships with key partner.

➢ Increased partnership revenues to the 2nd major source of corporate revenues, growing from 5% in Q1 to over 25% of Q4 revenue. Total Deep partner revenues for fiscal 2001 were U.S. $7M.

➢ Managed multi-disciplinary teams and assisted in creating vertical strategies, go-to-market solutions, and partner programs. Negotiated and drafted mutually beneficial agreements and strong business relationships.

STRATEGY MANAGEMENT CONSULTING LIMITED, Associate   1995–1999

Led Strategy-client teams in business development and strategy consulting projects to Fortune 500 companies in the United States in industries such as financial services, utilities, airlines, rail, government services, and mining.

Business Strategy

➢ Commissioned by an international airline to develop a product and labor strategy for their regional operations. Benchmarked competitors, interviewed employee groups, and modeled business economics.

➢ Prepared an integrated project management plan and government and interest groups negotiations strategy post acquisition for a major U.S. mining company.

➢ Created a de-averaged cost model for a major U.S. transportation hub in order to assess business and development opportunities eventually leading to a divestiture of the facility.

➢ Conducted a detailed analysis of mergers and acquisitions in the U.S. that provided the foundation and key conclusions for a Business Week feature article on this topic.

Marketing Strategy

➢ Conducted focus groups and recommended a targeted and tailored marketing offer, and improved brand repositioning of a major lending institution.

➢ Aided in a Strategic Choice Analysis™ market segmentation for the residential and small business market, and the commercial and industrial market for a major utility company.

➢ Analyzed the state operations of major bank and recommended a pilot strategy for alternative banking.

➢ Conducted an assessment of various customer relationship management outsourcing opportunities for a large municipality, resulting in an integrated call center with improved call response time.

➢ Developed and implemented a communications strategy and workforce rationalization plans for the merger of two real estate management services companies.

BUSINESS DEVELOPMENT: Bus. Dev. and Strategy Executive (cont.)

Process and Operational Improvement

➤ Restructured various operating units of major utility, costed out operations, assessed outsourcing options, and benchmarked competition and other industries.

➤ Reorganized several functions within rail company equaling projected savings of over $3M annually.

➤ Set up processes and prepared educational material for an internal training and development program and trained the internal consulting team at a major utility company.

POWER LAW FIRM   1991–1994
Articling Student, (1993–1994)
Summer Student, (1991 & 1992)

Completed articling rotations in corporate/commercial, intellectual property, civil litigation, and securities.

BRAND MARKETING INC.   1988–1990
Assistant Brand Manager

Conducted competitive category analysis, developed long-term brand strategy, allocated and managed promotional budget, and supervised the development of advertising for multiple brands.

➤ Produced an 8.9% sales increase in Health and Beauty Care territory.

YOUNG PAINTERS LTD.   **Summers 1985 & 1986**
Franchise Owner

➤ Received the Award as the top Manager in U.S.

EDUCATION AND PROFESSIONAL DEVELOPMENT

LAW SOCIETY OF U.S., Anycity, Anystate, (1994–1995)
Bar Admission Course

HOUSE UNIVERSITY, Faculty of Law, Anycity, Anystate, (1990–1993)
Bachelor of Laws

STATE UNIVERSITY, School of Business, Anycity, Anystate, (1984–1988)
Honors Bachelor of Commerce
Commerce Undergraduate Award; Marketing Award

Completed a wide range of professional development courses including:
5-day Solutions Selling™ course, 2001; Communications in the Consulting Craft, 1998;
Conflict Management Inc. Negotiation Workshop, 1997

MEMBERSHIPS AND AFFILIATIONS

Camp Fun, (*camp for children with cancer*)
Speaker to service organizations and corporate charitable functions, 2000–2001

Camp Fun, Counselor, 1998–present

Best Buddies of US, Board of Directors, Treasurer
Match intellectually challenged adults with college students, 1998–present

Best Buddies of US, Fundraising Committee, 1997–present

Charity Run, Prestige College Run Committee, 1999–present

Climbed Mount Kiliminjaro, Tanzania, Africa, 1994

State University Commerce Society, President, 1987–1988

US Humane Association Certificate for Valor, 1986

BUSINESS DEVELOPMENT: Bus. Dev. and Strategy

John J. Johnston
Business Development & Strategy

Summary **Action Catalyst, Problem Solver, Creative Thinker**

Top Skills

Gathering Critical Mass Marshalling internal and external financial, physical, and human capital to launch action.
Generating Buy-In Transferring enthusiasm for business programs & concepts to key external & internal stakeholders.
Relationship building/Team building.
Complex Knowledge Assimilation & Application Proven ability to rapidly absorb and apply highly technical subject matter. Superior interpolation and extrapolation skills.
"Big Picture" Analysis Full understanding of the interplay of biz factors, causation & linkage, mandate to bottom-line.
"Outside the Box" Thinking Creative lateral analysis combined with effective drill-down techniques. Original concepts. Problem solving.

STREAM CORPORATION, Vice President   **2002–Present**
Stream is a Limited Market Dealer. Stream has an FSE regulated affiliate in the UK and a branch office in New York.

Mandate: Develop Corporate Finance opportunities. Build network of highly qualified tech consultants to service clients.
Achievements:

- **Acquisition Pending.** Identified and opened discussions with an American company for acquisition by an Asian services firm. Discussions proceeding. To be combined with a U.S. acquisition and a Nasdaq RTO in process.

- **Funding Negotiation.** On behalf of an Asian investor negotiated funding terms for a European technology company. Details included valuation, special shareholding, co-investment rights, shareholding ratchets, special restrictions, etc.

- **Alliances.** Assembled consulting team including market and technical specialists and valuation expert. Negotiated services agreement finance firm.

DRV INC., Principal   **2000–2001**
DRV was established to provide an Internet-based Business-to-Business exchange and the opportunity to hedge price risk to the Semiconductor Industry.

Mandate: Conceive and draft Business Plan. Develop strategic alliances. Open funding opportunities.
Achievements:

- **Conception of Business Model.** Developed model to suit the needs of both the semiconductor and financial communities. Extensive study of regulated exchanges, suitable transaction mechanisms, and appropriate derivative contracts required for a successful market. Business plan author. Wrote a concise document to communicate the concept developed above. Inclusion of comprehensive market study and *Pro Forma* financials.

- **Initiate funding discussions.** Extensive discussions with Big Bank—ending in offer to employ the management team. Also, discussions with Saint Fund Management, (maintained interest in funding future activities) and York Securities (ending with an offer to fund).

- **Established partnerships** to provide technology with Other Big Firm (dealing at the Partner level and above), and Denmark's largest IT company with a global customer base, dealing with the CEO and Director of Financial Markets. Extensive discussions with the Other State Stock Exchange (dealings with Chairman& CEO and Executive Vice President Strategy).

BUSINESS DEVELOPMENT: Bus. Dev. and Strategy (cont.)

HARD BUCKX LIMITED, Assistant VP & Director (Marketing, Biz Dev)　　　　　**1998–2000**

Hard Buckx Limited purchased all assets of Wild Technologies (from the receiver) and was a turn-around operation.

Mandate: Support the president in the areas of strategy and planning, with a specific focus on Business Development, Marketing, and Technology Licensing.

Achievements:
- **Turnaround strategy author.**

  - Proposed and developed the company strategy to reactivate the networking division.

  - Wrote company long-run strategy and business plan. The plan helped the company to secure additional financing, in spite of high losses over the previous year.

- **Licensing.** Strengthened company product offering by licensing technology (OEM agreements).

  - Identified a low profile OEM supplier of Fax/RAS hardware to fill gaps in the company's line of products and offset technology weaknesses. Licensed for the company and negotiated interim OEM agreement. Initiated discussions through to agreement. STARR branded product won product of the year for 1998 (PCI Magazine).

  - Licensed WAN networking technology from Swiss company to support the networking product line. Effective door opener for sales. Initiated discussions regarding relicensing of this technology.

- **Sales and Channel relationships.**

  - Placed products with AUSA. Identified $10 Million opportunity with AUSA for fall promotion. The company achieved in excess of $3 Million in sales for 1998. Negotiated and closed sales to the account.

  - Identified retail agents across the U.S. doing business with the top ten computer retailers. Appointed Innovative Vanguard as agent to handle AUSA and other large retail chains. Negotiated agency agreement.

I-DIALOG LIMITED, Marketing Manager　　　　　**1996–1998**

I-DIALOG Limited (IDL) was a joint venture between South and Night Information Inc. IDL is the American market leader for archival online information, and NI is the largest provider of online information worldwide.

Mandate: Responsible for all marketing activity. Responsible for sales and profitability of CD-ROM business unit.

Achievements:
- Launched new Internet-based product line (IDL Talk) into the U.S.—top performance worldwide on this product.

- Negotiated all stages of a production and distribution agreement for the CD-ROM business unit that guaranteed growth of the business unit while doubling the profit over 1995 results. A two-year agreement guaranteed the company in excess of $500,000 profit and actual performance doubled minimum guarantees.

LIVE CORPORATION, President and Principal　　　　　**1993–1995**

LIVE Corporation published software products for sale to consumers, successfully penetrated U.S. retail channels for Tame software, and grew as a business from $0 start-up revenue to $400,000 per quarter over a 5-quarter period (60-70% GP). Products carried by 17 of the largest computer retail chains in the U.S., representing 2400 outlets and 70% of the software sold at retail.

THE MARKETING GROUP INC., Partner　　　　　**1990–1996**

The Marketing Group provided marketing consulting and sales agency services to software developers. One product became the leader in the institutional education niche in both the U.S. & Canada and lead to acquisition of the company.

BLUE DOG GROUP, Partner　　　　　**1987–1990**

Education　　State University of Anyregion　　　　Bachelor of Arts in Economics　1989

Hobbies　　　Oil painting, played professionally in blues band and wilderness camping.

BUSINESS DEVELOPMENT: BAD—Business Development

ALICE J. JOHNSTON

123 Learning Crescent
Anycity, Anystate
01010
(555) 999-1212

OBJECTIVE

To obtain a challenging position where my skills and abilities will allow me to grow as an integral member of an effective team.

SKILLS

* Computer experience including Windows 95, MS Office, Maximizer, and Internet Utilities
* Highly organized, motivated team player with excellent leadership skills.
* Detail oriented with the ability to obtain a high standard of work.
* Proficient in organizing workload to meet timetables and deadlines.
* Skillful in learning new methods and procedures quickly.
* Strong communications and interpersonal skills.

CAREER HISTORY

ABC COMMUNICATIONS- Any City

1996-Present **Business Development Manager**
*Generate leads, develop new business and upsell current clients
*Software sales - X Windows, NFS, Te[...]
  Portable Documentation Software
*Download leads from website and dis[...]
  and rest of the world
*Territory – Northern United States

1996 **XYZ MICROSYSTEMS**
Account Manager

* Provided Quotes for sales
* Maintained a daily call log.
* Generated new business contacts.

What's Wrong?
· Too long
· Too much wasted space
· Lackluster objective/profile or lack thereof
· No declared job role
· No accomplishments or specific and measurable results
· Uninspiring and boring
· Leaves a strange or weird impression or doesn't suit the industry

BUSINESS DEVELOPMENT: BAD—Business Development (cont.)

Alice J. Johnston - page 2

* Sales of computer hardware and software.
* Updated client listings through cold calls.

1994-1996   **LAWN CARE COMPANY**
Manager
*In charge of 20 employees in a call center environment
*Call center was to produce leads and generate business for
    for 21 franchises
* Manager of operations and productions
* Client base consisted of over 2000 clients.

EDUCATION

ABC COLLEGE - Any City, Anystate
1995   **Business Administration**

1989   **ANYCITY DISTRICT HS** – Any City, Anystate
High School Diploma

REFERENCES

Available upon request.

BUSINESS INTELLIGENCE & RESEARCH: Junior Research Assistant

ALICE J. JOHNSTON

Contact: (999) 555-1212 or alicej@yourname.com

Junior Research Assistant
Young, bright, diligent student looking for part time work in getting your endless research completed and your paperwork neatly organized.

EDUCATION

- Special Interest Certificate in Middle Eastern and African Studies
  (State University) – Current Grade point 4.0, expect to graduate April 2006

- Ta'lim-ul-Islam: Islamic Studies Certificate Program
  (The Shia Imami Ismaili Tariqah and Religious Education Board)

- International Baccalaureate Diploma – High School Diploma with Distinction

SELECTED WORK EXPERIENCE

Research Assistant State University, Political Science Department Assisting Dr. A Surashi with a book chapter on prospects for democracy in Pakistan and Turkey.	September 2004–Present (Part-time)
Student Assistant State University , Political Science Department Assisting Dr. W. Knight with his Children and War project as well as the academic journal Global Governance.	May 2004–Present (Part-time)
Bilingual Museum Guide Museum of Culture (Other State, USA) Guiding clients, working at the tourist information office, and conducting activities with children.	July 2001–August 2001 (Full-time)

SELECTED AWARDS

- State University Senate's Rising Star Award 2004
- Top Academic Student Award 2004
- Post-Secondary Youth Leadership Award 2003
- State University Academic Excellence Scholarship

SELECTED EXTRA-CURRICULAR ACTIVITIES

- Chair of the Anytown Youth Council (2003)
- Editor-in-Chief of *Youth Culture Magazine* (2002–Present)
- Elected to the State University highest legislative body in which students take part: Students' Union General Faculties Council (2004–Present)
- Vice-Chair of Internal Communications for the Communications and Publications Board of the Ismaili Council of (2003–Present)
- Chosen to be a Delegate and Representative at the world's largest university-level simulation of the UN, the National Model United Nations conference (to take place March 2005 in New York, USA)
- Feature Columnist for *The Journal*, the city's largest newspaper (2002–Present)

BUSINESS INTELLIGENCE & RESEARCH: Intelligence Manager

JOHN J. JOHNSTON

123 Learning St., Anytown, USA, 10101 /999-555-1212 (Ph/Fx)
johnj@yourname.com / www.johnj.com

OBJECTIVE: Business Intelligence Manager

HIGHLIGHTS OF QUALIFICATIONS

- Accomplished IT professional with an MBA in Marketing and 10+ years international experience working with multinational companies in the Telecom, Banking and Finance sectors
- A strong track record in sales, marketing, and business development, complemented with actual hands-on work in the design, development, implementation, and delivery of focused, responsive, and strategic business solutions; experience includes teaching and training at the university level
- Acknowledged expert in Data Warehousing, Customer Relationship Management and Business Intelligence
- Experienced professional in services consulting, database marketing analytic, fulfilment processes used for direct mail, email, and call center
- Flexible, responsible, self-motivated with ability to work under heavy pressure and multi-task
- Aside from English, fluent in Spanish and Italian

TECHNICAL SKILLS

- Advanced computer applications: MS Word, Excel, PowerPoint, Project and Publisher, Visio, Lotus Notes
- Functional knowledge of databases: Oracle, xBase, MS Access, MS SQL Server 2000, and MySQL
- Programming languages: Visual FoxPro, Clipper, Dbase IV, Turbo Pascal, and MS Cobol
- Multi-dimensional analysis, query & reporting tools: Cognos-Impromptu, SPSS
- Data Mining tools: Angoss-KnowledgeSeeker and SPSS-AnswerTree
- Familiar with: Front Page, HTML, Dreamweaver MX, Fireworks MX, SQL-Server, PHP-My SQL, and Linux environments

WORK EXPERIENCE

Big Bank

Business Intelligence Manager 02/00–10/03
- Developed, managed, and improved the Marketing Datamart
- Served as a key contact person with system operations and domestic business partners for requesting, developing, and managing required data extracts
- Interacted with required vendors for data processing preparation and analysis
- Developed insights and made recommendations based upon analysis and explorations

Major Achievements
- Led the strategic database marketing plan for the company, persuading the top management to increase the budget for new attraction, retention, and fidelity/loyalty actions that allowed the company to increase the customer retention rate by more that 10% after one year
- Achieved campaign results exceeding the targeted 50%, leading to net profits of over $1 Million per year
- Developed a data cleansing program which reduced the average mailing return rate from 12% to 5% resulting in cost savings amounting of $ 300K yearly
- Introduced the company to the advantages of CRM as a key factor in supporting sales channels and customers requirements

Telecom Inc. Anytown, USA

IT Projects Manager 03/98–02/00
- Led a multi-company team that implemented nation-wide the new company billing system, coaching end-users and managers in all the call centres and back offices of the company
- Managed the implementation of the Pre-Subscription Project for the deregulation of long distance services
- Collaborated as a team participant in the implementation of 'TravelPass' project (a multi-branding frequency/loyalty marketing program) and in the reengineering of the data warehouse data model

JOHN J. JOHNSTON
999-555-1212(Ph/Fx)

Database Marketing Manager   07/96–02/98
- Managed a multi-skilled team scheduling, prioritising and execution for querying marketing databases and extracting required information for database analysis during marketing campaigns
- Elaborated value-added information and reports for strategic business opportunities and doing an intensive use of Cognos-Impromptu and Angoss-Knowledge Seeker tools
- Designed the segmentation, scoring, and cross-selling models that allowed the company to solve the lack of knowledge of its business segments that increased significantly the sales after six months
- Analysed customers response using data mining tools and elaborated reports and proposals for improvement
- Participated actively in the maintenance of the data warehouse data model and in the improvement of the interfaces from the legacy systems

Data Warehouse Project Leader   03/95–06/96
- Designed, implemented and co-ordinated the development of the data warehouse for the company
- Designed detailed business requirements and analysed different technical solutions proposed by international vendors such as SHL Systemhouse, Cognos, Angoss, and RAC Marketing
- Managed multi-skilled teams of implementers from different suppliers, consultants, and software, communication, and hardware vendors for the project
- Introduced the data-cleansing concept as a key business intelligence success and recommended a detailed solution for the short- and long-term through data processing reengineering

Marketing Systems Analyst   05/94–02/95
- Provided assistance as required for marketing campaigns launch and implementation
- Administered, monitored, and audited the sales for small/medium sized companies according to plan
- Extended assistance to product managers, e.g., '0-800' and Plan TRUE products

Systems Analyst Programmer   07/92–05/94
- Partnered with Riddles Inc. as contractor; designed and executed the SIGLI project

Free Lance System Analyst   12/89–06/92
- Wrote programs for pharmaceutical, medical & insurance sectors throughout U.S.

EDUCATION AND PROFESSIONAL TRAINING

- **Master's Degree in Business Administration and Marketing** as assessed by World Education Services; Madrid, Spain, 1998–1999

- **Bachelor's Degree in Computer Systems** from a recognised university as determined by WES, Anytown, ST; Big University, Buenos Aires, Argentina, 1988–1991

Professional Development Courses

- Various courses in Data Mining, Data Modeling, Statistical Techniques and Methodologies, Data Warehousing, and Marketing
- Other courses in Investment Projects Preparation and Evaluation, Leadership, Effective Communication & Human Relations
- Italian Lingua Diploma, Lingua School, Buenos Aires, Argentina, 1997–2000

REFERENCES AND PORTFOLIO
Available upon request

BUSINESS INTELLIGENCE & RESEARCH: Research Intelligence

Alice J. Johnston MLS, CSC, MBA

Research and Competitive Intelligence Expert

123 Learning St., Anytown, USA 10101   999-555-1212   alicej@yourname.com

PROFILE

- Creator of internal strategies for information access (knowledge management)

- Expert in competitive business intelligence

- Experience in strategic marketing positions in the profit and non-profit sectors, with emphasis on direct response including web marketing

- Developer of a direct response marketing program at a NASDAQ listed company

RELEVANT EXPERTISE & ACCOMPLISHMENTS

Knowledge Manager/Competitive Intelligence Manager/Research Analyst

- Created internal company strategy for competitive and knowledge management initiative

- Analyzed and accessed relevant information from print and online database sources for various business initiatives and projects including pre-sales and marketing planning

- Designed and compiled competitive intelligence newsletters for clients, reporting on sector statistics, market segmentation, and business trends

Direct Marketing, Fundraising, and Marketing Strategy

- Developed a direct response-marketing program at an Internet company focused on advertising/marketing community. Using methodologies including client segmentation and list purchase, as well as creative development through new media and customer service initiatives to build relationship with clients including direct mail, direct email, and call centers. Responsibilities include management of virtual team of internal staff and outsourced suppliers

- Designed fundraising/prospecting program for non-profit seniors' residence/foundation

Training and Presentation

- Developed and delivered courses in three different programs at two community colleges. Including: Fundamentals of Electronic Commerce, Business Information, Database Searching, Value-Added (Information) Services, Research Methods

Project Management

- Proposed and developed list rental business, including development of an internal database with proposed revenues of 150K during the first year of operation

- Built and managed cross-functional team in two departments, and ten staff (at various levels) to implement project.

- Responsible for internal implementation plus working with external suppliers. Conducted supplier identification and proposal activity for projects.

EMPLOYMENT HISTORY

2002–Present **Smarty-pants Consultant Inc. Life Assurance**
Establish and manage competitive intelligence initiative in the market research area. Work with strategic planning and quality assurance in developing a competitive process enhanced by technological applications and information sources.

2001–2002 **Manager, Smarty-pants/Information Services, (Contract)**
Establish and manage competitive intelligence initiative and develop knowledge management program for access to information and resources at a pharmaceutical company.

State University. Strategic Management Study Group:
Non-Profit Retirement Residence Foundation
Analyze and forecast the 5-year plans focusing on seniors segment, retirement housing in the non-profit and profit sectors, long-term care, supportive housing/assisted living, government regulations and models, and fundraising.

Marketing and Public Relations Consultant. ABC Corp. (Consultant)
Implementation of marketing strategy including creation of marketing and PR collateral as well as competitive data for a wireless software company. Work with sales and business development in building B-to-B relationships with partners.

1999–2001 **Senior Marketing Manager, Direct Response, arabrand.com**
Developed and implemented direct marketing program for a dot-com company in the advertising/marketing sector using purchased and in-house lists to reach potential clients through email and postal campaigns.

Implemented list management business to bring in 150K the first year of rental.

1997–1999 **Instructor, State College and Local College**
Faculty of Business: Information Retrieval Services Program, electronic and Internet Commerce Program, and Library Techniques Program

Center for Creative Communications: Journalism program-Research Methods. Taught courses in e-Commerce, Business Information, Research Methods, etc. (Contract)

1996–1997 **Consultant & Knowledge Manager**
Provided competitive research services for various financial organizations, government agencies, and consulting firms

1992–1996 **Branch Manager, Anytown, Library**

1989–1992 **Manager, Information Centre, Crangle Communication-Marketing**

EDUCATION

2002 Master of Business Administration, State University. Major: Marketing
1979 Master of Library Science, Graduate School of Library Science, State University
1977 Bachelor of Arts, State University

CALL CENTER: Telemarketer

John J. Johnston

123 Learning St., Anytown, USA 10101 Tel. (999) 5551212   Email: johnj@yourname.com

Experienced Telemarketer: who works best within highly reputable organizations sponsoring and representing solid products and services.

Summary of Qualifications
- Powerful telephone skills, able to establish immediate trust and confidence
- Persistent, patient, and sensitive to customer's needs and apprehensions
- Effectively overcome objections to sales in a calming and convincing manner
- Excellent listening skills and eager to lean
- Ability to work under pressure

Work Experience

Telemarketer, ABC International   2004–2005
Telephone Sales
- Hit expected sales targets within first month of being hired; consistently stayed at or above quota

Telemarketer, direct sales department, Investment INC   2003–2004
- Telephone sales of financial and consulting services
- Research and resolve consumer disputes
- Provided technical and administrative support to General Manager in managing of individual and corporate financial assets for domestic and international customers
- Assisting in sales of different kind of investment products
- Maintain all expected company targets throughout employment
- Accept and process purchase and sale orders in accordance with approved procedure

Customer service representative, XZY Inc.   2000–2002
- Experience in financial and consulting services sales
- Collecting and analysis of information in industries and enterprises, preparation of publicly available financial information
- Analyzed and interpreted sociologic and media survey data
- Drew up contracts with customers and monitored payments

Media planner/Buyer, Tele Business   1997–1999
Telephone surveys
- Planned & executed advertising campaigns through TV, radio, outdoor, press & Internet
- Created pre-planning, post-campaign competitive and market analysis
- Initiated innovative strategies to increase brand awareness in the market
- Researched and acquired lists for direct mail efforts

Education
1993–1997   National Economics State University, BA

Seminars
Seminar on Increasing Sales   2000
Seminar on Public Speaking   1999

John Johnston
123 Learning St., Anytown, USA 10101
999-555-1212 johnj@yourname.com

CALL CENTER TEAM LEAD

SUMMARY OF QUALIFICATIONS:
I am a professional with the proven ability to combine customer satisfaction, information technology, and good business principles.
- 5+ years in support and call center environments
- 7+ years hiring, managing, and training staff
- Excellent Hardware Maintenance and Evaluation skills
- Project Management Experience – Application Maintenance and Development

WORK EXPERIENCE:

ABC Inc. - Team Leader, Call Center   Feb 2003 to Present

Responsibilities: Manage First/Second Level Support Help Desk (22 Analysts)
- 24 hour operating schedule (2000 sites worldwide)
- Support the hardware and operating systems (Win 95, 2000,XP,NT & Unix)
- Provide, install, and support all system software (POS Retail Support)
- Staff development, evaluation, and scheduling
- Configurations and development of system images
- Project Management/Project Deployment
- Develop and maintain all online documentation
- 3rd Level support and conflict resolution

XYZ Company - Team Leader, Help Desk   June 2001 to Feb 2003

Responsibilities: Manage First/Second Level Support Help Desk (8 analysts)
- 17-hour operating schedule (200 sites/2000+ users)
- Support the hardware platform (NT-AS400) and operating system
- Provide, install, and support all system software (POS Retail Support)
- Staff Development and evaluation
- Configurations and development of system images
- Testing all new hardware
- Project management/project deployment
- Develop and maintain all online documentation
- Problem resolution management

Law Offices Inc. - Coordinator, IT Department   Feb. 1998 to June 2001

Responsibilities: Coordinate all aspects of the help desk
- Training of help desk support staff and users
- Support 350 workstations, 11 servers, and 450+ users
- Support the hardware platform and operating system
- Provide, install, and support all system software; testing all new hardware
- Support and back-up administrator of accounting software: Elite - Informix
- Monitor all tape backups and off-site file restore procedures
- Creation and deletion of all user accounts
- Configuration and installation of all workstation desktops
- Software evaluation, installation, and implementation
- Develop and maintain all online documentation

CALL CENTER: Call Center Team Lead (cont.)

EDUCATION:

1999–2001   **State School of Information Technology**
           Microsoft Certified Systems Engineer

1998–1999   **ObjectArts Inc. - Microsoft Certification Courses**
           Mastering Microsoft Visual Basic 5.0
           Implementing a DB Design on SQL 6.5

1995–1997   **State College - MicroComputer Management Diploma**
           Business Accounting & Communication courses

1993–1994   **Advancement Institute - Computer Maintenance Technology Diploma**

SKILLS:

Technical/Applications:
Microsoft Certified Systems Engineer (MCSE, MCP, MCP + Internet)
NT. Workstation, NT Server 4.0 Administration, NT Server – Enterprise, TCP/IP, Internet Information Server IIS 4.0, Network Essentials, ACD

Operating Systems:
Windows NT Server & Workstation 4.0, Windows 2000 XP ME/ 98/ 95.x, AS400 some Unix, Novell (CNA/CNE material)

Software:
Lotus Notes, Enterprise Tivoli (Access Manager) Citrix Server, Peregrine, VNC, WordPerfect Suite Internet Explorer & Netscape, Various Anti-virus application (Norton, McAfee), Ghost, SQL, Informix, Remedy, PcAnywhere, ITR, ICE, Meridian Phone Systems

Past Experience:

7 years insurance industry	3 years hospitality industry
5 years retail industry	3.5 years legal environment (major law firm)

Personal Interests:
Downtime away from telephones - sea kayaking, nature walks, bouldering, and reading

123 Learning Ave.
Anycity, AS
10101

Phone 555-999-1212
Email johnj@yourname.com

John Johnston

Profile

CALL CENTER MANAGER - 7+ years of Sales and Call Center Management experience with special skill in personal selling and team selling up to 50% over quota.

Professional experience

ABC Business Systems   2002–Feb 2004
Call Center Manager

- Managed 5 outbound Call Center representatives, whose primary goal was to locate and cultivate new business via cold calling
- Responsible for $5 Million in annual sales
- Created call center environment by outsourcing technology and hiring staff in order to meet sales quota
- Provided sales and product training to call center team
- Created and executed marketing campaigns in order to increase sales pipeline
- Assisted in sales and product demonstrations

Tech Systems Inc.   2001–July 2002
Manager, Account Executives (Call Center)

- Managed 6 Call Center Representatives, whose primary responsibility was to account for $600,000 in annual sales
- Provide ongoing and initial sales and product training
- Implemented training course for new call center representatives in order to speed profitability
- Integral member of the project team which was responsible for the transition from territory assignment to vertical and name accounts
- Surpassed sales quota for 5 consecutive quarters
- Created and executed marketing campaigns in order to capitalize market segment
- Expanded sales territory from Northeast region to Southeast region

XYZ Systems Inc.   1999–Nov 2001
Sales Development Manager (Call Center)

- Responsible for $3 Million in annual sales
- Managed 5 sales development representatives whose primary responsibilities were to achieve $600,000 in annual sales
- Provided ongoing sales and product training to call center representatives
- Created and implemented training course and documentation for staff

CALL CENTER: Call Center Manager (cont.)

USBank Wealth Management   1997–Dec 1999
Manager, Call Center
- Managed 20 inbound call center representatives for both USBank's Securities and their Discretionary Managed Accounts
- Responsible for managing inbound call taken and talk time
- Provided call center representatives with the necessary information in order to provide superior customer service while expediting the call quickly
- Average representative was fielding 90 calls per day
- Integral member of projects
- Continuously met highest achievement awards for providing excellent customer satisfaction

Previous Roles
Call Center Sales, Call Center Support, Assistant Call Center Manager

Education   1993–1997   State University   Anycity, AS
B.A. Geography
- Minor Sociology

1997–1998   Financial Institute   Anycity, AS
- Series 7

Awards and Achievements
- Presented with Manager of the Year Award with Tech Systems for beating annual sales quota by 50%

- Awarded Certificate for Advanced Presentation Skills

- Honored with XYZ Systems Inc. Employee Dedication Award for locating, developing, and cultivating the largest deal in the history of the organization

Alice J. Johnston

123 Learning St., Anycity, Anystate 10101
Home: (999) 555-1212   Email: alicej@yourname.com

Bilingual senior call center manager with over 8 years domestic and international industry experience.

Skills Summary:

- Extensive call center managerial experience in blended (inbound/outbound) web-enabled call centers, both domestic and international.
- Management experience up to 200 call center agents.
- Proven record of producing substantial sales through improved customer relations and staff development.
- Solid understanding of the sales process and customer service.
- Strong business and financial acumen, along with analytical skills.

Professional Experience:

ABC Contact Centers (Farcity, Farland)   November 2002–February 2004
Director Operations, Call Center

- Directed ABC's, an American 3rd party call center with it's head-office located in Southwest Region, blended (inbound/outbound) call center, in Farcity, India, which grew to 100 seats (2 shifts) by year-end (2003).
- Oversaw the call center's expenses and payroll.
- Worked closely with the Quality Assurance department conducting daily monitoring and coaching sessions to insure company standards were being met, as well as handled escalated concerns and provided solutions to difficult situations.
- Identified the call center's training requirements and coordinated the fulfillment of those needs with the Training Director.
- Responsible for the scheduling, budgeting, and contingency forecasting models, and benchmarks performance standards to maximize resources quickly for volume changes and objectives.

Accomplishments

- Direct reports included 2 call center managers and 6 team leaders, plus 5 administrative staff.
- Increased the call center's $300K/month to $$750K/month through the implementation of policies and procedures.
- Created and implemented incentive programs that increased employee recognition and retention while promoting an achievement-oriented culture.

eCommerce.com (Nearcity, Anystate)   October 2000–November 2002
Internet e-tailer
Director of Sales, Call Center

- Supervised an operational team of 25 customer service representatives, in a 24/7 web-enabled inbound call center environment, located in Anycity, India (worked on-site).
- Ensured that the quality of all types of contacts, inbound/outbound calls, emails and web contacts, were meeting customer's expectations.
- Developed appropriate service strategies that support business objectives and provide value to our customers.
- Coached customer service representatives to improve their call-handling and communication skills thus enhancing customer service levels.
- Conducted new hire orientation and training.
- Monitored and managed call flows, volumes, and trends.

CALL CENTER: Call Center Executive (cont.)

Alice J. Johnston - resume - 2

Manufacturing Company (Anycity, Anystate)
Call Center Manager

April 1996–October 2000

- Managed operational team of 20–25 account representatives in a blended (outbound/inbound) call center environment.
- Completed a 6-month assignment in Europe establishing foreign operation.
- Directly involved in forecasting and setting sales quotas, while coaching account representatives to reach their fullest potential.
- Implemented performance measures (KPI's) relating to account representatives.
- Provided leadership, guidance, and coaching to achieve sale targets.
- Mentored team trainers to develop them to company's management standards.

Media Company (Anycity, Anystate)
Operations Manager

October 1994–April 1996

- Responsible for company's entire operation (i.e. acquisition of sites, installation of frames, selling of advertising space, etc...) in Texas and throughout western U.S.
- Restructured office to correspond with newly developed strategic goals and objectives.

Accomplishments

- Established entire Texas network from 876 frames to over 5000 frames.
- Reduced operational costs by 27% through implementation of installation standards, performance measures, financial objectives, and control systems.

Structube (Anycity, Anystate)
Store Manager

October 1991–October 1994

- Responsible for all aspects of managing a retail store including: scheduling, store security, customer relations, opening, and closing.
- Coached employees to increase sales.
- Exceeded 33 monthly sale quotas to obtain bonuses.
- Reduced inventory by 30% through more efficient ordering of stock.

Education:

Diploma, Business Management, ABC Career Institute (correspondence), 1995
Diploma, Advertising, XYZ National College (correspondence), Advertising, 1992
Diploma, Creative Writing, XYZ National College (correspondence), Creative Writing, 1987

Affiliations:

U.S. Professional Sales Association, since 1992
Periodical Writers Association of U.S., since 1991

CALL CENTER: Director of OP Call Center

Alice J. Johnston

123 Learning Drive, Anycity, Anystate, 10101   Residence: (555) 999-1212, Cell: (555) 999-1313
alicej@yourname.com

An experienced leader at the director-level with demonstrated skills in creating employee-centric organizations, particularly banking call centers. Extensive expertise in the design, and operation of help desks, call centers, and technology support organizations.

ACCOMPLISHMENTS

- Created a best in class help desk – AMERIBANK National Support Line.
- Implemented a structured quality/productivity management system for call centers. This resulted in a 20% increase in agent productivity and 40% improvement in quality.
- Introduced IVRs to improve customer service and productivity—a first in the courier industry. Reduced call handing cost by 90% with a payback of less than 3 months.
- Collaborated with national telecom carriers to develop new products and features. Introduced 1-800-GetItThere—the first national multi-site phone number in U.S.
- Launched the largest Internet-over-cable service in North America.

PROFESSIONAL EXPERIENCE

AMERIBANK   MAY 1997–JUNE 2004

Senior Director (1999–2004)

Reporting to the Sr. Vice President, Integrated Business Operations, provided strategic leadership to 3 business units through 7 direct reports & over 200 employees. Managed operating budget of $12 million.

National Support Line - Provided bilingual help desk support to all branches. Also provided directory assistance support to both the internal and external customers.
- Implemented an employee centric culture that resulted in best in class ranking by ABC & Co. for employee satisfaction, customer satisfaction, and agent productivity.
- Handled over 1 million product and procedural support calls each year.
- One of the lowest rates of casual absenteeism in the industry—less than 2% for last 3 years.
- Over the last 4 years reduced direct cost per minute by 5% per year.

Shared Services Group - Provided overall technology strategy and was directly responsible for: desktop hardware, applications & server support, learning & development, online information delivery, capacity planning & service level management, and internal communication.
- Designed & developed a complete web-based call center performance management system that resulted in productivity improvement of 30% for the help desk management team.
- Implemented the largest Problem, Incident, and Change Management System using XYZ's Service Center in AMERIBANK.
- Developed an in-house e-Learning Management System that resulted in a 30% reduction in training time for new hires and 20% reduction in training staff.
- Built an in-house web-based survey system that resulted in savings of over $200K while reducing turnaround time from 8 weeks to 2 weeks.

Procedures & Products Information Services – Created, published, and managed all content related to AMERIBANK's procedures and products.
- Using Six-Sigma process engineering methodologies, redesigned the request for content creation process. Reduced total time from 13 weeks to 4 weeks.

CALL CENTER: Director of OP Call Center (cont.)

Senior Consultant - AMERIBANK / New Networks (1997–1999)

Reporting to the Vice President, developed short-range tactical solutions and long-range strategy for voice systems.

- Responsible for creating business specific voice strategy aligned with business goals for various call centers and help desks.
- Successfully conducted Y2K certification for all voice systems for AMERIBANK. Developed and executed test scripts to verify Y2K functionality.
- Member of the technology forum for exploration, evaluation, and implementation of new voice and data technologies.

XYZ CABLE SYSTEMS LIMITED   1996–1997

Senior Director, Launch Division

Reported to the GM Operations with the mandate to build an organization comprised of sales, service, and field implementation to support national launch, offering Internet services over cable.

- Created & managed a sales & service organization with a mandate to meet aggressive targets for a brand new product.
- Responsible for the design and development of new sales, service, technical support, and network operation centers within accelerated time periods.
- Managed outsourcing agreements with external vendors to supplement the sales force for unexpected peak call volume during initial launch.

COURIER EXPRESS   1984–1996

Progressive 12-year career resulting in increased accountability as the company grew from 200 employees to over 4,000.

Regional Manager, Customer Service, Western Region (1993–1996)

Reported to the Managing Director, Customer Service, and managed the Western Region call center, which processed 8,000 calls per day and grew from 30 to over 100 employees.

- Implemented the first official multi-language (English, French, Cantonese) call center and supported the entire NA sales and service organizations with Cantonese & Mandarin language services.
- Developed a high performance work culture by implementing a qualitative and quantitative performance system (APMP)—a first in U.S.
- Improved quality attainment by 55% and productivity levels by 20%.

Country Manager, Communication Systems (1988–1993)

Reported to the Vice President, Information Technology Division (U.S.). Developed strategic direction for the foreign subsidiary's telecommunications needs. Responsible for the development and deployment of leading edge technologies that enhanced competitive advantage.

- Implemented the strategy for networks (SNA, LANs), midrange (Wang VS, AS400), desktops, voice (PBXs, ACDs, IVRs), and digital dispatching systems.
- Established short and long-term telecommunications service goals; implemented business plans and strategies to ensure alignment with corporate goals.

Manager, Customer Service (1987–1988)
Systems & Operations Analyst (1984–1986)

ACADEMIC BACKGROUND

MBA - University of Anycity - 1999

B.Sc. Computer Science - State University - 1985

Certified Process Engineering Specialist & Champion (Six-Sigma) - 2004

CALL CENTER: BAD—Call Center Specialist

Resume of:

John J. Johnston
123 Learning Street, Apt. #99, Anycity, Anystate, 10101
Tel: (555) 999-1212

Objective

To obtain a position in the area of sales/marketing/customer service where my education, background, and knowledge will be fully utilized and expanded

Computer Skills

- Microsoft Office (Word, WordPerfect, Excel, and PowerPoint)
- Lotus 1-2-3, Pagemaker, Project 4, MRP Max (Inventories), Basic 'C' Programming
- Software Used in Financial Services Companies—Coins, Link, Tracker, and Pathway

Personal Profile

- Well recognized for my consistent hard-work and professional conduct at all times
- Outstanding communication skills, extremely thorough, responsible, and reliable
- Good sense of humor, patience, and tolerance of others
- Strong ethics, leadership, and team-playing attributes

Work Experience

Sales and Marketing:
- Made cold calls and was successful in obtaining new clients
- Conducted telephone marketing surveys
- Promoted and sold electronic banking with information and demonstrations
- Helped resolve any customer problems
- Handled queries from ABC Financial's demutualization and processed sales and certificate requests
- Provided customers with detailed information on products and services
- Researched competitive products in order to evaluate competitors' streng
- Planned a marketing strategy that resulted in a significant awareness of se

Financial:
- Assisted several account managers with updating and maintaining option ensure compliance between the brokerage firms and the client's requests
- Helped two account managers with filing, organizing, labeling, and maili fund managers and pension companies
- Processed requests from Brokers for GIC redemptions and reinvestmen
- Logged commission clawbacks onto spreadsheet and helped with distrib
- Processed customer deposits, withdrawals, account updates, checks, bill
- Converted & distributed foreign exchange balanced cash, filed, and answ
- Identified and referred clients to the Personal Bankers for investment purposes

What's Wrong?
- Too many bullet points
- Lackluster objective/profile or lack thereof
- No declared job role
- No accomplishments or specific and measurable results

CALL CENTER: BAD—Call Center Specialist (cont.)

Page 2
Resume of:
John J. Johnston
Tel: (555) 999-1212

Employment History

2002 - 2003	**CSR - Call Center**	Staffing Temp Agency, Anycity, Anystate (Contract with ABC Mutual Funds)
2000 - 2002	**Assistant - Derivatives and Pension Funds GIC Redemptions and Reinvestments**	Any Temp Agency, Anycity, Anystate (Contracts with Any Trust & BankA)
2000	**CSR - Call Center**	Any Trust, Anycity, Anystate (Contract)
1998 - 2000	**Bank Teller/CSR**	BankB & BankC, Anycity, Anystate(Contract)
1993 - 1994	**CSR/Up Seller - Call Center**	ACompany, Anycity, Anystate
1989 - 1990	**CSR/Telemarketing**	TeleCompany, Anycity, Anystate
1976 - 1980	**Retail Sales**	Retail Clothing, Anycity, Anystate

Other areas of Work: Manufacturing and Food Services

Voluntary Work

Helped organize an environmental awareness conference (ISO 14000), participated in planning social functions for A.A.P.I.C. (American Association of Production and Inventory Control) and performed secretarial duties

Education

Present	**Enrolled in CPH**	US Securities Institute, Anycity, Anystate
2000	**Series 7 Certificate**	
1998	**Bank Customer Service Rep Certificate**	Burnside Heights School, Anycity, Anystate
1994 - 1997	**BSc in Business Operations (3.8/4 GPA)**	Institute of Technology, Anycity, Anystate
1984	**Secretarial Certificate**	Any College, Anycity, Anystate

Future Goals

To obtain a MBA and continue enhancing my education and experience

Hobbies/Interests

Cooking, music, movies, and shopping

References

Available on Request

CHEMIST LABORATORY & BIOLOGY: New Biologist

ALICE J. JOHNSTON

123 Learning Street, Anycity, Anystate 10101   555-999-1212   alicej@yourname.com

BIOLOGIST – with concentration of experience in environmental studies.

- Master of Science - State University 2002
- Bachelor of Science (Honors) - State University 2000

Government Environmental Agency   **June 2003–June 2005**
BIOLOGIST, Team Lead

- Planned and executed an investigation into mercury contamination in recreational fish from hydroelectric reservoirs, including the presentation of results.

- This project was part of the Federal Green Plan Toxic Contaminants Program and was successfully completed over a 2-year period. The purpose of this project was to determine the time required for mercury levels in reservoir fish to return to pre-impoundment levels following inundation and to determine any potential risk to recreational fisheries.

- Worked as part of a team of four as Team Lead.

State University, Biology Department, Anycity, AS   **Jan 2002–April 2003**
LABORATORY DEMONSTRATOR

Responsible for demonstration and instruction of university laboratory educational material to undergraduate students. Created new material and teaching aids around environmental biology.

January to April 2001	State University Biology Department, Anycity, AS LABORATORY DEMONSTRATOR
January to April 2000	State University Biology Department, Anycity, AS LABORATORY DEMONSTRATOR
January to April 1999	State University Biology Department, Anycity, AS TECHNICIAN
September to December 1998	State University Biology Department, Anycity, AS LABORATORY DEMONSTRATOR
May to September 1998	Oceans Sciences Centre Anytown, AS RESEARCH ASSISTANT

AWARDS:
- Fellow of the School of Graduate Studies (Awarded for outstanding achievement).
- Department of Biology Graduate Student Assistantship ($1500.00).
- Graduate School Travel Award ($300.00).
- Office of the Dean/Faculty of Science Travel Award ($250.00).
- Department of Biology Graduate Student Assistantship ($750.00).

PUBLICATIONS: Available upon request.

CHEMIST LABORATORY & BIOLOGY: Lab Technologist

John J. Johnston
123 Learning Street, Apt. 100, Anycity, Anystate 10101
Home: (555) 999-1212   johnj@yourname.com

PROFILE
A self-motivated and team playing **Medical Laboratory Technologist**, who excels in laboratory facilities that service a large and varied patient population. Specialized experience in the fields of hematology and the transfusion laboratory.

LAB SKILLS
- Platelet daily inventory projections and orders
- Inventory recall/retrieval of blood and blood products
- Assisting in the distribution of blood products to area hospitals
- Management of phenotype blood units
- Review of temperature charts, irradiation records, and B19 sample records
- Various hematological equipment operation
- Differential cell counts
- Phlebotomy techniques
- Routine blood bank procedures
- Cross matching donor blood units
- Various antibody screening techniques
- Data entry, organizational skills, and experience with Laboratory Information Systems

WORK HISTORY

Laboratory Technologist
Manufacturing/Production Laboratory - U.S. Blood Services-Anycity Centre
- Issues Department   December 2004–current

Medical Laboratory Technologist I
State Transfusion Services - Good Health Hospital - General Bench Technologist
- Independent shift and call work   June 2004–Dec 2004

Medical Laboratory Technologist I
Hematology Department - Good Health Hospital - General Bench Technologist
- Independent shift and call work   June 2001–June 2004

EDUCATION
Local College - Anytown, ST- **Medical Laboratory Science - Diploma, 2001**
State University - Anycity, AS - Area of Concentration: **Biology - Bachelor of Science, 1997**

CERTIFICATIONS AND RELEVANT COURSES
- Current SMLS registration
- Licensed practicing member of MLT
- Courses in transportation of dangerous goods, WHMIS, and GMP

CHEMIST LABORATORY & BIOLOGY: Chemist

01 of 02

Alice J. Johnston
123 Learning St., Anytown, USA, 10101
Tel: 999-555-1212, Email: alicej@yourname.com

Profile
Technically qualified laboratory **chemist** with extensive experience in **pharmaceutical and food product analysis using modern techniques, methods, and tools**.

Accomplishments
- Pharmaceutical laboratory experience and competent with sampling analysis using sophisticated equipment such as **HPLC, UV, TLC, Dissolution, Karl-Fisher**, etc.
- **Bachelor's degree in Chemistry**, Member of **The Chemical Institute of America,** and **HMS Society of Chemistry**
- Demonstrate the following technical skills:

  ✓ Prepared test samples and analyzed starting materials, in-process products and dosage samples for related compounds using instrumentation, HPLC, UV Spectrophotometry, Dissolution, TLC, Karl-Fisher, Poalarimeter, and wet chemistry technique according to the internationally established standards and regulatory requirements and completed comprehensive reports with technical data summaries.

  ✓ Investigated product quality and drug reactions complaints received from regulatory bodies, medical officers, and consumers. Reviewed pertinent data relevant to the complaint including batch records, product history, requests special testing, and examination of complaint and reserved samples. Prepared detailed investigation report and responded with justification.

  ✓ Assisted in preparation for regulatory and customer audits by gathering required documentation and contacts and participated coordinating departments contacts and provided information for the auditors.

  ✓ Participated in QA compliance initiatives including writing, reviewing, and revision of SOP's and ensured that all process improvement activities are in compliance with GMP's and quality standards.

- **Excellent report writing.**
- A team player with **strong work ethic** and commitment to internal, external regulations, and compliance.

Experience
Quality Controller   **Since August 2002**
Yummy Inc. (Food and juice manufacturing company)

- Preparation of test samples and analysis of manufactured products using modern laboratory equipment & chemical methods, comprehensive report writing and oral presentation as requested.
- Responsible for production line operation, reducing quality failures, non-conformance, and waste with vigilant action.
- Consistently perform in a proactive manner displaying "do it right the first time" attitude which is a "win-win" situation for the team and the department.

CHEMIST LABORATORY & BIOLOGY: Chemist (cont.)

Experience Cont:

Senior Analyst - Quality Assurance   **1997–2002**
Healthcare Ltd. - Sri Lanka
A reputed pharmaceutical company in South and East Asia specializing in manufacturing, sales, marketing, and distribution of antibiotics.

- Evaluated real time and accelerated stability studies for antibiotics strengths (Amoxicillin, Cloxacillin, Cefalexin, Erythromycin) and submitted details to regulatory authority for drug products registration purposes
- Handled internal and external customer complaints, quality failures, introduced competent solutions, and coordinated with the regulatory bodies in product recalls
- Assisted the laboratory team for instrumentation & wet chemistry technique and conducted training programs to the technical team
- Prepared audits and surveillance reports for management review and conducted appropriate follow-up as required

Quality Assurance Coordinator   **1992–1997**
Quality Assurance Assistant and Laboratory Technician - Sri Lanka
Worldwide Pharmaceutical Inc.

- Prepared test samples and analyzed drug products and excipients using modern instrumentation TLC, PH Meter, Karl-Fisher Titrator, polarimeter, HPLC, UV- vis spectrophotometer, dissolution tester, and wet chemistry techniques according to the established international standards
- Performed general maintenance and calibrated laboratory equipment according to the department's established calibration program
- Maintained stability testing programs accelerated and real time for products Analgesic (Panadol tablets Panadol liquid, Panadol for children tablets), Antacids (Actal tablets, Ph. Milk of Magnesia Tablets and liquid), Vitamin B liquid, etc. and submitted detailed technical reports to the regulatory and international bodies
- Prepared and submitted to management and to the head office the calculations of QA indicators as a monthly key business indicator

Education
Academic
- Bachelor's degree in Chemistry (Evaluated by World Education Services)

Professional Associations
- Elected Associate member of **American Society for Chemistry and Chemical Institute** in 2000
- Elected Graduate of **HMS Society of Chemistry** in 1996
- Elected Member of **HMS Society of Chemistry** in 2001

CITY PLANNING & GOVERNMENT: Government Research Assistant

John J. Johnston
1230 Learning St., Apt. 123 Anycity, AS 10101
(555) 999-1212 *email: johnj@yourname.com*

Bilingual Government Research and Campaign Assistant with experience creating reports on a variety of subject matter—from international relations to endangered species. Bright, willing, and hardworking.

EDUCATION	*Bachelor of Arts in International Relations and Spanish*	**May 2004**

City College – Anycity, Anystate

	Valedictorian, Learning High School – Anycity, Anystate	**June 2000**

EXPERIENCE

Committee on International Relations, Governmental Representatives   **January 2002–May 2002**
Intern
- Conducted research on a variety of foreign policy issues
- Compiled information on current US-EU relations for use by Committee specialists
- Attended hearings, briefings, and luncheons with policy experts and foreign guests
- Assisted with various administrative tasks including proofing testimony and assembling hearing materials

Institute of State and Local Government – Anycity, AS   **September 2001–December 2002**
Research Assistant
- Directed and assisted with projects including leading a student team in researching the impact of the Endangered Species Act on development in the Nature Valley
- Performed various duties such as writing articles for the *News Report*, surveying, assembling information for conferences, and other administrative tasks
- Chosen to oversee the fiscal analysis of Anystate schools

Friends for Local Community – Anycity, AS   **June–August 2001**
Campaign Assistant
- Organized various events for the Save the District campaign including bus trips to governmental hearings on redistricting
- Assembled volunteers to further the Save the District effort at area social events
- Contacted local political leaders in an effort to stay in touch with local needs

Youth in Government Program – Anycity, AS   **Spring 2000**
County Government Intern
- Attended several sessions with other local students regarding the operations of the Local County government
- Wrote a bill concerning smoking at indoor public restaurants that was presented and passed in a mock legislative session

LEADERSHIP

Student Council Vice President   **Fall 1998–Spring 2000**
Anystate Girls' State – Anytown, ST   **June 1999**
A weeklong simulation of state government that included committee work, discussions on patriotism, the role of women in the military, and other key issues

AWARDS

City College Scholar (4 year merit-based scholarship)	**2000–2004**
Most Valuable Student Scholarship	**2000–2004**
City College Distinguished Scholar	**2000–2001**

ACTIVITIES

Anycity International Relations Society, member	**2001–Present**
CMS Track and Field – 400m and 4x4 relay	**Spring 2001**
CMS Women's Soccer – midfielder and defender	**Fall 2001**

SKILLS

Proficient in Spanish; Familiar with French and Russian
Microsoft Word, Excel, and PowerPoint; Lexis-Nexis; Corel WordPerfect

CITY PLANNING & GOVERNMENT: Public Affairs Government

JOHN J. JOHNSTON

123 Learning Street • Anycity, AS 10101

(555) 999-1212 johnj@yourname.com

Staff Assistant with Specialty in Public Affairs and Research

WORK EXPERIENCE

OCTOBER 2002 – JANUARY 2003   *U.S. DEPARTMENT OF INTERIOR*   ANYCITY, AS
Specialist, Public Affairs, Office of the Secretary

- Coordinated media research, procured bios and informational summaries for the Secretary and DOI executive staff.
- Performed assignments for Assistant and Deputy Assistant Secretary including assistance with press releases, media advisories, and correspondence.
- Responded to direct requests from Secretary of Interior.
- Prepared press kits, maintained contact databases, and provided support at media functions.
- Prepared and distributed daily media clips to the Secretary and DOI executive staff.

FEBRUARY 2002 – OCTOBER 2002   *U.S. SENATOR LINDY LOOKY*   ANYCITY, AS
Staff Assistant

- Managed two constituent services, drafted constituent correspondence, registered constituent concerns.
- Responsible for front-office reception, data entry, and research.
- Entrusted with office-supply purchasing account, and managed office-supply inventory.

SUMMER 2001   *U.S. DEPARTMENT OF LABOR*   ANYCITY, AS
Intern, Public Affairs, Office of the Secretary

- Conducted broad research project gauging media coverage of Labor Secretary, spanning from Senate Confirmation to present, tabulated, and classified data according to several criteria.
- Assisted Deputy Assistant Secretary and Communications Director with necessary research and other tasks in fast-paced working environment.
- Maintained current event files, revised contact lists, and acted as interim receptionist.

SUMMER 2000   *ABC MANAGEMENT,* LLC   ANYCITY, AS
Fundraiser

- Solicited funds on behalf of the Fraternal Order of Police, Firefighters Association, and Paralyzed Veterans of America.
- Ranked consistently within the top 5 fundraisers.
- Received several recognitions for outstanding performance.

EDUCATION

- B.A. Degree, Communication Arts, Cum Laude. Ray College (AS), December 2001.
- Additional courses from Catholic University, and OST Grad School.

ACTIVITIES & HONORS

- RNC Volunteer, 2002, campaigned for AS State Republican Party (Anycity, AS).
- Graduate of the Leadership Institute's School of Broadcast Journalism.
- Recipient of the Leadership Institute's "Balance in Media Fellowship" Scholarship.

SKILLS

- Familiar with press tracking resources: Nexis, Bacon's, AP Wire.
- Strong interpersonal and organizational abilities.
- Excellent written and oral communication skills.
- Skilled researcher.

CITY PLANNING & GOVERNMENT: City Planner

JOHN J. JOHNSTON, BA (Hons.) MURP MCIP
123 Learning Street, Anycity, Anystate
Home (555) 999-1212   Work (555) 999-1414   Email: johnj@yourname.com

Planning and Development Manager with training and experience in Emergency Preparedness, Policy and City Planning Initiatives, Master Planning and Process, Traffic Flow, and other areas. Training in media relations and extensive experience dealing with print and radio media.

- Comprehensive experience with computers. Experience with transportation and simulation software.
- Experience with fiscal impact analysis techniques and demographic analysis.
- Extensive training in public speaking and debate including the presentation of complex policy and development control issues to the Planning Advisory Committee, City Council, committees, and the public.
- Extensive research experience and well developed writing skills including the preparation of policy papers, research studies, and development-related staff reports.
- Some knowledge of Spanish, French, and Thai.

WORK EXPERIENCE

MANAGER, PLANNING AND DEVELOPMENT   2004–Present
Anycity, Anystate, Development Services Department

- Project Manager for a major review of Anycity's Capital City Municipal Plan & preparation of the Master Plan.
- Continued responsibility for review of major development applications and a variety of short- and long-range policy initiatives.
- A Development Officer for Anycity.
- Member of Anycity delegation in the Federation of U.S. Municipalities Municipal Partnership Program between Anycity and the Municipality of Othercity. Responsible for assisting Othercity with preparing a corporate strategic plan, an environmental management plan, and establishing a community development planning process.

Other Responsibilities and Roles
- Participant in Anycity corporate strategic planning process.
- Involved in City and provincial initiative to protect Anycity sub-surface water supply.
- Member of an interdepartmental team exploring regionalized storm water management.

COORDINATOR, MUNICIPAL PLAN REVIEW AND SENIOR PLANNER   2001–2003
Anycity, Anystate, Development Services Department

- Responsible for the generation of policy documents including the review of zoning bylaw standards and municipal plan policies.
- Project leader for the Northwest Anycity Master Plan, Anycity Business Parkway Strategy, and the Northeast Anycity and Southeast Area secondary plans. Created the City's master planning process.
- Responsible for the review of major development projects as part of the development control function.
- Responsible for population, economic, and development trend analysis, review of the City's development standards and policies, and a residential marketing strategy.

Other Responsibilities, Roles, and Recognition
- Member of Anycity Regionalization Study project team that reviewed the impacts of a variety of regionalization and amalgamation options on the delivery of planning services. Conducted the fiscal impact analysis of various regionalization options on all City revenues and expenditures.
- Involved in transportation planning functions for the City. Prepared terms of reference and was a member of the Steering Committee for the Capital City Traffic Study. Member of Traffic Management Committee.
- Steering Committee member for the Capital City Leisure Study.
- Member of Anycity Fire Station Location Study team.
- Involved in property management issues for the City. Prepared and coordinated requests for proposals for the sale and development of a number of downtown and suburban properties for commercial and residential uses. Member of the City's Property Management Committee.
- Duty Officer for the Anycity Emergency Operations Group.

CITY PLANNING & GOVERNMENT: City Planner (cont.)

1997–2001	**SENIOR PLANNER**	
	Anycity, Anystate, Development Services Department	

1997   **PLANNING CONSULTANT**
Downtown Anystate

1994–1997 **INTERMEDIATE PLANNER**
Anycity, Anystate, Planning and Development

1994   **PLANNER**
Local District Planning Commission, Port Hawk, Anystate

1994   **TEACHING ASSISTANT**
Department of Urban and Rural Planning, Technical University

1993   **PLANNING INTERN**
Anycity, Anystate, Planning and Development

COURSES and TRAINING

1999   **Emergency Preparedness Eastern**
- Completed Basic Emergency Preparedness & Emergency Operation Center Mgt courses.

1996   **Geographic Information Corporation**
- Completed Introduction to Property Law in the Eastern Region course with excellence.

EDUCATIONAL HISTORY

1996   **University of Anystate, Anycity, Anystate**
- Completed coursework in Masters of Science in Engineering (Transportation Planning) Program.
- Completed continuing education courses in management.

1994   **Technical University, Anycity, Anystate**
- Masters Degree in Urban and Rural Planning.
- Recipient of American Institute of Planners Award (grad student with highest academic standing).

1992   **State University, Anycity, Anystate**
- Bachelor of Arts with Honors in Political Science.
- First Class Standing and Dean's List in Senior Year.
- Recipient of State Scholarship and Private Scholarship.

NON-ACADEMIC AWARDS AND RECOGNITION

1997, 1998	Certificate of Achievement from the U.S. Institute of Planners for Continuing Development.
1985 to 1988	State champion in Discussion Style and Impromptu Debate, and Model United Nations.
1985 to 1988	Provincial silver medallist in Impromptu Speech and Parliamentary Debate.

PROFESSIONAL AFFILIATIONS AND INVOLVEMENT

- Full Member of the American Planning Association.
- Occasional lecturer and employed as a marker for urban planning courses at the University of Anystate.
- Book review published in *Plan US*, September 1996.
- Articles published in *Plan US*, September 1997 and December 2000.
- Coauthor of case study of best practices in municipal development, Federation of Municipalities, 2004.
- President of the Anystate Assoc. of Planners, 2003, Secretary-Treasurer of the NB Planners, 1995 and 1998.
- Anystate representative on the Eastern Planners Institute Council and Secretary of API, 1999 to 2002.

CLIENT MANAGEMENT: Client Services Management

123 Learning St.
Anytown, USA 10101
johnj@yourname.com **(999) 555-1212**

John J. Johnston

Profile
Client Services Management with special interest in new media and interactive.

Career History
Big Data LLC   **October 1997–June 1999**
Big Data is one of the largest call center organizations in North America. It has been recognized as a Profit 100 and Fortune 100 company for five years, and has been rated one of the '50 Best Managed Private Companies'.

Account Executive/Client Services Manager   **April 1998–June 1999**
Responsibilities:
- Development and implementation of call center and e-commerce programs;
- Establish and maintain strong strategic relationships with corporate clients;
- Responsible for the management and development of multiple teams and agents;
- Partnering with clients from diverse industries, including e-commerce, advertising, satellite TV, government, tourism, not-for-profit, and associations.

Accomplishments:
- Chosen as "Best Client Services Manager" for 1998 among 12 managers;
- Responsible for 20% overall account growth and development of client base;
- Portfolio of accounts valued at more than $3,100,000;
- Creation of customized processes, reporting and data transmission procedures; and
- Provision of corporate seminars on effective use of software applications.

Business Development Coordinator   **October 1997–April 1998**
Responsibilities:
- Creation of all corporate communications and sales material;
- Design of multimedia sales and marketing presentations;
- Formulation of program profitability and cost analysis;
- Preparation of contracts and service level agreements;
- Control and verification of departmental expenditures;

Accomplishments:
- Successful bids to companies in the United States, Canada, and Mexico;
- Standardization and customization of responses to RFPs;
- Creation of Business Development prospect database; and
- Restructuring of three corporate network servers.

Murphy & Associates   **May 1996–September 1997**
Established in 1979, is owned by its employees, and is one of the world's largest insurance brokerage firms. Providing clients with insurance products, services, and solutions targeted to identified needs.

Program Coordinator
Accomplishments:
- 400% increase in client base across 4 states;
- Up-selling of numerous existing insurance benefit accounts;
- Development of numerous progressive benefit plan design innovations;
- Negotiation of client program renewals with reductions in premium; and
- Creation and organization of the annual User Group Seminar.

CLIENT MANAGEMENT: Client Services Management (cont.)

May 1995–April 1996   Student Federation of the State University

The Student Federation of the University, an incorporated company with revenues of over 5 million dollars per annum, is the official bilingual representative body of the undergraduates of the University. Serving over 18,000 members, the SFU provides services and employment for students, as well as researching political and social issues that affect its members.

Vice President - Finance

Responsibilities:

- Officer and Director of the Corporation;
- Member of the Corporation's Executive Board and Board of Administration;
- Senior finance officer responsible for all aspects of budgeting and finance for the SFU and the wholly owned subsidiaries,
- Supervision of Business Managers, Accounting & Client Services staff (20).

Accomplishments:

- Elected to this full-time position by the undergraduate population;
- Publication of the Student Planner, under budget;
- Negotiation and implementation of campus advertising campaign with New Ad Media;
- Achieved a surplus (totaling $151,000) for the first time in 9 years with a top line of 5 million;
- Design and implementation of the Risk Management Committee;
- Reduction of salaries by $30,000 through government programs and restructuring initiatives;
- Outsourcing of specific services, turning $250,000 annual losses into profitable ventures; and
- Reduced cost structure by negotiation favourable membership terms with the university's conglomerate buying group.

Languages   Spanish, English, & basic German.

Education   **State University September 1991–May 1995**

- Bachelor of Social Science in Political Science.
- Bachelor of Arts in Psychology.

Computer Skills   Excel, Access, Project, PowerPoint; Visio Professional 5.0; Database Management.

Extracurricular Involvement

Hide Park - Participated in the building of Hide Park's largest children's playground

Global Relief Fund - Fundraiser and participant in Annual Airplane pull

Police Community Center - Volunteer

Interests   Watching reality TV shows (particularly the *Amazing Race* and *Survivor*); planning dream trips to exotic locales as seen on reality TV shows; being around friends and family; running with my running group.

CLIENT MANAGEMENT: Client Services Director

JOHN J. JOHNSTON, M.A.
123 Learning St., Anytown, USA 10101
Phone: 999.555.1212   Email: johnj@yourname.com

SENIOR EXECUTIVE
International Perspective

- Dynamic, progressive, and results driven senior executive with an exemplary background of leading critical business units to achieve operational excellence. Driven to succeed, energetic and confident, visionary, solutions oriented, acknowledged for conceiving and executing unique strategies to streamline operations, enhance revenue, and extend global reach and increase profitability. Articulate, tactful, and diplomatic communicator and strong negotiator; relationship builder, inspirational and proactive leader who coaches, motivates, and empowers staff to deliver.

Core business competencies include:

- Customer Relationship Management	
- Marketing	- Change Management
- Sales	- Strategic Partnerships
- B2B	- Mergers & Acquisitions
- Business Reengineering	- New Business Integration

PROFESSIONAL EXPERIENCE

Cornwallis, London, United Kingdom (www.cornwallis.uk)   2002-2004
Held the following three progressively responsible positions:

CLIENT SERVICES DIRECTOR   2002-2004

- Instrumental in realigning business operations to meet the clients' defined requirements and propelling revenue though devising and initiating various strategies to improve the business to become the market leader in a highly competitive and restricted sector.

- Developed innovative client retention, communication and growth strategies for 3,000 demanding clients across the U.K. and Western Europe in various industries including: Telecommunications, Automotive, Pharmaceutical, Media, Public Relations, Financial Services, Banking, IT, Publishing, Government, Construction, Manufacturing, and Not-For-Profit.

- Participated in all business decisions as an active member of the 8 person Board of Directors.

- Controlled all facets of the international division of Cornwallis, expanding business and margins dramatically by increasing and enhancing the service offering.

Major Accomplishments

- Grew revenue per client by over 50% by establishing unprecedented rapport with clients, acquiring a complete understanding of their requirements and the ability to stimulate their interest in purchasing additional services over the competition despite a considerable price differential.

- Played a lead role in doubling turnover, tripling EBITDA and solely responsible for reducing the churn rate by 50% in the last three years, achieved, in part, through introducing new client care and sales strategies.

- Played an integral role in developing, executing, and marketing all the company's new services, significantly increasing the product line and differentiating Cornwallis from its competitors.

- Designed a high-speed multi-language translation service for the international clientele by sourcing and negotiating strategic relationships with other media monitoring and translation agencies across the world.

- Played the pivotal leadership role in integrating a competitor into Cornwallis. Process involved identifying and synergising the two distinct cultures and business practices, creating a unified client services philosophy to integrate operations without business interruption and no impact on service, and incorporating the best facets of both companies.

CLIENT MANAGEMENT: Client Services Director (cont.)

JOHN J. JOHNSTON, MA   Page Two

Client Services Director, Cornwallis continued...

CLIENT SERVICES MANAGER   2001-2002
- Reengineered Cornwallis's Client Services Department, which established it as the best in the industry for service and excellence, helping to accommodate service price increases and positioned the business for growth.
- Played a key role in building the business foundations and elevating clientele by actively sourcing and securing new business from existing clients.
- Delivered significant results and was rewarded with a promotion and a seat on the Board of Directors as the Client Services Director.

ACCOUNT MANAGER   2000
- Managed a portfolio of diverse clients and stabilized a concerned client base after an acquisition, preventing clients from contracting with the competition.

Relishing Inc., Anytown USA   1998-1999
PRINCIPAL
- Sales & brokering of vintage guitars to clients in Europe grossing over $200,000 each year of operation.

EDUCATION

State University
MASTER OF ARTS - History   1999
Special University Scholarship (SUS) 1997-98

BACHELOR OF ARTS, Honors - History   1997
Dean's Honour List 1997

PROFESSIONAL DEVELOPMENT

Big Company Consulting, Anytown, USA   2004
Mergers & Business Integration

ABC. Consultancy, Anytown, USA   2004
Team Building & Development

The Training Race, London UK   2002
Appraisal Interviewing

Training & Marketing Limited, London UK   2003
Finance for the Non-Finance Directors

Developmental Leaders Limited, London, UK
Big Ticket Selling   2002
Senior Management Course   2001

MEMBERSHIPS

Institute of Directors (IOD)   2002-present

Institute of Public Relations (IPR)   2001-present

Public Relations Consultants Association (PRCA)   2001-present

PERSONAL INTERESTS

Reading the front and business pages of three newspapers a day and the full weekend editions; drinking a good cup of coffee; visiting art galleries and museums; going for long walks around beautiful cities.

CLIENT MANAGEMENT: Director of Client Strategy

John J. Johnston

123 Learning St.
Anytown, USA
10101

Phone/Fax: (999) 555-1212
Email: johnj@yourname.com
Cellular: (999) 555-1313

Passionate, high-energy leader with a bias-to-action. A direct/interactive marketing professional with over 10 years of direct response and online marketing experience. Demonstrated expertise with all aspects of direct and online marketing including advertising, promotions, email marketing, usability testing, and research.

ToplerNet LLC (Division of Advertising Inc)
Director of Client Strategy,   Feb 2001–Present

ACCOMPLISHMENTS
- Lead client strategic development for all major accounts.
- Mentored team to become exceptional executers and innovative thinkers.

MAJOR ACCOUNTS:
Yummy Pet Food, Get It There Courier, Cheap Car, Big Brand Computer
- Yummy Pet Food: Strategized, planned, and managed development of www.yummy.com consumer facing website.
  - Planned and executed Yummy's first Customer Relationship Management (CRM) strategy, designed to increase consumer transition and loyalty rates. Includes advanced database, registration, profiling, and real-time analytics.
  - Developed and implemented a sophisticated analytics and reporting system designed to track, measure, and optimize communication's effectiveness.
- Get It There: Planned and developed an *extranet* based Sales Automation tool enabling Get It There sales executives to create custom presentations. Implemented a nation-wide print-on-demand saving Get it There more than $1MM / year in printing costs.
- Big Brand Computer:
  - Developed and executed more than 60 email marketing campaigns generating response rates 400% above industry average.
  - Created "first-of-its-kind" experiential product demo campaigns using rich-media 3D technology.

Grimsby Media Corporation (GMC)
Director of Client Services,   Oct 1999–Feb 2001

ACCOMPLISHMENTS
- Built, led, managed, and motivated a high-performance team of Internet advertising professionals.
- Strategized and implemented GMC's global advertising product-line including; broadband (audio/video), email, and IAB standard ad formats.
- Developed a suite of innovative online advertising ROI measurement tools.
  1. **Brand Impact Analyzer** – mines the 99.75% of data currently not being used by advertisers tracking "clicks." Measures the branding effectiveness of online advertising and calculates the true ROI of advertising dollars.
  2. **Post-Click Analyzer** – tracks consumers "beyond-the-click" measuring how well advertising is achieving "transactional" objectives.

CLIENT MANAGEMENT: Director of Client Strategy (cont.)

Joe Schemple Interactive
Group Account Director,   Nov 98–Oct 99

ACCOMPLISHMENTS
- <u>Led</u> the client service function (strategic planning and management of campaign execution), across multiple client accounts. Responsible for recruiting, performance evaluation, and team building.
- <u>Won</u> several Digital Marketing awards for work on Big Car website and online advertising campaigns.

MAJOR ACCOUNTS:
Big Car Brand, Big Name Bank, Rebopnell (Fake Margarine).
- Planned, developed, and executed Internet marketing and brand building campaigns, online promotions and advertising, permission-based email "dialogue" marketing, and experiential branding (feature content).
- <u>Big Car Brand</u>: Increased generation of qualified sales by over 300%. Generated print cost-savings of approximately $500,000 a year via development of online brochures in .pdf format.

Lower Prospect Advertising Ltd. (Tokyo, Japan)
Director of Interactive Marketing,   Dec 96–Sept 98

ACCOMPLISHMENTS
- Lead new business development, recruiting, and team building.
- <u>Generated revenues</u> in excess of targets for two consecutive years (in excess of ¥200 million - **USD $2.8 million**)
- Planned and managed all client interactive projects.

Dorhety Company Inc. (Tokyo, Japan)
Account Director,   May 94–Dec 96

ACCOMPLISHMENTS
- Planned, managed, and oversaw execution of all client interactive projects.
- Lead new business development resulting in over $2MM in sales revenues (unheard of at that stage of the Internet in Japan).
- Frequent speaker and presenter at industry conferences and seminars.

MAJOR ACCOUNTS:
Brown Cola, Duff Beer, Suds Beer, FIG Companies, FlyHome Air, and Photo Bop.
- Pioneered e-commerce in Japan with Suds Beer. Developed online sales of Suds Girl posters. Planned and developed the first-of-its-kind, live online event with the Suds Girls (live online chat) in the Suds "Cyber-Bar".

Grog Finance Corporation - Magazine Publisher (Tokyo, Japan)
Advertising Sales Executive,   Nov 93–May 94
- Recognized as #1 salesperson three consecutive months.

Ring Cellular/BlahBlurp Data   (Anycity, ST)
Sales Executive - Corporate Accounts,   Sept 86–Sept 89
- Awarded Salesman of the Month two consecutive months.

CLIENT MANAGEMENT: BAD—Client Services

JOHN JOHNSTON
(999) 555-1212 (mobile)
(999) 555-1111 (office)
Email: johnj@yourname.com

WORK-RELATED SKILLS

- ❑ Strong client, staff and project management
- ❑ Strong research and presentation skills
- ❑ Excellent analytical and problem-solving skills
- ❑ Excellent communication skills, both verbal and written
- ❑ Excellent organizational, analytical and management skills
- ❑ Knowledge of shareholder record keeping systems and the financial services industry.
- ❑ Proven track record in developing and effectively nurturing senior level client relationships
- ❑ Proven track record in managing high revenue, top tier clients
- ❑ Proven track record in meeting and exceeding sales lead quotas
- ❑ Unitrax and affiliated subsystems
- ❑ Web based products (Investortrax, Advisortrax, Marketrax, Navigator)
- ❑ Salesforce.com (web based Sales management tool)
- ❑ Web based Time/Labor management and Human Resource management products
- ❑ AS400 commands/Queries
- ❑ Thorough understanding of Microsoft Office suite of products

RELEVANT EXPERIENCE

2004-present   IT Company
National Account Manager, Client Services

- Report to Vice President Client Services
- Responsible for providing total relationship management (including growth, retention etc.) for a portfolio of regional/mid-market, national or strategic accounts
- Build relationships with Senior decision makers (C-Level) in client organizations to better understand client needs, short and long term strategic goals
- Responsible for annual business growth of company through addition of new customers and/or expansion of existing customers' business
- Manage contract negotiations/pricing agreements/Service level agreements
- Negotiate/Approve pricing analysis and recommendations for client portfolio
- Ensure the achievement of short- and long-range goals for growth as it relates management.
- Ensure retention risk is significantly minimized and/or eliminated
- Oversee the development and implementation of cost-effective and efficient current and future client requirements.
- Advocate on behalf of the client within the organization based on information through client meetings, to ensure that service issues are anticipated and proa
- Seek client feedback on product/service initiatives through: promotion of par and clarifying/reviewing survey feedback to ensure service levels are consiste
- Leverage available market data and analysis to develop potential sales and/or improved service offering to client based on assessment of their current servic product/service offerings
- Identify/Determine solutions for client's service related issues and identify op improved service
- Build strategic framework for facilitating resolution of critical service issues consistent allocation of internal resources (e.g. Service, Sales & Implementati up to client regarding resolution approach and timelines

What's Wrong?

- Too many bullet points
- Dense text—I'm too bored to read this all.
- Too long especially for your age and stage
- Lackluster objective/profile or lack thereof
- No declared job role

CLIENT MANAGEMENT: BAD—Client Services (cont.)

- Work collaboratively with Sales organization to identify opportunities/leads and generate revenue based on thorough understanding of the client's current operations and long term strategic goals
- Actively develop and promote best practice solutions within the client service environment

2000-2004   e-Investing Inc.
Client Manager/Senior Business Analyst, Relationship Management

- Report to Vice-President of Relationship management
- Develop and maintain customer relationships at a senior level through regular communication with clients
- Advise senior management on industry/product/customer requirements and their impact on company strategic direction
- Responsible for direct line management, resource recruiting, conducting performance appraisals, and staff development
- Work with Sponsors and Project Team members to define the projects within Project Scope Statements.   Activity includes defining goals and objectives, defining scope, defining factors critical to success, defining risk, defining communication lines, defining responsibility and accountability
- Lead and manage the execution of the project effort.   Responsibilities include project control and monitoring, management of expectations, status reporting, risk management, quality management, change management, and cost management
- Perform administrative closing activities to close off project work. Responsibilities include time and deadline analysis, identifying lessons learned, project recaps, and individual performance reporting
- Responsible for support of all Info Products including implementation/testing and management of Ebusiness product (web based) suite
- Liaise with other company departments to ensure present and anticipated customer needs are met.
- Participate in industry seminars, conferences, training sessions and user groups.
- Forecast revenues and budget preparation
- Responsible for meeting yearly sales lead quota based on fiscal objectives
- Responsible for pre and post sales support
- Provide project cost estimations to respective clients
- Provide detailed quoted developments outlining cost, time and quality
- Responsible for formulating gap analysis for prospects; lead/participate in sales presentations and demos

1999 – 2000   Mutual Funds Company
Manager Estates/Hedge Fund, Operations

- Responsible for providing service to investors, dealers and their legal representatives
- Research accounts and ensure documentation is received in good order for processing
- Provide for training and development as well as monitoring productivity and service levels of the team
- Re-create/Restructure estates department
- Research, write and maintain a comprehensive manual on policies and procedures for estate settlement requirements
- Act as a liaison between company, third party clients, Client administration and Client Services
- Review and update documentation and current estate manuals to ensure they meet current company policies as well as government and legal requirements
- Monitor the fund processing and completion of transactions for Global Opportunities III and American Opportunities funds

1997-1999   ABC Mutual Funds
Senior Estates Specialist, Operations

- Coordinate the flow of information between lawyers, accountants, executors, administrators, beneficiaries and or sales representatives acting on behalf of an estate, on estate settlement in either written or verbal form
- Read all estate documentation to determine if in order and request and/or perform all appropriate transactions to be completed to settle the account
- Investigate any problems on estate accounts and follow-up on all outstanding estate account settlement
- Act as a resource for estate administration, coach staff on matters in estate administration
- Responsible for ensuring that all necessary estates documents are received and that such documents comply with State and Federal requirements
- Responsible for ensuring that policies and procedures pertaining to estate administration are routinely updated

1996-2000   Anytown Community Center (Parks & Recreation)
Youth Program Director

- Select train and supervise part-time staff
- Ensure that government policies and procedures are adhered to by staff, participants and public
- Ensure program location meets government Health & Safety standards (necessary equipment and supplies are available and in safe condition)
- Communicate and work cooperatively with volunteers, community groups and other program staff
- Ensure effective public relations and problem resolution
- Take appropriate actions to deal with incidents, problems, and emergencies outlined in department policies and procedures
- Supervise and implement programs for participants (i.e. Sporting events, fund-raisers, etc.)
- Help to develop community peer organizations
- Involved in planning and coordination of sales/marketing activities

1993-1997   XYZ Financial Services
Client Service Supervisor, Sales/Client Services

- Supervise team of telephone sales and client service representatives
- Ensure that sales objectives are met through regular communication with customers
- Respond to telephone and written requests for product and administrative information
- Investigate account related problems
- Establish performance standards, evaluate performance, devise training and development plans, measure productivity and service levels

EDUCATION

1999-2003 **Central University** Somecity, Anystate
Bachelor of Arts - Public Administration and Governance

2001-2002 **Central University** Somecity, Anystate
Project Management Certificate Program

REFERENCES

Available upon request

COACHES & COUNSELORS: Career Management Coach

John J. Johnston
123 Learning St. Anytown, USA 10101• 999-555-1313• johnj@yourname.com

Career Management Professional
With over five years experience in Outplacement, Consulting, and EAP

- Conduct termination meetings in large corporations and counsel clients in transition
- Results oriented One-to-One Counselling, Coaching, and Mentoring
- Workshop design and facilitation from blue collar to management level
- Specialize in Information Technology, Manufacturing, and Financial Services sectors

PROFESSIONAL EXPERIENCE

VALUE COACH LIMITED, Consultant   **2001–present**
Coach and consult with over 150 clients from blue collar to vice president level on career transition and employment issues for mid-sized Career Transition firm. Consult on Termination best practices.

- Manage caseload for over 150 downsized and career-transitioning clients. Coach clients through all levels of search from self-assessment through to transition into new position.
- Coach and consult with VP's Human Resources and Managers through termination process for downsizings and cause reasons.
- Collaborated on the design and implementation of innovative middle management and blue-collar workshops. Delivered to downsized groups with across the board excellent feedback.
- Initiated and continue to lead monthly team building event resulting in a more cohesive, stronger consulting and administrative team.
- Manage off-site downsizing projects and plant closures including conducting specialized workshops and providing one-to-one consulting services and follow up.
- Provide retirement and entrepreneurship counseling to hourly and salaried clients.

ST. MARGARET'S EMPLOYMENT RESOURCES CENTRE   **1997–2001**
Career Counselor, 1998–2001
Provided results-oriented, career counselling to clients in gov't sponsored Career Centre.

- Maintained caseload for over 500 clients, designing unique action plans for each.
- Acted as lead in case conferencing meetings with team of counselors and for agency-wide planning sub-committee resulting in greater staff cohesiveness.
- Promoted and marketed agency resulting in the spearheading of new agency partnerships and increasing client intake totals by 10%.
- Researched, developed, and implemented new training which targeted specific group needs such as foreign-trained professionals and youth.

Employment Counselor/Facilitator, 1997–1998

- Developed & executed community partnership plan to over 50 groups ↑ resource centre attendance by 15%.

TVTOWN - Production Manager   **1988–1996**
Developed and managed budgets of up to $ .5 million, in consultation with producers for 30 television productions, co-productions and commissioned projects.

EDUCATION AND TRAINING

- **Honors Bachelor of Arts**, State University, 1986
- **Career Development Practitioner On-Line Diploma Program**, Local College

Conducting Job Search Work Team Groups, The Coach Corner; Success Leader's Training Program, Tiplady's Training Services Inc.; Needs Assessments, Adult Education Theory, Train the Trainer; Conflict Resolution; Teaching Adults; Crisis Intervention and Prevention.

CERTIFICATION and SPECIAL SKILLS
Certified Level B Tester, True Colors Level 1 Certificate, Life Skills Coach Certificate

COACHES & COUNSELORS: Art Therapist and Counselor

Alice J. Johnston
123 Learning Street, Anytown, USA 10101 999-555-1212 / alicej@yourname.com

"When the soul wishes to experience something, she throws an image of the experience before her and she enters into her own image."

EDUCATION

2000	**Postgraduate Diploma - Art Therapy (Master's Equivalent)** State University
1996	**Certificate in Art Therapy** Overseas School of Art Therapy, Scotland
1993	**Bachelor of Arts, Sociology** State University

CONTINUING EDUCATION

- National Community Crisis Response Team Training Certificate
- Addictions Training
- Grief and Bereavement Therapy
- Parenting Skills
- Critical Incident Stress Debriefing and SARS debriefing

RELATED SKILLS

- Knowledgeable and effective in working with cultural and social differences
- Strong communication and interpersonal skills
- Excellent organizational and time management skills
- Project management experience
- Work effectively as a team member and individually
- Excellent computer skills

EMPLOYMENT HISTORY

2001–present **Clinical Counselor,** Consultants Corp. (Employee Assistance Provider)

- Provide crisis intervention, single session and ongoing counseling to clients with diverse issues (eg. addictions, suicidal ideation, domestic violence, sexual abuse, depression & anxiety, parenting, eating disorders, grief, same sex relationships, self-mutilation, career development, dementias, caregiver stress, and trauma)
- Identify primary issues, enable the client to focus on obtainable outcomes and manageable action steps to lower stress, enhance coping abilities and develop individualized program plans addressing short and long term needs
- Identify related issues (e.g. financial stability, employment, child well-being, safety, parental communication), offer support, outline options, and refer to available community based resources
- Provide in-person group & individual critical incident trauma debriefings
- Participate in meetings and case consultations, ensuring a comprehensive approach to client assistance
- Provide peer support and assist in training/orienting new clinicians

1999–2001 **Research Asst.**, Center for Research: Violence against Women & Children, State U

- Managed a research project addressing the experiences of refugee children who witnessed war, from data collection through to data analysis
- Supervised the qualitative analysis for a national study addressing everyday violence in the lives of girl children
- Conducted in-depth interviews with innovative method: "photonovella"
- Analyzed data and identified, synthesized and coded emergent themes
- Co-authored peer-reviewed journal article: *Portraits of Promise and Pain*: a photographic study of Bosnian youth, Research, 32, 21–41
- Worked independently and met all required deadlines

Alice Johnston

COACHES & COUNSELORS: Art Therapist and Counselor (cont.)

- 2 -

1999–2000 **Art Therapist**
Child and Adolescent Psychiatry, Anytown Health Sciences Centre

- Utilized Art Psychotherapy for individuals and groups on an in & outpatient basis, addressing a multitude of issues (e.g. depression and anxiety, sexual abuse, eating disorders, schizoaffective disorders, psychosis, learning disabilities, ADHD & ADD)
- Developed an open group for children ages 6–17 that heightened social skills, self-esteem, healthy peer relationships, and addressed individual concerns
- Conducted assessments, charted patient progress, and wrote case summaries
- Assisted the therapeutic team with outpatient planning
- Co-facilited a closed group for teenage-girl victims of family sexual abuse
- Fostered excellent working relationships with therapeutic team and staff
- Participated in reflective family therapy sessions
- Competently carried out the duties associated with this student placement

1998–1999 **Art Therapist**
Anytown Alternative Secondary School

- Provided counseling for youth with emotional and behavioral issues (e.g., victims of sexual abuse, substance abuse, violence among youth, teenage pregnancy)
- Designed and facilitated group programs utilizing themed art therapy to address self-esteem
- Demonstrated knowledge and skill in directing and managing group dynamics
- Competently carried out the duties associated with this student placement

VOLUNTEER WORK

2004 **Member**
- Human Rights Watch

2004 **Fundraising Assistant**
- Jazz FM

2004 **Contributing Artist**
- Art for Life Art Auction for Women's Hospital and Grace Hospital

2001 **Fundraising Assistant**
- Run for the Cure for Diabetes Research

1995–1998 **Program Worker**
- Post Natal Depression Project, Department of Social Services
Provided emotional and practical support to spouse and children of mothers affected by post natal depression

PROFESSIONAL ASSOCIATIONS

- American Art Therapy Association, Professional Member

HOBBIES

- Painting
- Creative Writing
- Meditation

COACHES & COUNSELORS: Research Analyst & Organizational Consultant

John J. Johnston   Page 1

John J. Johnston, Ph.D. Candidate
123 Learning Street, Anytown, USA, 10101 Phone: 999.555.1212   Email: johnj@yourname.com

MISSION
To provide organizations with valid measurement and assessment for the purpose of identifying and optimizing talent, promoting employee well-being, driving organizational performance, and achieving peerless excellence in the service of all stakeholders.

COMPETENCIES

- Competency Modeling
- 360° Feedback Surveys
- Assessment Centers
- Multivariate Data Analysis

- Employee Surveys
- Structured Interviews
- Organizational Research
- Individual Assessment

WORK HISTORY

Research Inc., Research Analyst (Select projects)   2001–2003

- Designed a customer opinion survey, analyzed and interpreted data, and provided recommendations for brand repositioning for a major daily newspaper.
- Designed a survey of environmental opinions and behaviors, analyzed and interpreted data, identified segments in the general population, and provided recommendations to a government ministry for policy change and communication.
- Designed a survey of health care opinions and behaviors, analyzed and interpreted data, identified segments in the general population, and provided recommendations to a gov't ministry for policy change & communication.

Consultants Inc., Organizational Consultant   1995–2001

- Designed assessment tools for individual selection, development, and strategy alignment (i.e., competency models, 360° feedback surveys, assessment centers, structured interviews, etc.).
- Designed and managed organization-wide assessments (i.e., 360° feedback surveys, assessment centres, organizational climate/culture assessments).
- Statistically analyzed organizational survey data and provided recommendations to clients (univariate and multivariate analysis).
- Conducted validation studies of personnel selection tools and 360° feedback surveys.
- Conducted individual assessments of personality, aptitude, and leadership competencies (using 16PF, OPQ, MBTI, EAS, Watson-Glaser, structured interviews, assessment center simulations).
- Designed tools and resources for executive development.
- Served as a subject matter expert in psychology, data analysis, and measurement.

Research Inc., Research Analyst   1994–1995

- Statistically analyzed and interpreted national survey data (multivariate analysis).
- Coauthored a journal publication on the segmentation of Generation X values in America (supported the book *In the Bush* by Mark Rutherford).
- Consulted on employee opinion surveys for clients.

State University, Program Design and Evaluation   1994–1995

- As a team, evaluated and consulted on the revision of a chronic pain program for a private rehabilitation clinic.
- Consulted on issues of psychological assessment for a private rehabilitation clinic (i.e., evaluated their intake measures, recommended alternatives).
- Developed an applied practicum program for doctoral students in the Graduate Dept of Psychology, State U.
- Established liaisons between the Graduate Department of Psychology, State U, and public and private sector.

COACHES & COUNSELORS: Research Analyst & Organizational Consultant (cont.)

John J. Johnston   Page 2

EDUCATION

Ph.D. Candidate (Psychology), SuperState University   present
Master of Arts (Psychology), State University   1993
Bachelor of Arts *(Honors Psychology, Member of the Dean's Honor Roll, cum laude)*, State University   1998

- **Select Areas of Research:** Job Satisfaction, Job Characteristics, Burnout, Workplace Depression, Work Values, Perfectionism, Anxiety, Youth Values (Generation X), Cross-Cultural Self-Concept and Family Interdependence.
- **Graduate Courses:** Applied Practica (2), Research Practicum, Research Seminar, Univariate Statistics, Program Evaluation, Psychological Assessment, Personality, Social and Personality Development, Biological and Psychological Theories and Treatment of Major Clinical Disorders, Human Factors, History of Psychology.

PROFFESSIONAL STANDING & ACHIEVEMENTS

Coauthored Professional Journal Articles (e.g., APA)
Qualified for Level B Psychological Assessment (Personality, Aptitude, Vocational Interests, etc.)
Affiliate Member of the American Psychological Association
Presentations at Annual Conventions of the American Psychological Association

INTERESTS

Music Composition/Performance/Recording
Academic and Professional Reading/Development
Weight-Training/Cycling

COMMERCIAL REAL ESTATE: Commercial Lease Analyst

Alice J. Johnston

123 Learning St., Anytown, ST USA 10101 (999) 555-1212
alicej@yourname.com

Profile:

A Senior Lease Analyst in the Commercial Real Estate Division

Organized & attentive to detail; Analytical approach to assignments and enjoy problem solving; professional telephone manner; excellent communication skills and easily build rapport with new clients and colleagues; active team player and likes to take initiative.

Experience:

Senior Account Analyst, ABC Corporate Services   Jan. 2001–Present

- Abstraction of critical lease information including critical dates and tenant obligations
- Monthly reporting to client of critical date information
- Research and gathering of data for markets worldwide (i.e. comparable real estate rates; current competitor rates; other economic indicators)
- Set-up and subsequent implementation of client's portfolio in RE-Port database; training client personnel to access and use database for various purposes in a secure web environment
- Set-up and updating of real estate assignment in Assignment Tracking System; responsible for timely and diligent completion of all projects; ensured the collection and full execution of contractual documents, team member follow-up; project due diligence
- Negotiating leases, renewals, and expansions for National Corporate Client
- Workflow creation and customization based on client's internal processes

Accomplishments and Departmental Recognition

- Assisted with various Reporting assignments including Appraisal Report on more than 200 properties owned worldwide, Market Analysis of major cities and competitor rates for facilities leased nationally, Budget Forecasting for properties leased worldwide, Drive-time Analysis for potential consolidation project, Buyout Analysis for potential disposition, Highest and Best Use Analysis for potential acquisition and subsequent disposition of global portfolio
- Corporate Services Departmental Representative in marketing initiative; including review and revision of existing departmental brochures and design concept, participation in design of company-wide meetings and calls to review various draft materials and regular follow-up with marketing and design team to ensure timely execution and delivery of various departmental marketing pieces.
- Corporate Services Departmental representative for database and technology platform updating and corrections initiative

Commercial Real Estate Leasing Agent, Parkers Commercial Realty LLC. June 1999–Oct 2000

- Prospecting for quality leads involving screening calls of potential clients and presenting a series of questions
- Tracked all quality leads on Access Database system
- Meeting with clients to establish motivation, needs analysis
- Preparing and Negotiating Offers to Lease
- Showing properties to qualified clients

Personal Accomplishments and Initiatives

- Attending educational seminars and courses on topics (CCIM Breakfast meetings, Motivational seminars, Property Management Expo, Franchise Exhibition, Seminars on legal, financial, and practical topics & skills)
- Actively participated in weekly meetings and discussions on company business strategy and goals
- Developed and maintained comprehensive summary of available property throughout Anytown owned and managed by small private investors as well as larger institutions

Residential Real Estate Buyer Specialist, Big Realty Inc.   Jan 1998–May 1999

- Presenting and negotiating offers
- Prospecting for quality leads
- Conducting Open Houses
- Marketing of properties; designing advertisements and feature sheets
- Regularly showing homes to prequalified purchasers

COMMERCIAL REAL ESTATE: Commercial Lease Analyst (cont.)

Sales Assistant to New Homes Sales, Adler Homes   Nov 1997–Aug 1998
- Greeted visitors; introduced them to site; answered inquiries
- Prepared Offers of Purchase and Sale for negotiation
- Provided administrative support to sales personnel

Assistant to Brokerage, XZY Realty Inc.   Jan 1998–April 1998
- Designed ads for residential listings in local newspaper (biweekly)
- Answered all incoming calls and inquiries
- Daily upkeep of contact records and communication tracking; updating client database

Education:

1992–1996 State University: completed 4 years of undergraduate studies in Political Science and Art History (Several credits short of degree; not planning to complete at this time.)

1996: obtained membership and License to State Real Estate Association & Anytown Real Estate Board

1999: completed CCIM-101 Financial Analysis for Commercial Investment Real Estate
(Commercial Investment Real Estate Institute)

2002: completed CCIM-102 Market Analysis for Commercial Investment Real Estate
(Commercial Investment Real Estate Institute)

2003: completed CCIM-103 User-Decision Analysis for Commercial Investment Real Estate
(Commercial Investment Real Estate Institute)

Currently completing Series 7 course. Due to be completed March 2006.

Interests and Hobbies:

Toastmasters International, volleyball, Tae Kwon Do classes, painting and drawing, read extensively and enjoy attending art galleries

Technical:

Proficient with MapPoint (Geographical Information Systems), Excel, PowerPoint, RE-Port (Real Estate Portfolio Database), CATS (Colliers Assignment Tracking System), Contact Manager (internal database used to track client information and historical relationships with company personnel)

COMMERCIAL REAL ESTATE: Leasing Manager

Alice J. Johnston
123 Learning St., Anytown, ST USA 010101

alicej@yourname.com   (999) 555-1212

Commercial Real Estate, Leasing Manager and Business Development

SUMMARY: **"President's Round Table Membership Award"**
- **State College (Business Degree Program)**
- **Commercial Real Estate experience**
- **Proficient in Standard Sale and Lease Agreement and Real Estate contract law**
- **Detail oriented and organized**
- **Deadline oriented/superior multi-task skills**
- **Experienced team player**

EXPERIENCE: **Big Real Commercial Inc.,** Commercial Retail Sales/Leasing   **1/1995–5/2003**
Retail Advisory Group
- Development; Identify new projects, Buy/Sell and facilitate real estate transactions with Purchasers and Vendors
- Structure and assist financing in conjunction with client
- Specialization: Sales/Leasing and Pre-Leasing and developing commercial retail shopping centers and BTS projects i.e.: Big Bank, Bank Inc, Big Box Store, etc.
- Exclusively represented major retail clients re: real estate site selection mandates, sale/leasebacks and property disposition (North America)
- Developed and implemented network strategies in geographic region to ensure market leadership, i.e. local and national advertising, competitive analysis
- Maintain "Top Level" relationships with real estate community, developers and brokers; including attending national ICSC events
- Create customized sales/leasing/marketing materials
- Assist, architects with site plans according to Landlord/Tenant specifications
- Attend meetings with local municipalities and city officials re: zoning bylaws, environmentals, site plans and approvals

Achievements
- **Achieved "Round Table Membership Award"**
- **Held Market Leadership for region throughout my role**
- **Select Sale/Lease Transactions include (i.e.,)Big Box Store Inc., FabricsRUS, Restaurants Inc. Big Bank, Runners Inc., Bank Solutions**

Associates Inc., Project Manager   **8/1990–11/1994**
- Managed Development, Redevelopment, Renovation/Construction commercial–residential real estate projects
- Assist in evaluating, hiring and managing contractors, planning and design professionals
- Provide estimates of preliminary cost and assist in establishing development and construction budgets
- Oversight for ongoing construction activities, oversee contractors, manage construction schedules and monitor quality control on all projects
- Approve all construction bids/tenders
- Assist architects design/drawings re: floor plans, interior/exterior finishes and landscapes

Achievements
- **Brought all projects in on time and on budget**

COMMERCIAL REAL ESTATE: Leasing Manager (cont.)

A.B.C. Atlantic Corporation, Director of Leasing   **5/1987 – 8/1990**
- o   Syndicated value of 1 Billion U.S. dollars
- o   Assumed responsibility for leasing multi-property portfolio of shopping centers primarily located in south FL
- o   Produced sales presentation materials and advised leasing staff
- o   Provided monthly Lease Progress Reports to senior management and syndicated investors
- o   Formulated profitable lease inducements and creative leasehold improvement packages to key retail tenants targeted at underperforming centers

Achievements
- o   **Took the initiative to offer training sessions and discuss sales/leasing strategies with sales people – exceptional positive feedback and anecdotal improved results**

XYZ Limited, Management Intern/Leasing Manager   **10/1983–5/1987**

- o   Selected 1 of 5 among 1500 applicants to intern management/leasing representative with a major real estate development company
- o   Assisted in carrying out daily shopping center operations at Anytown City Center and surrounding strip centers according to policy and procedure manuals
- o   Assist hiring, training, evaluating, and managing property employees
- o   Assist senior leasing manager with leasing plans, proposals, broker liaison, tenant negotiations, and coordination
- o   Assist property manager with budget preparation, analysis, and management
- o   Assist financial reporting and fiscal control of assigned properties (i.e., outparcels, satellite centers)

Achievements
- o   **Initial project/task: Complete restructuring of Merchant's Association**
- o   **Result: A successful 150% annual rate increase to the Merchant's Association Fund**
- o   **Transferred as part of a 5 member Special Task Force to redevelop a multi-property portfolio acquisition of 26 regional shopping centers**
- o   **Pre-leased and developed 2 POWER centers totaling 1,500,000**

EDUCATION: **1983   B.A., State College**

AFFILIATIONS: **9/1990–Present   State Real Estate Association Member**

9/1983–Present   International Council of Shopping Centers Member

COMMUNICATIONS: Communications Management Professional

John J. Johnston

• johnj@yourname.com • 123 Learning St., Anytown, USA 10101 • (999) 555-1212

SUMMARY

• Goal-driven **Communications Management Professional.**
• Proven track record as editor, Web strategist, media relations professional, and project manager.
• Experience in writing and editing (news releases, articles, marketing collateral); project management (trade shows, seminars, event coverage) and directing publications and staff (newspapers, e-newsletters, and brochures).

PROFESSIONAL EXPERIENCE

Freelance Work
• Serving as freelance writer, copy editor/ producer and communications   Feb. 2002–Present
management consultant for previous employers and other clients. Clients include
ABC Inc and former employers MM Media.

MediaMap, Inc.
Online Editor/Content Manager   March 2000–Feb. 2002
• Managed strategy and production of all online editorial content. Supervised
editing, writing, and design staff for industry e-newsletter and company website.
Researched and wrote online daily media news. Coordinated marketing communication
and writing (press releases, direct mail, advertising, media relations).

Accomplishments: Reinvented newsletter offerings; grew readership from 3,000 to
27,000. Planned and wrote all content for new website. Managed all PR and
marketing communication activity during labor shortage. Revised all company
marketing collateral.

State University College of Communication
Adjunct Faculty member   Sept. 2000–Jan. 2002
• Evening instructor for professional writing and oral communication in Department of
State Communication, Advertising, and Public Relations.

Community Newspaper Company
Assistant Editor, Editor
Staff Writer, Newspaper   June 1998–March 2000
• Managed all content, from generating story ideas to layout and design. Supervised
reporters, columnists, and freelance writers and work with designers, production and
online staff. Maintained working relationships with community leaders, information
sources, and government officials at all levels. As staff writer, covered crime, municipal,
education, and transportation beats.

Accomplishments: Promoted from Staff Writer to Assistant Editor, March 1999.
Helped manage coverage of Cider Cup worldwide PGA golf tournament. Appointed
newspaper's Editor, Oct. 1999.

COMMUNICATIONS: Communications Management Professional (cont.)

State College
Adjunct Faculty Instructor   January–May 1998
• Designed syllabus for and taught Interpersonal Communication course.

State University College of Communication
Teaching Assistant, Senior Teaching Assistant, and Course Administrator   Jan. 1997–Jan. 1998
• Designed a freshman course syllabus, coordinated student orientation and activities
for 350 students. Hired, trained, and supervised a team of 16 graduate teaching
assistants. Taught a section of 20 undergraduate communication students.

Department of Foreign Affairs & International Trade
Assistant Project Manager   Jan. 1993–May 1995
• Recruited and organized American pavilions at trade fairs and missions to Africa.
Liaison with private sector, government agencies, media relations, and
embassy staff in South Africa.

Accomplishments: Managed American delegations for largest-ever government
trade show (Johannesburg). Helped produce first 'Team American' trade missions
(Zambia, Botswana, Namibia).

EDUCATION

State University College of Communication
Master of Science (communication, writing & editing)   December 1997

Overseas University, Spain   June 1993
(University-level Spanish-language studies)

State Memorial University
Bachelor of Arts (political science major, business administration minor)   December 1992

AFFILIATIONS AND SKILLS

• Bilingual (Spanish).
• Proficient in a wide range of word processing and online publishing software. Experience in CD-ROM
design.

John J. Johnston

123 Learning St., Anytown, USA * (999) 555-1234 * johnj@yourname.com

Expertise:

Business Communications: All forms of content (web, newsletter, column, internal messaging, brochures, reports, presentations, etc.)

Currently:

Communications Consultant, Parnelli's Partners

Clients include advertising and marketing agencies, communications consultants, corporations, community colleges, government agencies, and departments

Bleak Communications	Tony and Shoe Advertising	Sylvia Communications
AnyState Hydro	Bank Finance, Inc.	Safe Funds
Big Bank	Love Loyalty Miles	Television Production House
Other Bank	American Medical Association	Bus Services
Sal's Electronics	Nother Bank Investments	Garbage Haulers
Building Builder	Addiction Research Campaign	Labor Lumber
Pip College	American Cancer Society	My Best Financial

Columnist: *Small Town Life Magazine; Privately Owned Magazine; Convenience Magazine*

Experience:

2002–2003   **Communications Consultant, Nother Bank Investments**

Planned and executed messages and marketing campaigns on investing, mutual funds, and Nother Bank Investments.

Responsibilities included all aspects of corporate communications: annual reports, corporate profiles, sales and marketing brochures, fund commentaries, trade show material, internal and external sales and marketing presentations, fund manager interviews, business-building material for financial advisers, print advertising, website content, branding, and selection of appropriate media.

1995–2002   **Marketing Writer, Safe Funds**

Responsible for the preparation and maintenance of marketing material promoting investing and mutual funds in general, and SAFE Funds in particular. This included sales and marketing brochures, fund commentaries, corporate profiles, trade show material, presentations, fund manager interviews, business-building material for Safe advisers, print advertising, and website content.

Developed the concept and prepared all written material for SAFE's "Straight Talk on Investing" educational series. Prepared all materials for online and print publishing, including concept development and content for the SAFE Funds website at www.Safefunds.com.

Ensured consistent branding, design, and style; advised on marketing plans, messages, and selection of appropriate media.

COMMUNICATIONS: Communications Writing (cont.)

John J. Johnston Resume   Page 2 of 2

1986–Present   **Writer: Mass-market Magazine Articles, Books**

Reader's Digest   *American Living*   *Health Beat*
Anytown Business Magazine   *Environment Magazine*   *Homes and Forts*
Chicken Soup for the Resumes Soul

1982–1986   **Moore Photography: Commercial and Advertising**

Hooch and Mama   Humane Pets   CCL Industries
Papa Inc.   Beer Blast   Oil and Glue
Big & Name Brander   Elephant Trucks   Hand Cream Inc.
Special Place Hotel   Prestige Hotel   Burning Tires Not
Anytown Transit

1975–1982   **Writer & Presenter: Speaker's Bureau International**

Telephony   Birdland Training   WorkForce U.S.
Addiction Center   Region of Anytown   Polyglot
Capistrano College   Perks Construction, Ltd.   Rainforest
Department
Association of Law Clerks

Post-Secondary Teaching:

2004   **Curriculum Development & Instruction, State University, The School of English**
                 Business Communications

2003   **Instructor, Business Communications**
                 School of Business, Commerce Department

2002–Present **Instructor, Business Communications**
                 State College, Training and Development Division

1973–1996   **Instructor, Faculty of Education**
                 State University of Specialist Certificate, Guidance Program

Awards & Memberships:
Convenience Magazine - Nominated, "Best Column"
Trade Magazine Peach A. Parker Awards
Voting Member: Editor's Association of America (500 editing hours in the past 12 months)

Education:
Master's Degree: State University Communications & Psychology
Bachelor of Science Degree (Honors): State University

COMMUNICATIONS: Communications Professional

Alice J. Johnston

123 Learning St., Anytown, USA 10101
Phone: 999-555-1212 • Mobile: 999-555-1313 • Email: alicej@yourname.com

Marketing and Communications Professional
Creating Winning Promotion Strategies & Increasing Revenues

Motivated and results-oriented marketing professional with experience in all aspects of marketing and communications for diverse companies and industries. Negotiates partnering agreements and third party advertising that result in profitable projects and products. Managed several creative and marketing teams to produce a myriad of websites and print materials. Detailed analytical skills identify trends and create action plans to increase company and sales growth, reduce marketing costs, and increase brand exposure.

Areas of Expertise

- On/Offline, B2B/B2C Marketing
- Market & Competitive Research
- Trend Tracking & Data Analysis
- Copywriting & Press Releases
- Senior Management & Client Reporting
- Internal & External Communications

Career Highlights

- Created a data-mining division for an online educational marketing company and generated reports, not only for existing clients, but also for new/potential clients, which resulted in additional revenues of over US$200,000.
- Took an existing group of five directory websites and increased traffic up to tenfold in less than six months, resulting in 68% more site traffic with 54% less marketing costs.
- Developed and implemented a marketing program that vaulted a startup search engine to the #16 spot on Media Metrix's Top 50 within 4 months of launch.
- Created and maintained the first-ever intranet for Power Gen's Water Management Division and was responsible for the new look and feel of the entire PG family of websites used through late 2000.

Professional Experience

MARKETING RESEARCH MANAGER
Big Web Project, Inc. - (Online Educational Marketing Company Contract 10/02–02/04)

Compiled detailed regular reports on overall website activity, for a family of almost 30 sites, as well as detailed statistics on client-specific results. Provided the detailed analysis to allow executive management to develop the company's high-level marketing strategy. Researched and determined the demand for products and services offered by clients and competitors and identified potential markets.

MARKETING MANAGER
AXV Research Inc. - (Online Vertical Marketing Company 09/01–07/02)

Sourced and obtained paid & free methods (including search engine rankings, special page creation, opt-in email campaigns, banner and button campaigns, sponsorships, etc.) of driving traffic to the family of AXV Inc. websites; developed & maintained on and offline marketing campaigns—including online media buying and offline advertising planning & purchasing—and tracked and analyzed campaign results to ensure ROI.

INTERNET TRAFFIC MANAGER
Spin Doc Media - (Online Marketing Services Company Contract 01/01–08/01)

Developed and maintained online marketing campaigns for high-profile clients, highlighted by the first "blitz" of banner ads. Designed loyalty programs to retain current customers and generate new leads. Assisted with design and content of Spin Doc's sites. Liaised with Graphic Design and IT Departments to create user interface for company sites to influence visitor behaviour and maximize ROI. Managed online marketing department and was responsible for hiring new employees.

COMMUNICATIONS: Communications Professional (cont.)

Alice J. Johnston
- Page 2 -

CREATIVE DIRECTOR / WEBMASTER
Feel Good Inc. - (Health and Wellness Portal 08/00–12/00)

Designed, implemented, and maintained all network sites; liaised with 3rd party IT department to determine requirements that affected front end development of all web projects and tools; tracked and analyzed website stats to determine best-of-breed reporting tools. Designed all offline materials (sales, promotion, media, and marketing materials) and provided content that ensured all on and offline communications materials consistently met corporate design standards. Managed third-party outsource design and programming projects.

MARKETING MANAGER
kicks.com Inc. - (Startup Search Engine 10/99–07/00)

Managed a US$250,000 monthly budget to launch and promote their startup search engine to the #16 spot on Media Metrix's Top 50 within four months of launch. Designed the entire look and feel of offline marketing materials, from sales kits to a sixty-foot billboard. Assisted with trade show organization for Internet World 2000 Los Angeles and designed the booth graphics. Represented at the Internet World 2000 and Search Engine World Anycity to generate sales leads.

WEBSITE DESIGNER / PRODUCTION MANAGER
earthen.com Inc. - (Startup Design & 3D Chat Company 07/99–10/99)

Managed and created websites for clients of a corporate web design firm, from graphic design to copywriting to page layout including development of a touch-screen-based information site dealership kiosks. Redesigned earthen.com's 3D chat site and created an email-capable avatar. Designed client banner ads and CD art concepts. Sourced hardware and equipment and purchased software.

WEBMASTER / MARKETING DESIGNER
ZAP Inc - (Industrial Systems & Power Management 12-month contract 08/98–07/99)

Created and maintained first-ever Intranet for Power Management Division (4 plants in US, Spain and Puerto Rico). Created "Internet Best Practices" sites for Industrial Systems (parent division of Power Management—15 departments in total). Created page templates for all of GE - responsible for the new look and feel of Zap family of websites through to late 2000, including www.zap.com. Design the beta version of the Power Management online store front and Industrial Systems website.

ADVERTISING DESIGNER
AZC Communications - (Advertising Firm 03/98–08/98)

Created and developed custom print advertising and marketing materials for corporate industrial clients. Started the online marketing division of an established advertising firm, increasing revenue through creation of new product.

WEBMASTER / DESKTOP PUBLISHER
Fun Travel LLC. - (Travel Agency & Wholesaler 10/97–03/98)

Took existing website and print brochures from blah to wow. Revamped existing website to incorporate Fun Travel's products, brochures, and manuals to market trip packages. Created beta reservation storefront. Redesigned four-colour advertising brochures. Created ads for a wide variety of publications, as well as other marketing materials.

Education & Training

B.A., English	State University - 1995
Journalism Diploma	State College - 1997

- **Business Statistics**   State University - 2003
- **Business Report Writing**   State College - 2003
- **Java Certificate**   State College - 1998

COMMUNICATIONS: Marketing and Communications Specialist

Alice J. Johnston
Marketing Communications Manager

T • 999 555 1212   alicej@yourname.com
123 Learning Street, Anytown, USA 10101

A versatile **Marketing Communications Specialist** who transforms creative strategy into effective action with outstanding results.

Has developed and managed a wide range of highly successful, profitable initiatives within corporate and agency environments.

A resourceful, motivated team leader who balances big picture creative thinking with exceptional execution.

Proven talent for cultivating and sustaining partnerships with business and community groups.

EXPERTISE

- Developing marketing strategy
- Mobilizing people and resources
- Concept development, writing, editing
- Negotiating with contractors/suppliers
- Art direction, design and visual analysis
- Identifying new opportunities/partners
- Maximizing impact of marketing dollars
- Developing/managing projects and budgets
- Tracking, evaluating, and improving systems
- Providing exceptional levels of client service

PROFESSIONAL EXPERIENCE

Account Coordinator
ABC Group,
2002–2004
(Customer Relationship
Management/computer technology)

Within a CRM environment, managed a program awarding $5 million to customers across the Northwest U.S. Directed project managers and senior computer application developers to enhance functionality and efficiency of user interface. By remote methods, trained and supervised 4 fulfilment staff and project managers in another city. Proactively assisted 60 business reps with user technology and process. Ensured accurate processing of information and timely program delivery. Liaised with client's senior management, prepared client proposals, and initiated and prepared a comprehensive post-project evaluation.

Managed direct mail marketing projects and the warehousing and distribution of sales collateral.

Partner
Paladin Display Products
2000–2002

Provided marketing and communications services to clients such as *The l Sports Centre*, *Big Car Company*. Projects included corporate identity, websites, direct mail, newsletters, brochures, annual reports, and display products.

Launched a new business direction involving the wholesale distribution of imported fine display and tradeshow products. Starting from scratch with limited industry knowledge, succeeded in reaching and influencing decision makers to develop a national network of new clients and suppliers that form the foundation of *Paladin Display* today. In addition to driving sales, performed all entrepreneurial functions.

Communications Manager
WillTalk 1999
(translation, interpretation,
over-the-phone interpretation,
global operator services)

Handled communications materials, planned the revision of the corporate website. Improved the customer service standards of the translation and interpretation division and managed a staff of 5. Enhanced functionality and effectiveness of national translator/interpreter database.

Special Events Coordinator
The Theatre Centre
1996–1998

Raised over $200K annually coordinating fundraising events, including gala balls, theatre events, and *Brunch with Joe Schemple* in conjunction with volunteer committees of key business leaders. Handled advertising, communications materials, and sponsorship for events.

By initiating a series of effective new marketing strategies, achieved record-breaking numbers in net profits, silent auction profits and attendance for *The Theatre Centre's* 1997 *Blue and Red Gala Ball* in addition to the first waiting list in the event's 50-year history.

COMMUNICATIONS: Marketing and Communications Specialist (cont.)

Alice J. Johnston
Marketing Communications Manager

T • 999 555 1212   alicej@yourname.com
123 Learning Street, Anytown, USA 10101

Communications Coordinator
Centra Gas
1995 (contract)

Successfully launched a corporate community watch program to the media and public in collaboration with city police. Assisted with corporate communications. Analyzed sponsorship and donation requests, recommending to the CEO which proposals, to support and at what levels.

Project Coordinator
ABC Management Services
1995 (contract)
(marketing/advertising agency)

Developed and wrote sponsorship proposals, radio advertising and sales materials for logo licensing agency. Identified and solicited potential sponsors. Managed sales and delivery of limited edition commemorative prints. Pitched potential agency clients.

**Communications Coordinator
& Event Manager**
Renewal Corporation
1988–1995
(tri-level downtown development)

Attracted over 2 million visitors annually to a newly developed 56-acre heritage shopping and recreation site, formerly an abandoned riverside railway yard in the heart of downtown Anytown, and promoted it to become one of the State's top tourist destinations.

Developed communications, corporate identity, and advertising materials. A key player in terms of public, media, and tenant relations. Wrote and edited newsletters, annual reports, brochures, feature articles, media releases, event programs, sponsorship proposals, and post-event reports.

Liaised with television and radio production staff concerning live specials. Arranged photo shoots and acted as corporate photographer. Collaborated with designers and printers. Handled numerous sensitive and controversial issues.

From the ground up, designed and managed an extensive calendar of highly successful and popular events attracting hundreds of thousands of visitors annually. Every year added new and exciting components without increasing the budget by establishing and growing partnerships with groups and suppliers eager to showcase their products and services at our venue. Identified and solicited potential sponsors. Each year, recruited and managed an event coordinator to assist with in-house events.

Facilitated an annual calendar of 180 third-party events, working closely with business, cultural, sports, and non-profit organizations. Provided exceptional level of customer service resulting in an extremely high return rate of satisfied groups helping to establish a premiere event venue. Initiated/developed event application guidelines.

Initiated a series of fun open house presentations for groups interested in hosting events and significantly streamlining the event coordination process and increasing the number and quality of events.

EDUCATION

State University
- Bachelor of Fine Arts
- Marketing for Non-profit and Public Sector Organizations

State University Communications Program
- Advertising and Promotions, Effective Written Communications, Effective Oral Communications, The Art of Fundraising, Graphic Elements: Design and Production, Event Marketing and Sponsorship

COMPUTER SKILLS
- Lotus Notes, Entourage, Microsoft Office Suite including PowerPoint on both PC and Macintosh platforms

LANGUAGES, INTERESTS, VOLUNTEERISM
- Speaks English, French, and Italian
- Enjoys cycling, photography, design
- July 2004–present - Marketing communications volunteer with *The Pontification Foundation*

CONSTRUCTION: Construction Site Administrator

123 Learning Street
Anytown, USA 10101
Phone 999-555-1212

John J. Johnston

Email johnj@yourname.com

Site Administrator with Site Supervisor Experience - Construction Project Management

Qualifications
- Working knowledge in all areas of Construction Project Management
- Marketing, sales, research, development of building products and systems
- Experienced in office and field supervision in trade and contracting organizations
- Comfortable with PC, general software installation and applications
- Project Scheduler 7, AutoCAD 2000, and R-14

Employment
BUILDINGS LTD.   **Site Administrator**   Jan 2001 to Feb 2002
- Assist with contract negotiations
- Calculate concrete and masonry take-offs
- Prepare & distribute Purchaser additions & changes to respective trades
- Conduct inspections with Purchasers (PDI's)
- Source pricing of Purchaser's requests for additions or changes
- Organize and record minutes for weekly trade meetings
- Calculate and order the required quantities of concrete needed daily
- Prepare, issue, and record purchase orders for trades and completion slips
- Acting site supervisor as needed
- Order, review, correct & distribute architectural drawings to trades as needed
- Review architectural drawings to reflect Purchaser's request and updates

ABC HOMES   **Contracts Manager**   Feb 2002 to present
- Prepare hardwood take-offs, working drawings, scope of work for tenders
- Conduct final home inspection with purchasers
- Setup of contracts with Newstar system (REMS Enterprise)
- Purchaser upgrade estimating and pricing
- Permit application preparation and follow up
- Newstar contract maintenance
- Purchaser order preparation
- Invoice review for contract compliance
- Liaison with sales staff, sub-contractors, and site management staff
- Prepare, review purchasers' extras orders
- Contract negotiation assistance, preparations
- Site production monitoring
- Production list preparation with closing and project commencement dates
- Construction budget preparation and monitoring

Education
State College
1994–1995
Major: Architectural Technology

State Technical University
1995–2000
Major: Architectural Science, Project Management
Degree: Bachelor of Technology

- Familiar with SQL and HTML server, Microsoft Excel, Project, and PowerPoint, Newstar Rems, & Enterprise

CONSTRUCTION: Construction Engineer & PM

John J. Johnston, B.Eng., P.Eng.

Contact Coordinates:

123 Learning St.
Anytown, USA 10101
Tel: (999) 555-1212
Fax: (999) 555-1313
Cell: (999) 555-1414
Email: johnj@yourname.com

A Career Summary:

- More than 20 years of public and private sector facility and real estate management experience
- Skilled in work with large portfolio clients (public and private). $US 540 million acquisition of seven international properties, and public sector client with more than 3 million square feet of space
- Substantial service as Project Manager in public sector—from feasibility and planning studies to contract development/management, client service, and commissioning, financial forecasting, and maintenance program development
- Managed teams of up to 110 people (staff or consultants)
- Extensive private sector experience in engineering consulting and associated technical services
- Record-setting performance for profitability and delivery of project work to clients' satisfaction
- Ready for major assignment where strategic use of real estate resources sets the standard in industry metrics and client satisfaction

Start-to-Finish Leadership in Project and Facility Management Services:

- **Anytown Mun. - Project Manager, Capital Projects (Contract Position)** [*March 2000 to Present*]; project management for $12.9 million in capital projects; multi-project responsibilities covering feasibility and planning through to construction and commissioning, often for occupied/operational facilities; strong emphasis on client service; first-hand experience with public sector capital planning and facility management experience.

- **Regional Municipality of Anytown - Project Manager** [*March 2000 to May 2002*]; designed and coordinated four teams of consultants conducting building condition assessments, reserve fund studies, and preventive maintenance contracts covering 84 properties (fire/ambulance and police stations, day care centres, seniors retirement/health care homes, industrial, cultural, recreational, operations and administrative buildings), used Facility Management Software System to develop summary data for capital forecasting and scheduling as well as daily operations and maintenance activities.

- **City of Anytown - Consultant** [*May to June 2003*]; worked with ABC Management Group on Master Accommodation Plan, handling Preliminary Building Condition Report, Reserve Fund Study, Preventive Maintenance Report for each of five properties; more than 200,000 square feet of space.

- **County - Consultant** [*August 2002*]; worked with Asset Management Group on Master Accommodation Plan, handling Preliminary Building Condition Report, Reserve Fund Study, and Preventive Maintenance Report for each of 13 properties; more than 250,000 square feet of space.

- **ABC Consulting Engineers** [*July 1997 to March 2000*]; simultaneously served as Vice President, Business Development & Sales, Engineering and Management Division, and Vice-President, Business Development & Sales, Corporate; Vice-President and Principal-in-Charge of Special Projects; key responsibility was training of 70 engineering staff in business development (marketing and sales); included specialized training for staff working with corporate/large volume clients.
[*July 1978 to August 1989*]; Assistant Manager, then Manager of Building Science Services, after serving as Assistant Manager of Condominium Projects, and Project Manager of Building Science and Investigation Projects.

John J. Johnston, B.Eng., P.Eng.

Leadership in Building Engineering:

Delivered more than 20 lectures on issues such as:

- Audits
- Environmental considerations for development
- Facility management systems
- Real estate consulting services
- Dealing with deficiencies
- Use of thermography

Authored more than 35 published articles on:

- Property Managers and Consultants
- Reserve Funds and Capital Reserves
- Building/Facility Due Diligence Assessments
- Building/Facility Lease Audits
- Building/Facility Management Audits and Systems
- Technical Audits, Building Audits, and Condition Surveys
- Technical Audits - Pre-conciliation to Litigation to Mitigation
- Environmental Audits and Clean-up
- Technical Aspects of Parking Garages, Balconies, Cladding, Structural and Demolition/Environmental Clean-up

- **XYZ Consulting Engineers** [*August 1990 to July 1997*]; Principal; initially served as Senior Manager of Real Estate Consulting Service (Downtown Anytown), followed by Manager of the Building Science and Structural Engineering Division; then Manager, Business Development, Building Engineering Specialist.

- **BBBB Consultants LLC** [*April 1989 to August 1990*]; Established and led (as President) buildings, engineering, environmental and management firm; amalgamated with BBBB Consulting Engineers in 1997.

- **Big Tony's Contracting LLC** [*1968 to 1990*]; served as Property Manager for 52 residential and 4 commercial/industrial properties, including mortgage financing, rental leasing, handled outsourcing of maintenance service through contractual relationships; prepared and executed sale of properties attracting $36 million over two decades; [*1968 to 1978*]; project and construction management in family-owned residential, commercial and industrial construction business.

Professional Affiliations:

- Professional Engineers State (APES)
- Registered Consulting Engineer
- Association of Condominium Managers (ACM)
- American Condominium Institute (ACI)
- American Society for Civil Engineering (ASCE)

Formal Education:

- Pro-sell Sales Training [1999, 2000]
- Asbestos Abatement in Commercial and Industrial Facilities [1989]
- Applied Infrared Thermographic Training and Certification, View LLC [1987]
- Commercial and Industrial Thermography, State University [1980]
- Building Science Course, State University [1979]
- Thermography Training Course [1979]

B.Eng., Civil Engineering, State University [1978]

References:

- Available Upon Request

CONSTRUCTION: Sr. Exec.. Construction Manufacturing

John J. Johnston
123 Learning Street   Anytown, USA 10101
Phone: 999-555-1212 Cell: 999-555-1313 Email: JohnJ@yourname.com

PROFILE

An **Entrepeneurial Senior Executive** with over 27 years of innovation in the Construction, Manufacturing & Retail sectors. A strategic leader who develops effective management teams through mentoring, coaching and inspiring others. An imaginative team player who maintains a high level of ethics and integrity while driving profitable growth of the business.

SKILLS AND COMPETENCIES

✓ Strategic planner and visionary thinker
✓ Team builder with proven conflict management skills
✓ Excellent customer service and communication abilities

✓ Self motivating entrepreneur
✓ Problem solver who can manage a team through change
✓ "Win/win" negotiator who creates opportunities for partnership and alliance

CAREER HIGHLIGHTS

General Manager, Brightly Sunrooms (January 2004–Present)

Brightly Sunrooms is America's leader in sunroom sales and installations and is a subsiduary of Ultraframe UK.

Responsiblities: Business Management of the operation to include Profit and Loss.   In addition developed and implemented "Best Practice" solutions for the Sales and Marketing as well as the Operations of the American division.

- Established new benchmarks for managing the business
- Developed and implemented new policies and procedures utilizing a "Best Practice" approach to running the operation
- Established Human Resource weaknesses and either replaced or modified the roles of the staff
- Managed the Sales and Marketing Departments while redeveloping the website
- Managed the Operations side of the business (to include construction management)

Results: Collected 95% of the deliquent receiveables. Created a friendly & productive team environment. Turned the company around from a $450,000 loss to a breakeven position. Sales and lead generation have increased by 40% while the web site has improved lead generation by 25%. The American division is planning a 6% return on sales with a 12% improvement on Gross Margin while the sales will increase by 18% for fiscal 2005.

Chief Operating Officer, BIG Homes Ltd. (January 2002–January 2004)

Big Homes is an award winning home builder in the Greater Anytown Area.

Responsibilities: Address lack of policy, procedures and a budgeting process to control costs while managing company's expansion into land and commercial property development.

- Designed and implemented a Policy and Procedures manual for the field and office staff.
- Deployed new software applications to manage master design models, budgets, and production.
- Developed a new corporate ownership infrastructure to improve tax planning and operational flow.
- Established a Finishing Technician position to inspect homes prior to the Pre-Delivery Inspection in order to reduce deficiencies and increase customer satisfaction.
- Revitalized the corporate health and safety program.
- Negotiated agreements with banks, insurance companies, trades, and formulated land purchases.

Results: Increased sales volumes by 40% with an increase to the after tax line of 18%. Reduced deficiency claims by 50% with the average issue dropping from 73 days to 32 days.

Chief Financial Officer, The Group of Companies (December 1999–October 2001)

The Group is a national construction company and manufacturer specializing in developing big box retail outlets.

Responsibilities: Establish an infrastructure to grow the business, improve processes, and solve poor returns on revenue as well as the asset base.

- Prepared and managed fiscal budgets to achieve the business plan.
- Hired managers specializing in IT, Procurement, Engineering, and HR.
- Interpreted the financials and operational issues for the General Managers.
- Conducted operational and system audits to improve information flow.
- Developed an expansion program into the Southwestern U.S.
- Negotiated with sub-trades, banks, and unions and introduced a partnering strategy for suppliers.
- Developed tax planning programs to reduce future tax exposure.
- Improved the process of managing change orders from clients to the site supervisor and sub-trades to ensure approval process integrity was maintained and proper mark-ups were applied.

Results: Grew the business from $36 million to $100 million. A new Southwest division was created which generated an additional $5 million in sales. Fixed costs were reduced by 5% through streamlining the construction and manufacturing divisions while improving the overall cash management.

Chief Financial Officer, ABC Construction Company (1983–1990 & returned in 1998–1999)

Second largest sewer and watermain contractor in the state.

Responsibilities: Established and implemented the guidelines for the principals to flow from insolvency to profitability and then establish the organization's operational integrity.

- Developed a survival strategy to deal with the financial issues of insolvency.
- Auctioned off surplus equipment and negotiated a new banking line and bonding facility.
- Converted manual accounting system into networked accounting process and created a comprehensive job-costing program to effectively control spending.
- Filed Notice of Appeals and negotiated two settlements with IRS.
- Coordinated a new corporate structure featuring estate and personal/corporate tax planning for the family-owned business.
- Dealt with day-to-day issues including labor, union, construction and client negotiations.

Results: Grew revenue from $6 million to $80 million, increasing net worth of company from $0 to $10 million. Obtained an additional yield of 30% over auction guarantee, reduced fixed costs by 6% and created incremental profit of $300,000. Won $950,000 in tax appeals and established a bank line of $5 million with a $40 million bonding facility.

Area Owner and Developer for Anytown, POBOXES Inc. (1992–1997)

POBOXES Inc. is a one-stop shop for small business products and services.

Responsibilities: Start-up new franchise stores and grow area profitablity.

- Trained and developed franchisees in addition to owning and operating three business centers.
- Researched and developed new profit centers including desktop publishing, computer rentals, binding services and 24 hour copy access.
- Resurrected and operated the Anytown Advertising Association.
- Created and chaired the Regional Marketing Association.
- Aggressively sold new franchises and managed the implementation including site selection, lease negotiations, build outs, and training.

Results: Achieved a 20% increase in center profitability system-wide, winning a number of awards for achieving the highest sales in USA as well as winning Award for Public Relations within the international network of over 3,500 MBE franchisees worldwide.

Vice President and Partner, FOURDOORs Construction Company (1991–1992)

Provincial general contractor specializing in road building and concrete installations.

Developed an organization that generated a consolidated $13 million in sales within 12 months through a vertically integrated group of companies comprised of a paving company, an equipment rental company and a land development company.

EARLY EMPLOYMENT HISTORY

Controller, ABC Company Limited (1982–1983)

Operational Auditor and Systems Analyst, American Ltd. (1981–1982)

Auditor, BBB Credit Union (1980)

Auditor, Xyz Corp. (1979)

EDUCATION

- Graduated in 1979 from State Polytechnical Institute with a Bachelor of Technology specializing in Accounting, Finance, Computer Science, and Marketing.
- Certified Management Accounting Program (CMA).
- Various courses to upgrade auditing, accounting, management consulting, marketing, and salesmanship skills, as well as Personal Growth and Development programs by several notable speakers including Jim Rohn, John Bailey, and Anthony Robbins.
- Lifestream training program.
- Certified Toastmaster (CTM).
- Design/Build Course.
- Real Estate Financing Course.

PERSONAL INTERESTS & ACTIVITIES

Family, action and animated movies, squash, public speaking, and maintaining an active interest in my community.

CONSTRUCTION: Construction Project Supervisor

John J. Johnston

123 Learning St., Anytown USA, 10101 Phone: 999-555-1212   email: johnj@yourname.com

John J. Johnston has over 30 years of project involvement within the heavy industrial sector, and 20 years experience at the **Project Superintendent**, **Project Manager**, or **Construction Manager** level, including projects in excess of $50,000,000.00. This also includes **international experience**, and a working knowledge of the **Spanish** language.

This experience has included all aspects of a project from the original concept, feasibility and scope definition, to engineering, detailed design, project implementation, construction supervision, and commissioning to start up.

On-site responsibilities have included total project control and coordination for the project management team, along with **contract administration** for all service/equipment suppliers, multi-trade subcontractors, and the supervision for direct hire labor.

Industry experience has included **Pulp and Paper, Cement Manufacturing, Coal Fired Utility Stations, Mining and Smelting Operations, Steel Manufacturing, Aluminum Smelters, and Municipal Waste Incineration.**

Completed projects include the following:

Project Manager for **ABC Energy Corp.** at the Big Creek Power Station during the addition of 280 megawatts of Co-Generation. Projects included reliability upgrades to the base plant as well as tie-ins and BCP at the newly constructed Co-Gen facility. **(2000–01)**

Construction Manager during AAA project for conversion to High Consistency Bleaching at **Eastern Pulp**. Project included the engineering design, supply, for conversion of 4 bleaching towers. This included new bottom unloaders, upgrade of pumping and transportation lines, new chemical metering and mixing equipment, along with new dewatering equipment. **Project schedule was successfully implemented to meet with the mill production requirements, and to provide the necessary mill outages required by equipment suppliers and contractors. (1995–96)**

Project Superintendent at the **BBB Pulp Mill,** during the major plant expansion in 1989. Project included EPCM contracts for a Flakt Pulp Dryer and Heat Recovery System, Recovery Boiler Fans, and a double casing Flakt Electrostatic Precipitator, complete with a 250' freestanding stack. Additional equipment included Machine Room and Bleach Plant ventilation systems. **Site responsibilities also included the onsite Project team, equipment expediting, construction purchasing, Cost Control, direct hire labor, and the administration of multi-trade subcontractors.   (1989)**

Construction Consultant at **CCC Inc**, during the installation of Flakt Electrostatic Precipitator and the maintenance overhaul of the Flakt Pulp Dryer. Project included the design and supply of a new Flakt Electrostatic Precipitator, new ID fan, ductwork, throttle control, isolation dampers, and salt cake conveying system. **While on-site for this project, a dryer inspection was performed, and the related recommendations led to the initiation and execution of a substantial dryer overhaul during a planned mill outage. (1988)**

Work Experience: Since 1997 have been contracting as an Independent Project Manager on a project-to-project basis… successfully completed projects include the following:

2004 July–October: Working with the **A& S** Atlantic Regional office, proposal scheduling & preparation as well as Fall Shutdown supervision at various pulp mills in the maritime region.

2003–2004: Recently completed project at the **Cement LLC**, as **Site Supervisor** for **CCC Environment Inc.** on a EPC Project for the replacement of an Electrostatic Precipitator with a Bag House Filter. Replacement performed on a 28-day outage during the month of April 2004.

2003: On-site at **Northern Refinery** Comp. as **Project Scheduler/Subcontractor Coordinator** with **A&B** during annual maintenance outage. Project includes recertification of 3 Catalytic Reactors, 2 Heat Exchangers, and maintenance repairs to the related auxiliary equipment.

2002: On-site **Contract Administrator** at the **Anytown Bridge Project**. Project included bridge removal, site improvement, and construction of a new two span bridge. Project also included upgrading of the approach roadways, both east and west side.

February 2000–May 2001: **Energy Corp Inc.** as a **Project Manager** at their Big Creek Station during the addition of 280 megawatts of Co-Generation. Projects included maintenance planning and reliability upgrades to the base plant as well as tie-ins to the newly constructed Co-Gen facility.

October 1999–February 2000: **UMA DDD Constructors**, working within the Projects Proposals team, preparing Capital Cost estimates and proposals.

Feb 1999–October 1999: **Calibration Inc.** as on-site **Project Manager** during the construction of the Calibration Facility, the first of its kind in North America. Project included the decommissioning of old compressor station and rebuild to install new Meter Calibration Equipment.

November 1997–December 1998: On-site to perform a study on the dust collection system within the pellet handling equipment, batch plant, and pneumatic conveying to the extruder equipment.

September 1997–October 1997: **Project Manager** with **ABC Industrial** during a rebuild of gas scrubbing equipment, and modifications to the Nova Transmissions Compressor Station.

September 1995–March 1997: **Consulting Inc**, as **Construction Manager** within the Pulp and Paper Sector. Full responsibility for all project site activities including the onsite Engineering and Design team, Inspection and Quality Control, equipment purchasing, and the contract administration for equipment and service providers. Also included the commissioning and start up phases.

May 1993–August 1995: **E&C Inc.** as a **Project Manager**, within the Environmental Services group. Duties included initial customer contact, preparation, and presentation of proposal documents, through engineering and design stages, to the purchasing and installation and/or rebuild of air pollution control equipment.

May 1991–April 1993: Operated as a **Project Manager** for several projects in **Chile**.

October 1980–May 1991: **ABB Inc.** as a **Project Superintendent,** during EPC projects for supply and installation of Air Pollution Control Equipment, Pulp Dryers, and Pneumatic Dust Conveying Systems. Total site responsibility for purchasing, cost control, subcontractors and direct hire labor. This also included two years in the Ottawa office preparing and submitting Capital Cost proposal packages, and final negotiations to successful receipt of Purchase Order.

1973–1980: **Industrial Engineering Inc,** as a **Project Leader** for the design, fabrication, and installation or rebuild of industrial equipment.

1970–1973: **Steel Company Ltd**. as a **Mechanical Analyst** during a three-year program to establish a safe and clean working environment for employees, and for a contaminant free product.

Education: Completed a three year diploma program in Mechanical Maintenance

Technical: Construction Assoc. Gold Seal Certificate as Project Manager
Construction Assoc. Gold Seal Certificate as Project Superintendent
Licensed Construction Millwright
Licensed as an Industrial Mechanic

Have participated in numerous seminars, courses, and workshops, including the following:

Effective Project Management   HATSCAN Contractor Due Diligence
DNV Practical Loss Management   DNV Modern Safety Management
Budget Preparation and Cost Control   Estimating for Successful Projects
Involved with development and presentation of Project Management Seminar for State College
Experienced user of Microsoft Office components, including MS Project 2003

CORPORATE: Corporate Account Manager, Recent Grad

JOHN J. JOHNSTON
123 Learning Street • Anytown USA • 10101 Phone 999.555.1212 • johnj@yourname.com

PROFILE

Corporate Account Manager. Excellent relationship builder and problem solver.

EDUCATION

2004   **State University** - Bachelor of Commerce (Honors)

WORK EXPERIENCE

POST-
GRAD
2004

WWW, *Corporate Account Manager*

- Established a base of 100 actively worked accounts from across the US specializing in the pharmaceutical and biotechnology industries.
- Initiated and developed relationships with corporate customers to provide expert analysis of their IT requirements.
- Consulted with clients on a regular basis to help design custom IT solutions that provide value to both their company and WWW.
- Participated in weekly vendor training sessions to stay up-to-date with the changing technology.

Executive Development Center, State University, *Program Support Staff*

SUMMER

2003

- Coordinated and initiated daily activities for participants to help promote work-life balance.
- Ensured all aspects of classroom environment operated efficiently to maintain the strict program schedule.
- Facilitated contact between program participants and administration.
- Developed and managed fitness and lifestyle components of the program ranging from intense 3-minute "fit-breaks" to group sporting events.
- Gained insight and exposure to business executives from across the world.

SUMMER

2002

Residence Life, State University, *Assistant*

- Created and constructed resource boxes for over 80 incoming residence dons.
- Led Residence Life team in the coordination and planning of logistics for all training sessions involving incoming dons and residence staff.
- Played key role in coordination of the annual S.A.C.U.H.O. Institute (State Association of College and University Housing Officers) training session. Role included logistical planning, speaker coordination, and all technological aspects.
- Designed and arranged residence portion of Orientation Week for all incoming first-year students.

EXTRA-CURRICULAR ACTIVITIES

2002/03   **Creative Director – Motion Newspaper**
- Managed and coordinated all creative aspects of the successful launch of new undergraduate newspaper.

FALL 2002   **Events Coordinator – University Marketing Association**

AWARDS

2000   • *Valedictorian – High School*
2000   • *Memorial Scholarship – University entrance scholarship for academic excellence*
2000   • *Business Education Award – Highest graduating average in business courses*
2000   • *Old Boys Scholarship – Highest academic achievement for student entering State University*
2000   • *Aiming For The Top – Government tuition scholarship*

CORPORATE: Corporate Accounting Financial Analyst

Alice J. Johnston
alicej@yourname.com

123 Learning Road, Anycity, AS 10101
999-555-1212

Profile
Highly dedicated **Financial Analyst** with over 3 years experience with a Fortune 20 company and proven track record of resourceful problem solving

Computer Experience
SAP, Business Warehouse, Oracle, Access, Proprietary Software (COMETS, CARS, Concur, K-Central)

Professional Experience
Financial Institute   **August 2002–September 2005**

East Coast Financial Analyst   Anycity, AS   October 2001–September 2005
- Selected as Financial Data Lead for Eastern Business Unit Strategy Team
- Headed East Coast post-merger synergy tracking for regions and business unit
- Chosen member of Inclusion and Diversity team and subcommittee lead
- Chosen member of Safety Team and developed business unit Safety Manual
- Developed and delivered eight (8) financial tracking reports for field personnel
- Responsible for upkeep and maintenance of Access reporting database
- Assisted customers with billing problems as a result of SAP conversion
- Involved in generating multi-million dollar 2003 budget for Eastern Business Unit
- Developed and delivered rebate summary to twelve (12) franchisees
- Coordinated and assisted with recruiting efforts at local universities

Accountant II   Anycity, AS   March 2001–October 2001
- Promoted after eight (8) months
- Discovered over $250,000 in uncollected self-amortization monies
- Completed internal audit of over 500 self-amortization loan files
- Responsible for journal entries, calculating note payoffs, and billing customers for self-amortization loan program

Data Specialist   Anycity, AS   August 2000–March 2001
- Promoted after eight (8) months
- Assisted in customer account set-ups for acquisition, consisting of over 5,700 accounts
- Responsible for customer account set-ups and maintenance in billing and financial systems
- Processed NOAS forms and RIU forms

Education
University of Anystate   **August 2000**
- B.B.A. Business Management and Finance
- Cumulative GPA: 3.91/4.0 – Summa Cum Laude

Society for Human Resource Management   **April 2003**
- Completed Human Resource Generalist Certificate Program

Community Involvement
Literacy Council of Northern Region   **September 2002–September 2003**
- Volunteer Tutor for Adult Basic Literacy
- Student tutored won 2003 Outstanding Student of the Year Award

Breast Cancer Foundation   **November 2003**
- Raised nearly $4,000 for breast cancer research
- Participating in Breast Cancer 3-Day, 60 mile walk for awareness and research

CORPORATE: Sr. Corporate Writer

ALICE J. JOHNSTON

123 Learning St., Anytown, USA 10101 Telephone: (999) 555-1212   Email: alicej@yourname.com

PROFILE

*A versatile **Corporate Writer** with a diverse background in many different mediums and industries.*
Proven talent in creative concept development and keen ability to simplify and invigorate complex content.
A strong communicator across all organizational levels. Top-notch and imaginative presentation skills.

PROFESSIONAL EXPERIENCE

ACC FINANCIAL GROUP, SENIOR WRITER   2001–2002
- Planned and implemented creative projects and communication initiatives.
- Facilitated employee and client communications by creating and maintaining interactive website content for Intranet and Internet.
- Developed corporate executive presentations, speeches, letters, and invitations for brokers and customers.
- Promoted insurance related products and services through conceptualizing and writing marketing materials (ads, brochures, fact sheets).

Accomplishments:
- Created the strategy to publicize promotional items section of Intranet site to internal employees that included: internal marketing promotion; designing user-friendly site map including easily downloadable order form; setting price points and sell-offs; and writing item descriptions.
- Improved understanding between staff and the president by developing jargon-free executive communications, including speeches and written correspondence.
- Oversaw project management and strategy development in absence of department manager.
- Active committee member for campaigns in the initial stages of development; wrote campaign material and brainstormed fund-raising initiatives.

CCC INC., COPYWRITER   2000
- Developed marketing and promotional campaigns for Big Cereal Company Inc., State Lottery Corporation, and State College.
- Conceived advertising concepts and promotional writing through brainstorming sessions.

Accomplishments:
- Developed poster and radio promotional campaign for The Lotto Dream Machine that led to strong viewership numbers when promotion aired on national television.

SMITH & SMITH, SENIOR WRITER   1999
- Conceptualized and wrote advertising, marketing, public/corporate relations and promotional strategies for clients that included: The American Marketing Association, Big Car Company, Big Bank, Big Gas Company.
- Constructed clear and concise staff and client presentations, free of industry jargon, for corporate executives.

Accomplishments:
- Won a coveted RSVP award in 1999 for brand campaign.
- Obtained commitments for further business as a direct result of the success of promotional magazine inserts personally written for the Big Car Company 2000 Launch.

PUBLIC INTEREST INC., COPYWRITER/SR PR EXECUTIVE   1996–1999
Accomplishments:
- Instrumental in securing at least three new (or renewed) client contracts.
- Conceived and wrote an interactive CD-ROM for High Hill Wireless that targeted different publics from investors to customers worldwide and was translated into 4 languages. Content included history of wireless, company background, and in-depth wireless product and technology information.

BIG PUBLISHERS ASSOCIATION, PROMOTIONS COORDINATOR   1995–1996
Accomplishments:
- Managed and executed PR and promotional initiatives on behalf of over 250 American magazines.
- Tripled American magazine catalogue subscription sales by developing and aggressively marketing a sales-oriented catalogue, and changing format from black and white to full colour with creative advertising.

NNN INC. – MULTIMEDIA CD-ROM developer, COPYWRITER   1994–1995

ACADEMIC & PROFESSIONAL AWARDS: RSVP AWARD IN 1999 FOR BIG BRAND CAMPAIGN; STATE SCHOLARSHIP (FOR LATIN AND GREEK); STATE MEMORIAL SCHOLARSHIP (OVERALL ACADEMIC STANDING)

EDUCATION
Public Relations Certificate, State Polytechnic University
Honors B.A., English and Drama Specialist, Dean's List, State University College

CORPORATE: Corporate Planning Strategy, Midlevel

John J. Johnston
123 Learning Street, Anytown, USA, 10101
Home: 999-555-1212 Email: johnj@yourname.com

Corporate Planning Professional with aggressive and innovative marketing ideas to inspire growth and profitability.

Major accomplishments

➢ Developed the corporate business plan for a newly merged investment fund company with $2 billion of assets under management
➢ Participated in the introduction of a new brand of funds which now represents 70% of the parent company's net sales
➢ Managed the development of a new Extranet site which provides multiple functionality to the investment dealers who market the company's investment funds
➢ Developed a intercorporate marketing agreement to distribute insurance products which supplemented existing sales by approximately $6 million in annual premiums
➢ Managed all programs and marketing responsibilities in support of a $25 million per year insurance business which experienced 40% per annum sales revenue growth during my tenure

Professional experience

Cover Max Co., Director, Marketing & Strategic Planning   Nov 1999–Present
➢ Participated in the development of this new company's 5 year strategic plan and financial analysis
➢ Implemented overall Internet architecture
➢ Developed marketing plan with annual budget of $6 million in support of 3 mutual fund brands
➢ Currently focused on vendor rationalization which should result in $1 million/year cost reduction

Group Invest Inc., Product Manager, Insurance & Estate Planning   Dec 1997–Nov 1999
➢ Developed estate planning strategy targeted at retaining clients with over $100k in assets
➢ Negotiated intercorporate agreements with insurance companies which added $6 million/year to a $25 million/year insurance operation
➢ Participated in development of the company's client segmentation strategy

Group Invest Inc., Training Consultant   Sept 1997–Dec 1997
➢ Created training program on insurance planning implemented to 3,700 Representatives and which supported a 40% / year growth in sales revenue
➢ Participated in development of asset allocation program which became a key sales tool

Group Invest Inc., Marketing Consultant   April 1995–Sept 1997
➢ Developed and facilitated training seminar on financial planning for new and experienced Representatives
➢ Provided individual sales support on estate planning to approximately 50 Representatives per day

Group Invest Inc., Group Products Consultant   April 1994–April 1995
➢ Provided plan information and advice to over 10,000 pension plan and clients representing $1 billion in assets
➢ Provided individual sales support on group investment planning to approx. 20 Representatives per day

Big Insurance, Representative   Dec 1992–April 1994
➢ Built and serviced a client base of almost 80 clients and $4 million of insurance coverage

Education

State University Master of Business Administration - Marketing/Finance Major, Dean's Honor List 1998
State University Bachelor of Arts - Economics Major/Fine Arts Minor 1990

Interests and hobbies: Tae Kwon Do Black Belt; Downhill Skiing and Racquet Sports; Fine Arts, Painting, and Sketching when I'm feeling mellow.

CORPORATE: Business Management

John J. Johnston, MBA, PMP

Anycity, Anystate, 555 999 1313 (Cell), 555 999 1212 (Home), johnj@yourname.com

Seasoned Director of Projects and Businesses with over 20 years of experience in Consumer Financial Services, Telecommunications, and International Businesses

Career Profile

- ❖ Managed large and complex projects for major business clients in U.S. including, ABC, XYZ, internal customers, meeting stringent budgets and schedules delivery requirements.
- ❖ Launched the VISA cards business for AMERIBANK in Anycountry that became the largest cards business in the Middle Region. Budgets of up to $40 MM and profit of $10 MM. Installed the largest VISA neon sign in Anycountry, visible at Royal palaces creating niche brand awareness & brand loyalty.
- ❖ Deployed an offshore technology solution for AMERIBANK that allowed launching of cards business in multiple Asian countries saving $ 5 MM per launch and 2 years in time for each.
- ❖ Led multi-functional and multicultural teams of up to 125 members including senior managers.
- ❖ During major crises held fort to provide business continuity to AMERIBANK while dispersing team members locally and internationally to insure their safety and well-being.

Experience Summary

Project Management:

- ▪ Currently manages large telecommunication projects involving cross-functional teams of project managers, engineers, technology professionals, and operations, for major clients in U.S. for ABC Company. Includes networks, infrastructures, and systems.

- ▪ Projects for ABC Company ranging in value up to $10 MM and teams of 4–30 members have included, New Product Introductions, Strategic International Joint Venture, Data Center Transfer, Voice over IP, Unified Messaging, Enterprise Customers, Business Continuity, and Lease Migrations. Other projects included Logistics Systems, Website Development, Y2K audits, and systems and business projects.

- ▪ Led New Products Introduction projects for Consumer Products for AMERIBANK.

Business Management:

- ▪ As an international VP of AMERIBANK managed several business divisions in Anycountry. Launched major products including VISA cards, MasterCard, debit cards, and other consumer credit products. Achieved the leadership position for the bank in the Middle Region.

- ▪ The management of businesses involved marketing, advertising, technology, training, financial control, credit extension, and HR.

- ▪ Managed the relationship with major advertising agencies including XYZ, and Direct Inc. Also led the niche Marketing activities including culture shows, painting exhibitions, printing of culture oriented calendars, International Squash, and other activities.

Management, Business, & Marketing Consulting:

- ▪ As a self-employed business consultant in U.S., provided consulting and strategic business advice to various U.S. and International customers. Activities included the creation of international business relationships for CompanyUS, Technologies Inc. and the ABC Group International. The range of products and services included Turbines, High Tech equipment, and recruitment services.

- ▪ Developed the slogan, "Your bank in America", for ABC Bank US. Also advised a bank in Anycountry on its consumer business strategy.

- ▪ Advised the Travel Inc. to become the business leader in the Anycountry U.S. Travel market. Coined the slogan, "Wherever you want to go!"

Career Chronology

Senior Project Manager, XYZ-ABC Company   **Sept. 2000–Current**

The recent merger of ABC Company and XYZ has resulted in the creation of the third largest telecommunications business in U.S. The project management activity involves telecommunication, data, Internet, new product launches and deployments.

President, ABCD   **Oct. 1992–Sept. 2000**

As the self-employed president of own consulting company provided project management, strategic advice, joint venture, and business consultation to U.S. and international companies. Clients included CompanyUS, Technologies Inc. and the ABC Group International, and others.

Vice President, AMERIBANK   **Sept. 1980–Sept. 1992**

Joined the international division of the world's largest bank as a trainee officer. The Bank was known as Anycountry Bank. Obtained commercial and consumer credit training at various international training centres. Became a division manager before moving to U.S. on business immigration.

Marketing Coordinator, Trading Group   **Aug. 1977–Aug. 1980**

Trading Group is one of the largest trading houses in the Middle Region and Anycountry. A private multinational enterprise, the group today comprises 50 companies employing nearly 9,000 people, with over $ 10 BB turnover. My role was to provide market support and competition intelligence to the JV partners.

Research Officer, NewBank   **Jun. 1975–Aug. 1977**

Began my career at the bank's Research Division that was considered a center of excellence in Anycountry in business and economics research. The bank was later nationalized.

Education, Training, and Skills

Education   MBA   University of Anycity, OtherCountry
          B.Sc (Hons) Statistics   University of Anycity, OtherCountry
          Comprehensive Project Management   University of Anystate, USA
          Management Consulting   University of Anystate, USA
(University of Anycity's MBA is considered a program of excellence that is globally well-respected.)

Training

People Management:

AMERIBANK's Managing People For Middle Managers, Managing Expectations, and Leadership Training. Various Online ABC Company Management Courses in People Management & Leadership.

Banking, Credit, Cards, and Marketing:

AMERIBANK's core Corporate Credit Course, Consumer Credit Course, Credit & Risk, Small Business Credit, Selling Financial Services, Collection Management, Direct Marketing, and Credit Cards. Courses conducted by expert trainers at various international locations.

Knowledge and use of Productivity Tools:

MS Office, MS Project, MS Access, SAP, In-house PM system - NPTS

Interests and Activities

As a writer, poet, and citizen, I believe in helping to enrich society. I have contributed to various activities at the Local Community Reading Series, The Art Gallery of State, and Anycity Arts Gallery. My personal goals include writing a book on Northrop Frye in Urdu. Currently associated with:

PEN USA   *Member Writers in Exile Committee*
Writers Forum   *Director*
Writers Forum Group @ Yahoo   *Moderator*
Local Community Reading Series   *Patron Member*
Local Community Center   *Supporting Member (Name on the Wall)*
Art Gallery of State   *Supporting Member*
Mentoring a group of potential Project Managers.

CREATIVE ADVERTISING: Creative Director/Copywriter

John J. Johnston
123 Learning St., Anytown, USA 10101 • 999.555.1212 • johnj@yourname.com

CAREER RELATED SKILLS

Creative & Production • Skilled **Creative Director/Copywriter** with proven ability to develop concepts, write copy, design and execute creative. Expert in the development and management of brands. Proven project manager with excellent networking skills. Able to maximize budgets by means of effective strategic planning combined with expert knowledge of media and production.

Marketing Consultant • Experienced in the management of all aspects of the marketing mix including market research, market planning, and strategic development. Strong strategic and creative thinker. Able to develop on-target strategies that accomplish marketing/communications objectives. Experienced consultant to start-up businesses.

Communications • Good presentation skills and demonstrated ability to effectively communicate ideas. Comfortable presenting to large audiences. Adept in the art of persuasion and possessed of a knack for motivating and inspiring others. Good interpersonal skills and the ability to effectively communicate across organizational lines. Expert liaison.

CAREER HISTORY

Creative Director & Copywriter • Freelance • 1988–Present
Creative Director and/or Copywriter on a variety of freelance projects for agencies, arts organizations, government, and private businesses. Successfully conceive, develop, and supervise advertising efforts for clients. Direct, coordinate and manage all production activities including design, art, photography, and printing. Provide consultation in my fields of expertise – i.e., strategic planning, concept development, brand development, and copywriting. Full list of clients available on request. Includes Big Brand, Big Air, Tier One Cleaner.

Marketing Consultant • Contract • ZYX Transportation • May 2001–May 2002
In collaboration with the founding partners, wrote the business plan for this company seeking venture capital for the launch of a foot passenger, fast ferry service. Involved extensive research of the industry and marketplace to determine feasibility and to facilitate the development of business/marketing strategies. Performed an advisory and consultative role on all aspects of the business and carried out liaison with media, business partners, and prospect investors.

Director of Marketing • Contract • flybye.com • April 2000–April 2001
Hired to research the industry and write the marketing plan and develop a brand for this start-up dotcom specializing in immersive imaging. Designed the business model and wrote a strategic plan for the company's development from start-up. Formulated marketing and positioning strategies, named the company, developed the flybye brand and corporate identity, and acted as Creative Director in the development of the company's web site. Took the company "live" in December of 2000.

Creative Director • Contract • Advertising Inc. • August 1996–November 1997
Hired to act as Creative Director with a mandate to revitalize the creative department and improve the quality of work being produced by this agency specializing in recruitment advertising. Managed and directed the creative efforts of a department of six. Assumed responsibility for the presentation of all creative (spec work) to prospect clients, supported the Account Executives in their efforts to develop new business, and acted as liaison between established clientele, Account Executives, and the creative department.

Writer/Producer/Director • 1984–1988
Author of numerous short fictional works in a variety of genres – playscripts, filmscripts, novellas, poetry, and short fictional works. As *Producer*, controlled and directed all "non creative" aspects of theatrical "pre" through "post" production, including budget, production schedules, choice and acquisition of venues, contracting of production personnel, etc. As *Director*, coordinated the development of all creative elements of production – i.e., performance, set and costume design, lighting and musical score.

EDUCATION

State University, State College • English Literature Major • 1980–1984

REFERENCES & PORTFOLIO

Available on request.

CREATIVE ADVERTISING: BAD—Art Director

ALICE JOHNSTON
123 Learning Ave.
Anytown, U.S.A.
phone: 999 555 1212
e-mail: alicej@yourname.com

OBJECTIVE

- To obtain a challenging position in the interactive multimedia environment.

OVERVIEW

- Multi-skilled in various fields of visual communication, including advertising, graphic design, photography, and illustration.

COMPETENCIES

- **Advertising :**

    • Posses two years experience as Art Director in an award-winning
      advertising agency.

    • Have worked with major international clients such as CleanClothes for fabric
    softener (Flowers), detergent (Scrub), Cosmetic (Purty), PaperProducts Inc. for
    Cuties diapers, POWER for energy drink (Smasher), American Insurance Co.
    for various direct marketing insurance products, Hot Shoe Label,
    as well as national client such as Stupor, a pharmaceutical company.

    • Proficient in developing creative concepts into effective advertising campaigns
    in various media, such as TV commercials, print ads, point of sale materials and
    direct marketing materials.

    • Experienced in supervising the production processes o
    shooting through off-line and on-line, and printed materi
    color separation.

    • Experienced in delegating and supervising graphic desi
    and have worked with independent photographers and T
    to develop and enhance the advertising campaign.

    • Have working knowledge of marketing research.

- **Graphic Design :**

    • Familiar with PC and Macintosh computer platform.

    • Experienced in developing conceptual ideas and desi
    company profiles, posters, packaging, booklets, leaflet

What's Wrong?

· Too many unnecessary extras and/or irrelevant information and/or repetition
· Sends a mixed message
· No declared job role
· Too long
· Leaves a strange or weird impression or doesn't suit the industry
· Spelling, grammatical, or word choice errors

CREATIVE ADVERTISING: BAD—Art Director (cont.)

• Skilled in computer design applications including PhotoShop, Freehand, Illustrator, PageMaker, QuarkXpress and CorelDraw.

• Skilled in HTML.

• Aquiring skills in web design such as, Adobe Premier, Adobe Acrobat, Macromedia Flash, Quick Time, DHTML, and JavaSricpt

• Working knowledge of printing production processes.

• **Photography :**

  • Skilled in black & white and color photography.

  • Have working knowledge of B&W darkroom processes.

  • Skilled in digital photo retouching using PhotoShop application.

  • Placed third in photography contest sponsored by CoffeeChain and Family Gallery, exhibited in Family Gallery and Well-Known Mall.

• **Illustration :**

  • Skilled in using different kinds of media, such as colored pencils, ink, poster color, markers, water colors, crayons, and computer aided illustration applications.

  • Experienced in implementing conceptual ideas into an illustrations.

  • Work has been published for magazine covers, posters of theatrical performances, brochures, T-shirts, and E-cards

WORK EXPERIENCE

• **Assistant Art Director**, February 1999 (freelance)
American Film Production

• **Graphic Designer**, February 1999 (freelance)
Hotstuff Design Inc.

• **Art Director**, July 1996 - June 1998
Overseas advertising association with Big Ad Brand Worldwide,
Bombay, India.

• **Graphic Designer** , February 1995 - July 1995
Smaller Ad Co. Fort Cochin, India.

VOLUNTEER EXPERIENCE

- **Project Designer**, April - August 1997
  "Good Earth 1997", designed the logo for an event sponsored by Environmental Fund (EF) to preserve wild places in the world. From developing the concept, up to its final implementation as promotional items.

- **Project Designer**, March - May 1995
  "Cello Cello AIDS", designed the program for an event to build AIDS awareness, held by India AIDS Foundation (NGOs).

- **Project Designer**, July - August 1995
  Produced a slide presentation titled "Ancient Bridges in Kerela" from concept to finish for Fishing Museum in Kovalam.

EDUCATION

- Web Design Course
  On The Web Studio, Anytown, U.S.A.
  April 1999 - July 1999

- BA in Graphic Design,
  State University, Bombay, India
  Graduated in March 1996

PORTFOLIO on REQUEST

CREATIVE ADVERTISING: Design Consultant

Alice J. Johnston

123 LEARNING STREET ANYCITY, USA 10101 999-555-1212 EMAIL: ALICEJ@YOURNAME.COM

Education

State School of Continuing
Studies, Fall 2000
Intensive Multimedia Design
and Production

Art College of Design, 91
AnyCity, CA
BFA, Graphic
Design/Packaging
Honors

City College, 88
AnyCity, NY
Undergraduate Studies

Professional Experience

Alice Wonder Design Inc., NY   6/01-present
Founder, Creative Director
Creative strategy and brand design consulting and implementation.
Clients: Jewels Advisors, Make UP, Crazio, Money Dad, Jill Laboratories,
Luxury, Studio10 Lab, The PD Group, Art Int'l, The Street Group.

Auction Artist Inc., NY   10/99-11/00
Vice President, Design & Creative Services Creative Director
Responsible for the development of creative strategy and brand management
worldwide. Oversaw all creative execution, including all corporate design
guidelines, collateral materials, advertising, exhibit signage, window display,
and all catalog design-related projects.

Follows & Company, NY   11/94-7/99
Senior Vice President and Creative Director for a marketing collateral firm.
Led concept development and oversaw creative execution for a variety of
media including print collateral, new media, display, and packaging.
Clients: Credit Card Bank, Make UP, Anycity Global Bank, Dish Mobile,
Pocket Saving Bank, Trustworthy Investments Brokers, Big Tech, Online.com,
Creative! Inc., WOW Radio (classical), News Radio (news)
New Media: Europe Bank CD ROM, www.wowradio.com

Malbury Interactive Media, CA   6/93-11/94
Developer of screen graphics for Digital Video Titles.
Clients: Film Studio, Film Pictures, Firmament

Hot Dog Marketing, CA   9/92-6/93
Art Director for corporate accounts. Developed brochures and promotional
pieces.
Clients: PST Computer, Icy Sweets, Tennis Shoe, Electronic Corp.

Raja Display Inc., CA   10/91-7/92
Art Director for all exhibit graphics and all printed material for the company.
Clients: Belgium Trade Development, Film Studio, Home Theater Champ

Freelance Experience   8/90-3/94

Clients: Ocean Cruise, Tight Jeans Co, Firmament, Cute Car U.S.

Awards & Honors

Victor International Corporation, Distinction of Design Concept, 99
HOT STUFF, American Corporation Competition, 97: Dish Mobile
Brandweek, 96: Creative! Inc. packaging
Communication Arts Design Annual Award for Packaging, 99
Art College Scholarships, spring 92, summer 93, Fall 98
Anycity Women's Club Scholarship, 90
Christopher Baird Scholarship, 90
Vernon Studio, Ltd., Scholarship, 88

CREATIVE ADVERTISING: Creative Director

John J. Johnston – Creative Director
123 Learning Street, AnyCity US, 10101
H 999-555-1212 **C** 999-555-1313
johnj@yourname.com

EXPERIENCE

Conceptualize, design, and produce a variety of corporate communications material for print and screen. Projects include corporate identity systems, brand development, internet/intranet design, high end capability brochures, industry newsletters, conference and even collateral, stationery systems, business journals, invitations, advertisements. Direct and supervise all design projects from initial client contact through final press check. Oversee and manager designers, photographers and illustrators. Art direct and manager designs for out sourced projects. Collaborate with project managers and production managers to strategically plan projects to meet or exceed client expectations. Provide design and production consultation to business groups and clients.

- Strategically designed a series of 63 Angel Investments consumer brochure covers. The challenge was to reinforce the existing brand equity, incorporate new levels of information, and refine the design to target a more upscale investor.

- Designed and branded Angel Investments Wealth Management literature system. Oversaw implementation of design to include brochures, sales kits, flyers, and mailers.

- Designed and managed production of multi-faceted design system for *Compass Direct Asset Management Group.*

- Developed and designed *Upstairs,* a business journal targeted at top level management

- Designed and produced a high profile folder/brochure series for PJ Christopher Trust Companies targeted at high net worth clients.

- Coordinated and directed photo shoots of CEO's from Booze (New York) Electric (Tokyo), Mobile (Stockholm), Big Bank (New York), Rocket Science (London)

- Collaborated with photographers, Dave Rutherford, A. Weston, and Max Trout.

- Developed and designed Corporate Identity and collateral systems for various business groups of Big House Brand

EMPLOYMENT

Angel Investments Inc.
Senior Designer/Co-Creative Director   *April 2002–present*

Compass Direct *formerly* **Ben Eve & Perkins**
Art Director/Designer   *June 1999–December 2001*

Big House Brand
Art Director/Designer   *May 1994–May 1999*
Assistant Art Director/Designer   *August 1991–April 1994*

SOFTWARE

QuarkXpress, Adobe Illustrator, Adobe Photoshop

EDUCATION

Einstein Institute, 1985
Completed two years of study in Masters Program from Communications with concentration in Graphic Design

State Institute of Technology, 1981
Bachelor of Fine Arts, Graphic Design

AWARDS

2003 and 2004 winner **American Star Design Award**: Star and Stripes Graphic Design Event

CREATIVE ADVERTISING: Designer

alice j. johnston

graphic design + art direction

123 learning street
anytown, usa 10101
h. (999) 555-1212
f. (999) 555-2222
alicej@email.com
www.alicej.com

EXPERIENCE

SUNDARI MAGAZINES – CREATIVE COMMUNICATIONS, Anycity
design consultant – june 2003 to the present
associate creative director – march 2001 – april 2003
senior art director – march 2000 – march 2001
Manage all design direction for advertising and promotion for the following magazines:
CityWoman, CityGirl!, Out of City Style, Bows and Buttons, Countess, Fancy Name, The Sundari Collective and
City & Scene. Creatively direct and oversee all photo shoots. Art direct and manage six junior/senior designers.

art director – september 1996 - march 2000
Conceptualized and directed the design and execution for various promotion pieces for all fourteen magazines
as well as the Special Publications at the Sundari Collective. These projects included: advertorials – design
layouts, photo shoots, media kits, sell sheets, multimedia sales presentations, magazine/corporate brand
identity, logo design, stationary programs, invitations, and custom publishing.
Art directed and managed four designers.

CHURCHILL AND MUNROE, A PUBLISHING COMPANY, Anycity
senior designer – may – august 1996 [freelance]
Designed all promotion and marketing collateral for entire book division. Design included: presentations,
brochures, self-mailers, stationery, invitations, and logo design for company events and conventions.

TROUT GROUP, INC., Anycity
designer – april 1995 – may 1996
Created and developed promotional material for all design projects. These pieces included: marketing
presentations, company brochures, stationery, and invitations. Designed and rendered all presentations for
client meetings.

CIAO INTERNATIONAL DEVELOPMENT ENGINEERING & CONTROL, Italy
designer – may – august 1994   [internship]
Applied a new computer design program (MountainVIEW) to the completion of drafted plans, section details,
and 3D models for BBV office project in Milan, Italy.

EDUCATION
STATE UNIVERSITY
Major: Design and Environmental Analysis, B.S., January 1995

SKILLS
- Extensive experience of Macintosh computer applications: QuarkXpress, Photoshop, Adobe
Illustrator, PowerPoint, and Microsoft Word
- Extensive experience in all aspects of production, photo shoots, pre-press, and printing
- Fluent in Spanish
- Studied Adobe After Effects at the School of Images, Fall 2001
- Attended film-title design seminars with Max Trout and Freddy Jeddy at the Karina Miller Theater,
Spring 2000
- Studied advanced black and white photography with Miguel Sabatini at TAPP, Fall 1998
- Studied design with Stanford Fleming at the School of Images, Spring 1998

CREDIT & COLLECTIONS: Customer Service Credit Collections

JOHN J. JOHNSTON
123 Learning St., Anytown, USA 10101, TEL: (999) 555-1212
johnj@yourname.com

TARGET ROLE: **Bilingual Credit & Collection or Customer Service Representative.**

HIGHLIGHTS OF SKILLS AND ABILITIES:
- Excellent verbal & written communication skills in English & Spanish
- Comprehensive understanding of the General Accounting environments
- Highly motivated team player and committed to professionalism
- Possess strong analytical and problem solving abilities
- Extremely dependable in completing projects accurately, meeting Deadlines, and is a specialist in credit bureau reports
- Adapt to new systems and methods easily

EMPLOYMENT EXPERIENCE:

BIG BANK/CAPITAL BANK, Bilingual Collector   **Aug 2003–Aug 2004**
- Service lease contract and collect on delinquent accounts (approx. 500–700)
- Reconcile account either independently or at request of customer
- Pull credit bureau reports & refers to legal dept. for court adjudication
- Perform customer service by responding to inquiries and complaints
- Prepare paperwork for general inquiries, correspondence and refers to Asset Management
- Handled incoming and outgoing bound calls (approx 60-150 calls/day)

LINX CORPORATION, Bilingual Associate   **April 2001–Aug 2003**
- Responsible for contacting delinquent borrowers to collect on delinquent accounts
- To educate and motivate borrowers who have delinquent loans and resolve the delinquency
- To rehabilitate delinquent loan, educating and assisting borrowers on repayment methods
- Analyze borrower's financial condition and ability to pay
- Summarize and update the Account Management system for all activity

COURT FINANCIAL, Bilingual Collection   **May 1999–March 2001**
- Run the dialer with the team for collecting & reminding the past due balance on the lease
- Apply standard collection techniques while maintaining customer service
- Pull credit bureau report and refers to legal for court judgment

Incoming Administrative Collections
- Respond to basic customer questions and resolve customer issues
- End-of-lease activities and inquiries in regard to their account
- Meet standard measurements set for collection activity, coordination customer payments, and billing related activities
- Processing payments through pap, credit cards, and assistance on more complex transactions

CREDIT CORP, Courtesy Call Collection Officer/Tracer   **1997–1999**
- Produced weekly schedules for efficient account collection
- Pull various credit histories in addition to tracing residence and employment information regarding past due account holders
- Developed ongoing correspondence with clients and account

EDUCATION AND PROFESSIONAL TRAINING:
CERTIFICATE IN Collections and Customer Service (Training Workshop)   **July 2003**
CERTIFICATE IN The 7 Habits of Highly Successful People   **July 2002**

1999   **DIPLOMA IN BANKING AND FINANCIAL MANAGEMENT**
Commercial Business College, Anytown, ST, USA

1993   **Bachelor Economics**, National University of Overseas University
1988   **Diploma of Commerce and Administrative studies**, Overseas University

CREDIT & COLLECTIONS: Credit & Collections Management

Alice J. Johnston
(999) 555 1212
Email: alicej@yourname.com

Credit Adjudicator/Credit & Collections Management/Mortgage & Loan

HIGHLIGHTS OF QUALIFICATIONS:
- ❖ Strong planning and organizational skills with the ability to multi-task effectively
- ❖ Always looking for new opportunities for success while helping others to achieve their objectives
- ❖ Sharp problem solving and presentation skills
- ❖ Extensive knowledge of financial instruments plus operation & supervision of computer systems (Accpac, SAP, Excel, , DOS etc.) as well as knowledge of credit reporting systems; Dun & Bradstreet, Lumbermans, Equifax etc.
- ❖ Developed a sharply defined, critical mode of evaluating clients' needs

EMPLOYMENT HISTORY:
Collections Supervisor 2003–2004 Big Money
- ϖ First party person-to-person, collection accounts, supervising 2 regions at both the retail branch and call center environment(s).
- ϖ Organizational charts, weekly and monthly objectives, as well as monthly action plans, and performance appraisals for all collection staff concerned.

Credit Manager Feb 2002–Aug 2003 The Group
- ❖ Hired as part of the Management team compiled to set up new company.
- ❖ Developed the new team divisions through hiring, maintaining, and setting up new procedures.
- ❖ Proficient credit and collection expertise through interpersonal and communication skills. Self-directed motivation due to strong A/R skills and positive attitude.
- ❖ Effective liaison between clients, staff, sales, as well as management.

Credit Analyst Jan 2001–Dec 2001 Big POP   (Contract)
- ❖ Routine account interpretation and maintenance dealing with account issues outside perimeters.
- ❖ Analyzed, approved, and monitored receivables on average of 2.8 million monthly.
- ❖ Part of a national team that proactively governed all aspects of the credit and receivable function with collections kept to DSO of 32 days.

Credit Manager Mar 1998–Dec 2000 Taxi Inc
- ❖ Reporting directly to the CEO & President managing all credit and A/R functions.
- ❖ Responsibility for a minimum of 1000, (corporate & personal) accounts, receivables and billings of 850K to 1M on average monthly.

Credit Analyst 1998 Big Bank Finance (Contract)
- ❖ Provided extensive input to the Y2K project, which included adjudication of dealer applications.
- ❖ Provided vision and experience to approve (in minimum turn around time) a high volume of applications on new dealer accounts with proper advance procedures.

Credit/Collection Analyst 1997 Big Oil Company (Contract)
- ❖ Executed, planned, monitored, and evaluated a high volume of commercial accounts for over limit, past due, collection disputes, and credit references in the NGL and chemical divisions.
- ❖ Collection of all U.S. and Canadian based clients to adhere to their strict payment terms.

Mortgage Specialist 1996–1997 Mortgage Corporation (Contract)
- ❖ Responded to queries and mainly underwriting issues for Anytown regions.
- ❖ Analysis of incoming & outgoing calls- clients, branches, solicitors & agents in a rapid paced environment.

Manager Loan and Mortgages 1994–1996 ABC Bank
- ❖ Worked with brokers, real estate agents, bankers, and the general public.
- ❖ Maintained/acquired an equitable loan portfolio through reviews, delinquencies, adjudication, marketing.
- ❖ Solicited, prepared, underwrote, and placed construction, mortgages, and/or loans/credit instruments.

Assistant Manager Operations/Supervisor Customer Service 1988–1994
XYZ Bank/STR Bank
- ❖ Facilitated departmental seminars on systems, services, company benefits, accounting, and remuneration.
- ❖ Hired staff, scheduled workflows, verified & audited all work processes, orientation for 10 area branches.

EDUCATION AND PROFESSIONAL DEVELOPMENT:
- ❖ Member of the Anytown Chamber of Commerce
- ❖ FCI designation
- ❖ Communications, Time Management, Fundamentals of Accounting
- ❖ Addiction Research Level 1; Fundamentals in Psychology

Alice J. Johnston

(999) 555-1212   alicej@yourname.com

Profile

Highly Organized Finance Professional/Manager with 18+ years experience in a credit/customer service management capacity.

- Excellent prioritization skills and superior attention to detail.
- Productive leader who motivates and empowers staff to achieve success as a cohesive team and achieve performance excellence.
- Strong interpersonal skills and ability to develop rapport with both customers and colleagues. Flexible and adaptable to any work environment & able to swiftly master new systems & procedures.
- Expert in all aspects of the credit function through direct & indirect sales channels. Extremely effective cash flow management capability with reputation for ability in organization restructuring.

Professional Experience

Big Credit Inc.   2001 to 2005
Credit Manager, Retail

Recruited based on exceptional reputation as an industry expert. Managed the operations of a 20+ staff Credit department with annual sales revenue of $1.8 billion.

- Led a cross-functional team who managed the integration of two divisions to reduce cost and improve efficiency. Eliminated duplication of functions, realigned job descriptions, re-engineered processes, and arranged appropriate training to meet goals.
- Facilitated merger of retail and distributor departments and fostered effective relations between divisions, which created a cohesive team.

Accomplishments

- Improved Day's Sales Outstanding (DSO) from 32 days to 17 days by creating formal repayment plans with distributors and streamlining operations. Conducted extensive negotiations with top-tier clients.
- Negotiated repayment contracts with 60 distributors province-wide to increase cash flow attainment and decrease the DSO.
- Improved year-end retail account status of 96% from approximately 80% of current receivables value at $90 million.
- Achieved 100% of established objectives for 3 consecutive years.
- Managed up to 18 credit analysts. Prepared performance appraisals, conducted one-on-one discussions, and arranged appropriate training to meet goals.

St. Anthony's Hospital   2000 to 2001
Accounts Receivable & Collections Manager

Hired to ensure patient and non-patient claims and commercial carrier billings were managed promptly in accordance with policies and procedures. Managed 17 direct reports.

- Restructured department to reflect the integration of St. Anthony's reduced DSO from 120 to 78 days.
- Facilitated seamless departmental operations involving billings, cash application, collections, and monthly financial reporting.
- Served as direct liaison to senior management within hospital, participated in process improvement efforts, and represented hospital in province-wide meetings to nurture relationships with ministries, patients, and insurance companies.

CREDIT & COLLECTIONS: Credit Manager, Retail (cont.)

Alice J. Johnston   Page 2

ZYX Inc.   1996 to 2000
Credit & Accounts Receivable Manager

Facilitated the system conversion and transition to establish a Receivables department and oversaw the Credit and Collection department. Responsible for $25 million receivables.

- Managed department of 27 employees and coordinated 10,000+ accounts and 250 distributors.
- Centralized accounts receivable department, significantly enhancing organization, credit and collections, and customer service functions.
- Oversaw departmental reports, sub-ledger accounts, budget administration, and cash flow projections.
- Served as primary liaison between senior management and sales/retail staff.
- Led efforts for Electronic Data Interchange implementation.

Molly LLC.   1988 to 1996
Manager, Credit & Accounts Receivables

Managed three Credit Administrators' and one Leasing Administrator's cash management activities.

- Managed leasing portfolio, prepared monthly reports, and reconciled accounts receivable ledger at month-end and year-end.
- Instituted and maintained successful collection and repossession program through external parties and monitored current credit information for all distributor accounts and assisted controller in accounting functions.

Professional Affiliation

Credit Institute of America

Computer Skills

High level of proficiency with SAP R3, AS 400, Oracle, Lotus Notes. Microsoft Office Suite and SMS (Shared Medical Services).

Professional Development

- Credit & Collection
- Recruiting & Staff Training
- Time Management
- Accounting

- Financial Statement Analysis
- Dealing with Difficult Customers
- Dealing with Internal & External Customers
- Sales Strategies

Interests

Puzzles and word games (particularly New York Times Crossword); exploring different states within the U.S.; hiking and camping—best in the summer.

CREDIT & COLLECTIONS: Credit Senior Manager

John J. Johnston, F.C.I., C.I.C.P., Corp.S
123 Learning St.
Anytown, USA 10101

Residence: (999) 555-1212
Cell: (999) 555-1313
Email: johnj@yourname.com

Results-driven professional with more than 15 years of progressive global experience. Proven track record in credit collections, accounts receivable, billing, customer service, sales, and work order management for retail, manufacturing, distribution, and service-related industries. Project management and cross-functional team leadership skills, facilitating both internal/external customers to maximize A/R performance, collections, D.S.O. results, mitigate financial risk, and achieve departmental goals and objectives. Highly articulate and effective communicator; works well with individuals and groups on all corporate levels.

AREAS OF EXPERTISE

CREDIT COLLECTION MANAGEMENT	CONSTRUCTION LIENS	CHANGE MANAGEMENT
A/R MANAGEMENT	CUSTOMER SERVICE MANAGEMENT	POLICY & PROCEDURAL ADMINISTRATION
DEDUCTION/CLAIMS PROCESSES	SALES/WORK ORDER MANAGEMENT	CONTINUOUS IMPROVEMENT FACILITATOR
FINANCIAL RISK ANALYSIS	PROJECT MANAGEMENT	INTERNATIONAL FREIGHT FORWARDING
CONTRACTS MANAGEMENT	5-S IMPROVEMENT MODEL	PRICE NEGOTIATIONS

PROFESSIONAL EXPERIENCE

Customer Service Manager (Int'l./Dom.), XYZ LLC.   **2001–2005**
Corporate Credit Manager

Customer Service Manager Role
- Initiated numerous project action plans and continuous improvement programs.
- Reduced administrative work order lead times from 3 days to 4 hours.
- Streamlined the CSR team from 54 to 39 associates.
- Increased customer satisfaction rating from 2.3 to 4.1 out of 5, in 6 months.
- Developed effective CSR training programs for product knowledge and response time.
- Implemented a revised warranty program with tracking codes to identify root causes.
- Requested by the Sector President to take on the role of Customer Service Manager.

Corporate Credit Manager Role
- Implemented a complete turnaround of the credit collection, claims/deduction, invoicing and cash management programs/policies by quality control points, financial, and monitoring tools.
- Reduced DSO on average by 45.5 days, past dues by 56%, and total monthly A/R balance from $110M to $67M from 2001–2003.

Director of Credit, FIXTURES INC.   **2000–2000**
- Set in motion control points and monitoring tools to control and reduce claims.
- Centralized the invoicing process (outsourced) to reduce DSO by 2 days representing a cost saving of $100K per annum.
- Centralized cash application process that reduced over 5000 hours of processing time in 6 regions representing a cost savings of $80K per annum.
- Developed a private label credit card with a major bank to reduce the accounts receivable portfolio by 40%, thereby having a positive impact on DSO, cost of capital (EVA), and risks exposure.
- Centralized the credit department from 6 regions to 1, representing a cost savings of $120K and the reduction of 3 Credit Managers in Phase I.

CREDIT & COLLECTIONS: Credit Senior Manager (cont.)

Director of Credit Services, CHOW INC.   **1998–2000**
National Credit Manager
- Implemented a turnaround of the credit collection, claims/deduction, invoicing, and cash management programs/policies through a series of project action and corrective action quality plans. Promoted by the President to the position of Director of Credit for outstanding performance.
- Reduced DSO by 22 days and past dues by over 25% on $130M of monthly A/R for 2 divisions.

International Customer Service Manager,) MMM LLC   **1994–1998**
International Sales Development Manager
Credit Manager (Domestic/ International)
International Customer Service Manager Role
- Finalized global procedure for shipment of orders to over 65 countries.
- Coordinated the set-up of European and South American branch offices.
- Negotiated cost reductions with International freight forwarders.
- Initiated and chaired Customer Service Group, which included sales, distribution, and shipping and reported directly to the Senior Management Committee.

International Sales Development Manager Role
- Increased international sales within my established markets by 40%.

Credit Manager Role
- Improved current position of receivables from 64% to 98%.

Senior Management Consultant,   **1992–1994**
- Interacted with in-house collection teams to maximize accounts receivable performance.

International Sales Manager, Food Distributors Inc.   **1978–1992**
- **Also, General Credit Manager, Divisional Credit Manager, Asst Divisional Credit Manager**

PROFESSIONAL DEVELOPMENT
- Leadership Forum 2002 (Executive Program) – State University
- Financial Statement Analysis/Effective Accts Rec. Collections Certificate
- Customer Profiles/Producing Results with Others Certificate
- Public Speaking/Human Relations Certificate
- Dynamic Sales & Marketing Certificate

EDUCATION & TRAINING
- Diploma in Credit Management (F.C.I.), State University
- Studies in Business & Accounting, State University
- FCIB/NACM, International Credit and Risk Management program, with State University, C.I.C.P. designation (Certified International Credit Professional)
- Corporate Streamlining Designation (Corp.S) with Corporate Technology Company Inc. (3,500 hrs on-site systematic business/functional review)
- Registering for the Executive MBA Program - September 2005

Member:
- U.S. Credit Research Foundation
- Executive Finance Committee - Y.M.C.A.
- N.A.C.M. - National Association of Credit Managers

DATA DIRECT MARKETING: Media Relationship Specialist

ALICE J. JOHNSTON

123 LEARNING ST. • ANYTOWN, USA • 10101 • (999) 555-1212
alicej@yourname.com

AREAS OF EXPERTISE
- **MEDIA RELATIONSHIP SPECIALIST**
- 6+ years of strategy and communications consulting in the areas of marketing, PR, and event management
- Project management, writing, and editing

CAREER HIGHLIGHTS

Shared Services Bureau

Marketing Team Leader, Customer Relationship Management   **2002–Present**

Transformed a conservative communications team of four into a leading-edge, award-winning e-marketing machine that delivers unique campaigns including web ads, direct marketing, "on hold" IVR jingles, streaming video, and Flash.
- Increased customer usage of the Bureau's e-services by 150% over the previous year
- Achieved an 80% customer satisfaction approval rating on key strategic marketing campaign

Big Telecommunications   **1998–2001**

Communications Consultant, HR Strategy

Provided strategic communications advice and guidance to several HR leaders and their respective teams to support the implementation of a new "talent strategy" that focused on the recruitment, mobility, and retention of top talent.

National Marketing and Event Manager, Competitive Recruitment

Increased successful university recruitment by more than 20% over the previous year by developing and implementing a multi-faceted marketing plan that built relationships with, and attracted, top student talent to work for the company.
- Project managed the writing, design, and production of all university marketing collateral and websites
- Managed and supervised all student and new grad recruiting events

Media Relations Coordinator, Talent Market Branding

Implemented a strategic media plan to market the company as a great place to work and employer of choice.
- Developed pitches to major North American media and university press resulting in positive media coverage in numerous publications
- Wrote and edited news releases, media advisories, message boards, presentations, and speeches
- Co-facilitated and coordinated three highly successful media training sessions for key spokespeople

Assistant News Editor, Employee Communications

Researched, wrote, photographed, and managed the layout, production, and distribution of *Big News*, an 8-page biweekly newspaper distributed to more than 4,000 employees.

EDUCATION
- Completed the *Project Management Series* workshop offered by the Project Management Institute (PMI)
- Completed several business courses at State University
- Received an Honors BA in Mass Communications from State University

AWARDS
- 2004 Public Relations Society ACE award for the Public Sector Campaign of the Year
- Two Certificates of Achievement in innovation from Management Board of Cabinet (2002, 2003)

VOLUNTEER INITIATIVES
- Currently serving on the *Foundation for Youth Leaders* Board of Directors and leading its PR Taskforce that has successfully pitched news stories to newspapers and television
- Youth mentor to high school students involved in the South Anytown Youth Assembly (SAYA)

DATA DIRECT MARKETING: Manager

eCRM Internet Professional

(with 10 years B2B startup, E-consulting, Advertising-Marketing experience)

John J. Johnston
123 Learning St.
Anytown, USA 10101
johnj@yourname.com
Home: 999.555.1212

PROFILE Senior Manager in B2B dotcom environments—seeking e-commerce/Internet division of F500 firm or well-funded, pre-IPO with budget for Q401 profitability.

ACCOMPLISHMENTS **ENTREPRENEURIAL EXPERIENCE**
• Member of executive management team reporting to the Board of Investors for startup eCRM, B2B professional services, and internet infrastructure technology firm. Have met budget every quarter; on track for Q401 profitability.

DOTCOM MANAGEMENT EXPERIENCE
• Developed and staffed professional services organization from the ground up; defined function, created service offering. Forecasted department P/L; met budget and revenue goals every quarter since hire.

TURN-AROUND EXPERIENCE
• Successfully merged two agency offices within same metropolitan area - $31M and $12M P/L budgets, respectively. Combined front- and back-office functions; lowered total overhead by 23%.

CLIENT AWARDS & RECOGNITION
• Big Brand Store, Inc. - 1995 & 1994 "Partners in Progress" Annual Service Award for Innovation & Excellence.

EXPERIENCE **connections.com**   10/1999–Present

Vice President
PROFESSIONAL SERVICES
Major Clients: Big Zap; International Writers Group; TV Inc.; News Inc.
• Executive member of internet-infrastructure BSP management team.
• Maintain senior-executive level relationships for all clients.
• Possess managerial/budget responsibility across (2) professional service departments responsible for managing client relationships.
• Lead client "technology development, delivery, integration, & service consultancy" life cycle across entire client roster.
• Forecast, set & meet "organic growth" budget expectations for all department services and ensure client engagement profitability.
• Participate with Business Development in the prospecting & acquisition of new businesses.
•• *Led team responsible for attaining largest consulting engagement in company history.*
•• *Have attained or beat budget objectives for every quarter since hire.*

AD Agency Inc.   2/1998–10/1999

Managing Director
Major Clients: Fast Automotive/Motorcycle; ABC Computer; Big Movers Inc.; Technology Toys Industrial Equipment LLC
• Led 65 member account mgt staff in the overall operation & management of ad agency office; retained & developed agency relationships and office revenue within 85-plus account client base.
• Maintained budget, P/L, & profit.
• Grew existing business & cross-sold clients into other advertising, marketing research, Internet product, and service offerings.
• Maintained all senior-level client relationships on top accounts.
•• *Merged 2 offices & streamlined operational efficacy through organizational restructuring.*
•• *Led marketing & implementation efforts for new business efforts resulting in $11M of new billings during 1999.*

Ad Agency Inc.	5/1996–2/1998

Group Marketing Director
WESTERN REGION (6 OFFICES)
<u>Major Clients</u>: Big Brand Car Company; ABC Computer; Industrial Inc.
• Acted as agency's corporate marketing contact & Sr. consultant/strategist on top client accounts.
• Directed strategic planning efforts on agency/client business within assigned region.
• Supervised office Marketing Managers and managed their activity to ensure client growth, retention, and development.
• Created new services to differentiate agency from competition.
• Managed all Internet design & online media planning projects within Western region.
•• *Secured key agency Internet projects: ABC Site Design-Online Marketing-National Homepage Program-Field Agents.*

Ad Agency Inc.	6/1995–5/1996

Group Marketing Director
MIDWEST REGION (5 OFFICES)
<u>Major Clients;</u> Big Brand Car Company; ABC Computer; Industrial Inc.
•• *Secured key agency Internet project.*
•• *Awarded 1995 "Future Leader" award for service excellence and innovation in marketing strategy.*

Ad Agency Inc.	4/1994–6/1995

Marketing Manager
CHICAGO OFFICE
<u>Clients</u>: Big Brand Car Company; ABC Computer; Industrial Inc.
•• *Awarded 1994 "Future Leader" award for service excellence and innovation in marketing strategy.*

Ad Agency Inc.	3/1993–4/1994

Marketing Manager
ST. LOUIS OFFICE
<u>Clients</u>: Big Brad Car Company; ABC Computer; Industrial Inc.; Big Brand Cola Company

Ad Agency Inc.	8/1991–3/1993

Account Executive
<u>Client</u>: Big Brand Cola Company

EDUCATION

Bachelor's Degree
State University
Bachelor of Science - Business Administration & Marketing (Double Major)

Master's Degree
Southern State University
Prior Candidate for Masters of Science - Marketing Research

ADDITIONAL INFORMATION

<u>PROFESSIONAL AREAS OF EXPERTISE</u>
• e-Commerce Technology Solutions & Integration/eCRM Technology deployment (proprietary systems).
• Strategic Account Management/Client Relationship Development.
• Internet Advertising & Data Mining.
• Project Management & Reporting.
• Database Design & Administration/Sales Analysis & Demographic Segmentation.
• PC-based Geo-Demographic Mapping & Analysis.
• Marketing Research—Quantitative & Qualitative Methodologies.
• Excellent Presentation Skills—Keynote; Large/Small Group; One-on-One.
• Sales & New Business Development Acumen.
• Profit & Loss Business Management/Budget Creation & Financial Management.

DATA DIRECT MARKETING: Direct Marketing

JOHN J. JOHNSTON, MBA

123 Learning St.
Anytown, USA 10101

Phone: (999) 555-1212
Email: johnj@yourname.com

DIRECT MARKETING PROFESSIONAL
Driving revenue growth through effective analysis and market penetration

AWARD-WINNING DIRECT MARKETING PROFESSIONAL offering superior campaign coordination, advanced analysis skills, creativity, and a keen attention to detail. Career success founded on consistent ability to aggressively market product lines and effectively allocate resources in order to maximize margin and revenue gains. Organized and highly efficient with a goal-oriented "get it done" attitude. Excellent communication, relationship building, and leadership skills, with the proven ability to motivate and coach sales teams to reach targets. Expertise includes:

- Integrated Direct Marketing
- Market Analysis & Research
- Direct Mail/Database Marketing
- Trade Shows & Events

- Market Positioning & Development
- Strategic Market Planning
- Product Management
- Budget & Vendor Management

- Experience working with the pharmaceutical industry in North America -

PROFESSIONAL EXPERIENCE

CCC LIMITED
$70 million division of Spegelhaus, a €3.4 billion global multi-media publisher specializing in the health, corporate and financial services, taxation, accounting, legal, regulatory, and education markets.

MARKETING MANAGER, TAX SUBSCRIPTIONS   2002–Present

Hired to turn around the firm's second largest product group entering its 6th year of declining revenues. Challenged to re-strategize the entire direct marketing program and meet revenue targets. Scope of accountability encompasses all advertising, direct mail, promotions, retention strategies, market research and segmentation, agency relations, management of 35 trade shows annually, and control of a $350,000 marketing budget.

- Selected and worked closely with a single agency to rebuild an integrated direct marketing strategy with more structure, thematic consistency, and overall quality to the communication.

- Coordinated with sales reps to generate quality lists, identify top prospects, develop compelling sales scripts, and overcome rejections.

➢ **On track to reach $13 million target, the first time in 6 years for this product group.**

➢ Identified an opportunity to redesign and re-launch a previously introduced product to an untapped market—increased response rate, improved advertising-to-sales ratio, and **generated over $250,000 in new revenue.**

➢ Successfully remarketed a declining Tax product through a coordinated strategy of advertising, direct mail, and sales rep contact—product decline has stopped and showing **positive growth for 2004.**

➢ Met target of increasing retention of tax subscription by 1% through strategically timed retention communications and sales rep contact.

➢ **Adjusted pricing to offset printing costs** and bring CD/Internet costs in line with market prices and **slashed newsletter costs by $200,000.**

INTELE INC.
Telesales Division of Call Worldwide, an international leader in executive training, conferences, and seminars, specializing in pharmaceutical compliance, corporate strategy, human resources, and best practices.

INSIDE SALES EXECUTIVE   2001

Market research, sales, and business development position responsible for penetrating new markets and stimulating revenue growth. Successfully targeted, contacted, and secured seminar contracts with pharmaceutical companies throughout North America.

- Conducted in-depth sales calls to key corporate executives throughout North America, effectively identified and addressed specific business requirements, communicated benefits, overcame objections, and closed the sale.

  - ➤ **3-Time Winner** – Top Weekly Sales
  - ➤ **3-Time Winner** – Top Monthly Dialer

CREST GROUP
U.S. $1.4 billion division of Bloger Corporation, specializing in the publication and distribution of print, CD-ROM, and online legal information products and services.

DIRECT RESPONSE MARKETER   1995–1997, 1998–2000

Designed and implemented comprehensive marketing programs for the sale of online, print, and CD-ROM-based legal products to jurisprudential client-base throughout U.S. Controlled U.S. $350,000 marketing budget.

- Improved market positioning and penetration through development and implementation of an integrated marketing strategy employing direct mail, advertising, inside sales campaigns, author relations, media relations, trade shows, and package promotions.

  - ➤ Successfully generated over **U.S. $1 million in sales annually**
  - ➤ Consistently **exceeded sales goals while operating under budget** (2000: Sales +11%, Costs -42%; 1999: Sales +3.5%, Costs -30%; 1998: Sales +1.15%, Costs -52.5%)
  - ➤ Identified opportunity to implement 40% price increase on popular item, effectively generating over **$250,000 in additional revenue**
  - ➤ **Captured 30% of market** within first 9 months of launch against established market leader
  - ➤ Achieved one of the fastest sales of new crest titles while maintaining low cost-to-sales ratio— campaign material additionally won **Bronze Medal for Outstanding Direct Mail Marketing** (Midwest Direct Marketing Association)
  - ➤ **Increased estate publication sales 30%**

ACT CORP
Microsoft solutions provider offering custom software development services throughout the Midwestern U.S.

SALES & MARKETING MANAGER   1997

Hired to develop and market ACT's online, web hosting, and e-commerce services. Responsibilities included market identification, analysis, pricing, target marketing, trade shows, and sales.

- Identified core niche in wholesaling industry based upon comprehensive market analysis and research—worked closely with IT specialists to develop product and supporting marketing materials.

WEST GROUP, INSIDE SALES   1994–1995

  - ➤ **Award Winner** – Top Annual Referral Sales, Top Monthly Direct Sales, Top Dialer
  - ➤ **4-Time Winner** – Top Monthly Referral Sales
  - ➤ **2-Time Winner** – "Make a Difference" Award

EDUCATION

MBA, Marketing – State University   1993
B.Sc., Marketing – State University   1991

PROFESSIONAL DEVELOPMENT

Using Direct Response Marketing to Build Your Business – School of Business   2004
Integrated Direct Marketing – Ernan Roman   2000

DATA DIRECT MARKETING: Sr. Manager

Alice J. Johnston
☎ H: (999) 555-1212 W: (999) 555-1313 ✆ alicej@yourname.com

PROFILE

A **Senior Manager** with experience in implementing and managing **Customer Relationship Management (CRM)** programs, initiatives and systems, loyalty, relationship, and direct marketing strategies and initiatives, along with print production and project management. A respected leader and accomplished facilitator, able to pull together diverse groups of stakeholders and instill a sense of team spirit, while efficiently working towards a common goal. Excellent communication and presentation skills, promoting strong relationships with internal and external colleagues.

SUMMARY OF EXPERIENCE

BIG CLOTHING STORE INC.   2000–present
Sr. Manager, Customer Relationship Management (2001–present)
Strategic Development:

- Developed BCS CRM's 5-year strategic plan and achieved buy-in of key stakeholders, reporting to the VP CRM/Co-Chief Privacy Officer.
- Developed and received Senior Executive Committee-level approval for an enterprise-wide Customer Information Collection Strategy, ensuring standardized collection, maintenance, and use of data on over 11.5 million customers across multiple customer touch points.
- Developed and received approval for a corporate-wide Customer Contact Centre Vision Strategy, which would ensure an easy and seamless service experience for over 12 million customer contacts annually.
- Managed the offer and marketing strategy, technology implementation, and ongoing analysis of a 6-month kiosk pilot project, showing an 18% increase in average dollars per transaction for kiosk users.
- Developed a 7-year CRM Technical Blueprint, in collaboration with the IS group, to map out the ideal technical infrastructure in order to holistically manage customer relationships.

Leadership:

- Lead collaborative initiatives among business units, gathering requirements from over 30 key stakeholders across the organization to ensure CRM strategies and technologies are developed in alignment with diverse business objectives.
- Developed CRM component of BCS University's Trainee Program in order to educate 70,000 employees throughout the company on the value and importance of being customer-focused.
- Developed an internal CRM website with 4-tiered access in order to give unique levels of the organization a relevant snap shot of CRM activity.
- Acted as program manager for the $500,000 Privacy Compliance Project, responsible for achieving and maintaining compliance as of January 2004, and continue to own and manage the BCS Privacy Office.
- Lead the development of the consolidation of 2 major customer information sources into one central Customer Information File containing 8.5 million active customer records.

Loyalty Manager, BIG CLOTHING Loyalty Management (2000–2001)
Leadership & Strategic Development:

- Developed and managed the nation-wide launch of BCS Rewards, the company's first enterprise-wide marketing initiative incorporating all 3 retail formats (over 400 stores), and enrolling over 600,000 new customers within the first 4 months.
- Facilitated stakeholder development workshops of up to 50 people, ensured collaboration and buy-in across diverse areas of the business including Marketing, Operations, Communications, Finance, and HR.
- Developed Key Performance Indicators and managed their accurate tracking, analysis, and weekly publication, including the achievement of a 55% penetration of transactions within the first 4 months.
- Presented marketing strategy, ongoing status reports, and results to BCS's Executive Committee.

Project Management:

- Acted as the BCS Rewards business project manager, managed a $20 million budget and worked closely with the IS Project Manager to ensure all tasks were completed on time and on strategy.
- Developed training materials, to ensure understanding and buy-in of 58,000 front-line associates.

NICE FITTING JEANS. Inc.   1997–1999
Loyalty Program Specialist, Consumer Relationships Department
Project Management:

- Managed the nation-wide launch, ongoing operations, and marketing of NFJ's first loyalty card program as a global pilot project in 55 retail locations, testing the value of relationship marketing.
- Coordinated the installation of POS terminals in 55 retail locations for real-time capture of UPC data.
- Managed the $15 million operational, technical, creative & communication budget.
- Determined criteria for identifying the most valuable consumers and successfully executed 4 targeted communications over a 12-month period, achieving a 20% response rate.

Leadership:

- Coordinated training seminars for associates in 55 stores, and 25 third party call-centre phone specialists.
- Interpreted and presented statistical information to show the benefits of full store participation.
- Compiled information, including cost benefit analysis, and created comprehensive presentations that summarized findings, and explained ongoing proposals to store owners.

BIG DESIGNS   1993–1997
Production & Project Manager (1994–1997)
Design Studio Manager/Operations Manager (1993)

PROFESSIONAL DEVELOPMENT
Management 1: The New Managers Course, Executive Learning Center (2005)
Strategic Leadership, State University (2003)
Various CRM-related seminars/conferences including Gartner, AMA & AARM (2000–Present)
Print Production Level Two, International Business Education Center (1995)

EDUCATION
Bachelor of Arts, State University (1993)

INTERESTS
Planning last-minute jaunts to Europe and fondly reminiscing about past travel excursions.
Taking pictures of friends' babies while working on becoming an accomplished photographer.
Keeping on top of my life-long journaling habit.

ENGINEERS: Chemical Engineer Oil Refining

John J. Johnston, BEng
Tel: (999) 555-1212 – 123 Learning St., Anytown, USA 10101 Email: johnj@yourname.com

Chemical/Process Engineer
Experienced and educated in Oil Refining/Petrochemical/Polymer Industries, trained/certified in ISO-9002/ISO-14001/Engineering Standards

HIGHLIGHTS OF QUALIFICATIONS:
- 12+ years experience working as a Process Chemical Engineer
- Demonstrated ability to adapt and implement technological changes
- Proven knowledge with Total Quality Management (ISO9002), Energy Conservation, Environmental Management (ISO14001), and PHA Techniques (HAZOP)
- Strong background in process including commissioning, monitoring, optimizing, troubleshooting, revamping, executing performance/capacity test runs; managing projects and preparing process flow diagrams (PFD) and process & instrument diagrams (P&ID)
- Proven problem solving abilities, including root case analysis of operational problems
- Excellent knowledge of industry standards, specifications, and regulations
- Proficient in CAD, PRO2, Hextran, Pipe Phase, Hysis

PROFESSIONAL EXPERIENCE:

Applied Mathematics Inc. 2003–Present
Education Program, International Institute
- Teaching students to use Mathematics in Engineering and Technology
- Instructing in applied Mathematics for students

Senior Process Engineer in Energy Conservation (Combustion) 1999–2002
Big Oil Refining Co., Iran; Licenser: U.O.P. Co., U.S.A.
- Determined need for, designed, and managed a project to convert the refinery from fuel oil to natural gas consumption
- Revised and revamped fuel gas network to increase fuel gas consumption from 20,000 Nm3/hr to 200,000 Nm3/hr with PRO2 and Pipe Phase software
- Designed and purchased metering/regulating natural gas station and filter separator bank
- Programmed refinery fuel consumption/waste calculation with Excel software
- Revamped fired heaters to increase capacity by changing burners and purchasing high duty, low excess air, low NOx and COx, low noise, and low flame height burners

Accomplishments
- Achieved 88% reduction in fuel oil consumption and SOx emission with heater and boiler optimizing and fuel converting and saved $120,000,000 per year
- Defined and executed environmental protection projects and ISO-14001 programs and achieved 30% reduction in waste and flaring and saved $ 50,000,000 per year

Senior Process Engineer in Polymer (Synthetic Rubber) Plant 1995–1999
Big Oil Refining Co., Iran; Licenser: U.O.P. Co., U.S.A.
- Commissioned and de-bottlenecked Synthetic Rubber plant
- Designed latex tanks, vacuum evaporation vessel, and wastewater systems
- Calculated new recipe for synthetic rubber
- Selected flux oil as effective, safe, and environmentally friendly polymer solvent
- Programmed raw material consumption calculations with Excel

Accomplishments
- Produced extended oil for synthetic rubber production and saved $600,000 per year
- Designed C4 raffinate (a by-product) purification system to achieve 80% reduction in impurity and saved $1,200,000 per year

Process Engineer in Crude Distillation Oil & Lubrication Oil Plants 1991–1995
Big Oil Refining Co., Iran; Licenser: U.O.P. Co., U.S.A.
- Optimized Crude Oil and Lube Oil plants and calculated material and heat balance
- Performed modification on de-cocking system and inert gas production system.
- Simulated and revamped atmospheric/vacuum distillation towers with PR2 software

Accomplishment
- Increased Lube Oil plant capacity from 10,000 to 14,000 barrels per day with executing several test runs and revamping

EDUCATION:
- Bachelor of Science Degree in Chemical Engineering, from State University, which is recognized as Bachelor of Eng. Degree in Chemical Engineering 1990

- International Certificate in Environmental Protection, Institute of Urban Construction and Environmental Protection, sponsored by the UN 2000

TRAINING COURSES: 1991–2002

- Control Valves
- Pumps and Turbines
- Fired Heaters
- Quality Auditor Course for ISO-9002
- Management Training Course
- Supervision Skills
- HAZOP and What If in OHSAS 18001

- Environmental Protection System ISO-14001
- Dynamic Process Simulation (Pro 2) Software
- Cooperation Management and Proposals System
- Energy Management—Fuel and Wastes
- Safety System and Occupational Health
- Hextran and Pinch Technology Network
- Processes Interrelation of Refining Units

AFFILIATION:
Membership of World Energy Council

ENGINEERS: Civil Engineer, Midlevel

John J. Johnston, P. Eng.

123 Learning Street Anytown, USA 10101	Tel.: (999) 555-1212 Email: johnj@yourname.com

SUMMARY:

Experience in the land surveying (geodetic), structural and municipal engineering fields. Combined working skills in the areas of: Statistical Analysis, Surveying and Structural Engineering Designs (using hand calculations, AutoCad, and other 3rd party software), Staff Supervision, Construction Site Reviews, and the Writing of Technical Reports. Strong interpersonal skills.

HIGHLIGHTS OF KEY QUALIFICATIONS:

- Various work experience in the surveying, civil, and structural engineering fields, including: the analysis and presentation of scientific and statistical data to engineers, surveyors, and managers.
- Professional Engineers (P. Eng.) member.
- Ongoing professional development in engineering and computer based skills.
- Strong skills in: numerical analysis, site inspection, and technical report writing.
- Strong interpersonal and team working skills, and proven leadership skills.

(RECENT) EDUCATION:

Bachelor of Science (B.Sc.); Business and Land Surveying
University of State, (Current part-time studies)

Professional Engineer (P. Eng.), P.E.O. Exam Program
University of State, (Part-time studies; completed 1990)

ENGINEERING WORK EXPERIENCE:

ABC INC. (Consulting Structural Engineer)   Oct. 2003–Oct. 2004
Engineer-In-Training,   Engineering Staff

- Assisted in designing for: structurally loaded beams and concrete & steel composite beams, and the bearing capacity of concrete block walls. Assisted in designing the composite beam and concrete floor slab, for a car garage in a semi-detached townhouse. Checked for the compliance of multi-occupancy units for the applicable provincial fire regulations. Prepared comprehensive interim reports for various sites.

- Responsible for the numerical analysis of the window mullions' resistance to wind pressure loads.

- AutoCAD Versions 14 & 2000: structural design details; provided numerical analysis and site reports for the structural stability of a stone gabion wall.

JOHN J. JOHNSTON, P. Eng.
Tel: (999) 555-1212

NATURAL RESOURCES   Feb. 1993–Sept. 2002
Control Survey Analyst, Office of the Surveyor General

- Provided technical analysis of control network surveys, as performed by private and public agencies. Interpreted the overall surveying results using the Least-Squares Method, as submitted by the field surveyors for mathematical and statistical adjustments as sent to the M.N.R. Produced interim and final recommendation reports for the above analysis. Evaluated the horizontal and vertical geodetic control networks for over 25 towns, municipalities, and cities, including integrating all of the existing control stations for the city.

- Evaluated Requests for Proposals (RFP's), and the awarding of contracts for the scanning and digital storage of achieved maps, plans and other printed materials. Provided instruction and supervision to summer students, and to temporary staff.

MINISTRY OF NATURAL RESOURCES   May 1990–Jan. 1993
Civil Engineering Technician, Drafting Services
VARIOUS FREELANCE ASSIGNMENTS   Jun. 1987–May 1990
Civil Engineering Technician
XYZ ASSOCIATES LLC.   Jun. 1986–May 1987
Civil Engineering Technician, Office Staff

PROFESSIONAL AFFILIATIONS:
- Member - _Professional Engineers (P.E.)_, **P. Eng.**
- Member - Society of Professional Engineers (S.P.E.)
- Member -_Association of Certified Engineering Technicians and Technologists (A.C.E.T.T)_, **_Certified Engineering Technologist (C.E.T.)_**
- Associate Member - Association of Land Surveyors (A.L.S.)

COMPUTER SKILLS:
- "Lotus SmartSuite 2000": WordPerfect, Lotus 1-2-3, Organizer
- Fortran and BASIC programming languages
- AutoCAD (Ver. 14 & 2000)
- Operating Systems: Windows (Ver. 3.1, 95 & 98), WinNT 4.0, and MS-DOS Platforms
- M.C.S.E. Exam Program (Networking with NT 4.0)

AWARDS:
- National Key Honor Society
  State University Chapter, inducted in 1997
- Dean's Honor List, State University

FURTHER EDUCATION:
Bachelor of Arts (B.A.) Mathematics, State University (1990)

Diploma in Civil Engineering Technology, State College (1986)

HOBBIES & INTERESTS:
Reading, Music, Squash, Team Sports.

ENGINEERS: Professional Engineer

Alice J. Johnston, Professional Engineer alicej@yourname.com 999 555-1212

CAREER EXPERIENCE

Alice J. Johnston, PROFESSIONAL ENGINEER, Consultant   1994–Present

- **Working as a specialist in energy, environmental, and facility management for institutional and government clients. Providing services as a project manager, facilitator, and business administrator.**
- **Present Position**, 2000–Present, Project Manager/Engineer for State Power Generation. Working in Nuclear Plants on various specialized tool projects up to $3.5 million.
- Plant Manager for Island Government Plant April 1997–May 2000. Accountable for the safe and effective operation and administration of a 4000 kilowatt, refuse-fired cogeneration plant. Staff complement 38; annual budget $5.3 million.
- Chief Engineer, NewHospital.
- Chaired Energy Management Task Force, Anytown Chapter 1993–1997.

STATE UNIVERSITY, Director, Physical Plant   1988–1994

- Responsible for the planning, design, construction, operations, maintenance, and security of buildings and grounds. Population was 24,000, with 150 acres, and 3.2 million square feet of space. Physical Plant's budget, $30M with a staff of 155.
- Directed $58M of construction. Developed plans for $300M in new buildings.
- Created $29M in self-financing energy-saving projects.
- Completed a holistic examination of HVAC, control systems, and environmental systems for 15 university buildings.
- **Nominated Facility Manager of the Year**, 1992 by Building Owners and Managers Association. Designated as a Certified Facility Manager 1993.

CARBOY BOARD OF EDUCATION, Supervisor   1986–1988

- Responsible for maintenance and construction of facilities. Eighty buildings, 5.2 million square feet, population 29,000, Physical Plant's budget was $20M with a staff of 526.
- Directed the building of new schools. Completed 750-student Elementary ($5.9M) school. Coordinated construction of 600-student Elementary ($5.5M) school.
- Managed staff of 35. Started the introduction of female staff into the male dominated trades. Upgraded maintenance staff skills to reduce outside contracting costs.
- Directed the installation of 16 new $28,000 portable classrooms.
- Managed the $750,000 retrofit of junior kindergarten.

COMPUTING COMPANY, Manager, Electrical & Mechanical Maintenance   1984–1986

Managed a staff of 20 tradesmen. Built a retrofit team and a maintenance team. Retrofitted three buildings in 18 months. Developed operation and maintenance strategies for 5 buildings.

ABC ENTERPRISES LIMITED, Maintenance and Services Engineer 1978–1984

Managed a staff of 75. Member of the management team. Developed the energy management plans and budgets for ABC facilities in USA.

STATE COLLEGE, Teaching Master   1978–1978

Taught stationary engineering and first year engineering.

EDUCATION AND CERTIFICATION

Bachelor of Science, Mechanical Engineering, State University   1973–1977

- Certified Arbitrator (Construction) 1996
- Certified Facility Manager, CFM   1993

John J. Johnston

123 LEARNING ST., ANYTOWN, USA 10101 PHONE: (999) 555-1212 EMAIL: JOHNJ@YOURNAME.COM

A Senior Electrical Engineer with more than fifteen years of diverse and progressive engineering experience, domestic and international. Demonstrated strong problem-solving skills in engineering and co-workers issues to achieve optimum efficiency. Well organized and self-motivated, easily adapts to new situations.

BUSINESS EXPERIENCE

PIPE THIS LTD, Electronic Engineering/Operation Support 1998–2005

A major international oil and gas pipeline integrity service company. To be acquired by P.I.P.I. February 2005.

Reported to: Operations Manager. Responsible for providing operation support for different projects running around the globe. Included maintaining control of computers' functionality in the field while upgrading and updating to newly developed software and applications, modifying conversion configuration, and final tool release. Also included provision of on-call support for worldwide field projects. Member of Year 2000, and QA committees.

- Extended the scope of responsibilities to release IIT (Intelligent Inspection Tools) by achieving knowledge of modification, integrity, and operation of the tools in short period.
- Installed, upgraded, tested, and implemented software specifically developed to launch, calibrate, and test of High Resolution Magnetic Flux Leakage and Ultra-Scan tools to survey pipelines' integrity by developing specially tracking database.
- Updated embedded firmware of Inspection Tools and GPS (Global Positioning System) Time Base Marker System.
- Developed easy access prerelease test database to acquire different reference information.
- Acquired, translated, and analyzed surveyed data thorough quick learning new software.
- Participated actively in QA department MRB (Material Review Board) meetings, reviewing projects' NCRs, ECRs, ECNs, audits, vendors' qualification, and corrective-preventive actions.

Accomplishments
- Saved 70% time to recover control computers by categorizing & developing special purpose recovery backup.
- Reduced significant cost by upgrading & repairing more than 50 tools' control-computers.
- Improved operations technicians' skills by taking initiative to develop user manual and helping them to efficiently use control computers.
- Took initiative to reduce peak load by modifying and preparing tools for projects.
- Consistently received positive feedback from technicians in field locations grateful for my support.

BINGS ENGINEERING CO., SENIOR ELECTRONIC ENGINEER PROJECT MANAGER 1992–1998

An engineering consultant & construction company; instrumentation, automation, and construction fields.

Reported to: President. Responsibilities included performing electronic engineering consulting, providing technical and financial proposal, and project management. Actively involved in construction industrial, warehouse, residential, and sport complexes in excess of 500,000 S.F., as well as development, installation, maintenance, and operation of Foreign City Port (PSO), over a 9-year period, which included power distribution stations, heavy load electrical cranes, electrical transporting machinery and electronic control panels.

- Designed, programmed, and installed prototype micro controller system to control and optimize elevator travelling and eliminated the old multi board control system.
- Increased measuring standard by implementing micro controller and designed micro-scale measurement devices to acquire production line measurement digitally.
- Consistently demonstrated strong problem solving skills involving technical, financial, and employee issues in projects, ability to thoroughly analyze multi-task issues.

Accomplishments
- Increased efficiency and significantly reduced time spent on project financial estimation, accounting, book keeping projects to final balance, and profitability by developing and implementing special computer programs.
- Arranging extra meetings to discuss project's progress, ensuring client's expectations were met.
- Proven to be multi-task skilled engineer by taking initiative to obtain different engineering experience by cooperation with Power and Civil Departments, which led to proficient management of many projects within the company.

ENGINEERS: Sr. Electrical Engineer (cont.)

STATE UNIVERSITY OF SCIENCE & TECH / Electronic Research, RESEARCH ASSISTANT   **1998–1992**

Responsibilities include assist design, test, and implement of electro-optical and electro-pneumatic system and develop manual and test procedures.

- Contributed in research, simulation, design, and implementation of prototype Electro-Optical AM, FM, and PM modulators and electromechanical pneumatic steering system.
- Successfully designed and fabricated testers, simulators, and developed manual and test procedures.

EDUCATION

B. Sc. - Electrical Engineering - IUST (State University of Science and Technology) - **1988**
Specialized on Microelectronics and Circuits.

Recipient of Outstanding Engineering award - **1990**

SUMMARY OF TECHNICAL SKILLS

- Extensive knowledge of: Low power/low frequency analog circuit design, high performance static and dynamic logic design, Micro controller system design, Assembler programming language, PCB layout design, and Proportional Navigation System.
- Well experienced with electronic test instruments and installation, Ultra-Scan and MFL technology based survey tools, PC LANs and workstation Networks, MSWindows, DOS, Excel, Access, and PowerPoint. Familiar with DAQ analysis and design, Protel, Visual Basic, Java, ACAD, ORCAD, and Lab-View.
- Adept at learning new software, achieving new skills, and updating required knowledge to fulfil career qualifications.

COMMUNITY CONTRIBUTIONS

- National Baseball Team Player, Technical Committee Member, Chairman Umpiring Committee, and General Secretary 1984 to 2003
- International Hockey Federation coaching certificate 1980

ENGINEERS: Sr. Management Engineering Pro.

John J. Johnston MEng P.Eng. PMP
123 Learning St., Anytown, USA 10101 (999) 555-1212 johnj@yourname.com

EXECUTIVE SUMMARY

Senior Management Engineering Professional. Highlights include:

- **Technically Versatile** - BEng (Mech) & MEng (Elec), Certificate of Competency II (Marine Eng), patent holder, with additional experience in electrochemistry (fuel cells, semi-fuel cells, and fuel reforming) and nuclear engineering.

- **Professionally Adaptable** - 19 years direct management experience in a variety of fast-paced and demanding public and private sector roles as well as consulting. Managed diverse professional teams up to 75, budgets up to $17 million, contractors & sub-contractors in the engineering services, project/program management, and high-tech/R&D industries.

- **Eminently Dependable** - Excellent record for reliability, product delivery, project rescue, customer satisfaction. Secret (Level II) security clearance.

PROFESSIONAL EXPERIENCE

XYZ Company   2001–2004
A small public company developing fuel cell systems.

Director of Programs
Reporting to the CEO, managed multiple concurrent projects, day-to-day operations and personnel, financial and technical resources of an engineering group 20 strong, from technicians to PhDs, to meet diverse Company goals, objectives, and policies. Actively participated in the strategic and tactical business planning processes.
- Managed the design, build, global deployment, remote monitoring, and support of first-of-class revolutionary power generation systems (>$1.5 million) across three continents (Asia, Europe, and North America).
- Managed the Information Technology group, which delivered a real-time, internet-based remote control system for distributed power generation systems and all data aggregation, distribution, and security for XYZ's systems worldwide.
- Acquired new development contracts totalling $1 million and effectively managed a $6.5 million strategic contract, meeting all performance targets and expectations.
- Managed the doubling in size of the Engineering Group from 10 to 20 professionals.
- Ensured the delivery of a critical project by directly managing a strategic fuel cell simulator development project under extreme resource constraints. This project was finished in time for the intended international inverter competition and was completed under budget.
- Reorganized the engineering group to a more responsive and self-determining structure by training, mentoring, delegating, and promoting deserving individuals into positions of new responsibility.

ABC INTERNATIONAL   1995–2001
A large employee-owned company providing engineering services.

Program Manager   2000–2001
Reporting to the VP, managed the Information Technology program, consisting of 18 information technology professionals in the fields of IT security, Internet-based databases, VPNs, and project management support to multiple, concurrent federal government projects.
- Developed new markets by analyzing government initiatives, identifying linkages to company capabilities, developed a winning proposal for the competitive bid, and implemented the new Performance Measurement capability.
- Managed the relocation and consolidation of the IT group with the head office location without any significant interruption of the ongoing business operations.
- Provided all levels of support for sales, proposal writing, ranging from document final approval and QA through to actual initiating, estimating, and writing of proposals.

ENGINEERS: Sr. Management Engineering Pro. (cont.)

Project Manager   1995–2000

Reporting to the Project Director, managed a Defence Department Project Management Office (PMO) for various system development, integration, and procurement projects. This included all financial, technical/integration, and reporting/coordination aspects for multi-disciplinary technology-driven projects, such as:

- Resuscitated a $16.7 million project to replace all radiation detection equipment for the navy, army, and air force.
- Rescued an $8.4 million Nuclear Emergency Response equipment procurement project, completed on time and under budget, with improved service to the client. Major sub-projects include:
  - Re-equipped the ABC Nuclear Emergency Response action teams with enhanced, more cost-effective radiation detection equipment, on time and under budget.
  - Delivered, from initial concept to actual installation, a distributed radiation detection system to monitor nuclear submarines. This competitive procurement of a computer-networked, fully integrated, radiation monitoring system for the navy was completed on time and under budget.

NAVY Lieutenant-Commander (Engineer)   1975–1995

Project Manager, Fuel Cell R&D Program   1992–1995
Directorate of Marine & Electrical Engineering
Managed the navy's Fuel Cell R&D projects (totaling over $11 million), which included fuel cell technologies projects and other fuel cell, modeling, and related projects for DND, dynamic modeling of submarine propulsion systems and alternate fuel cell technologies.

- Identified and implemented an opportunity to salvage a promising R&D technology at reduced cost. As a result, a key technology remained in the United States, 8 high-tech jobs were maintained, and the project saved over $1.5 million, all within acceptable levels of risk.

Department Head, Marine Systems Engineering   1990–1992
Naval Officer's Training Centre
Managed the Marine Engineering division of the Naval Officers Training Centre, consisting of 7 engineers, plus support staff, to train over 100 naval officers/engineers per year.

- Delivered an accelerated audit and implementation of the new marine engineering classification standards and training system. This project was completed one year early, and reduced the classification training time by 33% and still exists today as the primary classification training system for all Marine Engineers.

Chief Engineering Officer   1988–1990
Directed the Engineering Department of over 75 technicians and professionals. Activities included the maintenance, operation, and refinement of all marine systems onboard a destroyer, including propulsion, power generation, and distribution, HVAC, hotel facilities, and damage control.

- Led the department from a chaotic, dysfunctional department to a cohesive, effective team helping to earn the best record for maintenance and reliability for ship's operations and the top engineering training record within Training Group Pacific.

EDUCATION & PROFESSIONAL AFFILIATIONS

Master of Electrical Engineering (Instrumentation & Control), Military College, 1986
Bachelor of Science (Mechanical Engineering), State University, 1979

- **Certified Project Management Professional (PMP), 2000**
- **Professional Engineer (P.Eng.), 1991**

OTHER ACCOMPLISHMENTS

- Published and presented 17 papers in international symposia (bibliography available upon request).
- Earned 2 patents in the solar power conversion field (details available upon request).

INTERESTS

- New technologies, exploring wireless world, creative writing, avid reader, rescuing strays & racing dogs.

ENGINEERS: BAD—Engineering Manager

John J. Johnston
123 Learning St
Anytown, USA 010101
(999) 555-1212
johnj@yourname.com

WORK EXPERIENCE:

04/99–present   **WALLY Division of The Plastics Group**

Engineering Manager - 06/00 through present
- Certified Six Sigma Blackbelt (received Six Sigma Blackbelt training).
- Conducted Six Sigma projects to investigate and eliminate sources of variation in injection molded components.
- Trained three employees as Six Sigma Greenbelts.
- Assisted in teaching a Six Sigma Champions' class for senior management.
- Coordinated daily activities of a project engineer and maintenance department.
- Prepared quotations (piece price and tooling) for injection molded components.
- Managed new product launches.

Coordinated tooling transfers from other plastics divisions and other molders.

Project Engineer - 04/99 through 05/00
- Responsible for specification and approval of mechanical design and material selection for production molding tools, coordinated sample part runs, supervised dimensional and cosmetic inspections, assisted in production launches.
- Assisted Quality Assurance department with QS9000 readiness as well as day-to-day quality concerns.

09/97–02/99   **Mass Newtype Inc.**

Project Engineer
- Planned and coordinated fabrication of prototype components.
- Sourced special tooling, materials, and hardware for prototype molds and prototype parts.
- Tracked and expedited fabrication to ensure timely completion of projects.
- Coordinated outside services (painting, engraving).
- Designed brackets, components, and jigs.
- Liaison with mold shops for quotes on tooling as well as design revisions on parts and molds.

11/95–05/97   **Injection Molding Systems.**

Project Engineer - Mold Division - Thincan Group
- Responsible for liaison between customers and mold division.
- Gathered all customer expectations and technical information required for design of molds.
- Tracked and expedited manufacturing to ensure timely completion of molds.
- Oversaw testing and troubleshooting of new and refurbished molds.
- Scheduled work for 17 mold designers.

11/87–01/95   **Auto Manufacturing Inc.**
Launch Manager - 06/93 through 01/95
- Provided expertise and advice to lighting design teams on headli[...] platforms.
- Responsible for specification and approval of mechanical design[...] molding tools, coordinated prototype part runs, and supervised d[...] inspections.
- Manager of Auto's design team (3 employees) during this time.

What's Wrong?
- Too many bullet points
- Lackluster objective/profile or lack thereof
- Uninspiring and boring
- No declared job role

ENGINEERS: BAD—Engineering Manager (cont.)

John J. Johnston 2-

Manufacturing Engineer/Design Engineer – 11/87 through 05/93
- Handled all design work and coordinated testing for engineering changes to automotive headlights.
- Supervised training programs for optical engineer and 2 mechanical designers.
- Program manager (assembly) for transfer of production of a high volume headlamp model from England to U.S.
- Responsible for generating CAD drawings and 3-D mathdata for headlamp components.
- Interfaced with optical designers, car platform engineers, and manufacturing team.
- Received training in automotive drafting practices, materials selection, testing requirements, and optical design.
- Received 3-D CAD training "CGS" system.
- Responsible for start-up and troubleshooting of 2 semi-automated assembly cells.
- Developed and optimized programs for 4-axis assembly robots.
- Designed and implemented jigs and fixtures for improved efficiency, durability, and ergonomics.

EDUCATION:
B.Sc. with Honors - Mechanical Engineering; State University.
Graduated April 1987 (received the "Francis Farrelly Scholarship" for academic achievement and the "Engineering Freshman Award" for intramural athletics).

Travel Sabbatical; 03/95 through 08/95.

INTERESTS: Skiing, motorcycling, charity work.

EVENT PLANNING: Junior Events Coordinator

John J. Johnston
123 Learning St., Anytown, USA 10101
999-555-1212 Email: johnj@yourname.com

Junior Events Coordinator looking to support diverse and challenging events.
- Exceptional writing, communication, and organizational skills
- Multimedia production and graphics design background
- Familiar with both creative and corporate environments

Work History
Cultural Dig   February–June 2003

I was an integral part of the organizing team responsible for the **Cultural Dig Creative Summit 2003,** one of the country's largest media events dealing with diversity. In addition to my regular duties I generated promotional material for Summit, edited MC scripts, and answered general inbound inquiries related to Summit programming. At Cultural Dig I held the following positions:

Associate Producer of Black & White
- Responsible for selecting and programming, both broadcast and independent submissions for spotlight screenings, and Q and A's
- Worked with TV and radio, religion TV, to create interactive forum for broadcasters to showcase programming to both industry experts and emerging creators
- Liaised with producers/creators to facilitate opportune environment for sharing of ideas

Pitch Coordinator, Pitch Contest
- Received and logged all pitches to the Cultural Dig *Open Door Pitch Contest*
- Liaised with all pitch entrants, judges, and trainers
- Part of selection committee that decided the 28 finalists in 7 categories
- Coordinated training sessions for 28 finalists at the CBC
- Helped facilitate training sessions, which included top commissioning broadcasters from major U.S. Networks
- Sat in on the Open Door Public Pitch at the Cultural Dig Creative Summit 2003
- Sat in on private judging discussions to decide winners held by top television producers and executives

Submissions Coordinator
- Received and tracked all submissions for the Creative Summit 2003
  Submissions included:
  - *Big Bank Scholarships*; *Story Clinic* (broadcast journalism and drama)
  - *Face T* (booked 1-on-1 meetings with applicants and network execs)

Insurance Inc. Summers through university
Customer Service Rep/Marketing
- Responsible for office admin. I also implemented a marketing program that resulted in a 10% increase in business

Student Achievements
- Produced short doc, "Monitor", which was nominated at 2002 State University Film Awards
- Produced 2 interactive multimedia projects that were chosen for year-end Fine Arts Cultural Studies show at Anytown Gallery, State University 2002

Interests: Reading (fiction, sociology, news, pop culture); Music (pop, jazz, instrumental); Sports (golf, boxing)

Education
- Honors Degree Fine Arts Cultural Studies, State University – Magna Cum Laude
- Certificate in Film Studies, State University (completion date: Dec 2003)

EVENT PLANNING: Event & Travel Planner

Alice J. Johnston
123 Learning Street
Anytown, USA 10101
Tel: 999-555-1212, Cell: 999-555-1313
Email: alicej@yourname.com

Event Planner and Travel Expert
specializing in conferences anywhere in the world

EXPERIENCE

Program Manager/Account Manager (Incentives & Conference Planners)
- Manage up to 5 programmes of varying formats at any time.
- Operate incentive travel, events, and conferences for groups of 6–500.
  - Interact daily with clients from financial, insurance, agricultural, architectural, security, medical, pharmaceutical, telecommunications, and technological industries.
  - Negotiate with suppliers to ensure the cost efficient use of resources.
  - Manage program suppliers and client in a timely manner for planning and operating hotel accommodation, transfers, air travel, group meals, activities, and producing print materials.
  - Supervise on-site implementation of program while fulfilling last minute client needs with venue staff.
  - Create and monitor budgets and expenses to ensure the programs meet client objectives.
  - Received Requests for Proposals and prepare full budget and descriptive outlines for programs.
  - Research and develop new concepts for proposals domestically and internationally.
- Operated inaugural web-based merchandise incentive program for 400.
  - Managed web architect and merchandise supplier for web-building and order fulfilment.
  - Worked daily with automotive client to monitor special requests and communicate with participants.
  - Control account receivables and disbursements.

Trip Planner (Dreger & Co.)
- Coordinated 20 expeditions and 7 active holiday tours.
  - Made reservations for and payments to 110 hotels, 75 activities, and 20 transportation companies.
  - Organized delivery of equipment and information for 100 departures of up to 26 people.
  - Researched, planned, and guided 9-day trip in Belize and Guatemala.

Assistant Travel Advisor (Tubb Travel)
- Assisted 8-person sales team.
  - Coordinated logistics of traveller information and sales of equipment for 4700 high-end clientele.
  - Aided with sales of tours to travellers, based on client request, dates of travel, and availability.

EMPLOYMENT HISTORY

2001–Present INCENTIVES INC. - Incentive Program and Conference Planning
1998–2001 CONFERENCE PLANNERS - Incentive Travel and Conference Planning
1994–1997 TUBB TRAVEL - World-wide Luxury Biking and Walking Tour Operator

SKILLS AND QUALIFICATIONS

- Have strong communication, service, organizational, planning, problem solving, and sales skills.
- Speak French as a second language; Hold EU Passport.

EDUCATION

1997 Deuxième Degré France Universitié - France, *Français Langue Etrangère*
1990–1994 Bachelor of Arts, State University, Political *Studies*

VOLUNTEER WORK AND PERSONAL HOBBIES
Playing beginner women's hockey; Hosting activities for members at my sailing club (as well as actually sailing); Committee Member on Food Drive event; Relaxing with a glass of wine and a friend.

EVENT PLANNING: Sr. Event & Meeting Planning

Alice J. Johnston
123 Learning St., Anytown, USA 10101
999-555-1212, alicej@yourname.com

SPECIALTY: Over 15 years of knowledge and expertise in both

Event and Meeting Production and
Multimedia Production Management

Personal Mission: To produce quality corporate communications projects on a single or multi-faceted level, on time and in budget.

Employment Experience

Senior Producer, Invisions Productions   **2002 to Present**

- Produce print and multimedia projects, live events, and meetings from proposal to art direction to implementation stages
- Create templates for production and budget management
- Participate in the theme and concept creative for various projects

Clients include: Big Bank, Hot Car Co. Bank, Luxury Cars, Postal Inc., HUGE Copies Inc., Big Oil, ABC Insurance, Party Mates, thekidsbenefit.com

Vice President, Backtalk Inc.   **2001 to 2002**

- Founded the 8-person interactive department
- Managed the creation and production of all Microsoft websites
- Managed the production of all projects including website creation, banner ads, interactive programs, meeting presentations, etc.
- Created a work progress and time management system for the creative & programming team
- Produced budgets and critical paths for all projects, average 10 or more projects per month, budgets ranging $1,000 to $50,000
- Produced revenue and expense reports for accounting purposes

Clients included: Harddrives Inc., Software LLC, Beer Co., Big Bucks Magazine, Telemar Inc.

Vice President, Pluvox Communications   **1998 to 2001**

- Cofounded a 7-person interactive company
- Created marketing and promotional strategies for the company
- Financial control of company revenue and investments
- 400% company sales growth from $150,000 to $6 million per annum in 2.5 years*
- Managed the company's daily operation
- Directed the employment of full-time and freelance workers
- Liaised with clients from initiation to completion of all projects including website creation, interactive CD ROM, meeting presentations, corporate identities, graphic design
- On site production of corporate meetings in various international cities
- While managing Pluvox, also held the position of Production Manager

Clients included: Body Lotions Inc., Netall, Big Tower, Chocolatiers, Clix Camera, Pharmaceuticals LLC

EVENT PLANNING: Sr. Event & Meeting Planning (cont.)

Director, Corporate Communications, Rainbow Communications   *1993 to 1998*

- Single handedly managed audio visual projects in all stages from proposal, concept, production to budget reconciliation
- Supervised all freelance writers, video producers, graphic designers, set designers, live performers, staging companies, and other suppliers
- Revenue of the division grew from $0 to $.5 million per annum in 10 years

Clients included: Big Bank, Chocolate lovers Inc., Pharma-sell Inc.

Early Work History

Media Liaison and Event Planner, Big Clients Inc.   *1991 to 1993*
Event Planner, Anytown Operations   *1989 to 1991*
Assistant Event Planner, Anytown Operations   *1989*

Education

School of Speech & Drama (State College)
Effective Communications courses

State College of Art, major in Communications and Design

State University BFA, major in Visual Communication

Interests

Reading; travel; organizing anything; getting a kick out of projects that end up under budget

EVENT PLANNING: Vice President Events

ALICE J. JOHNSTON
123 Learning Ave.
Anytown, NY, USA

Phone: (999) 555-1212
Cell: (999) 555-1313
Email: alicej@yourname.com

VICE PRESIDENT EVENTS

With 15 years experience in entertainment;
specializing in event marketing, promotions, and communications.

Key Accomplishments

- Creation of effective marketing programs and promotions.
- Concept development and implementation.
- Excellent reputation in the industry.

Background

Career includes experience at the Olympic Bid presentation (Overseas City), Anytown NBA Basketball Club, 1996 Olympic Games (Atlanta, GA), The Cohesive Games (Bigtown), and the Anytown NFL Football Club. Considered to be a professional, creative, and extremely organized executive who understands the market and gets the job done.

Areas of Expertise

- Event marketing
- Start up
- Strategic planning
- Financial management and budgeting

- Production and logistics
- Creative development and writing
- Public and media relations
- Corporate sponsorship

Career History

Vice President Events, Immediate Results Group   *Aug. 1999–Present*

Engaged by President to co-build an event management division that would successfully dovetail with his travel and incentive business. IRG employed 3 full time personnel at the beginning of my tenure.
- Implemented short- and long-term strategies designed to develop and grow existing relationships.
- Utilized my industry network to build properties.
- Created and implemented departmental structure and operational plans (i.e. event production, pitch documents, resource planning, etc.)

IRG now employs over 25 full time personnel and 30 seasonal employees throughout North America and manages over 20 programs annually.

Event Management Consultant (Project Summary)   *Sept. 1997–Aug. 1999*

- Project managed special events that included Beer Blast Evening Gathering, Mission of Achievement, Walk of Fame.
- Associate producer credit includes major vocalist Trudy Tingler's "Sing it Home" television special.
- Entertainment Producer for Men's Basketball and Women's Soccer at 1998 Cohesive Games.

Sr. Manager Game & Venue Operations, Anytown NBA Basketball Club   *Nov. 1994–Aug. 1997*

Hired by Lance McHenry to lead the game production and operations division. Challenged with the task of creating the public "face" of the club vis-à-vis the live game experience. Additionally responsible for developing the operations plan.
- Created and produced Anytown game day experience (look and feel, entertainment, contesting, partner programs, etc.)
- Established and maintained relationships with League, corporate partners, vendors, and consultants.

Hailed as the "Launch of the Year" by the news and entertainment media, the Anytown NBA Club was an unqualified success.

EVENT PLANNING: Vice President Events (cont.)

<u>*ALICE JOHNSTON*</u>
Career History

Hot Sport Producer, Olympic Games, Atlanta, GA (Special Project)   **1996**
Selected by the League as 1 of only 3 producers to accompany league officials to the 1996 Olympic Games.
- Produced hot sport games for men's and women's hot sport and medals ceremonies.
- Created and developed entertainment protocol plus script and rundown templates for production team.

PR & Promotions Manager, 1994 World Championship of Horseshoes   **Jan. 1994–Nov. 1994**
- Produced entertainment for horseshoe games at three venues.
- Promoted public relations opportunities to media and coordinated media events.
- Liaised with HSA on technical regulations and issues.
- Integrated media buying and promotional efforts into the corporate strategic plan.

Promotions Coordinator, Anytown Home Team Football Club   **Feb. 1991–Jan. 1994**

Account Executive, Looky Here Communications Inc.   **Aug. 1988–Feb 1991**

Independent Producer   **1983–1988**

Professional Highlights

Bid – Overseas City Presentation (*Overseas City*)	**2002**
Bid – Evaluation Committee Gala Dinner (*Anytown*)	**2002**
Sexy Lux Car (street festival) (*OtherTown*)	**2001–2003**
Luxury of Cars (luxury auto show)(*Othertown*)	**2001 and 2002**
Triathlon World Cup (*Anytown*)	**2001 and 2002**
Lux Car Party (Formula 1 Weekend) (*Othertown & CarTown*)	**1999–2003**
Walk of Fame (*Anytown*)	**1999**
Beer Blast Evening Gathering (*Anytown*)	**1998**
1998 Cohesive Games (*Bigtown*)	**1998**
Trudy Tingler's "Sing it On Home" (*Cheesetown*)	**1998**
NBA All-Star Game (*Anytown.*)	**1997**
1996 Olympic Games (*Atlanta, GA*)	**1996**
Anytown NBA Basketball -includes inaugural season opener (*Anytown*)	**199–1997**
B-ball Fest 3-on-3 (*Anytown*)	**1995–1996**
NBA Draft (*Anytown*)	**1995**
1994 World Championship of Horseshoes (*Anytown*)	**1994**
Anytown Local Team Football (*Anytown*)	**1991–1994**
Hopeful Food Sponsor Cycling Challenge (*Anytown*)	**1990**
Brent Buddy Softball Tournament (*Anytown*)	**1989–1990**

EVENT PLANNING: BAD—Event Planning

John J. Johnston
123 Learning Street, Anytown, USA 10101 (999) 555-1212

OBJECTIVE

To obtain a position in Event/Marketing/Sales

EXPERIENCE

BIG Baby. January 2000–Present
Event/Marketing Coordinator

Planning and executing all in-store and clientele events
Liaised with graphic designers in production of all Marketing materials.
Coordinated all marketing campaigns
Wrote Press Releases
Developed Marketing Calendar
Responsible for all New Store Events
Coordinated Direct Mail Campaigns
Liaised with journalists and newspapers in regards to stories and promotions.
Responsible for promotion, product development, and demographic research analysis
Purchased advertising space to promote events and promotions
Wrote advertising copy

Bet You'll Like It! January 199 –December 1999
Special Events Coordinator/Marketing Coordinator

Coordinated and Organized special events such as, reception's, open houses, anniversary celebrations,
business functions, fashion shows, and special days
This involved careful planning, organizing, analyzing coordination, and attention to detail.
Coordinated all marketing campaigns
Coordinated direct mail campaigns
Liaised with journalists and newspapers in regards to stories and promotions
Purchased advertising space to promote events and promotions
Wrote advertising copy
Acted as the direct contact for clientele

ABC Inc. September 1994–January 1997
Event/Marketing Coordinator

Assisted the Merchandise Manager through the onset of the catalogue, since this w
Booked all Newspaper and Magazine placements
Liaised with graphic designers in production of all marketing materials
Coordinated direct mail campaigns
Implemented print campaigns for the catalogue
Liaised with designers to produce catalogue
Purchased advertising space to promote events and promotions
Wrote advertising copy
Planning and executing all in-store and clientele events

What's Wrong?
- Too many bullet points
- Dense text—I'm too bored to read this all.
- Lackluster objective/profile or lack thereof
- No declared job role
- No accomplishments or specific and measurable results
- Too many unnecessary extras and/or irrelevant information and/or repetition
- Uninspiring and boring
- Leaves a strange or weird impression or doesn't suit the industry

EVENT PLANNING: BAD—Event Planning (cont.)

John J. Johnston
123 Learning Street, Anytown, USA 10101 (999) 555-1212

ABC Inc. September 1994–January 1997 Continued….
Event/Marketing Coordinator

Coordinated all marketing campaigns
Wrote Press Releases
Developed Marketing Calendar
Responsible for all New Store and other Events
Liaised with journalists and newspapers in regards to stories and promotions
Responsible for promotion, product development, and demographic research analysis

EDUCATION

State University 1992–1994
Bachelor of Arts Social Sciences

State University 1994–1996
Sociology

SKILLS

Strong personal and written presentation skills
Excellent analytical and organizational skills
Works well in team environment
Enjoys and thrives working under pressure
Microsoft Word PC
Microsoft Excel PC
Microsoft Access
Microsoft Power Point PC
Internet Explorer
Outlook Express
Microsoft Outlook
Familiar with STS

INTERESTS

Junior League of Events, Promotions, Internet Site, Marketing, Managing a team
Attending theater, opera, ballet, etc.
Reading
Sewing
Tennis
Golf
Skiing
Camping

REFERENCES

Available upon request

Alice J. Johnston

123 Learning St., Anytown, USA 10101 Tel. (999) 555-1212 Email: alicej@yourname.com

Award-winning Cosmetics Consultant looking for a Supervisory Role

EXPERIENCE

Mask, Big Name Store Inc. Cosmetics Consultant 2003–2005
- Participated with counter staff in planning and executing special events and promotions.
- Conducted consultations using Mask's computer and custom fitted products to meet individuals' needs.
- Completed training seminars aimed at providing tools to exceed individual sales goals and customers' expectations.
- Train new staff members in policies and procedures.

Accomplishments
- Many returning customers who ask specifically for my services and advice.
- Awarded **Mask Star Award** for the highest quality consulting.
- Was always staffed with new hires, as management trusted my training and support.

EDUCATION

State University, Fashion Institute of Technology, Presently Enrolled.

Bachelor of Science in International Marketing, Cum Laude, 2003
- Export practices and procedures for consumer and industrial products.
- Performance analysis. Audits for global firms with recommendations for future planning.
- Implemented plans to enhance marketing position.
- Training and staffing.

SKILLS

Computer skills:
MS Office, Photoshop, Adobe Illustrator.

Languages:
Polish (fluent), Russian (continuing studies).

INTERESTS

Other:
Piano, art, travel (extensively in Europe).

FASHION: Fashion Consultant

Alice J. Johnston

123 Learning St., Anytown, USA 10101 (999) 555-1212 alicej@yourname.com

High End Fashion Consultant and Sales Associate.

PROFESSIONAL EXPERIENCE

SERGE G. Fashion –

Sales Associate/Fashion Consultant   April 2003–September 2004

➢ Sold high end luxury garments to clients through accurate and astute assessment of client needs and overall product knowledge

➢ Collaboration with fashion consultants on approaches to securing, developing, and maintaining customer and brand loyalty and enhancing customer shopping experiences

➢ Analyzing sales and revenue reports

➢ Developed insightful knowledge or prêt-a-porter fashion

Professional Highlights and Achievements

➢ Exceeded monthly sales quotas by an average of 40%

➢ Highest sales within department for 2004

➢ Organized private shopping night for high net worth clients

Big Fashion Store –

Sales Associate/Customer Service Representative   June 2002–April 2003

➢ Sold high end luxury garments to a wide range of clientele

➢ Proven ability to recognize and respond to trends in the market

➢ Training and management of contracting staff

➢ Implementation of vender and department seasonal plans

➢ Attended product knowledge seminars by local and international designers to discuss product knowledge based sales strategies

Professional Highlights and Achievements

➢ Consistently exceeded monthly sales quotas

➢ Involved in the roll out of new POS system

➢ Selected by Flame as the "In-store Flame specialist" at Big Fashion out of 30 people

EDUCATION

International Academy of Design and Technology,
Fashion Design Diploma – Honors   2002

State Institute of Technology (NAIT),
Business Marketing Diploma – Honors   2001

Alice J. Johnston

123 Learning St., Anytown, USA 10101
(999) 555-1212 (home)   (999) 555-1313 (cell)

PROFILE: An energetic, career-oriented **sales and marketing Retail Fashion Professional**, with strong management skills. Offers creative and innovative strategies, tactics, and approaches by utilizing analytical and logical methods resultant in a strong capability for problem solving. Dynamic team oriented approach with strong people management skills. Able to motivate others, resulting in optimum productivity and performance. Strong negotiation and communication skills; action oriented with strong follow-up skills.

CAREER EXPERIENCE:

BIG BRAND NAME STORE MANAGER, COSMETICS & FRAGRANCES.   2003–Present
- Sales development & event marketing partnership with vendor base; sales growth of 15% per annum.
- Direction and training of over 110 commissioned sales associates. Negotiation, strategic planning, and development of individualized marketing plan with each cosmetic and fragrance vendor. Liaison between corporate buying office, store management, and vendor base.
- Awarded numerous store awards for sales achievement, customer satisfaction, and event marketing, in store marketing, and community involvement.
- Chair and/or member of numerous store, regional, and corporate committees and task forces.

BIG BRAND NAME STORE. SALES MANAGER, MENSWEAR.   2000–2003
- Sales development of all aspects of men's ready-to-wear, apparel, and furnishings. Direction and training of approximately 55 sales associates—commission and non-commission.
- Surpassed company expectations in sales, gross profit, expense control, inventory management, and customer satisfaction.

BIG BRAND NAME STORE, MERCHANDISE MANAGER, SOFT GOODS.   1998–2000
- Control of all aspects of merchandise management for women's and men's RTW, accessories, shoes, cosmetics, and budget divisions

BIG BRAND NAME STORE, STORE MANAGER.   1995–1998
- Complete control of full-line department store operation: sales development, markdown control, gross profit development, expense, and payroll management.
- Direction and training of over 250 selling and non-selling staff.
- Liaisons with company corporate offices, merchants association, community groups, and company task forces. Successfully directed and relaunched store through a $3.5 million renovation.

BIG BRAND NAME STORE, MERCHANDISE INFO/INVESTMENT MANAGER.   1991–1995

- Directing $200 million in computer automated merchandise purchasing per annum.
- Development and monitoring of $12 million expense budget centre and 45 staff.

BIG BRAND NAME STORE, ASSISTANT DIVISIONAL SALES AND MARKETING MANAGER, CHILDREN'S WEAR.   1989–1991
- Sales mgt of 16 stores resulted in net sales volume of $25 million; growth of 30% per annum.

DEPARTMENT CO., SALES & MARKETING MANAGEMENT.   1986–1989
- Rapidly promoted throughout career from entry-level floor management to regional management.

PROFESSIONAL TRAINING & EDUCATION:
1989 -   BIG BRAND NAME STORE - Preparatory Management Course
1986 -   Fine Arts & Design, Masters Degree, Fashion Institute of Technology
1984 -   Fashion Design and Merchandising Diploma, Honors State Polytechnic Institute

GENERAL INTERESTS: Martial arts, swimming, writing, painting, sculpting, cooking, and reading.
LANGUAGES: Fluency in English, Italian, and French. Rudimentary Spanish.
COMPUTER SKILLS: Proficiency in all Microsoft Office Applications, Lotus.

FASHION: Fashion and Retail Quality Control

John J. Johnston

123 Learning St., Anytown, USA 10101   Tel.: (999) 555-1212
Email johnj@yourname.com

PROFILE

> **Production and quality control in fashion management or operations**

HIGHLIGHTS OF QUALIFICATIONS

- Analytical and management skills with solid technical and creative knowledge, maturity, and flexibility.
- Building internal and external business relationships.
- Negotiating win-win agreement for deadlines/pricing.
- Directing multidisciplinary teams/projects: communicating targets, projects, goals, objectives and visions.
- Developing cost effective tools and marketing strategies.
- Creating and establishing new programs, initiatives, and processes.

PROFESSIONAL EXPERIENCE AND ACHIEVEMENTS

BIG FASHION INC   2003–Present
Sales & Marketing and Development Consultant
- Analyzed, distinguished, and improved marketing pitch for cross national advertising.
- Authored and executed an introduction letter about BF for national direct sales approach.
- Formulated and generated an introduction about BF services for 1st time encounters.

Undertook accountability for western U.S. sales in order to increase sales. Upgraded the marketing, corporate image, and presentation of BF. **Result**: Spearheaded the company's vision in a new direction and increased sales by 10% in one year.

Formulated proposals and mandates for presentation of tenderer and services. **Result**: Elevated the corporate image to new standards and facilitated sales closures.

Sold and prospected over $60,000.00 of consulting services and products with companies such as ABB, Le Fashion, Knutty Knitters, Confection LLC, and others. **Result**: Achieved targets, maintained and ensured BF's structure for continuous growth.

GIRLIE CLOTHING INC.   2001–2002
Quality Control Management
- Created, planned, and orchestrated operation start-up of Quality Control department.
- Planned, researched, documented procedures, hired staff, and implemented developed standards.
- Championed the development within the Quality and Buying department to address critical productivity, efficiency, and quality issues.

Researched standard grade rules and body measurements. Identified, researched, and implemented the Quality Control needs in order to function. **Result**: Set the foundation of quality control, as well as established the department based on industry standards.

Directed daily activities and weekly staff meetings. Planned and developed daily workload, analyzed daily activities, prioritized daily tasks, scheduled, and delegated the workload to staff. **Result**: Achieved daily set targets and also contributed to facilitating the efficiency and rapidity of the department with minimal negative impact.

John J. Johnston   **page 2**
BIG STORE   1999–2001
Production/Quality Management
- Revitalized the local production/quality department providing both management and operating abilities.
- Identified and implemented methods and procedures to enhance the quality of the finished products.
- Participated with the design department in all aspects of local research and development.

Developed a computerized costing chart. Researched and created all pertinent information required on the costing chart. **Result**: Increased accuracy and efficiency, reduced time, and allowed the possibility to review three profit margin scenarios at once.

Built relations with suppliers to strengthen and expand the technical resources needed in order to upgrade the quality of finished goods. **Result**: Partnership formed between customer/supplier, reduced costs and communication errors, increased garment quality thus increasing product sales at store level.

Negotiated prices with suppliers and reviewed all costs pertaining to services, raw materials, and accessories as well as analyzed historical profit margins on finished goods. **Result**: Reduced overall costs by 30% and increased profit margins.

ASPIRATION JEANS   1996–1999
Assistant Director of Production/promoted to Quality Control
- Planned, coordinated, operated, and followed-up on all weekly contracts.
- Initiated and designed a series of record-keeping, reporting, and innovative computer time management techniques to eliminate all production inefficiencies, streamline workflow, and enhance accountability.
- Authored policies and procedures and directed the design and implementation of ISO 9002 total quality management program, positioning the company as the first American wholesale fashion distributor to be accredited with ISO.

Established communication for sample production needs. Reviewed procedures and post-mortem report on previous season and implemented new procedures and tasks. **Result**: Eliminated costly errors through more effective communication between all parties involved and enhanced the quality of the season samples without affecting delivery dates.

Conceptualized a production workflow process and evaluated and documented processes. **Result**: A smoother, more efficient process while enhancing the performance and accountability of the personnel as well as the quality of the product.

PRIOR EXPERIENCE   1986–1990
Retail position in sales and customer service at:
- Skin Tight
- ABC Hardware
- Renovator Experts

EDUCATION AND SPECIAL TRAINING

Attestation - ISO 9000 series. QIT 9000. 1,2,3.	1999
Attestation - Priority Time Management-Priority Management	1997
Apprenticeship: June Ann Inc.	1992–1995
AEC in Fashion Design, International Design	1993
Continuing Education in Applied Arts, State University	1991
Graduate in Fashion Design and Merchandising-Consulting Italy	1990

LANGUAGES: Trilingual proficiencies in English, French, and Italian.

COMPUTER KNOWLEDGE: Computer literate, MS Office suite.

MEMBERSHIPS : Fashion Forward Foundation.

FASHION: Brand Seg. Clothes

Alice J. Johnston

123 Learning St.,   Res: (999) 555-1212
Anytown, USA 10101   Bus: (999) 555-1313

Profile:
Highly motivated and innovative Marketing Executive, with a proven ability to implement marketing strategies with strong bottom line growth. Excels at brand strategy in conjunction with corporate strategy.

Key Strengths:
® Strategic business planning and organizational strengths.
® Strong management skills.
® Creative, innovative, entrepreneurial, and practical.

SOFT & DREAMING CLOTHING COMPANY   **1999–PRESENT**
<u>Segment Manager – NICKIE</u>

Championed the development of Brand Segment Strategies to improve consumer equity and growth (sales, profit, share).

➢ Developed a Corporate Design Strategy, which provided structure for the design and development of all *NICKIE* product categories and fostered understanding of brand positioning and consumer targets across the organization
➢ Directed all *NICKIE* specific marketing activities through the introduction and development of advertising and promotional briefs (including in-store communications, mass media, 1:1 advertising, merchandising, public relations, promotions, etc.) that achieve all targets set out for the brand
➢ As a senior member of "Project Pyramid", worked with architectural design firms to lead the redesign of 7 original *NICKIE* Test Stores
➢ Responsible for a team of 2 Corporate Licensing Specialists and together increased licensing income by 24%

<u>Merchandise Manager – Youthwear</u>   **1998–1999**

Managed a team of five direct reports in the development and strategic direction of the Youthwear Apparel category.

➢ Prepared an extensive analysis of the Youthwear apparel category to strategically develop the fall product line. Incorporated market research, competitive information, account feedback, historical sales data, and in-depth SKU analysis.
➢ Reduced product costs, increased profit margins, and met retail price points on key products by developing alternate sourcing options.
➢ Rebuilt a team spirit within the Youthwear division.

BRIAN'S SPORTS EQUIPMENT   **1991–1998**
<u>Marketing Manager – Golf Products</u>

Lead a cross-functional team in the development and execution of long-range and annual brand strategies for five golf product categories.

® Achieved golf ball sales and revenue increases that consistently exceeded forecasts.
® Solidified relationships with U.S. counterparts and became a key member of the U.S. Steering Committee.
® Doubled golf glove sales within 2 years and increased market share from 6% to 22%.
® Employed American designers, domestic, and Far East suppliers to develop and launch a men's line of golf clothing that delivered 40% revenue growth in year two.
® Negotiated licensee contracts for retail apparel, retail golf shoes, and golf accessories, which in turn generated substantial bottom line growth.
® Introduced a successful, long-term direct marketing campaign with an active base of 40,000 targeted golf consumers. Developed mailing list, newsletters, contests for same.
® Directed the ad agency in the creative development and placement of strong consumer advertising and promotional campaigns. Lead the development and implementation of regional grassroots programs to support consumer-marketing efforts.

Product Manager – Team Sports   **1990–1991**
➢ Lead the development and strategic marketing of Team Sports products: baseball, football, soccer, and volleyball.
➢ Obtained product endorsements and negotiated contracts with several professional sports personalities and associations.

ABC BIG SPORTS INC.   **1988–1990**
Product Manager – In-Line Skates

Designed, developed, and introduced In-Line skates under the ABC brand name to the North American market.
® Lead a multifunctional team, including designers, graphic engineers, and mold makers to pioneer an innovative line of road skates for the North American market.
® Contributed to the growth and success of the category within North America.
® Captured 18% market share in year one.

KNOTS LLC
Product Coordinator   **1987–1988**

Managed the design and development of Rope Products totaling $34 million in annual sales.
® Developed a new clam pack design that substantially increased factory productivity and overall consumer demand.
® Secured the Department Store and Big Box Store Inc. accounts, which increased revenue by $3 million.

YOUR CAPITAL   **1986–1987**
Assistant Product Manager

Provided product support in the areas of Controlled Products (401k) and Mutual Funds.
® Preparation and evaluation of annual reports, Federal Budget Analysis, and product information booklets.
® Coordinated the broker sales incentive campaign, which increased holdings by 19%.
® Assisted in the development of the 1987 Federal Budget Analysis which received strong media recognition.

EDUCATION

1981–1985	Bachelor of Arts Honors Degree, State University
	Specialist in Urban and Economic Geography, English minor
1995	State University Direct Marketing Program
1990	Dale Carnegie - Effective Human Relations and Public Speaking
1987	Series 7

ACTIVITIES

Languages	English, German
Hobbies	Playing golf, any water activity, especially scuba diving, breast cancer fundraising

FASHION: BAD—Fashion Industry

Alice J. Johnston
999.555.1212

OBJECTIVE

To further pursue professional growth, through applying marketing and brand management experience.

SUMMARY OF QUALIFICATIONS

Experienced in many faucets of retail, marketing, & design. I have completed courses in: International Business, Marketing, Written & Oral Business Communications, Marketing Research, Consumer Behavior, Persuasive Selling, Retail Buying, Accounting, Retail Management, Photography, Graphic Design, Color Theory, Campaign Planning, Advertising Practices.

EDUCATION

STATE UNIVERSITY,
Marketing, Graduated with Honors
September 1997 - June 2001
GPA 2001: 4.08/4.33 - 94%

STATE SECONDARY SCHOOL,
September 1992 - June 1997
Secondary School Diploma, 1997.

WORK EXPERIENCE

RETAILERS WORLD LLC,
June – Present
Sales & Marketing Coordinator, Duties:

- Improve public relations within accounts for increased brand awaren
- Drive market research initiatives to ensure a competitive marketplace pos
- Manage account programs and promotions for all national account c
- Organize and coordinate trade shows nationally and regionally.
- Communicate and administer: pricing agreements, promotions and c
- Analyze and interpret national sales data to ensure optimum line perf
- Track catalog programs and analyze marketing initiatives for effective

SMART CLOTHING LLC
June 2001 – June 2003
Mens wear Marketing & Merchandise Coordinator. Duties:

- Coordinated all marketing activities for the division: direct mail, spec
  In store signage.
- Maintained accurate records of all coop, exclusivity, and in store sig
- Negotiated with vendors for terms, advertising dollars and special ev
- Developed and maintained vendor relationships through superior ve
- Adhered to financial commitments for marketing vehicles and moni
- Oversaw the development of advertising: editing, image and copy ap
- Project/Promotion Management: Events, launching, Private Shoppi

What's Wrong?
- Too stylized. I'm blinded!
- Too long especially for your age and stage
- Lackluster objective/profile or lack thereof
- No declared job role
- No accomplishments or specific and measurable results
- Spelling, grammatical, or word choice errors
- Too many unnecessary extras and/or irrelevant information and/or repetition
- Name is too small or address is too large or both

Evenings.Redeveloped product knowledge books and selling guides & pricing procedures for the Tailor-to Measure
program.
- Planned marketing objectives and corporate communications by season.
- Manage brands and private label development through analyzing sales and intervening with action plans.

ABC LLC,
May 1991 - June 2001
Assistant Store Manager/Advertising Manager. Duties:
- Coordinated all newspaper advertising and direct mailers for the retailer.
- Developed promotional objectives and designed corresponding in store displays and signage.
- Organized seasonal seminars with key vendors to educate clients.
- Developed master product catalogues and company policy literature.
- Managed and monitored inventory levels, accounts receivables and preferred customer accounts.
- Corresponded effectively with vendors and customers to achieve sales targets – strong understanding of retail channels.
- Responsible for the buying of exterior home fashion products.

FUN POOLS- Distributor,
November 2000 – November 2001
Marketing Consultant. Duties:
- Developed promotional objectives and launched promotional campaign.
- Created product identity and redeveloped product packaging.
- Identified prospective retailers within the US, for optimum positioning of the product.
- Provided strategic marketing and research support.

XYZ SALES AGENCY,
October 1999 - April 2001
Assistant Sales Representative. Duties:
- Business-to-Business sales experience.
- Prepared line list booklets, product knowledge booklets by brand.
- Assisted with the writing of orders and selling of merchandise.
- Represented the agency at the Anytown Fashion Exhibitors Market - Spring & Fall '99, '00.

SKILLS

Computer Software: Competent in Microsoft Outlook, Powerpoint, Access, Excel, and Word.
Knowledge Management: SMS, Cogno's Powerplay & AS400.
Communications: Strong interpersonal business skills and written business correspondence.
Language: English; general understanding of oral and written Spanish.
Graphic Design: Skilled in Adobe Photoshop, Illustrator, and Quark Xpress, manipulation and formatting.

MILESTONES

Key Note Speaker a tPeterson Awards Night - November 2002, Smart Clothing- Fall 01 Corporate Champion Award and Speedy Gonzales, Smart Clothing- Award 2000, Graduated with Honors, Fashion Alumni Award Recipient 2000, Award 2000, Deans List State University,
Member of the Honor Society, 1st place winner of the Smith Competition 2000,

FASHION: BAD—Fashion Industry (cont.)

1st place poster design winner of the Spring Designer's Fashion Show, 3rd place winner of the SPANGLE Communications Award 2001, Award of Excellence - 1998, 1999, 2000, & 2001, Entrance Scholarship to State University – 1997, The Woman's Award – 1997.

VOLUNTEER EXPERIENCE

Alumni Focus Groups, Assistant Choreographer for "Fashion Parade 2000",: Student Fashion Show, Annual Fashion Show for Breast Cancer Research..

INTERESTS AND ACTIVITIES

Pop Culture, Fashion, Interior Design, Visual Arts, Graphic Design.

REFERENCES

Available upon request.

FILM: Junior Production Coordinator

A L I C E   J .   J O H N S T O N   • • •   **JUNIOR PRODUCTION COORDINATOR**

999-555-1212 • alicej@yourname.com

INDUSTRY EXPERIENCE

QUENTIN'S INQUEST SEASON VII JULY 2004/December 2004	TV Series PM: Stan Peterson • PC: Alberta Torrez Position: 2nd Asst PC

QUENTIN'S INQUEST SEASON VII
JULY 2004/December 2004

TV Series
        PM: Stan Peterson • PC: Alberta Torrez
Position: 2nd Asst PC

KINGDOM COME
August 2003/May 2004

TV Series
PM: MJ House • PC: Michael Parker
Position: 2nd Asst PC

AMAZING OUTCOME
December 2002/August 2003

(permittee)

Feature Film
PM: Hubert Leehan • PC: Katie Nuric
Position Held: Office PA/2nd Asst PC

LAST TO LIVE
August 2002/November 2002

MOW
PM: Chuck Coverall • PC: Jacasta McKnight
Position Held: Office PA

SLEEPCATCHER
October 2001/June 2002
McKnight

(permittee)

Feature Film
    PM: KC Ogden • PC: JP Cantook/Jacasta

Position Held: Office PA/2nd Asst PC

RING OF FIRE
September 2001
Richards

            Feature Film (Green Screen)
PM: "Creature" McFeature • PC: Moby

Position Held: Office PA

HOTZONE
July 2001/August 2001
Richards

TV Series (Pilot)
PM: "Creature" McFeature • PC: Moby

Position Held: Office PA

DAGOBA
May 2001/June 2001
Montgomery

TV Series
        PM: Jed Rutherford • PC: Caspian

Position Held: Office PA

THEM
May 2001

Calls

TV Pilots

Feature Film
LM: Sandy Cohen
Position Held: Locations PA 2nd Unit Day

MAYBE I'M DEAD	1 Day Call	• LM: Nancy Simon
HEARING ME DEPARTMENT	2 Day Call	• LM: Natasha Lyon
UP AT THE LAKE	5 Day Call	• LM: Lucia Schaffer
MY BEST HAIRCUT March 2001/April 2001	6 Day Call Position Held: Locations PA	• LM: Lucia Schaffer

DAGOBA
Show Call
May 2000/December 2000

TV Series
PM: Manny Silthouse
        Position Held: Set/Locations PA/Key PA

SPACESHIP MINE
1 Week Day Call
April 2000

TV Series
ALM: Laird Hamilton
Position Held: Locations PA

ONE MONTH

TV Series

FILM: Junior Production Coordinator (cont.)

2 Weeks Day Call   ALM: Frank Baloney
March 2000   Position Held: Locations PA

cont'd

CERTIFICATION

- Member in IABTS 891
- Honorary Withdrawal in the DGC – BCDC – Production Assistant (#5214)
- ALM Apprenticeship Program Level I – Feliciano College
- Script Supervisor/Film Coordinator – Feliciano College
- Institute of Film Orientation Course – West Coast Film School
- Scheduling for Film and Budgeting for Film – Feliciano College
- Location Scouting – Feliciano College
- Basic Safety Awareness and Occupational First Aid Level I – SHAPE

BACKGROUND

Successful business in display, interior design, and design consulting:
- Display/Designer: 17 years experience in window and store display in a variety of retail settings: clothing, furniture, gift stores, trade shows, etc.
- Special Events: theme design and overall coordination of corporate and private events for For Every Event
- Interior Designer: décor/renovations; commercial projects include: design/completion of a clothing store – Look Twice in City Square
- Manager of the fabric department, store displays, and furniture sales at Wicker & Rattan
- Designer of kitchen, bathroom, and custom cabinets at Americ Kitchens
- Office Administration as well as Instructor of a Customer Service and Sales program for adults at Ameripro Employment Trainers Ltd.

EXPERTISE

- Ability to work in detail and manage a variety of ongoing projects simultaneously
- Creative organization, energetic, and imaginative—hard working, excellent team player with good interpersonal skills
- Excellent problem solving—remain calm under pressure
- Pleasant and professional manner
- Proficient with office machines and procedures
- Have Computer
- Will Travel!

123 Learning St.   (999) 555-1212 (H)
Anytown USA 10101   (999) 555-1313 (C)

Alice J. Johnston

Role   SCRIPT SUPERVISOR

Experience   1999–Present   Various Film and TV Productions
                  Script Supervisor

- Detail oriented, multi-faceted job requiring an organized, attentive, and accurate nature.
- Responsible for creating all of the editor's notes, camera logs, script breakdowns, and production shots.
- Overseeing and coordinating continuity from script to screen.
- Assisting the Producer in avoiding duplication and waste of services, i.e., reshoots, excess rentals, et al.
- Providing a daily statistical progress report for the production office.
- Providing the Editor's Log for the transfer house and the editorial department.

Partial List of Productions:

Burn Baby Burn (Feature Film)
LD Productions Inc., 2004
Producers: Paul Schafer, Dan Dickson, P. Pettigrew
Director: Jokeboy Slim

Dead Rising Fast (Feature Film)
Universal Pictures, 2003
Executive Producers: Douglas Smart, Pierre Sallow
Producer: Candy Jenkins
Director, 2nd Unit: Reuben Steward

Untitled Ron Murphy Pilot (Pilot for TV)
Script Supervisor
Periscope Productions Ltd., 2002
Director: Ron Murphy

Major Fool Hardy (Feature Film)
Script Supervisor, 2nd Unit
Nemar Pictures, 2002
Producers: Pete Peterson, Josh Brogan
Director: Paula Poppy
Me Against The World (M.O.W.)

FILM: Script Supervisor (cont.)

Script Supervisor
Bighouse, 2001
Producers: Fee MacDonald, Sarah Meharg, Sarah Moore
Director: Richard Taylor

Ouch I'm Hurt (Feature Film)
Script Supervisor, Emergency Replacement
Ouch I'm Hurt Ltd. Partnership, 2000
Producers: Pete Jenkins, Sally Formaggio, Cindy Solis
Director: Kim Jong
Prod. Mgr: Hunt Backstab

Running (a.k.a. Flaps) (Feature Film)
Script Supervisor, 2nd Unit
Richard Film Productions Ltd., 2000
Producers: Clay Spikins
Director: Jim Beam

Big Home Sally (Feature Film)
Script Supervisor, 2nd Unit / Script Co-Ordinator (Main Unit)
Wolf Love, 2000
Producers: Jenny Craig, Lena Horn
Director: Brian Bong

More Tears For Me (M.O.W.)
Script Supervisor
Fever International Inc., 1999
Producers: Mark Six, Julie Cooper
Director: Tony Grumps
Prod. Mgr: John Smith

Tears in a Valley (M.O.W.)
Script Supervisor, 2nd Unit
Back Bay Productions Co. Inc., 1999
Producer: John Tempo
Director: Darrel Montgomery

Education   1985   State University
- Bachelor of Arts, Psychology

Skills   Adept at various programs, including QuickBooks Pro, Excel, Microsoft Publisher, Quicktax, etc. Fast, accurate typing skills (i.e. 70 w.p.m.).

Alice J. Johnston

123 Learning St., Anytown, USA 10101 999.555.1212 Home alicej@yourname.com

Highly polished Executive Assistant with 11 years experience providing exceptionally high levels of personal and executive support, with the utmost in confidentiality. Unique knowledge of the entertainment industry.

SUMMARY OF QUALIFICATIONS

- Independent, self-motivated, highly organized, detail-oriented, and proactive professional.
- Excellent interpersonal, written, oral communication, and research skills.
- Coordination of intra-company programs, multiple function liaison.
- Special expertise in events planning, industry public relations, and report preparations.
- Exceptional ability to grow positive relationships with clients and colleagues at all levels.
- Well versed in entertainment "politics" and ins & outs of deal making.

PROFESSIONAL EXPERIENCE

BCA ENTERTAINMENT INC.   2001–2003

Executive Assistant to Executive Vice President/Chief Financial Officer

- Provided high quality support in loyal and discreet manner.
- Maintained professional and personal schedule and all appointments.
- Coordinated extensive travel arrangements, domestic and international.
- Managed expense account and recovery, financial reports, and all correspondence.
- Liaised with CFO's of 10 inter-company divisions.
- Administered/managed corporate credit cards for home office and field staff.
- Provided administrative backup for Chairman/CEO of ABC Inc.
- Interfaced with Human Resources department on senior staff benefit issues.
- Arranged all meetings and departmental off-site conventions and events.
- Acted as liaison and with stockbroker, accountants, and legal counsel.
- Tracked expense reports and invoices for 5 divisions to ensure timely approval.

BIG BRAND FILM & ENTERTAINMENT - (1994–2001)

XYZ HOME VIDEO 2000–2001

EA to Executive Vice President, Worldwide Sales, & Global Chain Supply

- Managed extremely active executive calendar.
- Arranged high-level domestic and international travel.
- Oversaw registration process, and traveled to manage yearly industry events/conventions.
- Maintained expense account with tracking to reconciliation.
- Liaised with all senior executive staff and major account executives.
- Provided administrative backup as necessary to President & EVP North America.
- Supported launching of Retail Rental Direct Program - March 2000.
- Ordered product monthly for field sales staff reps (150 domestic offices).
- Coordinated temporary recruitment activity for departmental direct reports.

FILM: Sr. EA Entertainment (cont.)

Alice J. Johnston.....page 2

XYZ HOME VIDEO 1996–2000
Executive Assistant to Executive Vice President, Worldwide Marketing
- Provided excellent administrative support to rapidly growing marketing division.
- Managed direct reports, administrative support staff of 30 assistants.
- Liaised with all XZY, departments, production companies/vendors.
- Secured artwork approvals for promotions with key accounts.
- Prepared Power Point presentations for special events.

XYZ STUDIOS 1994–1996
Executive Assistant to Senior Vice President, Theatrical Marketing
- Provided administrative support in fast-paced creative department for development of feature films.
- Coordinated high-volume daily communications, executive screenings, creative staff, and pitch meetings with high-profile industry professionals.
- Responsible for extensive travel arrangements domestic and international.
- Managed expense account and recovery.
- Interacted with finance, business affairs, and legal departments on preparation of travel arrangements and contractual payments.
- Liaised with story department on all script coverage.
- Created and maintained high volume script tracking system.

MRM, INC. 1992–1994
Legal Assistant to Vice President Legal, Business Affairs
- Supported legal/business affairs department in negotiation of long form agreements.
- Created and maintained multiple weekly status reports.
- Edited and processed all long form agreements, domestic and international.
- Managed writer contract payment schedules in accordance with agreements.
- Maintained heavy executive calendar with high domestic/international travel volume.

SEMINARS
Tom Hopkins' Sales & Marketing Boot Camps
John Maxwell Series ~ Leaderships Laws
Motivational and Self Improvement Seminars

FILM: BAD—Construction Model & Film

John J. Johnston

123 Learning St., Anytown, USA 999.555.1212 or 999.555.1313

CAREER GOAL
To achieve a challenging position in your industry and to use my creative
executive level of skills, to increase the success in the company, such as
yours.

EDUCATION
Construction Engineering Diploma, State College (1984 - 1987)

EMPLOYMENT HISTORY

ABC Film Productions Inc.
2003 - Present
    Position: Creator / Writer / Producer

    Creating / writing ideas, characters for scripts and episodes for Film and
    Television.
    Dealing with Producers and Production companies in United States, Canada,
    and abroad.
    Research, calling, and signing up sponsors for the projects.
    Research Executive Producers, Film / TV investors, Networks and meet with
    them, to close.
    Executive Director in marketing and sales

XZY MODEL INC.
1993-2003
    Position: Booking Agent / Scout, Promotions, Executive Director of
    Marketing and Sales

    Deal with upscale clientele from all over the world, NYC, LA,
    England, Milan, Germany
    Manage daily office functions, bookings, castings, promotions, model /
    talent searches, fashion shows, etc.
    Book, manage, and organize models for print, fashion
    shows, commercials, TV, film, fashion shows, and charity functions
    Set up model searches for scouting new faces and model development of
    portfolios.
    Conduct interviews, open calls, and auditions for models
    Create and design model agency promotional programs special events and
    shows.
    Recruit and train new employees.
    Acquire sponsorships and free media advertising f

AAA Distributing (Computer Wholesalers)
1990 to 1993
    Position: Personal Assistant to the head Executiv

    Responsible for taking orders from buyers and sel
    Negotiated with buyers and sellers with orders fr
    Dealt with corporate clients
    Promoted from London, England office to Europe an
    Europe for 12 months).
    Promotional and Sales presentations for new clien
    Responsible for working with existing clients and
    for new orders

What's Wrong?

- Too many bullet points
- Lackluster objective/profile or lack thereof
- No declared job role
- Sends a mixed message
- Leaves a strange or weird impression or doesn't suit the industry

FILM: BAD—Construction Model & Film (cont.)

Ace Auto (Brokerage Buying and Selling)
1988 to 1990

Position: Director of Buying/Selling

- Dealt with customers, wholesalers for buying and selling
- Responsible for the Florida Division (had to live there for six months per year to deal with the U.S. clientele)
- Dealt with brokerage firms/customs
- Public relations with upscale clientele (buyers and sellers)

XYZ Engineering Firm (1987 to 1988)

Position: Construction Engineer Technician

STRENGTHS AND SKILLS

- Constructive participation in both individual and team atmospheres so as to meet company objectives
- Solid public relation skills
- Excellent people, telephone, sales and marketing skills
- Effective in both relaxed and fast pace working environments
- Model/talent bookings, management, marketing and promotions work with upscale clients)
- An excellent knowledge of sales, fashion, and talent industry.
- A good encourager - like to help others
- Creative and teachable

ACTIVITIES AND INTEREST

- Working with the Youth Groups
- Events co-ordinating for fundraising.
- Acting and Working in the Film / Fashion Industry.
- Traveling.
- Kick Boxing, Volleyball , Tennis , Cycling.

REFERENCES AVAILABLE UPON REQUEST

John J. Johnston

123 Learning St., Anytown, USA 10101 Home Phone: 999-555-1212 Email: johnj@yourname.com

Head-of-the-class Bachelor of Commerce grad with entrepreneurial spirit, a great work ethic, and experience in small business consulting and banking looking for his first break into business and finance.

Education

State University *Graduate Bachelor of Commerce,* **2004**
➢ Placed 3rd overall at Q3C team-case competition 2003.
➢ Placed 3rd overall marketing management/travel and tourism bracket of the North Atlantic BUS competition 2001.
Denmark University - fall exchange program, Denmark 2002

Relevant Work and Volunteer Experience

University Small Business Consulting, Manager **2002–2003**
➢ Fourteen consulting projects were completed and $14,000 of total revenues acquired. Responsibilities as manager included acquiring and interviewing clients, creating the proposal and soliciting the required funding, and carrying out the consulting work including the writing, proofing, and delivery of the final report. Projects were team based (groups 2–3) and ranged from an economic impact study, to a marketing feasibility study, to business cases/plans, to a pricing/costing analysis (firm with an 8 million dollar budget). Was the recipient of the 2003 Small Business of the year award.

Big Bank, Implementation Coordinator **2002**
➢ Analyzed current clients using financial services offered through Big Bank's Corporate and Commercial Electronic Banking Services. This was part of the conversion process from an old (primarily paper-based system) to a new electronic based database system. Also, aided in the implementation of banking services for clients.

Community Learning Centre, Volunteer Consultant **2003**
➢ Provided research and strategic assistance for a business case required for adult distance delivery education in the Greater Anytown area.

University, Yearly Marketing Events Director **2002**
Aided in the amalgamation of the Marketing Association with the Marketing Association Conference (now the sole marketing entity at the University).

Commerce Cares, Advertising Director **2002–2003**
Promoted and marketed community services, events, and fundraisers for the less fortunate in the Anytown and global community. The organization doubled its total from the 2001–2002 campaign.

BUS, VP Finance **2000–2001**
➢ One of three cofounders of BUS, an international business competition. Primary responsibilities included monitoring finances, promoting BUS to delegates, and gathering recruits for the competition. BUS had a very successful first year of operation; 90% of University's delegates received a top-3 finish.

Other Work Experience

Anytown Day Camp, Sr. Counselor **2001**
➢ Dealt with problematic campers, created innovative camp activities, helped to lead Jr. Counsellors. Received top evaluation.

Personal Information
➢ Fifteen years of piano experience, 8 months of guitar, weight-lifting 3–4 times/week, squash, roller/ice hockey, golf. Travelling experience include; nine-weeks backpacking Europe, and excursions to Australia, New Zealand, Israel, Scandinavia, and Estonia.

FINANCE: Finance, Beginner

John J. Johnston, MBA (Candidate)

123 Learning St., Anytown USA 10101, Phone: 555-1212 Email: johnj@yourname.com

Profile: Futures Analyst & MBA Candidate with a concentration in Finance. Financial sector experience includes 4 years of research & analysis work for Chinese futures brokerage firm.

Work Experience:

Xinji Futures Brokerage Ltd., Shanghai, China   1999–2003
Ximji Futures Brokerage Ltd. is a futures brokerage company with a trading seat on the SHFE (Shanghai Futures Exchange). The company provides futures investment services for small and medium customers.

Futures Analyst   (2001–2003)
- Studied the market behavior of the traded products in SHFE such as copper, aluminium and rubber to explain and predict price changes using fundamental analysis and technique analysis tools.
- Provided clients with investment suggestions & advice; Wrote comments and articles.
- Studied and analyzed global market trends using other trading organizations such as the LME (London Metal Exchange) and COMEX as points of reference.

Selected Accomplishments:
- Used fundamental analysis and technological analysis to successfully predict the price trend for copper, following the events of September 11, 2001. This allowed clients to net a 5–10 times profit.
- Published comments and articles in China Futures Daily.

Risk Control Assistant   (2000–2001)
- Monitored and controlled the risks of various trading products.
- Reported on the risk conditions of each client to the manager.
- Provided management with risk control suggestions and ideas.

Selected Accomplishments:
- Avoided multi-million dollar losses for the company by accurately and quickly reporting client risk conditions.

Deputy Assistant   (1999-2000)
- Worked in the trading hall receiving and inputting client orders quickly & accurately.
- Coordinated with the risk control assistant to manage the risks for clients.

Selected Accomplishments:
- Allowed clients to maximize price benefits & minimize loss through timely feedback.
- Tracked trading details to help clients understand market changes and plan their investment strategy accordingly.

Part-time Working Experience: Campus Foods, a company on campus for catering.

Education:

Master of Business Administration   (anticipated)   2005
Major in Finance, State University

Bachelor of Economic Degree   1999
Major in International Finance Nanjing University of Science and Technology Nanjing, Jiangsu, China

Futures Career Qualification Certificate in Chinese Futures Market   2000

Personal and Community Involvement: Investing in futures & stock market; volunteer for Chinese Culture Center

John J. Johnston, MBA

123 Learning St. Anytown, IL (999) 555-1212   johnj@yourname.com

SENIOR FINANCIAL ANALYST

Skills and Achievements

◊   MBA with finance concentration. In-depth knowledge of financial and data modeling, capital markets, advanced statistical methods, and economic analysis

◊   Recipient of Flatbox award for business process reengineering leading to completion of market statistics program ahead of schedule and on budget

◊   Extensive experience in product development and support in data and wireless communications

◊   Developed forecasting models for PC components, such as liquid crystal display (LCD), allowing clients to meet financial objectives by effectively planning sales and inventory cycles

◊   Excellent verbal and written communication skills

Education

2002	Series 7 Honors, Securities Institute
2000	Master of Business Administration (Finance), State University
1997	Bachelor of Applied Science (Electrical Engineering), State University

Work Experience

Personal Sabbatical, (2001–Present)

◊   Engaged in continuous education. Attained Series 7 certification with Honors

◊   Conducted independent equity and investment research in the area of telecommunications

◊   Researched and built information technology applications using home wireless networking technology

◊   Volunteered in organizing and participated in community soccer activities

Senior Analyst, ABC Inc., (2000–2001)

◊   Promoted after six months to manage worldwide mobile computing program

◊   Led team of senior analysts in producing major research project addressing wireless LAN market

◊   Wrote research reports focusing on mobile and wireless computing to address client needs

◊   Presented technical and marketing product strategies at industry conferences

◊   Established key relationships with PC vendors to expand ABC's mobile computing program

Telecommunications Consultant, XZY Inc., (1998–1999)

◊   Led client team in assessing network management requirements and implementing a tailored UNIX-based network control system resulting in improved network management capability

◊   Developed and executed strategy to produce benchmark performance specifications for IP, ATM, Frame Relay, and X.25 switching products

◊   Provided on-site network system training and support for international telecommunications clients

◊   Spearheaded verification and release of customer-specific LAN/WAN applications, resulting in timely product delivery

Network Engineer, Indigo Inc., (1997–1998)

◊   Provided technical support for national network service provider deploying a multi-vendor platform including Big phone company allowing reliable network access

◊   Coordinated with equipment vendors and clients to consistently deliver innovative and prompt solutions in critical scenarios

◊   Studied network system requirements and presented documented network-level recommendations to improve customer efficiency, resulting in minimal network downtime

◊   Familiar with various UNIX-based and proprietary network management software packages

FINANCE: MBA Finance (cont.)

Internship Work Experience

Regulatory Specialist, Big Telecom, (summer 1996)
◊ Thoroughly researched compliance regulations on CDMA/TDMA wireless network products and facilitated regulatory approval accordingly

Hardware Tester, MMM Inc., (part-time 1995–1996)
◊ Performed initial testing on memory cards and collaborated with developers to perform failure analysis

System Administrator, Big Research Company, (summer 1995)
◊ Provided efficient, prompt support for voice switches in fast-paced design environment
◊ Designed, implemented, and maintained Internet-based software tool repository

System Administrator, Big Research Company, (intern 1993–1994)
◊ Developed and implemented traffic simulation tool for voice Advanced Intelligence System (AIS)
◊ Adapted Simple Network Management Protocol (SNMP) based software package to specific department needs and used to manage LANs and voice switches
◊ Developed technical training package for new-hire training program

Additional Information

◊ Competitive soccer player with participation in leagues in all over the U.S.
◊ Recreational interests include soccer, skiing, football, and running

John J. Johnston, B.Comm, C.A.

123 Learning Street, Anytown, USA 10101 Phone: 999-555-1212 Email: johnj@yourname.com

Executive Finance with specialty in overseas construction and operations.

PROFILE

- Experienced executive in financial and general management in America and overseas. Key member of bidding team that had an exemplary success rate.
- Developed and presented business plans for established and start-up organizations in an effort to arrange financing.
- Arranged project financing working with banks and government.
- Quantified the cost impact of economic damages in business/insurance claims.
- Variety of senior executive roles: Director, General Manager, VP Finance, and Controller.
- Private and public companies; joint ventures.

KEY SKILLS

- **Negotiation** – numerous agreements with customers, suppliers, bankers, investors, and joint venture partners; considerable collective agreement negotiation experience.
- **Managing through Adversity** – successfully led organizations through sale of businesses, cash shortages, and financial restructuring.
- **Interpersonal** – resolved difficult issues with partners, shareholders, customers, suppliers, and company personnel. Energetic motivator as team leader or player. Innovative thinker who works well under pressure. Develops a strong loyal following.

EXPERIENCE

Financial Consultant   2000–Present

- Involved in the preparation of a business plan for Shiny Gold Inc. (TSX-SGR) to obtain financing to launch a gold jewelry company.
- Played a key role in the preparation of a business plan to obtain government assistance and other financing for ABC Inc., an animation and multi-media company.
- Engineered the required financing ($1,200,000) to construct an Irish Pub (Irish Pub Inc.).

Pipe&Pipe LLC.   1996–2000
V.P. Finance & General Manager

- Large diameter pipeline construction across U.S. with sales of $50,000,000–$100,000,000 annually.
- Negotiated extremely lucrative compensation for management team and set up the new company which was 100% owned subsidiary of Bypass Bridge Limited.
- Had unbroken string of very profitable contracts, earned over $20,000,000 in 3 years.
- Negotiated accelerated invoicing (weekly) and payments (immediate) from the client to alleviate a tight cash situation created by the parent company.
- Set up a joint venture with another company which provided necessary financial guarantees on project when the parent company filed for bankruptcy (contract earned $12,000,000). Also convinced the client and unions that parent's bankruptcy would not hinder our ability to finish the project.
- Upon completion of the above-mentioned project, worked with the receiver to sell company.
- Secured project financing/bonding/insurance and negotiated key contracts with clients and subcontractors.
- Set up large equipment leasing contracts ($10,000,000–$20,000,000).

FINANCE: Construction Finance (cont.)

V.P. Finance, XYZ Pipe Inc.   1989–1996

- Large diameter pipeline across U.S. and bidding on overseas work.
- Contracts awarded were up to $100,000,000 in volume and all were profitable.
- Established excellent credibility with bankers by providing current (daily) information on contract progress to ensure concurrence with all borrowing covenants.
- Inaugurated annual seminars with field superintendents and foremen to ensure timely information flow between the job and head office and outlined the impact certain field decisions had on the bottom line (i.e. the amount of increased production required to justify overtime).
- Negotiated joint-venture agreements and ensured reporting structures were in place to satisfy U.S. partners. Worked with Export Development Corporation and affiliates to determine financial assistance available for overseas bids.
- Assisted legal team in quantifying cost impact of business dispute with partner.

V.P. Finance, MMM Pipelines Inc.   1982–1989

- Large diameter pipeline construction across U.S.
- Sewer and water main construction in the Anytown area.
- Arranged unique tax deal that saved the company $2,000,000–3,000,000.
- Developed equipment program that helped to determine an economical disposal policy (i.e., when to stop repairing and sell).

V.P. Finance, Pipelines International   1979–1982

- Overseas pipeline construction, working in the Middle East.
- Set up tax companies in Holland and Switzerland through which money would flow from our company in Iraq to an affiliate in the U.S. with virtually no taxes.
- Coordinated the wind down of the Iraqi company and the disposal of its assets to a Turkish company.

Controller, ABC Pipelines   1975–1979

Assistant Controller, ABC Products Ltd.   1973–1975

EDUCATION

- **B. Comm from State University.**

FINANCE: Finance, Portfolio Management

JOHN J. JOHNSTON

PROFILE

Senior Management Professional in institutional asset management.

EDUCATION

2005–Present   University of Western Region, Top Business School   Anycity, AS
- Currently enrolled in the Executive MBA program

1998–2001   Association of Investment Management and Research   Anycity, AS
- Completed the Chartered Financial Analyst (CFA®) Designation

1993–1997   State University   Anycity, AS
- Bachelor of Arts, Urban Systems

EXPERIENCE

2003–Present   Northern Capital Management   Anycity, AS
Vice President
- Develop relationships with public and corporate pension plans resulting in fund growth of 120%.
- Market synthetic indexing and market-neutral fund of hedge funds products.
- Support existing clients with data, performance reporting, presentations, and education.

2000–2003   Strong Investments Ltd.   Anycity, AS
Portfolio Manager
- Co-managed a $300 million equity and fixed-income portfolio.
- Performed quantitative and qualitative analysis on portfolio investments.
- Executed due diligence on new ideas and current holdings, including management and customer interviews, site tours, and industry analysis.
- Launched and co-managed the first leveraged fixed-income hedge fund in U.S.
- Appeared in both television appearances and national newspaper interviews.
- Transacted over $5 billion in government bonds, U.S. Treasury Bonds, and repurchase agreements each year.

1997–2000   Young Commercial Real Estate   Anycity, AS
Associate
- Acted on behalf of corporate and institutional clients in asset purchases, dispositions, and leasing.
- Performed cash flow analyses, asset valuations, and due diligence in support of complex real estate transactions.
- Worked with a senior partner to produce the highest revenue of any team across the country in 1997 and 1998.

LICENCES AND MEMBERSHIPS

- Currently registered with the NFA as an Associated Member.
- Holder of the CFA® Designation and member of the Anycity Society of Financial Analysts.

123 LEARNING ROAD • ANYCITY, ANYSTATE • 10101
PHONE 555-999-1212 • FAX 555-999-1313 • EMAIL JOHNJ@YOURNAME.COM

FINANCE: CFO & VP Finance

ALICE J. JOHNSTON

123 Learning St., Anytown, USA 10101
Res: 999-555-1212   *alicej@yourname.com*

A Finance Executive with diverse background in the investment industry including institutional and retail investment businesses, and buy-side and sell-side firms. Recognized as a business builder with a solid background in investing. Designs and implements strategies around lines of business and empowers and motivates sales forces to sell with confidence.

CAREER OVERVIEW

XYZ INVESTMENTS   1999–2004
Vice President, Program Manager, Mutual Fund Wraps

- Bottom line responsibility for growing mutual fund wrap programs: mandate covered four programs, including the Big Plans Investment Program™ and wraps for international clients.
- Led a team of up to 3 marketing professionals for assets under management ranging from $3B to $8B.
- Designed, implemented, and delivered sales force education programs and materials to multiple domestic and international sales forces, including stock brokers, financial planners, and investment counsellors.
- Responsible for compensation, pricing, relationship with external investment managers, reporting, and administration.

Vice President, Strategic Initiatives, Private Client Division

- Business Champion in the rollout of an $80M portfolio management system (Linklet) to 3,000 brokerage users.
- Led diversity program for 8,000 employees at XYZ Investments, including strategic client markets and people strategies. Led a team of 12 executives representing XYZ Investments units to set diversity objectives and implement cultural change.
- Team member mandated to bring consistency to the multiple asset allocation and discovery processes across XYZ's NA businesses. The objective was to implement consistent language (e.g., conservative, moderate, aggressive) to describe clients and to translate those terms into consistent asset allocations, while allowing for different fulfillment in each business.
- Within sales effectiveness for XYZ Investments (works with managers to coach sales forces and grow the business), partnered with XYZ Banking to lead the referrals program between banking and investments sales forces.

Selected Achievements

- Grew mutual fund wrap assets by $2.5B over 2 years by:
    - Improving education, fees and communications, such as market commentary;
    - Introducing a reward program for the IAs;
    - Working in the branches with the IAs to sell (up to 3 weeks/month); and,
    - Supporting internal wholesalers and a Help Desk.
- Managed the budget for a period of the three-year roll-out of Linklet and developed and implemented the training program. This involved project management, communication with the sales force, focus groups, and prioritizing deficiencies.
- Using Cultural Assessment study, led a group of 60 in interviewing more than 500 employees and leaders to assess XYZ Investments' state around diversity and to develop and implement a plan for improvement. Employee perceptions showed a 6% improvement in the way XYZ Investments managed diversity over 2 years.
- Providing the basis for some of the recent restructuring at XYZ, supported leaders in making cultural change in two pilot projects. The objective was to present XYZ as a single solution provider, rather than referring clients among different businesses as a series of discrete service providers.

BROCK DOBEY   1997–1998
Director, Global Custody Consulting Services, North America

- Mandated to build a custody consulting practice for North American institutional clients.
- Worked with an international team and supported by an analyst.
- Focused on product development and sales: $500K revenue in year 1.

FINANCIAL INC.   1990–1997
Client Service Executive, Funds (1996–1997)

- Created, developed, launched family of DC funds.
- Determined vehicle structure and nature of investments.
  - Created marketing materials, managed media.
- Assisted with sales and serviced accounts.
- Corporate public relations including media relations and advertising.
- Initiated, implemented an appropriate funds governance process.
- Developed, implemented issue-focused reporting.

Client Executive, Asset Consulting (1990–1996)

- Asset consultant for 7 institutional retainer clients from $80M to $1B.
- General issues included liabilities, asset mix, manager research.
- Specialized in derivative products, real estate managers/vehicles, and directed brokerage.

INVESTORS LIMITED   1989–1990
Partner

- One of three to start up an investor relations consulting business.

ABC ASSURANCE   1984–1989
Equity Analyst/Portfolio Manager

EDUCATION AND PROFESSIONAL DEVELOPMENT

- **Honors Bachelor of Commerce**, State University, 1984
- **Series 7 Securities Course**, 1985
- **PDO Exam**, 1996
- Published a number of articles for industry periodicals

OUTSIDE INTERESTS AND ACTIVITIES

- Head, Strategy Committee of the Labron Charitable Foundation, dedicated to helping families fight cancer with dignity and determination.
- Member of the Sculpture's Guild.
- Member of Anytown Bicycling Network.

FINANCE: Sr. Financial Executive

Alice J. Johnston, CA

123 Learning Street
Anytown, USA 10101

Home: (999) 555-1212
Email: alicej@yourname.com

PROFILE

A **Senior Financial Executive** with extensive experience in multinational organizations. Recently completed a challenging acquisition and the related integration of personnel, best practices, and systems. Managed corporate reengineering and downsizing, directed system implementations, specifically J.D. Edwards, Prism, and SAP financial and customer service applications. Redefined the related business process.

BUSINESS EXPERIENCE

Big Management Inc.   1999–2000
Chief Financial Officer and Vice President, Finance
Directed all facets of Finance, facilities management and procurement as the business grew from $600 million to over $1.3 billion. As a member of the Board of Directors and two other subsidiaries, played an integral role in the development and implementation of strategies and objectives.

- Participated in the due diligence and strategic planning of the acquisition and integration of SHL Systemhouse. Efforts yielded a stronger negotiating position on settlement and financial data meaningful to the ongoing management of the amalgamated entity.
- Directed the local implementation of the new corporate business model, moving the operation and related financial support from a geography focus to a Global Line of Business delivery model.
- Consolidated and streamlined Finance and other functional areas and former to generate cost effective support to the merged operational entity. This process emphasized the retention of best practices and best employees, while mitigating significant variance in culture and compensation.

ABC INC.   1985–1998
Director of Finance and Administration (1995–1998)
Managed the Finance and Administration department, including financial planning, corporate accounting, tax, payroll and fringe benefits, pension and savings plans, office services, customer service, including credit and collection, sales order management, and information systems. As a member of the operating committee, played an integral role in the development and implementation of the company's strategies and objectives. Reported to the President.

- Created and led task forces to solve customer issues arising from parent company initiatives including distribution centre outsourcing and global business process integration.
- Directed the local implementation of new system applications, specifically Pyramid and Prism, while minimizing the impact to internal and external customers.
- Designed job functions to provide value-added activity to the company, assessing process, and contribution to the company.
- Managed the ongoing downsizing of the Finance and Administration function from 45 to 20 people while continuing to achieve all company goals within the stated time frame.
- Consolidated the Finance and Administration functions of business units into a U.S. "campus," resulting in greater synergy within the total organization.

Alice J. Johnston   Page 2

Manager, Financial Reporting and Legal Administration
Corporate Secretary (1990–1995)
Managed a staff of twelve professionals who performed all corporate accounting functions including capital asset management, promotional fund and advertising accounting, inventory accounting, and cash disbursements. Coordinated legal administration for marketing and sales management.

- Reduced audit fees charged by external auditors through enhanced communication of issues and a proposal of alternate audit methods.
- Controlled operating costs of all functional areas by assisting in the forecasting of costs, providing timely reporting, and identifying potential cost savings.
- Successfully streamlined the accounting process by focusing on value-added activities.
- Initiated organizational changes within the department to provide greater exposure, challenge, and cross training to employees. Supplemented this process with management skills training to enable the team to better deal with evolving business trends and issues.

Manager, Financial Planning (1988–1990)
Managed four Financial Analysts. Prepared and presented short-, medium-, and long-term business plans.

- Analyzed product and trade marketing activities and provided critical assessments, yielding more cost-effective business results.
- Implemented customer based profit and loss statements generating more actionable financial information.
- Organized, planned, and implemented changes to the financial management process as manufacturing operations were eliminated.

Manager, Internal Audit, North America/Asia-Pacific (1985–1988)

Smith & Thompson, CHARTERED ACCOUNTANTS   1979–1985
Client Manager

EDUCATION

Chartered Accountant   1981

Graduate Diploma in Accountancy, State University   1981

Bachelor of Commerce, Accountancy, State University   1979

Professional Development
Helping Others Succeed   1997
Behavioural Interviewing   1997
Managing Through Change, Career Consultants, Inc.   1997
Strategic Presentation Skills, Dale Carnegie   1995
Effective Management Programs   1994–1989
The Race Beyond, Tom Peters   1994
Principled Centred Leadership, Stephen Covey   1994
TMG Tax Updates   Various

Memberships
Certified Public Accountants
Institute of Certified Accountants

FINANCE: BAD—Finance & Securities Executive

John J. Johnston
123 Learning Trail
Anycity, Anystate
10101
Home: (555) 999-1212

SUMMARY OF QUALIFICATIONS:

- Great team leading skills
- Superior analytical skills
- Excellent customer service skills
- Strong communications & interpersonal skills
- Self-motivated, enthusiastic, and focused

EDUCATION

- 35 years in the securities industry
- Served 1 year as Chairman, 2 years as Vice chairman of the Trading Policy committee for the Stock Exchange
- Served 1 year on the Stock Exchange Disciplinary Committee
- Served as the Chairman of the Brokers Committee for the implementation of CDS
- Officers and directors course
- Industry Courses such as the Series 7, Conduct and Practices Handbook

WORK EXPERIENCE:

Securities Corporation
(March 2004–Current)
- Acted as an independent consultant
- Worked exclusively on a fraud investigation
- Worked with legal counsel regarding various legal claim
- Negotiating client settlements

Bleak Securities Corporation
(September 2003–March 2004)
- Chief Operating Officer
- Recruiting advisors – 6 advisors in 6 months
- Grew Bleak from $250,000,000 to $450,000,000 in 6 months
- Turned first profit in the history of the company – 4 out of 6 months t[...]

Own Consulting
(July 2002–September 2003)
- Acted as a consultant to Securities Corporation to assist in credit probl[...] operation
- Uncovered a multi-million dollar fraud
- Worked with legal counsel to devise a strategy

US Securities Ltd.
(September 1995–November 2001)
- Worked as a retail/institutional trader and salesperson
- Assisted in corporate finance transactions, such as proxy solicitations, [...] reorganizations

What's Wrong?

- Too much information about out-of-date or inapplicable jobs
- Lackluster objective/profile or lack thereof
- No declared job role
- Leaves a strange or weird impression or doesn't suit the industry

- Handled all marketing for the proprietary trading system
- Designed a brochure for Institutional Sales department
- Principal contact for the back-office operations area
- Resolved all administrative difficulties, some dating as far back as 12 month
- Provided assistance and guidance to other members of the firm when they requested
- Arranged for securities loans for customers

ABC and Company
(April 1986 to June 1995)

- VP, Director and Chief Operating Officer
- Member of the executive committee
- Wrote the corporate "Policy and Procedures" manual
- Ultimate designated person for compliance and corporate governance purposes
- Chief contact for external counsel and accounting /audit firm
- Led the opening of 2 branch offices in Anycity and Somecity
- Interviewed all prospective portfolio managers
- Managed and developed a staff in excess of 60
- Maintained good financial controls as both staff and client number expanded dramatically
- Secretary of the firm, taking and maintaining minutes from all executive committee and board meetings

Equity Trading Company
(March 1977 to June 1986)

1983–1986 Director Equity trading

- Implemented pro-trading operation, whereby traders could trade on the firms capital base
- Handled all equity trading for the company, and responsible for reporting on all equity accounts
- Managed a staff and traders and administrative personnel totalling approximately 50

1980 to 1983: Director of Operations

- Responsible for entire operations department, including all branch offices
- Indirectly responsible for contracts, client accounting , securities processing and security, cash management, stock records, and dividends
- Staff of approximately 260 nationally
- Hired and trained my replacement for the position of Securities Manager

1977 to 1980: Securities Manager

- Managed the securities department, which included cash management, stock, bond, and money market cages. Also responsible for cash management with receipts and disbursements in excess of $1 billion daily
- Set up the first stock lending operation in U.S., which subsequently has become a very profitable area for all investment dealers
- Acted as chairman of the Brokers Committee for the implementation and development of the U.S. Depository for Securities
- Converted the company to Bulk Segregation from the old safekeeping system
- Handled new issue settlements, reconciliation of daily clearing and settlements

1976 to 1977: Operations Assistant

- Reconciled old dividend record; recovered excess of $160,000 in unclaimed dividends & coupons
- Went to Anycity to clean up unreconciled dividend problems, task took approximately 6 weeks
- Went to Somecity to clean up unreconciled position, lasted 1 week and left and associate there for 6 weeks to ensure the system and training were complete

FINANCIAL PLANNING: Financial Services Rep.

Alice J. Johnston

123 Learning St. Anytown, IN 10101 alicej@email.com (999) 555-1212

Profile	**Personable, professionally poised and focused Financial Services Representative with a developed portfolio of high accuracy mathematical and computer skills**

- An extremely positive individual with the capacity to make service targets feel that their needs are the number one priority
- Outstanding history as a loyal employee, wide-ranging exposure to demanding transaction processing environments, and a highly developed work ethic
- Self-reliant, self-motivated, ambitious, rapid assimilation capacities; profound customer service, business, and loyalty development skills
- Professional, courteous, honest, and reliable
- Strong attention to detail; knowledge of financial services and products

Work experience

2000–present   Kim Jong Inc.
Branch Services Specialist 2 - (2004–present)
Branch Services Specialist 1 - (2003–2003)
Field Supervision Administrator - (2001–2002)
Branch Office Administrator - (2000–2001)

- Responsible for achieving company mission of delivering superior financial services to businesses and consumers; support 'Delighting Customer' concept
- Full understanding of Operational Processes, Securities Information, Foreign Exchange, Account Opening, Account Status, and Reporting
- Handle a portfolio of accounts by reviewing information regularly to ensure the safety of these transactions; handle high volume of incoming calls and emails
- Process transactions accurately with maximum efficiency in a high-volume environment in accordance with the policies, procedures, and regulatory guidelines while minimizing risk
- Review transactions for accuracy; endorsements, proper identification. Maintain strict attention to detail, providing outstanding service resulting in notable client satisfaction
- Identify sales opportunities and promote a full range of services by strong marketing effort and prompt personal service
- Keep customer status updated and performed reconciliation
- Effectively utilize all reporting and information systems to provide pertinent analysis for planning and re-projections
- Train, motivate, and mentor new associates

Education

- 2005 – Financial Management Advisor Designation (FMA)
- 2004 – Wealth Management Techniques (WMT), Securities Institute
- 2003 – Series 7 Securities Course (ASC), Securities Institute
- 2003 – Conduct and Practice Course (CPH), Securities Institute
- 2003 – Professional Financial Planning Course (PFP) Securities Institute
- 2000 – Bachelor of Management Degree – State University
- 1997 – Diploma – Accounting – Community College

Interests

Running cross country, learning about food and wine, and cooking

FINANCIAL PLANNING: Senior HNW Financial Planner

John J. Johnston

Mailing Address: 123 Learning Street, Anytown, USA 10101
Phone: (999) 555-1212 Fax: (999) 555-1313 Email: johnj@yourname.com

CAREER PROFILE

A dedicated Financial Service Professional, I have built my career over the past eleven years around meeting the needs of personal and corporate clients through developing and implementing both domestic and international investment, financial planning, and trust and estate solutions in partnership with other BBBC businesses and external professionals.

WORK EXPERIENCE

BBBC FINANCIAL GROUP

Senior Manager, International Services, Global Private Banking (Level 52) Oct 1999–Present

Responsibilities:
- Support all internal BBBC Financial Group sales channels & Int'l Wealth Management business
- Maintain strict Risk Management protocols covering compliance and Know-Your-Client details required for each client.
- Manage the sales process of all internal and external partners with respect to all Int'l Wealth Management solutions being offered to clients in the geographic territory.
- Work with High Net Worth (HNW) families and corporations ($1–5 million + in assets) to develop customized solutions to meet identified opportunities of through a comprehensive range of products and services. These sophisticated solutions include trusts, company formation, Discretionary Investment Management, Non-discretionary Investment Management, Brokerage, Banking, and Credit Solutions. Solutions are developed through completing customized client profiles covering such topics as Investment Strategy Formulation, Estate Planning, Tax Planning, Financial Planning, and Family and Business Succession Planning. All products and services are offered both internationally and domestically.
- Develop new business for the above-mentioned Financial Solutions by promoting referrals from key delivery channels including BBBC COI relationships, both internal and external, and from existing clients. This represents approximately $50 million of net new assets annually.

Selected Accomplishments:
- Contributed to the establishment of new annually recurring revenue of $1 million over my 2-year term. This represents $100 million of new client assets.
- Improved efficiency by implementing a new Due Diligence documentation system

Senior Advisor, BBBC Investments (Level 42)   October 1998–September 1999

Responsibilities:
- Marketing of investment management and fiduciary services and consultative investment sales
- Providing training to all internal staff including Private Banking Senior Client Advisors, Business and Personal Banking Account Managers, and Investment Advisors with respect to opportunity spotting, and referring clients for Wealth Management Services.
- Work with High Net Worth (HNW) families and corporations ($1–5 million + in assets) to develop customized solutions to meet identified opportunities of through a comprehensive range of products and services.

Accomplishments:
- Develop new business for the above-mentioned Financial Solutions by promoting referrals from key delivery channels. This represents approximately $50 million of net new assets annually.

FINANCIAL PLANNING: Senior HNW Financial Planner (cont.)

John J. Johnston   2

Financial Advisor, BBBC Investments (Level 32)   November 1996–September 1998

Responsibilities:
- Work with Affluent and High Net Worth (HNW) families ($100,000–5 million + in assets) to develop customized solutions to meet identified opportunities of through a comprehensive range of products and services. All products and services are offered both internationally and domestically.
- Maintain a relationship with a portfolio of target 300 Affluent and High Net Worth clients by providing thorough, efficient, and quality service. Using a personal and confidential approach, manage a portfolio of clients requiring sophisticated levels of banking, credit and other financial solutions, both domestic and international. Proactively coordinate the relationship by teaming with other experts within BBBC Financial Group, acting as quarterback to ensure a seamless client experience.
- Document complete client profiles and financial plans in order to develop and recommend solutions for identified opportunities for domestic and international services. Participate in portfolio and/or credit reviews as appropriate.

Selected Accomplishments:
- Achieved 177% of sales objective for Investment Management and Trust business (domestic and international) placing in top 5% in the U.S. in the 1997 fiscal year.

Assistant Manager, International Services, BBBC Trust (Level 22)   September 1995–October 1996
Responsibilities similar to those of Senior Manager, International Services above.

Client Service Officer, BBBC Trust (Level 22)   May 1993–August 1995
Responsibilities included providing financial advice and relationship management to affluent clients, consultative investment sales, and marketing of investment services.

EDUCATION

- **Masters of Business Administration (MBA)**   **(December, 2000)**
  State University part-time, Concentration in International Management and High-Tech.
- **Bachelor of Commerce Degree (B. Comm.)**   **(May, 1993)**
  (Magna Cum Laude, Honors)
  State University, *Double Major in Finance and Management, top 5% of graduating class.*

PROFESSIONAL DEVELOPMENT

- **Association for Investment Management and Research (AIMR)**   **(2004)**
  Regular Member of the Association
- **Society of Trust and Estate Practitioners (TEP)**   **(2000)**
  Full Member of the Society of Trust and Estate Practitioners
- **Personal Financial Planner (PFP)**   **(August, 1997)**
  Designation received from The Institute of American Bankers
  Mentor for PFP candidates, 1998, 1999, and 2000
- **Series 7**   **(July, 1992)**

AWARDS

- BBBC Funds Inc. – Mutual Fund Sales Award   1995 & 1997
- BBBCl Trust 401K Transfer-In Award   1995

COMMUNITY INVOLVEMENT

- **National Institute for the Blind**
  Member of Crocus Campaign Committee, 2002/2003
  Member of the District Board of Directors
  Chairperson, Fundraising & Communication Committee, 1999/2001

FINANCIAL PLANNING: Financial Services VP

JOHN J. JOHNSTON

123 Learning Dr. ◆ Anycity, AS◆ 10101 ◆ Tel: 555 999 1212 ◆ Email: johnj@yourname.com

PROFILE

A senior **Financial Services Industry Executive** with 25 years of successful and diverse experience managing complex operations and changes. Senior management roles span Information Systems, Operations, Electronic Banking, and Retail Banking. A leader of major change initiatives in IT and financial services. Recognized within the industry as highly competent at effectively linking people, processes, and technology to deliver lasting and significant change. Recognized for the ability to:

➢ Lead highly complex and strategic business and technology change initiatives
➢ Evolve business from strategy through to implementation, building the operating organization and business processes, and leading the operating environment after implementation
➢ Present key ideas and plans to Management to gain approval and alignment around key business strategies and objectives
➢ Develop internal & external strategic relationships to rally diverse groups to common goals

KEY BUSINESS STRENGTHS

- Complex project and program management
- Innovative change management
- Operational general management
- Technology development

- Business strategy and execution
- Relationship management
- Coaching/mentoring/building teams
- Ability to sell ideas and concepts

CAREER HISTORY AND ACHIEVEMENTS

CREDIT UNION, VICE PRESIDENT, INFORMATION SYSTEMS & OPERATIONS   2003–2004
Reporting to the President and CEO, led the rebuilding of the IS function in the company. This included instituting IS disciplines in Change Management, Project Management, Operational Service Level Management, and Procurement processes. Responsible for leading a team of 80 full-time staff in Operations, Business Analysis, Application Development, and Back Office.

KEY ACHIEVEMENTS:

- Recruited new leaders for the IS and PMO functions and rebuilt these teams, aligning them with the organizations business strategy and goals
- Renegotiated our Banking Services Agreement, reducing our annual expenses in this area by over 30% per annum
- Implemented several change initiatives resulting in significant improvements in service availability for ABMs, POS, and Branch Delivery Systems, enhancing our ability to service our members and generate revenue
- Led the transition team in the completion of Phase I of the merger process, across (8) workstreams covering all facets of the company, resulting in the presentation and approval of the Amalgamation Agreement by the Board of Directors
- Established the Phase II Project team and methodology for the implementation planning phase of the project

FINANCIAL PLANNING: Financial Services VP (cont.)

COMPUTER INC., PROJECT EXECUTIVE   2002-2003

Provided consultative services in conjunction with Business development teams, Solutions Architects, and the Self-Service delivery team in the areas of mid-range systems, outsourcing, and business process reengineering to create solutions for several Financial Institutions.

KEY ACHIEVEMENTS:

- Led and/or participated in the due diligence process on several outsourcing bids and solutions for FI clients
- Utilized as the Retail Financial Services SME in a consulting role to FI clients
- Developed a new transaction based pricing model for FI clients

US BANK OF COMMERCE   1978-2002

Vice President, 1997-2002

Reporting to the Executive VP, led the launch and operations of Bank's home banking application.

KEY ACHIEVEMENTS:

- Led the release of the home banking launch over a private, proprietary network and the internet creating 2 channels to 1 internet banking capability
- The capability was so successful in customer adoption and usage measures that it was recognized as the leader in PC and Internet banking by Online Bank Report and was ranked 3rd in North America behind Citibank and Bank of America
- Achieved the 5-year business plan in terms of customers acquired, transactions completed, positive financial impact to US Bank within the first 2 years of operation
- Integrated the release of the brokerage and insurance internet applications with banking, offering customers a single site to conduct multiple line of business financial transactions

Director, Systems Development, 1995-1997
Manager, Systems Development, 1993-1995

Reporting to the Vice President Technology, led large teams of internal systems developers and external vendor resources creating and reengineering applications.

KEY ACHIEVEMENTS:

- Led the design, build, and successful implementation of the initial PC Banking capability. This program was completed from start to implementation in 5 months
- Led the design, build, and successful implementation of the reengineering of the ATM system. This program of 4 projects resulted in the creation of new business functionality in support of the Bank's overall retail branch strategy

Manager, Production Support, 1990-1993

KEY ACHIEVEMENTS:

- Reengineered the operation environment to restore service levels for the VISA merchant system, prior to this work service levels had been consistently under target for 6 months

Manager, Processing Centre, 1988-1990

KEY ACHIEVEMENTS:

- Automated the output processing to eliminate paper output, saving $1.0MM per year

- Various positions in Branch Banking and HR leading to above appointment, 1978-1988

PROFESSIONAL DEVELOPMENT

Project management & lifecycle methodology; negotiating skills; certified facilitator for leading

INTERESTS

Quality time with family; sailboat racing; scuba diving; reading; skiing

FINANCIAL PLANNING: BAD—Investment Advisor

Alice J. Johnston

Objectives:

The opportunity to utilize the extensive experience in business, sales, marketing, finance, and relationship building.

Personal Profile:

- Integrity, honesty, loyalty are a cornerstone of my personal & business life
- 21 years experience in sales, marketing, business, and the art of entrepreneurship
- 15 years experience in managing staff and business
- 14 years of motivating, educating, and addressing clients and staff both one on one and through group seminars or large events.
- Lifetime of leadership, compassion, and charitable work
- Client orientated with a focus on quality of service
- Top Producer with every organization involved with
- Managed over $90 million in assets
- Have proven to be able to sell a wide variety of products and services with a keen knack to adjust to changing sales situations
- Able to jump start a stagnant sales community
- Able to motivate staff with high energy while providing a nurturing environment
- Self starter and able to work with little or no supervision letting results speak for themselves

Skills & Experience:

Sales

- Owned and operated business at age 19. Responsible for all
including inventory, staffing, banking, and all responsibilities
operation of small Business, sold business in 1988.

- Top performing sales professional in all organizations I hav
including a member of the Chairman's Club.
- Management of staff to provide results comes easy
- Mastered the art of closing and cold calling.
- Able to transfer knowledge to new salespeople to generate
- Professional sales expert at cultivating leads, follow up, and
relationships. Understanding client's needs and acting upon t
- Able to evaluate a situation and work toward a successful in
- Expectations of above-average results are always met
- Meeting targets is a requirement

Marketing

What's Wrong?
- Too many bullet points
- Dense text—I'm too bored to read this all.
- Too long
- Too much information about out-of-date or inapplicable jobs
- Lackluster objective/profile or lack thereof
- No declared job role
- Too many unnecessary extras and/or irrelevant information and/or repetition

FINANCIAL PLANNING: BAD—Investment Advisor (cont.)

- Have been responsible for growing and managing business from a early age, a bottom-up management style of marketing including all aspects of marketing, telemarketing, media, client appreciation seminar events, letters, correspondence, and leading major marketing campaigns. Working in a retail environment early in my career helped master these skills. Understand distribution and system requirements to implement
- Able to market tangible and known tangible products and services.
- Able to provide to staff guidelines and marketing strategies to help them become successful
- Understand marketing plans from budgets to implementation
- Inventing and implementing new marketing ideas
- Searching out solutions to forward the big picture for the organization

Leadership/Management

- Have managed staff of up to 20 individuals, and large market areas
- Managed 28 locations and the staff to provide above average results
- Responsible for screening and accessing prospective candidates, and supporting them through their sales career
- Provided educational, motivational, and topical orientated seminars to staff, clients, and prospective clients
- Spoken to groups on a wide range of topics and material
- have marketed through direct sales, advertising, leads, cold calls
- have lead through example for sales and marketing success

Additional Skills

- Competent in Word, Lotus, Microsoft Office, Maximizer, and a wide variety of software for business and banking
- Understand financial reports and statements
- Vast knowledge of accounting, taxation, and tax issues
- Accomplished marketer and motivator, very much a team player and/or leader
- Quick learner and able to adapt to any situation quickly
- Have been involved in Trust/ Insurance marketing in the past 3 years
- Knowledge of all aspects of business from sales to shipping

Employment History:

2003 - Present Kingdom Enclave Inc.

Vice President Sales, Marketing, Business Development – responsible for the implementation of all aspects of sales including managing a sales staff of 20. Responsible for the management of marketing department including strategies and execution. Responsible for sale of large territories on a large scale basis. Clients include Big Gold,

Football Team, Interactive, Crippen and many of the professional sports teams in North America.

1998–November 2002 Big Bank Group

<u>Vice President/Senior Investment Advisor</u> – managed $60 million in assets, approximately 600 clients responsible for all aspects of creating growing and maintaining the business. Sold and retired from business November 2002.

1997 - 2000 Another Bank (Smaller Bank of Region)

<u>Vice President/Senior Investment Manager</u> – managed $90 million in assets, approximately 600 clients responsible for all aspects of creating, growing, and maintaining the business. This was a new branch opened by myself grew from zero dollars in revenue. Also included managing 5 other branches of Another bank. (Top 5 in organization was on chairman's club)

1995 - 1997 Region Bank of U.S.

<u>Manager Investment Services</u> – Newly created position which I was responsible for opening 16 branches of Region Bank branches, included finding new business and closing leads, managing staff, educating staff through seminars. Recruiting new individuals to fill positions in the branches I opened. (Top 5 producer in organization) Responsible for the marketing and implementation of the new position and was required to bring in new assets for bank, lending, trust, and securities

1991 - 1995 Bank of Another Region

<u>Personal Investment Manager</u> – Newly created position which I was responsible for 18 branches of Another Region Bank. Included sales of financial services products, educating staff, hiring staff, recruiting staff, and maintaining sales quota's and goals. (Top 5 producer)

1990 - 1991 Technical Stuff American

<u>Senior Commercial/Educational Sales Representative</u> – new position created to sell directly to the education market. Responsible for first sale to the State University in Southwest. Area included all of Southern Region (Top producer in U.S.) this position a provided me with extensive knowledge of hardware and software for personal computers.

1988 - 1989 McDonald & Beard

<u>Junior Investment Advisor</u> – first year in investment business, top rookie for first year.

FINANCIAL PLANNING: BAD—Investment Advisor (cont.)

1985 - 1988 Owner of business operation sold in 1988

Nookey's – this was a limited company in which we sold groceries, furniture, sporting goods. I was responsible for sales, marketing, accounting, staffing, and all aspects of maintaining a growing business, which did $ 1million in sales year over year.

Education:

- Graduated Grade 12 Southern Elementary Secondary (Honors)
- A variety of sales and management courses from Dale Carnegie to leadership (entire list can be provided)
- Financial planning courses
- Series 7, and courses or credits to continue to keep license active

Accomplishments:

- Valedictorian of my graduating class 1985
- Top sales and marketing producer and member of Chairman's Club
- Work with many charities including the Breast cancer drive where I raised $20000 in one lunch hour for Breast cancer research

Contact Information

Address: 123 Learning St.
Anytown, USA
10101
Telephone: (h) 999-555-1212
(c) 999-555-1313
alicej@yourname.com

FOOD SERVICE & RETAIL STORE: Bar or Retail, Non-University Grad

Alice J. Johnston

123 Learning St., Anytown, USA 10101
(H) 999-555-1212   alicej@yourname.com

**Bright, energetic and hardworking Retail and Service Person.
Ready and willing to work hard — and extra hours — as I save up for a trip around the world next year.**

Employment History

Bar Assistant *(part-time) - Pink flamingo [public house]*   **June 2003–present**
Duties from taking and preparing drinks orders, using electronic till, waiting on tables, to inventive cocktail creation and promotion development.

Sales Assistant *(full-time) – K& M [fashion/retail]*   **Sept 2003–present**
Extremely rapid-paced work assisting customers (with good product and campaign knowledge); achieving set sales incentives through target display techniques; using company policy combined with personal discretion in giving refunds/exchanges; overseeing stock delivery; working varying and often unsociable hours.

Sales Assistant *(part-time) – Spades [fashion/retail]*   **1999–2003**
Assisted and advised customers implementing good communication skills; handled responsibilities such as stock-checking and refilling; developed new marketing strategies (using personal knowledge of target customers); influenced open-minded buying for a wide market.

Also:
Babysitter *– for two local families*   **2002–2003**
Cared for four children aged 4–8, including food preparation, bathing, and dressing, as well as entertaining!

Voluntary:
Veterinary Assistant (voluntary) – Parrots to Ferrets Veterinary   **1997–1999**
Aided veterinary surgeon in consultations and operations, dealing with clients (in person, and over the telephone), as well as their animals; responsible for animal surgery aftercare; maintained accurate client records, responsible for premises appearance and cleanliness (including sterilization of equipment).

Education & Qualifications
Straight-A High School Graduate
Also:
- Certificate in Basic Food Hygiene (Chartered Institute of Environmental Health, 2001)
- Attendance voucher for completed 'Save a Life – Adult Course' First Aid Course

Interests & Hobbies

Creative Arts – language, literature, fashion, and drama. Heading a make up team for theater. Poetry (recognized in national competition); Classical Clarinettist with bent for jazz and blues.

FOOD SERVICE & RETAIL STORE: Food & Beverage

John J. Johnston

123 Learning St., Anytown, USA 10101
(999) 555-1212 Email: johnj@yourname.com

Food and Beverage Server Resumé

- Able to establish quick rapport when dealing with customers
- Shows understanding, patience, and fairness to customers & fellow employees

EMPLOYMENT EXPERIENCE

Food & Beverage Attendant, **Young Lovers Resort & Spa, Australia**   Nov 2003–Feb 2004

- Responsible for barista duties in tourist restaurant for up to 10 hours per day
- Conducted bar duties for multiple resort functions including precise preparation of cocktails, draught, wines, and top-end liqueurs
- Managed up to a 20 table section during any given shift
- Served both private and business functions of up to 240 people per function

Accomplishments

- *Highly praised for the skills in the art of espresso preparation and customer flair*
- *Quickly mastered Point Of Sale system (Maxial) in one shift and thrived in new environment*

Server, BRIAN MacLeod Golf Links   April 2003–September 2003

- Performed opening and closing duties on a daily basis for the member-lounge facilities
- Served both personal and professional functions of up to 180 people per function
- Planned and arranged all amenities for private and business functions

Accomplishments

- *Mastered restaurant Point Of Sale system (Squirrel) within two shifts*
- *Quickly developed personal relationships and key contacts with various members*

Grocery Clerk, GROCS Inc.   June 1994–April 2001

- Supervised and delegated duties of up to five employees during a eight hour shift
- Responsible for opening and closing store four times per week
- Administered daily dairy and frozen food orders for "just in time" deliveries
- Trained new employees on day-to-day operational responsibilities
- Designed and assembled attractive displays to promote weekly specials

Accomplishments

- *Directed full receiving duties including scanning, computing, and bookkeeping of all incoming inventories, plus managed between eight and twenty incoming vendors per day*
- *Executed a new pricing system in 2 stores over a 2-week period and achieved a 98% price accuracy rate on 20,000 items*

HIGHLIGHT OF SKILLS

- Completed 11-month trip across 4 countries gaining experience working abroad in different cultures
- Completed Responsible Service Of Alcohol Training course
- Completed the Smart Serve program in April 2003
- Completed The Cocktail Training Course

VOLUNTEER WORK AND ACTIVITIES

Fund Raising for Cystic Fibrosis   Sept 1997–1999
Student Walk Home Attendance Team (S.W.H.A.T.)   Sept 1999–April 2000

FOOD SERVICE & RETAIL STORE: Customer Service, Beginner

John J. Johnston
123 Learning St., Anytown, USA 10101 (999) 555-1212

Customer Support and Customer Service Rep

HIGHLIGHTS
- Proven ability to work well within a team environment or independently
- Excellent computer skills plus Desktop Publishing, Graphics, CAD and a number of accounting packages
- Strong interpersonal skills; demonstrated integrity and dependability

Computer Support Skills
- Provide technical support for computer related issues/problems
- Responsible for ensuring customer data input information entered efficiently and in a timely manner
- Experienced in computer repairs and hardware/software installations

Sales/Customer Service Skills
- Experienced in telephone sales for Big Telephone Company Inc.
- Able to effectively deal with irate customers ensuring needs were met
- Cash register and cash handling experience including credit/debit cards
- Responsible for inventory control, pricing goods, stocking shelves, merchandise displays
- Took orders and served food and beverages

EMPLOYMENT EXPERIENCE

MacDonald Ltd.	Sept. 2003–Present	**Technical Support**
AAA International	July–Sept. 2003	**TSR – Sales**
Gerard's Restaurant	March–Oct. 2003	**Bartender**
Reg. Security Services	June 2002–June '03	**Security Guard**
Refills Inc.	Oct. 2001–June '02	**Customer Service**
Computer Store	January–April 2001	**Computer Repair**
Fast Food Restaurant	Mar. 1999–June '01	**Customer Service**

EDUCATION
State College of A. A. & T.   **Computer Engineering Program**
Completed first year

CERTIFICATES/ACHIEVEMENTS
- ✓ Military Basic training, Military Gunner Certificate
- ✓ First Aid
- ✓ S.H.A.R.P. training (Sexual Harassment & Racial Prejudice)
- ✓ Encounters Leadership Program

VOLUNTEER EXPERIENCE
Security - Sate College sponsored events
Coached elementary girls floor hockey
Assisted coaching - minor hockey

FOOD SERVICE & RETAIL STORE: Retail Sales Associate

ALICE J. JOHNSTON

123 Learning St, Anytown, ST USA 10101   999-555-1212   alicej@yourname.com

---

Retail Sales Assistant manager-level experience. Excels at retail management duties such as training, display, marketing initiatives, and tracking numbers.

EDUCATION

Honors Bachelor of Business Administration - Major Marketing, State University 2004
• State University Entrance Scholarship

EMPLOYMENT EXPERIENCE

Retail Sales Representative, Spare Inc, Anytown Mall, Dec '99–April '05
• Track daily and weekly sales figures for head office
• Received and organized incoming stock in an orderly fashion
• Designed displays for new stock
• Provided excellent customer service through strong interpersonal and communication skills
OVER & ABOVE
• Manage staff in absence of supervisor
• Trained new employees by walking them through orientation and store operations
• Developed a tracking list to update inventory

Personnel Administrative Assistant, L.A.S.E.R. Eye Institute   May '01–Sept '02
OVER & ABOVE
• Developed a contact list to increase and generate new business
• Initiated and implemented new polices for the office administrative staff, including a training manual for new employees
• Assisted in the decision making process for marketing strategies which included determining target market regions and promotional material
• Accountable for daily activities in the absence of the education manager

Customer Service Representative, ABC Office Supplies   May '00–Sept '00 (Seasonal)
• Provided customers with information about products and sales throughout the store
OVER & ABOVE
• Created point-of-purchase displays, increasing impulse purchases.
• Trained new employees on products and store operations.

Assistant Manager, Big Scoop   May '96–April '99
• Assisted in the preparation of products and special orders
• Received a promotion from customer service representative
OVER & ABOVE
• Managed staff in absence of supervisor
• Trained new staff on store operations

VOLUNTEER EXPERIENCE

• Anytown Business Co-op Club - September '00–April '02

INTERESTS: Learning more about fashion and retail; reading Vogue, Seventeen, and other fashion and lifestyle magazines for new trends; TV shows about design; tennis

FOOD SERVICE & RETAIL STORE: Retail Account Manager

John J. Johnston

123 Learning St., Anytown, USA 10101 Phone: (999) 555-1212

CAREER PROFILE: Skilled Account Manager with over 10 years of sales experience and 6 years buying experience. I offer a prospective employer a strong work ethic, computer literacy, and dedication to meet objectives on time with a positive bottom-line impact.

EMPOYMENT EXPERIENCE:

ABC Inc., Account Manager, 1995–Present
- Account Manager representing 10 companies for housewares, hair accessories, lawn and garden, small electrics, golf, paper products, giftware, personal care, & cleaning products
- Responsibility for approximately 100 accounts, consisting of mass merchants, department store, specialty retail, drug chains, and distributors

Responsibilities include: Presenting to buyers product for regular listings, promotions, and special buys; analyzing each account and selecting merchandise best suitable for their assortment; working with buyers to crate category plan-o-grams within the space available.

Strategy: Develop merchandising strategies for best presentation of product
- Control stock levels in various retails outlets, monthly counts, and reorders; analyze competitors product for quality, price assortment, and presentation

Trade shows: Solicit new business customers, outside gift shows; set-up and work trade shows, present new product to current customers and source potential clients.

ACCOMPLISHMENTS:
- Constantly surpassed annual revenue goals by 20%
- Opened approx. 50 new accounts, consisting of wholesale distributors and retail chains
- Implemented plan-o-grams that have proven to be excellent programs and produced increased sales to the customer
- Gained respect from all buyers due to my work ethics and dedication to each customer

MMM – the kitchen collection, Buyer, 1990–1995
- Purchased all merchandise, plan promotions, special events, seasonal buys for chain of 34 stores—negotiate price, terms, and programs
- Develop new product and Junors exclusive products
- Attend domestic and foreign trade shows in search of new products

ACCOMPLISHMENTS:
- Reduced $2,000,000 inventory overstock in 1 year
- Achieved highest sales increases in Junors history, exceeded sales increases by 20% each year
- Increased turnover by 1% the first year, and 2% every year after
- Introduced new product categories (small appliances, giftware)

DeVONS LTD., Merchandise Assistant, 1985–1990
ACCOMPLISHMENTS:
- Coordinated the first, and most successful, DeVONS Bridal Event
- Coordinated a number of events, vendor work shops, ceramic fair, and appearances

EDUCATION:
- American Business – State Polytechnical Institute
- Negotiation Skills – Retail Council
- Retail Direction Seminars

FOOD SERVICE & RETAIL STORE: BAD—Customer Service

Alice J. Johnston
123 Learning DR. Anycity ST10101
(555) 999 1212
;alicej@yourname.com

Objective
To obtain a position as a Servicing Associate Inbound/Outbound Position in a

company that offers a challenging environment and a professional growth.

Skills
. Excellent customer services.
. Well adapted to handle irate customers.
. Advanced computer skills (windows 98,XP/NT, MS office, Internet explorer).
. Exceptional communication skills and telephone manners.
. Creative and resourceful problem solving and decision making skills..

Employment History

Chicken To Go (OPD.call center)   2003~till to date
Customer Service Representative/Order Taking
. Greeted customers by utilizing Customer Courtesy Code with every interaction.
. Resolved customers problems in professional and understanding
manner. .
. Took order over the phone and Procesed them accurately and
efficiently
. Performed additional duties as required ,(e.g,Trained new staff
members to perform CSR also performed Miscellaneous administrative tasks as
assigned).

Client Calls (call center)   2002-2003
Customer Service Representative
. Answered inbound calls.
. Handled customer inquiries including account information, billing inquiries and suggesting the appropriate
plans
. Answered technical questions and solved dial-up networking and connectivity issues.
. Contributed to the internal solutions database. Performed customers relations duties.

Calls People (Telemarketing)
Sales Representative
. Outgoing calls to selected customers
. Meet monthly targets
. Assissed customers need to advise for best package plans.

Education
. Graduated from District C.I. Anycity Anystate.
. Currently enrolled in a call center and customer service skills certif

Highlights of qualifications
. Strong organizational skills;
. Worked effectively in fast paced teal environment in retail industry.
. Advanced keyboarding skills with a typing speed of 50 words perm

What's Wrong?
- Lackluster objective/profile or lack thereof
- Spelling, grammatical, or word choice errors
- Name is too small or address is too large or both
- Uninspiring and boring

HEALTH & BODYCARE: Nurse, 5 Years

123 Learning Street
Anytown, USA 10101

Home: 999-555-1212
Cell: 999-555-1313

Alice J. Johnston
Highly motivated, caring, compassionate, with high levels of energy and stamina

Profile

A **Registered Practical Nurse** who cares for clients by drawing on my interpersonal strengths and five years of experience working with chronically ill people. Dedicated and high achieving student of the Practical Nursing program. Effective communicator with meticulous attention to detail. Fluent in four languages (English, Greek, Portuguese, and Spanish—conversational).

Relevant Experience

Registered Practical Nurse
The Villa, Long-term Care Facility   **May '03—present**
Duties Include:
- ✓ Administering medications
- ✓ Providing wound care
- ✓ Monitoring vital signs and blood glucose
- ✓ Providing personal care
- ✓ Documenting residents' progress
- ✓ Processing doctors' orders, etc.

Visiting/Community Nurse and Support Worker
Nurses on the Go   **Jan. '00—Jan. '04**
Duties Included:
- ✓ Working with chronically ill clients, with conditions such as Parkinson's, Alzheimer's, Multiple Sclerosis, COPD, Diabetes Mellitus, Heart Disease, CVA, Mental Illness, Cancer, etc.
- ✓ Providing wound care, medication management, injection administration, catheter and colostomy appliance application and care, staple removal, parenteral feeding, personal care, performing active and passive exercise routines, and documentation.
- ✓ Providing palliative care on a number of occasions.

Special Award: Recipient of the Nurse on the Go Award for Service - '01.

Practical Nursing Program, Student   **Jan. '02—Dec. '02**
During the Practical Nursing program I was exposed to the following clinical environments:
- • **Seacrest** (Chronic Care Facility for the Elderly)
- • **J.F.K. Rehabilitation Centre** (Chronic Care)
- • **Northeastern Hospital, Cardiac Unit** (Acute Care Facility)

Education

Registered Practical Nursing Diploma (GPA 3.8 out of 4.0) **   Dec. '02
State College

Personal Support Worker Certificate (GPA 4.0 out of 4.0) **   Jan. '02
State College

Palliative Care Course (final mark A+) **   Dec. '01
State College

** Certification achieved with 100% attendance

Interests

Reading books on Religion and Philosophy; Philanthropy within my community.

HEALTH & BODYCARE: Speech Pathologist

Alice J Johnston

123 Learning St., Anytown, USA 10101   (H) (999) 555-1212

PROFILE: **Passionate Speech-Language Pathologist**
- 15 years of experience with the adult and geriatric populations.
- I am known among my colleagues as a warm, open, and caring person who speaks her mind and listens to others with equal respect.
- I am also a clear communicator who puts technical & complex information into laymen's terms, and who writes—if can you believe it—one page reports.
- Above all, I am a tireless, committed advocate for patients, families, and colleagues.

WORK EXPERIENCE:

Rose Center for Geriatric Care   **June 1991–present**
Position: Speech-Language Pathologist

Caseload:
Adult & geriatric populations presenting with communication and/or swallowing disorders associated with stroke and other neurogenic & progressive disorders, in Rehabilitation, Day Treatment, Palliative Care and Complex Continuing Care

Day-to-Day Patient-Related Care:
* Assessment, treatment, and management of communication disorders for individuals and groups
* Assessment & management of dysphagia, including Videofluoroscopy of the oral & pharyngeal phases of the swallow (modified barium swallows)
* Consultation, therapy programming with family, nursing staff, and interdisciplinary teams
* Participation in patient care rounds, family conferences & interdisciplinary team meetings

Additional Center-wide Responsibilities:
* Participate in strategic planning sessions, in departmental meetings, and hospital-wide operational planning meetings
* Provide in-service training for hospital staff, Nursing students, Medical, and Dental residents
* Supervision of Speech-Language Pathology graduate students for two month placements

Special Achievements:
* Co-chaired the Tube Feeding Task Force which developed Clinical Practice Guidelines for feeding tube insertion and for reassessment of feeding tubes in Complex Continuing Care residents
* Developed the Goal Program for the Rehabilitation Unit
* Co-created the Adaptive Communication Service and integrate "Communication Circles," a new method for delivery of communication services for communicatively-complex residents
* Co-created a special-textured diet for Dysphagic patients, with two Dieticians
* Ongoing work with HR to maintain good Labor Relations between Professional Staff & Management
* Continue to receive cards/letters of thanks and other positive feedback from patients & residents, their families, other team members, and hospital staff, including the CEO of the Center

West Park Hospital   **January–June 1991**
Position: Speech-Language Pathologist
Special Achievement—Developed & implemented Videofluoroscopy protocol with radiology

Big Hospital   **Oct. 1989–Dec. 1990**
Position: Speech-Language Pathologist

City Rehabilitation Centre   **July 1987–Sept. 1989**
Position: Speech-Language Pathologist
Special Achievement—Chairperson of the "Family Evening Stroke Program"

RECENT PRESENTATIONS AND OTHER INITIATIVES:

Nursing Gerontological Association Annual Conference   **Nov. 2002**
  Presented the Tube Feeding Task Force's Clinical Practice Guidelines for Enteral Feeding

Grand Rounds (Center-wide, multidisciplinary education rounds)   **Sept. 2002**
  Presented model for "Communication Circles"

Capistrano College   **June 2001, July 2002**
  Guest lectured to occupational therapy & physiotherapy aide student on "Communicating with
  People with Dementia"

Occupational Therapists' Interest Group   **March 2002**
  Guest Lecture—"Unable to Assess Secondary to Aphasia" on how to modify OT assessments
  for assessing aphasic, and other communicatively-impaired, patients

Central Negotiating Team—Hospital Professionals Division of SAOW   **Dec. 2002–present**
  Elected to SAOW team to negotiate province-wide contract with the State Hospital Association

Private Practice   **Ongoing**

EDUCATION:

Master of Science, Communication Disorders - 1987
State University,

Bachelor of Arts, Honors Linguistics - 1984
State University

Undergraduate courses, Linguistics and Psychology - 1980–1983
State University

PROFESSIONAL ORGANIZATIONS/AFFILIATIONS:

Registered/Certified Member of:
- State Association of Speech-Language Pathologists and Audiologists (SLA)
- American Association of Speech-Language Pathologists and Audiologists (ASLPA)
- College of Audiologists and Speech-Language Pathologists (CASLP)

THINGS I ENJOY WHICH AREN'T SPEECH-LANGUAGE PATHOLOGY:

Sunshine, the beach, gardening, yoga, reading, and motorcycle riding (think Grace Kelly on a Harley)

HEALTH & BODYCARE: RMT Massage Therapist

Alice J. Johnston R.M.T., B.Ph.E.

tel: 999-555-1212   123 Learning St., Anytown, USA 10101

A Registered Massage Therapist and Physical Education graduate with strong interpersonal and communication skills combined with extensive diverse experience with individuals with special needs, especially children.

PERSONAL ATTRIBUTES

- Innate desire to comfort people
- Strong interpersonal, communication, and listening skills
- Compassionate, caring, and motivated

MASSAGE THERAPY BACKGROUND

Self-Employed

• Therapeutics Massage	2003–present
• Private clients and retirement home residents	1997–2003

Prelude   2003–2004
- Working with regular clients in a day-spa setting

Feeling Good   Physiotherapy Clinic   1998

VOLUNTEER EXPERIENCE

Children's orphanage   1993
CENTRAL AMERICA

Centennial Nursery School – special needs children   1992

Camp Giggles counselor – camp for children with cancer   1990–1993

Swim for Better Health Center – rehab swimming program   1990
for children

EARLY WORK EXPERIENCE

Underwater Diving School   1994–1999
- Working as a PADI Scuba Instructor in Bay Islands, HONDURAS

EDUCATION

State School and Teaching Clinic   1995–1996
    Registered Massage Therapy Program

State University   1988–1992
    Bachelor of Physical and Health Education

HEALTH & BODYCARE: Medical Education Health

John J. Johnston

123 Learning Street
Anytown, USA 10101
(999)555-1212 (W)   (999)555-1313(H)

October 2003 to Present

Professional Experience

ABC Inc.
Continuing Medical Education Manager

- Manage a staff of six Continuing Medical Education associates.
- Work closely with product managers in the development of new and innovative Continuing Medical Education programs by using needs assessment surveys.
- Conduct needs assessment surveys to aid in the development of new and innovative Continuing Medical Education programs.
- Work closely with Regional and District Managers in the development of annual and quarterly Continuing Medical Education business plans.
- Maintain accurate record keeping of $1,500 000 Medical Education Budget (national) and provide product managers with regional and district updates of program activity.
- Establish and maintain close relationships with major teaching institutions and professional medical organizations.
- Provide effective follow-up strategies for sales representatives upon completion of a medical education event.

Selected Accomplishments and Professional Highlights

- Designed and implemented a continuing medical education strategy to support the launch of our new antidepressant which attracted over 120 Psychiatrists from across America.
- Elected to the planning committee for the annual American CME symposium which attracted 135 CME providers from across the US.
- Designed and implemented a new CME management system for sales representatives and a separate management system for district managers.
- Designed and implemented a new CME management system for district managers.
- Instrumental in creating a presence for ABC Inc. on the internet via 3 different websites specific to our therapeutic categories.
- Wrote a monthly internet column for *AP Med*, a new periodical for family physicians.

HEALTH & BODYCARE: Medical Education Health (cont.)

September 2002 to
October 2003

ABC Inc.
Continuing Medical Education Associate

- Work closely with District Managers in the development of annual and quarterly Continuing Medical Education business plans.

- Maintain accurate record keeping of $100,000 Medical Education Budget and provide regional and district managers with updates of CME program activity.

- Support sales representatives in effectively planning and implementing continuing medical education programs.

- Work closely with speakers and facilitators to ensure sales representative objectives are met, negotiate speaker honoraria.

- Attend numerous CME events and conventions to critically evaluate and critique ABC Inc. speakers.

May 1999 to
September 2002

ABC Inc.
Pharmaceutical Sales Representative

- Developing and implementing an effective territory management system.

- Organization and administration of continuing medical education events for pharmacists and physicians.

- Educating and motivating physicians to maintain support of the ABC's product line.

- Establishing quarterly goals and objectives to ensure attainment of total annual territory sales targets.

- Maintaining accurate physician/pharmacy records.

- Collecting competitive information for ABC's head office to aid in the development of product marketing strategies.

Significant Achievement

In my first full year as a ABC's Pharmaceutical Representative (2000) I was awarded "District Representative of the Year" as selected by my District Manager and the National Sales Manager.

Education

Bachelor of Physical Education and Science, State University (1996)

Masters Degree, Physical Education and Sport Administration, State University (1998)

Professional Appointments

Alliance for Continuing Medical Education

- Organization Member
- Member of the Planning Committee for the 1998 Annual Meeting

GHAC Subsection for Continuing Medical Education

Organization Member

Outside Interests

All sports, looking at great art in small art galleries, messing around on my computer with new games and programs.

John J. Johnston

123 Learning St., Anytown, USA 10101
Email: johnj@yourname.com

Tel: (999) 555-1212/Cell: (999) 555-1313

PROFILE
Sales—Over 12 years of experience in sales management, sales, & pre-sales support for enterprise-wide, mission critical technical solutions to fortune 1000 corporations in various markets. Seeking executive opportunity in sales and marketing for a highly energetic company requiring a self-directed, goal-oriented, problem-solver in a technically demanding environment.

Business Experience

Jan 2000–present

Vice President Sales, USA, *MEGA Inc.*
Managed American sales team and developed vertical market strategies to sell MEGA end-to-end security solutions for: Financial Services, Telecommunications, ISP/ASP, Healthcare, and Government markets. Member of MEGA Integration team representing sales in three acquisitions: combining compensation, sales staff, & business plans. Developed MEGA sales process to implement best practice methodologies and implement sales tools. Planned and executed sales training program to improve selling efficiency. Grew revenues by 100% each quarter and targeted key large accounts including: Big Phone Company USA, Wireless USA, Government of USA, and others. Responsible for developing sales strategy for Public Key Infrastructure (PKI), Security, and Storage solutions.

Director, Secure Network Storage Division, *MEGA Inc. (Off-site Data Technologies)*
Responsible for sales of online backup and recovery solution for Eastern USA. Developed business plan and targets for rapid growth through leveraging major channel partners. Developed channel partner start-up model and required marketing and sales collateral. Target key partnerships with telecommunication providers, ISPs, and IT solutions providers.

Mar. 1997–Nov. 1999

Sr. Account Executive, Northeast US, *Commune Inc.*
Responsible for sales and marketing of Enterprise Wide Risk Management solutions for financial institutions in USA and Northeast US. Solution based sales that involved software licenses, support, software integration, and third party products. Prepared territory business plan to increase revenues and exposure within the territory. Exceeded targets by 20% and increased territory revenues by over 400% delivering $3M in sales in the first year. Increased prospects from a handful of unqualified accounts to a fully developed sales funnel with over 30 targeted accounts.

Nov. 1993–Mar. 1997

Sr. Representative, Business Development, *My Data Inc.*
Responsible for software services and solutions business development for industrial automation, aerospace/defence and financial markets with additional geographical responsibility high-tech region. Personally achieved growth over 33% yearly compounded and exceeded quotas by over 20% every year. Managed one business development representative responsible for Big Power Company and provided mentoring and guidance for two new sales recruits. High-growth targets were achieved by signing exclusive partnership agreements with large customers and by leveraging alliances with third party software product providers.

Jan. 1990–Nov. 1993

Account Manager, *XYZ Prototypes Inc.*
Initiated and managed office with sales and technical support focus for GUI design tools for customers North Central U.S. Achieved 130% of first year quota. Maintained strong presence in aerospace and defence, while starting new customer base in process control, automotive, and financial markets.

HIGH TECH: Sales (cont.)

Pre-Sales Support Engineer, *XYZ Prototypes Inc.*
Responsible for international pre-sales support. Obtained largest revenue base of all pre-sales employees during the two-year period. Set-up and managed Australian distributor. Trained and provided technical support to distributors in Northern Europe and Asia. Managed global distributo in: Australia, Sweden, UK, and Germany.

May 1987–Aug. 1988   **Technical Sales Engineer,** *AC Electronics Inc.*
Sales & technical support for AC graphic display products for finance industry. Financial applications products group achieved $12M in sales for financial products, a 25% increase over the previous year. Managed distributors for state financial market.

Business Awards
1997	Commune Sales Award—Recognizing Excellence in Exceeding Quota
1996	CUBIE My Data Quota Club
1995	CUBIE My Data Quota Club
1994	CUBIE My Data Quota Club

Business Training
1999	Sales Training—e-business Solution Selling, Sales Methodology, and Customer Management courses
1996	Management Skills for new supervisors—SPAR University
1996	Opportunity Management—American Computer Marketing Consultants
1995	Leadership Skills—SPAR University
1994	How to Get Results with People—CareerTrack

Education
1988-1989	Masters Engineering, State University—Mechanical Engineering (CGPA 4.0/4.0)
1983-1987	Bachelors Engineering State University—Mechanical Engineering (Top 10% of class)

Academic Awards
1986	Academic Scholarship
	Awarded for maintaining an academic standing in the top 5%
1984–1986	Faculty Scholar
	Received for maintaining an academic standing in the top 10%
1985	NSERC research grant for summer session

Languages   French: spoken

JOHN J. JOHNSTON

123 Learning St., Anytown, USA 10101
Home: 999-555-1212; Cell: 999-555-1313; Email: johnj@yourname.com

CAREER PROFILE

A resourceful, innovative, and entrepreneurial General Manager with over 15 years of management experience in starting, managing, and growing a successful high-tech company. Results-oriented team leader who has built trust-based relationships with suppliers, employees, customers, and partners. Comprehensive P&L responsibility including a successful track record of controlling and reducing costs, increasing gross margins, outsourcing non-value-added functions, and improving company profitability. Wide-ranging public company knowledge and experience including raising capital, initiating and maintaining a NASDAQ listing, completing SEC filings, overseeing the audit process, and participating in annual general meetings. Graduate of the State School of Management's International Executive MBA program.

BUSINESS EXPERIENCE

Pebbles SEMICONDUCTOR   1987-2001

Pebbles Semiconductor was founded in 1987 to design and sell PC-based logic analyzers and in 1989 the company shifted its focus to the design and sale of custom integrated circuits. By the end of 2000 the company was trading on the NASDAQ National Market System with annual sales of over $11M, with a workforce of over 50 employees worldwide. A partial list of the company's customers included Space Center, Big Hydro, Ministry of Defense, XYZ Company.

President (Shareholder)   2001

Reported to the Chairman of the Board with the mandate to negotiate and complete the sale of the company to Smart Corporation, a publicly traded state company. The sale was completed in September 2001.

- Partnered with the Chairman of the Board to structure and negotiate the terms of the sale. Worked with legal, accounting, and investment banking professionals to create, assemble, and review the due diligence documentation.

- Successfully implemented an employee retention strategy that resulted in an employee retention rate of over 95% through the completion of the sale. Worked with customers, partners, and suppliers to provide a smooth transition of the business.

Chief Operating Officer (Shareholder)   2000

Reported to the CEO with responsibility for product development, operations, sales, and information systems.

- Introduced a new product development and planning process which included leading cross-functional teams that were responsible for product definition and development, marketing and sales strategy, and operations planning.

- Negotiated the purchase of $500,000 USD in third party intellectual property rights licenses to be incorporated into the company's products and negotiated the purchase of over $2.5M USD in hardware emulation tools and electronic design automation (EDA) software licenses. These initiatives significantly reduced the product development and verification times as well as increasing design reusability.

- Conceptualized and introduced a new sales management initiative, including the implementation of a comprehensive design win tracking and forecasting database, aimed at increasing revenues per key account as well as expanding market penetration into new accounts. Realigned the compensation plan in support of these new goals.

- Researched, evaluated, and successfully implemented the enterprise resource planning (ERP) software from JD Edwards that was used to process sales orders, generate financial statements, and facilitate business planning through the sharing of real time business information.

General Manager (Shareholder)   1993-1999

Reported to the CEO with responsibility for operations, sales, and information systems.

- Negotiated manufacturing supply agreements with Chunk, Kim Electronics, and Jong Electronics to manufacture the company's integrated circuit products.

- Successfully implemented a continuous cost reduction program with each manufacturing supplier and devised and implemented the pricing strategy for all product lines for sales directly to OEMs and through distribution channels. These initiatives resulted in increasing gross margins of 53%, 62%, 69%, and 70% from 1996 through 1999 respectively.

- Boosted sales by 1600% from $600,000 in 1993 to over $10,000,000 in 1999. Increased sales and gross margins resulted in company reporting a profit in 1993, 1994, 1998, and 1999.

HIGH TECH: General Manager (cont.)

- Negotiated a third party logistics supply agreement to outsource the bulk purchasing of the company's integrated circuit products as well as the inventorying, handling, repackaging, and shipping of the products as per customer orders. As a result of this agreement the company was able to free up more than $1.5M in cash that was no longer tied up in inventory. This agreement also allowed the company to support significantly higher sales volumes without incurring additional personnel or fixed costs.

- Managed the complete overhaul and updating of the company's entire information systems structure to support future growth and information sharing requirements.

Chief Financial Officer and Secretary (Shareholder)   1994-1999

Reported to the CEO with responsibility for finance, corporate reporting, and human resources.

- Instrumental in taking the company public, in 1994, through a reverse merger with a state-based pubic shell. Integral in raising $1.5M USD through a private placement in 1995 and an additional $5.5M USD through a private placement in 1998. Completed all the required SEC filings on time and was successful in qualifying the company for a listing on the NASDAQ National Market exchange.

- Successful in negotiating a $250,000 line of credit with the bank, minimizing bad debts, managing costs and expenses, implementing capital asset purchase guidelines, and managing cash flow. In 1999 was successful in obtaining a Dun & Bradstreet rating of 3A1 the highest rating for a company of that size.

General Manager (Equity Partner & Member of the Board)   1989-1993

Reported to the President with responsibility for sales, operations, and finance as well as managing the Pc/La business unit.

- Increased sales by negotiating distribution agreements in the United States, Japan, Israel, Finland, England, Greece, and Italy. Negotiated an agreement with Onlineinfo to sell the Pc/La through its catalog which increased Pc/La sales by 100% from 1992 to 1993.

- Instrumental in negotiating the company's first manufacturing supply agreement with National Semiconductor Corporation (NSC) to manufacture its integrated circuit products. Assisted in the negotiation of a marketing and distribution contract with NSC that netted the company $2.4 million over an 8-year period.

- Successfully increased total product sales by 160% from 1989 to 1993 while maintaining an average gross margin, across all product lines, of 73%. Defined and instituted expense control policies and procedures that resulted in the company remaining profitable from 1990 through 1993.

- Set up the company's entire financial infrastructure and negotiated a $250,000 bank loan that was repaid over 3 years.

Equity Partner and Member (Board of Directors)   1987-1989

One of four founding partners of the company. Complete profit and loss responsibility for the Pc/La logic analyzer product family.

- Instrumental in the launch of the Pc/La into the marketplace including writing the graphical user interface, diagnostic and test software, writing the user manual, and spearheading the development and preparation of promotional materials.

- Negotiated Pc/La distribution agreements in the U.S., Canada, Germany, France, and Australia to allow access to a broader base of customers resulting in sales of $220,000 in 1989.

Software Group Leader   1986-1987
Senior Software Designer   1984-1986

EDUCATION AND PROFESSIONAL DEVELOPMENT

International Executive MBA, School of Management   2003
Project Management Course, State University   2000
Bachelor of Science (Computer Science), State University   1980

Member, Department of Computer Science Industry Advisory Board, State University
Secretary & Member of the Board of Directors, State University Alumni Association
2002 Arbor Award recipient for volunteer service, State University

HIGH TECH: BAD—Sales

JOHN J. JOHNSTON

123 Learning Rd, Apt 111, Anycity ST 10101

(555) 999 1212 C
(555) 999 1414 H

OBJECTIVE

To obtain a senior role with a leading services orientated organization, providing an opportunity to apply skills and interest in sales, promotions, and customer service.

SUMMARY

Aggressive & enthusiastic hi-tech sales professional with an 8 year track record of sales. Dynamic and motivational team leader with the ability to bring individuals to function as a team. Results oriented, competitive performer, and a team player.

CAREER HISTORY

ABC Consulting, Anycity, Anystate
*Account Executive-SAP Practice (*Sept 1 2002 to December 2002)
- Identified new SAP clients throughout the United States
- Partnered with Big 5 Consulting firms
- Assisted in the recruitment of high level candidates
- Have great contacts within the SAP market.

National Trucks, Anycity, Anystate
*Recruiter-Exporter (*November 2001 to Present)
- Assisted with the location process of identifying product to be shipped overseas
- Understanding what the customer wants from a foreign prospective
- Dealing with high level calls (President CEO etc)

Smith Associates, Anycity, Anystate
High Tech Recruiter- Hardware and Software (July 1997 - August 1999)
Consultant- High Tech Sales (August 1999 - October 2001)
- Qualified for President's Club 1999* 2000 (* first President's Club as a company)

DataPro, Anycity, Anystate
Recruiter- Hardware and Software (August 1995 - May 1997)
- Was hired to generate new leads through cold calling.
- Worked with the sales team to ensure candidate flow.

Grocery Inc, Anycity Anystate
Warehouse Help- Feb 1995 - May 1995)
EDUCATION

What's Wrong?
- Lackluster objective/profile or lack thereof
- Uninspiring and boring
- Name is too small or address is too large or both

HIGH TECH: BAD—Sales (cont.)

State University, Anycity
B.A. - May 1993 Political Science

INTERESTS

Reading, traveling, music, food
Enjoy golf, squash, rollerblading, soccer, cafes

Alice J. Johnston MBA

123 Learning Street, Anytown, USA 10101 Tel: 999-555-1212 Email: alicej@yourname.com

Management or Trainee for Hotel. Energetic self-starter with global experience.

PERSONAL PROFILE
- Passionate about the hospitality industry, qualified with specialized hospitality education, with extensive guest service experience
- Planning of tactics and timely execution; capable of multitasking and meeting deadlines; strong work ethic and adaptable to many tasks
- Delegation to appropriate support roles and excellent follow-up; respect for colleagues and customers; positive attitude, interacting with people in a constructive and professional manner
- Good interpersonal communication skills, both written and oral; computer literate, comfortable with computerized working environment, quantitative work, and data processing

WORK HISTORY
Sales Executive, 5-Star Hotel, China, February, 2002–April, 2003

- Experienced with Fidelio system, achieved excellent service standard and guest satisfaction with attention to detail, devotion to guests and hotel
- Responsible for support functions for the Director of Sales & Marketing, and supervised five Sales Coordinators
- Participated in ensuring the smooth operation of the division, assisted Director of Sales & Marketing working with Regional Sales Office in submitting Annual RSP, updating the Marketing Plan, and the Sales & Marketing Manual
- Maximize business opportunities, deliver quality service & products, involved in initiation, development, implementation, & ongoing adjustments to the Customer Loyalty Program
- Assisted with department operations and staff training, completed cash reconciliation, and ordered select merchandise

Started as a Sales Assistant, and was promoted to Sales Executive four months later. Made significant contributions to Sales teams, especially in situations dealing with English speaking VIPs. One of the only 2 5-Star Hotel supervisors selected to attend the International Training Program for "Taking Sales Managers to a Higher Level", (completed the training in June 2002).

EARLIER WORK HISTORY
- **Local Weekly News Broadcaster (Part-time)**, EL Broadcasting Station, China, Sept 2000–Dec 2001
- **English Simultaneous Interpretation (Part-time)**, China, May–Sept 2001
- **Research Assistant (Part-time)**, Cheng Travel Agency, China, Nov 2001–Sept 2002

EDUCATION
MBA in Hospitality and Tourism Management, State University, 2003–2004
- Scholarships: Winner of University Graduate Scholarship 2003 & 2004
- Teaching Assistantships: Professor Frith, (Wines); Professor Barns, (Managerial Skills)

Major Courses: Hospitality Marketing, International Tourism & Tourism Marketing, Hospitality Policy, Services Operations Management, Business Research Methods, Managerial Skills, Financial Accounting

B. HTM, Shenyang Normal University, 1998–2002
One of Top 5 students who received Diploma of Honor at graduation

COMPUTER SKILLS: SPSS, Computer Network, Research Applications (Internet)
LANGUAGE PROFICIENCIES: Native Language Mandarin, some knowledge of Cantonese; speak and write fluent English

HOTEL & HOSPITALITY: Resort Sales Executive

John J. Johnston

123 Learning Street, Anytown, USA 10101
PHONE: 999-555-1212   EMAIL: johnj@yourname.com

MISSION

To continue developing a long-term career within the ever-diversifying hospitality & tourism industry. Apply my tour and leisure knowledge, hotel training, skills, and formal education to execute sales and/or operations roles.

EMPLOYMENT EXPERIENCE

Resorts of the Big Mountains, Director, National Sales   *July 2003–Current*

- Create and lead the National Sales team, developing and penetrating new market segments within regional, national, and international markets. Efforts encompass Tour & Travel, Leisure, Incentive/Group, and Corporate segments

- Contract new package and product offerings including daily scheduled transportation routes to RCR destinations. Develop unique packages for AAA and CAA travel agencies. Grow Internet marketing/leisure opportunities with distinctive U.S. FIT partners

- Cultivate strategic relationships with traditional and non-traditional partners, diversifying distribution channels to increase year-round revenue streams. Develop sponsorship and partner opportunities that secure marketing funds, co-op revenue, and business-growth for the organization

- Develop a national sales budget and strategic plan to ensure all facets of the team are productive and profitable. Increase yield at all resorts, growing business volumes, and attain company goals

- Effectively target strategic and tactical travel agent partners to position Resorts of the Big Mountains ahead of the competition, increasing market-share annually by identifying unique products

- Seek and create analytical systems to measure team successes and develop analysis that measure and forecast business volumes on annual productions

Hotels & Resorts, Lake Wherever, Sales Manager, Tour & Travel   *2000–2003*

- Responsible for achieving $19 million Tour & Travel revenue by aligning with long-term tour and leisure partners targeting inbound business from European and Global markets

- Key contributor and joint author of the Marketing/Strategic plans; completed monthly sales commentary and revenue analysis of tour and travel market. Pro-actively assessed trends.

- Regional Sales Champion and multi-property seller for German and UK markets, selling and forecasting within the region. Travel included tradeshows, travel seminars, and presenting educational, training missions to FIT and Leisure partners

- Increased leisure group business, and winter/shoulder-season business in excess of 15% each season

- Attended bid presentations, securing 3 Ski Councils and growing ski club business three years in a row

Antlers Properties   *1995–2000*

Sales & Marketing Manager 1997–2000

- Worked within a dynamic team, implementing sales and marketing strategies to increase year-round business for five accommodation properties targeting all market segments

- Created Leisure and Tour Development Plan to grow annual room-nights

- Increased tour and leisure room revenue by 10% annually

- Attended trade and travel events for markets including tour and leisure in Europe, the U.S., and Canada

Tour/Group Desk Coordinator 1996–1997

- Worked as a central resource to Food & Beverage, Revenue Division, and Tour Sales by collating and issuing detailed communication
- Event Manager for functions and sales packages such as WinterStart Night Run. Increased sales opportunities to maximize Revpar

Front Desk Supervisor 1995–1996

- Senior duties included people resources, staff management, and training
- Created guest-recognition program to increase hotel revenues, brand loyalty, and account management processes

Dizzy Brewery, Assistant & Relief Manager   1988–1993   Essex, England

- Completed fast-track management program in public-house management and operations. Acted as General Manager and Relief Manager

RELATED ACCOLADES & TRAINING

2000–2003   Resorts of the Big Mountains - State-wide, U.S.

- Prospecting for the 2000s
- Account Development Management and Strategies
- Situational Selling
- Making Effective Presentations
- Delphi Conversion
- Leader of the Month, September 2000

1993–1995   State College, Coventry

- Graduated HND Hospitality, Hotel & Tourism Management
- Moey Cup – Student of the Year 1994
- Graduated MBII – British Institute of Innkeepers
- Completed 6 month work placement in Bavaria, Germany

1991–1993   Royal Windsor College - Essex, England

- Graduated National Diploma, Hotel and Hospitality Management
- HCIM – Food Safety

INTERESTS

- Aviation, global travel, checking out other resorts and inns for "research", mountain/road biking, skiing, and increasing my experience by learning from industry leaders within the tourism industry

MISCELLANEOUS

- Solid understanding of spoken German and basic written skills. Basic spoken French

- Completion of private pilot training and striving for commercial pilot's license

HOTEL & HOSPITALITY: Hotel Marketing, Vice President

Alice J. Johnston

PROFILE

Marketing Executive Specializing in Hotel and Tourism. Possess over nine years of communications/marketing experience backed by a journalism degree and certificates in both public relations and tourism marketing. Skilled in negotiating, writing, and developing innovative marketing strategy.

RELEVANT EXPERIENCE

Nights Slumber, Vice President, Marketing   **June 1999 to Present**

ABC Inc. is the master franchisor responsible for providing marketing, sales, and operations support to over 80 Nights Slumber properties nationally. The three-person marketing team is responsible for all national/regional marketing, advertising, promotion and public relations initiatives for the Night Slumber brand as well as for providing advice and consultation to franchisees on property-specific marketing, advertising, promotion, and PR activities.

- Progressed during three-year tenure from Marketing Manager to Director of National Marketing to Vice President, Marketing.

Key Campaigns
- Launched image campaign after determining the need to address perception versus reality of brand in terms of product quality. The primary component of the campaign, "The Bomb!" television spot, was recipient of Finalist Certificate at New York Festivals Television & Cinema Advertising Competition.
- Sought strategic marketing alliances to generate awareness of the Nights Slumber brand and reduce pressure on national marketing budget in exchange for room nights: Garnered logo exposure on 1.2 million bottles of Rid All and through $1M advertising buy; With KIDSTV received 20,000 kid packs for distribution at all hotels during peak family period; With Credit Card Inc., received logo/product exposure as part of national contest targeted at 260,000 cardholders with tendency to purchase travel and travel-related products.
- Created annual tactical promotions targeted at corporate and leisure audiences. For business travelers: "Stay 3 nights, receive free $40 gift certificate for Big Box Business; Stay 8 nights, receive 9th night free and stay 12 nights and receive $50 car rental coupon."

The City of Anytown, Special Events Office, Acting Marketing Manager March 1998 to June 1999

Division within Anytown responsible for producing signature events and festivals, enhancing Anytown's image as a whole. The marketing team is responsible for all marketing activities related to the promotion of the events.

- Progressed during tenure from Marketing Coordinator to Acting Marketing Manager.
- Garnered over $1M in media support for the 1999 Celebrate Anytown Street Festival including live coverage, editorial support, live liners, pre-produced spots, live remotes, and contesting opportunities. Marketed event to increase visitation over the previous year (625,000 attendees in 1999 and $7,519,895 direct spending in AT versus 400,000 attendees in 1998).
- Actively pursued a promotional relationship with the Anytown Transit Commission, a first for the division, including exposure in in-vehicle communication pieces and on subway station billboards.
- Acted as spokesperson for both events.

Alice J. Johnston

The City of Anytown, Office of the Mayor, Communications Coordinator   **Feb 1998 to March 1998**
- Wrote speeches for the Mayor's speaking engagements including Big Theater opening, restaurant opening, and carbon monoxide detector campaign.
- Provided communications assistance to the Director of Communications.

The City of Anytown   **May 1993 to February 1998**
Chief Administrator's Office, Information & Communications Officer

The Chief Administrator's Office guides the Corporation and advises council in its development of policies and services. The Information & Communications Office provides communications advice and consultation to all departments within the city of Anytown.

- Progressed during tenure from Intern to Junior Information Officer to Information Officer to Information & Communications Officer.
- Developed and executed transit advertising campaign designed to explain role of municipal government to residents.
- Secured media coverage of launch of the Big River Pedestrian/Cyclist Bridge.
- Wrote news releases, public service announcements, backgrounders, fact sheets, website copy, newsletter articles, and communication campaign proposals as required.

VOLUNTEER EXPERIENCE

- August 2000 to Present, Member, Domestic Marketing Committee and Member, Regional Marketing Initiatives Sub-Committee, American Tourism Commission.
- February 1993 to December 1999, Member and Volunteer International Association of Business Communicators (IABC).
- June 1996 to February 1997, Volunteer, SMARTRISK Foundation, Member, Special Events Committee.

ADDITIONAL EXPERIENCE

- Served as Volunteer Reporter for Access Cable Channel 13.
- Delivered two presentations on media relations to students enrolled in State College's Sport & Event Marketing Program.

EDUCATION

- Certificate, Tourism Marketing, 1997, State University.
- Certificate, Public Relations, 1993, State College of Applied Arts & Technology.

B.A.A., Journalism, Print Major, 1992, Ryerson Polytechnic University

PERSONAL INTERESTS

Baking - especially brownies, cakes, and cookies; entertaining friends to eat up all said brownies, cakes, and cookies; boxing and golfing to burn off remainder of brownies, cakes, and cookies; culinary mystery novels.

123 Learning St., Anytown, USA 10101
(999) 555-1212 (B)   (999) 555-1313 (R)
alicej@yourname.com

HOTEL & HOSPITALITY: Director of Operations

John J. Johnston
123 Learning St., Anytown, USA 10101
Home: (999) 555-1212 / Cell: (999) 555-1313 / Email: johnj@yourname.com

Director of Operations, Hotel Industry

I have acquired extensive multi-unit Operations, Marketing, and Sales expertise. A disciplined, honest, and team-building motivator, I have a hands-on leadership style and an approach to management focused primarily on attaining predetermined objectives within an entrepreneurial, professional, and mutually respectful environment.

BIG HOTELS, Director, Operations and Marketing   2001–2005

- Brought to Anytown on a two-year contractual agreement, my role was to act as a link between property managers at four resort hotel operations under my immediate supervision based private ownership group.
- In 2003, record high revenues were posted at locations through initiatives aimed at creating new— or solidifying existing—relationships with local, regional, and international tourism industry operators and development of package-segmented and targeted-marketing initiatives.
- Initiation, development, production, and distribution of new brand image and corporate identity campaign which included new in-room and internal stationary, signage, brochure, advertising, collateral material, and assorted promotional items.
- Consultative role and due diligence process to the 2002 purchase of a preexisting full-service hotel and partial implementation of procedures applicable to seasonal and transient staff.

ABC HOTEL, Anytown Airport, General Manager   1998–2000

- Contributed to the pre-opening preparations of a new 135-room full-service luxury hotel operation linked via indoor skywalk directly to Airport terminal.
- Developed and collated the operations' pre-opening manual in accordance with criteria originating from and dictated by *BrandsHotels,* the franchisor, and personally coordinated the data input and assimilation into the GEAC (property specific) computer system.
- Recruited, selected, and trained Hotel Department heads; build morale and a team spirit.
- Report to private ownership, maintain entrepreneurial spirit at hotel level, assume responsibility and accountability, implement business plan, and ensure adherence to guest service protocols, etc.

BIG INNS, Supervisor, Operations & Marketing   1995–1998

- Full start-up and ongoing daily supervision of 12 new hotel operations
- Search, interview, selection, and recruitment of local management and support personnel, provide pre-opening training, initiate motivation and retention techniques, reprimand and terminate, etc.
- Formulate and implement business plans, ensure compliance to quality control standards, establish pro-formas and budgets, revenue projections and P&L statements, and supervise daily operations.

TRIP'S OVER! CORP., Supervisor, Northern Operations   1991–1995

- Initiate and maintain all relationships with regulatory authorities to ensure full legal compliance.
- Multi-unit site selection and evaluation, monitoring progress of construction development, purchasing and ordering of all FF&E requirements for over 40 new hotel projects located throughout the Northern states with subsequent supervision of up to 20 individual locations.
- Management staff recruitment, selection, training, and retention for new locations.
- ❖ **STATE UNIVERSITY: MASTERS – COMMUNICATIONS**
- ❖ **STATE UNIVERSITY: BAC. SOC. SC. (HONORS – INT. RELATIONS)**

- ✓ University Management Institute: Anytown, USA
- ✓ American Hotel & Motel Association: State University
- ✓ Big Inn Management Institute

John J. Johnston

123 Learning Ave, Anytown, ST * (999) 555-1212 * email: johnj@yourname.com

MBA student with experience in HR Generalist Roles looking to specialize in HR strategic initiatives

EDUCATION

2003   **Master of Business Administration Fast-Track (Co-op)**

State University   Concentration(s): Strategic Management

2002   **Bachelor of Commerce (Honors)**

State University   Concentration(s): Finance/Operations Management

EMPLOYMENT EXPERIENCE

Human Resources Generalist   August 2003 –Current
Dumbry of North America

• First line response for both hourly and salaried employees in a non-unionized environment
• Responsible for running the Temporary Part-Time Employee Program, Dumbry Pension Plan, company sponsored special events
• Recruit, interview, facilitate, and organize orientation and training for both hourly and salaried employees
• Conduct wage reviews for various job classifications, perform cost/budgeting analyses that serve as the basis for the implementation of new program & operations implementation as well as policy creation/amendments (surveying and budgeting)
• Amend policies, procedures, and job descriptions (for both hourly and salaried employees)

Human Resources Generalist (Co-op)   Fall 2002
Big Car Company

• Designed and implemented a more efficient Medical Surveillance System by improving upon existing resources; Helped improve plant compliance rate from 73% to 100% during co-op term
• Designed and implemented new MS Access employee attendance tracking system by improving upon existing resources; Helped improve plant controllable absence percentage from 5.7% to 5.3% during co-op term
• Performed Health and Safety Audits, distributed prescription eyeglasses forms, issued licenses, issued safety locks, booked driver medicals, generated employee attendance reports, fallout claims, issued letters of identification and layoff notices, created and distributed the monthly newsletter—"CAR Talks"

Diagnostic Imaging Assistant   Summer 2001
Steveson Health Alliance

•   Purged, consolidated, and reorganized patient X-ray files for both campuses of the SHA
•   Retrieved, prepared, and couriered patient files/charts as needed
•   Monitored file status and extracted patient information via the Star Navigation Computer System

COMPUTER SKILLS

•   Pear Tree Software (PTS) & BPCS v. 8.2 (Enterprise Resource Planning tools)
•   Highly proficient in Microsoft Office 2000 (Word, Excel, PowerPoint, Access, Outlook)
•   Proficient in Corel Office 2000 (WordPerfect, Quattro Pro, Corel Presentations)
•   SPSS Version 10.1, MyHRIS; Familiar with HTML and Web Page Design

ACCOMPLISHMENTS & ACTIVITIES

2002–2003 Maintained an A average in the State U Fast-Track MBA Program
1998–2002 Major grade point average of 11.04 (A-) overall for degree in Business Administration at State U

Fast-Track Representative - MBA Society Executive Committee (SU)   2002–2003
Co-coordinator - Walk Safe, State University   2001–2002

HR: HR Professional, Midlevel

Alice J. Johnston, SPHR

123 Learning Street • Anytown, USA • 10101
HOME 999-555-1212 • WORK 999-555-1313 • EMAIL alicej@yourname.com

PROFESSIONAL PROFILE

A Human Resources professional with a broad range of experience in a variety of sectors. Demonstrated strengths in program alignment with business objectives, partnering with the business, and sound decision-making. Loves mentoring and team building while achieving organizational goals.

- 8 years varied HR experience
- MBA, BA, SPHR
- Results orientation with pragmatic & consultative approach
- Bottom line focus & business perspective
- Strong analytical thinker & problem solver

- Relationship builder & client orientation
- Strong influencing & negotiation skills
- Proven supervisory/managerial skills
- Valued for one-on-one coaching, mentoring & team building skills
- Strong assessment skills

PROFESSIONAL EXPERIENCE

CORPORATION OF THE TOWN OF ANYTOWN   2001–present
(Public sector—municipal; 725 full-time and 500 contract and seasonal employees; unionized)

Staffing Manager/Senior HR Advisor, Human Resources   2001–present
Responsible for leading a team to provide flexible and responsive staffing services, job evaluation, and advice regarding succession planning, compensation, retention trends, restructuring, labor relations, performance management during a period of organization-wide restructuring.

- Contribute, as a Senior HR Management Team member, to department's overall direction to ensure services meet evolving needs of a rapidly changing and dynamic organization.
- Provide strategic human resources advice and leadership regarding numerous restructurings, Contact Center start-up, diversity initiative, HR departmental reorganization, senior management recruitment, HR process, and technology improvements.
- Partner with Community and Fire Services Business Unit to provide a full range of HR initiatives and services to support their strategy including staffing, manager counseling, labor and employee relations, performance management, organizational design, compensation.

BIG OIL LIMITED   1995–2001
(One of the largest producers of crude oil and the biggest refiner and marketer of petroleum products; 18 billion dollars of revenue in 2000; 6500 employees)

Training and Development Consultant, Human Resources   1999–2001
Promoted to this position to provide consulting in the areas of needs assessment, design, delivery, and course evaluation for corporate programs and client driven initiatives.

- Managed and delivered a five phase, mixed design format management training program to develop skills of new managers. Received consistently strong ratings.
- Provided leadership and project management for launch of new diversity program.
- Developed a mentorship program for Human Resource employees.
- Led the design and implementation of the annual new employee orientation.

BIG OIL LIMITED (continued)

Human Resource Consultant (Automotive, Marketing), Human Resources   1997–1999
Provided advice and coaching as an internal consultant and member of the business management team in change management, employee relations, recruitment, retention and talent management, succession planning, performance management, manager counseling, team effectiveness, diversity, variety of reorganizations, and HR communication messages. (300 employees)
- Evaluated by client executives as being their most effective HR advisor two years in role.
- Partnered with the business and HR to ensure successful roll out of HR programs and initiatives.
- Anticipated HR issues emanating from business plans and worked with senior management to develop and implement proactive solutions.
- Led two attrition and retention projects resulting in target group attrition reduction and the development of high impact tools (values vs. performance surveys, focus group methodology, employee forums, career planning models) adopted by other groups.
- Provided advice regarding a variety of reorganizations (outsourcing, centralization, and group terminations) to ensure supportive work environment, employee productivity, high redeployment levels and to reduce corporate risk during the changes.

Recruitment Supervisor, Human Resources   1995–1997
Managed five staff and a budget of $600,000 to drive and sustain a high quality and volume of recruitment (particularly campus) activity for the organization, while focusing on staff workload, marketing, technology, process streamlining, and metrics.
- Reorganized work group to upgrade skills to better meet evolving needs of business.
- Leveraged technology (website, report customization, recruitment hot line) to increase efficiency, to reduce costs, and to broaden the company's appeal to its target candidates.
- Customized and delivered behavioral interviewing workshops across the company.
- Streamlined campus recruitment process by leading team in process mapping and analysis.
- Successfully influenced policy changes and national consistency in recruitment practices.
- Enhanced campus recruitment marketing strategy by using focus groups, changing ad agencies, and developing new ad campaign.

STATE UNIVERSITY   1993–1995
Project Manager, Clancy School of Business

INTERNATIONAL CONVERSATION CENTRE (Tokyo, Japan)   1988–1990
Business and Conversation English Instructor

EDUCATION
MBA (Human Resources), State University
BA (Psychology), State College
- SPHR, Human Resource Professional Association
- PHR candidate (anticipated end of 2006)
- Additional: MBTI professional qualifying certification, DDI Targeted Selection Behavioral Interviewing Trainer and Administrator

HR: Sr. HR Account Management

ALICE J. JOHNSTON SPHR, GPHR

123 Learning Circle
Anycity, Anystate 10101

(555) 999-1212
alicej@yourname.com

PROFILE

Senior level Manager or Account Manager with HR and Training background. Provider of superior service when my creative management style and leadership skills can be used to impact company performance customer relations, employee retention, and profitability.

QUALIFICATIONS

19 years of progressively increasing responsibility and experience in:

- Coaching
- Establishing Systems
- Economizing
- Problem Solving
- Leading People
- Making Decisions
- Establishing Procedures
- Analyzing
- Coordinating Activities

ACHIEVEMENTS

Coached and advised for job advancement, built trust and rapport in providing job performance counseling. Directed performance improvement process, analyzed skills, education, and goals to provide guidance and coaching. **Results:** Strong competent team, increased job satisfaction, reduced turnover, and provided internal career path opportunities. *(ABC Professional Services, Easy Solutions Inc.)*

Utilized **problem solving** skills to create automated solutions to manual tasks. Researched processes, desired outcomes, format of data, available systems to develop database and spreadsheet solutions to previously pencil and paper procedures. **Results:** Reduced data entry and processing times by a factor of ten and increased data integrity by 25%. *(Health Plan of Anystate)*

Established procedures for new candidate application, testing, new hire orientation, and training. Coordinated staff, information, forms, documents, government requirements to develop efficient processes and procedures. **Results:** Candidate pool became deeper and better-qualified, new hire processing time reduced by 75% while 95% of all paperwork errors were eliminated. *(ABC)*

Led the efforts of 10 staff that supported a workforce of up to 950 employees. Formulated written standards of performance, executed training plans, coached individuals, created reward and recognition programs, encouraged career development, utilized corporate resources. **Results:** High productivity and morale, quality performance, low turnover, and consistently met or exceeded customer expectations for 9 years and counting. *(ABC)*

Analyzed budget goals and performance to consistently meet or exceed profit and expense expectations. Monitored monthly expense records and income statements, researched alternative supply and service providers, provided incentives to staff and encouraged creative ideas. **Results:** Consistently profitable, improved direct margins from $1.92 per hour to $4.10 per hour in less than 18 months. *(ABC)*

Coordinated the efforts of staff and customer to develop safety training and certification procedures. Created a customer acceptable, OSHA compliant training process for basic safety. Developed early return-to-work, modified work, and ergonomic assessment programs. **Results:** Reduced Worker's Compensation incident rating and lowered premium rates, received wage rebates, reduced lost time hours and recordables. *(ABC)*

PROFESSIONAL EXPERIENCE

Program/Account Manager
ABC Professional Services   Anystate   1993–2003
Managed the on-site temporary labor program, headcount ranged from 200 to 950 with revenues from $10 to $35 million annually. Managed a staff of 10 which administered payroll, benefits, training, workers compensation, recruiting, employee relations, policy development, orientations, and record retention. Coordinated staffing and employee relations efforts with over 200 using managers and supervisors. Consistently met or exceeded revenue, profit, and margin goals while maintaining a comparatively small staff with very little turnover. Successfully built rapport and trust with executives to entry-level manufacturing employees.

Employment/Training Administrator
Easy Solutions, Inc.   Anystate   1990–1993
Employment and recruiting administration for both exempt and nonexempt, technical, clerical, and temporary contract labor. Policy development, review and change, AAP/EEO plan and goal creation. Negotiated temporary labor contracts. College recruiting, workforce planning, interview training, overall HR support, and project work. Self-managed work team training and facilitation. Included were assessing, developing, and implementing team training, facilitating teams through the evolution of change to self-managed work teams, and administering both the written and video versions of Job-Training-Instructions.

Human Resource Specialist
HealthPlan of Anystate   Anystate   1989
Comprehensive Human Resources support to seven individual health care centers, including staffing and recruiting, employee relations, EEO/AA, compensation and benefit administration, training, and development.

Area Personnel Manager
CellPhone Inc.   Anystate   1986–1989
Personnel and Employee Relations representative for all of second shift at the Anycity sites (approx. 1000 employees). Managed a wide variety of employee relations issues, benefits and salary administration, employee counseling, internal placements, and administration of policies and procedures.

Personnel Specialist
CellPhone Inc.   Anystate   1984–1986
Coordinator of Human Resources Information Systems for the Group Personnel operations, career counseling, generated all computer reports, special projects, newsletter editor, coordinated operations review materials, trained personnel to operate Macintosh computers. Coordinated all internal staffing through a posting and bidding system.

EDUCATION

BS Business Administration   State University   Anycity, AS
Earned SPHR and GPHR designations (IIHR Institute)

HR: Sr. HR Professional

Alice J. Johnston PHR

123 Learning St.
Anytown, USA 10101

Tel: (999) 555-1212
Email: alicej@yourname.com

PROFESSIONAL GOAL

A senior role on the management team leading the vision for Human Resources; with the opportunity to leverage other business skills.

BUSINESS EXPERIENCE

HR Transformations   October 2002–present
Owner
Leverage background and experience to provide HR consulting expertise to both public and private sector clients, including Beer Inc, Corp Foods, Big Bank, Huge Book Store.

Intranet Inc. - An internet professional services company   January 2000–October 2002
Vice President, Human Resources and Marketing
Led the vision and strategy for Human Resources and Marketing, including managing two teams of six Marketing and 14 HR professionals.

- Created HR processes, structures, and programs for a fast-growth company, resulting in 300% customer service improvement, 30% higher employee satisfaction rate, and reduced voluntary turnover by 25%.

- Hired and developed a skilled and highly motivated HR team. Only VP to have zero voluntary turnovers in past two years during a period of high industry turnover.

- Developed a performance and compensation management philosophy and approach based on external market benchmarking and an objectives-based process versus a "wheel of fortune" approach. Received 100% participation and strong feedback that initiative improved morale and increased productivity.

- Led the M&A work on two acquisitions. Integrated all people systems for maximum ease of transition with zero turnover.

- Led a major downsizing effort from design to implementation in order to achieve profitability. Several other companies in our venture capital fund have used our model for their own downsizing.

- Spearheaded the marketing of a new service offering in the internet industry, a mutual funds communication tool that increased Intranet's profile as an industry leader in financial services and led to eight expressions of interest and three sales.

Huge Communications USA   August 1996–January 2000
Manager, Organizational Development
Accountable for all core HR processes, with a team of three direct reports, including: recruiting, training, compensation, benefits, pension, relocation, and administration. Responsible for establishing critical HR systems and processes within the organization, and providing HR consulting to customer account teams, with special focus on employee relations, recruiting, training, and organizational development issues.

- Designed and led the process for developing the three year vision and strategy, resulting in quarterly reviews of tactics and company wide cascading of strategy.

- Led the Organizational Change Team for the restructuring effort of the organization, including infrastructure reconfiguration, work process reengineering, and cultural shift.

- Designed and implemented broadbanding compensation system, to align with new company values, culture, and goals.

Alice J. Johnston   page 2

MacConsultants   Nov 1995–Aug 1996
Contract Consultant
Provided Human Resources consultation.

BIG Company INC.   1984–1995
Employee Relations and Training Manager, 1991–1995
Human Resources Department
Provided HR generalist expertise to specific business units. Developed and implemented the training
strategy, with special focus on needs assessment, design, and facilitation.

- Led the transition plan for the organization, after a downsizing, in response to low morale. This plan
  included a seven year corporate strategy and directing a team to create the Vision 2000 transition day.
  Feedback said over 80% of participants felt "very committed" to the company.

- Decreased turnover to zero from 30% and increased morale in Pharmaceuticals Division, by completing
  an Organizational Development Assessment, which led to the recommendation and implementation of a
  six-point plan.

- Transformed the Training function to a needs-based, strategic approach, through needs analysis and
  designing workshops for specific skills. Increased overall average workshop rating from 3.4 to 4.2 out
  of 5.0.

Community Projects Director, 1991
The Alliance for a Drug-Free America
Reported to the President: responsible for developing outreach programs in the community, with emphasis
on corporate initiatives.

Commercial Production Manager, 1989–1991
Marketing Services Department
Ensured the objectives of the Brand's creative strategies were achieved by consulting with the Brand
Department and Agencies on 30+ creative strategies and commercials ($2MM budget) to establish cost, and
resolve creative issues.

Relocation Coordinator, 1986–1989
Human Resources Department
Developed and interpreted relocation policy; and relocated employees. Changed relocation function from
partial service to full service for 200 employees annually with $2MM budget. Ratings from employees
rose from average 2.5 to 4.0 out of 5.0.

Marketing Department Assistant, 1984–1986
Marketing Department

EDUCATION

State University Scholarship, 1980–1984; Hon. B.A. English and Drama
PHR designation from IIHR
Part-time studies in Psychology at State University
Part-time courses towards GPHR through IIHR

OTHER ACTIVITIES

- Volunteer facilitator of leadership program at personal development company
- Marathon training
- Started up and participate in a book circle, a film club, and an investment club

INTERACTIVE: Project Manager, Beginner

John J. Johnston

123 Learning Street, Anytown, USA 10101   999.555.1212   johnj@yourname.com

PROFILE: Junior design Coordinator and Project Manager with deep interest in leading edge interactive content. Works well in collaborative team environment and motivates "creatives" to contribute their genius on time, and on budget.

EXPERIENCES

Project Manager, Anytown Film Center   2004–2005

Mythical Legends (Interactive Installation)
- Collaborated with a group of 4 residents assuming the role of project manager and content producer
- Researched the various aspects of the life and mysterious death of filmmaker Jed Degoba to incorporate into a script for this interactive installation
- Ensured that schedule and deadlines were met within the group
- Gathered and organized production deliverables

Accomplishment: The exhibit won rave reviews in local and state papers with specific mention of the layout.

On-Site Account Manager, Southern Graphics based at ABC USA   2002–2004

- Worked as a liaison between designers, customers, and internal operators to ensure that the criteria for a specific design was met
- Coordinated the entire print production of primary and secondary artwork
- Prioritized and scheduled jobs in each department in order to manage tight deadlines and maintain this 2.5 million dollar account

Accomplishments: Brought each stage of project in on time and resolved outstanding priority issues within design team.

Editorial Intern, *Big Culture Magazine*   2002

- Proofread articles and checked the consistency of the layout prior to hitting the press
- Assisted editorial staff in conducting interviews and gathering info for feature articles
- Updated contacts for various nightclubs, bars, and social clubs in order to keep the daily listings organized and relevant

EDUCATION

Anytown Film Center   2004–2005
Interactive Arts and Entertainment Program

State University, BA, Major: English Literature   1999–2002

TECHNICAL SKILLS

- In-depth knowledge of project managing software such as FileMaker, AS400, Virtual Ticket, Job Manager, and Dot Project
- Extensive knowledge of Final Cut Pro, DVD Studio Pro, HTML design programs Dreamweaver, and GoLive along with MS Office
- Working knowledge of Adobe Illustrator, Photoshop, and Flash MX
- Ability to type 65 words per minute

INTERESTS

- Producing electronic music, Study of pop culture and retro culture, Writing poetry and prose

Alice Johnston

123 Learning Avenue, Anycity, AS 10101
(h) 555-999-1212 (w) 555-999-1313
alicej@yourname.com

Profile:
An **Advertising Account Supervisor** with traditional advertising experience AND insights into interactive and new Internet business. Creates lasting client relationships with existing Internet clients and helps to strategize bold new directions with substantial futures.

Employment History:
Top Notch Advertising, July 1998–Present
Supervisor (October 1999–Present)
XYZ Wireless

- Played a key role in the rebranding of ABC Wireless to XYZ Wireless as a member of a team of three that has since expanded to twelve people. Simultaneously launched the overall rebranding *"Imagine"* campaign, while introducing a secondary tier of product focused outdoor and magazine advertising as well as a third tier of tactical advertising in newsprint and radio.
- Created a smooth account transition from AdMart Partners to Top Notch Advertising by completing a National campaign within the first month of acquiring the account (including two television spots, five print ads, and four radio spots).
- Developed the strategy and executed the *"Fun Theatre"* campaign including web banner advertising, PR, and traditional advertising.
- Managed Account Executives and Account Coordinators on multi-disciplined accounts which include Relationship Marketing, Public Relations, and Interactive Advertising.

Account Manager July 1998–September 1999
National News

- Launched *National News*, the first new national newspaper to be printed in 15 years by utilizing each domain of the agency including PR, Events & Sponsorship, Interactive, and Relationship Marketing. This project required complete communication and consistency between all divisions of the agency. Working with the Account Director on the *"rollout"* strategy, a national campaign was created and launched. This campaign helped *National News* gain a six-day average paid circulation of 273,000 within seven weeks causing *The Old News* circulation to drop 27%.
- Coordinated with Hot Swing several large parties from a minimum of 120 CEO's at the home of Pro Golf star to 1200 advertising industry people at the media launch of National News
- Integrated new procedures for a product that was new to both Southern Inc. and Hot Swing Advertising. This involved creating all new processes including budget control of four Hot Swing sister companies, developing traffic procedures, devising new methods to manage media planning and buying.
- Received Certificate Award from *2000 Marketing Awards* for Newspaper Single "Correction Ad."

Print Technologies

- Working directly with the CEO of Top Notch Advertising, launched the English and French portion of a worldwide rebranding campaign for Printing Corp's new company Print Technologies.

ABC Consumer Healthcare

- Involved in the strategic development of Children's Cough Medicine, other medicines. Developed new television and print creative for other medicines.
- Instrumental in the initial research of Allergy Medicine required to introduce Allergy Medicine over the counter in U.S.

INTERACTIVE: Advertising (cont.)

Alice Johnston ——————————————————————————————
123 Learning Avenue, Anycity, AS 10101
(h) 555-999-1212 (w) 555-999-1313
alicej@yourname.com

careersite.com
- Developed a pitch presentation for Com Digital. The intent of the project was to create online television advertising that would be "bootlegged" and emailed around the world.

Trendy Technologies
- Developed U.S. creative in conjunction with Top Notch Tech.

Small Ville
- Donated time and resources to develop a compelling print and Direct Mail campaign for the Small Ville Athletic Centre

New Advert Inc., January 1997–June 1998
Account Coordinator
Car Dealers Association
- Twice coordinated and produced the yearly sales rally for 800 car salesmen. This included a formal meal, prepared speeches, and the presentation of the upcoming year's advertising campaign.
- Maintained the current promotion on the dealer website.
- Executed newsprint, radio, and television campaigns, solely managed all financial budget reports.

Cool Drinks Beverages (Tomato Juice, Apple Juice, InstaMix, FruitJus)
- Instrumental in the launch of Tomato Juice outdoor campaign (Awards finalist) which pioneered wild postings and chalk art advertising.

InstantDoc (PainRelief, Children's PainRelief, BackRelief)
- Contributed to the development of InstantDoc's first website http://www.InstantDoc.com/
- Controlled and maintained the budget control report.

Car Worldwide, June 1996–December 1996
Account Coordinator
FastCar
- Adapted Southern U.S. creative for the Northern U.S. Market.
- Created proposal and managed the FastCar Marketing Program.

Education
1997–1999   Institute of Advertising, *Advertising Agency Practitioner (AAP)*
1995–1996   Art College, *Faculty of Business Advertising Program*
1992–1995   University of Southern Region, *Bachelor of Arts Degree, Major in Sociology*

Business Courses
November 1999   Institute of Advertising, *The Principles of Business Writing*
November 1998   Computer Training Centers, *Intermediate Excel Version 97*
June 1998   International Limited, *Presentation Skills*

Additional Information
Level 1 Certification   Ski Instructors Alliance
Level 2   Certified Tennis Instructor

Interests
Snowboarder and Ultimate Frisbee player; Secret love of Scrabble

---

Alice Johnston

JOHN J. JOHNSTON

123 Learning St.   (999) 555-1212
Anytown, USA 10101   johnj@yourname.com

SUMMARY OF QUALIFICATIONS

Self-motivated and results-driven **Internet Sales Professional** with exceptional management skills and extensive experience in purchasing, marketing, advertising, promotions, budgeting, forecasting, inventory control, customer and vendor relations, and the recruiting, hiring, training, and motivation of personnel. Thrives in a challenging "start up" environment. Energetic leader possessing a fantastic ability to win over accounts and to significantly grow revenue within each account. Demonstrated talent for discovering ingenious ways to acquire and retain accounts by developing customized programs to meet the specific needs of each client.

PROFESSIONAL EXPERIENCE

PEOPLE FINDERS LLC –   **January 1999–Present**
Outside Account Manager/Sales Representative
Selected due to outstanding leadership skills to play a key role in opening of a new satellite office for a fast-paced, dynamic Internet company that primarily assists *Fortune* 1000 companies in their hiring efforts. Research, identify, and contact key decision-makers within large corporations in order to increase sales for the company. Actively participate in the interviewing, hiring, and training of all new associates.

- Recently promoted to a channel sales rep. Responsibility will be calling on the medical industry.

- Consistently exceeded sales quota while maintaining one of the lowest client turnover rates in the company by supplying a high level of customer service and follow up; continually rank in the top 20 percent of the company sales force in terms of sales.

- Generated additional revenue and reduced call lead-times by implementing fax- and email-based programs that enabled sales force to meet team sales goals.

- Successfully closed one of the largest revenue-producing deals in company history, generating approximately $150,000 in annual revenue.

- **Management Awarded**—Won the 1999 Award for **"Constant Positive/Team Attitude"** for strong ability to excel in a team environment & exude positive overall attitude within ever-changing Internet/"dot com" arena.

- **Management Awarded**—2nd Quarter 1999; **"Working Outside the Box"** – a unique award for "creative thinking" and "uniquely" contributing to sales force while achieving monthly and yearly sales goals.

ACC USA –   **August 1997–January 1999**
Southeast Territory Sales Manager
Chosen to deal with executive-level decision-makers at regional and corporate retail headquarters to secure profitable programs and in-line product assortments for a $1 billion housewares manufacturer. Managed corporate accounts within a territory. Supported a wide range of accounts, including hardware, housewares, lawn and garden, and office supply stores. Key accounts included Waccamaw, Simms Distribution, Independent Stationers, and U.S.O.P. Created and implemented marketing promotions for prospective customers and drafted, forecasted, and evaluated monthly business plans.

- Increased annual sales from $1.8 million to $3.2 million through aggressive acquisition of new accounts and expansion of existing business to key accounts.
- Utilized extensive cold calling and effective sales techniques to secure new business with regional accounts such as Creamers Brothers and Big Guy's Hardware.
- Resourcefully created and executed category management programs based on individual accounts, SKU assortments, seasonal programs, and special promotions to boost company revenue.

INTERACTIVE: Internet Sales (cont.)

JOHN J. JOHNSTON

123 Learning St.   (999) 555-1212
Anytown, USA 10101   johnj@yourname.com

SUPER STORE –   **January 1996–August 1997**
Store Buyer   August 1996–August 1997
Promoted to establish new vendor contacts and to vigorously pursue substantial discounts with vendors to increase store sales and company profit. Maintained existing vendor relations to ensure proper product assortment, inventory levels, and discounts. Frequently reviewed categories and sell-through of products.

- Revamped three departments—Kids, Kitchen, and Luggage—through the complete redesign of each department and elimination of under-performing products.
- Achieved maximum discounts, allowances, and rebates from vendors by working with each vendor to develop a strong rapport and create a "partnership" mindset.

Store Manager   January 1996–August 1996
Brought in to open a 20,000 square-foot store location, including the hiring and training of all "start-up" store employees and the supervision of more than 17 full-time and part-time personnel. Continuously maintained the payroll budget and various expenses relating to start-up and operation of the store.

- Accelerated store sales from zero to approximately $1 million within eight months by developing effective store promotions and thoroughly training new sales associates.

SECURITY INC. –   **June 1994–January 1996**
Sales Representative   Jun 1995–January 1996
Fully responsible for acquiring residential home security accounts through company-provided and self-generated leads in a high-volume environment for the world's largest provider of commercial and residential security systems.

Customer Service Specialist/New Associate Trainer   June 1994–June 1995
Diverse duties included working with Premier and National commercial and residential accounts, managing "at-risk" or special attention accounts on a dedicated phone. Performed classroom training for new and veteran associates.

AWARDS AND RECOGNITION – HEADHUNTER.NET

- Selected as **"Best Sales Rep"** by Training team during the December 1999 Sales Training Seminar.
- **Management Awarded**—2nd Quarter 1999; **"Working Outside the Box"**—a unique award for "uniquely" contributing to sales force while achieving monthly and yearly sales goals.
- **Management Awarded**—Award for **"Consistent Positive Attitude"** in 1999.
- 04/00—Completed AMA (American Management Association) training for the New/Prospective Manager.

COMPUTER SKILLS

- Windows 95/98
- Microsoft Word
- Basic HTML
- Microsoft Excel
- Outstanding Internet Knowledge
- Microsoft PowerPoint
- Various Internet Applications

EDUCATION

STATE UNIVERSITY –   **March 1994**
Bachelor of Arts in Psychology, Minor in Marketing

INTERACTIVE: Marketing Communications Specialist

Alice J. Johnston

123 Learning Road, Anycity, Anystate 10101   (555) 999-1212 (Home)   (555) 999-1313 (Work)

Convergent Marketing Communications Specialist with experience in leading start-up and turn-around operations

---

EMPLOYMENT HISTORY

Success Advertising Ltd   **Jan 1994–Present**
Anycity, Anystate
Managing Director, SuccessInteractive (2000–present)
Media Director, Success Advertising (1997–2000)
Media Director, Success Worldwide (1994–2000)

- Founded SuccessInteractive. Manage as autonomous business unit
- Responsible as media director of Success Advertising and Success Worldwide for driving integrated marketing communications strategies for all Success clients
- Headed the 6th largest media operation in U.S. with 60 employees

Achievements

- Developed SuccessInteractive as a stand-alone profit center and achieved profitability from year 1. Grew from 0 (1995) to 65 (2001) employees and $8MM revenue
- SuccessInteractive named to Top 10 Digital Agencies in 2001 by Marketing Magazine. Won 20 National and International Creative Awards in 2001
- Pioneered direct response media planning and buying in U.S. and developed U.S.'s first and largest response media operation
- Appointed Media Director of Success Advertising in conjunction with Success Worldwide and SuccessInteractive responsibilities in 1997
- Expanded Success media business form $120MM to $220MM during tenure as joint Media Director

Media Associates Ltd   **Dec 1990–Jan 1994**
Anycity, Anystate
Media Director

- Responsible for developing, managing, and strategic direction of the media department

Achievements

- Developed Media Department within creative boutique agency
- Successfully moved media businesses from large buying independents to in-house department
- Built business from zero to $35 MM media billings

Media Specialists Inc   **Feb 1990–Dec 1990**
Anycity, Anystate
Vice President, Account Director

- Directed largest group of accounts within agency representing almost 2/3 of revenue
- Hired to manage relationship with largest client who had placed account under review

Achievements

- Secured relationship with review account

INTERACTIVE: Marketing Communications Specialist (cont.)

Resume	Alice J. Johnston

Southern Newspaper Group, Marketing Division **April 1988–Feb 1990**
Anycity, Anystate
National Account Manager

- Represented national chain of newspapers to agencies and direct accounts
- Managed $45MM territory

Achievements
- Built business by 20% during each year of tenure
- Recipient of Rep of the Year Award 1989

Fun Advertising Ltd. **May 1986–April 1988**
Anycity, Anystate
Media Group Head

Black Advertising Ltd. **May 1984–April 1986**
Anycity, Anystate
MIS Manager
Media Supervisor

White Advertising Ltd. **Nov 1982–May 1984**
Anycity, Anystate
Media Assistant

Classic Country Club **May 1980–Aug 1982**
Anycity, Anystate
Club Manager

EDUCATION
University of Anycity
Bachelor of Science, Biology Specialist

OTHER ACTIVITIES AND INTERESTS

Board of Directors Pops Orchestra
- Privacy and Ethics Committee
- Task Force on Consent

Board of Advisors LoveTV Entertainment Inc.
- Marketing to Children Subcommittee (2001)
- Internet Privacy and Ethics Code Subcommittee (2000)
- DRTV and Teleshopping Council Executive (1999–2001)
- DRTV and Internet Council Executive (1995–1999)
- Fall Interactive Conference Committee (1994–97)
- Media Directors Council (1997–2000)

Director of Advertising Club of Anycity (1990–1994)
Frequent Speaker on Interactive and Direct Marketing
Collecting 19th Century Art and Antiques

2 of 2

INTERACTIVE: BAD—Internet Operations

123 Learning St. Anytown, USA 10101
(P) 999-555-1212 (C) 999-555-1313 ● E. johnj@yourname.com

JOHN J. JOHNSTON

OBJECTIVE

Secure full-time, permanent employment in business development, with a progressive Internet company.

SUMMARY OF QUALIFICATIONS

An intelligent, dynamic, responsible, and highly motivated individual, that is spanish/english bilingual, with tremendous leadership ability and team-building skill, having 4 years of university education and over 7 years of professional experience, in sales, marketing, finance, health sciences, and pharmaceuticals. Specifically - managed promotions for a global consumer electronics manufacturer, managed key accounts for both a logistics firm and a clothing design and manufacturing agency, worked as an investment advisor for a large retail financial services dealer, currently manage day-to-day operations for a pharmaceutical packager, and functioned as a personal trainer while studying at university.

EDUCATION

Sep. 1999 - Aug. 2001   *State University – Anytown, ST*
B.Sc. – Physiology and Psychology
- Completed 3rd year of combined honors degree
- Vice-President, Alpha Fraternity
- Member, SU pre-Med Club, STU Investment Club

Sep. 1996 - Apr. 1997 *Twisdon College @ Out of State University – Anytown, ST*
B.A. – Economics and Spanish
- Completed 1st year of program
- Attended Twisdon's bilingual campus
- Member, OofS Investment Club

RELEVANT PROFESSIONAL EXPERIENCE

Feb. 2004 - Present   *Pills for Health Packaging Ltd.*
Operations Manager – Production and Project Manage
Reporting to the President, duties include day-to-day m
scheduling, and production staff. Manage the flow of pr
packaging facility. Manage materials and component p
and provide consultation to the agency, client, and supp
producing new packaging solutions. Create client proje
the business forecast and contribute to company growth
soliciting new business. Work with industry leaders suc
AllergyMeds, Cool, SneezeFree, Fancy, and Partis.

What's Wrong?
- Dense text—I'm too bored to read this all.
- Too Stylized. I'm blinded!
- Lackluster objective/profile or lack thereof
- Name is too small or address is too large or both

INTERACTIVE: BAD—Internet Operations (cont.)

Jan. 2003 - Feb. 2004   *The American Clothing Group Inc.*
Account Manager
CWG operates as a private label clothing design and manufacturing company, serving both retail and corporate clothing markets. Reporting to the Executive Vice-President, basic responsibilities included generating leads, and identifying opportunities for new business as well as forecasting growth opportunities for the existing client base, and developing and carrying out client-specific sales and marketing plans. Specifically, attended client meetings, guided creative team, created project budgets and timelines, and managed client projects from material procurement to final production. Worked with clients such as Deets, MMP, Cool Man Golf, Discount, Department Store, Big Breweries, and Cola Co.

Sep. 2001 - Dec. 2002   *Happy Financial Services Inc.*
Finance & Investment Advisor
Operating as a self-employed broker, responsibilities included prospecting and growing a client base, and provided full financial planning guidance to affluent individuals, by promoting a full range of products and services, including investment vehicles such as stocks, bonds, mutual funds, guaranteed investments, and also protection products, such as life, health, and disability insurance.

Jan. 1998 - Aug. 1999   *DGN Marketing Services Ltd.*
Account Manager
DGN operates as a logistics management firm that specializes in the warehousing and distribution of marketing, and sales support material, and managing call center operations for various industry leaders. Reporting to the Vice-President of Sales and Marketing, responsibilities included the day-to-day management of 7 key accounts that together contributed $4 Million in annual sales. Also responsible for forecasting account potential, and up-selling of managed accounts. Specifically, prepared and managed project timelines, participated in account growth strategy, developed client relationships, and managed the account teams by being the liaison between suppliers, internal operations and the client. Worked with teams from Big Cars, Big Bank, Bunch Letters, Sailors, Wine Country, Cola, Beer, HotStuff, Partis, Chocolate, and FastFood.

INTERESTS

Activities include, working out, playing organized sports, reading business biographies, investing, and cooking.

INTERESTING JOBS: Photography, Recent Grad

Alice J. Johnston

123 Learning St. Anytown, USA 10101
(999) 555-1212   (999) 555-1313
alicej@yourname.com

Young professional photographer with great eye captures your special moments on film. Custom printing and framing available.

Professional Photographer, Alice J.'s Photography   2002–present

I have owned and operated my photography business for the past two and a half years. I specialize in Wedding and Events photography (30 weddings and 30 happy brides).

Also enjoy doing portraiture (babies and adults) and nature photography.

For more information and an instant portfolio, please visit my website at
www.alicejjohnston.com

Other Photography Work Experience

Photography Seminars, State College   2002–2003
- Spoken to 5 classes yearly (with two sessions each) about my photography business and the photo techniques I use.

Assistant Photographer/Darkroom Technician, Flash Photolabs   1999–2001
- Worked for two years as a first assistant and darkroom technician.   My responsibilities included color and black and white printing, color and black and white film development, helping customers, assisting during photo shoots, invoicing, training, and assisting during photo workshops.

Assistant Framer, In A Square   2000–2001
Photolab Technician, One Hour Developers   2001

Education

- **Professional Photography Diploma**
  Academy of Photography   2001–2002
- **Business Course**
  Academy of Photography   2001–2002
- **Fine Arts Degree** (incomplete)
  State University   1996–1999

Awards: **State College Fine Arts Award**

Volunteer Experience:

Visual Editor, *Chronicle Magazine for the Old Girl's Association*
- Volunteering my photography and editing services to yearly magazine that focuses on 20 portraits of exceptional women. 2002–2005

Travel Photography: England, France, Holland, Budapest

List of photography exhibitions on request.

INTERESTING JOBS: Designer, Furniture

•••John J. Johnston•••••••••

123 Learning Ave.
Anycity, ST

Res: 999*555*1212
Email: johnj@yourname.com

Profile ————————————————————————————

A **DESIGNER** with over 10 years leading one of America's most innovative furniture design firms. Has a passion for good design wherever it's found—be it Gehry's Guggenheim or a garbage can in Paris. Excellent at problem solving affordable and innovative solutions.

Key Qualifications ————————————————————

- 10+ years working in the design industry; creating furniture lines, designing trade show booths, wholesale, & retail showrooms
- 8 years leading a team of designers and workers
- 3 years running a retail furniture and design store; customer service included giving everything from product explanations to home decorating advice
- 12 years using materials ranging from steel, wood, glass, coroplast, fabrics, & lighting
- 10+ years of designing and producing marketing materials; brochures, postcards, business cards, website

Career Experience ————————————————————

Zang   **Founder / Designer & Shop Manager**   **Sept 1991–Aug 2004**

www.zanghome.com (html version recommended)
Co-owner and operator of a small-scale furniture design and manufacturing company based in Anycity, ranging from home furnishings to the design of corporate offices. Clients include: Brand Name, Art Gallery of AnyState, National Gallery, Museum of Contemporary Art (California), Furnituremaker.com, Picasso, Pink Vision, and Urban Styling.

During my time with Zang, I led over 100 design projects. We wholesaled to companies across North America and Japan and eventually opened our own retail store in downtown Anycity. My partner and I were also completely responsible for all marketing and promotion.

Selected Accomplishments
- Turned an unwieldy, ugly auto shop garage of 40 years into a sparkling retail store on a trendy Anycity street; the store was covered on TV ("The Hot Zone") and recommended in Anycity's Best Shopping Guide and the National paper
- Zang gained international & national media including: *National* paper, *Herald, Gazette, Design Mag, Metro Mag, Style In Home, House & Office, Bride Guide*
- Recently led modern office design and project delivery for office in Miami, FL; provided guidance and custom furniture to PR firm in Anycity
- Hot Anycity restaurant "HAL" had custom made Zang stools, tables and lighting as well as a Zang design concept of "2001 Space Odyssey"

Education: Honors BA (History and English), State University 1990

Personal Interests: Learning more about environmentally friendly & energy efficient building solutions; kayaking in Back Bay; sketching ideas for a future modern house and a new shelving system for the guest room; NEXT PERSONAL PROJECT: totem poles

INTERESTING JOBS: Director, Center on Aging

John J. Johnston, Ph.D.

Phone: 999-555-1212 ext. 118   Cell: (999) 555-1313

Director, Public Policy Think Tank

Current Positions

11/01–   **Director, Center on Aging**
Research and write reports, policy briefs, and fact sheets examining the opportunities and challenges of an aging society. Organize experts for policy briefings and symposiums. Design and conduct research projects involving quantitative data analysis. Respond to press, policymakers, and general public queries on policy issues related to domestic and global aging issues.

Editor, *Aging & Policy News*
Conceptualize and develop topics, recruit expert authors, and manage production for Center's monthly publication focusing on aging-related policy topics. Recent issues have addressed pension reform; age discrimination; end-of-life care; technology and aging; and geriatric care workforce issues.

Education

Ph.D. (Sociology, Specialization in Aging and Human Development). State University, Dec 1997.
Dissertation: Boom or Bust?: The Impact of Population Age Structure on the Economy.

M.A. (Sociology). State University, Dec 1993.

B.S. (Psychology, Philosophy). State University, May 1991.

Other Professional Experience

06/98–11/01   **Research Associate, Center on Aging**
Conducted data analyses for the Center's reports on *Healthy Aging*. Led data analyses research on the impact of low health literacy on health care use and health care costs.

09/92–12/97   **Teaching Assistant, Department of Sociology, State University**
For *Introduction to Sociology, and Statistics* courses.

05/95–08/95   **Research Assistant, Center for Demographic Studies, State University**
Investigated predictors of early retirement in Health and Retirement Study dataset.

Select Publications (full list available on request)

Reports:
Johnston, John J (2002). "Aging and Health in America."
Johnston, John J (2000). "Hearing Loss: Preparing for the Baby 'Boom'."
Center on Aging. Available (and more) at: www.assa-aging.org

378 | THE COMPLETE BOOK OF RÉSUMÉS

INTERESTING JOBS: Director, Center on Aging (cont.)

Articles:

Johnston, John J (2003). "Training Physicians in Geriatrics." *Aging & Policy News*, Vol.10 (No.2).

Johnston, John J (2001). "Social Networks and Healthy Aging." *The Journal of Aging Research*, 51(4): 207-229.

Select Presentations (full list available on request)

- (2004). "Policy Challenges in an Aging Society." Presented at the 2004 Annual Meeting of The Aging Society of America. San Francisco, March 2004.

- (2004). "The Future of Work and Retirement." Presented at The Center for Voluntarism, Corporate Retiree Volunteer Programs Exchange Conference, Alexandria, VA, November 2004.

- (2004). "The Macroeconomic Impact of Aging." Chair of session at the 2004 Annual Meeting of the America Demographics Society. Boston, MA, April 2004.

- Johnston, John, Peter Pumpkin, and Percy Schoolyard. (2001). "The Effect of Population Age Structure on the Economy." Presented at the 2001 Annual Meeting of The Aging Society of America. Chicago, IL, March 2001.

- Johnston, John, Peter Pumpkin, and Percy Schoolyard. (2000). "Do Pharmaceutical Purchases Determine the Dow's Destiny?" Presented at the 2000 Annual Meeting of The Aging Society Of America. Washington, DC, March 2000.

Congressional Briefing

Planned & organized a Congressional briefing on "Older Workers in a New Economy," held 2002.

Media (2003/2004)

Work cited by journalists and columnists in local, regional, and national publications, including the *Herald*, the *Times*, the *Chronicle, Aging Magazine, Health House Magazine*, among many others.

Grants

- NorthWest Foundation, *The Future of Senior Centers*, $650,000, John J. Johnston (Principal Investigator), 2004–2008.
- Chimney Institute of Aging and Health, *Aging and Health in America (Chartbook)*, $150,000, John J. Johnston (Principal Investigator), 2001–2002.
- The Association for Retirement Research, *The Challenge of Retirement Planning*, $40,000, John J. Johnston (Co-Principal Investigator), 2002.

Awards and Honors

- Big Drug Company Dissertation Award, June 1996.
- Institute for Population Research, Research Award, May 1995.
- State University Summer Research Award, June 1992.
- State University Graduate Fellowship and Full Tuition Scholarship, Sept. 1991–May 1995.

John J. Johnston page 2 of 2

INTERESTING JOBS: Games Operation Supervisor

123 Learning St., Anytown, ST USA, 10101 (999) 555-1212 johnj@yourname.com

John J. Johnston

Operations Supervisor

With unique experience handling large leisure and tourist attractions. Expertise in hiring and staffing and running a huge operation with upwards of 1900 employees and averaging 100,000 people per day including revenue collection and crisis control.

America's Wonderful World, Games Operations Supervisor   **1995–2005**

Responsibilities Included:
- Supervision of four Seasonal Operations Supervisors, twenty-six seasonal supervisors, and over three hundred line employees;
- Profitable operation of over sixty games locations;
- Maintain control of cost of sales, supplies, and labor expenses;
- Oversee cash control procedures, revenue collection, coupon tracking, and cash outages; as well as assisting in the completion of revenue, labor, and capital budgets for the future seasons;
- Organization and implementation of preseason and ongoing training sessions for all managerial levels;
- Assist with interviewing and hiring of Seasonal Supervisors and Linestaff; review and approval of performance appraisals and staff evaluations;
- Dealing with and solving guest, staff, and emergency related problems;
- Representative of Games Department on the Resale Joint Health and Safety Committee.

Accomplishments:
- Received seven promotions since beginning in 1995;
- Conceived weekly seasonal management operations meetings in order to increase communication between full-time management as well as between the individual games areas;
- Helped to plan, manage, and implement numerous motivation events for Merchandise and Games Linestaff and Supervisors;
- Assisted in creating, initiating, and monitoring the Games Workplace Inspection Program, raising safety levels and staff professionalism;
- Proposed and implemented many changes to paperwork and information recording procedures which has led to greater efficiency in processing everything from park finances to staffing and payroll.

EDUCATION:

State College   Graduated April 1995
Sport & Event Marketing Program (Postgraduate)
- Internship with BSN - Big Sports Network

Accomplishments:
- Successfully completed twelve courses with an overall GPA of 3.72. They included: Marketing Management, Sport & Event Planning and Management, Communications for Sport & Event Marketing, Sales & Presentation Skills, Media Applications, Financial Management, Database Marketing, and Licensing & Merchandising.

State University   Graduated April 1994
Bachelor of Business Administration (BBA) - Honors Program Specializing in Marketing
Accomplishments:
- Successfully completed six Marketing courses for specialization.

SUPPLEMENTAL EDUCATION: Blitzie's Presentation Skills course – May 1998.

INTERESTING JOBS: Geographer and GIS Specialist

John J. Johnston, BA

123 Learning St. ♦ Anytown USA ♦ 10101 ♦ 999.555.1212 ♦ johnj@yourname.com

ENTRY-LEVEL GEOGRAPHER AND GIS SPECIALIST

SUMMARY OF SKILLS

- In-depth knowledge of MapInfo 6.5, MapBasic 6.5, CanMap 5.1, ArcView, ArcGIS, SPSS
- Strong critical thinking, analytical, research, and problem-solving skills
- Able to work as a team and independently, detail oriented, personable, and responsible
- Proficient in report writing, presentations, and project management
- Excellent verbal & written communication, interpersonal, and organizational skills
- Educated in performing numerous GIS tasks including: querying, buffering, geo-coding, digitizing, clustering, generating reports, segmentation, conducting demographic analysis

EDUCATION

School of Geography, State University, Anytown (1999 to 2003)
- Bachelor of Arts in Geographic Analysis
- Specialized in GIS and Retail Analysis
- Attended a series of conferences in Paris over a period of nine days. Topics covered location/urban analysis, GIS, tourism, environmental management, transportation, international trade, and industrial development
- Courses include: Research Design, GIS, Advanced Applications in Remote Sensing & GIS, GIS in Decision Support, Analytical Techniques I & II, Geo-Demographics, Int'l Marketing

PROJECTS

Demographics, (September 2001 to December 2001)
Perceptual Mapping
- Assignment entailed a perceptual mapping of the entire Greater Anytown Area
- Various clusters were established and mapped in terms of ethnicity, age, gender, education, and average income

Information Systems, (January 2002 to April 2002)
Constraint Mapping
- Purpose was to develop new industrial sites in the Creek Anytown area
- Various raster and vector representations were looked at and an analysis and depiction of the data was also completed
- Conducted research; collected and entered data into the system
- Project concluded that new industrial land must be located on flat land with immediate access to highways and along railways; presented to instructor and fellow classmates

Remote Sensing & GIS, (January 2003 to April 2003)
Visualizing Socio-Economic Surfaces
- Digital Elevation Models (DEMs) and Thiessen Polygons were created in order to visualize the distribution of females in the labor force for natural sciences and engineering, in the City of Anytown
- Project concluded that the distribution of females in the occupation of natural sciences and engineering, directly correlated with the distribution of the wealthier people in the City of Anytown; presented to instructor and fellow classmates

PROFESSIONAL EXPERIENCE

Big Construction Inc., (April 2004 to Present)
Site Manager
- Responsible for the planning and utilization of manpower and equipment
- Provide necessary guidance and support to enable the effective control of daily operations
- Plan and coordinate the production process
- Liaison with city inspectors, architects, and designers
- Maintain relationships between company and clients

Eco-logist, (January 2004 to April 2004)
Data Specialist
- Responsible for the verification of American wide environmental and real estate locations
- Involved with the update and maintenance of environmental risk databases

Big Bank ETS Service Desk, (August 2002 to August 2003)
GIS Specialist
- Responsibilities included the support, maintenance, & customization of MapInfo
- Participated in the monthly creation of maps and reports
- Updated and maintained a variety of databases using Access, MapInfo, and Excel
- Administered various mapping requests from internal clients

Anytown District School Board Planning Section, (Sept. 2002 to Apr. 2003)
GIS Consultant
- Member of a team responsible for creating student generation yield factors for public elementary schools in the City of Anytown
- Executed various GIS statistical techniques using SPSS, MapInfo, ArcView, and Excel
- Conducted formal analyses using the results of the study

XZY Construction Inc., (July 1996 to August 2002)
Laborer/Administrative Assistant
- Involved in administrative responsibilities such as invoicing, filing, and banking
- Entailed the transportation of material and operating heavy machinery

XYZ Retail Store, (November 1998 to May 2002)
Receiving Department
- Progressed from general labor to temporary weekend supervisor
- Dealt with a variety of customers, personnel, and superiors

INTERESTS
- Attending AAG (Association of American Geographers) meetings regularly
- Ball Hockey League, Canlan Ice Sports Hockey League, Intramurals
- Travels include trips to Brazil, France, Portugal, Spain
- Volunteer Tutor – Central High School

INTERESTING JOBS: Animation Art Director

John J. Johnston

Apt 111, 123 Learning Ave. Anycity, AS   10101
telephone: (555) 999-1212 email: johnj@yourname.com

ANIMATION Story Developer and Design with quirky edge. Top skills are cooperation, leadership, self-motivation, and enthusiasm—not to mention creativity!

WORK EXPERIENCE:

Story Productions Inc. (August 2004–currently)
Freelance story developer/designer (full-time)
- Developed character profiles and episode summaries for a prospective children's television show entitled *Wicked Freddy* by Andrew Smith.

Revolution Animation (April 2004–August 2004)
Art Director (full-time)
- Served as a liaison between the production designer and the building department on the Christmas special.
- Oversaw the construction and installation of small-scale sets and props, to ensure they met the needs of the designer, animators, lighting, and building crews.

Revolution Animation (June 2003–March 2004)
Production designer (full-time)
- Designed locations, props, and graphics for the stop-motion animated television series *The Wrong Coast* for ABC Theater.
- Oversaw the creative aspects of sets and prop construction, after completion of design drawings and client approvals.

Chuckie Animation (May 2002–April 2003)
Freelance story developer/designer (full-time)
- Codeveloped two prospective children's television programs with Chuckie Animation. Provided character profiles, designs, and episode summaries.
- Assisted in the adaption of the children's book *Norbert Book* by Robert MacDonald into an animated feature-length film project.

Department Inc. (Fall 2001–Spring 2002)
Freelance Artist (part-time)
- Designed logos for children's clothing line.
- Responsible for meeting stylist's requirements, providing conceptual roughs, revisions, as well as final clean line and color prints.

Association for Community Living (1993–1999)
Relief worker for mentally handicapped Gentleman (part-time).

EDUCATION:
University of Anycity – Hon. B.A. Biomedical Ethics (completed April 1997)
- Art College – Classical Animation (completed April 2002)
- Art College – Art Fundamentals Certificate (completed April 1999)
- Familiar with Adobe Photoshop, Illustrator, Premiere, After Effects, SoundEdit 16

EXTRACURRICULAR ACTIVITIES:
- Residence Council President, New College, University of Anycity
- Recipient of Cartoon and Galleries Volunteer Association Animation Scholarships
- Hobbies include guitar playing, singing, camping, hiking, film, photography, and painting

Alice J. Johnston

123 Learning Street, Anytown, USA, 10101 • 999-555-1212

PROFILE: **IT Sales Associate**

STRENGTHS:
- ❖ Sales experience for a major international software and hardware vendor.
- ❖ High personal standards, excellent listening skills, strong communications and relationship-building skills.
- ❖ Strong "solution-sales" skills; appreciation for the need to translate technology into return on investment for the client.

EXPERIENCE:

Big Computer Inc, Sales Specialist/IT Specialist   2004–present

- ❖ Selling enterprise systems management, service management, and Self Service solutions to medium and large companies.
- ❖ Manage relationships, deliver presentations, prepare proposals, architect solutions, and handle client concerns.
- ❖ Work with reseller partners.

Achievements:
Considered a key asset to selling team for presentation style.
After first few months began hitting quota and above.

Bigtel Networks, Hardware Simulation/Software Verification

Summers '03, '04
- ❖ Created a practical simulation environment for functional processor cards.
- ❖ Automated the regression testing of switching software using Expect and TCL scripts.

Achievement:
Designed and maintained a company Intranet website still in use for company communication.

EDUCATION: **BscE Mathematics and Engineering, Honors**   **2004**
STATE UNIVERSITY

PERSONAL INTERESTS: Reading up on sales techniques in books and magazines; web design for friends; visiting family near the ocean.

IT: Sr. IT CIO

John J. Johnston MBA, PMP

123 Learning St., Anytown, USA, 10101
Email: johnj@yourname.com, Phone: (999) 555-1212

Sr. IT PROGRAM DIRECTOR - PROFILE SUMMARY

Experience in Program/Release Management with a budget of $400 million over 5-year program at The Bank of ABC. Experience in the establishment and supervision of IT Program Office with a budget of about $200 Million at Southern Tel Billing Inc. International experience in project management, experience in e-business CRM, and other mainframe applications.

Recognized for exceptional leadership, process improvements, and organization building skills. 5 years of programming experience ranging from mainframe applications to web development. Exceptional at communication between clients, departments, sr. management, and teams.

WORK EXPERIENCE

Big Bank, Senior Release Manager   April 2003–Aug 2004

Responsibilities: **Establishment of Release level PMO**. Project Management of Release 2 of the BB connect program. BB connect is an enterprise-wide, high-visibility, mission-critical sales and service application development project. Release 2 is a part of 5 year vision budgeted over $400 million. It is composed of 6 multimillion-dollar projects with teams from various BB biz units and tech organizations.

- Supervision of 6 IT Project Managers, 6 Business PMs, and release level staff.
- Supervision of day-to-day release level activities and process improvements (revision of status reports, time sheets, executive reports). Development and management of release level charter, risk management plan, Integrated WBS, and other project documentation.
- Relationship management with vendors, partners, IT organizations, and business units, status reporting to executives and BB IT PMO.

Southern Tel, Technology Group
Senior Southern Tel Billing Program Manager   Sept 2000–Nov 2002
For the Project Management Office (PMO)

PMO Establishment: Established project management office for Southern Tel IT Billing Organization. PMO supervised billing projects estimated at $200 Million in 2002, improved IT efficiencies of a highly outsourced, projectized matrix organization, streamlined PM practices, improved project tracking, and reporting structure.

Developed RACI (Responsible, Accountable, Contributing, Informed) matrix/chart to define roles and responsibilities for different IT functions. Established centralized location for documentation, created PMO website to establish centralized web based electronic repositories for knowledge management.

Workforce Consolidation: Conducted organizational wide analysis and recommended consolidation of Electronic Billing Systems organization and its operations for increased efficiency and reduction in cost.

Consumption Reduction (Cost Reduction Initiative): Supervised identification and completion of cost reduction initiatives by retiring servers, reducing hardware dependencies, print reduction, and introduction of new technology.
Project Director (Prime Integrator)

IT Outsourcing Initiative (Software / Hardware Transition to Partners)
- Senior Project Manager who supervised Project Mangers from DPS, Venture, and Southern Tel to successfully outsource application support to Venture and hardware services to DPS on time within budget.

Desired State Retail Billing Project Management Office (PMO)
- Established Project Management Office for Desired State Retail IT Billing Organization. Implemented project management processes to manage legacy systems' replacement with new software technologies.
- Developed Mission and Vision statements for PMO, developed centralized skill-set repository, supervised creation of process improvement documents, & evaluated tools for Knowledge Management incl. Documentum & Idiom.

Face's Cosmetics March 2000–Aug 2000 (Contract)
E-commerce Project Manager, International Information Services Department

Responsibilities: Development, implementation, and documentation of International e-business strategy & initiatives, CRM, and project management.
- Led a team of 25 resources with a budget of $500, 000 to deliver Face's first International B2B & B2C e-commerce solution on time within budget.
- Developed International e-business strategy, evaluated IBM's websphere, Intershop's Infinity, Microsoft's Site Server for global/regional implementation.

ABC Inc. (Big Airline Inc.)
Consultant and Programmer   Sept 1998–March 2000
- Developed and maintained mainframe COBOL, JCL and PL/I, & DB2 applications, performed enhancements in revenue accounting systems of major airlines.
- Performed Y2K upgrades, authored documentation, and coordinated Y2K system check for PRAS department.
- Developed PRAS e-commerce Intranet website to distribute financial reports and info to various airlines. Created documentation, revised application manuals, and archived legacy information.

COMPUTER SKILLS
Languages: JavaScript, VBScript, CGI, ASP, HTML, Visual BASIC, Pascal, COBOL, JCL, UNIX, PL/I, SQL, Ada, XML, XSL.
Software Tools: Doors (Requirement Management Tool), PARTS, MS Front Page, Visual InterDev, Access, Project 98, Microsoft Office 2000, SAS, SABRE, Object Manager, Adobe PhotoShop, TSO, Visio, ORACLE E-business Suite 11i, Microsoft Site Server.
Operating Systems: OS390, Windows, UNIX, VMS, TPX, CICS, DOS

CERTIFICATION
Project Management Professional (PMP), Project Management Institute (PMI), July 2001; Certified Internet Webmaster (CIW).

EDUCATION
State University: Executive Education in Leadership Concepts, 2002.
State University: *Master of Business Administration*. Major: Management Information Systems.
State University of Other State: *Master of Human Relations*. Major: Organizational Development and Communication.
State University: *B.S. in Business Administration*.

TRAINING
Southern Tel Corporation: Prime Integrator training, Project Management/Management training, Doors training, ABT Workbench training.
EDS: Change Management Training/Problem Management training.
City Community College: 21 credit hours of Computer Science courses. Major: Mainframe programming languages and operating system.

HONORS AND AFFILIATIONS
- Published article about Internet and the future of e-commerce, 1999.
- Merit Scholarship, Residential Assistant Scholarship.

IT: Sr. IT Program Director/Project Manager

John J. Johnston, M.B.A.
123 Learning Street, Anytown, USA, 10101
Telephone: (999) 555-1212   Email: **johnj@yourname.com**

Executive with international success in creating **world-class operations.** Accomplished in P&L management, strategic planning, business process reengineering, business development, and operations. "Specialty" is helping start-up companies flourish in a very competitive environment by providing front-line technical strategy on challenging and complex Worldwide Enterprise deals.

Innovative thinker who partners technology with business to achieve corporate objectives.
• Saved 15% on multimillion-dollar budget reducing reliance on outsourcing new technology infrastructure.
• Delivered $400K annual savings by transforming organization into a client-server environment.

Problem solver who consistently improves revenue, efficiency, and the bottom line.
• Generated $2,500,000 savings by bringing outsourced software development in-house.
• Slashed time to process reporting from 2 days to 4 hours by reengineering reporting procedures.

Creates vision and gains cross-functional consensus while transforming IT into a strategic business partner.
• Produced $195K savings by streamlining development processes and utilizing standardized methodologies.
• Served as Chief Executive Officer and Director of a fully reporting, (NASDAQ listed) Traded Public Corporation

Professional Career Experience

The Turbo Group Inc., *venture capital financial services company, 2000–present*
Senior Vice-President, Information Technology,
& Chief Information Officer (C.I.O.)
• Provided a homogeneous, web-based infrastructure solution, (ERP) system to access their disparate data sources
• Effected front-line technical strategies on challenging and complex worldwide enterprise deals, while driving organizational change to reduce reliance on outsourcing, thereby reducing capital costs of technology infrastructure expenditures by over 15%
• Improved sales process by implementing a "Customer Relationship Management" (CRM) application
• Played key roll in integrating operations into parent company following merger. Reduced support costs 30%

Big Tool & Tire Corporation, *major retail organization, 1999–2000*
Technology Solutions Delivery Manager
• Directed Y2K lifecycle for an organization with operating revenues of 5.9 billion, 45,000 employees, and 1,000 retail locations
• Human Resource oversight of Technology, Development, and Support personnel of 600+
• Sign-off authority/Divisional Business Unit Budget responsibility of $45,000.000

Shadows Limited, *information technology consultants, 1985–1998*
President – Chief Executive Officer
• Primary Consultant for State Government (Finance, Attorney General, Health, Lands and Forests), Comp Ltd., State Info Work Group, Systems Corp, and other Fortune 500 Corporations
• Lead team that generated $8,000,000 in annual billable fees
• Directed the supervision of corporate Development and Support personnel, 25 Resources
• Managed long-term budgets, multimillion dollar oversight

BMM International Industries Corporation, *international constructers, 1981–1985*
Executive Vice President
• Member of team responsible for negotiating 2 joint venture contracts between China and a Western Corporation

Other Executive Duties: served as a past Officer and member of the Board of Directors of a number of publicly listed and traded corporations. These corporations's trade on the NASDAQ over-the-counter bulletin board market (OTCBB).

Education: Bachelor of Science (B.Sc.) – Major – Biology – 1977
Master of Business Administration, with Distinction (M.B.A.) – Major – Computer & Info Systems Mgt – 2000

IT: BAD—Sr. Financial IT

Alice J. Johnston
123 Learning St.
Anytown USA
10101
(999) 555-1212

Employment Background

Jan. '97 - Present   Digital Renewal

    Nov. '97 - Present   *Vice-President, Infrastructure*

- Responsible for Finance/Accounting, Legal, Human Resources, IT, Facilities, and Administrative departments, including CFO and HR Director. Furthered the establishment of Human Resources and Finance. Development of Strategic Plans for the company in conjunction with Marketing/Sales and Development VP's. Ensure implementation of Strategic Plans and Action Items. Ensure development and management of budgets for all reporting departments. Operational management of IT, Facilities, and Administration. Executive Sponsor for Process Improvement company-wide. During this time the company has grown from 90 to 140 employees. Oversee continued growth and operational effectiveness of departments within sphere and company. Currently on Transition Team to re-structure and improve the Development area and develop an additional 28,000 sq.ft. of office space

       Jan. '97 - Nov. '97   *Director, Information Technology & Facilities*

- Participate in the Strategic Planning Group to develop business strategies to address the growth, business development, human resource, financial, and technology needs of the company
- Led the Operations Group in the development of action items to support the strategies generated by the Strategic Planning Group and ensure their completion
- Build and maintain an Information Technology Department and Infrastructure from the ground up to support a wide range of customer requirements and technology platforms
- Develop IT Strategies and Plans to ensure future requirements and service levels are met
- Manage and coordinate use of human, budgetary, and equipment resources to maximize return on investment and quality of service
- Coordinated design and construction of 11,000 sq. ft. addition to office space
- Build and maintain a Facilities Department and Infrastructure

Jun. '89 - Dec. '96   ABC Financial

    '92 - Dec. '96   *Manager, Computer Services*

- Established and maintained the Computer Services department
- Responsible for Mainframe/Data Center, LAN, WAN, PC and Commun[...] operations, purchasing and related contracts
- Compass' Data Center study evaluated NN Financial's Data Center as [...] efficiency and quality of service
- Led ING North America team in the development of a voice communic[...] Life Insurance Companies
- Participant on the team that developed the RFP and in-house counter pr[...] outsourcing of all North American data centers

Employment Background, continued...

Manager, Computer Services, NN Financial, co[...]

What's Wrong?

- Dense text—I'm too bored to read this all.
- Too long
- Too much information about out-of-date or inapplicable jobs
- Lackluster objective/profile or lack thereof
- No declared job role
- Name is too small or address is too large or both

IT: BAD—Sr. Financial IT (cont.)

- Participant on the team that negotiated the data center outsourcing agreement/contract ($20M/year for 10 years)
- Development and management of a departmental budget of $4M
- Coordinated research into technical and procedural improvements, new technologies and strategies, including the development of Business Cases, vendor evaluation and contract negotiation. Manage implementation.
- Manage and develop departmental staff, including Mainframe Operations and Scheduling, Support Desk, Office Systems/Training and Network Analysts
- Ensure that the department achieved or exceeded business and customer technology service requirements
- Coordinate with Human Resources, Finance/Accounting and Legal as necessary to ensure operational effectiveness and compliance with financial policies and contract and employment laws

'90 - '92   ***Supervisor, Office Systems***

- Hire and supervise Office Systems staff responsible for LAN, Workstations and Phone System
- Development and management of departmental budget
- Ensured SLAs were met or exceeded
- Develop business cases and plans for the implementation of new technology or changes to existing technology, and manage their implementation
- Ensure service contracts, etc. were in place and favorable. Negotiate as appropriate
- Provide 3rd level support to Office Systems staff on technical problems
- Coordinate resolution of major system problems

'89 - '90   ***LAN Network Administrator & Information Center Consultant***

- Responsible for the day-to-day operations of the network
- Recommend and implement new technologies
- Provide user support

'88 - '89   Skills Development

Systems Officer (Contract)

- Develop statistical forecasting spreadsheet templates
- Software Testing
- User Support

'87 - '88   Big Bank

Junior Production Services Analyst

- Produce nightly production and test batch schedules and ensure appropriate operations completion
- Recovery of lost reports and job re-runs
- JCL changes
- Documentation for Support and Batch requirements
- Mainframe and PC User Support
- Network monitoring and problem resolution
- Coordinate resolution of system failures

Employment Background, continued...

'84 - '87   <u>XYZ Co.</u>

'86   ***Data Collection Computer Services Supervisor***

- Supervise department staff to ensure completion of duties and resolve problems
- Ensure processing of data collected from Diaries and People Meters
- Implement People Meter System and coordinate with field staff
- Test changes to batch and on-line systems
- Coordinate with Data Entry and IT Operations for timely completion

'85   ***Database Specialist***

- Ensure integrity of data
- Test changes to batch and on-line systems
- Make manual changes to data as required
- Coordinate with Data Entry for timely completion

'84   ***Office Clerk***

- Supervise part-time students to ensure accuracy and timely completion of duties
- Data entry
- Error checking and resolution
- Filing

Education

- Completed 2 years towards a Combined Specialist in German & Spanish, Minor in English
  State University, 1984
- Graduated Scholar
  1982
- A variety of Management and Technical courses
  1985 - Present

Languages

English:	Fluent written & spoken
Spanish:	Fluent written & spoken
German:	Fluent written & spoken
French:	Intermediate

Other Interests

Reading, Scuba Diving, Golf, Cooking, Gardening, Travel

References   Available upon request

Alice J. Johnston

123 Learning St. Anytown, USA 10101 (999) 555-1212

Journalist, Writer, and Researcher with background in business, current affairs, and beat reporting in both print and TV.

JOURNALISM AND MEDIA EXPERIENCE

Researcher/Writer, WOW Television News   March 4, 2002–Present
- Helped the editorial team with research and administrative duties.
- Wrote news stories for WOWnews and WOWnews International.
- Supervised editing of news reports, voice-overs, and clips.
- Interviewed sources for reporters.
- Coordinated current affairs satellite feeds.

Reporter, *The Anytown Business Journal*   April 2001–November 2001
- Reported daily city business news for anytownonlinenews.com.
- Responsible for keeping website information updated and prioritized.
- Wrote retail, marketing, and technology stories for the weekly paper.

Editorial Student Trainee, *The Anytown Herald*   September 2000–April 2001
- Monitored fifteen police, fire, and ambulance scanners to provide breaking news stories.
- Wrote news and feature articles for the daily paper on strict deadlines.
- Adapted to evening, weekend, and overnight shift-work.

General Assignment/Student Intern, *The Smallertown Spectator*   Oct.–Dec. 2001
- Worked as a general assignment reporter for the Metro section.
- Wrote community, health, education, and crime stories for the daily paper.
- Worked on computer assisted reporting articles and investigative features.
- Reported on the municipal and federal elections.

News Editor, *The University News*   September–October 2001
- Led a group of twenty writers to venture beyond their previous reporting experience.
- Wrote news, entertainment, and feature articles for the weekly paper.
- Generated story ideas to fill six to eight pages of news per week.
- Increased readership with investigative articles regarding safety on campus.

Writer/Editor, *Global Stratagems*   May 2000–August 2000
- Reported and copyedited for a daily website and telephone broadcast.
- Wrote feature articles for bimonthly business magazine.
- Covered breaking news stories, such as the security breach hearings, and produced radio features.

Freelance Journalist 1996–Present
Published in:
- *Ear Magazine*
- *The Anytown Sunshine*
- *Boost Magazine* (an international magazine for young women)
- *FEMALE Magazine*
- *The SouthAsia Journal*
- *ThinkTank* (a marketing magazine)
- *The Smalltown Reporter*

Assistant to the State U. Students' Administrative Council
State University October 1999–April 2000
- Assisted in publicity and media relations for State U events.
- Helped organize *Barriers Protest*: a protest against tuition increases and student poverty.

Assistant Organizer of the National Science Fiction Expo
Dagoba Marketing June 1999–September 1999
- Worked with a team to plan one of the largest pop culture events in the U.S.
- Wrote press releases and communicated with local and national media.
- Created a database of media and corporate contacts for future trade shows.

OTHER EXPERENCE

Crisis Line Worker – Volunteer, The Local Sexual Assault Center
February 1996–April 1999
- Counseled sexual assault survivors on the crisis line.
- Accompanied survivors to the hospital, police station, and court.

Administrative Assistant, Medium Bank
Operations and Technology, Corporate Services Summer 1996, 1997, and 1998

EDUCATION

2001 - Bachelor of Journalism. *State University*.

1999 - Honors Bachelor of Arts – Sociology. *State University*.

References and portfolio available upon request.

JOURNALISTS: Journalist, Midlevel

John J. Johnston

123 Learning St., Anytown, USA 10101 (999) 555-1212 johnj@yourname.com

---

PROFILE

Energetic, creative, accurate journalist and writer with more than 5 years experience in newspaper and magazine (conventional and electronic) writing; demonstrates deep respect for deadlines; experienced communicator and a visual thinker. Thrives on a team, and enjoys challenges like launching and building a new publication or company.

Specialty areas include: business, marketing, lifestyle, and music reporting

---

EMPLOYMENT HISTORY

Main Beat Magazine, contributing writer   April 2002 to present
Anytown-based bimonthly trade publication for American marketing industry.
www.mainbeatmag.com
- Beat: youth marketing trends, sports, music, promotional strategies, Western U.S. region, and technology.
- Duties: conceive, report, and write 4–7 stories per issue, ranging from short news pieces and quick hits to profiles and features; develop contacts across North America and Europe; update Promo Files section each issue; track down art, graphics, and/or charts for every story; headline writing; and research and develop stories for upcoming issues.

Businessmen Quarterly.com, senior writer   April 2000–March 2002
Anytown-based online daily read in more than 42 countries covering e-business strategy-related news for senior executives.
www.businessmenquarterly.com
- Beat: B2B e-business and e-commerce trends.
- Duties: establishing and expanding contacts across North America and abroad; writing stories in a clear, lively, magazine-style format; writing Q&As; keeping up-to-date with technology and e-commerce news; managerial duties, including weekly meetings discussing how to improve readership and site quality; editing duties like scouring the Web for news, editing other writers' work, and maintaining Public Relations contacts.

Americancontent Magazine, music department editor   February 2000–May 2000
Anytown-based online lifestyle magazine covering issues like sonic diversity and American identity.
www.beme.net
- Beat: American and international music & artists and issues surrounding electronic music.
- Duties: editing other writer's work; establishing contacts with record companies; writing columns, features, and CD reviews; and keeping current on music trends, new artists, and concert dates.

Freelance Writer, 1997 to present – features and stories have been published in…

- *BBB Biz Magazine*, an e-business magazine distributed nationally with a readership of 114, 000. Have written several magazine features since the publication launched in January 2001. Topics include: wireless hacking, online youth marketing, trends in the online automotive sales space, and web banking in U.S. Leveraged and acquired sources across the country. Considered a preferred contributor.

- *ThePoly-tech News*, campus newspaper at State Polytechnic University. Contributed news and music articles. Website editor from September to November 2001. Responsible for layout, extra online content, editing, and updating.

- *Big Plastic Valley North,* Contributing writer.

- *BBB Scene*, an Anytown-based urban music and lifestyle magazine. Contributing writer and music department editor from debut issue in September 1997 until it folded in May 1998. Duties included: news reporting and feature writing; CD reviews; suggesting and pitching editorial content; and light editing and design suggestions.

- *The Squeaker*, a community newspaper. Contributed music articles.

EDUCATION

- Bachelor of Applied Arts, Journalism from State University May 2002.

STRENGTHS

- Strong interview and research skills – focusing on details.
- Versatile and practised writing style – news and features, Web writing.
- Time management and multi-tasking.
- Intuitive Internet research skills.
- Online reporting specialist with over three years of writing for the Internet.
- Excellent computer skills, with experience using IBM and Macintosh systems.
- Specialty areas:
  - Music reporting and reviewing, and feature writing.
  - American marketing and advertising industry.
  - Technology and related areas generally referred to as e-business.

PERSONAL INTERESTS

- Music: especially North American scene, obsessed concert fanatic, owner of over 500 CDs.
- Hockey, movies, cooking, camping, and the "great outdoors."
- Internet journalism and surfing for work-related content and news, and for recreation.

JOURNALISTS: Editor

123 Learning St.
Anytown, USA

Alice J. Johnston

(999) 555-1212
alicej@yourname.com

Profile

- 7 years **writing** experience and 4 years as an **EDITOR**, including 2½ years in a production-for-Web environment plus extensive editorial and promotional copy work
- Eighteen months hands-on experience with HTML coding and web publishing software
- Proven record of adding to skill set & new responsibilities through on-the-job training

Work History

On-line Editor, Office Products Associated

OPA is an industry association representing the interests of approximately 700 firms across America, including retailers and manufacturers.   April 2001 to present

Responsibilities:

- Editing, management, and writing of all online content for the redesign of the association's web properties
- Daily content updates using Dreamweaver, HTML, Microsoft Access, & proprietary software
- Writing and editing of official communications, including promotional material, releases to members, and a weekly bulletin
- Supervising and assigning junior writers

Accomplishment: Creation/editing and management of all content for the online **Office Products Training Center**, a new product recently purchased for the education of more than 1,000 employees

Business Editor, Skyblue.com

Skyblue.com is the website of America's largest national bookseller, and caters to online buyers by providing detailed product information.   January 2000 to October 2000

Responsibilities:

- Wrote/edited all content in the business, personal finance, and computers sections, including feature stories, reviews, synopses, and teaser blurbs
- Attained and coordinated freelance feature writers
- Conducted audio and print interviews with various nonfiction authors
- Occasionally wrote promotional material for advertising campaigns

Accomplishment: Developed and implemented original content strategy, including feature stories and a roster of respected business and personal finance columnists, which provided a unique incentive for return visits from online book buyers

Editor, *State Purchasing Guide*

SPG is a trade magazine that has catered to purchasing officials in all levels of government across America for more than 30 years.   September 1998 to January 2000

Responsibilities:

- Conceived and acquired all editorial content, including graphics, news, company profiles, case studies, and technology/product overviews
- Tools included QuarkXpress, Photoshop, and Acrobat
- Communicated with all internal departments, as well as printers, advertising clients, corporate communications, and PR agencies

Accomplishment: Became the magazine's first editor to assume all editorial desktop production, including layout, scanning of materials, and electronic manipulation of photos and documents. This both saved the time and effort of the office's production manager and ensured a more creative and conscientious approach to the magazine's design.

Reporter, Production Assistant, *State Business Journal*

The SBJ is a highly respected weekly newspaper catering to the business community, and was the model for the Business Journal.

August 1996 to July 1998

Responsibilities:
- Wrote news articles, profiles and features, cutlines and headlines
- Weekly copyediting and editorial production on Mac platform with QuarkXpress

Accomplishment: Compiled detailed history and economic aspects for the issue of a quarterly *Business Visitor's Guide*

Accomplishment: Researched and compiled a 96-page directory of companies in the high technology sector for an annual *Book of Lists*

Associate Editor, Writer, *Anytown Magazine/Anytown Business Magazine*

These titles were glossy magazines catering to the upscale market. Anytown Magazine *covered local news, politics, fashion, and trends, while* Anytown Business Magazine *covered economic news and profiled local companies and businesspeople.*

April 1995 to November 1996

Accomplishment: Researched and wrote various full-length features, including Anytown's first <u>Top 40 Under 40,</u> for both *Anytown Magazine* and *Anytown Business Magazine*

Accomplishment: Eventually assumed responsibility for coordinating all freelance writers, photographers, production, and advertising staff as Associate Editor, *Anytown Magazine*

Computers More than eight years of desktop/web publishing and word processing with several proprietary and consumer programs, including QuarkXpress, Dreamweaver, FrontPage, Adobe Photoshop, Illustrator and Acrobat, Access, Excel, WinZip on both Mac and PC platforms.

Education

State College - Print journalism Honors diploma, May 1995
- Winner, Margaret Graham award for scholastic achievement
- Third-place winner, College Association Language and Literacy contest

Interests

- Walking, cycling, and swimming
- Fostering homeless cats and kittens through Anytown Cat Rescue
- Performing with the amateur theater company The Sandy Singers. I am also a member of the Board of Directors

LAW: Junior Law Associate

Alice J. Johnston, *Hon. B.A., LL.B./LL.L., M.A. Candidate*

123 Learning St., Anytown, USA 10101
Cellular: (999) 555-1212, alicej@yourname.com

JUNIOR LAW ASSOCIATE

EDUCATION

LAW SOCIETY OF AMERICA
- *Called to the State Bar, July 2004*
- *State Bar Admission Course, 2001*

OUT OF STATE UNIVERSITY
- *Civil Law Degree, 2002*

UPPER CRUST HALL LAW SCHOOL
- *Bachelor of Laws, 2001*
- Specialization in International Law

STATE UNIVERSITY
- *Master's of American Politics and Policy Candidate, 2003*
- *Honors Bachelor of Arts, 1998*
  - Double Major: International Relations & Peace and Conflict Studies

DISTINCTIONS & AWARDS

- **Rotary Ambassadorial Scholarship** - *Finalist, 1995*
- **Anytown's Catholic Children's Aid Society Scholarship,** *1994–1995*

LEGAL WORK EXPERIENCE

Pringle & Mckay, Attorneys,
Junior Associate (October 2004–present)
- Civil litigation-driven practice
- Work focusing on components of civil litigation legal files including drafting affidavits, pleadings, attending on motions (from time to time when instructed to do so), and legal research on various files

Ottley, Mankey & Dupra: ASSOCIATES,
Articling Student (January–June 2004)
- Rotated through Litigation, Criminal, Real Estate, Corporate/Commercial, and Immigration law
- Conducted research, drafted documents, investigated facts, interviewed, attended court sessions, filed court documents
- Wrote two newsletters on: (1) identity theft and, (2) how to deal with the police
- Gained practical legal experience within the context of a boutique firm

Percy & Taylor ASSOCIATES,
Articling Student (May–October 2003)
- Worked within Corporate/Commercial and Litigation practice areas
- Assisted with the incorporation and organization of a corporation, annual meetings, and ordinary corporate procedures; and, engaged in problem analysis, advising, investigating facts, legal research, planning and conduct of a matter, file and practice management, negotiation, drafting, writing, and advocacy (conducted negotiation of a small claims court matter, which I successfully settled)
- Gained practical legal experience within the context of a large real estate corporation

EXTRACURRICULAR ACTIVITIES

REPUBLICAN PARTY
Volunteer & Member (2003–present)

UPPER CRUST HALL THEORY & PRACTICE OF MEDIATION
Participant (2000)
- Developed an understanding of the utility and impact of mediation within the context of contemporary dispute resolution developments in State
- Gained an understanding of mediation through seminars, simulations, and placements in the small claims courts

DEBATING SOCIETY   *Member (2000)*

COMPETITIVE MOOTING Lerner Internal Mooting Competition Participant (1999)

PRE-LAW SCHOOL EXTRACURRICULARS

STATE UNIVERSITY:
Political Science Department *Research and Admin Assistant (1996–1998)*
Political Science Department *Research and Admin Assistant (Summer 1997)*
Varsity-Campus Student Newspaper *Staff Writer (1997)*

NORTH AMERICAN MODEL UNITED NATIONS, *Assistant Director (February 1997)*
- Disarmament and International Security Committee
- Wrote discussion paper on subject of international disarmament

CHILD HELP SOCIETY, *Relief Staff (1994–1996)*
- Worked within a group home for teenage girls

STATE UNIVERSITY: W.O.W. 77.5 FM, Campus Radio
Elected Student Representative (1993–1995), Elected Treasurer (1994–1995)
Advertising Director (1992–1993)

LAW: Lawyer

ALICE J. JOHNSTON

123 Learning St., Anytown, USA 10101 ♦ Phone: 999.555.1212 Email: alicej@yourname.com

EDUCATION AND PROFESSIONAL DESIGNATION

Called to the Bar, July '03

LL.B., State University, Faculty of Law ('99–'02)

Ph.D. Program, State University, Institute for Studies in Education, Philosophy of Education ('98–'99) Completed coursework component

M.A., State University ('95–'97) (Co-op Program)
Thesis: *Liberal Citizenship and Citizen Virtue: A Critical Analysis of William Smith's Purposive Liberalism*

B.A., State University, Joint Honors in Anthropology and Sociology ('90–'94)

ACADEMIC ACHIEVEMENTS AND AWARDS

Civic Fund Summer Fellowship in Public Interest Law, Pro Bono Students of the United States, State University, Faculty of Law (declined) (2001)

Johnston A and Schemple, J, **"On the Meaning of Law"** in (ed.) *Thoughts of the New World*, Anytown, State: Thinking All the Time Society. Presented at the 46th Annual Meeting of "The Thinking all the Time Society" (May 2000).

MacDonald Entrance Scholarship, State University, Faculty of Law (1999)

State Graduate Scholarship, State University, (1998, 1999), State University (1996, 1997)

Outstanding Achievement in Graduate Studies Award, State University (1998)

State University of Graduate Scholarship (1997)

Faculty of Arts Special Merit Scholarship, State University (1995)

RELEVANT EXPERIENCE

STAFF LAWYER
Apr. '04–present

Family Court, Superior Court of Justice,
• Provide legal research and opinions to the Senior Judge of the family court
• Prepare materials related to the education of judges, practice, and procedure in the Family Court and expansion of the Family Court
• Liaise extensively with the Bench, Bar, and other family law-related associations

RESEARCH LAWYER
Nov. '03–Dec. '03

Office of the Lawyer,
• Researched and wrote memoranda for litigation on a project-by-project basis

JUDGES LAW CLERK
Sept. '02–Sept. '03

Superior Court of Justice,
• Researched and wrote pre- and post-hearing memoranda on wide range of legal issues
• Edited judgments, speeches, and articles
• Observed trials, pre-trial conferences, and motions in family, civil, estates, & criminal matters

CASEWORKER
May '01–Dec. '01

Anytown Community Legal Services, Landlord and Tenant Division
• Responsible for intake and all subsequent written and verbal communications with clients
• Provided legal advice and other information to clients, negotiated agreements between tenants and landlords, represented clients at State Rental Housing Tribunal

INTAKE OFFICER
Oct. '00–Apr. '01

Family Court Project,
• Assisted individuals in filling out appropriate court documents and forms for a variety of family law problems

- Provided general information about the court process and other court services to individuals who did not qualify for Legal Aid

INTERN
'99–'01

Justice for Children and Youth
- Processed client intakes and assisted with litigation preparation
- Created a resource list used by clinic lawyers to refer clients to appropriate advocacy groups

OTHER EXPERIENCE

Research and Writing

RESEARCH ASSISTANT, *Professor A Peterson*, State University, Faculty of Law (May '01–March '02)
- Performed research in the area of international law with a focus on labor rights
- Edited manuscripts, performed literature searches, read and summarized relevant articles and documents

ASSISTANT EDITOR, *Journal of Women and the Law*, Faculty of Law, State University ('00–'02)
- Critically evaluated the content of papers that had been accepted for publication in the journal

ASSISTANT EDITOR, *State University Faculty of Law Review*, Legal Theory Cell ('99–'00)
- Critically reviewed submitted papers and presented paper evaluation to the senior board

Community Work

MEMBER, *East Diehl Tenants Association* (May '01–present)
- Attended monthly meetings and participated in the organization and implementation of activities designed to improve the lives of tenants in East Diehl
- Monitored and responded to inquiries on "Bad Landlord Hotline"

MENTOR, *Community Action Partnerships in Service Learning, Anytown Intergenerational Partnerships* ('98)
- Worked with a team of mentors in two grade-four classrooms in downtown
- Helped the children plan and implement a food drive for their community

HOSPICE CAREGIVER, Calcutta, India (Mar.–May '95)
- Volunteered at charity mission; provided basic daily care giving activities in an orphanage and a facility for mentally and physically ill women

ENGLISH TEACHER, *New Model Primary School* India (Dec. '94–Mar. '95)
- Created and implemented grade three curriculum in English, social studies, and mathematics courses

Extracurricular

MEMBER, *Law Union*, Faculty of Law, State University ('00–'02)
- Projects included: curriculum reform and a review of administrative policy on laptop use
- Worked with the Career Development office to increase the availability of information about career and volunteer opportunities in public interest law

MEMBER, *Women and the Law*, Faculty of Law, State University ('00–'02)
- Participated in organizing and running various awareness and fundraising events
- Created a resource list of topical websites and December 6th events for the white ribbon and petition campaign

MENTOR, *Faculty of Law Mentor Program* ('00–'01)
- Mentor to a lawyer from England who was seeking professional accreditation in this state

LAW: Lawyer, Midlevel

John J. Johnston
123 Learning Street, Anytown, USA 10101 999.555.1212, johnj@yourname.com

---

EXPERIENCE

STATE OF WISCONSON, MINISTRY OF THE ATTORNEY GENERAL
Assistant Crown Attorney, 2000 to present
- Prosecuted a variety of cases including commercial frauds, criminal organization charges, and homicides before the Wisconsin Court of Justice and the Wisconsin Superior Court of Justice.
- Received "Exceptional" rating for excellence in prosecution in 2002 from the State of Wisconsin.
- Led team of law enforcement officials in prosecuting America's largest credit card fraud.

TIPLADY MACDONALD RUTHERFORD BRAY
Associate Lawyer, 1999
- Argued motions and assisted with trials before a variety of courts and tribunals on behalf of firm clients (including telecommunications providers, auto makers, and chartered banks).
- Interacted directly with CEOs and general counsels of Fortune 500 companies.
- Worked on files involving the following issues: breach of contract, securities disputes, patent infringements, international conflict of laws, labor law, and product liability.

HAPSBERG SHYDOCK MILLS AND MAY
Student-At-Law, 1997–1998
- Completed eight-month rotation in the Litigation Department and a four-month rotation in the Corporate Department.
- Argued motions and wrote memos on the following issues: breach of contract, secured lending disputes, corporate taxation, labor law, and commercial real estate disputes.

EDUCATION

BARNEY CASEY SCHOOL OF BUSINESS
Masters in Business Administration (M.B.A.), 2004
- Dean's Honor List: 2002–2003, 2003–2004.
- Scored 740 on GMAT (98th percentile).
- Summer internship with Layne and Company in 2003 advising American auto parts distributor on corporate finance, strategy, and operations.

STATE UNIVERSITY, FACULTY OF LAW
Bachelor of Laws (LL.B.), 1997
- Scored 169 on LSAT (98th percentile).
- Elected Class Representative, Students' Law Society, Editor-In-Chief, *Status Quo* magazine.

UNIVERSITY OF WESTERN WISCONSON, NIETZSCHE COLLEGE
Bachelor of Arts (B.A.) (Honors History), 1994
- Recipient, Christopher Sweeney Scholarship for Academic Excellence, 1990–1994.
- Dean's Honor List, 1990–1994.
- Elected Class Representative, University Students' Council.

OTHER

LANGUAGES
- Certified by the Ministry of the Attorney General as fluent in Spanish.

COMMUNITY INVOLVEMENT
- Nietzsche College Development and Community Relations Committee (1998–present): Responsible for targeting young alumni in fundraising efforts.
- Columnist and financial adviser, *Highlights Magazine* (1998–2000): Wrote column and assisted publishers with financial planning and helped them implement a successful exit strategy.

INTERESTS
- History buff, listening to music on my iPod, reading when there's time, golf as much as possible.

John J. Johnston
123 Learning St., Anytown, ST USA 10101
johnj@yourname.com 999-555-1212

SUMMARY

An **Electronics Engineering Technologist** with extensive experience in an ISO 9002 qualified electronic manufacturing and customer service environment. Well-organized and detail-oriented with strong interpersonal and problem solving skills. Special strengths in technical support, document control, and MRP. Enjoys being a team player as well as taking leadership.

CAREER HISTORY AND ACCOMPLISHMENTS

Data Systems Inc.   **1997–2000**
A worldwide supplier of data communication equipment for WAN and LAN based internet networking technologies.

Hardware Technologist, Product Development Group
Responsible for creating and maintaining bills of materials, production documentation, engineering change control, and introduce new products to manufacturing.

- Trained production staff in the final assembly and testing of new products.
- Successfully introduced new products from design engineering to subcontract manufacturing.
- Coordinated engineering changes in a cost effective manner.
- Gained experience in field service of new products.
- Prepared and maintained assembly/test instructions and compliance engineering documentation.
- Created and maintained bills of materials accurately in the AS/400 MRP system.

BIG COMMUNICATIONS INC.   **1994–1997**
A leading manufacturer of Wireless LAN products—Wireless ISA, MCA, PCMCIA, Ethernet and Token Ring Access Point, and Bridge using DSSS/FHSS radio.

Document Control Coordinator, Manufacturing Engineering Group
Responsible to manage and implement engineering change requests, administration of bills of material, review and control production documentation.

- Controlled and administrated production documentation, including hardware/software data management, source control documentation, test and assembly procedures.
- Chaired engineering change meetings and coordinated Engineering Change Orders (ECO) in a timely and cost effective manner from materials perspective.
- Created and maintained bills of material accurately with many ongoing changes.
- Increased productivity by implementing product configuration to customer requirements in the MAX - MRP system.
- Interfaced with engineering, purchasing, and marketing to resolve manufacturing issues.
- Established good working relationship with subcontractors and OEMs.

MANUFACTURING: Technologist (cont.)

JOHN JOHNSTON   Page 2/2

R& D INC   **1982–1994**
Manufacturer of Data Networking products—X.25 packet switches, T-1/E-1 multiplexers, modems, and statistical multiplexers.

Test Engineering Technologist, Manufacturing Sustaining Group   **1992–1994**
Responsible for technical support to all levels of the production and service departments; including troubleshooting, maintaining, and commissioning functional test stations, revise test documentation, purchasing equipment, evaluate and recommend processes and methods for increased productivity, quality, and future requirements.

- Simplified and improved test procedures and provided leadership role in technical activities.
- Successfully integrated test equipment and trained technical and production staff at Corporate Headquarters.
- Improved cycle time for networking products.
- Controlled documentation database to ISO 9002 quality standards.
- Trained 20 team operators and junior technicians on safe operation of test equipment and increased knowledge of company products.
- Backed up Production Supervisor when required.

Intermediate Technologist, Test and Customer Service Departments   **1982–1991**
Responsible for testing and troubleshooting high-speed modems, multiplexers, and 68000 microprocessor based X.25 packet switches to the component level for customer and field returns.
- Provided detailed test report upon completion of customer unit.
- Exceeded or met product quality and customer delivery goals through proper planning and organization.
- Prepared yield reports and analyzed data in order to implement and/or recommend corrective actions to quality concerns.
- Initiated action and liaison with Engineering to resolve test/design problems.

EDUCATION

Completed following courses at State College,   **1988–1997**
Leading & Team Building, Management Services.

* ISO 9000 Documentation	* UNIX	* Technology of LAN
* ISO 9000 Management	* DOS	* Intro to C Programming
* Design for Manufacturability	* VAX/VMS	* Excel, Access
* Statistical Process Control		

State College of Applied Arts and Technology,   **1982**
Electronic Engineering Technologist Diploma (With Honors)

State Collegiate Institute, State Scholar Award   **1979**

AWARDS

CodeExcellence Award for **Total Customer Satisfaction
and profit improvement.**   **1993**
Special recognition for contribution made in achievement of   **1993**
ISO 9002 registration and **outstanding teamwork** in the
successful launch of new products.

MANUFACTURING: Manufacturing Manager

John J. Johnston
123 Learning St, Anytown, ST ▪ 10101 ▪ (Cell) 999.555.1313 ▪ (Email) johnj@yourname.com

SALES LEADER
~ Specializing in Manufacturing and Industrial Products ~

Well-respected and extremely motivated individual eager to serve in the capacity of Sales Manager. Quickly establishes positive client relations, resulting in continuous Key Account customer loyalty. Tenacious nature closes the toughest sales. Refined leadership qualities establish team cohesiveness, optimizing corporate goals. Meticulous regard for detail and accuracy with strong follow-through skills. Establishes plans, goals, and processes to assure that strategies are competitive, effective, and protective of long-term success. **Core Attributes include:**

Client Relationship Management	**Quota & Goal Attainment**
Partnerships & Strategic Alliances	**Sound Decision Making**
Product Development	**Staff Leadership & Motivation**
Contracts & Negotiations	**Regulatory Compliance**
Strategic Marketing	**Recruiting & Training**

CAREER PATH

MANAGER   1998–2004
DHH Corporation
Retained to provide operational, outside sales, product development, and safety training for this furniture manufacturing firm. Maintained client relations with important accounts. Relied upon for solid problem solving capabilities in this fast-paced setting.
- Revamped employee compensation protocols. Introduced a performance-based remuneration structure, instead of the former hourly wage. Resulted in daily quota rising from just 60 units to 250 pieces.
- Ensured compliance for gov't & environmental permits for both equipment and chemicals.
- Granted complete autonomy to source suppliers, negotiate pricing, and purchase manufacturing products.
- Oversaw ordering procedures, shipment and delivery tracking, and inventory needs.

OUTSIDE SALES REPRESENTATIVE   1993–1998
ABC Moving
Achieved highest ranking sales in department, superseding results of 15-year veterans. Trusted with decision-making power in problem solving and the provision of extraordinary client relations.
- Presented corporate marketing initiatives and estimates for large corporations.
- Delivered in-house presentations and surveys for international & domestic moving services.
- Employed computer scanner and laptop in performing estimates, explaining services, and managing inventory.
- Efforts rewarded by increasing sales volume from $100k per month to $200k per month.

CUSTOMER SERVICE/FLEET MANAGER
Initially retained as a Customer Service/Fleet Manager with accountabilities for ensuring full care of 30 tractor-trailer units. Respected for consistently making effective use of all available resources in fleet management & clear communications to clients on delivery schedules.
- Revamped tracking drivers' licenses and vehicle insurance permits were due by introducing an auto-renewal notification application using Excel.

EDUCATION & SPECIALIZED TRAINING
INDUSTRIAL/MECHANICAL DIPLOMA- Major: Applied Mechanics. *State College*   1985–1989

Other Courses: Dealing with Problem Employees, Employee Motivation, & Hire & Develop Employees.
TECHNOLOGY: Excel, PowerPoint, and hardware/software installations and upgrades.
HOBBIES: Ice hockey, extreme 4X4 off-road adventuring, old boat restoration, & home/auto repair.

MANUFACTURING: Lean Manufacturing Engineer

123 Learning St.
Anytown, USA 10101

Phone: (999) 555-1212
Fax: (999) 555-1313
Email: johnj@yourname.com

John J. Johnston

Profile

Process Engineer - Lean Manufacturing, Industrial Engineering, Teams, and Quality Systems

Career Summary

- Twelve years of progressive responsibility and leadership in manufacturing.

- Competent team builder and Kaizen leader in both union and non-union environments.

- Accomplished at leading the implementation of Cellular Manufacturing and Continuous Flow.

- Key assignment involved lead role in implementing lean in an automotive plant.

Professional Experience

12/03–Present **Power Adaptor Inc.**
Lean Manufacturing Engineer
- Kaizen leader for biweekly action workouts ranging from SMED, to Value Stream Mapping
- Leader of project to implement lean manufacturing in a product sampling room, where orders taken via the internet are picked and shipped
  - o As part of project, developed a lean (one-piece-flow) filling, labeling, and packaging cell
  - o Implemented a Kanban signaling system to schedule cell outside of SAP
- Implemented lean manufacturing in a chemical testing laboratory
- More than $400,000 savings recorded in first 6 months

06/02–12/03 **Engines Corporation, Chassis Group**
Lean Manufacturing Engineer
- Shortened lead time on machining lines by 70% via SMED, Kaizen, and Kanban implementation
- Improved plant OEE (uptime) by 10% in one year
- Leader of SMED, and 5S teams – reduced one changeover from 6 hrs. to 20 min.
- More than $750,000 savings recorded over last 12 months
- Implemented a plant-wide visual TPM system

07/00–03/02 **Bowmen Incorporated**
Sr. Industrial Engineer
- Functioned as internal consultant for various divisions
- Shortened Product Development time for Extensions from 6 weeks to 10 hours
- Reduced platinum shop leadtime by more than 30%, saving more than $1 million
- Trained engineers in Lean Manufacturing and Value Stream Mapping

01/99–07/00 **BBB Systems – Thermal Division**
Global Manufacturing Systems Engineering Team Leader

- Team Leader of 6 Worldwide Lean Implementation Facilitators
- Guided cross functional teams using the Manufacturing System Design (MSD) Process to
    o Develop Lean Manufacturing systems for new and existing products
    o Identify manufacturing system best practices and common-ize globally
    o Identify and eliminate waste from the MSD and Product Development Processes
- Divisional trainer in Lean Manufacturing, Lean Cell design, and Value Stream Mapping
- Coordinated the development of common manufacturing systems and processes (templates)
- Reduced annual capital investment by more than $11 million
- QS9000 Coordinator for Mexican operations

12/93–12/98 **Blast Automotive Systems – Thermal Division**
Advanced Industrial Engineer

- Developed labor standards, workstations, facility layouts, and product timelines for North American, European, and Asian operations including HVAC assembly, injection molding, compressor machining and assembly, and heat exchanger manufacturing
- Used computer simulation to develop manufacturing operations from the ground up
- Developed, implemented, and provided on-going training for and Excel based line balancing system used world-wide
- Developed, via simulation, a material supply labor balancing system
- Developed spreadsheet macro to help cube out every day LTL truckloads

8/92–12/93 **LEE USA Pharmaceuticals**
Industrial/Quality Control Engineer

- Implemented a computer based preventative maintenance system
- Audited for compliance to FDA regulations (GMPs), developed Standard Operating Procedures
- Supervised clean room production and maintenance teams

7/92–11/92 **NIC Consulting INC**
- Built a static simulation model of NIC's armature shaft production system. Evaluated scheduling, manning, and machining alternatives. Reduced leadtime by 65%

Special Skills   Able to speak French and Spanish at a conversational level.

Education   **B.S. Finance, Anticipated 2005** GPA 4.0
State College

B.S. Industrial Engineering, 1992
State Institute of Technology

Interests and activities   Currently seeking APICS certification
Hockey, juggling, history buff (military), Oscar-worthy films, starting home projects.

MANUFACTURING: BAD—Inside Sales Rep

1

John J. Johnston
123 Learning Street,
Anytown USA 010101
Telephone No. (999) 555-1212

OBJECTIVE

To secure a position and to add to the on going success of the company.

PERSONAL SKILL

- Excellent leadership qualities
- Ability to work well with others and or on my own
- Excellent time management and organizational skills
- Public speaking
- Problem solving skills
- High computer literate

WORK HISTORY

July – Present
2003

Valve & Fittings
Inside Sales Rep

- Maintaining inventory levels
- Customer service
- Quoting and Order Entry
- Updating product information on server
- Creating new contact data base
- Creating customer cross reference catalogue
- Monthly and weekly reports using crystal reports
- Summarising technical information for company knowledge base

April-October
2002

Click Electric Supply
Inside Sales Rep

- Maintaining inventory levels
- Achieving monthly sales and profit quo[...]
- Customer service for current accounts
- Creating new customer accounts
- Delivery of products
- Branch banking (deposits, account bala[...]
- Finding and setting up new supplier acc[...]
- Estimating for new commercial job con[...]

What's Wrong?

- Too many bullet points
- Too much wasted space
- Lackluster objective/profile or lack thereof
- No declared job role
- No accomplishments or specific and measurable results
- Uninspiring and boring
- Spelling, grammatical, or word choice errors

2

January-April *2002*	*Cable Systems* *Inside Sales Rep*

- Telemarketing for new and existing customers
- Setting up new accounts, collections, and promotion of new products
- Booking of work orders

1999-2001 *Wild Fire Protection*
Inside Sales Rep

- Achieving monthly sales and profit quotas
- Customer service for current accounts
- Finding and developing new accounts
- Estimating for new commercial job construction.
- Maintaining inventory level
- Involved in having products approved by CSA, UL, ULC
- Involved in creating new products

1995-1998 *Wild Fire Protection*
Shipping and Receiving

Warehouse duties included:
- Shipping and receiving
- Pulling and packing orders within a 24 hour time period
- Maintaining inventory levels

EDUCATION

1998-1999 *State College*
1ˢᵗ year of electronic engineering
1992-1997 *St. Lucia's Secondary School*
Secondary School Diploma

COMPUTER SKILLS

Knowledge in both software and hardware. Software programs include:
- MS Word
- Excel
- Cbs System
- Business Visions 32
- Scala
- MS Publisher
- Various Photo Editor
- Maximzer
- Crystal Reports

References available upon request.

MARKETING: Marketing Assistant, Beginner

John J. Johnston

123 Learning Street
Anytown, USA 10101
Phone: (999) 555-1212
Email : johnj@yourname.com

Marketing Assistant

EDUCATION

Bachelor in Business Administration, Major in Marketing /Management, graduated summa cum laude
State University

2002–2003

Diploma in Business Administration, graduated with honors
State College

2001–2002

Diploma in Marketing, graduated with honours
State College

1999–2001

EMPLOYMENT EXPERIENCE

Marketing Assistant, CoEd Communications Inc.

2003

- Actively persuaded contestants applying for a national award program, increasing amount of sign ups by 20% from previous year
- Conducted market research to promote and distribute educational programs
- Helped train company personnel in the Microsoft Project software suite

Marketing and Administrative Assistant, ABC Securities Corp.

June 2000–2002

- Coordinated and cohosted educational seminars and social events for clients and prospects, thereby improving prospect possibilities and exceeding client expectations
- Developed and implemented direct marketing campaigns for leads and prospects, resulting in a twofold increase in the number of leads
- Expanded customer service and satisfaction by handling client inquiries with diligence and courtesy
- Efficiently performed administrative duties on a timely basis, allowing the company to become more organized and better equipped to handle more significant issues
- 1st event coordinated as a Marketing assistant was profiled in May 2001 issue of *Get the Edge* magazine

Distribution Coordinator/Problem Solving Clerk, Medics Laboratories

June–Sept 1999

- Coordinated and tracked samples leaving dept., resulting in better department procedure and reliability
- Resolved various non-routine situations, such as lost samples and unsatisfied customers, providing better customer service in a speedy and effective

Telemarketer, Association for Consumers of Anytown

Summer 1998

- Conducted market research surveys to determine consumer behaviour patterns allowing the department to improve marketing and sales efforts

Circulation Distribution Clerk, Bubble Business Communications

Summer 1996, 1997, 2000

ACTIVITIES

PHAU Youth Committee

2000–present

- Organized activities such as retreats and debates for children and youth for the 2000 International Conference

Tutor "Lunch-Box Learners"

2002

- Assisted students within the community in developing reading and comprehension skills

JOHN J. JOHNSTON

123 LEARNING ST. • ANYTOWN USA • 10101
PHONE (999) 555-1212 • CELL (999)555-1313
JOHNJ@YOURNAME.COM

Field Marketing Manager

Excels in motivating teams, public speaking, and creating excitement. Well-traveled with understanding of technology, culture, and the current youth generation.

FINANCIAL & ESTATE PLANNING INC., ADMIN ASSISTANT   Dec 2004–current

- Assist in the creation of client proposals and business plans, qualified leads, and organized business records.

CONSUMER IMPACT MKTING, NATIONAL FIELD MANAGER   2003–May 2004

- Managed over 25 Exxtreme Gamers reps across US who routinely visited a variety of outlets that showcased Exxtreme Gamers products.
- Began on the Big Cola Account but was quickly elevated to the Exxtreme Gamers program.
- Consistently trained, motivated the reps along with controlling aspects of payroll, expenses, incentive, and working budget.
- Strong public speaking was a necessity along with advanced analytical and business skills required for both roles.

ABC GROUP/S&MG, MARKETING/PROMOTIONS   May 2001–May 2003

- Involved in various programs including Big Soda Challenge (2000), World paper.com, and Crazy shoppers. All of the above programs required excellent individual skills, energetic public interaction, and comfort working alone under limited supervision.
- Top Coordinator Award Big Soda Challenge.

XYZ CONSUMER HEALTH, RESEARCH ASSISTANT   May–Sept 2001
ABC INC., MANAGEMENT TRAINEE   May–Aug 2000

Focused on training in management techniques and skills. Involved in internal audits, payroll, marketing activities, and web page design.

May–Dec. 2004   **World Travel**
Backpacker/Working Traveler

- Traveled extensively through Australia and several countries in South East Asia.
- Gained unparalleled education in geography, culture, and the tourism industry.

2000–2004   **State University**
B.A. Media Information Technoculture (Science Tech State)

Other Interests & Experiences:
Certified PADI scuba diver; Level II ski coach, Level II ski instructor
Memberships: Big Guy Golf and Country Club, GS Ski Club.
Previously – an actor in 6 commercials and a sitcom.

MARKETING: Marketing Manager, Junior

Alice J. Johnston

123 Learning St., Anytown, USA, 10101 (999) 555 1212
alicej@yourname.com

CAREER PROFILE: Marketing Manager looking to apply diverse marketing experience in consumer magazines and STATE EMBA education in a marketing position for a multinational publishing/media company.

EDUCATION

Master of Business Administration, *The Joint STATE EMBA*, July 2005
- The program schedule allows for full-time employment.
- The Joint STATE Executive MBA offers the combined strengths of the two top US business schools (*Business Week* 2003).

Master of Arts, *State University*, July 1998

EXPERIENCE

Marketing Manager, consumer tech magazines, *Classified, Anytown*   2000–2005
- Recruited to manage marketing activities and new product development of the Media division. Scope of accountability included: marketing budgeting responsibility for new product & business development, building strategic partnerships, brand leadership, marketing strategy development, and implementation.
- Developed and implemented print and online marketing strategies and activities for the launch of media websites
- Launched Research Reader Panel project in partnership with the top research company

Advertising Director, *Independent Media Publishing (Recognizable Household Magazines)*
Oct 1998–Jun 1999
- Created and implemented marketing and advertising revenue generating strategies for *Household Magazine* and special regional projects

Senior Advertising Sales Manager for Fashion Guru, *Independent Media Publishing*
Jan 1996–Sep 1998
- Sold an average of 80% of all advertising for each issue of *Fashion Guru* magazine
- Participated within the sales team in a groundbreaking special project: *Guru 850*, an 850-page special edition. Personally sold 200 pages for this issue.

Advertising Sales Manager, *Independent Media Publishing Ltd.*   Jan 1995–Jan 1996
- Sold an average of 40% of all advertising for each issue

COMPUTER AND LANGUAGE LITERACY
- **Computer -** Lotus Notes, Advanced Excel, PowerPoint, basic HTML
- **Language -** French (fluent), German (beginner level), Russian

ADDITIONAL INFORMATION
- Member of AMA (American Marketing Association), GIMP (Group of Interactive and Marketing Professionals)

MARKETING: Sales & Marketing Manager

John J. Johnston
123 Learning St., Anytown, USA   999.555.1212   johnj@yourname.com

Summary

A·successful **Sales/Marketing Manager** having a proven track record creating new business development initiatives and key account management. Work experience includes delivering innovative solutions in retail & commercial sales, marketing & advertising, new business channel development, CRM programs, resulting in significant revenue expansion and increasing the bottom-line profitability for employers.

Key Strengths

- Extensive experience planning, organizing, and managing complex projects.
- Ability to create & implement accurate budgets, generate revenue, & increase profitability.
- Excellent interpersonal people-skills and strong customer-service focus.
- Strong communication and interpersonal skills. An excellent hands-on manager.
- Methodical and detail-oriented.

Core Competencies,

• Business Development	• Business Leadership	• New Product Launches
• Budgets & Forecasting	• Process Management	• Sales & Trend Analysis
• Trainer/Team Builder	• Strategic Planning	• Distributor Management
• Customer Retention (CRM)	• Administrative Skills	• Project Management

Experience

STICKY WICK LTD.
Sticky Wick is an industry leader in the prepress design and production of adhesive labels for national name brand packaging.

Marketing Manager   2003–2004
Responsibilities included conducting research of target markets and potential business channels within various packaged goods industries.
- Managed two direct reports in the marketing department.
- Targeted new markets, opportunities, and accounts in the health food and beer industry.
- Successfully acquired over $1 million of new business through the development of professional RFPs-RFQs and contract negotiations.
- Key accounts top-of-mind awareness of the company's core capabilities was raised from 1 of 3,000 suppliers to *Top 25* supplier status through marketing campaigns, that included sampling, direct mail, advertising, sales proposals, customer seminars, and a new corporate brochure.
- Implemented a CRM program to support the sales funnel development efforts.

BOONE & COMPANY, INC.
Boone & Co. is a publicly traded (2002 sales, $60 million) printing company.

Sales/Marketing Manager   2002–2003
- Managed two direct reports. The product line was expanded by two major new services early in 2002. Successfully developed promotional and marketing initiatives that improved revenues and increased profitability.
- The 18-person sales force was trained and supported by the marketing team to grow profitable market share in a highly-competitive environment.

MARKETING: Sales & Marketing Manager (cont.)

- 2 -

TRUDY COMPANY, INC.   1979–2002
TRUDY is one of the world's foremost innovation companies. Employed by TRUDY in various progressive roles of responsibility from 1979 until 2002, with a 2-year period in 1983 when I returned to school to earn an MBA degree.

Sales Manager/Key Account Manager – Office Products   1998–2002
- Progressed through three divisions before being recruited to the Office Products Division by the Vice-President, Consumer, and Industrial Products Group, and reported to the Business Manager, Office Products.
- Was promoted for building this division to the largest in the company (2002 sales, $80 million).
- National Account Managers supported 5 of the top 10 accounts for the company.

District Sales Manager – Office/Promotional Products   1994–1998
- Recruited by the Vice-President of the Industrial & Consumer Sector to the largest corporate division ('94 sales, $35 million) to turn around a 6-person sales force that supported dealers and end-user customers in the office products and advertising specialty markets. Sales went from 2% to 13% growth.
- Developed the Sales Core Competencies Program for the 345-person sales force.

Marketing Manager – Occupational Health & Environmental Safety   1986–1994
- As a supplier of industrial personal safety equipment, targeted two key markets to grow sales. Grew both the welding (30%) and agricultural (20%) categories.
- Applied to the government for a $40,000 grant to produce a training video to educate pipe fitters on the importance of using respiratory protection. Sent out 4,500 training videos ordered by customers to raise pipe fitters' awareness of our products. Trial was initiated by providing a free sample with each video. 30% growth resulted, plus a key competitor retrenched from the welding market as the campaign captured over 90% of the disposable respirator category. TRUDY translated the program into five languages for global use, and the program was recognized at the annual TRUDY Marketing Excellence Awards.

Marketing Supervisor – Business Communications Products   1985–1986
Educational Sabbatical – State MBA Studies   1983–1985
Market Research Analyst   1980–1983
- Highest producing Analyst: completed over 90 market research projects on markets and competitors in both consumer and industrial markets.

Education

State School of Business, Masters of Business Administration, 1985
State University, Bachelor of Arts (Economics), 1978

Interests

Learning to surf, horseback riding, reading trend analysis books.

ALICE J. JOHNSTON

123 Learning Ave., Anytown, ST, USA   999-555-1234 (h)   999-555-1313 (w)
alicej@yourname.com

A GET IT DONE PROFESSIONAL: Versatile marketing/communications specialist with proven success to manage a diverse range of projects from vision and strategy through to execution and delivery. I look for innovative ways to bring freshness to delivery and have earned the respect from colleagues for my effortless way of keeping the team motivated and excited.

KEY QUALIFICATIONS

- Seasoned veteran of communications with over 15 years of executing quality marketing initiatives
- A creative professional with a sharp eye for detail who is able to grasp new concepts quickly and manage time productively, always deadline ready with best results
- In-depth knowledge of print, design, advertising, and marketing principles
- Superior analytical and organizational skills to manage data and understand brand and target market
- Experienced in costing and budgeting
- Media expert, having dealt with senior journalists, publicists, and VPs of advertising and marketing

CORE SKILLS AND ACCOMPLISHMENTS

PROJECT MANAGEMENT
- At the peak of Banner, managed 16 magazine editions in one year under three different brands
- Directed and executed all production on three hardcover books for international distribution
- Managed and created the brand extension for a Spaceship fan club and magazine (10,000+ members)

RE-BRAND, LAUNCHES AND SPECIAL EVENTS
- Led recent rebrand and redesign of *Banner* magazine to shift from an older demographic to the university and college market
- At Banner Licensing, created and launched events on behalf of Kaye Entertainment (Power Monkeys), Gathering Media (Bananas), and Fairgate Pictures (Spaceship) for potential licensees. High impact and "buzzed" about events led to increased revenues
- Delivered fun and sharply executed events to promote the State Arts Council and TVState

PUBLIC RELATIONS
- Generated publicity for the book launch of *Movies of our Time* and *Leading Ladies* by calling the "right" people and staging unique parties. Coverage included print, broadcast, and produced book sales
- Developed relationships with publicists/agents in New York and Los Angeles to get one-on-one interviews. Currently work with VPs of advertising and marketing in the film industry to create awareness of product

COMMUNICATIONS
- Produced close to 30 print projects for the State Arts Council and TVState including corporate brochures, annual reports, and special one-off editions
- At Banner Licensing & Promotions, reviewed all advertising, marketing, and promotional materials for content and clarity prior to client approval

BUDGETING
- Responsible for operating budgets for each edition of Banner magazine
- All special events were successfully executed within budgetary restrictions

MARKETING: Marketing & Communications (cont.)

EMPLOYMENT HISTORY

Banner Media Inc., Managing Editor and Marketing Manager   1993–current

Currently, Banner Media publishes a national entertainment magazine distributed into university and college newspapers six times yearly. In its earlier days, Banner had a number of divisions including licensing, promotions, book and magazine publishing, and a nationally syndicated entertainment radio program.

Banner magazine

- Research, develop content, assign, edit, and direct all production through to publication and distribution

Accomplishments

- Initiated a number of special issues to attract diversified advertising base
- Successfully keep the brand fresh and deliver a creative product on time and within budget

Other Projects

- Banner Licensing & Promotions – Special Events/Marketing Manager
- *Spaceship Fan Club* Magazine – Managing Editor
- *The Picture Show* Magazine – Managing Editor

Banner Publishing, Production Manager   1990–1992

- Managed production on three hardcover books including content research, photo approvals, manuscript fact-checking, proofreading, and display writing; approved layouts, film output, and printing proofs

Project Message (Owner and Operator)   1984–1989

Leveraging my entrepreneurial spirit and experience in marketing/communications for several arts institutions, I lent my expertise to a variety of initiatives including the State Arts Council, TVState, Banner Media, and other various publications.

- Managed special events and media/press coverage to promote/publicize TVState and the State Arts Council
- Produced close to 30 print projects (corporate brochures, annual reports, special edition booklets)
- Researched, fact-checked for various publications including National paper *Purposes* and *Banner* magazine

State Arts Council, Visual Arts Program Assistant   1980–1983

- Completed background research on more than 1,000 grant applications (per year) by analyzing proposals and writing historical/financial assessments required for Council approval. Managed and catalogued all application support material (from artists and arts publications) for adjudicating procedures

Art Gallery of State, Extension Services – Special Projects Assistant   1979

- Coproduced more than 25 contemporary art exhibitions circulated to provincial galleries by coordinating programs with artists and gallery directors. Completed research and coproduced brochures and catalogues to publicize and promote exhibitions

Office Experience   1972–1978

- Worked in a variety of office settings in supporting roles for: Royal State Museum, Lakebeam Community Centre, Mathers May and Meryl Law Office, and Big Bank Personnel

EDUCATION

State University, Magazine Journalism   **1987–89**

Capistrano Collegiate, Business & Commerce   **1972**

Cannestoga Collegiate, Secondary School Diploma   **1971**

COMPUTER SKILLS

Microsoft Office Suite including, Access, Excel

PASSIONS

Taking dogs from the pound for a walk as a volunteer, planting seeds in my garden and watching them come up while sitting in my back porch armchair, reading 2 to 3 newspapers a day if possible.

John Johnston BSc., MBA, P. Eng

123 Learning Street, Anytown, ST 01010 *Tel: (999) 555-1212 Email: johnj@yourname.com*

Director-level Marketing and Business Strategist with practical background in manufacturing, wireless, telecom, and digital broadcasting. Excels in start up situations, new divisions, and ventures.

KEY STRENGTHS

- Expertise and versatility in all facets of the business cycle including budgeting, pre-sales planning, marketing, account management, operations, & post-sales support in organizations ranging from start-ups to multi-nationals.
- Skilled communicator with well-honed interpersonal skills based on a strong collaborative approach and focus on conflict resolution & diplomacy.
- Exceptional customer service focus with the keen ability to build and enhance customer relationships.
- Effective manager with a proven track record of recruiting, developing, motivating, and leading staff.
- Highly results oriented with extensive project management experience on complex, technical projects.

PROFESSIONAL EXPERIENCE

2003–Currently   *Big Entertainment Inc.*   **Director, Business Affairs & Marketing**

- Established and oversaw corporate policies, strategy, and tactics as a member of the senior management team of a newly established producer of digital branded multimedia content.
- Developed and directed the implementation of online marketing strategy & tactics including; e-commerce, mass email marketing, interactive gaming (award nominated) & websites to promote individual production (award nominated), & overall corporate marketing objectives.
- Led the execution of corporate communication, public relations, and customer service activities and provided critical support for corporate marketing initiatives.
- Secured production funding from government and private sources and consulted on contracts & business practices.

2000–2002   *Not Your Average Networks*   **Director, Sales Engineering**

- Provided grounded leadership in helping build a start-up company during extremely challenging economic times.
- Defined objectives and established mandate of a newly created sales engineering department responsible for providing technical and business support to sales executives of multiple product lines across North America.
- Recruited, staffed, and managed department, developing it into a high performance team that was instrumental in achieving corporate revenue and earnings targets.
- Led cross-functional integration ensuring product development met market needs and enhancing customer support.
- Prior to promotion, acted as a senior project manager working closely with clients at all project stages in defining project scope, budget, and schedules, managing implementation, and gaining satisfactory closure.
- Planned, assembled, and managed virtual project teams of programmers, content developers, graphic and designers ensuring project deliverables met/exceeded customer expectations while optimizing company business objectives.

1998–2000   *BIG Wireless Network*   **Sr. Manager, Marketing Operations**

- Ran the operations group of a $150M+ division selling products & services to wireless service providers.
- Achieved operational excellence by strategic hiring, team building, and the personal and professional development of staff enabling the division to surpass financial targets and customer objectives.
- Initiated improved coordination of cross-functional groups enhancing focus on customers & divisional bottom line.
- Led the analysis and implementation of business process improvements increasing responsiveness and profitability.
- Primed the market analysis, forecasting, and planning optimising divisional strategy of customer and product mix.

MARKETING: Director, Marketing (cont.)

John Johnston BSc., MBA, P. Eng

| 1995–1998 | *Big Cellular Company* | **Manager, PCS Planning & Data** |

- Managed mission critical projects for Big Cellular's launch of mobile Personal Communications Services (PCS).
- Acted as the principal marketing resource for product functionality, positioning, and internal & external training.
- Championed marketing interests in cross-functional teams of engineering, technology planning, sales, and channel distribution driving the definition, business case development, and roll-out of PCS products and services.
- Modeled, and optimized distribution and pricing strategies as part of creating budgets & long-range financial plans.
- Prior to promotion, provided marketing and sales support to national accounts in the role of senior market analyst.
- Managed cross-functional teams and coordinated inter-company activities to deploy new service offerings.

| 1991–1995 | *BIG Wireless Network* | **Marketing Manager, Eastern USA** |

- Generated, sold, and implemented multi-million dollar proposals to both established customers and new accounts resulting in significantly surpassing regional budget targets.
- Supported regional sales force on commercial, market, and product issues for portfolio of cellular products.
- Presented in-depth product and market information to customers facilitating the roll out of new products & services.
- Prior to promotion, established the Marketing Operations department as part of a new joint venture in the role of a senior marketing operations specialist.
- Generated marketing proposals for American cellular operating companies with the ultimate responsibility for ensuring conformance to customer, engineering, commercial, and contractual requirements.

| 1986–1988 | *Consulting Civil Engineer, Contractor* | **Site Superintendent, Field Engineer** |

EDUCATION & PROFESSIONAL DEVELOPMENT

1998–2000	*Foundation Skills for Managers*	Networks
May 1991	*Master of Business Administration*	State University
May 1986	*B.Sc. in Civil Engineering*	State University

PROFESSIONAL ASSOCIATIONS

| January 1995 | *Licensed Professional Engineer* | Professional Engineers |

ACTIVITIES AND INTERESTS

- Member of the Group of Internet Marketing Professionals (GIMP).
- Part-time instructor at a local Business School teaching advanced-level courses.
- Active volunteer: i) coaching sports teams, ii) participating on elementary school councils & iii) teaching English to American immigrants.
- Continuing education in creative writing.
- Postgraduate studies in Belgium & traveled extensively throughout Europe, Turkey, North and Central America.

MARKETING: BAD—Summer Marketing

(1)
John J. Johnston
123 Learning Street
Anytown, USA 10101
Phone: (999) 555-1212
Fax: (999) 555-1313
Email: johnj@yourname.com

OBJECTIVE

To obtain a summer position in the field of Marketing or management.

WORK EXPERIENCE

Anytown Parks and Recreation, 2001 - 2003

- Lifeguard- Maintain a safe and pleasant place for adults and children to swim.

ABC Renovations Inc.
General Labor

- Assisting in the construction trade

Construction and Remodelling- Summer 2004
- Analyzing Blueprints
- Construction of exterior and interior projects.

Action June - Sept 2003
- Organized and ran "Drive Straight" with the cooperation of the Community Council on Impaired Driving.
- Attended Numerous Golf Tournament and events raising Alcohol Awareness
- Responsible for corporate sponsorship and fundraising throughout the State

Community Council on Impaired Driving (CCID) Jan- Sept 2003
- Co-op Position
- Writing letters to press, memos and pursuing corporate funding
- Working on PSA's and public relations letters..

EDUCATION
sophomore at the State University pursuing Marketing and Managem

AWARDS
National Lifesaving, CPR, Swimming Scholarship

CV: John J. Johnston
Date: 25/07/2005

What's Wrong?

- Too long especially for your age and stage
- Lackluster objective/profile or lack thereof
- No declared job role
- Spelling, grammatical, or word choice errors
- Name is too small or address is too large or both

MARKETING: BAD—Summer Marketing (cont.)

(2)

SKILLS

Team Player My six years on the East Town Swim Team and my 2 years in The Aquatic Club, it has taught me the importance of being a quality team member. Working cooperatively, watching out for my teammates, offering a helping hand when needed are skills applied daily.

Hard-Working Involvement in community service, extracurricular activities, and being a great student has taught me the importance of setting priorities in my work, leisure, and studies so I can maintain quality performance in all areas.

Diplomatic Leader After being apart of the athletic counsel, I have developed a leadership style that empowers the team as a cohesive whole instead of simply as a group of individuals.

Strong Communicator Participated in class lectures where I learned to prepare and develop my thoughts before speaking them and then to state my case logically and persuasively.

ACTIVITIES

- Track Team, Team Member, fall 1999 - spring 2000.
- Athletic Counsel, Counsel Member, spring 1998 - spring 1999.
- East Town Swim Team, Team Member, 1996 - 2001
- Town Aquatic Club, Team Member, 2001 - 2003
- State University of Denver 2003- Present
- Active Member In Church
- History Fair, 2000

VOLUNTEER EXPERIENCE

- Food Bank - Fall 1995
- Simpson's Farm - July 1997, 1999, 2000
- Heart And Stroke – Feb, 1999, 2000, 2001, 2002, 2003
- Eastern Swim Club – 1996-2001
- Town Aquatic Club – 2001- 2003
- Swim-A-Thon- Spring, 1996-2003
- Special Olympics- 1999-2000
- Race for a Cure - 2003
- Big Brothers and Sisters - 2003
- Community Council on Impaired Driving - 2003
- Walk For a Cure – 2003-2004

INTERESTS

Reading, Helping Others, Sports, Computers, Business, Swimming

John J. Johnston – Mathematician & Statistician

123 Learning Street
Anytown, USA 10101

Telephone: 999-555-1212
Email: johnj@yourname.com

Education **Master of Science** in **Mathematics** State University
Bachelor of Arts in **Economics** at State College

Computer Skills SQL, STATA, Minitab, C/C++, Java, Excel, Certificate in SAS

Experience

Big Financial, Financial Advisor (2002–Present)
- Provide funding for security lending.
- Arrange loans and mortgages for clients.
- Assess the needs and provide income protection plans for families.
- *Manage clients' investment according to their risk tolerance, style, and preferences.*
- *Assist clients in speeding up their house down payment, retirement, and education fund planning.*

Gamehead, Statistician (2001–2002)
- Conducted statistical consulting projects for casinos concerning game performance and spending behavior.
- Analyzed gaming software behaviors using both SAS and Excel. Researched genetic algorithms for strategic games.
- Conducted statistical analyses on horse racings, sports, and industrial trends of gaming.
- Provided excellent client oriented consulting for investors, clients, product development, and management teams.
- Responsible for the research and development of random number generator.
- Studied and complied gaming regulations of various jurisdictions.
- *Assisted in streaming and other Internet projects and improved run time performance of games.*

GBV Network, Mathematician (1999–2000)
- Responsible for all statistical analysis of the product performance on different hardware, operating systems, connection speeds, and data types.
- Designed and managed various data sets for clients' websites.
- Conducted statistical studies on clients' websites concerning demographics, hits, and visitor behavior.
- Managed the development of Mpeg4 and participated in Mpeg4 Industrial Forum meetings.
- Coordinated correspondence with various organizations, ISO, ITO, ANSI, W3C, MPEG.
- Designed and developed software development cycle and testing procedures.
- Designed and developed ITO H261 and a GSM-slide-show in Java.
- *Improved 90% of the raw code run-time performance of Fast Fourier Transform algorithms.*
- *Trained two new programmers.*

Office of Planning and Budget, State University, Research Assistant (May 1997–August 1997)
- Researched the rate of retention, graduation, alumni giving, and application yield of the University using SAS.
- Conducted segmentation analysis to validate findings and assisted in developing tactical performance indicator.
- Established this position and introduced new statistical techniques, logit regression to the Office.
- *Results were used for conferences within the University.*

Mathematics Department, State University, Teaching Assistant (January 1997–May 1998)
- Conducted a three course planning and evaluated seventy student performances.

Volunteer

Local Political Party, Fundraising Co-coordinator, (November 2003–Present)
- Conduct data analysis of all the fundraising direct mail appeals. Function as the chief statistician/database manager.
- Write summaries reports, interpret results, and provide recommendations for future donor segmentation.

Go Club (chess), Secretary (December 2001–Present), Fundraise for the 2004 Anytown Open tournament, now the second highest prized tournament, increased club membership by more than 500%.

Tax Clinic at Community Centre (2003), Assisted low-income families to file taxes.

MATHEMATICIAN: Senior Consultant

John J. Johnston

123 Learning St.
Anytown, USA 10101
Email: johnj@yourname.com

Dept. Stats & Actuarial Sciences, SU
TEL (999) 555-1212   (W)TEL (999) 555-1313 Ext. 888
FAX (999) 555-1414

Instructor and Senior Consultant
Department of Statistical and Actuarial Sciences, State University (SU)

A graduate of the US's leading Actuarial program, who embraces 10 years of professional experience of modeling development, data management, and analysis in engineering, insurance, and public health, in the Far East and US. Honed by the comprehensive understanding of mode applied mathematics, statistics and actuarial science, and frontline working experiences in two different cultural environments, can examine and absorb large amount of qualitative & quantitative data, constantly scans the processes for potential problems and opportunities for improvement, and is adept at communicating and coordinating with internal and external levels of the organization. Assertive, hardworking, innovative, and a long-range thinker with an excellent strategic vision. Key mathematical modeling and consultancy skills include:

Data Mining Techniques for Nonparametric Data – Risk Analysis and Management – Project Design & Development Strategy – Financial Analysis – SAS and SQL Programming

---

Education

Department of Statistical and Actuarial Sciences, State University – Anytown,
Masters of Statistics (focus on the Actuarial Science), 2004
- Well-rounded training of life, finance, pension, and risk management
- Two year project focused on insurance industry data mapping, data analysis, and mortality construction of pension plans
- Member of the Society Of Actuaries (SOA) project (2002–2004, UWO)
- Consultant at State-Lab, State University

China University of Mining – Beijing, China
PhD of Applied Mathematics, 1992
- VP External, Graduate Student Union, 1989–1991
- Two year scholarship reward from the Department of Resources, China

---

Professional Experience

Instructor, Senior Consultant, and Research Associate, Department of Statistical and Actuarial Sciences
State University (2000–Present)
- Give lectures for the third year undergraduate students:
  - ✓ Course: Applied Statistical Computing: SAS and its applications in statistics & actuarial science.
  - ✓ Achievement: (1) Teaching SAS coding.
    (2) Notes for the course (11 chapters) and lab guide.
    (3) Obtained high marks from the students' evaluation.
- **Consult for clients from different departments in the State University:**
  - ✓ Department of Applied Mathematics and the Department of Human Ecology, University:
- Communicating with internal clients to understand the nature of the projects, setting the solid and measurable objectives of the projects, allocating the resources, & set timeline for each project lead.
- Providing instructions, advice, and assistance for the analysts when it comes to the major milestones of the clients' project.
- Coordinating between analysts, internal researchers, related functional departments, corporation management, and external coworkers in Department of Civil Engineering, State Hydro to assure effective cooperation.

John J. Johnston

123 Learning St.
Anytown, USA 10101
Email: johnj@yourname.com

Dept. Stats & Actuarial Sciences, SU
TEL (999) 555-1212 · (W)TEL (999) 555-1313 Ext. 888
FAX (999) 555-1414

- **National Science Research Inc.:**
  - ✓ Scope of the project: Develop the mathematical models for the pension plan mortality rate using local likelihood and data mining approaches.
  - ✓ Propose a standard model for the mortality rate calculation in the insurance industry.
  - ✓ **Achievement: The model can describe the pension plan mortality rates from 79 North American companies and will be accepted and used widely once it is published.**

- **Actuaries LLC**
  - ✓ Aim: Construct the mortality tables for the usage of insurance companies. The results will be published annually.
  - ✓ Achievement: Create the mortality tables for the retirees and the actives by life and by benefit amount separated by females and males. The SAS codes are made the various tables.
  - ✓ **Awarded: Bonus awarded from each of the participants.**

- **Stochastic and dynamic modeling the data of State Hydro electric:**
  - ✓ As a coinvestigator, I was involved in several areas such as analytical models, computing simulation, comparison, & modification of the models with the experimental data.
  - ✓ Cooperation with other researchers at the Wind Tunnel Lab.
  - ✓ Associate Professor, Development of Mathematics, Big University, China (1994–2000)

- Gave the mathematics, calculus, algebra, and statistics for all departments in the university.
- Won the funding from the National Nature Science Foundations of China (NNSFC).
- Won the Outstanding Young Student Funding from Government.
- Awarded by the Government for the Excellent Young Teachers (1995).
- Awarded by the University for the Excellent Young Teachers (1994).
- The established models recognized by publication in several famous international journals.

Postdoctoral fellow
Department of Mathematics and Mechanics, Other University, China (1992–1994)
- Independently made a computer program for the computing consulting company to record their customers' information and calculate the necessary information.
- Designed and developed a program for industrious data management allowing the immediate consideration of all risk factors involved in particular segment of the company, thereby greatly facilitating the profitability assessment of the product.

Professional Examinations – SOA exams

- 1, 2, and 4 passed

Computer Skills

- Advanced level in MS Office Environment including Excel, Access, PowerPoint
- Statistical packages: SAS, S-plus, R, SPSS plus Fortran, C++

Other Academic Activities

- 1999 Dept. of Math., University, UK, Fellowship

Publications

- Available upon request

MATHEMATICIAN: BAD—Finance Specialist

John J. Johnston PhD.

Address: 123 Learning St., USA, 10101 Phone number: (999) 555-1212
johnj@yourname.com

RECENT WORK EXPERIENCE

Mathematics Inc., Senior Financial Engineer (1998–today)

- *Value vs. earnings at risk optimization case study*
  The modern approach to asset / liability management is based on an adequate
  measurement of both value and earnings at risk. The earnings approach is based on a
  static balance sheet while the economic value approach takes into account changes in
  the balance sheet either by incorporating new business or closing unprofitable
  businesses. This difference gives rise to a trade-off between both approaches. The
  objective of this case study is to assess the inter-temporal nature of this trade-off
  through the simulation of both the balance sheet and income statement of a
  commercial bank.

- *Big Bank, Mexico - credit risk management project.*
  I am responsible for the successful implementation of a credit risk system for their
  loan book. The project involves measuring counterparty and portfolio credit risk for
  both commercial and retail loans as well as the implementation of a limit system
  across the different business areas of the bank.

- *Stocks Inc.*
  My involvement in this project is to provide a methodology for generating risk based
  spreads for all illiquid instruments that are quoted in the Mexican Stock Exchange.

- *National Bank Inc.,*
  As a major state development bank it provides funds to non-bank financial
  intermediaries but bears the credit risk in case the ultimate borrower defaults. We
  created a loan valuation prototype to assess counterparty credit risk.

- *Big Italian Bank, Italy*
  I created a credit risk simulation model to measure counterparty and portfolio credit
  risk for a derivatives book. (interest rate and currency swaps and FX forwards)

- *Big Bank, USA*
  The project involved the application of the CreditMetrics me[...]
  credit risk of a portfolio of long-dated corporate and sovereig[...]
  emerging markets. Credit risk was decomposed into default a[...]
  we assessed the sensitivity of the loss distribution to various [...]

What's Wrong?
- No declared job role
- No accomplishments or specific and measurable results
- Too many unnecessary extras and/or irrelevant information and/or repetition
- Uninspiring and boring

Banco Franco (1990–1998)

- *Financial planning*

  I was responsible for the implementation and monitoring of the financial and business plans of the different areas of the bank and assess their contribution to the bank's overall profitability. This responsibility also entailed the assessment and valuation of new lines of business for the Banco Franco such as the introduction of new mortgage products, complex debt issues in international markets, streamlining of back office operations, restructure of service fees across assets and liabilities, etc.

  I was also responsible for providing balance sheet and income statement forecasts to the board of directors and executive committee of Banco Franco on a quarterly basis.

- *Valuation of mortgage loans*

  Mortgage loan projects required the analysis and assessment of migration patterns in the portfolio to forecast the behavior of past due loans, the valuation of mortgages for low-income housing and provide reliable numbers on the potential outstanding balance due to the negative amortization characteristics of these loans.

- *Structuring of new mortgage products*

  During the low inflation growth period of 1990–1994, we introduced a new loan product into the market that had a profitable effect for the bank and at the same time preserved borrowers' liquidity.

- *Loan analysis models*

  As the person responsible for financial analysis and valuation, during 1995–1998 I was in charge of providing senior management with a detailed assessment of the impact that the different government restructuring programs would have on the bank's financial statements.

- *Investor relations*

  I was responsible for the drafting of offering memorandums and investor prospectuses as well as for the generation of the relevant financial information required by regulators (SEC) and international investors. This task also required the reconciliation of the bank's financial statements to U.S. GAAP.

SCHOLARSHIPS AND AWARDS RECEIVED

- ABC Foundation Scholarship
- State Scholarship
- State University Scholarship

EDUCATION

- **State University, PhD. Program in Economics**
- **Instituto Tecnologico, BA, Economics (magna cum laude)**

MATHEMATICIAN: QA Coordinator

John J. Johnston

123 Learning St., Anytown, USA, 10101 (999) 555 1212 johnj@yourname.com

A highly motivated, results-focused QUALITY ASSURANCE professional with extensive experience in economics, statistics, data analysis, and public policy. International experience. Advanced skills in Microsoft Office products, database, and statistical packages. Resourceful problem solver with proven ability to bring quick resolution to challenging situations as well as building lasting relationships with executives and staff.

EXPERIENCE

08/03–present Quality Assurance Coordinator   ABC Oil Exploration LLC
- Develop ongoing quality assurance and compliance reporting against company policies, procedures, and internal controls. Coordinate inputs and communicate to Business Unit users via company intranet
- Verify propriety and coordinate account reconciliation process in Financial Controls and Accounting Dept
- Produce strategic quality recommendations to optimize business performance
- Prepare accounting closure schedule. Coordinate inputs and deadlines to achieve group best practices
- Prepare and maintain quarterly performance reports for Financial Controls and Accounting Dept
- Coordinate responses to Control audits and assist in collating and submitting supporting documents
- Assist in special projects (quarterly Due Diligence, Business Continuity, Central Group reporting, etc)

04/02–07/03   Sr. Data Analyst   *ABC Healthcare Services, Inc*
- Developed business optimization solutions for clients applying statistical and marketing tools
- Set up surveys/studies and pulled survey results for a call center using Sawtooth WinCati, Ci3, and SPSS
- Recoded, processed, transformed, and archived survey data using SPSS, SAS, MS Excel, and MS Access
- Produced ad hoc analytical reports using MS Access/SQL and posted output to the website
- Planned automation of tasks in a call center and ensured that deliverables meet accuracy and timeliness
- Operated existing models and developed new statistical solutions to measure client's performance
- Dealt with monthly trainings, day-to-day client interaction, and hardware/software issues

01/01–05/02   Research Assistant   *State University, Department of Economics*
- Responsible for data collection, library research, data maintenance, manipulations and transformations
- Performed economic and statistical computations using SAS, SPSS, Stata, and MS Excel to understand consumer spending. Produced regression analyses for integrating public programs and business strategies
- Composed and edited qualitative research reports for internal and external distribution
- Developed and upgraded economic databases using MS Excel, SPSS, and MS Access/SQL

03/99–08/00   Economist   *European Union's Technical Assistance Program*
- Collected foreign trade data and procedures from various official authorities (ministries and agencies)
- Performed analytical analysis of foreign trade regime in Istanbul. Generated market research reports on WTO Agreements on Agriculture, Subsides, Technical Barriers and delivered to WTO Secretariat
- Consulted government officials on a variety of the WTO requirements (technical barriers, import and export licensing of goods and services, taxation, customs valuation, agricultural and industrial subsides, and patents)

07/97–08/00   Research Associate   *Turkey Academy of Science, Economic Institute*

EDUCATION

05/02	**Master of Arts in Economics**	*State University,*
12/99	**Diploma in Labor Economics**	*Academy of Science, Turkey*
06/96	**Honor Diploma in Economics (Equivalent to US BBA)**	*State Economic Institute, Turkey*

COMPUTER SKILLS
- Office: MS Excel, MS Power Point, MS Access, and Harvard Graphics
- Database: Sawtooth CATI, Win CATI, MS Access, and SQL language
- Statistical programs: SAS, SPSS, Eviews, Stata, Minitab, and Limdep
- Internet: PERL, HTML, MS FTP, and Javascript

INTERNSHIPS: Economic Assistant Intern   *Office of United States Senator* 05/01–08/01
RELEVANT COURSES: Chartered Management Accountant, The Chartered Institute of CMA, 07/04–enrolled
ACHIEVEMENTS: Freedom Support Fellowship; Yorkshire Seminar "Urban Problems" Alumni

John J. Johnston

123 Learning St., Anytown, USA 10101
Phone: (999) 555.1212 Email: johnj@yourname.com

Talented Media Administrator and Designer

o **Corporate Branding:** Corporate Identification, Website Design, Audio-Video Production, Interactive CDs
o **Software Testing:** Development of Test Plans for Unit testing, Functional testing, System Integration of Cross platform and Client/Server applications

o Short learning curve for new technologies and environments
o Excellent time management with strong organization skills and ability to prioritize tasks and manage resources
o Can work on assigned projects independently while contributing to positive team communications and environment

WORK EXPERIENCE

Media Administrator
Clean Water Agency, Anytown January 2003–Present
o Recorded and edited variety of videos, and animations for social events, security procedures, and wastewater treatment methods – Adobe Premiere, Photoshop/ImageReady, Macromedia Flash, MS PowerPoint
o Created posters and collages from original sources for CWA's events – Adobe Photoshop, Illustrator
o Designed and created the community Facilities intranet site – Hand coded HTML, DHTML, and JavaScript
o Photographed construction sites and created .gif images for client to see work that has been done – Adobe Photoshop, ImageReady, PanaVue ImageAssembler

Additional Initiatives
o Created, modified, and improved existing Access databases, and Excel spreadsheets
o Created and updated safety manuals, documentation books, and active fields forms - Adobe Acrobat, MS Word, Excel
o Trained employees in video editing, document and database updating

Multimedia Designer
Big Chicken – 2002
o Developed interactive CD-ROM for Big Chicken including Business Plan presentation: Provided digital photos and included motion graphics, video, game, and interactive elements - Macromedia Director and Lingo scripting, Adobe Photoshop

Graphic Designer
Recital Hall Conservatory–2002
o Violin Recital - Designed concert tickets and plackets - Adobe Illustrator, Photoshop, QuarkXPress

NEW MEDIA: Multimedia Designer and Admin. (cont.)

John J. Johnston   Tel: (999) 555.1212   Email: johnj@yourname.com

Web Designer
State College – 2001
- Girl Group, website redesign
  The original site redesign included new design concept, choice of color, and topography to give the site a new look and feel
- Bearwear Gear, website design (Flash and HTML version)

Software Tester, Romania
VIS Company, (1997–1999)
- Designed and maintained test cases
- Performed Cross-Platform (Win 95/98 – NT 4.0) testing of Retail Management System, Windows based, client server application
- Reported test results and recommended product quality improvements
- Reviewed Functional Specifications for completeness, consistency, and accuracy

SKILLS

- Operating Systems: Mac OS X, Windows XP/2000/NT/9x
- Software Packages:

Adobe Photoshop	3D Studio MAX	QuarkXPress
ImageReady	Strata 3D Pro	Cool Edit
Illustrator	Macromedia Flash	Sound Forge
Premiere	Director	MS Office (Word, Excel, Access
After Effects	Dreamweaver	PowerPoint, Visio, FrontPage)
GoLive	Fireworks	Lotus Notes
Acrobat	FreeHand	

- Script Languages:

HTML (Advanced Level)	ActionScript (Intermediate Level)
DHTML (Advanced Level)	Lingo (Intermediate Level)
JavaScript (Advanced Level)	VB Script (Beginning Level)

- Photography: Photography development and effects techniques

EDUCATIONAL BACKGROUND

Multimedia Design and Production - Diploma
(2000–2002) State College

Surveillance Engineering - Diploma
(1995–1998) College of State, Romania

PERSONAL INTERESTS

Web design for friends; drawing and animation; choral singing; running.

NEW MEDIA: Business Development

John Johnston

123 Learning Street, Anytown USA 10101
Cell: (999) 555-9999 ■ Email: johnj@yourname.com

PROFILE: *Interactive Media Supervisor/Business Development Strategist with extensive, diversified experience in the advertising industry; a proactive, results-driven producer adept at developing and implementing comprehensive planning initiatives, strategizing to analyze future business potential, coupled with expertise in all areas of media planning, seeks an opportunity that fully capitalizes on this background while providing further career growth and advancement potential as merited.*

ATTRIBUTES:
- PROVEN BUSINESS DEVELOPMENT SKILLS
- CONSISTENT PRODUCER/QUICK TO LEARN
- EFFECTIVE COMMUNICATOR/NEGOTIATOR
- PROACTIVE, MULTI-TASKING TEAM LEADER

EXPERIENCE:
05/03 to Present

THE DEAN AGENCY
Initially recruited by this leading advertising agency as a Senior Media Planner assigned to the Interactive Group, as a result of top performance and exceeding company expectations, earned a promotion to my current position.

Media Supervisor - **INTERACTIVE GROUP** (04/04–Present)
- Direct a staff of seven and manage all interactive advertising for major accounts *(Overnite Deliveries, Insurers R Us, Big Box Furniture, etc.)*; hire, train, and develop staff.
- Meet with clients to introduce interactive advertising concepts; work closely with our creative department to develop online banner, pop-up, and other advertising concepts.
- Present concepts for client approval; develop projections for anticipated advertising results.
- Coordinate all aspects of interactive advertising campaigns.

Senior Media Planner - **INTERACTIVE GROUP** (05/03–04/04)
- Revamped, organized, and grew this virtually nonexistent department from $650K to over $25MM in annual media billings.
- Trained and developed staff in all areas of interactive media advertising.
- Worked closely with existing accounts to educate them on interactive advertising potential.
- Created and presented innovative interactive advertising concepts that earned client approval.

10/01 to 05/03

A BUNCH OF GUYS ADVERTISING
Initially hired as a Senior Media Planner by this major agency that specialized in direct response advertising. Thereafter, was appointed to the Business Development Team to explore revenue-generating opportunities.

Business Development Strategist/Senior Media Planner
- As *Business Development Strategist*, conducted competitive analysis with prospective clients to determine the most effective approach to earn their advertising business.
- Created targeted promotional materials for usage in presentations to specific accounts.
- As *Senior Media Planner*, managed client advertising campaigns *(Big Drug Company, Consulters Inc etc.)* in various media including print, television, direct mail, interactive, and radio.
- Tracked direct response results; compiled statistics for presentation and recommendations to clients.
- Conducted professional presentations to clients both individually and as part of a team.
- Conferred with client senior management to develop methods for optimizing advertising results.

08/00 to 10/01

FAB-EURO ADVERTISING
Hired from college as an Assistant Traffic Coordinator assigned to the FUEL: North America Interactive Department, earned subsequent advancement to Assistant Media Planner.

Assistant Media Planner (04/01–10/01)/*Traffic Coordinator* (08/00–04/01)
- Planned, researched, and trafficked interactive campaigns for a key client (Computer Giant).
- Examined client websites; researched relevant content areas and target audience of sites to structure on-line campaigns; allocated ads on preferred web sites to reach specific audiences.
- Negotiated advertising rates, placements, and impression levels for campaigns.
- Analyzed and optimized campaigns weekly to ensure best performance results.

EDUCATION: **State University**
BS Speech Communication / MINOR: *Business* (GPA: 3.67)…Graduated May 2000

TRAINING:
- ACCOUNT MANAGEMENT
- DART RICH MEDIA TRAFFICKING I, II
- ATLAS DMT

SKILLS: **DFA Manage; HTML; CorelDRAW; Photo Paint; Internet; Interactive Research Tools**
PERSONAL: **Motivated…Problem Solver…Organized…Creative…Resourceful…Confident…Inquisitive**
INTERESTS: **Wine tasting tours; expanding my wine collection; reading the latest recommended fiction**

NEW MEDIA: Associate Media Director

Alice J. Johnston

123 Learning Street
Anytown, USA 10101

(999) 555-1212
email: alicej@yourname.com

SUMMARY

Experienced Media Executive with over 18 years in the advertising industry. Successful in negotiating large corporate conjunction deals and promotions. Ability to establish long-term client relationships. Works well under pressure while meeting tight deadlines. Excellent managerial and training skills. Excellent communication skills.

WORK HISTORY

BEIDEL COMPANY LIMITED   1988–1999
Associate Media Director   (1993–1999)
Media Supervisor   (1990–1993)
Senior Buyer   (1988–1990)

Selected Accomplishments
- Negotiated and executed on-air/in-store hockey promotion for the past three years. Negotiations included on-air time, production of commercials, prizing, and legal approvals. *Results included* gaining additional shelf space with key accounts, increasing vendor list, and increased sales results.
- Negotiated and assisted in the design of added value website packages resulting in increased sales for with over 4,000 hits on each of these websites.
- According to industry auditor, successfully executed competitive television buys for the past six years.
- Spearheaded and negotiated large 52-week conjunction deals with television stations.
- Established television planning cost guides for all accounts for the past eight years.
- Trained and supervised media department buying staff of 10.
- Member of Management Leadership Committee and Coordinator for in-house computer system (1998–1999)

ABC ADVERTISING   1981–1988
Media Buyer

BENES & GERRARD   1979–1980
Assistant Media Buyer

MILLS and MAGEE   1976–1977
Assistant Media Buyer

EDUCATION

Bachelor of Business Administration, State University, 1978
Marketing Degree, State College of Applied Arts and Technology, 1976

INTERESTS & ACTIVITIES

- Power walking, cycling, gardening, aerobics, traveling
- Conversational Spanish course

John J. Johnston, MBA

Address: 123 Learning St., Anytown, USA 10101
Telephone: (h) 999-555-1212 (c) 999-555-1313 (w) 999-555-1414
johnj@yourname.com

PERSONAL PROFILE

An ambitious leader with strong team, communication, and interpersonal skills, coupled with 6 years experience in media strategy, sales, and marketing.

CAREER HISTORY

2003–2004: XYZ Broadcast, Business Development/Sales Strategy

XYZ Broadcasting is the largest privately owned multimedia company in America. Its primary business activities are in traditional radio broadcasting and ancillary services such as radio syndication and national sales representation.

- Currently working on four projects with senior management to improve and develop more efficient sales processes across Standard's owned and operated stations.
- Responsible for identifying and establishing opportunities for direct relationships between clients and Standard Broadcastings National Sales division (IMS), with the intention of building these into 'key accounts.'

2002–2003   MBA – State University,
Specialist in Strategy and Marketing

- Graduated in top 5% of class
- Academic curriculum consisted of courses in corporate finance, strategy, operations, marketing, statistics, accounting, and economics.
- Completed year ending dissertation analyzing the different production incentives used throughout the world to attract film and television production.

1999–2002   CCC Television Inc., National Account Executive

CCC Television is America's preeminent broadcast company with a leading position in conventional, specialty, and digital television operations

- Initiated the creation of CCC's first **Sales and Marketing Strategy Team**. Working directly with senior management our team critically examined CCC's business practices to improve efficiencies within the marketplace and generate new revenue opportunities. The initial project developed a strategy that netted an addt'l $1.5 million by focus on those programs that had a low level of commercial sale.
- Instrumental in formulating yearly **key account plans** for clients. Established a **preferred supplier** relationship between clients and CCC, elevating them to the number one billing position amongst CCC's advertising group.
- Awarded gold medal at Marketing Awards 2001 for **best television campaign of the year** for the relaunch of the Big Car Company.
- Successfully rebuilt relationship with disgruntled agency upon arrival at CCC, increasing revenue from a low of $9 million to $18 million over a two-year period.
- Brokered national airtime across CCC's 25 television stations to a client base worth in excess of $20 million.
- Achieved ranking of **Exceeds Expectations** on all performance reviews.

NEW MEDIA: Media Strategist (cont.)

1997–1998   Office Talk Corp., National Account Executive
Office Talk is a news and entertainment network, operating throughout North America, providing programming & advertising to affluent professionals via wireless, flat paneled screens in corporate towers.

- Set up sales systems and marketing packages for the initial stages of OT's launch in new sections of the North American marketplace.
- Responsible for developing relationships with key decision makers at both advertising agencies and client level.
- Generated revenue through advertising sales and the creation & execution of tactical marketing campaigns. **Consistently one of the top revenue generators in advertising sales.**

ACADEMIC HISTORY

1994–1998   BA Honors, Mass Communications, State University

- Accepted for academic exchange to University of New Zealand in to study media and communications.
- Graduated with **Distinction.**

PERSONAL ACHIEVEMENTS AND HONORS

- Squash: Chosen to represent U.S. at New Zealand Teams Championships in 1997 and American Teams Championships in 1998.
- Selected by Government to be member of International Economic Development Group 2002/03.
- Awarded research grant by Alumni Association for dissertation regarding global film and television production incentives.
- Commissioned by Big Insurance Inc.'s head office to develop and present a market feasibility study for a flexible mortgage based product within the European market.

INTERESTS

- Reading, squash, music, golf, and financial markets.
- Currently taking lessons to improve Spanish language skills.

NEW MEDIA: Digital Production Manager

ALICE J. JOHNSTON | 123 Learning Street · Anytown · USA · 10101
999.555.1212 · alicej@yourname.com

PROFESSIONAL QUALIFICATIONS:

Detail-oriented, organized, and dependable individual with 3 years of computer and marketing experience. Excellent communication, interpersonal, and leadership skills. Proven ability to work efficiently in both independent and teamwork environments. Ability to manage multiple tasks and priorities and comply with all Company Policies and Procedures. Quick learner with an ability to rapidly achieve organizational integration, assimilate job requirements, and employ new methodologies. Energetic and self-motivated team player/builder. At ease in high stress environments requiring superior ability to effectively handle multi-task levels of responsibility. Solid written and oral communication skills in English and Spanish.

Proficient in the following areas:
· E-commerce
· Web design/development
· Graphic design
· Marketing and advertising
· Designing printed materials
· Pre-press production

EDUCATION:

Bachelor of Business Administration
State University   2000

· Major: Marketing (3.6/4.0 GPA)
· Minor: Information Systems
· Cumulative GPA: 3.3/4.0
· Association of Systems Management

Associate Degree of Technical Studies
State University   2002

· Major: Digital Imaging and Web Design
· GPA: 3.6
· Dean's List

Associate Degree of Information Sciences
State University   2002

· Major: Computer Networking Systems
· GPA: 3.6
· Dean's List

A+ Hardware Certification Course
State College   2000

CAREER OBJECTIVE:

A Digital Production and Design management role in the field of e-commerce web development and new media.

PROFESSIONAL EXPERIENCE:

Digital Production Manager
Checkers INC;   8/2000–12/2002

· Designed sales catalogs, flyers, and product newspapers
· Coordinated the process of digital and pre-press production
· Photographed products and maintained image libraries
· Design of internal & external artwork/graphics/advertising for sales materials and websites
· Digitally edited images
· Maintained relationships with advertising and printing agencies
· Maintained products and client database
· Created and implemented online advertisements

Web Designer and Computer Graphics Specialist
Feldstein Inc;   5/1999–5/2000

· Developed corporate websites from design to completion
· Created navigational structure and maintained all websites
· Designed graphics for print and electronic media
· Digitally created artwork for product engraving and packaging
· Integrated photography and movie clips
· Implemented online advertisements and banners
· Developed and maintained image libraries
· Tested site functionality and usability

COMPUTER & SOFTWARE SKILLS:

· Microsoft Office Suite	· Macromedia HomeSite
· Adobe Acrobat	· Macromedia Dreamweaver
· Adobe PageMaker	· Macromedia Fireworks
· Adobe Illustrator	· Macromedia Flash
· Adobe Photoshop	· Macromedia FreeHand
· Adobe InDesign	· QuarkXpress
· Adobe Premiere	· CorelDRAW
· A+ Hardware	· HTML, CSS, CGI
· PHP, MySQL	· JavaScript

· ME/NT/2000/XP/MacOS,
· Novell, TCP/IP, FTP, POP3, SMPT, TELNET, DNS

SPECIAL PROJECTS:

· Detailed online portfolio and resume that demonstrate my professional background, education, and skills can be viewed at this address.
(*http://portfolio.johnston.com*)

NEW MEDIA: Media Manager

John J. Johnston
123 Learning St., Anytown, USA 10101

johnj@yourname.com • Work 999-555-1212 • Home 999-555-1313

Senior Manager - Qualification Highlights

Online Marketing I have been a leader in the online marketing/advertising field for almost 10 years (my first online buy was in 1994) and bring a wealth of knowledge about the Internet and its capabilities and limitations. I have managed online divisions at Jefferson LLC, Interactive Inc. and Bickers & Sons. I have been responsible for online campaign strategies through creative development down to execution and analysis.

Advertising Sales I was the highest performing Account Executive with Stock Media in online advertising sales. Thus I thoroughly understand the intricacies and nuances of moving clients to campaign based executions though customer service and experience.

Management I have over 2 ½ years of departmental management experience over my career. I have managed departments with as many as six employees. I'm experienced at developing departmental strategic vision, process implementation and revenue projections, building and motivating teams to reach goals, and dealing with day-to-day staff issues. I have trained and managed assistants & planners for over 14 years.

Media Planning and Buying In 14 years developed and executed media strategies for some of the largest companies in the US. Planned and executed campaigns in all forms of media from TV, Radio, Newspaper, Magazine, Online, Direct Response, and all variations of out-of-home.

Employment History

Jefferson LLC, *Media Manager*   2002 to Present

A full service advertising agency that specializes in Healthcare, Pharmaceutical, and Lifestyle advertising. With over 150 employees across North America, Jefferson provides Media, Creative, and Production services to clients.

Working closely with clients to move traditional pharmaceutical companies, versed in professional trade (talking to doctors), to more consumer-focused advertising campaigns. Direct supervision of a media planner and a media buyer.
Highlights

- Developed an Online Marketing competency within Jefferson that has seen new business growth of $250,000 in revenue in two years.
- Developed, launched, and continue to grow the first consumer advertising campaign in the Oral Contraceptive category. Highly strategic media executions (national television sponsorships and cinema advertising) have helped propel this brand to number one in its category within two years, while generating awareness levels of 86% against the target audience.
- Developed and executed the launch of GrainShop cereal in the US. Used specialty television stations like Bodies Network and Busy TV to exceed sales expectations by +35% in a flat, highly competitive cereal market.
- Contributed to the development of the Effects (www.effectme.com) website. The website has won the IPA gold award for best non-branded pharmaceutical website in North America 2004. Employed online marketing tactics like search engines, banners, and sponsorships to acquire 20,000 new visitors per month.

Stock Media, *Sr. Account Executive*   2001 to 2002

An online financial information website with 450,000 visitors per month. Widely supported by financial institutions, banks, investment companies, and brokerages.
Responsibilities included increasing advertising sales revenue through client service and prospecting.
Highlights

- Top selling Account Executive with sales of $160,000
- Increased revenue from existing client base by 12%
- Increased revenue from new business by 100% (42% coming from advertisers outside the financial sector). Secured clients like Online buying .COM, Big Insurance Inc., Anytown Tourism
- Trained fellow sales staff on building solution driven campaigns that meets the clients overall business needs, and becoming a trusted partner in the advertising process

John J. Johnston

123 Learning St., Anytown, USA 10101

johnj@yourname.com • Work 999-555-1212 • Home 999-555-1313

Bickers and Sons, *Director, Online Marketing and Response Media* 2000 to 2001
A full service advertising agency specializing in Direct Response, Online, and Database Marketing. Providing services to clients like Banks Inc., Big Telephone, American Tourism.

Responsibilities included strategic vision, process implementation, agency integration, and management of a team of six online professionals as well as for all clients' online campaign strategies from end to end. Heavily involved in new business development and expanding the revenue of the current client base.
Highlights
- Able to establish and develop a new online marketing department within the existing Direct Response agency, while building the department to six employees and revenues to $500,000.
- Developed and executed the BIG Golf vacation promotion (that is still running today) with online contesting and fulfilment. Secured 2,000 contest entrants per flight despite a stringent entry requirement.
- Contributed to one of the first "Convergent" media executions for Big Telephone using media like Television, Newspaper, Magazine, and Online. Contributed to the first ever execution of a Newspaper "gatefold" (securing the full front page of the newspaper for client advertising).

Interactive Inc., *Associate Media Director* 1999 to 2000
All online media planning, buying, and strategic analysis, as well as all tracking and optimization. I also assisted in creative development, production, and new business development.
- Contributed to the development of www.doggyvitals.com, a global pet portal promoting pet food brands.
- Launched online-based financial site. Employed unique media placements and creative executions to secure new account sign-ups.

NYPP, *Sr. Media Buyer* 1998 to 1999
Execution of media buys (broadcast, print, and outdoor), pre- and post-buys analysis and maintenance of buys. I was also responsible for the development of four junior buyers.

Listen & Deliver Group, *Sr. Media Planner* 1997 to 1998
A full service advertising agency.
Produced unique media executions for Big Beer Store (wrecked cars on outdoor posters) and Software Inc. (Newspaper belly bands in the form of a growth chart for School Bus software).

Apokipsi Advertising, *Sr. Media Planner/Buyer* 1995 to 1997
All media planning and execution for traditional media, as well as direct marketing and online marketing.
- Developed an advertising model that incorporated all media disciplines to achieve the optimal media mix. The incorporation of traditional brand advertising with direct response and online created a synergistic approach to media strategy, similar to what is being done today with convergent media.

Big Brand Inc., *Media Planner/Buyer* 1990 to 1995

Education

State College 1991
Certificate, Creative Advertising
State College 1989
Certificate, Marketing

NOT-FOR-PROFIT: Group Home Worker

ALICE J. JOHNSTON
123 Learning Dr., Anycity, AS 10101 Ph. (555) 999-1212

Crisis Counselor and Not-for-Profit Administrator

Bright, warm, engaging not-for-profit worker who specializes in working in crisis situations.

EMPLOYMENT EXPERIENCE

Sabbatical/Parental Leave – Took a break from working to have my two children and care for them full time 2002–2005

Crisis Line Coordinator
Management and administration of statewide 24hr. crisis line
Supervision, scheduling, and evaluation of 30+ staff. 24-hour emergency support.
Employee relations, staff recruitment, change management.
Assaulted Women's Helpline, Anycity, AS
March–October 2002

Training, Resources and Outreach
Development of statewide database. Staff training, community relations.
Assaulted Women's Helpline, Anycity, AS
January–March 2002

Crisis Counselor
Issues of domestic violence, incest, sexual assault, and harassment.
Assaulted Women's Helpline, Anycity, AS
August 1997–December 2001

High School Outreach Counselor
Women's Sexual Assault Helpline of North Region, Anycity, AS
November 1999–June 2000 (contract)

Youth Worker, Student Placement and Volunteer Supervisor
Crisis intervention, client advocacy, and residential management and administration in a coed emergency shelter for homeless youth.
Local Youth Center, Anycity, AS
February 1997–May 1998
Internship: September 1996–January 1997

Youth Counselor/Street Outreach Worker
'Out of the Cold' Program for Homeless Youth, Anycity, AS
December 1997–April 1998 (contract)

Internship Support Worker: Gay and Lesbian Youth Residence
Children's Aid Society of Anycity; group home for youth in long-term care
February–April 1996

A. Johnston   resume as of January 1, 2006   AS   Page2/2

EDUCATION

Honors Bachelor of Arts in English Literature
University of State Anycity, AS 1990–91
University of Anycity Anycity, AS (Graduated with Honors) 1992–1995

Assaulted Women and Children's Counselor Advocate Program
Local College Anycity, AS 1995–1997

VOLUNTEER EXPERIENCE

Group Facilitator and Crisis Line Counselor
Anycity Rape Crisis Center Anycity, AS. October 1995–September 1997

Child Support Worker (children who have experienced violence in their homes)
Localtown Interval House Anycity, AS. May–September 1996

Advocacy Committee Member
Localtown Women's Advocacy Group Anycity, AS. 1996

PROFESSIONAL DEVELOPMENT

Liability and Reporting as it Relates to Violence Workshop, Faculty of Law, University of Western
Region. June 2002

Suicide Risk Assessment Training, Distress Center Anycity. July 2002

Group Facilitation Training, North Region Abuse Program, Anycity, AS. February–March 2000

Abnormal Psychology and Mental Health, State University, 1998

Crisis Prevention and Nonviolent Intervention, Certified October 1996

Speaking engagments:

Teen Issues and Abuse, Children's Hospital, Teen Clinic. March 1998.

Elder Abuse: Issues and Future Directions, U.S. Naturopathic College. March 1997.

Further professional development and references available upon request.

NOT-FOR-PROFIT: Director of Marketing, Fundraising

John J. Johnston
123 Learning St. Anytown, USA 10101
Phone: 999/555-1212 Email: johnj@yourname.com

Marketing Director with Special Understanding of Not-for-profits

Skills

- Brand Management
- Strategic Planning, Marketing Strategy
- Advertising
- Media Relations
- Project Management
- Research and Analysis

- Managing External and Internal Relationships
- Creative Development
- Writing and Editing
- Strong Interpersonal and Presentation Skills

Employment History

2000–Present   **Director of Marketing, Big Umbrella Charity Org**
Strategic Planning and Marketing Strategy
- Develop and oversee branding and marketing strategies, in collaboration with the Vice President, Marketing and Communications
- Work as part of the senior management team with Peterson & Co. to develop a strategic plan laying out a new direction for the organization
- Develop advertising strategies and creative as the principal liaison with advertising agency, Whyte and Zohar
- Oversee marketing of special initiatives, such as 211

Research
- Facilitate research, prepare recommendations, and report to senior management as principal liaison with research house, Strategic Counsel

Management
- Oversee committee of senior marketing professionals, including marketing professor at State University, Steph Palazzi, partner at Big, and Steve Trout, head of marketing for ALL Year Hotels
- Manage seven person in-house team producing more than 200 print pieces each year, populating three websites, and providing communications expertise to the organization
- Solicit donations of media space

Key Accomplishments

- Fundraising increase from $60.25 million to $81 million, a 33% increase in four years
- Increase in value of donated advertising from $3 million to $5.25 million over two years
- Increasing correlation, as indicated by tracked research, between exposure to advertising and propensity to give
- Movement from needs-based to empowerment messaging, especially through development of the "Your Money" advertising campaign
- Launched 211, an information and referral line, with the aim of driving traffic within call center capacity. Delivered targeted call volumes, allowing for a 98% call answer rate, and establishing a 211 service as one of the busiest in North America
- Secured probono services of Bick for an additional two years beyond original mandate of three years

1999–2000   **Marketing Manager, Big Umbrella Charity Org**
Implemented marketing strategies. Targeted multimedia appeals to general and target donor groups. Guided production of all print material, participated in research development and analysis, and generated creative and strategic writing. Worked with advertising agency to produce creative and generate donations of free advertising space for this creative.

1997–1999   **Publicist, Writer/Editor, Big Umbrella Charity Org**
Joined Big Umbrella as publicist and helped generate $4 million in news coverage. After six months, moved laterally to Marketing Dept. as writer/editor. Responsible for quality and content of all marketing communications. Generated creative direction and strategic wording for approximately 200 print pieces, among other duties.

1994–1997   **Information Officer, State Police Department**
Provided media expertise to members of the force, fielded inquiries from reporters, wrote press releases, fact sheets, brochure material, and articles for *The SM Review*.

1989–1992   **News On A Wire Editor**
Wrote local, regional, and national news stories for ABN, a national radio newswire service. Conducted research and interview to generate original news and worked with stringers to create regional news packages.

Education

1986–1989   **Bachelor of Applied Arts, Journalism**
State University

1998–1999   **Certificate, Creative Copywriting**
State College

1999   **Survival Skills for Managers**
Mica

2001–2001   **Presentation Skills I & II**
Mica

Personal Interests: Writing for fun and for myself; hang gliding, bungee jumping and other extreme experiences; interviewing strangers at parties to keep journalism skills in shape.

NOT-FOR-PROFIT: Sr. Manager, Fundraising Development

Alice J. Johnston

123 Learning St., Anytown, USA 10101   (999) 555-1212   alicej@yourname.com

PROFILE

Experienced **Senior Manager in Fundraising and Not-for-Profit Development** who values integrity and professionalism and boasts relationship building, leadership, and strategic-visioning skills.

PROFESSIONAL EXPERIENCE

λ Angels on Earth 1999–2004
Angel's is a transitional shelter that offers training and employment programs for homeless and at risk youth.

Manager of Development, Mentorship Network, 2002–2004

Partnership Development and Fundraising
- Formed an advisory council for the One to One Mentorship program with representatives from Board Of Trade, Big Gas Distribution, and Center for Holistic Mental Health.
- Developed proposal—Result: $50,000 from National Crime Prevention for salary & program supplies of 1-2-1 Mentorship Coordinator.

Program Development
- Researched and developed the Peer Mentorship program and One to One Mentorship program with evaluation based on logic models and surveys.

Management
- Hired and managed two Mentorship Coordinators and one Follow-up Support Worker.
- Created the vision for mentorship, training, and employment programs that led to a strategic framework.

Manager of Partnership Development, 1999–2002

Partnership Development and Fundraising (selected)
- Successfully articulated new opportunities to potential partners; established and ensured successful outcomes for unique multiple partnerships across numerous sectors, achieving goal of funding, creating, and implementing programs that benefited all parties.
- Launched a business, the Angel Print Shop, in partnership with Rotary Club, Graphic Resource, Bridge Printing, and State College. Total of funds and in-kind donations was $50,000.
- Developed the Film Training program with the National Association of Broadcast Employees and Film and Television Producers Association. Total funds for youth salaries were $100,000 over three years.
- Developed and secured funding for the Landscaping program with State College, Landscape Anytown, Federal Department of Training, Colleges, and Universities, with funds of $56,000.
- Created the Culinary Arts program with State College, Colleges, and Universities, and restaurants like Star Hotel, train youth as cook apprentices with Job Connect.
- Contributed to HR Development proposal for training programs, which raised $1,700,000 in its first year.
- Developed successful proposals to foundations, government, associations, and corporations to benefit partnership creation resulting in increased funding, equipment, expertise, training, and careers.

Program Development
- Researched industries & identified partnership opportunities for training & employment for homeless and at-risk youth.
- Created training and employment programs for culinary arts, landscaping, network administration, web design, print shop, child and youth worker, and film industry.

Management
- Hired and supervised Social Enterprise Coordinator and Network Technology Instructor.
- Developed and continue to refine Angels on Earth as a new model. As member of the management team contributed to integrating the often competing interests of the shelter, life skills, and employment programs.

...2

λ Big Bank DEVELOPMENT CORPORATION, 1992–1998

BIG BANK is the US's second largest financial institution and BIG BANK Development was a wholly owned subsidiary, which managed and developed the bank's real estate assets.

Consultant—Retail Leasing, Commerce Square and Atrium Center

- Created merchandising strategy and tenant mix. Completed the leasing of Commerce Court retail with two large restaurant locations and unique retail establishments; for glass windows on the Bay, undertook a two-year re-merchandising program that helped prepare the property for disposition.
- Analyzed proformas for offers to lease; assisted in setting up procedures for retail section of BIG BANK Development Corporation and negotiated the offers to lease.
- Established links with the brokerage community and cohosted events for the brokerage community with office leasing staff.
- Liaised with Marketing, Construction, Property Management, Lease Administration, and Accounting Departments to ensure the efficient operation of the buildings.

λ Collosal Developments Ltd., Anycity, 1985–1992

At the time of my employment, Collasal was one of the largest global real estate developers with flagship buildings in New York, Tokyo, London, and Toronto.

Director of Retail Operations

Marketing & Advertising
- Developed 5-year marketing plan (annual budget of $800,000).
- Hired market research and advertising agencies. Worked with the agencies to create strategy and the implementation for television, radio, newspaper and print campaigns, direct mail, newsletters, and brochures.
- Worked with a publicity company to create the first Corporate Running Race in Anytown. Disseminated media materials and generated free media coverage.

Management
- Formulated and implemented a strategic plan to reposition buildings through marketing and promotion, new merchandising mix, and working with new and existing tenants, leading to increased revenue.
- Managed the retail operations staff for the complex, including the budgeting, the lease proformas, negotiation of the legal documentation and database for retail leasing prospect system.

λ Big Tele, 1980–1985

Computer Communications Group, Sales, 1983–1985

- Sold computer data network lines to Fortune 500 companies.
- Recognized with the Presidents Award for sales in my division.

Real Estate Manager, 1980–1985

- Revised a multimillion-dollar budget preparation; bought, sold, and leased residential, commercial, and office properties.

EDUCATION & PROFESSIONAL DEVELOPMENT

2004	**In-depth Group Facilitation** Collaboration in Community Development
2001	**Program Effectiveness Organizational Development** United Way of Anytown
1999	**Overview of Fundraising Management** State University
1982–1988	**Evening Business Administration Program** State University
1976–1978	**Government Operations: Legal Administration** State College

ADVISORY & VOLUNTEER POSTS

Volunteer   **Well being** (a cancer support center) 1995–1996

OPERATIONS: Plant Manager

John J. Johnston B.A., CET

123 Learning St., Anytown, USA 10101 H # (999) 555-1212 / C# 999-555-1313 e: johnj@yourname.com

PROFILE: Plant Manager and Senior Manager Operations

➢ 20-year veteran with comprehensive experience in Strategic Planning, Plant Turnaround, and Operations as we as total Supply Chain Management, with full P&L responsibility for staffing and sales mgt.

➢ Brought facilities back to profitability and to meet all RIO targets.

➢ Well-versed in corporate strategy, manufacturing processes, and Continuous Improvement to increase Operatic Profits while decreasing costs; strong background in transportation, retail, automotive services, and aerospace industries.

➢ Skilled in project management, team leadership, and the control of materials, plant safety, and QA.

➢ New product introductions from prototype to production, scheduling, delivery, & customer support.

➢ Effectively hire, train, and mentor Senior Managers and Sales teams in product lines, policies, and procedures; proficient in Lean Manufacturing, Kaizen, 5S, PDCA, QS9000, ISO14001, JHSC.

EXPERIENCE:

ABC Inc., <u>Plant Manager</u>   2004–present

- Report directly to the VP of Operations, dotted line to the COO/President
- Manage and direct all plant Operations with 140 employees in a unionized environment
- Full P&L and capital budget responsibility and responsible for turn key operations
- Working to improve other plant operations in other locations

Accomplishments

- Improved productivity by 55% in 3 months
- Reduced scrap by 10% which is ongoing
- Reduced inventory by $150,000.00
- Improved inventory turnover by 25% (10-12.5) ongoing

ZYT Design, <u>General Manager</u> – Reported to the President   2002–2004

- Managed and directed all manufacturing, engineering, and production activities for this designer and manufacturer, with full P&L responsibility for all operations.
- Determined costs and priced new product line for maximum profitability.
- Oversaw unionized and non-unionized production staff to support sales staff.
- Conducted extensive research on appropriate materials to use in producing a new product line.

Accomplishments

- Developed and launched a new product line within 4 months that had previously been attempted for 4 years.
- Implemented a new digital graphics department.

Busy Company, <u>Operations Manager</u> 2000–2002   1994–2002

Promoted to this role after successes as Manager of Process Manufacturing:

- In charge of manufacturing with P&L responsibility for this $70 million operation with 210 employees.
- Managed new projects, capital justification, MRO, APR's, product quality, progress reports, budget forecasting, month-end reports, staffing, documentation, production, engineering, and plant efficiency.
- Brought facilities back to profitability and met all RIO company targets.

Accomplishments

- Took control of operating expenses and instituted procedures that raised plant operating profits from a negativ to $1 million within 5 months, achieving #1 plant ranking out of 5.
- Reduced equipment-operating costs by 30%.
- Improved plant efficiency to 85% and reduced downtime to less than 2%.
- Implemented MP2, Inventory Control System, and Cost Control programs, as well as Kaizen, C.A.T., and work cells that increased productivity and reduced plant costs by more than 40%.

Manager of Process Manufacturing & Plant Maintenance 1999–2000

- Responsible for plant P&L with sales of $80 million and burden cost of four plants with total sales equaling $250 million
- Worked with both union and non-union plants, as well as assembly line modifications in a union facility.
- Eliminated shutdowns by establishing monthly targets.
- Increased the life of tooling and reduced replacement costs through use of cryogenics, titanium nitrate coating, and higher quality material where needed.

Accomplishments

- A $2 million savings in first year by reducing $18 million in plant burden costs of 4 plants to $16 M.
- Designed and implemented plant budgets control system, use of MP2 and improved operating costs with a savings of $650,000 per year.
- Reduced tooling frequency turnover by 50%.
  Decreased welding tip consumption by 50% using higher quality tips that resulted in less downtime.
- Reduced plant-operating costs by 40%.

Manager of Engineering & Continuous Improvements 1996–1998

- Improved plant efficiency to 85%.
- Reduced tooling frequency turnover by 50%.
- Decreased machinery-troubleshooting time by 75%.
- Successful in reducing plant downtime to less than 2%.

Senior Manufacturing Engineer 1994–1995

- Modified equipment to improve efficiency and reduced bottlenecks; saving $1.8 M in 1st year.
- Improved and modified tooling and increased longevity by more than 200%.
- Increased equipment output by 277% from 1000 pieces to 3600 pieces per shift.
- Increased productivity by 80% on sub and final assembly lines.
- Reduced plant's RPPM's from 15,000 to 50.

Self Employed 1991–1994
Technologies Inc. Engineering Services R&D 1985–1991

FORMAL EDUCATION:

➢ State University - **B.A. Degree – Industrial Technology**
➢ State College - **Diploma – Technologist in Engineering Industrial Instrumentation**

CONTINUED EDUCATION:

- Financial Training for Managers – Management
- Performance Appraisals/APR Training – Management
- Lean Manufacturing
- Kaizen; PDCA; 5S
- Environmental Management Systems Internal Auditing; Value Stream Mapping
- ISO14001 Awareness Training/KPMG; QS9000
- Supervisory Management Certificate – State College

OPERATIONS: Director of Operations

John J. Johnston

123 LEARNING STREET ♦ ANYCITY, ANYSTATE ♦ 10101 ♦ HOME: (555) 999-1212 ♦ CELL: (555) 999-1313
EMAIL: johnj@yourname.com

Senior/Executive-level Operations Manager. A positive-thinking, results-orientated, and team-spirited professional recognized for proactively exceeding organizational mandates over the past 23 years.

CORE COMPETENCIES

- ➢ Account relationship management
- ➢ Customer service and retention management
- ➢ Business development and expansion
- ➢ New process rollout development
- ➢ Start-up & turnaround management
- ➢ Operations management

- ➢ Multiple-project/location management
- ➢ P&L responsibility
- ➢ Team/organizational leadership
- ➢ Production and efficiency optimization
- ➢ Staff training, development, empowerment
- ➢ Logistics and warehouse management

PROFESSIONAL EXPERIENCE

Hitech Inc.   **Anycity, AS**   **11/2003 to 11/2004**

Opened in 1996, Hitech Inc. is a privately owned computer/electronic depot service company servicing "third party" service companies as well as major manufacturers, with annual revenues of $7 million.

Vice President Operations
- ➢ Utilized learned skills to improve workflow and streamline operations via process reengineering in order to increase quality and reduce costs.

  - ✓ Developed KOR (Key Operating Reports) to measure performance and identify areas of concern.
  - ✓ Instituted "New Product / Process Implementation" process to ensure that customer requirements were addressed and monitored.
  - ✓ Reengineered processes to drive a "customer focused" work flow.
  - ✓ Responsible for the creation and implementation of ISO 9001 compliant processes and procedures.
  - ✓ Senior lead in ISO 9001:2000 certification (audit to take place January 2005).

Electronics Global Services   **Anycity, AS**   **06/1999 to 06/2003**

Founded in 19XX, Electronics is a $26 billion company which is one of the world's largest supply chain management companies providing design, manufacturing, and post-manufacturing services that help make brand-name electronics companies more competitive.

Senior Planning/Purchasing Manager
- ➢ Led a team of eight Production Planners and four Purchasing professionals supporting a $44 million revenue base. Collectively responsible for the process development, production planning and procurement, to support a production floor of 375 technicians, ensuring a smooth flow of JIT (Just In Time) materials. Supported customers such as ABC (worldwide), Computer Inc, Software Ltd.

  - ✓ Developed short / long range "what ifs" and material impact reports.
  - ✓ Ensured closed loop feedback to end customer, internal team and management.
  - ✓ Capacity / manpower reviews and WIP balancing to meet revenue forecasts.
  - ✓ Monitored work order aging to ensure customer commitments were being met.
  - ✓ Rough cut capacity planning.
  - ✓ Developed & instituted "Supplier Evaluation Program" to monitor, track, and report on supplier performance.
  - ✓ Supported the "New Product / Process Implementation Team" identified costs, kept within budget.

- ➢ Led the joint rolling production schedule with ABC U.S., which identified parts availability and existing order shortfalls (shortfalls were minimized dramatically).
- ➢ Facilitated projected schedule changes, which in turn generated incremental revenue and increased customer satisfaction levels, supporting the vision of "doing what we said we would do."
- ➢ Capitalized on the internal repair process reducing the Materials Costs Per Unit by $56 (62%).
- ➢ Developed initiative to source parts from six alternative suppliers from one, and to strengthen the purchasing power in Midwest Region by utilizing a combined volume with a sister plant resulting in a 56% reduction in the purchase costs of OEM parts.

John J. Johnston

Senior Program Manager
- ➤ Managed all aspects of Electronics' business relationship with eight major customers. (ABC-four business units; Computer Inc.; Computer Inc Financial Services; Investment Group)

    Key responsibilities:

✓ Customer Satisfaction Index (CSI)	✓ Tactical account business leader
✓ Customer Complaint Resolution Process	✓ Priority management
✓ Customer Issue, coordination, resolution	✓ Team issue escalation
✓ Direct interface with customer at all levels	✓ Forecast management
✓ Develop business relationship	✓ Performance metrics management
✓ Contract maintenance and management	✓ Program P&L management
✓ Develop new business	✓ Conflict management

- ➤ Developed a comprehensive model for the personal computer leasing industry (end of lease) to grow the existing business and develop new opportunities.
- ➤ Approached ABC Global Finance with a unique business plan, which was embraced, subsequently generating $4 million in revenue for 2002.
- ➤ Utilized a variation of the same plan with Computer Inc Financial Services and achieved $1.5 million.
- ➤ All customers grew annually not only in revenue and profit but, just as importantly, in customer satisfaction (achieved greater than 95 percent satisfaction for all customers).
- ➤ Generated $15.5 million in revenue for 2002 from existing client base.
- ➤ Recognized for exemplary performance and over achieving targets for 12 consecutive quarters.

XYZ Technical Services Inc.   Anycity, AS   11/1991 to 05/1999

Business Unit General Manager
- ➤ Recruited as the Sr Procurement Specialist for the creation & direction of the purchasing team.
- ➤ Selected by Senior Management to restructure and turn around an under-performing, unprofitable business unit, which led to the promotion to General Manager.
- ➤ Renegotiated the rental agreement with the landlord to a more favorable lease saving $100,000.
- ➤ Initiated new business lines; developed and installed a new asset management and billing system to track business unit's productivity and revenues along with client assets (system is still in use today at Electronics Global Services).
- ➤ Drove the business increasing customers, volumes, and revenues subsequently leading to the outsourcing of distribution services.
- ➤ Completely managed facility with ownership of production, logistics, purchasing, HR, and education.

ABC Ltd.   Anycity, AS   08/1981 to 11/1991
Senior Procurement Specialist
- ➤ Held numerous roles leading to Senior Procurement Specialist.

RECOGNITION/AWARDS
- ➤ Recognition for over achievement (accelerated bonus payments 12 quarters in a row) – Electronics Global Services
- ➤ Top Performer of the Year – XYZ Technical Services (1997)
- ➤ Key Contributor Award (3) – XYZ Technical Services
- ➤ $115,000.00 Suggestion Award – ABC Ltd.

EDUCATION / TRAINING

Professional Development
- ➤ Polytechnical Institute - Technical Mathematics; Community College - Advanced Electronics, Creative Writing Skills, Industrial Mathematics, Production Planning and Scheduling, Project Management, Principals of Buying, Principals of Successful Negotiations

Corporate Education
- ➤ Effective Comm Skills, Effective Negotiations, Program Management, CFT Training (Customer Focus Team), Fundamentals of Inventory Control, Finance, Kaizen, Six Sigma Lean, ISO

OPERATIONS: COO Operations

JOHN J. JOHNSTON

123 LEARNING ST., ANYTOWN, USA 10101 (999) 555-1212 JOHNJ@YOURNAME.COM

Profile: An effective, value-building **Executive** with a broad knowledge base acquired in senior sales, marketing, and operational capacities in both large and small business settings. Entreprenuerially oriented with significant start-up, reengineering, and expansion experience gained in service, technology, and manufacturing (OEM) organizations. A seasoned and pragmatic businessperson who has the ability to take strategic concepts at the edge of market innovation. An open and effective communicator capable of fostering confidence, respect, and loyalty throughout the organization. An action-oriented motivator who creates a winning team by personally delivering results.

Professional Experience

ABC LLC   *May 2004–Present*
Chief Operating Officer

ABC is the leading Structured Finance Trading system designed for highly complex financial instruments. Retained by the CEO of this rapidly growing software vendor and services outsourcer to develop a strategic plan to grow company without significant equity dilution. Significant achievements include:

- Drove the sales pipeline by 100%
- Restructured and aligned the functional reporting lines
- Developed and executed the strategic business plan
- Increased margins on software licenses by 35%
- Improved service delivery, and revenue per billable head by 156%
- Cut client acquisition costs 31%

Timmons Data   *October 2002–May 2004*
Senior Vice President, Integration Services

Timmons Data is a global $2.5 Billion IT Services organization providing systems integration, IT solutions, and network infrastructure to Fortune 1000 companies. Primarily focused on Financial Services, Automotive, Retail & Consumer Goods, and Energy industry sectors. Senior executive hired to turn money-losing division to profitability, drive revenue through direct, indirect, and alliance channels, and create a sales centric culture. Solutions offerings included Branding User Experience Interactive Sites, Portals, Enterprise Content Management, EAI/WebServices, Custom Applications, Application Management Services. Specific achievements include:

- Reduced monthly loss from $1.2M to 100K profit in 5 months
- 23% growth rate Q1-Q4, first time in 24 months for the company
- 47% increase in pipeline health
- Restructured go-to-market solution group resulting in 56% diversity increase in revenue
- Implemented account planning process resulting in 24% increase in client revenue and reduction in total cost of sale
- Developed repeatable fully architected solution offerings by industry sectors
- Achieved 39% of year targets through recurring revenue streams

Big Corporation
May 1998–May 2002

Strategic Planning and Marketing Officer (SVP)
Vice President, Sales, Strategy, and Business Development
Vice President, M&A, Healthcare

Big is the result of an initial acquisition of XYZ LLC acquired in March of 1998. Following the transaction, identified four key markets and developed respective strategies specifically to service e-business initiatives. Executive "evangelist" for positioning *Big* with multi-tiered CRM, e-commerce, e-business, and collaboration offerings. Chief marketing officer globally establishing brand awareness, demand creation, and sales support. Participated in the acquisition of five organizations (total revenues of $217MM including CRM analytical engine, campaign management, and email management tools) and personally led the sales and marketing integration activities. Subsequently, became lead executive in developing a Healthcare Services acquisition strategy. Reported directly to the Chairman & CEO. Responsible and accountable for driving sales from $14.5 million in 1998 to $384 million in two years.

Key accomplishments:

- Attained $10 Million in revenue first year
- Hired, trained, and managed a direct sales team
- Developed and executed channel strategies for extended sales team
- Participated in the acquisition of 5 companies
- Developed, managed, and executed a multimillion dollar marketing budget

XYZ LLC, Inc.
March 1997–May 1998

Vice President, Sales and Marketing

Responsible for all sales, marketing, and client management;

- Achieved $12.5 million revenue in first fiscal year
- Developed and executed go-to-market strategies, brand awareness and product evolution
- Achieved 140% of forecast revenue, 137% EBITDA in 1997
- Achieved 117% of forecast revenue, 106% EBITDA in 1998
- Negotiated multiyear, multimillion dollar service agreements

Track & Field Inc.
October 1993–December 1996

General Manager, Apparel-Global

Assumed a General Management role for a strategic business unit after developing a business plan (on a consulting basis) for a new manufacturing division of the world's leading hockey equipment manufacturer in the fall of 1993. Led a new global Apparel Division. Full P&L responsibility including sales, marketing, distribution, and operational management on a worldwide basis. Staff of 62 plus a distribution network of 25 agencies.

- Achieved Sales of $US23 Million in first quarter of launch (132% of target)
- Developed and accountable for complete new distribution network, globally; 52 sales reps, 25 agency agreements
- Negotiated international licensing agreements with the NHL, IIHF, IHL, NHLPA, Universities and Colleges

MMM International, *Principal Consultant May '86–September '93*

Big Group of Companies, *Vice President, Business Development & Client Services Sept. '84–May '86*

Big Retailer LLC, *National Marketing Manager June '81–Sept. '84*

EDUCATION

State University, Honors Bachelor of Commerce, Marketing, and Finance
- State University, Project Management, Finance, Computer Science
- Big Copies, Sales Management
- International "The Change Leader" Executive Course

OPERATIONS: BAD—Operations

Alice J. Johnston
123 Learning Street
Anytown, USA, 10101
Home: (999) 555-1212 Email: Alicej@yourname.com

OBJECTIVE

To obtain a challenging position and grow within a progressive organization where I can utilize my expertise and be part of an effective team. To achieve sales targets and corporate objectives!

HIGHLIGHTS OF EXPERIENCE

MMM Corporation
Operations Manager
May 1, 2003 - Current

Job Description:

1 Manage all internal departments
2 Develop new opportunities for expansion
3 Develop target accounts with sales team and work together to retain business
4 Outside sales
5 Develop media relations/marketing programs
6 Build strong business relationships with national accounts
7 Adhere to all corporate policies and programs
8 Represent Corporation at trade shows and corporate events
9 Develop internal procedures to reduce costs and improve quality
10 Train all sales staff
11 Achieve sales targets and expenditure budgets
12 Oversee day to day operations and logistics
13 Negotiate contracts at senior level
14 Prepare employee evaluations and negotiate compensations
15 Review all financial reports
16 Oversee 6 direct reports and 22 secondary reports

ABC Media
Plant Newspaper/Auto Plant Magazine
District Sales Manager
July 2002 - March 2003 (layoff)

Job Description:

1 Outside Sales within North America
2 Analyze key accounts and propose key strategies for meeting cli
3 Attend all trade shows / conferences
4 Develop sales Power Point presentation
5 Negotiate and develop advertising programs
6 Establish a strong business relationship with existing and potenti
7 Work with members of the sales team to develop new revenue ge

What's Wrong?
· Too many bullet points
· Too long
· Too much wasted space
· Lackluster objective/profile or lack thereof
· No declared job role
· No accomplishments or specific and measurable results
· Uninspiring and boring

material
8   Assist in the collection of overdue accounts if necessary
9   Achieve sales targets

XYZ Inc.
Daily Commercial News/Construction News
National Account Representative
October 1, 1994 - July 2002

Job Description:

1   Analyze accounts and develop strategic plans to increase customer share
2   Access proposed target accounts to maximize sales to national accounts
3   Promote company at trade shows/conferences
4   Cultivate strong senior-level business relationships within specific accounts
5   Design, Layout, and approve program material
6   Collect overdue accounts if necessary
7   Negotiate and develop contract agreements
8   Analyze industry trends and develop sales strategies
9   Develop and implement sales budgets
10   Develop sales presentations, i.e. print material & electronic
11   Network through all aspects of the construction industry
12   Implement and assist in the development of internal systems
13   Liase within the specifiers, architectural, municipal and engineering sectors

Accomplishments:

1   For the past six years, consistently **over achieved all sales budgets**
2   Consistently hit target accounts
3   Developed print/electronic corporate presentation

The JOB News/New & Resale Homes
Account Executive/National Operations & Sales Manager
February 1986 - September 1994

Job Description:

1   Organize, approve, and implement trade shows
2   Develop promotional campaigns i.e. radio, bus shelters, print material
3   Develop rate specifications and cost analysis
4   Coordinate 6 regional franchise operations
5   Liaise with regional sales managers
6   Develop sales compensation packages
7   Analysis and prepare sales budgets
8   Negotiate sales contracts and programs
9   Recruit and prospect new client base
10   Motivate sales teams (approx. 80 staff members)
11   Staff and train sales force
12   Implemented internal network systems
13   Coordinate distribution locations
14   Outside sales

Education:

OPERATIONS: BAD—Operations (cont.)

State College 1998–2000
Business Management Certificate
Human Resources and Management

State College 1985–1987
Business Administration
Major courses: Accounting, Financing & Sales

Market Street Secondary School 1981 - 1985
Grade 12

Skills

Power Point, Excel, Microsoft Suites, Maximizer, Admarc, Priority Management

Hobbies:

Reading, skiing, and swimming

References:

Upon Request.

John J. Johnston

123 Learning St., Anytown, USA 10101
999.555.1212 (Cell) johnj@yourname.com

Over eight years of progressive **Pharmaceutical Sales** experience, ranging from OTC to pharmaceutical, and most recently biotech. Consistently surpassed sales targets due to excellent communication and interpersonal skills in concert with customer fidelity, empathy, and focus. Recently was Sales Rep of the year, two years running.

PROFESSIONAL EXPERIENCE

ABC INC., 1996–2005

Better Bones Specialist 2004–2005

1. Achieved 135% growth over 2004 in a hyper-competitive marketplace through innovation and tenacity.
2. Optimized utilization of Infusion Access Coordinators through facilitation of relationship building between the rheumatologists, receptionists, and coordinators.
3. Developed preceptorship programs to foster trust and provide an opportunity to address hidden concerns.
4. Developed continued medical education events focused on physician's needs.
5. Developed relationships within "patients support programs" by incorporating Better Bones treatment into their model of optimal patient management.
6. Further developed essential sales skills, specifically probing to uncover the physician's hidden objections and concerns.

Pharmaceutical Care Specialist 2003–2004

1. Achieved 107% of Therxa sales forecast in spite of established competition.
2. Launched and achieved a 105% of forecast for Protextone (antihistamine).
3. Developed fruitful relationships with allergists, respirologists, dermatologists, and OB-GYNs in Greater Anytown area, including the Health Network, through value added sales calls.
4. Demonstrated leadership skills by providing support and guidance to Primary Care Representatives working within my area of responsibility.
5. Maximized return on investment for continued medical education events by developing value added events and thorough follow up with attendees.

Pharmaceutical Care Representative 1998–2003

1. Achieved an average of 102% of sales forecast over 4 years.
2. Promoted to Care Specialist for outstanding work.

Pharmacy Care Representative 1996–1998

Achieved 103% of sales forecast in 1996 and 118% of sales forecast in 1997.

GRAYS Franchise Owner/Operator   1989–1994

1. Increased sales and reduced cost to position the business second in its category.
2. Increased repeat customer base.
3. Created promotional ideas to capitalize on special events and drive business growth.

PROFESSIONAL DEVELOPMENT: OTC, Accreditation, Immunology, Pneumology, CCPE; Peer Mentoring Program, Kelly Ann Cowan Management Consultants

AWARDS: Sales Representative of the Year (Two times from 2001–2005)

EDUCATION: B.Sc. Biology Major, State University

PHARMACEUTICAL: Sales Rep., Advanced

John J. Johnston
123 Learning St., Anytown, USA 10101 Phone: 999-555-1212 johnj@yourname.com

Pharmaceutical Sales Representative with Track Record for Delivery. Eager to learn and capable of teaching. Strong skills in making group presentations to health care professionals. Ensures delivery and execution of the customer service plan.

Education

Bachelor's Degree (June/1997)   State University
State College of Pharmacy - Program recognized by Pharmacy Examining Board of America

Work Experience

Abu-Dhabi Hospital, Abu Dhabi, UA
Marketing Manager (January/2004–November/2004)
*Marketing and medical services manager for the hospital.
*Responsible for managing all hospital sales and income.
*Responsible for the media relations and advertisements for the hospital and for promoting the hospital's services and facilities to the public and medical community.
*Responsible for recruiting visiting doctors from around the world.
*Member of the board of directors for Abu-Dhabi Medical Group.
*Expanded sales & marketing team from 1 to 6 representatives.
Increased the hospital's revenues by 44% during my time with the hospital.

ABC Pharmaceuticals, Abu Dhabi, UA
Medical Sales Representative (February/2002–December/2003)
*Responsible for promotion of products such as anti-inflammatory, respiratory, and anti-infective products
*Acting as a team leader for the erectile dysfunction line (PDE5 Inhibitors-Chuep)
*Implemented training course for new recruits—speeding profitability.

XYZ Pharmaceuticals, Abu Dhabi, UA
Senior Medical Sales Representative (January/2001–February/2002)
Responsible for medical promotion of NSAID's, H2-blocker, anti-infective, and respiratory medicine lines.

IRON Pharmaceuticals, Abu Dhabi, UA
Medical Sales Representative (November/1999–December/2000)

Professional Qualifications

Training Courses *A Step Ahead for Experienced Medical Representatives, Impact Consulting and Training Solutions, 2003.
*Speeding Profitability training course, professional selling skills training course, 2003.
*Product training in fertility and enuresis lines, 2000.
*Product training in anti-infective, H2 blocker, NSAID, and respiratory tract drug lines, 1999.

Affiliations Pharmacy Examining Board, Eligible to Enter the Evaluation Examination in 2005, from March/2004 to Present

Volunteer Work **The Memorial Cancer Run**, Registration Coordinator, February/2002–November/2004

Interests Scuba diving and snorkeling; traveling through the mid-west, also best beaches and coral reefs in the world.

PHARMACEUTICAL: Pharmaceutical Liaison

John J. Johnston, Ph.D.

Pharmaceutical and Research Expert/Liaison

- Knowledge of Pharma Discovery targets, research priorities
- Expertise in collaborations/partnering practice/licensing
- Established network in American science and biotechnology
- Thorough science and business preparation

Professional Experience

Acting Research Liaison Manager, ABC Firm (2002–2004)
- Responsible for integrating ABC International Discovery research with science in US
- Supported US Alliances in Biotechnology and Academia
- Co-managed academic alliances over $2MM
- Participated in scientific collaboration committees
- Implemented SR&ED taxation leverage; scholarships; strategic investment

Research Liaison Officer, XYZ (2001–2002)
- Led Business Development Activities for novel technologies
- Designed, negotiated awards program with leading research societies (AIHR, CSC, NSERC)
- Chaired collaboration meetings including leading Swedish (ABC) and US scientists' collaboration in GI disease

Recent Invited Lectures

BIG North	'Partnering with ABC' Ottawa, Canada, Dec '04
Bio Tech Brunch, BIO 2004	'ABC Licensing' San Francisco, June '04
Bio Pharm	Annual meeting 'Alliances Panel Lecture' Chicago, April '04
Bio Finance CFO Roundtable	'Biotech partnering, supporting deals' Seattle, June '03

Training

ABC Business Intelligence: Competitive Intelligence training, Anytown, AS, 2001 and 2004
Legal/Intellectual Property Workshops: Semi-annual workshops, Global Discovery Alliances, ABC PLC, since 2002
Basic Licensing: Association of University Technology Managers AUTM, 2002

Education

Doctor of Philosophy (Ph.D.)
2001, State University, Faculty of Health Sciences
- Concentration: molecular physiology of cardiac and skeletal muscle cells
- Thesis: Transcriptional regulation of HSP70 and striated muscle phenotype

Masters of Science (M.Sc.) 1997, State University

Bachelor of Physical Education (B.Ph.Ed.Hons.) 1994, State University

Committees and Councils

- American Research-Based Pharmaceuticals (Rx&D) Biopharmaceutical Committee
- Advisory Council, Masters of Biotechnology Program, State University (2002–2004)
- President's Advisory Committee: The Finnoula Institute for AHS (2002)

Phone: (999) 555-1212   johnj@yourname.com

PHARMACEUTICAL: Account Director

ALICE J. JOHNSTON

123 Learning Street, Anytown, USA 10101 Email: alicej@yourname.com Res: (999) 555-1212

PROFILE

Results-oriented **Account Director in the health and pharmaceutical field** with exceptional client and project management skills. A versatile team player who takes a creative approach to problem solving. Effective communicator at all levels of management. Special strength in managing client relationships and developing and implementing business strategies.

CAREER HISTORY

GET A LIFE, Account Director   **June 2003–Present**
A full-service marketing and communications agency specializing in the health care industry. Part of an international group of companies specializing in both traditional and health care advertising.

Responsibilities
1   Develop and grow business within existing agency accounts.
2   Member of core branding team. Assist with yearly brand plans and strategies.
3   Active in all new business pitches. Responsible for integrated interactive strategies.
4   Strategize on a broad range of interactive tactics including: websites, e-Details, PDA applications, Continuing Medical Education, Online Media, Direct to Physician, & Direct to Consumer Advertising.
5   Lead on all active interactive projects.

Accomplishments
- Key member of pitch team responsible for winning a new $8M account with a large international pharmaceutical company.
- Created a PDA strategy to help pharmaceutical sales reps with the physician detailing process. The client has since bought PDAs for the entire team and are in the process of implemented the first detail.
- Assisted in the creation of an e-Detail strategy for a pharmaceutical company launching a new product. Worked closely with global marketing team on interactive launch strategies.
- Created a Direct to Consumer (DTC) interactive advertising plan for the launch of a new pharmaceutical product in Canada. Worked closely with the client's PR department to ensure integration of all launch strategies.

GETIT.NET, Senior Account Manager   **June 2001–April 2003**
An Internet consulting and development company specializing in global e-business solutions and online media for pharmaceutical companies.

Responsibilities
1   Develop and grow business within identified accounts through consultative selling and effective relationship building.
2   Strategize on account activities including Consulting, Marketing, Builds, and Maintenance.
3   Act as the client advocate as well as the internal team leader by showing a focus on client needs, attention to detail and focus on quality through the development lifecycle.

Accomplishments
- Managed the design and development of a site segmented to support DTC and Healthcare Professional (HCP) initiatives for the launch of a new innovative contraceptive product.
- Consultant to the central eBusiness group, for all strategy, build and marketing initiatives.
- Director for all projects worldwide associated with new contraceptive product. There were twenty-five initiatives at different stages of development.

ALLOVER.NET   1998–March 2001

An Internet consulting and development company specializing in global e-business solutions in the financial services and emerging markets sectors.

Manager, Business Development/Client Relations

Responsibilities

1   Source, solicit, and secure targeted clients for top line revenue generation.
2   Partner with potential clients to assess their needs, desires, and strategies in order to structure and sequence e-commerce initiatives.
3   Determine pricing and profit margins for client proposals.
4   Manage client relationships ensuring quality of contracted deliverables and securing follow on opportunities.
5   Create, facilitate, implement, and manage sales initiatives and report results to senior executives.

Accomplishments

- Program managed an initiative to consolidate seven lines of business websites for a large full-service US banking consortium. Project mandate covered the development of a common branding and user experience design for all lines of business and the implementation of site tools including: a content management system, single login capability, personalized site concierge, and online application tools.
- Achieved sales of 1.9 million in booked revenue within the first six months as a Business Development Manager.
- Established a high level alliance with sales professionals from Boone & Co., the parent company, within assigned territory. This collaboration resulted in access to high-level client relationships and partnerships, several proposals and the booking of 2 million in revenue.
- Acted as a Solutions Selling coach, providing guidance, mentoring, and evaluation for participants learning the sales process.

Proposal Specialist

Accomplishments

- Designed and managed the creation of a knowledge management intranet which pulled together all company reports, case studies, proposals, and client information to facilitate the presales process. This initiative resulted in a more consolidated central approach to proposal creation, reducing effort, and increasing sales.
- Designed and managed the creation of a sales funnel database that was used to forecast revenue and improve the sales process. This project resulted in more accurate forecasting for operations management, improving resource management, and financial projections.
- Managed a proposal for the creation of an Electronic Document Delivery system for a large US mutual fund company in conjunction with two other lines of business. This proposal resulted in a research and development project to create the system.

EDUCATION AND TRAINING

Bachelor of Education, Anystate Teaching Certificate - State University
Masters in Text and Performance Studies - State College/University of the Academy of Dramatic Arts
Bachelor of Arts Honors - Concentrations in Drama and Russian - State University

1   Pitching to Win - The Joe Rogan International Group
2   Solutions Selling - No Boundaries Communications Inc.
3   Project Management Training - Networth

PHARMACEUTICAL: Sr. VP Bio and Pharmaceutical

John J. Johnston
123 Learning Street, Anytown, USA 10101 Res: (999) 555-1212 Email: johnj@yourname.com

---

Senior Sales and Marketing Executive in Life Sciences & Pharmaceutical Field

ABC Scientist   **2001–2004**
Senior Vice President Sales and Marketing: Anycity, AS

Represented both ABC Scientist and its corporate parent ABC Inc. in an internationally senior management role. Global business responsibilities included Sales, Marketing, Government Relations, Customer Support, Operations, and Business Development.
Accomplishments
- Increased revenues by 38% in FY03 to $440 million
- Signed business development deals for product commercialization
- Developed sales and support distribution channel strategy
- Instrumental in opening 'emerging markets'
- Moderator and keynote speaker at Embassy in Japan
- Organized ABC involvement within India, Japan
- Spearheaded and implemented key initiatives: Major account program, branding, CRM, website redesign, order generation, order fulfillment contracts, and international agreements
- Established and hired key director positions in sales, marketing, and support

ABC Technologies Inc.   **2000–2001**
Worldwide Marketing Manager, Life Sciences Division: Othercity, AS

Responsible for ABC's Marketing department for the bioconsumables and services product lines. Core focus included marketing and sales channel management in addition to full profit and loss accountability.
Accomplishments
- Increased sales by 40% in first six months
- Signed major business development deal
- Restructured department; reducing costs by 15%
- Established sales distribution channel strategy
- Implemented successful branding and major account program for capital equipment and supplies in Life Sciences market

ABC Technologies Inc.   **1999–2000**
Vice President and General Manager, Chemical Analysis Group

A General Management role, responsibilities included sales, marketing, operations, and support for ABC Technologies' American operations.
Accomplishments
- Double-digit revenue and operating income growth in first year of operation
- Implemented key strategic partnership between universities/colleges and pharmaceutical industry

Winifred Mathers LLC.   **1983–1999**
Vice President and General Manager, Chemical Analysis Group: 1998–1999
General Manager responsibilities as listed below with additional responsibilities to represent HC-LLC in a senior management capacity.
Accomplishments
- Member of HC-LLC's senior management council
- Global 'second' for percentage growth increase
- Led business units to a worldwide "Number 1" customer survey rating
- Implemented Sales Channel model with North America's first sales agent
- Nominated for "Top 40 under 40" in National magazine

General Manager, Chemical Analysis Group: 1995–1998
Accomplishments

- Achieved double-digit growth annually, with year one achieving 32% growth
- Led the first successful reorganization of sales and support operations under business managers; an operational first internationally
- Top country for laboratory computer and software support sales
- Finished in Top Five countries worldwide for sales performance

District Sales Manager, Analytical Instruments: 1989–1995
Accomplishments

- Double-digit sales growth
- Made Top Ten District list in Americas for sales achievement
- Implemented Pharmaceutical Industry program, resulting in unprecedented growth: from 300K in FY89 to 3.29 million in FY94

Technical Sales Representative, Analytical Instruments: 1985–1989
Accomplishments

- America's Top HPLC and Laboratory Data Systems sales representative, FY89

Technical Computer Sales Representative, Computer Systems Organization: 1983–1985
Accomplishments

- Attended the first sales High Achievers' Club in FY85
- Top Computer sales representative in district

Scientific Inc, Sales Representative   **1981–1983**

ABC LLC, Laboratory Technician   **1981**

Education/Professional Development

2003	Global Leadership Management	State Institute
2002	Executive Management Development	State University
2001	Sales and Marketing	School of Business
2000	Leadership at the Speed of Change	State University
1999	Running Cross Boundary Business	WM, Out of State
1999	Managing the White Space	Rummler Brache Group
1998	Managing Channels of Distribution	State University
1981	**Honors Bachelor of Science**	**State University**

Associations/Memberships/Task Forces

1995–Present	Board of Directors, Partners for a Drug Free Community
2003–Present	Board of Directors, Anytown Biotechnology Initiative
2003–Present	Board of Directors, State College, BCART
2003–Present	Board of Directors, Region Biotechnology Cluster

Speeches

2004	Pharma New Technology	Bio Conference Australia
2004	ABCs of Drug Discovery	Embassy Japan
2003	Biomarkers in Drug Discovery	Embassy Japan
2003	Large molecule development	State Institute China
2002	AMAP Guest Speaker	State University
2001	PLT Keynote Speaker	State College

PMP: BAD—Project Manager

John J. Johnston, CD PMP

123 Learning St.
Anytown, USA 10101

Phone (999) 555-1212
johnj@yourname.com

Profile

A collaborative, PMI Certified Senior Project Manager with multi-industry experience specializing in quality management and business process improvement. An accomplished leader who assures successful project delivery within defined scope and budget through the enablement of an empowered team.

Experience

July 2003 - Present   Big Bank Financial Inc.

Program Manager, Credit Risk Solutions, Enterprise Technology Solutions

Basel II Commercial Banking Technology Projects

Role: Program Manager

Program Manager for high risk mission critical projects aimed at upgrading the Big Bank Commercial Bank computer systems in preparation for the Basel II Accord. Encompasses internal project teams from three distinct business and technology units and two external consulting firms. Program encompassed the design, development, and implementation of Peoplesoft EPM data warehouse and Ab Intio ETL. As well, upgraded to existing legacy source systems to support the compliance requirements of the Basel II Accord. Improved management processes and provided program/project management mentoring to business and project managers. Completed Program 24.5% below anticipated cost without sacrificing functionality and quality.

Infrastructure Upgrade Project

Role: **Project Manager**

Upgraded physical server complex (7 HP DL850) and migrated associated systems from NT6 to Windows 2003 Server. Completed with no impact to production systems.

Project Manager, Implementation Management Office

XYZ Group Financial
Role: **Program Manager**

Program Manager for key organizational project. Supported project teams from across all business segments (national and multi-national) and provided mentoring to junior Project Managers. Program is being conducted within a business segment that lacks strong project management experience and awareness. Successfully overcame this by introducing best practices in program management and by providing consultative support to business segment leaders.

Regulations Reporting , Group Finance
Role: **Project Manager**

Project Manager and consultant to business segment leaders through the selection and procurement of a vendor system providing Risk Weighted Asset and Capital Adequacy Reporting functionality. Introduced best practices in project management.

Implementation Management Office
Role: **Project Manager**

Assisted in the enhancement of project management documentation, methodology, and training. Provided mentoring to junior Project Managers.

What's Wrong?

- Dense text—I'm too bored to read this all.
- Too stylized. I'm blinded!

John J. Johnston, CD PMP

123 Learning St.
Anytown, USA 10101

Phone (999) 555-1212
johnj@yourname.com

March 2000 - January 2003   **ABC Projects Ins.**

Project Manager

ISO 9001:2000 Certification
Role: **Project Manager**

Initiated, planned, and executed the primary corporate project to achieve ISO 9001:2000 certification. Project included the definition and establishment of an intranet document management system sufficient to ensure satisfactory control over the critical quality documentation. Project was successfully implemented and certification achieved on first audit.

Corporate Information Systems Contract Management Project
Role: **Project Manager**

Led an executive level team in the defining and documenting of ABC's Corporate Information Systems Contract which details the legal separation between ABC and client in respect to developed information systems.

May 1997 - March 2000   **ZYY Consulting**

Project Management Consultant

Provided project and program management services.

Developed and implemented a new evaluation program for Army Reserves.

Developed and implemented training programs for Hospital Company.

1983 - 1997   **Armed Forces**
                         Various Locations

Combat Arms Officer

Commanded soldiers in training and operational units

Managed recruiting efforts.

Managed professional training in military skills and quality management.

Provided Human Resource Management to over 100 personnel.

Education

- *Project Management Professional*
- *Project Management Advanced Certificate*
- *Big Bank Financial Group Project Management Certificates*
- *Total Quality Management Facilitator Certificate*
- *Business Process Quality Management Certificate*
- *ISO 9001:2000 Internal Auditor*
- *State University Executive Program on Quality*
- *Officer Professional Development Program*
- *Advanced Armored Officer*

PMP: Project Coordinator, Junior

Alice Johnston
123 Learning St.
Anytown, ST

999 555 1212 Res
999 555 1313 Cell
alicej@yourname.com

PROFILE

An experienced, enthusiastic, and determined **Project Coordinator who takes ownership of her projects,** possessing proven interpersonal, communication, and organizational skills. Successful at coordinating and executing **Recruitment, HR Consulting, Technology, and Marketing Projects for** small to medium-size organizations. Aspiring to expand working on **larger projects in diverse functions** within a growing professional services company.

PROFESSIONAL EXPERIENCE

Project Coordinator   **Jan 2003–Feb 2004**
Pepper Partners Inc. – Executive Search & HR Services
My clients have included Religion &TV, Brain candy cartoons, Big Bank etc.

Responsibilities:

Recruiting

- Liaise with client lead on client's requirements and define expectations.
- Source potential qualified candidates via web, directories, and publications.
- Conduct reference checks on potential hires and manage offer process.
- Prepare PowerPoint slides for presentations and participate in client proposal prep.
- On consulting assignment, worked at client site, conducted employee interviews, and developed their employee manual.
- Go the extra mile & create employment contracts for clients as a value added service.

Office Management

- Act as the network administrator and security officer and manage the relationship with the company's technical outsourcing company's Project Manager.
- Update database with candidate resume & contact information & track project cycle.
- Manage budgets and track expenses on spreadsheets; manage financial reporting on both projects and company overall.
- Facilitate interviews and client/team meetings.

Special Projects

- Assist with design of company website and manage edits to content.
- Managed online project from inception through marketing and implementation.
- Create plan of action with deliverables and MS Project timelines for completion and provide explanation of variances. Monitor and follow-up on issues/actions log.

Accomplishments:

- I have acquired **strong business knowledge by managing diverse projects**, interacting with key client executives, and by actively networking.
- Being the CRM database specialist, I **reduced the cost of training** for new consultants by taking it on myself.
- **I reduced the expenditure on IT support by 50%** by learning, taking over, and managing the day-to-day IT functions.
- My recruitment **projects are completed speedily with a turn around time of one week to one month.**
- **Generated revenues** by actively promoting and selling our online resume service.

Alice Johnston

1 of 2

Office Coordinator   Jan–Dec 2002
ICU Partners Inc. – Executive Search & HR Services
As the first full-time employee at this start-up company, I built the administrative function from the ground up.

Responsibilities:

- Created new employee orientation package and developed all office procedures and processes.
- Scheduled and facilitated team meetings, drafted agendas, prepared and distributed minutes, followed up on issues and action items.
- Managed IT functions including network, individual workstations, and the CRM database.
- Managed day-to-day operations (bank deposits, mail, invoicing, and filing).

Accomplishments:

- Sourced and administered company's benefits plan.
- Launched a performance review process that continues to be used today.
- Created and maintained a document storage system (hardcopy and electronic files).
- Trained new consultants on the recruitment process and CRM database.
- Succession planned my own position by documenting my function and training a competent replacement.

COMPUTER SKILLS

- Proficiency with MS Office (PowerPoint, Excel) and MS Project
- Proficiency with Microsoft 98, 2000, and XP Operating Systems

EDUCATION

Honors Bachelor of Science (November 2001)
State University
Specialist: Psychology; Minor: Sociology

Certificate in Human Resources Management (In progress)
State College
6 of 10 courses completed, achieving a grade of A in each

AFFILIATIONS/PROFESSIONAL DEVELOPMENT

Registrations Coordinator	GIMP (Group of Internet Marketing Professionals)	2003
Effective Self-Marketing	Professional Development Seminar	2003
Leadership Training	Professional Development Seminar	2003
Effective Self-Promotion	Professional Development Seminar	2003
Pushing your Comfort Zone	Professional Development Seminar	2003
Your Extraordinary Edge	HRAA Conference	2003

INTERESTS/ACTIVITIES

Cooking Indian food, nature walks in the great outdoors, yoga, current affairs, business, finance & investing, continuous learning, and networking.

PMP: Project Manager

John J. Johnston, PMP, B.Sc. Eng.	123 Learning St. Anytown, USA 10101 Tel.: 999-555-1212 Home ◆ 999-555-1313 Mobile Email: johnj@yourname.com

Profile Summary

Highly versatile and seasoned **Project Manager** with more than 18 years of management experience in engineering, financial, and communications industries. Strong business acumen and understanding of information systems technology: internet hardware software and related B2B applications. A creative, analytical thinker who makes sure the job gets done. Professional project team leader who is comfortable using empowerment and participative leadership as well as a directive style in order to reach maximum effectiveness and efficiency.

Expertise

Scope	Time	Cost	Risk	Integration
• Initiation • Planning • Definition • Verification • Change control	• Activity definition • Activity sequencing • Activity duration estimating • Schedule development • Schedule control	• Resource planning • Estimating • Budgeting • Control	• Planning • Identification • Qualitative analysis • Quantitative analysis • Response planning • Monitoring & control	• Project plan development • Project plan execution • Integrated change control

Products & Solutions	Business Management	Technology HW & SW
• E-commerce • Intranets • Web security • Legacy systems integrations • Customer DBs mngmt • Voice, data, wireless • Billing systems • CRM	• Partnerships & alliances • Process analysis • Process reengineering • Process control • Rational unified process • New product development • Product launch & marketing	• Limtur • DB2/SQL • W 95/98 & NT • UNIX • Web security protocols • Web database interface • IBM DB2 • IBM Visual Age 2/4 • IBM MVS-OS/390 mainframe • IBM WebSphere

Professional Experience

Sr. Manager of Programs, New Products, and Services Development Department
Another Telephone Corp, 2000–2002

- Led a group of 20+ direct and indirect reports, PMs, functional project leads and business analysts, in management of strategic corporate initiatives. Managed $3 mil. annual budget for new products and services development and implementation.

- Improved project and product life cycle management support adapting them more to corporate capability, customer needs, and service cost reduction.

- Hands-on project managed development and implementation of new products, services, and programs using 20+ cross-functional team effort and different business management platforms, while linking customer databases, internal and external suppliers across the enterprise. Ensured team's adherence to the budget, schedule, and scope. Received directions and reported regularly on progress, obstacles, and potential solutions to VP level executive sponsor.

Sr. Manager of Programs con't...

- Promoted across the corporation business and project management best practices and methodologies. Presented to Senior Leadership Team, corporate governing body as well as to operating level staff in number of departments. Developed Accelerated Iterative Development methodology for programs.

- Hired, performed evaluations, led, and supported direct reports in business process, project management, and professional development.

- Technology: IBM WebSphere Application Server 2.0.3/4.0.1 (J2EE, XML, XSL/XSLT, Xalan XSLT processor, Xerces parser, SAX/DOM, JAXP, Swing, Java Servlets and Enterprise JavaBeans, JMS, Java Mail), IBM VisualAge for Java 2/4, IBM WebSphere Studio Application Developer 4.0 (Java Server Pages – JSP, Java Servlets, Data Beans), IBM WebSphere MQ 5.3/MQ Series 5, BEA WebLogic 4.5.1/7.0, CICS Transaction Server for OS/390 1.3, Netwise RPC Tool 3.1, PL1, IONA Orbacus 3.1.3, Calico 3.1 e-commerce framework, Borland JBuilder 7, WebGain Studio/Visial Café 4.0, IBM DB2, Sybase 11/12, Oracle 8i, MS Windows NT 4.0/2000, Solaris 7, Sun O/S, Rational Rose 2002, CyberCash/TouchNet Payment engine for credit card processing, Entrust Java Dev. Kit, iPlanet 4.1 Web Server.

Selected projects

Wiredup Program. E-commerce B2B integrated offering of services and products to business customers. Includes telecommunications services, equipment, business applications. IS development utilized IBM WebSphere Studio Application Developer 4.0, Web Security Protocols (SSl, PCT, SET) and Web Database Interface (ODBC, JDBC, ADO/RDS). Data has been stored on IBM MVS-os/390 mainframe and 11 Sun/OS servers located nation wide. Portal architecture based on J2EE standards. Partners include corporations like Big Name, Brand Name, My Name.

Managed capital budget of $2.4 mil., team of 50+, requirements analysis, scope planning and definition, business case analysis, funding approval, development lifecycle, equipment procurement, technology integration, troubleshooting, post implementation review, and lessons learned.

Any Distance program. Bundled services of Local, Long Distance, and Internet product lines. Offered to business customers across the nation. Integration of 14 different billing platforms residing with regional dominant service providers with feeds into billing raters, and production of one cumulative e-bill for the service.

Managed capital budget of $1.1mil. team of 27+, external project team leads and business partner consultants. Resolved extensive and complex issues related to revenue performance, credit verification, customer discounts and credits, customer database management. Delivered program six weeks ahead of schedule.

Sr. Project Manager, Corporate Project Management Office, Big Telephone Inc., 1998–2000

Responsibilities, operating capabilities, and activities

- Responsible for corporate support of infrastructure initiatives servicing data and voice product lines. Based on projects that have utilized variety of technologies corporate network was upgraded and improved effectively enabling interfaces with variety of business partners as well as acquired companies.

- Hands-on project managed number of initiatives, successfully leading cross-functional teams of 20+ members through development cycle of network management and applications management related projects. Acted as PM of last resort for critically derailed projects and as PM of first choice for mission critical developments.

- Technology: LAN, WAN, PSTN, IPVPN, VoIP, ATM, FR, BPX, ISDN-BRI, TLS, MNS, xDSL,VPoP, SONET, OC1, OC3, OC12

PMP: Project Manager (cont.)

Selected Projects

APS – TLS. Initiative provided the enterprise with national expansion of the network reach offering to business customers state of the art Transparent LAN Service (TLS). Teamed up with Big Communications as business partner, this No.1 corporate priority was completed ahead of schedule and in time for Sales Launch of business 1999 year. This was a first phase in massive program of APS network expansion. Project required integration of NOCs, rollout of CPE installation and Customer Service Support centers. Network supplied by Big Name (modular access routers).

Managed capital budget of $1.8mil and 35+ cross-functional team through full development lifecycle.
Ensured AS 400 billing system data integrity while linking customer databases across the enterprise. Supported Procurement department in goods and services acquisition, vendor management.

Enhanced Toll Free service and Voice Test Lab

The project is part of the assets integration after the acquisition. I managed integration of Enhanced Toll Free (ETF) platform as well as creation of Voice Test Lab from site selection to implementation user training and hand over to the users. ETF service was a complex initiative developed in parallel with Calling Card service project which made it very constrained and challenging to manage.

I managed capital budget of $2.8 Mil. and led 30+ cross-functional project team made of functional leads and Vendor SMEs. Service was offered over AS400 billing platform with e-bill utilizing BAS application.

Project Manager/Consulting Engineer   1984–1996
Responsibilities of Project Manager/Consulting Engineer on domestic and international projects. (*More detail about those assignments will be provided upon a request as they are older than five years.*)

ACHIEVEMENTS

President's Award of Performance Excellence – Another Telephone Corp.
Developed Accelerated Iterative methodology which established new corporate record in Time-To-Market
Certificates of Excellence –Big Telephone Inc.
Corporate reorganization mission critical product and services according to expected quality under the budget.

EDUCATION
Project Management and General Management
- **PMP Certification,** Project Management Institute, USA
- **Master's Certificate in Project Management** - School of Business and Management, State University
- **Seven Habits of Highly Effective People** - Franklin Covey Institute
- **Performance Coaching** - Performance Coaching Inc.
- **Presentation Advantage** - Franklin Covey Institute
- **MS Project, Advanced** - Knowledge Alliance
- **Project Management Course** - State University

Functional technology and business training and Financial training
- **AVVID Applications and IP Telephony** - Telephone Systems.
- **Business IP Services** - Another Telephone Corporation
- **Rapid Business System Requirements Analysis** - Power Plus Systems
- **Mastering Telecommunications Fundamentals, Voice, & Data** - Rivers Technologies Inc.
- **Mission Critical Marketing** - State School of Business.
- Series 7

Engineering

B.Sc. Engineering, University of Overseas Country

MEMBERSHIPS & ASSOCIATIONS
PMI- AS, USA
SLF - Strategic Leadership Forum

John J. Johnston, PMP, B.Sc.Eng.
Tel. 999-555-1212
Email: johnj@yourname.com

PR & PUBLIC AFFAIRS: BAD—PR

JOHN JOHNSTON
123 Learning Ave.
Anytown, USA
10101
(999) 555-1212

Highly motivated marketing/communication specialist, works well in pressure positions, detail and organizationally minded. Excellent communicator, writer and manager, French/English bilingual, good interpersonal skills. Looking for a challenging team position with long-term growth potential.

Education

1992 - 1995
Bachelor of Applied Arts - Radio and Television Arts
State Technical University, Honors Graduate

1989 - 1990
French as a Second Language Diploma
Université de France, France

Relevant Work History

11/04 - 07/05 – <u>Public Relations Supervisor</u> – Everyday Communications
Building the healthcare team at a senior level. Focusing in on new business development, media relations, strategic planning, and senior client counsel. Senior management team member.

03/04–11/04 - <u>Public Relations Supervisor</u> – Weston Montague Derbyshire
Responsible for new business, brand development, and all activities of 4-person PR team. Includes media relations, strategy development, writing, budget management, video news release production, strategic designed and execution of multi-faceted marketing plans. *Reporting directly into the president. Clients included fashion/beauty, healthcare, food, and not-for-profit clients.*

04/02 - 03/04 – <u>Marketing Communications Supervisor (promoted from Manager)</u>, Manly Marketing Group
Responsible for design and development of new Marketing Communications Department with staff of three. Duties included all public relations activities, including strategy, design and implementation, client and media relations; all advertising and tra[...] coordination and development of major press activities and public sp[...] This position was responsible for all internal and external communic[...] detailed liaison with large parent company. *Projects included: critical inter[...] campaign, national launch of proprietary study, Olympic PR around Sydney, 1 y[...] Lake Games, and complete redesign of corporate image and advertising and comp[...] and electronic).*

PR & PUBLIC AFFAIRS: BAD—PR (cont.)

03/01 - 04/02 - <u>*Public Relations Consultant*</u> *– Talk of the Town Inc.*
Responsible for strategic development of communication and media relation strategies for Electronic Brand and Software Brand. As a high-tech consultant, responsibilities included press release writing, success story pitching, media training, key message development and general marketing/communication consistency in message. *Key personal relationships developed with clients and key journalists. This position was very much an extension of the clients' own marketing/communications team.*

01/00 - 03/01 - <u>*Public Relations Account Executive*</u> *– Nice Lady & Associates*
This position encompassed both high-tech (Electronic and software companies) as well as consumer-focused and not-for profit clients. Duties included maintaining and developing media relationships, intense customer liaison, extensive writing and organizational duties as well as complete client management from budgeting to multi-national event planning. *With a roster of seven full-time clients, diplomacy, organizational proficiency, and high turn-around time was required constantly. This position was very detailed focused, and required the ability to do many things at once.*

10/98 - 01/00 - <u>*Marketing Director, Regional Shopping Center*</u> *– Semi-Big Local Mall*
Full marketing plan development from conception to delivery. Increased sales during 12-month period by over 500%. Key marketing plans included direct mail, customer loyalty and satisfaction programs, and retail incentive plans among the dozens that were implemented. Responsible for all marketing and communication messages delivered during a public 10-month renovation process. *Exceeded in obtaining positive press and improved corporate image considerably. Wrote and directed majority of radio spots and provided strategic direction on all advertising. Responsible for staff of seven including hiring and review procedures. Great deal of community/charity/volunteer board work involved in this role.*

03/98 - 10/98 - <u>*Promotions Manager & Community Liaison*</u> *-   WOW Radio*
This maternity-leave position required aggressive sales coordination efforts for the stations' clients including special event planning, marketing consultation, script writing and general communications counsel. All marketing plans and community initiatives were coordinated and developed through this position. Corporate communication/station imaging also played an important role.

04/96 - 03/98 – <u>*Account Services Representative*</u> *– Tourism State Associates*
Advertising and marketing firm based on small eastern coast state. Lead account responsibilities included account traffic, press proofing, production assistant, advertising sales support, and general office duties. *A small agency, our main account was State Tourism and as a result, much of the position required government liaising.*

Related Experiences
- Doula: volunteer labor and delivery coach
- Other volunteer work includes: Boy Scouts, AIDS Committee Anytown
- Freelance wine consultant

References and portfolio available upon request

Alice J. Johnston

123 Learning Street, Anytown, USA 01010 (999) 555-1212 alicej@yourname.com

Junior PR Rep

An enthusiastic, experienced planner and promoter who can operate calmly and efficiently under pressure and within deadlines. Willing team member who can take the ball and run with delegated tasks and make independent decisions if necessary. Comfortable taking leadership role, speaking, and giving presentations. Familiar with all aspects of a campaign—print, billboard, radio, TV, Web.

Education

State University   2001–Present
Bachelor of Public Relations, Cooperative Education   (Graduation, April '05)

Experience

Marketing/Communications   **Jan–Apr 2004, Sept–Present**
Assistant
  Big City Partnership
- Developing marketing and communications collateral
- Extensive research and writing for several publications (including newsletters for national and international audiences and press releases)
- Website management (including writing for the Web and daily website updates)
- Working with investors and public relations agencies in developing an investor relations communications strategy
- Working with public relations agencies to develop a new marketing campaign to be used in all mediums including print, billboard, television, and radio
- Media monitoring and segmentation

  Accomplishments
- Won praise from clients for Web writing and for creative newsletter articles

Communications Coordinator   **May 2003–Aug 2004**
 Sport Center Anytown   **(some contract work)**
- Writing articles for monthly and quarterly newsletters, annual, and board reports
- Website management (including updating website daily in French and English)
- Writing letters for SCA President and Athlete Services Manager
- Tracking and researching athlete results, coordinating daily media monitoring
- Writing profiles and conducting interviews with athletes and coaches for website
- Managing the SCA database and developing survey questions for SCA publics
- Responding to media requests and assisting with event planning

  Accomplishments
- Developing one-page marketing documents for athletes seeking corporate sponsorships; one came back to thank me personally for helping land his deal
- Developed an annual survey for SCA affiliates; survey still used by SCA

PR & PUBLIC AFFAIRS: PR, Beginner (cont.)

Alice J. Johnston Learning St., Anytown, USA 10101
(999) 555-1212 alicej@yourname.com

Experience Continued...

Manager/Cheerleading Coach   1999–2004
Cheer Extreme
- Administrative and registration responsibilities
- Planned fundraisers (raising over $8,000), special events and parent meetings
- Planned/choreographed cheerleading camps and classes for up to 40 participants

Gymnastics Instructor   1997–2003
Gazelles Gymnastics Club
- Answered questions and informed parents about the club's programs
- Organized and planned gymnastics classes for large groups of participants
- Hosted/planned group birthday parties and day camps for up to 30 participants

Master of Ceremonies   Aug 2002 (other state)
Cheer Expo
- Hosted expo and delivered presentations for the entire event (attendance 4,000)
- Formulated advertising techniques and promotional techniques with exhibitors
- Responsible for assisting exhibitors and facilitating networking opportunities

Photographer Assistant   2000–2002
Photodelic
- Organized over 500 children for individual and team photographs
- Distributed and advertised photo packages to more than 400 clients
- Documented and verified all necessary information for photographers

Public Relations Courses/Projects

- Developing a complete communications plan and case study (2003)
- Developing collateral for media kits and fundraising packages
- Developing/presenting a strategic communications plan for a request for proposal

Qualifying Skills and Accomplishments

- Functional in Spanish
- Proficient in PowerPoint, Adobe PageMaker, and Photoshop

Community Services and Awards

- Assisted Coast-to-Coast for Cancer in organizing an event in Anytown (2003)
- Volunteer coach of Happy High School Cheerleading Team (2002–present)
- AAA all-star/AUAA all-conference player - Varsity Soccer Team (2001–present)

John J. Johnston

123 Learning Street, Anytown, ST USA, 10101 * 999.555.1212 * johnj@yourname.com

COMMUNICATIONS ♦ PROMOTIONS ♦ PUBLIC RELATIONS DESKTOP PUBLISHING ♦ EVENT PLANNING

ACCOMPLISHMENTS

COMMUNICATIONS & PUBLIC RELATIONS:

- Successfully conducted a 3-month Communications Audit and prepared a Communications Strategy for St. Lucia's Cathedral, Anycity, ST.
- Designed & developed a procedures manual and tracking system database for Big Store's Head Office, Corporate Incentive.
- Wrote feature articles for the Downtown Business Association of Anycity's newsletter to promote bars and restaurants in the downtown core.
- Produced, assembled, & distributed Media Kits to 150 communications outlets & mediums across America to prepare for the September Public Awareness Campaign for Muscular Dystrophy.

PROMOTIONS & EVENT PLANNING:

- Co-planned the General Meeting for Muscular Dystrophy (annual 2-day gathering of 1000+ chapter members).
- Launched Food Drive for Anycity Food Bank (raised over 2,500 lbs of food), Valentines Day Candy-Grams Blitz and Corporate Christmas Bash for Telecenter.
- Organized & launched Dine-a-Round London 2002, on behalf of the BBB Group.
- Produced a Marketing/Trade Show Launch for Oliver Imaging.
- Organized and launched 18 Stakeholder Outreaches, Focus Groups, and Technical Workshops, comprised of mayors and decision-making delegates, held in various municipalities throughout the state.
- Planned, promoted, and executed 3 divisional retreats, 3 conferences, 3 Intranet training seminars, 15 learning events, and 4 charity campaigns.

DESKTOP PUBLISHING:

- Designed and produced all promotional collateral used in pre-post event advertising (brochures, flyers, posters, web pages, and invitations for monthly learning lunches, biannual retreats, training seminars, awareness campaigns, conferences & special fundraising, and charity events).
- Acted as Webmaster/Administrator for FFPD Intranet website: (wrote and edited copy, managed all users & editing authority) created and posted online surveys, training pages, & resource links, post-event survey statistical analysis; creative designer for graphics and page layouts.
- Co-facilitated content management application training sessions for content providers, developed training, & reference material for ongoing sessions.

PR & PUBLIC AFFAIRS: Director of PR (cont.)

WORK EXPERIENCE

Projects Officer, Corporate & Quality Service Division   Sep 2004–Present
Anycity, ST

Communications & Community Relations Coordinator   Feb 2004–Aug 2004
Anycity, ST

Junior Coordinator, Fiscal & Financial Policy Division (FFPD) Oct 2002–Jan 2004

Communications & Special Projects Assistant   Apr 2002–Jul 2002
Muscular Dystrophy (National Office)

Team Leader, MD Org   Mar 2000–Apr 2002

Big Store Head Office   Oct 1996–July 1999
Corporate Account Coordinator

EDUCATION

Corporate Communications & Public Relations   Post-Graduate Diploma
State College   April 2002

Travel and Tourism   Diploma
State College   1992

DESKTOP PUBLISHING APPLICATIONS

- QuarkXpress
- HTML
- FrontPage

- PhotoShop 7.0
- PageMaker
- Microsoft Office Suite

- Dreamweaver MX
- Illustrator
- PowerPoint

SPECIALIZED TRAINING & SKILLS

Event & Project Management   ◆   Facilitation   ◆   Negotiation

Analytical Problem Solving   ◆   Conflict Resolution   ◆   Crisis Communications

Research   ◆   Writing   ◆   Editing   ◆   Proofreading

Speech Writing   ◆   Press Releases   ◆   Script Writing

PR & PUBLIC AFFAIRS: PR and Promotions

John J. Johnston

123 Learning St., Anycity, ST, 10101   Mobile - Anycity (999) 555-1212   Work - Othercity (777) 555-1313   johnj@yourname.com

Results oriented Communicator with key strengths in strategic communications planning, project management, proactive media relations, issues management, and client counsel.

BCB Capital Markets USA, *Communications Advisor, Othercity*   Nov 04–present
Promoted to principal communications counsel for BCB Capital Markets USA. Mandate includes developing communications strategy and programs for BCB Capital Markets with a major focus on building brand through proactive media relations and acted as principal media contact and spokesperson for BCB Capital Markets USA. This role includes issues management and reputational counsel for BCB's North American executives and working with counsel to develop North American media policy for equity research analysts.

BCB Financial Group, *Manager, Media & PR and Corporate Comm. Advisor, Sponsorships, Anycity*   June 03–Nov 04
Took on a full time role, acting as a primary media contact and spokesperson for BCB Financial Group, both acting as a communications consultant within BCB to ensure that the communications strategies for each business platform within the enterprise are aligned with BCB's overall objectives and developing and managing strategic media and pr programs for BCB Capital Markets, BCB Investments, and BCB Systems & Technology. Sports sponsorship principal communications counsel (internal and external) included Olympic Games, American Soccer League, Athletics U.S.A., Freestyle Ski Association, and Snowboard Federation.

Accomplishments
- Managed BCB Investment's 2003 and 2004 RRSP media relations campaign and achieved over $1.3 million in earned media in 2004, surpassing nearest competitor by over $500,000. BCB was the only bank to witness an increase in its share of voice (60% increase) among the major banks.
- Worked closely with BCB Sponsorships to launch BCB's new Olympic marketing campaign over the summer of 2004. Media coverage surpassed targets by more than 70% in August 2004 and achieved more than $1.7 million in earned media. Awarded a gold medal by Score Magazine for Olympic marketing campaign. Sponsorships emerged as BCB's most visible source of favorable exposure.
- Media coverage for BCB Capital Markets in August 2004 reached its highest level in two years, surpassing previous levels by 46%. Year-to-date, media coverage has increased by over 14% as a result of coverage of underwriting and its role in M&A advice. In contrast, other major banks saw an average of 26% less coverage.

Pepper Consulting, *Principal, Anycity*   May 02–June 03
Primary Client: BCB Financial Group
Secondary Clients: Quickly Method (branding counsel) and Sullivan Custom (media relations counsel)

Accomplishments
- Revitalized BCB Systems and Technology/e-Business media relations program and increased media coverage by 41% for Fiscal 2003 (Plantex).
- Worked with B2B-TV, CP24, and WOW NewsNet to develop regular weekly BCB Investments TV interviews.
- Judge (2001–2004) for North American Public Relations Society annual PR Awards.
- Coordinated BCB's Trading Floor media camera (direct feed from BCB's trading floor to international broadcasters) that has significantly increased BCB's broadcast media coverage. In the twenty months of operation, the BCB media camera has garnered the equivalent of over $6 million in advertising dollars. The BCB media camera communications plan won a Randy Quarin award in 2003.

Hollaback International, *Consultant, Financial and Technology Communications Practice, Anycity*   Nov 99–April 02
Roles included counselling senior executives on corporate communications strategies including media training, key message development and speech writing, and developing and managing targeted media relations programs. The programs resulted in significant coverage for clients including PPE, Mighty Thoughts, and In2itive.

Education/Professional Development
Einstein School of Business – *Financial and Managerial Accounting Seminar*   Anycity, ST 2003
American Investor Relations Institute – *Fundamentals of Investor Relations Seminar*   Anycity, ST 2001
Capistrano College – *Corporate Communications Post-Diploma Certificate Courses*   Anycity, ST 1999–2000
UK School of Economics – *Specialization in European Economics*   London, England 1996

University of Anytown - *Bachelor of Commerce with Honors in Marketing*   Anytown, ST 1992–1997

- Travelled extensively through Canada, Europe, and the U.S.; enjoy windsurfing, snowboarding, mountain biking, squash, skiing, and running
- Member of Golden Road Ski Club and Anycity Lawn and Tennis Club

PROCESS ENGINEER SIX SIGMA: Consultant

123 Learning Street, Anytown, USA 01010   **John Johnston**   Phone: (999) 555-1212
Email: johnj@yourname.com

Professional Profile

An accomplished professional consultant with over nine years of experience across the high-tech and management consulting industries. Has leveraged strong interpersonal, analytical, and production skills and capacities to successfully manage and execute high-profile projects in the areas of:

- Marketing Strategy
- Performance Measurement and Improvement

Employment Experience

Big Insurance Company   *Senior Consultant, 2002–Present*

- Led product team in joint development project. Created a health insurance product to be used in the settlement of toxic waste mass torts. Produced and/or coordinated production of all material required for business case and product development. Business case for pilot, including ten year projected financial statements, reviewed and approved at Big Insurance Company's highest levels. Regulatory approval granted in AS state, generally regarded as the most demanding.

- Led Six Sigma (Quality) project to improve performance for application processing. Collected and cleaned two years of data for statistical analysis of cycle-time variation across thirty variables. Presented findings and nine categories of solutions to senior management, who redirected substantial resources (capital and people) for implementation in all categories. Midway through implementation, cycle time has been reduced by 33 percent.

- Conducted a market assessment and created a market entry strategy for a U.S. software/service provider to enter new markets. Final report presented to the board who provided the "go ahead." Implementation in progress.

- Partnered with Big Company Equity to value an early-stage equity opportunity in an emerging insurance industry information and technology provider. To management's surprise, returned "no-go" recommendation, which was upheld after scrutiny.

- Authored an industry best practices report as part of a large, global life insurer's due diligence process for a $50M backoffice technology investment decision. Findings contributed to a significant redirection of the project.

- Interviewed, mentored, and managed business students employed as Associate Consultants. Established framework and tools for goal-setting, performance evaluation and 360° feedback. Garnered overwhelmingly positive feedback from students.

The ABC Group   *Consultant, 2001–2002*

- Assessed industry attractiveness for the largest business unit of a $5.2Bn U.S. manufacturing company. Collaborated with senior management to set an intellectual agenda that enabled strategic decision-making. Undertook required materials preparation, which entailed primary and secondary research, and then the analysis, synthesis, and presentation of findings. Results, included in a package presented to the board, contributed to a complete change in strategy.

- Designed and built a market segmentation framework for pharmacy e-communications efforts at the U.S. division of a $45Bn drugstore company. This framework was endorsed by senior management and implemented in planning of over $50M in spending for 2002.

- Executed a comprehensive quality of service (QoS) survey of 1,400 customers within a $1.8Bn business line. Achieved a four-week turnaround time from the "go-ahead" decision to completion of data analysis.

John Johnston

Employment Experience (continued)

Xyz Consulting   *MBA Summer Associate, 2000*
- Contributed to the building of a business case for a multimillion-dollar investment at a large American telecommunications company by deriving a benchmark cost per bill across North American telecos.

Enterprise Systems   *Business Analyst & Project Manager, 1996–1998*
- Managed projects and conducted analysis for software implementation across sales and marketing divisions. Consistently generated reference accounts, critical for sales as success stories.
- Implemented a process for addressing technical problems, which reduced diagnosis time by 90 percent.
- Represented and communicated client and implementation requirements as part of the five-person product development team that set strategy and development goals for all software products.
- Facilitated all meetings with senior management, resulting in milestone or project sign-off.

Small Company Incorporated   *Account Manager, 1993–1995*
- Succeeded, as part of a three person sales team, in doubling this PC networking manufacturer's revenues each year.
- Developed a territory analysis and forecasting strategy, enabling the company to switch to individualized compensation.

State School of Business   *Class of 2001*
- Master of Business Administration
  Dean's Honor List (Awarded for Academic Standing in Top 10 percent of 1st Year MBA, Class of 210 People)
- *Legacy Scholarship (Awarded for Academic Achievement and Contribution to College Community)*

State University   *Class of 1993*
- Bachelor of Arts, Honors

Six Sigma Quality Program,
"Six Sigma" is a collection of tools, principles, and methodology that is used to drive measurable, customer-focused continuous improvement throughout the company. **Big Insurance Company** *grooms demonstrated talent with advanced Six Sigma training.*
- Black Belt Certification   *In Progress*
- Green Belt Certification   *Awarded in 2003*

Community Involvement and Recreational Interests

- **Camp Healing Hands** (summer camp for children with Cancer), Volunteer Camp Counselor
- **State School MBA Management Consulting Club**, President, *1999–2000*
- **State School LEADER Project** (Barcelona), Business Instructor and Site Leader, *1999–2000*
- **Member, Art Gallery of Anytown**
- **Big Brothers**, Big Brother, *1996–2001*
- **Interests & Activities:** Alpine skiing, snowboarding, canoe tripping, squash, watching DVDs, and reading current fiction when I've pulled a muscle

PROCESS ENGINEER SIX SIGMA: Senior Consultant

123 Learning Avenue
Anycity, Anystate
10101
555-999-1212

ALICE J. JOHNSTON, ABCP

SUMMARY (RANGE OF EXPERIENCE)

Alice is a Senior Consultant in the Anycity office who specializes in Enterprise Wide Risk Management, Process Improvement, and Project Management. Since joining the firm, Alice has been dedicating herself to facilitating control assessments by using state-of-the-art tools and techniques. She is also responsible for effectively assessing and identifying risks, performance gaps, process mapping, and minimizing exposures and leveraging opportunities to drive shareholder value.

Prior to joining ABC, Alice worked as a Six Sigma Black Belt for International Financial Data Service, where she was responsible for the development and facilitation of process improvement strategies for the areas of Operations, Human Resources, and Learning & Development. She has also held a position as Senior Manager of Client Service at XYZ Asset Management Corporation and was responsible for the call center amalgamation and the deployment of Six Sigma. Alice is a certified Associated Business Continuity Planner and certified Six Sigma Black Belt. Alice is a member of the American Society for Quality and is a certified Six Sigma Black Belt.

EDUCATION

Bachelor of Commerce (Honors), State University
Certified ISO 9000 Internal Auditor
Certified Six Sigma Black Belt
Associate Business Contingency Planner Certification

AREAS OF SPECIALIZATION

❖ Change Management
❖ Revenue Assurance
❖ Process Improvement
❖ Project Management
❖ Business Continuity Planning
❖ Risk Assessments
❖ User Acceptance Testing
❖ Customer Relationship Management

SOFTWARE EXPERTISES

❖ MS Project Manager
❖ MS Visio
❖ ACL
❖ Minitab
❖ MS Office
❖ Lotus Notes

❖ Access Database
❖ Statistica
❖ MS PowerPoint

PROFESSIONAL AFFILIATIONS

American Society for Quality
Disaster Recovery Institute

EMPLOYMENT HISTORY AND RELEVANT PROJECT EXPERIENCE

ABC Co LLP
Senior Consultant–Sept 2001–present

- Assessed and implemented risk management methodologies for various clients.
- Facilitated and developed a risk management database for high-valued clients.
- Provided constructive input on various contingency plans.
- Worked on various process improvement initiatives with clients.
- Managed a large-scale process review for a procurement department for a large telecommunications company.
- Reviewed management expense systems for a large-scale pharmaceutical company.
- Provided clients with an in-depth review of their processes and determined performance gaps.
- Developed and reviewed test plans.
- Developed tools for Business Impact Assessments and Vulnerability Risk Assessments.
- Held key project management position for some key clients.
- Facilitated, developed, and implemented a risk management database for a high-value client.
- Provided clients with an in-depth review of their processes and identified performance gaps.
- Developed Business Impact Assessments and Risk and Vulnerability Assessments.
- Conducted diagnostic assessments to determine cost reduction for proposed implementation of a quality program.
- Conducted policy and procedure review against industry bench marks.
- Developed a project management framework for internal staff to assist in engagements.
- Led and facilitated revenue assurance projects for various clients the resulted in $1.2 million dollars in billable revenue.
- Trained Six Sigma Green Belts and reviewed Black Belt projects.
- Coached and mentored Green Belts and Black Belts.

123 Learning Avenue
Anycity, Anystate
10101
555-999-1212

ALICE J. JOHNSTON, ABCP

XYZ Asset Management Corporation
Senior Manager-Client Services   March 2001–Sept 2001

- Successfully completed a process review for two separate call centers.
- Reengineered call center processes for greater efficiency and decreased resolution time for Advisor issues.
- Developed internal Service Level agreements to support the new processes implemented.
- Developed a Training Manual for new associates Operation wide.
- Developed a management reporting system for Operations.
- Examined in-house products and conducted an in-depth cost analysis pertaining to our trading system.
- Developed quality control measures to sustain gains made through process improvements.
- Modified tracking system to meet user requirements.
- Reviewed and modified the scheduling model for both centers.

International Financial Data Services
Project Manager-Six Sigma   April 2000–March 2001

- Led Six Sigma project teams and mentored and developed Green Belts on the principles of the methodology.
- Developed, purposed, and facilitated process improvement strategies for the areas of Operations, Human Resources, and Learning and Development.
- Provided Senior Management with quarterly presentations on current projects and project findings.
- Implemented measurement systems reviews for pre-existing performance measures.
- Used statistical tools to effectively analyze the data collected and developed accurate process improvements.
- Identified and implemented best practices based on benchmarking industry leaders.

International Financial Data Service
Fund Liaison   Dec 1999–April 2000

- First point of contact for our International Client.
- Dealt with and resolved escalated issues by the client and liased with internal departments and vendors to find remedies.
- Maintained an accurate log of all inquires and issues for management reporting.
- Designed and developed monthly performance reports for clients.
- Responsible for all Ad Hoc requests and provided clients with information regarding system enhancements.

References upon Request

Anycity, Ontario
Nov. 1996 to June 1998

PROCESS ENGINEER SIX SIGMA: Director, Process Eng.

John Johnston (999) 555-1212

123 Learning Street, Anytown, USA 10101 johnj@yourname.com

PROFILE
Organizational alignment: Lean Management, Six Sigma (January 2004) E-Business certified, communication, knowledge transfer, performance improvement and redesign, sales development

AREAS OF EXPERTISE

- Over seven years of experience in project management and directing change leadership, performance improvement programs for large-scale engagements in various industries. Focus is with strategic change integration planning and implementation, communications strategy and design, organization and job impact, communication strategy and execution, executive alignment and sponsorship, project team training, capability transfer program development, business readiness assessment.

- **Organization Effectiveness/Program and Project Management**: *Extensive use of continuous improvement tools (lean, Six Sigma) and business process improvement*. Balanced Scorecard; business case development; process redesign.

- **Change management:** Leadership alignment, train the trainers, communication, skill matrix, gap analysis, org. redesign.

WORK HISTORY AND ACCOMPLISHMENTS

BIG CONSULTING COMPANY   July 2000– present

Director, Process Strategy and Operations

Managed teams of consultants in the implementation of new performance solutions. Developed new accounts. Developed methodologies and tools.
LEAN and Pull system: Analysis of manufacturing capabilities and business process improvement. Strategic manufacturing alignment using Enterprise Level Lean Methodology (Modeling, corporate and business level consolidation, manufacturing strategy). Business process reengineering and asset plant maintenance–TPM, Preventive maintenance. *Business Case development*. Strategic alignment: corporate and business level. Balanced Scorecard. Performance management.

Program management: Led teams of clients and consultants in the development of change management program for large, global organizations.

- Set up program management office (PMO), including tools, resources, communications, coaching, planning, and budgets. Led global deployment teams, responsible for changes to processes and roles, training, communications, and support. Supported multiple projects and team leads in project and team management.

Change leadership and process reengineering: For various clients, led change management and process improvement for procurement/sourcing, operations and maintenance, and field office processes. Developed client print and gap analysis.

- Led process redesign teams distributed across core processes, resulting in integrated, rationalized, process flows across the organization.

- Managed redesign of process, organization structure, supporting technology, and job design for global leaders. Conducted analysis of existing processes, redesigned processes and roles, implemented supporting organization structure, identified opportunities to optimize technology utilization.

- Managed definition of organization redesign options. Conducted analysis of existing organization structure and interviewed senior management; synthesized findings into assessment of current organization structure and culture; conducted root-cause analysis of current organization structure and culture; presented assessment during facilitated redesign session, and assisted with facilitation of organization redesign session; developed and implemented structural and cultural improvements.

Change management: Created a centralized change management group to drive the smooth implementation of the changes. The group was created to provide subject matter expertise in change execution, learning and education, behavioral measurement and metrics, and communication. Developed a change management Toolkit as a consistent foundation of tools and knowledge from which to drive change within the business units.
In addition, the team developed and/or implemented the following:

- **Change Management Roadmap** – A guide to when and with whom each of the tools should be used.
- **Change Readiness Assessment** – A survey tool to determine the business unit's preparedness for the impending changes.
- **Maturity Model** – An assessment tool to measure progress of the organization as it moves from awareness to adoption.
- **Communication Strategy and Plan** – A structure to define overall communication objectives, key messages, communication channels, and timing of communications.
- **Training Strategy and Implementation Plan** – A tool to define overall training objectives, required capability, education channels, and timing of education.
- **Capability Transfer Strategy and Individual Capability Transfer Plan** – A tool to ensure capability was shared across the change management group with the work streams and business units. Change accomplished through targeted measurements.

John Johnston (Continued)   Page 2

BIG PAPER COMPANY INC.   **1998–June 2000**
North American leading company in the sales, marketing, and manufacturing of fine paper, packaging, and forest products with annual sales of $7 billion U.S.

Project Manager, Organization Effectiveness and Performance

- Implemented continuous improvement approach throughout the organization (24 plants) on productivity improvement.
- Reduced lead-time, inventory, and non-value activities.
- Standardization of work processes.

HOMECARE WORLD   **1990–1998**
Worldwide leader in the sales, marketing, and manufacturing of leading brands (Cleaner, Scrubber, Waxer, Lifer) for the household and industrial cleaning markets.

Distributor (Assistant, Area Vice President)   **1993–1998**
Revitalized the entire sales, customer service, and marketing function with emphasis on organization alignment. Developed and delivered management training in effective leadership and in market and competitive analysis.

HIGHLIGHTS:

- Achieved market penetration in excess of company objective.
- Identified and implemented performance measurement systems for customer service, product development and distribution, and developed monitoring solutions. Scorecard.
- Introduced Business Process Improvement in reducing deliveries, inventory levels; as well as proactive strategic planning.

Director of Training   **1990–1993**

- Trained and developed the distributors' sales force on specific products and applications. Developed training programs in organizational development.
- Developed and adapted training programs and customer service.

Account Manager: Achieved outstanding growth in my region, recovered $2M loss; managed the third largest distributor relationship in U.S.

EDUCATION:

> **School of Business, State University**   **1995**
> Master Subject: Organizational Fit. Configurations and Performance. Decision
> and Operations.   **(MSc)**

> **State University**
> Bachelor of Science and Public Administration   **(BSc)**   **1986**

TRAINING:

- Six Sigma Black Belt – Big Consulting Company (January 2004)
- E-Business certification
- Hyperion software – balanced scorecard and performance management
- Fluent in English and Spanish. Excel, MS Project, Visio, PowerPoint, Project Management

OTHER ACTIVITIES: Currently President of SU Network for Anytown (Alumni Association).
Member, Historical Society. Speaking at conferences and seminars regarding process improvement (More Research Institute).
Hockey pick up games, history buff, DIY house improver.

PRODUCT DEVELOPMENT & LAUNCH: New Product Manufacturing

John J. Johnston

123 Learning St., Anytown, USA 10101
Cell phone: (999) 555-1313 / Home phone: (999) 555-1212
email: johnj@yourname.com

Profile

Product Manager and Application Engineer who excels at introducing new products into manufacture. Also have strengths in planning and implementing strategies to improve and enhance performance and profitability. Manages reports with respect and motivates through tapping into each employee's passions and drives.

Summary of Qualifications

- More than ten years of experience in the Electronic and Electro-mechanical fields, in Automotive & Manufacturing
- Excellent capabilities in Program Management and Application Engineering/Technical Sales
- International, large-scale Project Management/Sales Management which involved frequent travel to countries including Germany, England, Hong Kong, and China
- Proficient in manufacturing software like Comet Top, MFG/PRO, XPPS and SAP
- Knowledge of QS-9000, ISO-9000, ISO-14001, and TS-16949. Fluent in Spanish and some German (30 percent)

Professional Experience

Sales Manager/Application Engineer ABC **2003 to 2005**
ABC manufactures electric precision harnesses and electro-mechanical assemblies for DC electric motors. Processes: Plastic over molding, Electro-welding, Laser-welding, High-speed wire cutting, E-Testing, Automatic & Manual Assembly. Reported to CFO with four departments reporting to me.

- Promoted business opportunities with current and new automotive clients for Electro-Mechanical products.
- Led and/or actively participated in cross-functional project teams. Responsible for the project execution within the concept defined in the proposal phase. Generate of detailed Gantt-Chart and follow-up with all tasks of a custom manufacturing-type project (design, purchasing, installation, start-up, and production), to ensure timely completion within budget and satisfying quality requirements according to QS-9000 and ISO-14001 standards.
- Managed programs from RFQ to PPAP: Interface with customers to analyze the design, application, and development of the new and/or existing custom-made products; Confirm customer requests and propose possible solutions by active coordination with the engineering department, production personal, and top management; Provide to internal departments BOM, Drawings/Sketches for quotation and negotiation; Quotation & Negotiation; Perform Technical as well as Commercial Presentations to the customers; Coordinate the assembly and delivery of samples for Prototypes purpose, Test and Approval processes; Main contact for customer requests and the coordination of customer engineering design changes, production program changes, and material requirements.
- Continuous search for new component suppliers to negotiate prices and conditions for our customers as an effort of Continuous Improvement (Cost-reduction). Responsible for purchase orders and prices administration.

Project Leader/Product Engineer Blerb Innovations **2000 to 2003**
Blerb Innovations design and manufacture Telephony Consumer Products. Processes: Plastic Injection, Printing of plastics, Electronic Assembly: Solder paste printing; Glue application; High-speed SMD Automatic assembly; Re-flow oven; Automatic insertion for axial and radial components; Manual insertion; Wave-soldering; E-Testing. Design: PCB's; Firmware; Software; Industrial Design of new products; Design and constructions of Injection molds. I reported to the New Product Introduction Manager and had four departments reporting to me.

- Led introduction to Manufacture Project from kick-off meeting to SOP and first delivery.
- Involved in the development of new products providing feedback to Design and Marketing areas to improve manufacture performance and productivity. Generation of Gantt Charts and follow-up with all the tasks of a manufacturing-type project (purchasing, design, installation, start-up, and production) to ensure timely completion within budget and satisfying quality requirements according to ISO-9000 and ISO-14001 standards.
- Loaded in Computerized System BOM to share with internal areas (Purchasing, Material, Manufacture, Testing, etc.)
- Coordinated purchasing and delivery of components and raw material according of Launch program (Prototypes, Engineering samples, Approval run trail, and Production programs).
- Coordinated of: Design and construction of E-Testing Fixtures and Software; Technical changes; Continued improvement of manufacturing processes to reach reductions in time and cost.

Program Manager **ZIPPY Automotive** **1999 to 2000**

ZIPPY Automotive designs and manufactures Electronic Control Modules for the automotive industry. Processes: Electronic Assembly: Solder paste printing; Glue application; High speed SMD Automatic assembly; Re-flow oven; Manual insertion; Wave-soldering; Mechanical assembly; E-Testing.

- Led multidisciplinary project team with the responsibility to introduce into Manufacturing of Automotive Electronic Control Modules. Guaranteed the project execution within the concept defined in the proposal phase. Assured products met internal as well as customer specifications. Liaised with customer Engineers Technical Changes and with customer Logistic area Delivery Program Changes during Mass Production.
- Responsible for generation of detailed Gantt chart and follow-up, with all tasks of a custom manufacturing type-project (design, purchasing, production, installation, and start-up), to ensure timely completion within authorized budget and under quality requirements according to QS-9000 standard.
- Coordinated Continued Improvement activities in Manufacturing Process to reduce cost.
- Responsible for on-time deliveries coordinating sea/air freights. Ensured friendly and efficient relations with customers as well as the satisfaction of our services. Hired and managed necessary human resources for the project.
- Responsible of one chapter of Internal Quality System according QS-9000 standard.

Technical Sales Unit Manager **XYZ Company** **1994 to 1999**

XYZ designs and manufactures Electronics and Electro-mechanics (Mechatronics) products for the automotive industry. Processes: Design and construction of Injection Molds and Stamping Dies; Plastic Injection; Insert Injection; Overmolding Injection; Electric welding; Ultra-sonic welding; Automatic insertion for axial and radial components; Manual assembly; Wave-soldering; E-Testing.

- Promoted business opportunities with current and new automotive clients for Electronic and Electro-Mechanical products.
- Managed programs from RFQ to PPAP: Interface with customers to analyze the design, application, and development of the new and/or existing custom-made products; Confirm customer requests and propose possible solutions by active coordination with the development/engineering department, manufacture personal and Top Management; Provide to internal departments BOM, Drawings/Sketches for quotations and negotiations; Quotations; Negotiations; Technical Presentation to the customers; Coordinate the assembly and delivery of samples for Prototypes purpose, Test and Approval processes; Main contact for customer requests and the coordination of customer technical changes, production program changes and material requirements.
- Administrated of Purchase Orders and Prices. Collaborating in Forecast and Sales Plan issues.
- Coordinated many projects at the same time for big clients such as American Car, European Big Car, Asian Car, with the last one being an example of my dedication since I improved the percentage of NAFTA content, reduced costs, reduced imports by 70%, and at the same time turned our company around to become profitable in a matter of a year.
- Generated new business for our company by landing contracts with difficult clients who'd been impossible to sell to in the past, such as European Car where we sold our alarm systems for most of their vehicles.

Education and Training

BSc Engineering Degree in Electronics (SU) 1994

- Local Area Networks-LAN ; Telecommunications through optical fiber (UNAM) 1991
- QFD-Quality Function Deployment (ITESM) 1992
- Effectiveness Project Administration (Technology Training) 1993
- Time Administration Program (SolutionsInc.) 1993
- Statistics Process Control (ABC) 2002

PRODUCT DEVELOPMENT & LAUNCH: Product Manager Computer Product

John J. Johnston – Product Manager
123 Learning Street, Anytown, USA 10101   (999) 555-1212

Technology Marketing   Consumer Products   Marketing Communications

---

Product Manager, Home Computer products, X Software LLC
June 1999–Present

Responsible for all domestic and international marketing strategy, retail planning, and execution for HappyGreetings, Home Computer Publishing, and Home Publishing Premium products. Responsible for product messaging, packaging, PR strategy, SKU management, product promotion, and Web.

Achievements

- Effectively executed long lead and short lead PR tours at product launch—improved weekly PR reporting process tools by creating master schedules and easier to follow planning documentation
- Working with channel team to ensure that channel programs are executed and products are well stocked throughout holiday times; hit optimized levels of product each Christmas season
- Launched new At-Home Program product across North America with penetration in all markets (radio, TV, print) to a "**Best Ever**" launch of a new product
- Launched international product localizations for France and Germany

Worldwide Product Marketing Manager, X Software Geography products
May 1997–June 1999

Responsible for worldwide finished goods, including domestic products and international.

Achievements

- Zippy Streets/Trip Planner Value bundle achieved #1 publisher status (from #4) in December 98. We are #1 in Great Britain and France
- Developed product positioning, PR key messages, and new for Streets & Trips 2000; updated packaging for 2000 editions in Europe
- Developed all domestic and international sales collateral materials—demo scripts (internal and external) reviewer's guides, fact sheets, etc.
- Achieved leverage in WinCE group—Streets & Trips 2000 benefited from $2.5+ million awareness campaign at not cost
- Seasoned agency experience—work with variety of vendors for PR agency, Web marketing, advertising, and promotions

Product Manager, X Software LLC
June 1995–June 1997

Clients: Kids, Personal Interest, Creativity, DreamCreator
Responsible for all facets of product management including demand generation, channel tools, public relations, and measurement programs.

Achievements

- FY97 Holiday portfolio marketing program—promotion
- FY97 Back to School Distribution promotion
- NT Workstation national advertising program
- Phase II customer loyalty program execution, fulfillment, and measurement
- Created a National PR gaming tournament in colleges and universities

February 1994–June 1995

Marketing Communications Manager, X Software

Advertising, Direct Marketing, Loyalty Program, Measurement
Competitive tracking, Research, Event Recommendation, Media analysis
North American Synergy responsibility, U.S. collateral management in Canada

Achievements

- Product PR, execution, and measurement for Microsoft Home consumer products
- Manage outside agency vendor relationships and internal processes to ensure effective execution of program components (advertising, public relations, database management, customer profiling, fulfillment, and program measurement)
- Leading the North American Synergy program for connections between key products and partnerships; buy in from all major partners

Account Supervisor, Smith & Smith, LLC   December 1992–February 1994

Achievements

- Key contact/manager of advertising projects in agency
- Led in communication recommendations, creative development, and project supervision of team members
- Two days per week on-site at Copies, Inc. developing national and district programs with managers
- International responsibilities include establishing/maintaining information network with S&S offices in South East Asia, Hong Kong, and Americas
- Developed reviews for Copies, Inc. international network—key liaison with S&S NY.

FDR Advertising Inc., Account Executive   June 1986–June 1991

Education

October 95/96	Spanish Language Studies, State University
July 94	Advanced Direct Marketing, State University
March 94/95	Worldwide Direct Marketing Workshops
October 93	Creative Strategy Workshop
March 93	Supervisor's Workshop
1986–1989	Certified Advertising Agency Practitioner Designation, Institute of American Advertisers
1983–1986	Diploma of Advertising Studies, State College of Applied Arts & Technology

Affiliations and memberships
Professional Photographer's Network

Interests
Photography—nature, faces, and especially underwater; scuba diving; organic gardening

PRODUCT DEVELOPMENT & LAUNCH: Senior Product Manager

JOHN J. JOHNSTON

123 Learning St., Anytown, ST, USA 10101 * Home: (999) 555-1212 * johnj@yourname.com

---

Senior Marketing and Product Manager
With nearly 10 years experience in
• **Start-up & High Growth Companies** • **Internet** • **New Product Development**

Experience includes

Market & competitive analysis	Product strategy and roadmap
Market requirements	Product lifecycle management
Positioning and messaging	Marketing communications
Channel management	Public speaking and training

1. **A product strategist and key member of the marketing team** with extensive knowledge of new product and market development.

2. **A participative manager who builds consensus** and brings strong organization, communication skills, and a logical decision-making process to solving problems.

3. **A proven team leader and troubleshooter** with highly developed analytical, organizational, and strategic planning skills.

4. **A manager that embraces fast-paced and emerging businesses** with a proven track record in both private and public companies.

BIGBASE SOFTWARE (NASDAQ: BBSW)   1998–Present
Senior Product Manager
Senior product manager responsible for developing and executing strategy for e-service suite of products. Reports to Senior VP of Product Management.

- **Full product management responsibility** for "All Base Communication Server" *(a suite of customer relationship applications for email Management, Live Collaboration, and Outbound email Campaign Management)*, and "E-service Analytics."
- Worked closely with engineering—from product concept to launch—to develop functional and design specifications, make technology decisions, and manage project timelines.
- Negotiated legal and financial aspects of third party license and OEM technology agreements.
- Bigbase agreed to merge with Brains Communications (NASDAQ: Brains) April 2001.

Quasi-soft Inc. (Acquired by Bigbase in 2003)
- **Managed all aspects of product management** for three products: *EmailContact, LiveContact,* and *Campaign.* Developed and launched new products in highly competitive market.
- Instrumental in winning major accounts including Big Bank, Mobile Phone, S&S Inc.
- Filled in for CEO and represented company as speaker and discussion panelist at many analyst and industry events such as Internet World, CTExpo, CRM Expo.
- Managed the collection, analysis, and distribution of competitive and market intelligence. Presented regularly to CEO, senior executives, and sales force.
- **Awarded Quasi-soft *Outstanding Achievement* award.**

JOHN J. JOHNSTON

123 Learning St., Anytown, ST, USA 10101 * Home: (999) 555-1212 * johnj@yourname.com

SoSoft Technologies, Inc. (Merged with Bigbase 1999)
- In a startup environment, handled product management, marketing, and communications for *EmailContact* product.
- Worked closely with engineering and managed entire product lifecycle—from product inception, to business case, requirements gathering, through development and market launch.

JESSICA INTERNET SERVICE   1996–1998
Business Manager
Managed dial-up and high-speed (DSL) Internet Service with revenues of more than $10 Million.

- Created and executed strategy for emerging Internet protocol applications and services.
- Initiated, developed business plan, and successfully launched small business Internet access and hosting service including local content and directory website.
- Managed staff of two. Hired, trained, and developed marketing and product management personnel.

Marketing Manager
- Key member of the management team that **grew the business from start-up phase to largest and fastest growing provider** in the state.
- From scratch, set up and managed VAR and reseller distribution channel accounting for more than **80% of sales after year one**.
- Managed relationships with outside creative, research and promotions agencies.

WEST CORPORATION   1995–1996
Sales and Marketing Associate

- **Excelled as a top sales representative** with the second highest closing percentage in the company.
- Significantly **increased sales efficiency and closing percentage** through initiation and implementation of an Internet-based sales contact and follow-up system. The system was adopted as the standard for all sales teams North America wide.

BIG BULL & ASSOCIATES   1992–1995
Founded Design/Build construction firm generating $250,000 in sales by year three.
- Year over year **sales growth of greater than 250 percent.**
- Managed entire design and construction process—from client needs assessment and concept development, to working plans, permits, and construction project management.
- Negotiated and contracted with numerous subcontractors and suppliers.

EDUCATION
Executive and Professional Development:
Social Style/Producing Results with Others, ListenGroup (2000)
Leadership Management International (2000)
Practical Product Management, Pragmatic Marketing Inc. (1999)
SU Continuing Studies (1996-98)

History BA, State University (1992)

PUBLISHING: Director of Sales

ALICE J. JOHNSTON

123 LEARNING ST. • ANYTOWN • USA • 10101 • PHONE: 999-555-1212
CELL: 999-555-1313 • EMAIL: ALICEJ@YOURNAME.COM

INTRODUCTION:

I am a client-focused, relationship-passionate Director of Sales with an exceptional ability to use creativity, mentoring, and leadership to deliver win-win solutions to grow business.

ACHIEVEMENTS:

- Have developed sales kits, presentations, and databases to launch several new media businesses, both online and offline. I also introduced these businesses to top advertising agencies as well as to clients across a variety of platforms and demographics from students, to small business professionals, to the pharmaceutical and elder-care categories; in all cases bringing new revenue streams to life.

- Created the business model into the commuter newspaper market. Recruited, hired, and trained my team of sixteen and delivered over One Million Dollars in net revenue within five months. (Big City Today)

- Conceived the business plan for a brand extension for *Big Life Magazine* – the **AnyCity Services**. Managed this plan from conception to reality— delivering the second most successful brand extension in the history of the magazine.

- Created several multimedia sponsorships and partnerships to grow business for clients via the **Big Life, AnyCity Services,** and several sponsored and partnered events in the city. I was able to grow revenue for our business, as well as raise money for partnered non-profit organizations.

- Created the concept of Multimedia (Convergence) sales for **Big Media Inc**. I delivered on that idea, resulting in a brand new and extremely profitable department for **Big Media Inc**. Conceived and sold the first ever multimedia program in Anystate, including print, broadcast, and online media properties for just short of one million dollars. Renewed this program for over Three Million Dollars by its third year.

- Web-business savvy, I built the business plan and then launched **Electric Bookshop USA**, an online resource for elementary and midlevel students and teachers. This is a subscription based, online library targeted to schools, school boards, and governments. I hired and trained the sales team and delivered revenues in excess of expectations.

PROFESSIONAL EXPERIENCE:

Business Development and Marketing Consultant: January 2001–present
Business Development consulting, contract publishing, developing databases, presentations, media kits, sales programs as well as strategic business plans to deliver revenue for **ABC Communications**, **XYZ Capital, Microsoft Network, The Decision, Everyday Consumer Health Care.**

Vice President Sales & Marketing: May 2000–November 2000
Big City Today a division of **Camp Newspapers Ltd**. - Developed the revenue plan for the hired team of sixteen to execute the advertising sales for **Today**, delivering $1 million (net revenue) in just five months.

Advertising Director & Associate Publisher: March 1998–April 2000
BigLife Magazine - Managed a National and Retail sales team of ten. Attained strenuous revenue targets in a tough media marketplace. Conceived the revenue plan and executed the launch of the **Anycity Services**—the second largest brand launch in the magazine's history.

Director of Sales: 1993–1998
Electric Bookshop USA - Developed the sales plan, then hired/trained sales team to launch this brand new service in Canada; **Account Manager**: Highest achieving account manager for two years consecutively.

Account Manager: 1989–1993
The Easy Reader Inc. - Winner of several awards including the Chairman's Cup for outstanding sales and creative solutions.

Director Advertising Sales, Account Manager: 1987–1989
MyCity Magazine

Director Advertising Sales, Account Manager: 1979–1987
Trade and Consumer publications.

EDUCATION:

State University
- Honors BA - 1975–1979

VOLUNTEER EXPERIENCE:

Wanapao Boys & Girls Clubs – Member of the Corporate Opportunities Group to raise funding for this amazing support club since September 2003.

Arts Council Anytown – Member Executive Committee & Board of Directors since 1999. Actively involved in both fund raising and marketing to raise both support and profile for the arts in our city.

Perspectives – A corporate organized art exhibition in support of women's and children's shelters in Anytown–Advisory Board Member since 1998.

Special Olympics – Fundraising and event assistance.

Paraplegic Association – Put together relay team raising over $10,000.

PUBLISHING: BAD—Publishing and Entertainment Account Executive

ALICE J. JOHNSTON
E-MAIL: ALICEJ@YOURNAME.COM 123 LEARNING ST. ANYTOWN USA 10101
(999) 555.1212

Publishing and Entertainment Account Executive – Cheerful, bright, and 100% dedicated to team success.

EXPERIENCE

ABB Entertainment   March 2004 – Present
Account Executive, East Coast

- Worked as part of a two-person sales team that earned 1st place sales award for 4th Quarter and 2nd place award for 2004 annual Consumer Sales
- Strategize with major agencies –as well as direct clients – to develop advertising opportunities that align with their campaign objectives and goals
- Implement and execute integrated unique sponsorship for clients such as Huge Cola Beverage company
- Provide analysis and optimization reports to improve performance for active campaigns
- Manage day to day contact for agencies and clients
- Monitor campaign reporting to ensure ABB could recognize full revenue from current campaigns

Edge   October 2002 - March 2004
Media Strategist

- Responsible for daily maintenance of Copy Inc, Big Batteries Inc. and Far CountryTourism online advertising campaigns.
- Prepare and present media plan and analyses to clients.
- Plan, negotiate and purchase online media placements for Copy Inc's products.
- Implement and negotiate unique, cost effective media opportunities.
- Analyze and optimize campaigns on a daily & weekly basis to ensure campaign success.
- Responsible for trafficking and tracking all campaigns thru DoubleClick's DART and Atlas DMT.
- Analyze media data to provide weekly reports and post analyses to clients.

XYZ Magazine   May 2001 – Sept 2002
Sales Coordinator

- Coordinate and support the work of 3 sales people, including Associate Publisher.
- Create and distribute monthly Newsletter with circulation
- Assisted Creative Director in the XYZ mannequin presentation, booth, and video wall at MAGIC 2002.
- Create proposals for clients and track insertion orders for weekly issues.
- Organize and update ACT database.

EDUCATION

1996 - 2000   State University
BA, Communications. Financed 70% of college education through sports scholarship.

SKILLS

Proficient with Excel, PowerPoint, DART, Atlas DMT, @ [...] Solbright

---

What's Wrong?
- Too much wasted space
- No accomplishments or specific and measurable results
- Too many bullet points
- Spelling, grammatical, or word choice errors

John J. Johnston

123 Learning St., Anytown, USA 10101   Home: 999-555-1212 – Mobile: 999-555-1313
Email: JohnJ@yourname.com

PROFILE: A technology literate **Publisher** with marketing and operational experience. An experienced sales coach and mentor. A hunter and closer. A strong relationship builder and champion of teamwork who is flexible and resourceful with the knowledge to thrive in an increasingly convergent business world.

EMPLOYMENT HISTORY

Big Man Publications, National Sales Manager   **Jan 2004 to Present**
Hired on contract by a start up publication to develop a strategy to sell advertising to national accounts for a group of regional retail magazines targeting the baby boomer demographic. Easy LifeStyles is published in six regions reaching 217,000 Anystate homes. Local retail advertising makes up 75 percent of the revenue.
Accomplishments
- Advised name change of magazine to better represent the demographic.
- Introduced new editorial features to broaden the advertising base.
- Prepared proposals and edited sales letters for sales reps.
- Sold retail and national accounts into magazines.

Media Boxes Communications, Associate Publisher/Director of Sales   **Oct 2001 to Dec 2003**
Hired on contract to publish and sell advertising for two business publications, plus booth space for one b2b trade show.
Accomplishments
- Increased ad sales in *Office Life* by introducing new ad formats.
- After one year was given additional responsibility as Director of Sales for Builder & Renovator Expo.
- Increased sales for *Builder* by 20 percent over 2002 show.

BBB Industrial Communications, Publisher and major shareholder   **1993 to 2000**
(Joint venture with premiere publishing company)
Published two b2b magazines and one Internet site. *New Equipment News* and *The Publisher's Book* and **stop.com**.
New Equipment News is a product tabloid serving the Industrial market. As publisher, I managed a large sales territory, a staff of six, and a contract sales team of eight sales agents throughout the United States.
Accomplishments
- Took a money losing publication and within two years showed a profit by increasing sales while lowering costs.
- Increased ad revenue year after year.
- For seven years I grew market share and competed against two of America's largest b2b publishing companies.
The Publisher's Book & **stop.com** was a compendium of advertising rates and data with market focused editorial. Stop.com was a dynamic interactive website with advertising rates and data on American media options.
Accomplishments:
- Developed a hybrid publication from conception to launch.
- Created three national editions serving different market segments. Daily newspapers, television, and the Internet.
- Initiated an online interactive research system with ComQUEST, an industry research company.
- Designed and created an online data mining system to collect more accurate data at a greatly reduced cost.
Result: At height of company success, I sold my shares to my partner.

Ports Incorporated, Sales Rep to Group Publisher, Construction Information Group 1985 to 1993
Group Publisher
Directed a staff of 25 publishers, editors, & sales people with responsibility for operation of seven b2b publications.
Accomplishments
- Developed and launched a cross-market publication focusing on energy management that generated 63 percent profit.
- In 1992 I won Ports' most profitable revenue generating idea award.
- Relaunched a money-losing magazine and within two years took it from losing $280,000 annually to making a profit.
Advertising Sales Rep to Publisher
- Year one - As a sales rep, exceeded budget expectations first year and was promoted to Advertising Sales Manager.
- Year two - Sales team exceeded publication sales budget, was promoted to Associate Publisher.
- Year three - Exceeded sales budget, lowered operating costs, and increased profit, promoted to Publisher.
- Year four - Exceeded sales budget, lowered operating costs, and increased profit. Promoted to Group Publisher, newly formed Construction Information Group.

EDUCATION: BA (Industrial Sociology)   State University
CONTINUING EDUCATION: State University - Macro Economics
Ports Inc. - Numerous courses and seminars in leadership, sales management, general management, conflict resolution, succession planning, strategic planing, circulation strategies, print production, and magazine layout.
PERSONAL INTERESTS: Keeping abreast of various publishing and Internet initiatives—looking for the next breakthrough; reading (of course) a variety of books and magazines; training to run a marathon this year.

PUBLISHING: Editorial Assistant

ALICE J. JOHNSTON

123 Learning Avenue, 1A • Anycity, Anystate• 10101
(home) 555.999.1212 • (work) 555.999.1414 ext. 111 alicej@yourname.com

PROFILE

Editorial Coordinator/Assistant Editor with both non-fiction and fiction experience. Great at author relations—keeping them happy and on deadline. Detail-oriented and excels at schedule-making and tweaking.

EXPERIENCE

Readingbooks, Inc.   Anycity, AS   Feb 2004–current
Assistant Editor/Editorial Coordinator
• Create and maintain editorial schedules for 140 titles.
• Set deadlines for manuscripts and help to develop titles.
• Copyedit and proofread manuscripts, book covers, publicity press materials, and marketing projects.
• Communicate with authors to discuss editorial changes and direction of manuscripts.
• Compile and edit the trade and gift catalogs.
• Update the company to changing book specifications on a weekly basis.
• Serve as a liaison to production, publicity, and sales.
• *Promoted from Editorial Assistant to Assistant Editor in October 2004.*

Readingbooks, Inc.   Anycity, AS   Oct 2002–Jan 2004
Production Coordinator
• Bid and awarded marketing, sales, publicity, and trade show projects to the most cost-effective print vendor.
• Generated schedules for and monitored the progress of projects from design stages to final printed product.
• Fulfilled demand for titles by bidding out and scheduling reprints.

EDUCATION

State University at Anycity, ST   2002
• B.A., English with a focus in advertising.
• GPA: 3.55 on a 4.0 scale.

ADDITIONAL KNOWLEDGE

Computer programs: QuarkXpress, Photoshop, Illustrator, Microsoft Office (Excel, Word, and Project), FileMaker Pro, Acumen.

FAVORITE BOOKS/AUTHORS READ THIS YEAR: Anything by David Sederis; *Obliviously on He Sails*; *The World Is Flat*; *Never Let Me Go*; *Pride & Prejudice*; The Philip Pullman series.

Alice J. Johnston
123 Learning Street, Anycity, AS 10101
555.999.1212   alicej@yourname.com

EXPERIENCE:

| **Mass Media Corporation** | **Anycity, AS** | **May 2000 to Present** |

9/2003 to Present

Senior Editor

- Developed and launched 3 new imprints/series in the last four months, which significantly improved profit margins.
  - Created logos, names, vision, and focus.
  - Worked with parent company's existing content and other divisions to streamline the process.
  - Constantly researching the marketplace needs and adjusting efforts accordingly.
- Led new product development committee with parent company editorial department.
- Expert in repurposing existing content to bring it to the marketplace with a new look and feel.
- Negotiated all new contracts with an average savings of 26 percent below budget.

3/2003 to 9/2003

Acquisitions Editor

- In charge of all aspects of acquiring and developing Anything Brand.
- Acquired over 30 titles during this six-month period.
- Under my direction, Anything Book brand grew 44 percent in retail sales since 12/2001.
- Developed marketplace relationships and research analysis to maximize success of new products.
- Developed new profitable subset brands in the ANYTHING series.
  - Parent's Guides
  - Breed Specific pet series
- Created successful series marketing materials that had a direct impact on sales and marketing efforts.
- Headed the brand growth initiatives for the ANYTHING KIDS' series which resulted in a 28 percent increase in sales.

12/2001 to 3/2003

Associate Acquisitions Editor

- Acquired over 30 series titles per year.
- Developed a working publishing strategy, vision, and schedule for acquiring the ANYTHING KIDS' series.
- Top research skills used in extensive market analysis to compile new series title ideas.
- Flexible enough to acquire titles for alternative markets while continuing to champion titles in the trade.
- Set deadlines, reviewed manuscripts for acceptability, and served as contact between author, agent, and publisher.

3/2001 to 12/2001

Project Editor, Series Acquisitions

- Acquired over 30 series titles during this period. Negotiated contracts, set deadlines, and served as primary contact between author and publisher. Prepared manuscripts for production, guiding books through the production process.

5/2000 to 3/2001

Editorial Assistant/Associate Development Editor

- Conducted thorough review of accepted manuscripts. Worked closely with authors and acquisitions editors to shape and develop manuscripts to adhere to series tone, style, length, and overall vision. Reorganized manuscripts, line edited, proofread, and engaged in extensive rewriting.

EDUCATION: Bachelor of Arts in Mass Media and English, 1999

9/1995 to 5/1999   **Capistrano College**   Anycity, AS

- Major in English, Minor in Sociology
- Promotions director and on-air talent for RMU, Capistrano College radio.
- Capistrano College Public Relations office by writing press releases, writing copy for the College Website, and working closely with the staff to coordinate photo shoots and charity events.

9/1997 to 12/1997   **University of State**   Anycity, AS

- Intensive study of English course work, culture, and history.
- Lived with a diverse group of students and built intercultural communication skills.

PURCHASING: Material and Logistics Manager

John J. Johnston, P.Eng.

(999)555-1212   johnj@yourname.com

Materials and Global Logistics Manager

- ♦ Six Sigma & 'Lean' Trained (pursuing Blackbelt)
- ♦ Restructured 3 organizations
- ♦ Expert at process improvement work
- ♦ Proven track record of delivering cost savings
- ♦ Completed SAP & Oracle implementations

- ♦ State University Engineering graduate
- ♦ Experience in 4 industries
- ♦ Manager with Big Electricity, ABC, XYZ
- ♦ Project manager in corporate & volunteer environments
- ♦ Significant strategic planning experience

Materials & Global Logistics Manager

Big Electricity Inc. (Power Management industry)   July 2002 to Present

Key responsibilities: Inventory strategy & management of 2 businesses; Forecasting
Develop materials and distribution models; Manage all material transition plans for headquarters
Day-to-day shipping, receiving, warehousing, & distribution management for headquarters
Transportation & distribution strategy for division (4 plants: 2 in USA, 1 in Canada, 1 in Europe)

- Created inventory strategy & targets; reduced active inventory by 50%, doubled turns
- Developed new materials model for contract manufacturers; Changed supply & distribution model for inbound materials
- Implemented $200K savings in transportation in first 3 months
- Proposed & executed plan to save USD $1.2 million in transportation (focus: global)
- Created division's outbound and inbound freight policies
- Increased shipping throughput by 30%; Reduced receiving time by 50%
- Key team member in Six Sigma Blackbelt project to save $1 million through supplier transition
- Increased customs compliance by 70%; Created importer of record matrix for the business to assist shippers
- Selected & executed a 3 PL solution; Introduced new broker
- Managed execution of 3 hour/day reduction in shipping processing time; implemented in 6 weeks (focus: global)
- Introduced warehouse plan to increase current storage space by 40%

Operations Manager

ABC Furniture Group LLC   Oct 2001 to Feb 2002

Key responsibilities: Member of senior management team of this 65,000 ft^2 distribution center
Day-to-day customer service, operations, QC, logistics, safety & HR management
Manage 30 direct reports

- Implemented packaging project; the redesign was stronger, more efficient on the line and saved money throughout the supply chain (reduced cost of packaging by 40%, decreased cube in trailer & decreased storage requirements)
- Created staffing plans; Changed hiring & on-boarding process; Revamped pay practices
- Developed plan to increase efficiency, quality, and output of assembly operations
- Completed assessment & plan to improve utilization of warehouse space, increase picking rate, & decrease unloading time
- Introduced & rolled out process to evaluate employee performance
- Developed a safety program & safety training plan; initiated forklift certification program

Materials & Logistics Manager

XYZ Manufacturing LLC   Jan 2000 to Aug 2001

Key responsibilities: Day-to-day logistics, supply chain & materials management (300 raw materials worth $50 million)
Manage partnership with suppliers (100 global raw material vendors & 3 carriers)
Manage 9 direct reports and 32 indirect reports

- Team lead in North American project to save transportation costs & improve speed of distribution; project saved over $1 million & reduced transit time by 1 day; project received Division's Operations Excellence award
- Executed 3rd party mgt of raw materials; ↓ capital tied in inventory & ↑ operational flexibility (saved $250K)
- Introduced, developed, and rolled out process to evaluate supplier performance; planned & performed supplier audits
- Developed and implemented an internal quality information system (completed in 3 months)
- Optimized space utilization of warehouse by introducing racking, increasing current space utilization by 90%
- Leader of Six Sigma greenbelt project to simplify cross border shipping process; supervised 2 greenbelt projects

John J. Johnston, P.Eng.

(999)555-1212   page 2/2   johnj@yourname.com

Logistics Planning Manager
Big Paper Company   May 1997 to Jan 2000

Key responsibilities: Raw material & production planning ($150 million, 15 machines, 3 businesses)
Day-to-day inventory, capacity, deployment, contract manufacturing, & supplier management
Communication cross-functionally and to upper management
Manage 12 direct reports

- Project Manager for SAP Demand & Supply implementation (MM & PP modules); completed project in the shortest time & with the most successful startup in category; maintained current high levels of customer service through transition
- Reduced overtime (from 14% to <5%), inventory & cycle times (50% reduction in papermaking cycle time)
- Change management leader for MRPII integrated planning, achieved almost Class A rating in 6 months (streamlined work processes, increased cross functional communication, reduced rework, drove more accountability & ownership)
- Participated in setting site operating strategy; chaired site meetings; led cross functional teams
- Facilitated department teambuilding sessions; transitioned team to new work system

Category Supply Planner
Big Paper Company   May 1997 to May 1999

Key responsibilities: Develop 18-month American capacity & inventory plan
Resolve North American paper products supply chain issues
- Site leader at Sales & Operations Planning (S&OP) process (making business strategy and supply & demand decisions)
- Improved rough cut capacity planning (RCCP) analysis & what-if simulations

Quality Information System Manager
Big Paper Company   June 1996 to May 1997

Key responsibilities: Integrate & standardize site's Quality Window (QW) system
Comanage 12 reports (7 full time, 5 co-op students)
- Developed & implemented lab information system
- Completed design of site QW system & received buy-in from all key players
- Initiated & developed ergonomics action plan for safety in Quality Lab

COMMUNITY LEADERSHIP
Oct 2002 to Present   Vice Chair of Planning, Planning & Evaluation Portfolio

EDUCATION
Mar 2001 to Present   **Pursuing Certified Production & Inventory Management (CPIM) designation;** *APICS*
April 2000   **Professional Engineer (P.Eng.) designation**
Dec 1999   **Certificate in Intercultural Studies;** *State University*
May 1996   **Honors Co-op Bachelor of Applied Science in Systems Design Engineering;** *State University*

TRAINING
- Zenger Miller Leadership 2000
- Six Sigma Greenbelt training
- Dupont STOP program
- Zenger Miller Team Leadership
- Coaching/Mentoring
- SAP
- MRPII

- Lean Manufacturing
- Managing Employees
- U.S. Customs 101
- European Customs
- Communication Skills
- Providing Effective Feedback
- Systems Management

- Fundamentals of Purchasing
- Integrated Supply Management
- Supplier Development & Audit training
- Ergonomic Assessments
- Time & Stress Management
- Diversity Training
- Continuous Improvement

ASSOCIATIONS
Member of Professional Engineers
Member of Purchasing Management Association

PURCHASING: Purchasing Manager

John J. Johnston

123 Learning St., Anycity, Anystate 10101
Cellular: (555) 999-1212, Home: (555) 999-1313, johnj@yourname.com

Purchasing Manager known for company dedication and loyalty. Excellent at reducing purchasing costs and fostering morale through mentorship.

WORK EXPERIENCE

Purchasing Manager   1999–2003
ABC Autosport, Anycity, ST

- Manage sales accounts with extensive client contact
- Perform due diligence on new product lines
- Research, plan, and execute company strategy to counter competitors in industry
- Develop and implement corporate policies and procedures resulting in increased productivity

Accomplishments:

- Implement foreign currency-hedging program resulting in significant reduction of earnings volatility
- Authorize all purchases, handle bids, negotiate contract pricing, and carry out technical research resulting in increased inventory turnover by 67 percent
- Consolidate purchases resulting in substantial cost reduction and ability to finance 25 percent of purchases interest free
- **"Most Dedicated to the Success of the Company"** in 2002 in recognition of my dedication, perseverance, and contribution to profitability

Accounts Representative   1992–1999
Bay Credit & Financial Marketing Services, Anycity, ST

- Negotiate payment agreements with delinquent clients in a high-pressure environment
- Tabulate & analyze employee statistics
- Form & support corporate relationship with credit rating agencies, banks, and credit unions
- Assist with implementation and transition to a new computerized system

Accomplishments:

- Mentor for trainees
- **Employee of the Year** in 1995 in recognition of my spirit of initiative, flexibility, professionalism, enthusiasm, and devotion

EDUCATION

- **Certificate in German Studies, in progress**   2003
  University of Anystate, Anycity, ST

- **Bachelor of Arts, Economics**   1998
  Minor Equivalent in Business Studies
  State University, Anycity, ST

INTERESTS

Learning new languages; driving anywhere on the (open) highway; trying the latest video games.

LANGUAGES & COMPUTERS

Fluent in English, Spanish; Conversational in Arabic, German
Proficient in Excel, Access

PURCHASING: Sr. Procurement Manager

John J. Johnston

123 Learning St. • Anytown, USA 10101 • Home: 999-555-1212 • johnj@yourname.com

SENIOR PROCUREMENT MANAGER

With Expertise to Reduce Cost and Improve Supplier Quality, Performance, and Commitment

Dynamic, results-driven professional qualified by extensive experience, a broad-industry background, top-notch procurement knowledge with high caliber qualifications in the following key business areas:

Supply Chain Management	Surplus Equipment, Inventory, & Materials Recovery
Strategic Global Sourcing	Systems Integration
E-Commerce Integration	Market Analysis, Forecasting & Planning
Consortium Operations & Management	MRO & Capital Equipment

PROFESSIONAL EXPERIENCE

Purchasing Manager/Senior Buyer, WELL KNOWN PRODUCTS INC. 2003 to 2005

Aggressively researched and recommended cost savings possibilities based upon negotiations, new sources, substitutions, and continuous process improvement. Established and implemented standards programs for IT equipment, computer peripherals, facility services, lift trucks, office furniture, office supplies, office papers, cellular telephones, telecommunications, and forms. Negotiated capital equipment purchases for improved delivery, performance criteria, pricing, spare parts, start-up assistance, terms, and training.

1. Developed & administered various supplier bid seminars with full RFQ and performance criteria matrix.
2. Analyzed & evaluated bid quotations to assure quality, capabilities, service, & total cost of ownership.
3. Monitored appropriate market pricing and supply, and reported changes or conditions that could affect the company's procurement position.
4. Utilized AS400, Prism, and Microsoft Office 2000 software for daily procurement activities.
5. Participated as a cross-functional team member with Production Planning, Quality, Traffic, Engineering, Marketing, and Finance to ensure supplier service and delivery through effective communication and negotiation of objectives.
6. Developed MRO and raw material budget and established standard cost for all purchased raw materials.
7. Monitored raw material cost to budgeted cost; took appropriate action to correct negative variances.
8. Worked with Production Planning to keep inventories on purchased materials at desired levels.
9. Reduced raw material & MRO inventories with MRP system, consignment, & JIT vendor stocking programs.
10. Wrote standard operational procedures for the procurement of raw materials, MRO goods and services, and facility related subcontract labor services.

Results – Utilized the best b2b platforms and e-commerce websites for strategic global sourcing, supply chain, excess inventory reduction, purchasing card sourcing, and asset recovery. Generated cost savings of $1,005,012 annually while improving supplier performance.

Purchasing Manager, BIG PURCHASER INC. 2000 to 2003

Managed daily purchasing functions for BPI clients (small- to medium-sized U.S. corporations). Procured capital equipment, direct materials, MRO, and various support services. Daily activities include research, forecasting, RFQs, purchase order generation, expediting, lead-time reduction, negotiation, and cost-reduction analysis.

1. Negotiated contracts for commodities including IT equipment, computer software, office equipment, office furniture, office papers, office supplies, freight, MRO, steel, telecommunications, and travel.
2. Utilized Microsoft Office 2000 for daily communication, RFQs, and cost-reduction analysis.
3. Practiced and implemented current procurement techniques for maximum cost reduction.

Results – Generated average cost savings of 20-24 percent for each CPI client. Improved supplier lead time and performance through market analysis, forecasting, and planning.

PURCHASING: Sr. Procurement Manager (cont.)

John J. Johnston Page Two

Purchasing Consultant/Consortium Manager, PURCHASING SUPPORT SERVICES 1997 to 2000

ABC Group – Coordinated efforts among Fortune 500 corporations to form ABC Group Purchasing Consortium. Members include Stickems Inc. XZY Labs, Cheapy Airlines, Big Deliveries LLC, Huge Foods Inc.

1 Researched and gathered market data for various commodities.
2 Guided consortium members in choosing commodities that generated greatest cost-reduction benefit.
3 Sorted annual expenditures and data by member companies.
4 Invited and presented competitive bid seminar to major suppliers with national distribution capabilities.
5 Compiled bid responses, completed cost/analysis benefits, & presented bid analysis to member companies.
6 Negotiated final supplier agreements and implemented unique market sensitive pass-through escalating/de-escalating pricing programs.

Results – Supplier flat-line pricing was achieved for car rental, office equipment, and office papers resulting in $230,000 average cost savings for each member company.

Murphy Jones – Consulted with Murphy Jones in regards to their Asset View Purchasing Module.
1 Participated in the beta testing of the purchasing module program.
2 Researched Murphy Jones's competition in the procurement software marketplace.
3 Created detailed analysis of critical improvement areas for MJ to remain competitive or gain.
4 MJ improved upon Asset View Purchasing Module and established unique procurement call center.

Eastern Commerce – Assisted in the development of an online bidding system for Eastern Commerce.
1 Designed system with drop down menus for MRO commodities, which include brass, chemicals, fittings, lumber, pipes, valves, shipping supplies, steel, and industrial valves.
2 Integrated online access for national suppliers and buyers in all industries for true competitive pricing.

Office Furniture Group – Structured and coordinated central purchasing process for Office Furniture Group, Inc.
1 Produced purchasing policy manuals for the centralized purchasing department and fifty-five satellite offices.
2 Created OFG standards program for equipment, furniture, supplies, hardware, software, & security systems.
3 Initiated and executed bid process for procurement of various items.
4 Utilized IBM AS400, JD Edwards, & Microsoft Office to complete purchasing duties.
5 Established and maintained national contracts.
6 Reduced annual expenditures by $ 440,000.00.

Purchasing Manager/Senior Buyer, EMERGENCY SUPPORT SERVICES 1995 to 1997
Developed and maintained central purchasing program utilizing AS400 computer system. Wrote, revised, and updated current purchasing policies to maximize time and efficiency.

Purchasing Manager/Materials Manager, BIG INDUSTRIAL INC. 1982 to 1990
Results – Established 92 percent service level utilizing a $300,000 inventory to generate $17,000,000 in sales annually.

EDUCATION

Bachelor of Science – Business Administration   **State University College**   1994

Certificates: State University - Inventory Control & Record Accuracy
GMP Institute - cGMP / QSR 820 Workshop

PURCHASING: Sr. Purchasing Manager MBA

ALICE J. JOHNSTON

123 Learning Avenue • Anycity, ST • 10101 • 555-999-1212 • alicej@yourname.com

Senior Manager in Purchasing and Process Realignment with MBA. Excels at data-tracking, minimizing overheads, and reducing costs without any expense in quality.

Education

PRESTIGE SCHOOL OF BUSINESS, University of Southern Region, Anycity, ST

Master of Business Administration – Dean's Honor List   2001

Bachelor of Arts in Honors Business Administration   1997

Professional Employment

FITTING PACKAGING INC., Anycity, ST   May 2001–December 2001
Consultant (contract)

- Led a newly created sales team concentrating on retrofitting and refurbishment.

- Analyzed and documented all Made2Manage system processes and functionality using MS Office Suite and Micrografx Flowcharter. Also documented all processes and functionality for Engineering Database (customized).

- Investigated system errors and data inconsistencies. Developed changes to existing processes and procedures in order to optimize workflow and improve system productivity.

- Led and managed a team project that successfully reduced obsolete stock by over $157,000.

ABC COMPANY, Anycity, ST   1998–2000
Senior Purchasing Agent / Supervisor, Supply & Materials

- Effectively negotiated improved supplier contracts that reduced the cost of purchases by 20% and strengthened key supplier relations to achieve the annual cost-savings objective.

- Led and managed the timely implementation of ABC's Wire Management program, which cut lead times, minimized transportation costs, and improved employee satisfaction.

- Trained key purchasing users in the functionality of SAP R/3 client server to decrease implementation costs.

- Expedited material delivery and solved emergency part problems in order to alleviate customer plant shutdowns.

XYZ GROUP, Anycity, ST   1997–1998
Inventory Analyst, Consumable Products

- Analyzed current inventories investment and forecasted future consumable inventory demand, then used data to maximize inventory turnover and increase available cash by $30,000.

- Developed the Consumables Forecast Tracking system to evaluate the accuracy of sales forecasts, which improved the calculation and allocation of commissions.

Achievements & Accomplishments

Dean's Honor List, University of ST/Prestige School of Business   1994–1995, 2000–2001

Contributing case writer, "Purchasing & Materials Management" textbook by Dr. Dean Parnelli   2001

Purchasing Management Association of U.S.'s (PMAUS) "Certificate in Purchasing"   2000

M. Smith Scholarship Award for Excellence in Operations Management   1996

Leadership Experience

Leader, ABC's TOPs Supply Chain Management Program   1999–2000

Coordinator, U.S. Bank World Market's Summer Student Program   1996

Manager, Educational Outreach Program for the U.S. Solar Vehicle Team   1995

President, The Entrepreneurial Society of ST   1995

Skills and Interests

Proficient with computer platforms: MS Office, Lotus Applications, SAP R/3, AS400, BPCS 3.0, Made2Manage

Enjoy sailing, alpine skiing, racquetball, and worldwide traveling (most recently China).

RECRUITERS: BAD—Recruiter

Alice J. Johnston
123 Learning Rd. Suite #123
Anycity, ST 10101

(555)999-1212
alicej@yourname.com

OBJECTIVE

Looking to secure a challenging and rewarding position as a bilingual recruiter in a professional environment where my past experiences and skills can be utilized towards fulfillment of recruiting.

EDUCATION

Polytechnic University
Marketing

1998
Anycity, ST

EMPLOYMENT HISTORY

Recruit Personnel
Recruiter

Nov 02- Jan 03
Anycity, ST

Recruiting and selecting appropriate candidates.
Ensure consistent documentation of interviews, provide candidate assessments, meet daily deadlines.
Respond to candidates, follow up with managers, and conduct reference checks, selectively reviewing resumes.
Maintain a contact database and interview scheduling.
Develop and maintain relationships with clients to obtain a clear understanding of their staffing requirements.

LUXURY CLOTHING
NARS – COSMETIC COUNTER MANAGER

Interviewing staff for the Nars counter.
Responsible for scheduling of staff.
In charge of all bookkeeping, inventory, and ordering of supplies.
Maintaining and successfully achieving monthly quotas.
Keeping in contact with clientele and updating them on new products.
Organizing national makeup events and doing up to $8000 in sales da

What's Wrong?

· **Sends a mixed message**
· **Too much information about out-of-date or inapplicable jobs**
· **Too many unnecessary extras and/or irrelevant information and/or repetition**
· **Leaves a strange or weird impression or doesn't suit the industry**

HIGHEND CLOTHING (UPPER CRUST CENTER)
PRETTY – COSMETICS COUNTER MANAGER

1999-2000
Anycity, ST

Responsible for all bookkeeping, inventory and ordering stock.
Keeping in contact with clientele and updating them on new products.
Performing makeovers on a daily basis.
Bookings for major events, such as weddings.
Performing skin analysis, and recommending skin care products.

VALUE ADVERTISING
OFFICE MANAGER

1998-1999
ANYCITY

In charge of recruiting and hiring of staff.
In charge of staff payroll.
All accounts receivable and payable.
Contracting and marketing for company.

KICK KARATE AND FITNESS HEALTH CLUB
ADMINISTRATION AND ACCOUNTING MANAGER

1995-1998
Anycity, AS

Responsible for all accounting and bookkeeping.
Developed marketing strategies for promotion.
Overlooked advertising development and promotional material.
Prepared advertisement for newspaper layouts.

ALTERNATIVE ARTS
MANAGER

1998-1995
Anycity, AS

In charge of recruiting and hiring of all staff.
Responsible for purchasing and merchandising of the gallery.

Handled the bookkeeping and all A/P and A/R.

RECRUITERS: Tech and IT Recruiter

Alice J. Johnston

123 Learning Avenue Apt. 123, Anycity, Anystate, 10101
Phone: 555-999-1212 Cell: 555-999-1212   Email: alicej@yourname.com

Technical and IT Recruiter

CAREER PROGRESSION:

Tech People Systems, Inc., TECHNICAL RECRUITER, Engineering/IT   2003–2005

As Technical Recruiter, partners with senior line-of-business management in our high-growth Service Provider, Enterprise, and Channel sales teams to establish and satisfy quarterly hiring priorities across the country. Specific responsibilities include:

- Delivering aggressive and creative online and traditional sourcing services in a fast-paced, high-volume environment in the search for experienced optical and IP sales and pre-sales engineering talent who possess solid backgrounds in the networking industry.
- Aggressively exploiting the recruiting systems, qualify and screen prospects, act as a point of contact for third parties. Develop Campus recruitment programs currently at University of State, Intercity University, and the University of Anycity.
- Coordinating interview scheduling, interview feedback, reference checking, pre-hire paperwork, the hiring approval process as well as offer preparation and presentation.
- Communicating the recruitment processes to internal client groups.

Telecom Group, TECHNICAL RECRUITMENT CONSULTANT   2002 (Contract)

As Recruitment Consultant for Network Services, responsible for the full recruitment process and staffing the Operations and Engineering departments. Areas of recruitment encompass multiple technologies in the areas of voice and data communications including UNIX, ATM, SONET, POS, CISCO, DACS, CSU/DSU, PBX, Meridian, Centrix, Trunking, SS7, PNNI, TCP/IP, OSPF, RIP, EIGRP, etc. Responsible for sourcing and staffing approximately **50+** staff from newspaper advertising, Internet recruitment, and referrals. Other responsibilities include:

- Initial requirements assessment to employee induction.
- Establish strong client relationships across network services within various levels of the department from manager to senior VP. Advise managers on the recruitment process.
- Develop recruitment strategies and ad placement with the hiring managers.
- Recommend position salary grades and conduct job evaluations as required.
- Source, identify, and shortlist candidates based on hiring requirements. Conduct in-depth interviews and reference checks.
- Develop total compensation recommendations with hiring manager.
- Complete and process recruitment paperwork and statistics.

Multi Tech Ltd, CONSULTANT (IT Division)   2001 (Contract)

The services provided by Multec consist of permanent and contract placement, IT, engineering, and project realization. Value added by providing intensive guidance for both employer and career seeker.

As Consultant, responsibilities include:

- Business dev, account management, direct and indirect recruiting, career fairs, & trade shows.
- Qualification through intensive phone interviews as well as in-person tech & profile evaluations.
- Reference checks and closing.

Applied Technology Solutions, ACCOUNT MANAGER/RECRUITER   1999–2000

Responsibilities as above.

Computer Personnel Ltd., IT RECRUITER   1997–1998

As Information Technology recruiter for this large and successful recruitment firm, responsibilities included market research, client liaison, personal interviews, and sales. Achieved an average revenue of 105 percent of quota per month. Other activities included lead generation, cold calling, presentation, and closing. Other activities:

- Assessed technical skills and marketability of candidates represented. Screened applicants to appropriate jobs and conducted references during the entire recruiting life cycle. This encompasses a wide range of information automation tools including Object-Oriented, Client-Server, and Mainframe technologies.
- Utilized database information stored in Lotus Notes 4.6 operating under Windows NT 4.0/95 and running on an in-house Ethernet LAN with 60+ users. MS Office applications are used for various administrative duties, including Microsoft Word, and Excel.
- Conducted search and recruiting activities on the web using various sites including Headhunter.net, JobShark.com, Globecareers.com, Monsterboard.com, and CareerMosaic.com.

Department of Fisheries and Oceans, Science Branch, BIOLOGIST   1995-1997

EDUCATION:

1997   **Master of Science**
                State University

1995   **Bachelor of Science (Honors)**
                State University

HARDWARE/SOFTWARE: Unix, VAX/VMS, Windows NT 4.0, Windows 3.11/95, Minitab 6.02, Minitab 7.0 for Windows, SigmaStat, SigmaPlot, Quattro Pro, Lotus 1-2-3, Lotus Approach, Lotus Notes 4.6, CorelDRAW, MS Office, WordPerfect Suite

RECRUITING SOFTWARE: Lotus Notes 4.6, Resumix, Bond Adapt, Personic – Easy Access

RECRUITING TECHNICAL SUMMARY (Brief): Mainframe, MVS, Tandem, Honeywell Bull, UNIX, Windows NT, AS/400, BaaN, SAP, JD Edwards, PeopleSoft, DB2, Natural/Adabas, Oracle, Sybase, SQL Server, Access, Cobol, RPG, PL/1, C/C++, MFC, Visual Basic, FoxPro, PowerBuilder, ActivX, COM/DCOM, Corba, Booch, UML, OMT, Jacobson, ATM, SONET, POS, Switches, Routers, Hubs, Voice/Data Communications, Meridian, Centrix, PBX, Trunks, SS7, TCP/IP, RIP, OSPF, PNNI

CERTIFICATIONS:
1999   ISO 9000/9001 Training
1997   W.H.M.I.S. Safety Course

TRAINING:
2000   Cisco Overview: Products and Vision
2000   Cisco Networking, Basic Introduction
2000   Introduction to Telecommunications Workshop

RECRUITERS: HR Recruiter

Alice J. Johnston
123 Learning Avenue, Anycity, ST 10101 (555) 999-1212 email: alicej@yourname.com

PROFILE
A dynamic and resourceful **RECRUITING PROFESSIONAL** with a demonstrated ability to motivate and inspire others through energy and enthusiasm. Contributes to organizational and placement success through charisma, versatility, and integrity.

CAREER HISTORY

MOBILE INC., Recruitment Consultant   **July 1998–present**

Reporting directly to the Sr. Vice President of Corporate PMO/Information Technology, solely responsible for high-volume recruitment for a client group size of 370 employees including 60 hiring managers. Responsible for managing the tasks and supervising the day-to-day activities and performance of one full-time Recruiting Assistant.

Key Accomplishments:
Recruitment

- Screened, evaluated, and recruited candidates for positions ranging from Programmer Analysts to Sr. Project Managers and technical Directors filling 85 percent of roles within 3 weeks or less.
- Conducted effective telephone and face-to-face interviews using Mobile's behavioral interviewing methods and participated in technical assessment interviews.
- Prepared formal documentation and flowcharts for all CPMO/IT hiring managers that provided information on the recruitment workflow and processes.
- Effectively utilized a variety of applicant sourcing methods such as the company's electronic resume search bank (RESTRAC), various career websites, search firms, referrals, advertising, etc.

Training, Reporting, and Other

- Coached client groups and hiring managers on the recruitment process, Mobile's interviewing methods, recruitment techniques, and compensation practices.
- Produced analytical recruitment reports in order to record and track statistics to gain an insight into hiring trends and to employ more effective recruitment strategies.
- Prepared a profile of the Information Technology department outlining the company's internal System Development Life Cycle Methodology (SDLC) and the roles of each division and their respective positions. This document is used as a marketing tool for search firms assisting with employment searches.

THE DATABASE INC., Recruiter (Contract)   **July 1997–May 1998**

Responsible for high-volume, multi-level recruitment and selection activities, utilizing behavior-based interviewing techniques with emphasis in Information Systems.

Key Accomplishments:

- Evaluated and recruited candidates for multilevel positions by assessing individual and organizational fit using behavior-based interviewing techniques.
- Determined appropriate, cost-effective strategies through recruitment process from initial request to the induction process, while providing coaching and training to hiring managers as required.
- Effectively provided one-on-one coaching and guidance to employees with respect to opportunities for growth in new positions within the organization.
- Conducted research and provided valuable input on the assessment of information systems technical tests used to screen applicants' knowledge base.

ABC COMPANY, HR Administrator   **August 1993–November 1996**
Responsible for the recruitment and selection of positions in Information Technology, Finance, Accounting, Logistics, and Purchasing.
ABC COMPANY, Customer Service Administrative Assistant   **August 1991–August 1993**
Various office positions as a temporary full-time employee   **1989–1991**

EDUCATION: Bachelor of Science Degree – Psychology, State University

CAREER DEVELOPMENT & SPECIAL TRAINING: Targeted Selection Certified Interviewer from Development Dimensions International (DDI); Advanced computer skills and experience in Visio, Windows NT, PeopleSoft HRIS, RESTRAC, Lotus.

RECRUITERS: Recruiting Manager

John J. Johnston MA. B.Sc.

123 Learning Rd, Anycity, Anystate 10101   (home) **555-999-1212** (cell) **555-999-1313**
Email <u>johnj@yourname.com</u>

RECRUITER AND RECRUITMENT MANAGER WITH SPECIALTY IN HEALTHCARE & IT

HIGHLIGHTS OF QUALIFICATIONS

➢ MA Psychology in Behavioral Science with Honors (July 1999)
➢ 16 years experience as a Recruiter in a high-volume recruitment agencies incl. Fortune 500
➢ 12 years experience in Business sales & client building contracts
➢ Business diploma in Human Resources & Recruitment
➢ Strategic thinker with strong development orientation, able to identify and achieve priorities
➢ A natural gift for working and understanding recruitment management

EMPLOYMENT HISTORY

Director   2001–2004
Major Staffing Inc.   Anycity, AS
➢ Responsible for recruiting and selecting candidates to a large client base
➢ Supplied over 760 candidates to the USA over 3 years. Supplied over 1,290 candidates covering Health Care Catering & IT sectors. Incl'd Fortune 500 companies
➢ Responsible for building and maintaining the resume database while being able to recruit & maintain qualifying candidates
➢ Preparing candidates for immigration & visa screening for the USA; teaching and preparing candidates for the NCLEX TOEFL & TOEIC.

Probation Officer   1991–2001
National Probation Services   Anycity, AS
➢ Counseling unemployed people & set up contracts with companies to hire candidates who attended our job clubs. Working with child abuse victims and families helping them try to understand the abuse and how to cope with assault; writing Court CPA, CPR, and EPS before sentencing of offenders
➢ Teaching employment awareness at our drop-in center to young adults from the ages of 15 years and up
➢ Alcoholic and Drug Counsellor; setting up 56-week programs of one-on-one personal help
➢ Set up work training for individuals seeking full- or part-time work while on probation

Director   1989–1999
Great Care Services Limited   Anycity, AS
➢ Developed company whose main goal was to assist individuals in finding work
➢ In charge of 12,850 part-time contracted tender employees & 1,900 full-time employees to a 42-client base within the USA
➢ In charge of 86 full-time staff members, which consisted of 40 recruiters, 15 office support staff members, & 31 managers covering all client contracts

EDUCATION
State College of Business, *Diploma in Business Management*   1990–1991
➢ Human Resources Management, Business Management

University of Anycity, *MA of Behavior Science*   1997–1999

New Possibilities Trust College, *B.Sc. Mental Health Nurse Psychology*   1993–1996

VOLUNTEER: Social Worker/Recruiter program for Community Center   2002–2003
➢ Working with & the setting up of employment club & social. Funded by the Umbrella Charity of Anycity, and supported by Anycity.

SALES: Sales, Beginner

John J. Johnston
123 Learning Ave., Anytown, ST. USA (999) 555-1212
johnj@yourname.com

Young, hungry sales professional seeking the opportunity to join an early-stage venture. Prefers to work an undeveloped territory on a compensation model that rewards performance over plan.

ACCOMPLISHMENTS
- Finished 2004 at 147 percent.
- Responsible for 15 percent of company revenues in 2003.
- Signed startup.com's largest license deal—$3.5M, competing against Brand.
- 2004: Closed 3 enterprise deals within 9 months. Total revenue of $5M.
- President's Club 2001, Hawaii.
- Awarded "Rookie of the year 2000" at Enterprise Software for sales.

EMPLOYMENT HISTORY

Startup.com Vice President Sales   Jan 2003–Nov 2005
Startup.com is a venture capital funded services company with a vision to become the leader in the B2B integration/web services space.

* Recruited to drive revenue through personal sales while scaling out a national sales force.
* Hired a national sales force of 40 reps within first 6 months of operation.
* Exceeded targeted burn rate of $500K/month by 230 percent!
* Successful at selling to 6 out of 8 sister companies within the VC portfolio.

Enterprise Software Inc. Account Executive   2000–2003
Enterprise Software Inc.—headquartered in Anytown, ST—is the leader in the WOW marketspace, a solution which combines all of the best functionality of B2B, B2C, CRM, eRM, ERP, SFA, PSA, in either an ASP or ISP environment, which can be accessed mobility using WAP, GPS, and IMAP technologies.

* Pioneered the midwest, prospecting and closing new business opportunities.
* Wins include: Big Bank - $3.5M Big Brand - $2.2 Big Drug - $2M

EDUCATION/CAREER DEVELOPMENT

World-renowned Copiers Training: Full 10-course program.

State School of Personal Development: Leadership, Motivation, and Excellence.

Ivy League School of Business, MBA, 1999
New York State University, BA, 1997
GPA: 4.0

LIFE OUTSIDE OF WORK

* Golf and gardening
* President of an Investors Club of two. (Wife is Vice President)

John J. Johnston

123 Learning St. * Anytown, ST, USA * 10101* Telephone: 999-555-1212
Cell: 999-555-1313 * email: johnj@yourname.com

Profile: Client Relationship expert who excels at solution-based sales and account management.

Key Qualifications
- 8+ years of selling to high level executives and Fortune 500 companies
- At ease with cold calls and networking, while skilled in building existing relationships
- Personable and well-organized with the ability to work in a multitask environment
- Fluent knowledge of 2 languages: English and Spanish

Work Experience

BIG COMMUNICATION INC., Sales Agent, April 2002–Present
Responsibilities: Delivery of Optical Ethernet Networking Solutions to clients across Eastern U.S.
Penetration of Fortune 500 Companies.

Achievements:
- Delivered Eastern American WAN Service to Perogies Textile Company.
- Provided BIG BOX STORE U.S. a Fiber Campus Network environment to facilitate their supply chain management requirements.
- Opened the first government account for Suburb Hydro, a private Source Solution to AES (Alternate Energy Source U.S. Limited).
- Replaced existing ISP with Hydro Broadband Internet Services to clients such as PeopleVision.

CORP-NET – Tubby U.S., Account Manager, February 1999–January 2002
Responsibilities:
Responsible for acquisition and retention of profitable revenues within a target market from new and existing enterprise customers.
Selling to "C" level executives by providing cost-effective, bottom-line solutions.
Worked with international organizations to implement wide area networks (WAN), storage, hosting, and security solutions to manage critical data.

Achievements:
- Attained 136 percent of quota over 3-year period.
- Won President's Club for Sales - 2000
- 1st in Branch Data Sales - August 2001
- 1st in Branch Voice Sales - July 1999, February 2000, & April 2000

XYZ, INC., Account Representative, March 1997–February 1999
Responsibilities:
Responsible for sales, financing, and managing a large current and potential client base, daily quota of 25 cold calls and 2 demonstrations. Mentoring and training new hires during 2nd year of employment.

Achievements:
- Attained 114 percent of quota over 2-year period.
- Won President's Club for Sales - 1998
- 1st in Branch Sales - Q1 of Fiscal Year 1999; 2nd in Branch Sales - Fiscal Year 1998
- 1st in Branch Sales - November 1997, March 1998 & June 1998
- Attained Anytown Branch Rookie Sales Record during first three months of employment

SKILLS/TRAINING: Proficient computer skills in PowerPoint and Funnel Management Applications (Smart Sales, ACT). Completed Ethernet Networking training; Executive Level Contact Sales training; Data Application Training

EDUCATION: STATE UNIVERSITY: Bachelor of Arts, Psychology Major, 1993

SALES: Lead Generation Specialist

John J. Johnston
Lead Generation Specialist
999-555-1212
johnj@yourname.com

Providing a growing organization new business development solutions and strategies through research, marketing, and lead generation initiatives.

Summary of Qualifications

Sales
- Over 10 years experience in Inside Sales and Lead Generation
- Experience generating and nurturing qualified leads in the high-tech/dot-com industries, primarily by telephone and email
- Energetic cold calling and prospect courting techniques
- Comfortable dealing with all levels of an organization, from CEOs to DBAs

Research
- Lead acquisition from Internet, print, and other media sources
- Established network for market research and prospect identification
- Client and Individual identification through needs analysis and interviewing

Marketing/Advertising
- Direct mail campaigns (including mail merge and campaign tracking)
- Lead acquisition from Internet, print, and other media sources
- Radio and print advertising, Internet promotion
- All aspects of Seminar hosting, including planning, invitation, follow-up, registration, design, and presentation

Management and Administration
- Experienced in staff management, training, and growth nurturing
- Worked with various databases and CRM applications, including implementation, maintenance, data cleansing, and system improvements

Work Experience

Round the Bend Business Views   **Market Intelligence Associate**   **2003–2004**

Target Verticals included Pharmaceutical, Health Care, Financial, Manufacturing, Utility, and Government

- Generated Qualified Leads and Opportunities for target verticals in an assigned territory for an international Performance Measurement and Management software firm
- Conducted cold prospecting calls, timely follow-up calls, and email marketing initiatives
- Researched organizations and champions through Internet, trade publications, and subscription databases (Hoovers, Leadership Directories)
- Conducted validation and qualification of champions and subordinates to evaluate opportunity potential, primarily interacting with CFOs, Human Resource Executives, CIOs and IT Directors and Performance Measurement Managers

Results: Created over 120 Qualified Leads and $500,000 in sales in first fiscal year

In addition:
- Initiated calls and marketing campaigns for trade shows and seminars
- Trained individuals on Market Intelligence team in research and prospecting techniques
- Worked with Sales & Marketing teams to develop new Marketing Campaigns
- Maintained and updated marketing collateral documentation files and database

John J. Johnston
Lead Generation Specialist

999-555-1212
johnj@yourname.com

J & J Associates   **Sales & Marketing Consultant**   **2002–Present**
- Built action plan to penetrate competitive IT Recruiting marketplace through organized lead generation, effective prospecting techniques, and improved marketing collateral
- Identified and qualified candidates for specific sales opportunities across several different verticals and conducted market research in specific industries, collect and analyze the information
- Developed and initiated Marketing Strategy to effectively establish new leads, maintain the current customer base, and renew old relationships for a material-handling equipment-training company
- Launched direct contact marketing campaign to ISPs and CLECs across North America to promote new technologies and business opportunities
- Initiated direct marketing and cold call campaigns for Web Development contractor
- Contacted clients to evaluate satisfaction and analyze current needs and market trends
- Conducted initial interviews with candidates to analyze compatibility with client needs
- Administration of database and CRM applications (PAD, ACT 2002, FileMaker & CRM software) including integrity, growth, implementation, reports, and training
- Fostered a Customer Centric approach

ARP Group   **Sales and Marketing Manager**   **1999–2001**
- Oversaw the marketing and sales lead generation function for ARP Group Inc.—a data warehouse software and consulting firm
- Conducted cold prospecting calls, lead qualification and development, and prepared prospects for the outside sales force, generated leads in many different industries across the board, including government, natural resources, insurance, financial, health, pharmaceutical, and manufacturing
- Redesigned the marketing package, designed and implemented advertising and directing mail campaigns, planned Data Warehouse and Performance Management Seminars
- Trained staff in Internet research and promotion
- Designed a reporting structure for access and accountability
Results: More effective lead generation leading to company growth of 25 percent

The Views Mirror Corporation   **Inside Sales Rep**   **1998–1999**
- Generated qualified leads in the Central U.S. region for a multi-platform data transformation software company
- Maintained a minimum daily call rate (55) in a call center environment and consistently exceeded targets of 12 qualified leads per month

RightSearch Inc.   **Telemarketing Supervisor**   **1997–1998**
- Designed telemarketing strategy, including scripts, target markets, database implementation, and call/contact objectives
- Hired and trained 9 telemarketing/CSR reps in technique and customer satisfaction
- Supervised team of 6 cold calling and generating leads from area businesses for a local site launch and consistently exceeded department quotas of 50 appointments per day

1994–1997	Big Store Inc.	Maintenance Supervisor
1989–1993	Inter Security	Security Supervisor
1987–1989	Big Box Corp	Receiving Manager

Education

| Marketing | State College | 1986 |

Interests   Creative writing, music (guitar, vocals, songwriting), baseball, personal development

SALES: B2B Sales and Marketing Exec..

ALICE J. JOHNSTON
123 Learning Street
Anytown, ST, USA 10101
Res: (999) 555-1212
Email: alicej@yourname.com

CAREER OBJECTIVE: To plan and direct sales and marketing activities of a mid-sized company, utilizing my entrepreneurial background and extensive B2B marketing experience with developed abilities in problem solving and strategic planning. This will contribute to expand an organization's marketplace and help them look beyond their current capabilities.

PROFESSIONAL PROFILE: A creative, entrepreneurial marketing executive with over twenty years experience in the conceptual sales and marketing environment, supported by a university degree and significant professional training. Key strengths include:

- Concept Developer
- Business-to-Business Marketer
- Results-Oriented Implementer

- Motivating Leader
- Persuasive Communicator
- Project Manager

SELECTED ACHIEVEMENTS:

- Created and built one of America's largest specialized advertising agencies and worked with some of the country's largest and most prestigious companies. Clients billed twelve times the national average for the industry. Raised the bar for client service. The agency's account personnel were highly sought after by other agencies. (Media Inc.)

- Rebranded and repositioned a small publishing company, helping it to become a leading American B2B publisher. Created a new image through advertising and the design of a new slogan, better representing the publication's new focus. Personally introduced the new look to the CEOs of some of America's largest companies. Within two years the advertising income from the publication had grown from less than $2 million to almost $14 million annually. (Media Inc.)

- Helped create an e-commerce training site that averaged 30,000 hits a month, strictly through viral marketing. The site became so popular that it was sold within eighteen months to a multinational company who used it to promote their own learning products. (News Nine)

- Worked with one of America's most respected magazine publishers to create a section devoted entirely to international trade. Was responsible for the design of the section, the content, and the advertising sales. First month ad sales were in excess of $100,000. The section has remained virtually unchanged for twelve years. (News Nine)

- Created a sales training program that stressed customer awareness and retention. Marketed the product throughout the state as an off-site, instructor-led seminar series and also offered customized in-house packages. The program was very well received and resulted in a number of long-term relationships. (Media Inc.)

- Negotiated an equitable compensation arrangement between two sales operations within the same organization, diffusing a potentially volatile situation. Both sides were convinced that any money given to the other side would negatively affect their income. Created a win-win scenario by getting each side to agree to concessions. (Consulting Corp.)

- Created a new image for a non-profit school for troubled kids and designed a comprehensive marketing plan, enabling it to create an additional revenue stream from the huge North American and Asian markets. With the addition of a website and promotional material, the school was able to attract over three times the number of students. As a result, they could hire more qualified staff and embark on an ambitious expansion program. (Media Inc.)

ALICE J. JOHNSTON

PROFESSIONAL HISTORY:

Vice President Business Development   Media Inc., 2003
- Design new products geared to specific industry groups
- Source and generate all company new business and client acquisition
- Approach and secure partnerships with companies with a synergistic product or service

Vice President/Managing Director   Media Inc., 2002
- Secured existing client base
- Sourced and generated all agency new business and client acquisition
- Reestablished agency credibility in the industry
- Created and managed the execution of all client yellow pages marketing and advertising programs
- Hired and managed qualified, senior Account Management

Principal   News Nine Studio, 1996–2001
- Planned strategy and set the direction for the agency
- Sourced and generated all agency new business and client acquisition
- Liaised with an average of four clients annually and did their business & marketing planning
- Created and managed the execution of all client marketing and advertising programs
- Hired and managed independent and/or freelance creative and IT personnel
- Negotiated with suppliers for equitable pricing and terms

President   News Nine Studio, 1988–1996
- Directed strategic planning, business, & marketing plan writing
- Implemented new business development and client acquisition
- Hired and managed all account and creative personnel
- Provided creative direction for nine national advertising programs annually
- Managed complete P&L responsibility, with final budget approval

Principal   Consulting Corp., 1986–1988
- Generated all business for the partnership, hired, and trained additional personnel
- Wrote P.O.S.T. training courses, conducted hotel seminars, and on-site training
- Created America's only advertising-based directory including fax, toll-free, telex, and phone

National Sales/Marketing Manager   Communications Inc., 1980–1986
- Member of the Executive Committee responsible for managing day-to-day operation
- Had four direct reports and fifty-three total staff members, did all hiring and training
- Designed the sales compensation plan, incentive program, and commission plan
- Prepared all sales forecasts for the company plus sales and marketing budgets
- Created all marketing and advertising and hired the company's first advertising agency

Sales Representative   Call-Me Limited, 1975–1980
- Sold directory advertising

EDUCATION/ADVANCED TRAINING:

B.A., Philosophy   **State University, 1975**

Editing & Proofing Chicago Style	Brainbench Online, 2000
Strategic Marketing	State Executive Institute, 1997
Strategic Leadership Practices	ASAS Management, 1995
Six Thinking Hats Workshop	ASAS Management, 1992
In Search of Excellence	Tom Peters, 1986
Building High Performance Teams	Ken Blanchard, 1985
The One Minute Manager	Ken Blanchard, 1984

SALES: National Account Manager

John J. Johnston
123 Learning St., Anytown, ST, USA, 10101 (999)555-1212 (cell) johnj@yourname.com

A proven Sales Leader with management training & demonstrated success in managing top performing sales teams to overachieve on corporate revenue objectives. A strategic thinker with strong relationship building, financial, persuasion & negotiating skills.

Big Credit Card Inc. 1988 to Present

National Account Director, October 2000 to Present
Responsible for leading a team of 12 Account Managers nationally in the expansion of a $250M customer portfolio. Specific focus on market share growth and customer retention.

Accomplishments:
- 2004 Graduate of Management Development Program (School of Business – State University 2004): *Nominated and accepted to attend this exclusive program for the top 12 Big Credit Card Inc. management performers*
- 2002 President's Club Winner: Awarded to the top 2 percent of company worldwide for exceptional accomplishments
- Led sales team to attain 35 percent revenue growth and 98 percent client retention
- Developed and coached employees in the areas of product knowledge, positioning, technology, financial, sales strategy, and key account management
- 25 percent of employees received corporate recognition for top performance in 2001
- Developed Market alignment strategy leading to increased efficiency and productivity within account management team

National Account Manager, December 1997 to 2000
Key account manager for $65M portfolio of the company's largest accounts.

Accomplishments:
- Developed and implemented strategic account plans which resulted in 100 percent account retention in portfolio
- Exceeded all growth targets and new sales quotas as assigned
- Successfully cross-sold and leveraged new products to generate incremental revenue within existing account base
- Effectively negotiated key contracts with strategic vendors to generate significant client savings and increase corporate profitability

Technical Consultant (Corporate Services), July 1996 to December 1997
Consulting with customers on the use of technologies to manage travel & entertainment.

Accomplishments:
- Conducted 100+ multimedia boardroom presentations to existing & prospective customers
- Chaired ACTE (Association of Corporate Travel Executives) seminar on the use of technologies in business
- Provided full product demonstrations of all Big Credit Card Inc. products, including software and Internet products
- Played key role in 'best and final' presentations, leading to signings of strategic accounts

Special Skills: Excel, PowerPoint, Lotus Notes, Act for Notes, Siebel – My Client (CRM)
Awards: 2004 Nominated & Accepted to Management Development Program; 2002 President's Club
Education:
4th Level Certified General Accountant (currently pursuing)
Accounting and Financial Management Diploma, State College (1998)

SOFTWARE: BAD—Business Analyst Software

123 Learning St.
Anytown, USA
10101
(999) 555-1212
alicej@yourname.com

Alice J. Johnston

Profile

Business Analyst and Manager with extensive project management, business analysis, and financial industry background in the software industry.

Software Industry Work Experience

ABC Resolution Inc.   Mar '00–Dec '01
Engagement Manager, Professional Services
In this project management role, I worked on key customer implementations of ABC's wireless banking and brokerage products for major financial institutions,

I developed and executed project plans: including resource planning, contingency planning, risk management, forecasting, and budgeting. During this time, I:

- promoted a cohesive, unified project team, internally and externally
- understood, prioritized, and managed units of work, delegated tasks accordingly
- managed customers' expectations and scope; followed change control process
- adhered to tight delivery dates and escalated issues as warranted while proposing corrective actions to promote swift resolution
- contributed to RFPs and customer legal agreements (e.g., Statement of Services), and monitored and satisfied contractual obligations with customers

Sr. Business/Systems Analyst
In this senior BA role, I worked as part of ABC's Professional Services division and within ABC's Development group to understand and define both the business and technical requirements for various ABC products, including their internet based aggregation product, their internet and wireless based alerts application, and their wireless banking and brokerage products. While working in Professional Services, I was assigned to major customer projects. During this time, I:

- analyzed, defined, and created documentation, including project scope, gap analysis, & detailed specifications
- understood and adhered to business and technical product and project scope in all written and verbal communications
- ensured acceptance of documentation from all ap
- validated quality of product by participating in or development cycle, including assisting with QA
- interacted with customers professionally and know
- managed customer expectations
- helped define a company-wide development and
- assessed potential products for possible inclusion

What's Wrong?

- Too much wasted space
- No accomplishments or specific and measurable results
- Too many bullet points
- Too long especially for your age and stage
- Too much information about out-of-date or inapplicable jobs
- Too many unnecessary extras and/or irrelevant information and/or repetition

SOFTWARE: BAD—Business Analyst Software (cont.)

BIG Company   Mar '98–Feb '00
Sr. Business Analyst

In this senior BA role, I worked within BIG's customer services division and their software development lab to define, gather, and document various product requirements, including their enterprise CRM Corepoint Banking Solution which encompassed Internet, Contact Center, Branch Sales and Teller solutions that targeted the global financial industry. My customer engagements included on-site assignments at Overseas Bank in U.K. implementing our Internet solution implemented our Contact Centre application. During this time, I:

- worked with planning, development, and customers to deliver enterprise CRM financial software targeting the global financial industry

- gathered requirements for all phases of software development

- documented requirements, including creating use cases and use case diagrams

- validated product quality by participating in UI reviews and assisting with QA

- helped acquire new business by presenting at customer briefings, conferences, and trade shows, by demonstrating our products, and contributing to RFPs

Big Company Footprint   Jan '91–Feb '98
Business Analyst

In this BA role, I worked on both internal projects and on customer implementations. Internal assignments included the conversion our sales tools from DOS to Java, and the creation of an online discount brokerage application as part of a complete financial planning prototype. My customer-specific projects included a six-month on-site assignment at Overseas Bank in Hong Kong to implement our branch sales Visual Banker product, and an on-site Visual Banker engagement at Big Bank in Anycity. During this time, I:

- gathered, defined, and documented functional specifications for various internal and external projects

- analyzed, defined, and created gap analysis documentation

- designed a wizard style UI for our financial sales tools product appropriate for North American online banking customers

- defined requirements that met specific geographic needs

- designed user interfaces appropriate for both the Asian and North American markets

**Brokerage Industry
Work Experience**

Stock Company Inc.   June '86–May '91
International Sales Administrator

- managed company's international retail and institutional client accounts

- received, executed, reported, and settled buy and sell trades of stocks, bonds, and money market instruments for all international clients

- arranged daily foreign exchange transactions

- reconciled international customer account positions on a daily and monthly basis

Securities Cage Manager

- supervised securities cage staff

- hired, trained, and reviewed cage personnel

- balanced in-house security inventory positions

Money Makers Inc.	'84–'86
Reorganization Administrator	

Little Bucks Limited	Jan '84–Sept '84
Securities Cage Supervisor	

XYZ Limited	Sept '81–Dec '83
Contracts Administrator	

Education/Training

Aug '01	• MS Project 2000
Feb '01	• Project Planning and Control
May '00	• Communication and Effective Meeting Skills
Dec '99	• Technical Introduction to MQ Series Workshop
Nov '99	• Object Oriented Analysis & Design Using UML & Java
Nov '99	• PASA '99 Workshop (demonstrator & attendee)
Oct '99	• Effective Presentation Skills Workshop
Aug '99	• Rational Analyst Seminar
Apr '99	• Financial Services in the New Millennium Conference & Workshop
June '98	• Business Process Modeling & Analysis Workshop
May '98	• 1998 User Interface Update - Human Factors International
Sept '97	• Usability & Ergonomics Update
May '97	• CTI World Conference & Workshop
Feb '97	• Dale Carnegie Course
Jan '97	• BIG Campus Workshop
June '96	• Performance Support Systems Seminar
1982 - 1988	• Various IDA courses including: Supervisor, Introduction to Operations, Reorganization, Contracts, Clearing
1981	• State College - Business Certificate

Business Skills

• Adobe Acrobat	• MS Word	• MS Project	• SnagIt
• Freelance Graphics	• MS FrontPage	• MS IE / Netscape	• Visio
• Lotus Notes	• MS Outlook	• Rational RequisitePro	• WinZip
• MS Excel	• MS PowerPoint	• Rational Rose	• WordPro

Awards

ABC Outstanding Achievement Award - Jan '01

BIG Peer Recognition Awards - July '99, Mar '99, Jan '99

BIG Value in Performance Award - Sept '97

SOFTWARE: Software Training

John J. Johnston
123 Learning St., Anycity, Anystate 10101 johnj@yourname.com 555-999-1212

Technical Trainer and Computer Based Training Developer:
- Extensive experience analyzing training needs, developing and delivering classroom, computer, and web-based training materials
- Utilize post-baccalaureate coursework, as well as tech and hardware knowledge to create course curriculum, catalogue employee help resources, and maintain training records
- Utilize expertise in Microsoft Office Suite, Adobe Photoshop, and Macromedia products to enhance students' training experience

EXPERIENCE:

Clarity, *Trainer - Precision Marketing Institute*   **Anycity, AS**   **4/2003—Present**
Deliver application & software training to clients & staff in classroom and virtual settings
- Develop computer and web-based training applications and develop and update training materials and documents
- Consult with sales team to deliver customized training
- Assist with design and production of all training materials
- ***Clarity has been recognized and ranked as a top training school in AS by several magazines and newspapers***

Pure Healthcare, *Technical Trainer CIS*   **Anycity, AS**   **10/2001–12/2002**
- Manage Computer-Based-Training Authorware development project
- Led classroom training sessions for CliniVision and Crystal Reports software
- Create & develop web/computer training interactive applications using Macromedia Flash
- Develop and present ideas to improve and update the CliniVision software
- Develop training materials & create documentation on CliniVision and Crystal Reports
- Assist users in isolating problems, support users after application implementation
- Test functionality of all aspects of CliniVision software

Art Web Den, *Trainer, Web Developer*   **Anycity, AS**   **9/1999–6/2001**
- Lead classroom training sessions for all applications used by clients
- Assist users in isolating problems, support users after application implementation
- Develop training material and documentation for applications
- Develop web and computer based training applications using Macromedia Flash

Big West World, *Consultant*   **Anycity, AS**   **6/1999–9/1999**
- Compose and edit web pages for curriculum development based on traditional class materials and texts using Netscape Communicator and Adobe PhotoShop

Eastern University   **Anycity, AS**   **8/1998–5/1999**
Graduate Assistant

EDUCATION:
Eastern University, Anycity, AS, 1999
Post-baccalaureate Coursework
M.A. History with European Concentration (5 credit hours remain for completion)
- ***Distinguished Graduate Student for History Program***
- ***"Excellence in European History" Scholarship***
- Published in Historia (Award winning EU History Journal)

University of State, Anycity, AS, 1998
Bachelor's Degree - B.A. History – U.S. Concentration

SKILLS: Microsoft Office Suite, Seagate Crystal Reports, Adobe Photoshop, Macromedia Studio MX, MapInfo, Cool Edit Pro, HTML

John J. Johnston

123 Learning Street, Anytown, ST, USA 10101
tel: (999) 555 1212 (h) or (999) 555 1313 (c) *email:* johnj@yourname.com

Senior Executive - Software and Computer Industry

Profile:

An entrepreneurial-style executive with over 25 years experience in the computer and software industry. Passionate about keeping companies ahead of change curve with flair.

Cofounded Software City Corporation without investment capital and succeeded in managing its growth to over $28 million in revenue and 15 offices around the world. During this time, managed its successful IPO on the New York Stock Exchange and subsequent rounds of financing.

Excels at managing companies through growth and restructuring. Keeps morale high through mentoring and effective incentives.

Professional Experience:

General Manager, California Dreaming Networks Inc.   *1999–2003*
Responsible for all non-R&D related activities for this startup company in the telecom sector, which has been developing a fixed wireless solution for 'the last mile.' Activities involved HR, business development, office leasing/planning, finance, etc.
Key Achievements:
- Managed the growth of American operations from 15 employees to over 180 over the course of 3 and a half years
- Hired and recruited, mentored and managed the majority of hires and employees
- Managed 3 office moves (upgrades) in three years with a minimal disruption to productivity

Consultant, Pastoral Properties   *1998–1999*
Reported to the CEO of one of the world's largest commercial property management companies. Developed and established strategy and direction for the IT department.
Key Achievements:
- Successfully selected a new ERP system
- Defined direction for the IT dept over the advent of interactive websites

President/CEO/Chairman, Software City Corporation Inc.   *1976–1998*
Founded and developed Software City Corporation with one partner and no investment capital. Software City is a leading supplier of application development technology and business intelligence tools for management analytics and is a profitable publicly traded company.
Key Achievements:
- Managed growth from incorporation to over $28 million revenues
- Managed IPO on the NY Stock Exchange
- Managed second round financing and two acquisitions
- As Chairman, managed the transition of two CEOs and company restructuring

Analyst Programmer, Software Development Manager, Large Tel
1974–1976
Performed feasibility studies for a variety of real-time operating systems for Large Tel and supervised a staff of approx. 30 programmers.

Systems Analyst/Corporate Consultant, Brand Electronics   *1970–1974*
Designed and implemented many commercial applications for a variety of industries.

Computer Operator, Programmer, Team Leader, Department of Health   *1960s*
Learned basics of computing and programming on early mainframes and early small business computers.

Appointments:

Shareholder and Director   **Software City Corporation** (Software City.com)
Software City is a profitable publicly traded software company. Its product lines include tools for business managers and IT professionals together with industry leading ERP solutions. It has customers around the world and has been established since 1976.

Director and Volunteer   **Helpful Foundation for Youth**
Helpful Foundation is an organization with a focus on helping youth at risk, such as street kids, by teaching them new skills such as sailing and boat repair. It is based at Local Yacht Club.

Personal:

Sailing (racing): Actively involved in yacht racing and have won trophies for regattas and offshore long distance races. Also participated in a North American championship regatta.

SOFTWARE: Software Developer

John J. Johnston

123 Learning St., Anytown USA, 10101, Phone: (999) 555-1212
Email: johnj@yourname.com

Senior Software Developer with 8 years of experience in development of large-scale applications.

OBJECTIVE: Contract Position

HIGHLIGHTS

- Experience in **C++/Visual C++, JAVA,** and **SQL**.
- Object-Oriented Analysis and Design (**OOA/OOD/OOP**) **applied UML methodology**.
- **Internet** and **B2B** development: **JAVA, JMS, Servlets, JDBC, XML/XSL, CORBA, CGI.**
- **Multithreaded** and **multplatform** programming (Windows, POSIX, and JAVA threads).
- **Network** programming through **sockets** (Berkley and JAVA).
- **Real-time** experience in **VoIP** applications (RTP/RTCP).
- Technical competence in wide range of **Telecommunication Technologies**.

SKILLS

Languages:	**JAVA, C++** (MS **Visual C++** including **MFC** and **STL**), **XML/XSL,** C
Databases:	**Oracle 8.0.6/8.1.6**
OS:	**Windows NT, UNIX** (HP 11, HP 10.20, SunOS 4.x, Solaris 2.x)
Compilers:	Visual C++ 6.0, HP aCC, Sun/Solaris CC.
Protocols:	**TCP/IP, UDP/IP, SNMP, H.323, RTP/RTCP,** HTTP, **DNS**
Tools:	Rational Rose, Continuus 4.5, SourceSafe, Remedy, SoftIce/WinIce, VtoolsD
Other:	**ORACLE 8.1.6 MQ (Java), JMS, Servlets, JavaBeans,** Swing, JDBC, DOM, **CORBA**

EXPERIENCE

Senior Software Developer   **1999–Present**
AXY Software

Project: Order Management System.
Java1.2.2, JMS, Oracle8.1.6 MQ, JDBC, Servlets, XML/XSL, DOM, CORBA – Java IDL, Sockets, UML with Rational Rose, Continuus.

The project included design and implementation of several connector applications for the web-based Order Management System (the upstream system). Each connector was designed for a specific type of external application (downstream system). Each connector was a listener on a message queue established by the Order Management System (ORACLE 8.1.6 Advanced Message Queues were used). The connectors converted Order Management System data (messages) into appropriate format/protocol supported by the external downstream system (CORBA, HTTP, TCP/IP). Java Messaging with XML payload (SUN JMS) was used as a messaging system.

- Analyzed existing tools/systems/protocols and provided a proof of concept. ·
- Designed and implemented TCP-based connector to General Purpose External Application (TCP/IP based connector, JAVA sockets).
- Designed & implemented CORBA-based connector Automatic Service Activation System.
- Designed & implemented HTTP based connector to Inventory Management System.
- Extended existing XML API of Order Management System.

Project: Product Integration Server.
C++, STL, XML/XSL, DOM, Sockets, multithreading, NT/HP10.20/HP11, Continuus.

The project involved development of dynamically loaded interfaces for interconnection of different external systems. The interfaces were loaded as shared libraries (UNIX) or DLLs (NT) into the core server application and provided a communication channel between different external systems (businesses). The payload of B2B services/requests was XML document.

- Implemented different interfaces for Integration Server (**C++** and **STL**).
- Designed & implemented synchronization mechanism for integration server & external applications.
- Handled concurrency problems in a multithreaded system of Integration Server.
- Resolved connectivity problems between Integration Server and external systems.

John J. Johnston   page 2

Senior Software Developer   1997–1999
Big Communications Inc.

Desktop and group videoconferencing systems designed for IP networks. Developed on Windows 95/NT platform. The product is H.323 protocol compliant. Transport protocols used for VoIP transmission are RTP/RTCP.

- Designed and implemented **multithreaded C++** applications on **Windows** platform for videoconferencing system (video and audio over IP).
- Developed inter process communication API based on **Memory Mapped File** and **Windows Messages** (**Visual C++, MFC**).
- Designed, implemented, and tested the mechanism of synchronization of video and audio packets of **Real Time Protocol** (**Visual C++, MFC, VtoolsD**).
- Responsible for adding functionality into existing **VxD** driver (**Visual C++, VtoolsD**).
- Analyzed communication protocols requirements for application design.
- Provided application maintenance and support.

Intermediate Software Developer   1995–1997
Research & Design Inc.

SNMP-based network management station. The system allowed doing a remote setup and management of routers and smart bridges.

- Designed, implemented, and tested **SNMP-based network management** applications in **C++** for **UNIX** and **Windows.**
- Provided software solutions for automated discovery of **MIB** of network devices and fast copy of device configuration (**WinSNMP, Visual C++, zApp, multiplatform**).
- Developed **Java** client (Java Applet) for **web network management** system.
- Provided **CGI** scripts on a server side of the **web network management** system.
- Designed and implemented local **DNS server** in **C** for **UNIX** (SunOS 4.x, Solaris 2.x).
- Tested and maintained C++ and Java applications.

Software Developer   1993–1995
NNN Research Lab

- Developed and tested applications for signals processing in **C** for **UNIX** (SunOS 4.x).
- Implemented GUI application for visual representation of experimental data (Motif/X-WINDOWS).
- Used mathematical models for noise reduction, filtering, and statistical analysis of results.

EDUCATION

Master of Science in Computer Science   1998
State University

Bachelor of Science in Computer Science   1992
Institute of Radio Engineering, Electronics and Automatics

COURSES
- Understanding TCP/IP, Telecommunications Research Associates   2000
- Object Oriented Design for C++ Programmers   1998
- JDK1.1 – Advanced Internet programming   1997
- Networking, RAD Data Communications   1996

PERSONAL SKILLS
High motivation and responsibility, creative and skilled in problem solving, goal oriented, hard working, good learning ability, good communication skills

SOFTWARE: Sr. Software Developer and Architect

T: (999) 555-1212
C: (999) 555-1313

John J. Johnston
JOHNJ@YOURNAME.COM

123 Learning St.
Anytown, ST 10101

Objective

SENIOR SOFTWARE DEVELOPER & ARCHITECT *THAT LIKES TO CONTRIBUTE TO THE HEART OF AN ORGANIZATION.*

Summary of Qualifications

- EXPERIENCED IN LARGE SCALE, CONCURRENT, AND MULTITIER SOFTWARE SYSTEMS, USING A VARIETY OF TECHNOLOGIES
- COMFORTABLE IN ALL OF DEVELOPMENT, TESTING, DESIGN, ARCHITECTURE, AND ANALYSIS
- LANGUAGES: EXPERT IN JAVA, C, C++. PROFICIENT IN XML, PERL, SHELL TOOLS, DELPHI, PL-SQL
- PLATFORMS: UNIX (HP-UX, SOLARIS, LINUX), WINDOWS, ORACLE, SYBASE
- MIDDLEWARE: J2EE (WEBLOGIC), TIBCO, DCE-RPC, CORBA, XML-RPC, HTTP
- PROVEN MATHEMATICAL ABILITY AND PROBLEM SOLVING SKILLS

WORK EXPERIENCE

Senior Developer/Architect   *Big Pay Inc.*   *January 2002–November 2002*

- Designed and led three-person implementation team on new XML messaging layer servlets for J2EE/Oracle based real-time electronic payment financial app, using a test-driven methodology
- Designed and prototyped next generation architecture of our core financial services product with one other architect to solve problem of multiple versions of business logic operating simultaneously in a clustered J2EE environment (Weblogic) while serving conservative financial clients
- Debugged threading issues in our JNI interface to Entrust PKI toolkit, and converted our XML processing servlets to use a pipe/daemon based protocol instead
- Worked around bugs in Weblogic Message Driven Beans queue notification using an Oracle backing store
- Updated funds transfer batch job to support new commission structure using Java, JDBC, and PL/SQL stored procedures
- Designed and wrote various session and entity EJBs

Professional Services –   *XYZ Inc.*   *July 2000–December 2001*
Developer/Architect

- Provided creative solutions for Internet companies (ISPs, Telco, domain name processing) on our provisioning and billing product in both presales and delivery situations
- Architected, designed, and led three-person implementation of complete native Java API to C++ server to support clients using J2EE technologies for the Amdocs Product group
- Designed and built novel implementation of real-time pricing, and provisioning interface for Tucows in dynamically loaded C++
- Modified billing & real-time rating system to support Mobile custom requirements using PL/SQL, and C++, making changes to our core product
- Developed simple unified process for source control (CVS), build management, and deployment for Professional Services solutions
- Developed tools to support this process using shell tools, Perl, and Solaris packaging tools

Head of Development   *Be New Media*   *December 1999–June 2000*

- Developed prototype for web content hosting business using Linux, Apache, MySQL, and Perl (LAMP)
- Provided technical expertise to business decision making process, including participation in marketing, financing, business development, and planning activities

Work Experience – continued

Lead Developer *Sussex Transmedia* *December 1998–October 1999*
- Lead technical team in developing new DirectX (Win32) turn-based strategy game using C and Delphi
- Mentored junior technical staff
- Designed and developed rendering engine, networking protocols, and graphics effects

Programmer/Analyst *Big Bank & Dominion Securities* *December 1995–December 1998*
- Maintained real-time systems for foreign exchange (cheque and note) rate capture, and calculation which also distributed those rates to internal clients, international information bureaux (Reuters, Telerate, etc.), the Big Bank retail network, and Internet trading using C, C++, Sybase, TIBCO, Motif, SNA, 3270 emulation, and various in-house custom technologies
- Handled all aspects of extended these HP-UX based FX systems to support money market, and precious metals rates, from analysis, through design, implementation, testing, and deployment
- Handled all aspects of extended our HP-UX, Motif, TIBCO, and Sybase based real-time money market trading system to support custom splits for complex bought deals, providing analysis, design, implementation, testing, and deployment
- Integrated third party Repo trading system into our global trading system in London, Sydney, Toronto, and New York
- Developed application servers and user interfaces for real-time financial trading systems using C, C++, Motif, Excel (w/ custom plugins), TIBCO, Sybase, and DCE-RPC.

Program Manager – Co-op *Big Software* *May–August 1993*
- Coordinated multilanguage issues between Word, Excel, and PowerPoint groups
- Developed dictionary and installation policy for French and German version of MS Office 3.0
- Managed small text resource translation (French and German) project
- Managed inclusion of Clip-Art gallery in BS Office 3.0
- Evaluated several third party software products considered for inclusion in BS Office

Lead Programmer/Analyst – Co-op *Imaging Inc.* *August–December 1992*
- Took new Motif/UNIX based medical imaging product from functional specification through design, prototyping, development, and the initial stages of testing
- Delivered C/C++ based prototype to international trade show
- Worked closely with Imaging's European client's engineers and managers

EDUCATION AND RESEARCH EXPERIENCE

Honors B. Math, with *State University* *December 1994*
distinction (Dean's Honor list)
- Double Major – Computer Science and Pure Mathematics
- Top 100 prize in Putnam mathematics competition (among North American mathematics undergraduates)

Research assistant *January–August 1995*
- Developed symbolic linear algebra functionality for the MapleV software package
- Improved special function handling in MapleV

Research assistant *May–August 1994*

Overseas University *Hungary* *January–May 1992*
- Term abroad in pure mathematics (geometry and hyper-graph theory)

SPORTS: BAD—Sports Operations

Alice J. Johnston
123 Learning St. Anytown, ST, USA 10101 (999) 555-1212

OBJECTIVE

To obtain a challenging position within the sporting goods industry that will utilize my strong operational, sales, retail, and managerial skills to their fullest.

EMPLOYMENT HISTORY

WORLD SPORTS   **Anytown USA**   **Sept '97–Present**
Operations Manager
Responsibilities included
- Supervision of Customer Service and Warehouse Staff
- Trade Show budget planning
- Attendance at all major trade shows
- Office troubleshooting (cost reductions, efficiency standards)
- Sales throughout North America
- Implementation of new projects
- Supervision of Sales staff at all trade shows
- Hire, train staff and contractors
- Trade show marketing and advertising
- Implementation of new procedures
- Trade Show booth design and layout
- Trade show logistics
- Design and implementation of all P.O.P and T-shirts
- Execution of all sales presentations

RIDES, INC.   **Dec '96–Aug '97**
Sales Representative
Responsibilities included
- Sales throughout North America
- Assisted in product development
- Created several databases to increase efficiency
- Attendance at all major trade shows
- Assisted in graphic choices
- Designed mass mailers and faxes

What's Wrong?

- Too many bullet points
- Too much information about out-of-date or inapplicable jobs
- Too much wasted space
- Lackluster objective/profile or lack thereof
- No declared job role
- No accomplishments or specific and measurable results
- Name is too small or address is too large or both

Resume of Alice J. Johnston cont....

RETAIL INC.   Jul '95–Jan '97
Manager/Store Opener
Responsibilities included

- Managed retail staff
- Opened new four stores
- Trained and hired all staff
- Implemented sales goals and targets (individual, store)
- Merchandised
- Ordered product
- Assisted in buying
- Bank deposits
- Implemented several policies and procedures still used there today

BIG SPORTS   1985–1995
Merchandising Manager/Buyer
Responsibilities included

- Managed small staff
- Opening and closing of store
- In-store merchandising
- Creation and design of P.O.P and window displays
- Sales and cashier
- Assisted in buying and creating seasonal programs

EDUCATION

STATE COLLEGE   1993–1995
Sporting Goods Business Diploma
Major courses included Marketing, Sales, Economics, Merchandising, Organizational
Behavior, Financial Statistics, Small Business Management, and Computers (literacy in
Microsoft Excel, WordPerfect, Access, PowerPoint, Publisher, as well as Lotus 123,
CorelDRAW, and The Print Shop).

HOBBIES/INTERESTS

I enjoy playing many sports on a competitive level: baseball, soccer, golf, and volleyball.
On a recreational level I enjoy swimming, snowboarding, fishing, and in-line skating.
Other hobbies include poetry, computers, and philosophy.

REFERENCES

Furnished upon request.

SPORTS: Jr. Sports Manager

123 Learning Ave, Anytown, ST   AliceJ@yourname.com   (999) 555-1212

Alice J. Johnston
Junior Sports Manager

EDUCATION
- Bachelor of Science in Business Administration *Cum Laude*, State University, 2001
  Marketing Major, Communications Minor

EXPERIENCE

Big City Sports, LLC   Feb. 2003–Present
(Zephyrs Triple-A Baseball, Anytown Timbers A-League Soccer, ABC Park)
Community Outreach Manager
* Organized and implemented programs designed to connect the company and teams with the surrounding community—fulfilled donation requests, arranged player and mascot appearances, scheduled front office speaking engagements, led park tours, and coordinated participation in local service organizations.

Client Services Coordinator
* Managed eleven existing sponsorship accounts with responsibility for all advertising, promotions, event coordination, hospitality, signage, & end of season summary reports highlighting each sponsor's park exposure.
* Coordinated Community Outreach Program for the Zephyrs Baseball Club—arranged visits for local community organizations to each Saturday home game, provided Kid's Club memberships to local Boys and Girls Club, arranged player visits to children's hospital, and Police Activities League (P.A.L.).
* Designed marketing materials such as flyers, discount, & VIP cards for promotional nights at the stadium.

Luxury Suite Box Manager
Managed luxury suite boxes for all events at ABC Park. Functioned as the primary point of communication and coordination for all annual luxury suite box holders and nightly suite box renters. Additional responsibilities included concierge staffing, serving as a liaison between suite holders and other departments at the park and ticket distribution.

FIFA Women's World Cup
Functioned as Park Liaison between FIFA Match Commissioner, park operations, & the City Sports Authority.

State University Athletic Department   2001–2002
Athletic Department Intern
* Assisted Ticket Manager in daily functions of ticket office—issued tickets to campus sporting events utilizing the Ticketmaster network, worked as a will-call representative at various games held on campus, and closed out credit card and check deposits at the end of the day. Designed database for tracking men's basketball season ticket holder upgrades, as well as managed existing men's basketball ticket waiting list. Still in use today.
* Co-coordinator of women's basketball game day ticket operations.
* Helped develop team-marketing plans with the Marketing and Promotions staff, as well as prepared a proposal for women's basketball/retirement center promotion to be implemented the following season.
* Varsity Softball Game-Day Manager—served as contact person and supervisor for all home softball games.
* Worked with freshmen student-athletes as an academic mentor, meeting on a weekly basis to go over schoolwork and discuss various problems or issues concerning the transition from high school to college.

Varsity Softball Pitching Coach
Worked with five (5) varsity softball pitchers on improving their existing pitches, as well as developing new pitches. Provided advice & motivation to players in regards to both the physical and mental aspects of pitching.

ATHLETICS/ACTIVIES
Full Scholarship Division I softball pitcher – State University   1997–2001
- Team Tri-Captain (2001); Big East Athletic Conference's Aéropostale State Female Scholar-Athlete of the year (2001); Female Scholar-Athlete of the year (2001)
- Academic All-American District 2 1st Team (2001); Academic All-American 2nd Team (2001)
- 2nd Team All-Big East selection (2000); 2nd Team All-Northeast Region selection (2000)

ACA (Athletes for Community Action) Executive board member (1999–2001)   1998–2001
Habitat for Humanity, retirement center renovation project – Pennsylvania (2000), weeklong retreat (1999)

T. (555) 999 – 1212 Email johnj@yourname.com
123 Learning Avenue, Anycity, Anystate, 10101

John J. Johnston

Profile

Sports Agent and Marketing Coordinator.

Experience

Sports Agent, Basketball Association   2002–2004   **Anycity, AS**

- Negotiated and maintained over 5 million USD in basketball and marketing contracts for professional basketball players in the U.S. and in Europe.
- Increased clientele list from 3 to 22 in 2 years.
- Contributed on numerous athletic industry national and international marketing campaigns, working on these campaigns on both the behalf of the involved athlete and the brand.
- Worked daily to increase the level of professional relationships I had, using my employer as an introduction, and then connecting on my own to solidify and grow the relationship.
- Made daily contacts and kept strong relationships with high profile NBA team personnel, coaches, general managers, and players; did this by being professional, prepared, and concise.
- Was 24 hours per day, 7 days a week, 365 days per year accessible to each and every athlete we represented. Dedicated to each individual's success; at the same time keeping balanced with a hectic schedule.

Event Planner, Local Ball Park   2001–2002   **Anycity, AS**

- Organized Large-scale community-based events for a city run facility.
- Handled all PR and Marketing of each and every event.
- Organized and negotiated contracts from the NBA team using our facility for training camp to province wide coaching clinics.
- Worked on non-profit community building and based events for the youths of the area. Ran basketball clinics, workouts, and spring leagues.
- Met with vendors, sponsors, and participants daily to balance each aspect while at the same time adhering to a budget.

Residence Life Don, State University   2000–2001

- Organized several community-building events to enhance each student's first year of the university experience.

In Store Retail Assoc., Athletic Footwear   2000–2001

Education

1997-2001   State University   Anycity, AS

- Honors BA in English with a minor in Communications
- 4-year varsity basketball player

SPORTS: Sports Senior Sales

John J. Johnston

123 Learning St., Anytown, ST USA 10101 * 999-555-1212 johnj@yourname.com

Profile: Results-oriented, sales executive with over 20 years of experience selling a wide range of media products including the Olympics, sports properties such as entertainment programming, news, and radio. Has successfully launched new media outlets and rebuilt existing ones. Responds positively to changing markets conditions.

Sales and Marketing Experience

BBR Marketing and Sales	**1991–2004**
Sports – Account Manager	2001–2004
Olympic Marketing and Sales – Manager	1995–2001
Network Sales – Sales Team Manager	1993–1995
Newsworld Sales – Account Manager	1990–1993

- Initiated and secured the sale of over 25 Olympic Sponsorship agreements including several new sponsors. Over $60 million in sponsorship sales from 1996–2004.
- Led Olympic participation sales effort and achieved over $180 million in total sales in Olympic broadcasts from 1996–2002.
- Created multimedia Olympic consumer and trade promotions. Integrated the broadcast features seen on television with a complementary Internet feature.
- As Sales Team Manager 1993–95, grew territory by over 10% and made it one of the largest territories ($30 million annual sales—15% of the total corporate revenue). In 1994, despite a 3 month NHL Lockout, maintained total billing in territory in the fourth quarter by attracting new feature film clients.
- As Sports Account Manager secured and maintained long-term clients in premier professional sports properties. In the past three years, contributed to 10% annual sales growth of the Hockey play-offs.
- Doubled annual sales revenue to over $10 million and quadrupled the number of clients. This was achieved through a prospecting and presentation process to the agencies and clients in which audience research indicated that buyers of their products and services were more likely to be viewers.

Earlier Work History

Broadcast Sales - National Sales   **1987–1990**
Sold sponsorships of syndicated television and radio programs.
BIG BIZ - Account Manager   **1986–1987**
- Led business unit of 14 that successfully restructured a $24 million annual advertising media buying strategies, client gained nearly a 20% improvement in ad cost efficiency.

Admiral Supply - Partner   **1984–1986**
- Self-employed business consultant
Chute Broadcast Sales - Account Executive   **1983–1984**
- National television and radio sales.
TKO All News Radio - Account Executive   **1981–1983**
- National radio sales.
Binman Advertising - Account Executive   **1979–1981**
- Responsible for day-to-day ad operations.
Smith & Goby - Associate Media Director   **1973–1979**
- Managed business unit of 20 and oversaw ad planning and buying for key accounts.

Personal Interests and Associations: Member (Past) Board of Directors, Knights Minor Hockey League; Cancer Society—Canvasser; Board of Directors—District Ratepayers Association

Education/Training: Bachelor of Arts—Economics, State University 1971
Trintock International—Sales and Presentation Courses; The Art of Negotiation—Ross McBride Sales Training; State University—Marketing & Sales Seminars; State College—Intro to Marketing

JOHN J. JOHNSTON

123 Learning Road, Anycity, Anystate 10101
TEL: (555) 999-1212 email: johnj@yourname.com

Profile

An energetic and ambitious **Sports Marketing Executive** with a strong focus in the areas of account management, sponsorship planning and strategy, event, and project management. Comfortable in a range of sports promotion and marketing events and organizations over international boundaries.

A highly motivated manager possessing strong skills for client servicing, organization, and relationship building.

Professional Experience

Johnston Entertainment/The Fun Tour   Anycity, Anystate—2000 to 2005
Director

As a regional marketing company in operation for over five years, the responsibilities focused on servicing and consulting clients regarding corporate sponsorship strategy, hospitality, and event planning. Corporate clients included the NBA team, Insurance Company, Marketing International, ABC Capital Inc.

Accomplishments:
- Planning and execution of over 250 regional events from 1997 to 1999
- Increased revenues 50% within the second year of operation
- Acquired sponsors for The Fun Tour, raising over $150,000 in funds and contra, sponsors included Cooltaste Breweries, Soft Drink Inc, Investment Group
- Scheduled all events, secured venues, developed a marketing/advertising budget
- Produced marketing and promotional campaigns with local television and media
- Developed and implemented The Fun Tour corporate sales package and brochure (2002–2004 distribution 150,000)

Athletic Sports Marketing/Tennis USA   Anycity, Anystate—1995 to 2000
Marketing Executive

A key member of the sponsorship marketing and execution team for International Players Association, National Tournaments, and Cup tournaments.

Accomplishments:
- Participated in the management and planning for Tennis USA's operations (sponsorship sales/servicing, signage, hospitality, site preparation, and ticket sales)
- Developed and implemented sponsorship and promotional programs; pro-ams, corporate tennis days
- Generated corporate sponsorship for tournaments ($150,000 within the first 12 months)
- Ensured that corporate sponsors understood and realized the full value of their sponsorship dollar (media, corporate hospitality, signage, and leveraged programs)
- Developed an extensive database on more than 25,000 companies used on all Tennis USA direct mail campaigns, fundraising, and sponsorship sales initiatives

SPORTS: Sports Marketing (cont.)

ABC Communications Inc.   **Anycity—1992 to 1995**
Account Director

Codeveloped and executed sporting events in U.S.; including ATP Tour, PGA Tour, and the Beach Volleyball Circuit.

Accomplishments:
- Developed and sold corporate sponsorship packages for all of the above properties (total value of sponsorship sold was in excess of 1 million U.S.) sponsors included U.S. Bank, Automobile Maker, TV Channel, Cooltaste Brewery, Soft Drink Inc.
- Developed marketing and promotional campaigns with broadcast and media
- Serviced both title and secondary sponsors throughout the above tournaments
- Codeveloped and executed the Beach Volleyball Circuit which included twelve events in eight countries over a four month period

XYZ & Associates/A&B Enterprise Inc.   **Anycity, Anystate—1990 to 1992**
Leasing Manager

US Trust Company/Real Estate Brokerage   **Anycity, Anystate—1987 to 1990**
Sales Executive

EDUCATION
BA, State University, Anycity, Anystate   1984–1987
Sociology Major, Marketing Minor

Community College, State Real Estate Association, Anycity, Anystate   1987–1988
Industrial, Commercial and Investment Disciplines
Property Management

Local College, Anycity, Anystate   1987–1988
Anystate Real Estate Association License

Associations: Health Foundation, Anystate Golf Association, Tennis Open,
              Anystate Tennis Association, Anycity Basketball Foundation

Interests: Sports! Competitive golf, tennis, squash, biking, snowboarding, and skiing. In non-sports pursuits: history and traveling.

Alice J. Johnston, English & ESL Teacher

123 Learning St., Anytown, USA 10101   **999.555.1212**

English & ESL Teaching Experience *

1998–2004   **English**   *Jefferson C.I.*   **Grade 11 College**
Focus: Grammar, paragraph structure, essay structure, essay format, editing, test writing skills

Feb.–June 1997   **English (Adult)**   *Grace C.I.* **Night School**   **Grade 12**
Focus: Literature, essay writing and structure, rewriting, Independent Study mentorship

1997–1998   **ESL**   *State Collegiate*   **Levels 2, 3 ESL**
Focus: Grammar, reading, language study, remedial, multilevel instruction

1996–1997   **English, ESL**   *Dracard C.I.*   **Grade 9, Grade 11 ESL**
Focus: Advanced ESL language study, integrating language study into higher level writing

Feb.–June 1996   **English**   *Memorial C.I.*   **Grade 12 Adv.**
Focus: Essay portfolio, test and exam writing preparation, rewriting, literature, timed writing

Mar.–Aug. 1995   **ESL**   *State College*   **Grade 12 Adv., ESL, ESD**
Focus: College preparation, language study (all levels, multilevel ESL), test writing

Sept.–Dec. 1995   **English**   *State Memorial C.I.*   **Grade 10, Grade 12 Adv.**
Focus: Writing structure and style, language study, literature, media, organization

Nov.–Dec. 1994   **Business English**   *Wallace Simpson C. I.*   **Grade 11, 12**
Focus: Writing for business, letters, proposals, informative essay structure, remedial

Dec.–June 1994   **Adult Day School**   *Wallace Simpson C. I.*   **Guidance Course**
Focus: Personal writing process, discussion, personalized study
* Other than State College, all schools listed above are with the Anytown District School Board.

Other Work Experience
2000–to date   **Flow Yoga Teacher** (over 200 adult students; various studios)
2001–to date   **Specialized Workshops for Adults: Wellness & Lifestyle Coaching**
1994–1976   **Hilltop S.S. Night School: Occasional Teacher**
1986–to date   **Private Tutor: ESL, Essay Writing, Organization,**
1994   **Computer Education Coordinator** *Computer Center*

1993–1994   **Bachelor of Education**   1988–1992 **Honors B.A.,** *Dean's Honor Role*
    I/S - English, Drama   *AQ* - ESL Part 1   Major - Classical Studies
    State University   State University

TEACHING: New Teacher

Alice J. Johnston

alicej@yourname.com
123 Learning St., Anytown, ST, USA 10101
(999) 555-1212

OBJECTIVE : **To be a reliable, competent, and professional teacher and an experienced, role model traveler teaching a summer course abroad.**

LANGUAGES :
English (mother tongue), French (fluent), Portuguese (fluent), Spanish (conversational)

EDUCATION :

Sept. 2004–present

State University
MASTERS OF EDUCATION in Language, Culture, and Teaching
FULL-TIME STUDENT and T.A. for a First Year Humanities Course

- Currently working on course work; research interests include critical multiculturalism, globalization and education, and pre-service teacher education

1994–1999

State University
BACHELOR OF EDUCATION - Secondary English and History

- National Honor Society, Dean's Athletic Honor Role, CGPA: 3.7

PROFESSIONAL EXPERIENCE :

Jan. 2005–present

Hampton School for Girls
SUPPLY TEACHER: fill in for teachers as needed.

Aug. 2002–June 2004

Sao Paolo American School (South America)
TEACHER: Taught grade 6, 10, and 11 English and grade 9 World History.

- Participated in the development of K–12 social science curriculum
- Organized and led leadership and group building retreats for students
- Acted as advisor for the Junior class as it raised over $5000 and organized the senior prom
- Worked with colleagues from both South American and American programs to align curriculums
- Aligned grading practices and rubrics within the English department
- Supervised students on community service outings to help children in the slums
- Used course-web as a tool for student learning and parent-teacher communication

Sept. 2000–June 2002

St. Mary's Secondary School
TEACHER: Taught grade 9 English, grade 10 History, grade 11 English, and OAC English at an academically focused urban high school. Worked with course-teams to organize and implement new state curriculum.

STAFF ADVISOR: Peer Mentor Program. Assisted student leaders in coordinating, planning, and running a program to help grade nine students integrate into high school. Led an outdoor training retreat for new 'buddies.'

State Collegiate Institute

Mar.–June 2000

TEACHER: Taught grade 9, 10, and 11 English at a wonderfully multicultural (40 languages spoken) urban high school. Facilitated learning for many E.S.L. students and youth at risk.

Sept. 1999–Mar. 2000

State College

L.T.O. Supply Teacher: Took full responsibility for two grade nine geography classes for a period of four weeks and worked as a substitute teacher for a variety of subjects.

Oct.–Dec., 1998

Anytown Middle School

STUDENT TEACHER (remote placement): Assumed full teaching responsibilities for grade 7/8 English, grade 7/8 General History, grade 9 English, and grade 10 History.

- Participated in parent-teacher interviews

PROFESSIONAL DEVELOPMENT:

2002–2004

- Led staff-development workshops on <u>Student Led Assessment of Learning</u> and the application of research on <u>Creative Writing</u> as a teaching strategy.
- Participated in a two-day workshop on Application of Research Studies on <u>Assessment</u> of Student Learning.
- Participated in a two-day workshop on <u>Peer Coaching.</u>
- Attended a one-day workshop on <u>Curriculum Assignments</u> in order to promote student achievement and success in <u>Advance Placement</u> programs.

WORK RELATED EXPERIENCE:

Fall 1997–Spring 1998

Students for Literacy *Youth at Risk Center*

VOLUNTEER: Planned recreational and literary activities with a group of 14–17 year old males under the Youth Protection and Young Offenders Programs.

Fall 1997–Spring 1998

Sexual Assault Center of State University

VOLUNTEER: Completed 30 hours of training for the OUTREACH Public Education Program and then led discussions with high school and college students.

OTHER WORK EXPERIENCE:

Anytown Museum and Historical Society

LIBRARIAN/RESEARCHER: Completed and responded to general and genealogical research requests using primary sources, kept inventory of the resource library, and assisted visitors in their research.

ADDITIONAL ACTIVITIES AND INTERESTS:

<u>TRAVELING</u>: Alone and in small groups to South America, Central America, Central Europe, Scandinavia, Northern Africa, South East Asia, and beyond!

<u>SPORTS</u>: Varsity figure skating 1994–8, dance (Latin and hip-hop), aerobics, weight training, spinning, biking, hiking etc.

<u>CREATIVE SIDE</u>: Acoustic guitar, vocals, piano, song-writing, poetry writing.

TEACHING: New Teacher, Elementary

Address: 123 Learning St.
Anytown, ST, USA 10101

Telephone: (h) 999-555-1212
(c) 999-555-1313
Email : johnj@yourname.com

John J. Johnston

Junior Elementary School Teacher

Summary of Qualifications

- Committed to Professional Development. Demonstrate diversity in professional educational opportunities.

- Two years exciting and rewarding experience in inner-city schools.

- Success creating a collaborative and cooperative student-centered learning environment; experience with team-teaching in a variety of forms.

- Enthusiastic and creative. A dedicated team player in the school community.

Education

Bachelor of Education, Elementary Program   2003
Saint Stephanie University, Anytown, State

Cooking Diploma   1998
Anytown Community College, Anytown, State

Certificate in Business Administration   1996
Saint Stephanie University, Anytown, State

Bachelor of Arts Degree, General Studies   1995
Saint Stephanie University, Anytown, State

Teaching Experience

Substitute Teacher   April 2003–Present
Anytown Regional School Board

Tutor   June–August 2003
English Language Arts, Grade 1/2 and Mathematics, Grade 5/6

Pre-Service Teaching Experience

Grade 2   September 2002–April 2003
- Mentor Teacher: Linda Market
Eastern Memorial/Back Bay School, Eastern Memorial site, Anytown, State

Grade 5   January–April 2002
- Cooperating Teacher: Penny Kind
Water View Elementary School, Anytown, State

Grade 2   October–December 2001
- Cooperating Teacher: Tim McDogal
Water View Elementary School, Anytown, State

Volunteer Experience

CREATE Art Education Workshop Volunteer   2002 & 2003
Eastern Memorial/Back Bay School, Anytown, State

Grade 3 Classroom Volunteer   2000–2001
Jack Hamilton Elementary School, Anytown, State

Resource Center Volunteer   2000–2001
Winterwoods Elementary School, Anytown, State

Primary Classroom Volunteer   2000–2001
Winterwoods Elementary School, Anytown, State

John J. Johnston   **2**

Professional Development/ Certification Training		
Cardiopulmonary Resuscitation and First Aid		2003
(Saint John's Ambulance, Anytown, State)		
Second Step: A Violence Prevention Program		2002
Irondale Conflict Resolution Workshop		2002
(Water View Elementary School, Anytown, State)		
Peer Mediation Training		2003
Issues of Abuse Workshop		2003
Focus on Belonging Workshop		2003
Creating a Culture of Care Workshop		2003
True Colors Workshop		2003
Creating and Supporting Safe School Communities P.D. Series		2003
Project Wild		2002
Developing Algebraic Thinking and Problem Solving, grades 2–5		2003
(Saint Stephanie University, Anytown, State)		
The Bully, the Bullied, and the Bystander		2002
(Driekers University, Anytown, State)		
Active Young Readers		2001–2003
(WaterView Elementary and Eastern Memorial School)		
Association of Science Teachers Conference		2002
Mathematics In-service, grades Primary-2		2002
School Improvement Plan Development		2002–2003
(Eastern Memorial/Back Bay School, Anytown, State)		
WHMIS Training		1997
Level 1 Food Safety Training Program		1997
(Anystate Community College, Anytown, State)		

Computer Skills

Software: M.Y.O.B, Excel, PowerPoint, Inspiration.

Peripherals: Digital Camera, Scanner, and LCD Projector.

Non-Teaching Employment History	
Woodland Golf Club	June 2003–Present
Food and Beverage Waiter	
Soho Bistro and Bar, Anytown, State	July 2002–Present
Food and Beverage Waiter	
Café Cool, Anytown, State	1994–2002
Operator and Managing Partner/Head of Kitchen	

Interests and Activities	
Provide catering services for small parties	1998–Present
Played percussion for four-piece band, Anytown, State	1995–1999
Served as Outdoor Education Assistant, Camp Meegwich	1992
Skiing, Cycling, Camping, Writing, Painting, Gardening	

TEACHING: Teacher Facilitator

Alice J. Johnston

123 Learning St., Anytown, USA 10101 (999) 555-1212
phone message (999) 555-1313; email alicej@yourname.com

Profile

As an enthusiastic, motivated **Teacher, Facilitator, and Workshop Leader**, who believes that global education is an integral part of any classroom experience. Possesses the critical success skills in facilitation: establishing goals, priorities, and integrity based on academic learning, training, and teaching plus long, varied practical workplace experience—especially with diverse cultures, races, organizations.

Teaching Experience

Anytown District School Board, Secondary School Teacher   1999 to present

State Collegiate Institute: *Full-Time*
I enjoy teaching at an inner city school of over 700 multicultural, multiracial, income diverse students. I teach Business Studies (BOH 4M, BOA, BBI, BDE, TIK, DIC; English Language and Literacy (EPS3, ENG 4U, 4C, 3U, 1D1, 2A, 2P); and History (2A).

State Collegiate: Adult Continuing Education Teacher   1999 to 2002
State Collegiate: Continuing Education, Summer School Teacher   2001

Additional Teaching Projects   1999 to 2004

- Instructor for Joint Venture: Local Construction Labor Union's apprentices to develop preliminary School-to-Work transition training (1999)
- Junior Achievement Liaison Teacher, State Collegiate (1999 to 2002)
- Member, Grade 10 Civics Curriculum Review Committee (2001)
- Writer, Big Publication Corporate Profiler, Secondary School, pilot program for Business Studies, cross curricular learning activities in Guide (2001)
- Board Member and Team Leader, STEA (Science and Technology in Education Alliance), Teacher's Kit, for State Science Grade 7 Unit (1999 to 2004)
- In-school Presenter to Staff, on Resources for Cross Curriculum Literacy (2004)

Selected Facilitation Experience: A Few Typical Assignments

Alice J. Johnston Enterprises, Independent Consultant   1995 to 1999
Based on my earlier Operations and Marketing experience at Department Store and Real Estate Shopping Centers, I worked as a consultant providing guidance to both public and private companies and enabling management change.

***AXY, USA*, Fundraising Analysis for Education (1996 to 1998)**
Surveyed individual, corporate, and internal support for major gifts program for Sir Monty Green College; facilitated discussions with volunteers; provided counsel for the launch.

In a different environment, gathered business-wide, educational requirements of employees for Human Resource Executives in the Pulp and Paper Association. In the face of global competition, assessed member CEOs' interest in establishing a common, industry Learning Foundation.

Alice J. Johnston, Facilitation Resume Cont page 2/2

Associate, Consultants Inc., **Strategic and Technology Services** (1995 to 1997)
Facilitated a national conference of employees (managers) to develop a new work culture that blended trends, values, customers, and technology.

Manager, Consultants Inc., **Communications** (1994 to 1995)
Led workshop groups of managers nationally to assess problems and develop solutions for a better balance of work and personal life. Presented report to executive, resulting in more work flexibility, education, and internal communication.

Voluntary Leadership in Education and Training

- Leadership to improve adult learning, equity integration, and assessment practices (1996 to 1999)
    - Board of Trade: Board Director, Unit Chair Human Resources, Co-Chair Education & Training Committee, Member Environment Committee
    - Anytown Training Board, Executive Member, Business
    - State University, School of Retailing, Member, External Committee, and Distance Education Degree Project
- Presentations and Facilitations to Annual Industry Conferences (1991 to 1997) such as Retail Council, Society of Association Executive, International Group of Shopping Centers

Education

MA in Psychology, State School of Professional Psychology, 1996
BA in English Language and Literature, (4-year program) State University, 1963

Other Training and Certification

- College of Education, Certificate of Qualification: 1964
- Honors Specialist: English, 1999
- Graduate, Series 7, 1986

Professional and Personal Development

- Member of Institute of International Affairs since 1972
- Member of Anytown Association of Business and Economics since 1986
- Favorite books read recently: *Fire and Ice: The United States, Canada and the Myth of Converging Values* by Michael Adams, *What Went Wrong?: The Clash Between Islam and Modernity in the Middle East* by Bernard Lewis; *Bel Canto* by Ann Patchett

TECHNICAL: Technical Writer, Sr.

123 Learning St., Anytown, USA 10101 • 999-555-1212 • johnj@yourname.com

John J. Johnston

A publishing professional specializing in content writing and editing, desktop publishing, layout, and design. Dedicated to delivering "the goods" on time and being responsive to your needs. Personable, with a flair for applying creative and artistic talents, I have extensive experience with pre-press production and project management facilitation.

WRITING AND EDITING	• I edited and produced three newsletters (a weekly, monthly, and a bimonthly) according to strict deadlines for Coorswell, Tommy Pro Publishing.
	• Rose to challenge of writing technical documentation for MPPS, efficiently delivering software manuals and online help on a timely basis, as well as coordinating the publication/production process. Vice President and Director of R & D personally commended my work.
	• Edited standardized assessment tests for MPPS, which required working independently, as well as liaising with professionals and authors and understanding behavioral psychology.
	• Helped develop a knowledge base and improve the dissemination of information at Grovel & Groan, along with providing end-user documentation.
	• At Freddy Kruger Ltd., came in cold to new subject matter and tight deadlines. Interviewed subject matter experts then wrote and edited documentation praised by senior staff.
FACILITATION OF PROJECT MANAGEMENT AND QUALITY ASSURANCE	• A release of "buggy" software at Grovel & Groan required documenting over 300 problems, tracking and testing these issues, writing solid, dependable workarounds on an ongoing basis, and maintaining close contact with technical support representatives who were relating customer complaints.
	• Facilitated collaboration between technical support and Amgone Group clients by developing an implementation guide, which helped clients navigate through complex software and set up their property management systems.
GRAPHICS & LAYOUT	• Created graphics, flowcharts, drawings with Photoshop, Illustrator, and Visio.
	• Designed, implemented, and maintained several online Help systems.
	• Snapped and created/altered screenshots for inclusion in print and online documentation.
SOFTWARE APPLICATIONS	• FrameMaker, PageMaker, QuarkXpress, Photoshop, Illustrator, RoboHelp (Classic and HTML), RoboDemo, MS Access, PowerPoint, Excel, Acrobat, Visio, Dreamweaver, Front Page, SnagIt, Visual SourceSafe.
CREATIVE FLAIR	• Recently illustrated a children's book entitled, *Harry the Hippo Goes Flippo*.
	• Past accomplishments include illustrating CD covers, as well as providing illustrations for T-shirts and posters for bands and charities.
	• Used creative talents to illustrate and help design a company newsletter.
EDITORIAL PRE- AND POST-PRESS PRODUCTION	• Worked arduously as a copyeditor/paginator to help produce two editions of a weekly suburban newspaper serving the Poughkeepsie/Arlington area.
	• Organized PDF files, graphics, and fonts for sending documentation to printers.
	• Liaised with print personnel to ensure production went smoothly, and finalized and approved galleys for printing.

123 Learning St., Anytown, USA 10101 • 999-555-1212 • johnj@yourname.com

WORK EXPERIENCE:

Amgone Group   January 2003–April 2004
Documentation Specialist

Documented new features and procedures on an ongoing basis, producing marketing literature, creating graphics, and maintaining the company website.

Skills applied: Writing, editing, desktop publishing, webpage creation, and liaising between departments.

Freddy Kruger Ltd.   May 2002–November 2002 (Contract)
Senior Technical Communicator

Employed on a contractual basis in the Jason Initiative project documenting various end-user guides for an internal system based on Michael software.

Skills applied: Writing and editing, extracting and conveying information from subject matter experts, understanding accounting practices, and desktop publishing.

Grovel & Groan Software Inc.   November 1999–April 2002
Documentation Writer/Editor

Employed in the Products and Development department writing end-user and marketing documentation for Amookus Attorney, a legal case-management software program.

Skills applied: Writing and editing, working under pressure to meet tight deadlines, multi-tasking, and desktop publishing.

Multi-Hach Systems Inc.   March 1997–October 1999
Technical Writer/Editor

Employed in the Research and Development department writing/editing software and technical manuals for psychiatric and professional standardized assessments.

Skills applied: Writing and editing, working independently and meeting tight deadlines, displaying a flexibility to take on many projects at once, and writing user documentation.

Coorswell, Tommy Pro Publishing   July 1995–March 1997
Production Editor

Was primarily responsible for the production of three newsletters for subscribers in the legal community: *The Weekly Digest of Civil Purport; The Digest of Law;* and *The Digest of Environmental Assessment.*

Skills applied: Editing, desktop publishing skills, and organizing a heavy workload to meet tight deadlines.

The Suburbaniac Newspapers Ltd.   July 1994–July 1995
Copy Editor/Paginator

Copyedited columns, news stories, and articles and used QuarkXpress to paginate The Poughkeepsie Suburbaniac and The Arlington Suburbaniac, weekly community newspapers serving large portions of the Greater Poughkeepsie/Arlington Area.

Skills applied: Adhering to strict deadlines on a tight weekly schedule; copyediting and desktop publishing skills.

POST-SECONDARY EDUCATION:

State College   September 1998–March 1999
Technical Communication I and II

State University   September 1986–May 1989
BA in English

State College   January 1983–May 1986
Diploma in Humanities

HOBBIES/CREATIVE ACCOMPLISHMENTS:

1   Drawing caricatures and illustrations. I have designed CD covers, T-shirts, and coffee mugs.
2   Playing acoustic guitar, singing, and songwriting (I have written songs that are performed by a local punk band). I play harmonica too and regularly attend open mic nights.

TECHNICAL: Technical Writer

Alice J. Johnston

123 Learning Ave., Anytown, USA (999) 555-1212 alicej@yourname.com

Skills & experience

- Plain language and technical writing
- Stylistic, structural, and copyediting
- Clear visual design
- Project planning and management

- Web writing, design, and usability
- Teaching, training, and facilitation
- Assessment and testing of print information
- Fluency in English and Spanish

Computer skills: Proficiency in both Windows 2000 and Lotus Notes 5.0 environments; basic skills in HTML coding and webpage design; regular use of Inter- and intranet publishing and search tools, scanners, OCR software, and relational databases. Conversant with and quick to learn new applications.

Areas of specialty

- Organizational communications (internal and external)
- Guidelines, policies, and procedures
- Health information and medical instructions
- Forms, questionnaires, and educational materials
- Information for diverse audiences, from basic level to sophisticated audiences

Recent writing, editing, & consulting
*(Staff positions are in **bold italics**)*

Our Kids USA (PPP [April to July 2002])
- Edited plain language safety and policy information for PPP partners and the public.

State University Health
National Eating Disorders Information Centre (NEDIC [May 2002])
- Revised *An Introduction to Food and Weight Problems* to improve clarity.

The Kid's Hospital (TKH)
Health Communication Service, Centre for Health Information and Promotion (December 2000 to March 2002) *Plain Language Writer/Educator*
- Developed information to educate patients and families at TKH; collaborated with internal clients on design, illustrations and field tests for print, web and other media; presented and developed resources on plain language for TKH staff.

Independent Living (May to December 2001)
- Conceived and developed design for multisection manuals, both for consumers and IL staff; revised new and existing policies to improve clarity.

Origami Ltd. (May 2001)
- Adapted a medical instruction booklet into plain language for a layman audience.

Alice Johnston – Recent writing, editing & consulting (continued)

Anytown Training Center (June 2000 to February 2001)
- *Smoking cessation resources for low-literacy readers (3 separate publications):* rewrote materials in plain language and consulted on design; conducted field tests with sample readers, reported on and incorporated findings; trained public health staff on clear language principles.

American Health Network (AHN [December 1998 to October 2000]**)**
Writer/Communications Consultant
- *Frequently Asked Questions (FAQs):* managed project to develop over 350 questions and answers for consumers and health providers, to be posted on the AHN website.
- *Internal Communications:* wrote or contributed to internal style guides, newsletters, clear language and design guidelines, and procedural documents for staff and partners.
- *Development of AHN website:* wrote, edited, and ensured quality of explanatory and facilitative text; advised on design and other user-centred aspects.

Training, presentation, & publication

AnyStateToday, WKRP (October, 2002) • Guest on phone-in show about plain language

Plain Language Group (September, 2002) • *Biennial Conference;* Co-Chair and lead on Communications

Health World (May 2002) • *Designing Clear Health Information on a Limited Budget;* speaker

Anytown's Center for Literacy (March 2002) • *Clear Communication: Skills for Reaching Diverse Audiences in Healthcare Settings;* guest presenter and full-day trainer of 35 nurses and other clinical staff at General Hospital

International Patient Conference (June 2001) • *Health Literacy* breakfast presenter

Capistrano College, School of Media (September to December 2000) • *Public Relations and Presentation Skills;* course instructor

Related activities

Plain Language Group (1999 to present) • Member

Technical Communication Society (2000 to present) • Member

State U • (2000 to present; *expected graduation in spring, 2006) Master of Education,* Adult Education • (1988 to 1992) *Honors Bachelor of Arts,* Spanish Language and Literature; graduated with Distinction

HTML Writers' Guild (2001) • Accessible Web Design online course

Regional Literacy, Board of Directors (1997 to 2000) • Vice President 1999 to 2000; Chair, Personnel Committee 1998 to 2001

TECHNICAL: Technical Manager

John J. Johnston

123 Learning Street, Anytown, ST, USA 10101   Tel: (999) 555-121   johnj@yourname.com

PROFILE: **TECHNICAL MANAGER** – Great with compelling applications using sound development practices in environments that recognize the benefits of a lightweight (and rapid) development process.

SKILLS: Strong object-oriented design/architecture/programming (OOD/OOA/OOP) skills (including use of design patterns, continuous integration, unit tests, and test based design)
Extremely proficient in Java, Visual J++, C++, Visual C++, C, Visual Basic, and Pascal
Trained in UML/Design Patterns (by RADSoft, www.radsoft.com) and have made extensive use of UML diagrams to assist with design work (using GDPro, Rational Rose, and Visio)
Trained in CORBA and have designed/implemented many CORBA services (using both Java/C++ language bindings) with ORB's from both Borland (VisiBroker) and Iona (ORBIX)
Very strong database skills including Relational Databases (Oracle, MySQL, PointBase, DB/2-UDB) as well as pure Object Databases including both POET, and Versant
Solid understanding of OLE/COM (particularly event sinks using OLE Automation Servers)
Operating systems worked on include: Windows NT/9x, Sun OS/Solaris 2.5/2.6, AIX, OS/2, Macintosh System 7.x, HP-UX, Digital UNIX, IBM VM/CMS, IBM MVS

WORK EXPERIENCE:

Software Technical Project Manager
ABC Inc.
July 2001–Current

- Lead software developers, quality assurance, product engineering in the deployment of major wireless back-end components on behalf of ABC's customer base. Also provide design/development/mentorship as required

- Recently completed the successful management of a major application development test/deploy to O3 Ireland for a wireless Group application which will be released to their customer base shortly (http://www1.o3.ie/business/voice_and_business_services/group)

- Designed/developed/deployed a very successful application for O3 Ireland known as the 'Hello' SMS (Short Message Service) that allows pre/postpaid wireless subscribers to initiate calls back to them, from other wireless subscribers. O3 now experiences over 170,000 Hello's every single day within their network (http://www1.o2.ie/products_services/mobile_services/hello)

- Primary languages/platforms include Java on Windows NT and UNIX/Solaris (Java 2 SDK 1.3.1/1.4), JUnit testing framework, StarTeam source control, and CORBA 2.3 (VisiBroker for Java v4.5), Oracle 8i (8.1.7) and the Jakarta Ant Java build/deploy framework

ABC Inc., develops network billing infrastructure and associated applications for mobile carriers. ABC is quickly becoming the dominant network application/infrastructure provider for mobile carriers in Europe.

Technical Team Lead/Software Architect
XYZ Media Inc.
July 2000–June 2001

- Worked as software architect responsible for designing/developing a virtual channel mechanism for use with XYZ's MicroJava set-top box platform (with both enhanced and interactive television). This virtual channel mechanism provides XYZ Media with a tool to build virtual channels and to specify and publish a variety of content to those channel(s)

Technical Team Lead/Software Architect (Continued)
- Worked as technical team lead on a series of regional websites which XYZ had been contracted to design, develop, and implement on behalf of Sports Channel (this included: leading the design and development of a series of back-end components to support the administration and view of dynamic webpages using Java Servlets/JSP, on the regional web sites; overseeing the deployment of those sites to the customers production system – including all configuration management issues; directing team members on work items and deliverables)

- Primary languages/platforms included Java on Windows NT and UNIX/Solaris (Java 2 SDK 1.3.1), Java Servlets, Java Server Pages with JavaBeans, MySQL/JDBC on WebLogic

- XYZ Media Inc., develops interactive websites for large scale media companies and is moving aggressively to become a major content producer/provider for the rapidly growing interactive TeleVision (iTV) space

Senior Software Engineer, Info-Look Corporation   **1995–April 2000**
- Designed and implemented a protocol/application independent communications layer (which supports SNA/TCP-IP and local connections) using 100% Pure Java in order to support Info-Look's enterprise level data transformation software and to provide support for JDBC BLOB's and CLOB's within Transformation Server for PointBase

- Designed and implemented a 100% Pure Java compatible expression parser/tokenizer/evaluator for Info-Look's latest data transformation server product which supports all JDBC compliant relational database systems (including PointBase, Inprise's J/DataStore, and DB2/UDB), using Sun's parser generator tool JavaCC (now being maintained by Metamata Inc.)

- Primary languages/platforms included Java on Windows 95/NT (Visual J++) and UNIX (Sun's JDK 1.1.8/1.2.2)

- Info-Look develops and sells a complete line of enterprise wide tools for transforming and mirroring data across heterogeneous computing and database platforms

- Developed a Win95/NT DLL using Visual C++ that extends Algo's Visual Basic compatible macro language to provide dynamic inquiry of COM/OLE 2.0 automation objects for outgoing callback interfaces so that event sinks may be established for these interfaces. This functionality replicates a feature used in Visual Basic for Applications (i.e., the "WithEvents" language construct)

- Primary languages/platforms included C++/Visual Basic on NT/UNIX (Cygnus GNU C/C++ compiler on Sun Solaris, Digital UNIX, and HP-UX) and Visual C++ for Windows NT

Senior Software Engineer, Systems Limited   **Oct. 1992–Nov. 1995**
- Designed and developed new feature sets for Systems automated facilities mapping (AM/FM) tool, including a platform independent raster graphics engine, a digitizing driver for large scale graphics tablets and a more efficient C-spline algorithm

- Developed a series of low-level display drivers for Systems first generation AM/FM tool which allowed users to run the product on many different display sub-systems under DOS and OS/2 (sub-system support included EGA, 8514/A, XGA-1/2, SVGA using Video PMI)

- Primary languages/platforms included C++/C/Assembly language on OS/2 Intel and C on UNIX (Sun OS and IBM AIX)

Software Engineer, Isolation Systems Limited   **Oct. 1991–Oct. 1992**
EDUCATION: **BA-Computer Science**, State University (1991)

TECHNICAL: Technology Director

John J. Johnston
123 Learning St., Anytown, USA 10101; (999) 555-1212 Email: johnj@yourname.com

SUMMARY

An energetic, motivated, **Technology Director** with a positive, contagious energy who builds teams, creates relationships, and earns trust with his clients. Strong communication, interpersonal, leadership, and customer service attributes as well as a diverse information technology background.

Extensive experience in strategic planning, project management, information systems development/support/maintenance, budgeting, performance and change management, policy and standards programs, as well as senior management roles at both an organizational and individual team level.

PROFESSIONAL EXPERIENCE

ABC Consulting Services Inc. - Established May 2003

Securities Ltd. (CDS)   **December 2003 to May 2004**

- Reporting to the CIO SVP of Technology and Operations, created a strategy to reduce the external vendor software budget.
- In conjunction with the VP of Tech Operations, CDS Finance, & all the CDS external vendors established a detailed inventory of existing software & respective billings.
- Completed a 3-year strategic plan to reduce the software budget by 25%, reduce the number of software vendors by 50%, as well as increase and update the software used by the CDS Technology team.

Securities Ltd. (CDS)   **June 2003 to November 2003**

- Developed an all-inclusive end to end organizational Testing Strategy. Implementation included development of the policies, methodology, standards, and procedures.
- In addition, the creation and setup of a centralized test support services team, financial chargeback process, environments, tools, defined roles, and a training plan.
- Contract extended to develop an IT procurement process. Conducted data gathering interviews with the top ten vendors as well as the senior IT & Finance mgt team.

Big Bank of Commerce   **1987 to 2003**

Director - Technology & Operations Support Services   **(2000 to 2003)**
- Created and managed a team of 45 staff that supported the consolidated Technology division with information technology solutions, project management, administration support, and management information services.
- Expanded client base by 300% in the first 12 months with no increase in costs or FTE using automation and consolidation of processes.
- Designed, developed, and implemented an online management information report builder system. This system was built in house at a cost savings of over $700,000 and six months sooner than the submitted proposals of two highly regarded external vendors.
- Created a master facilities plan for the technology team including the negotiation of three new leases with external vendors based on multiple clients future growth needs.
- Creation of an internal Client Satisfaction survey resulting in increased client satisfaction results and improved operational efficiencies across the client base.

Director - Commercial & Specialty Business Systems   (1998 to 2000)

- Reporting directly to the Vice President, had direct responsibility for 2 major lines of business in the org as a member of the Commercial & Specialty Business sr. mgt teams.
- Responsibilities were at a senior management level working with the business clients and the Technology teams in the smooth execution of both project delivery and production support. These two lines of business had a mix of technologies including legacy systems.
- End to end accountability for the budgets, recruiting, facilities, training, performance management, career planning, coaching, expense management, staff retention, and resource planning was successfully managed for the 180 members of the portfolio.

Resource Manager - Technical Services and Offshore Systems   (1995 to 1998)
- Manage a resource portfolio of approximately 60 technology professionals including project managers, database analysts, programmers, testers, and technical specialists.
- Resource planning with business and project execution partners to staff projects across all of the Technology division.
- Managed automated tracking of resource utilization which produced base lines used to improve and maximize work on billable project activities.

Program Manager – Systems Development Standards Program   (1992 to 1995)
- Created the Standards Program for the Systems Development division.

Project Manager - Direct Deposit Accounts (DDA)   (1990 to 1992)
- Project manager for the Delivery Task Force project with a project team of 14 and a budget of $1.6 million over an 18-month period. The project was completed 3 weeks ahead of schedule and 9% under budget.

Senior Programmer/Project Leader Clearing & Check Processing   (1987 to 1990)
Big Bank - Intermediate Database Analyst   1984 to 1987

PROFESSIONAL DEVELOPMENT
Extensive leadership, technology, project, people, and change management training.
- Personal Mastery Executive Management 3 Year Program
- Organizational Development Resources (ODR) Change Management
- Tooling the Partnership - Business Group
- Quality Assurance Institute - Standards Development Program

SOFTWARE TOOLS
- Familiarity with HTML, internet technologies, & protocols
- Programming languages include COBOL, REXX, VBA

MEMBERSHIPS
- Association of Professional Computer Consultants (APCC)
- Project Management Institute (PMI)
- Quality Assurance Institute (QAI)

ACTIVITIES
Time with family, volunteer coach for community sports teams, and travel to exotic places like India, Nepal, and the Galapagos Islands.

TELEVISION: Producer Writer for TV

John J. Johnston
123 Learning St., Anytown, USA, 10101
phone: 999-555-1212   email: johnj@yourname.com

Producer/Writer/Researcher for Television and Film

Work Experience

Producer/Writer – TV, June 2002 to Present
- Writer/Researcher – series concept outlines for 2 Big Companies Films Inc.
- Associate Producer/Writer/Researcher – "Icebergs" – Storyline Entertainment
- Coproducer/Researcher – "POWS." Storyline/Historical Channel - In development
- Writer/Researcher – "Dead Dogs Calling" – Storyline/Graphic Pictures
- Project Coordination – corporate film – Office Transition Team

SCCC Solutions Manager, Dec. 2000 to June 2002
- Wrote proposals, "discovery" documents, and high-level functional specs.
- Managed development of marketing material; responsible for communication with clients and partners.
- Defined & planned online projects; budgets ranging from $20,000 to $6 million.

Media Contract Work, ABC Advertising Inc., 1996 to 1998
- Wrote content for websites, presentations, marketing materials, and videos.
- Market research, delivered marketing surveys, reviews, and recommendations.
- Conducted research meetings with corporate and government clients, conference participants, college and university faculty, and military IS personnel.

Account Manager, Big Communications LLC, 1995 to 1996
- Wrote proposals and did creative & budget planning for Internet, video, CD-ROM, and print projects.
- Wrote Internet content, promotional, and training materials.

Independent Writer/Producer, 1993 to 1995
- Wrote scripts, retained writers and story editors.
- Raised broadcast and private development funding to develop original series concepts.
- Conducted "pitch" meetings with network executives.
- Negotiated development contracts.

Technical
- HTML (basic), FrontPage 2000, Visio and Director, Photoshop, Flash.
- Experience with the rational process for project definition and deployment.
- Experience with various non-linear editing suites.

Education & Training
State University – B.A. (Hons. English Lit.)
Drama Studio UK – Post Graduate Program
American Film College – Television Producers Program
State Polytechnic University – Business of Film courses
University Extension Courses – Writing, Acting, Directing for the Camera

TELEVISION: Senior Marketing Research Television

Alice J. Johnston

Research, Projects Manager – 2005
ABC Media Company

Research Manager – 1998–2003
Young Children Programming

Director of Strategy & Research – 2004
Communicado Inc.

Sales & Research Coordinator – 1992–1998
Radio & TV

Director of Research – 2003–2004
AZY Broadcasting LLC

Buying Assistant 1986–1992
Big Retail Store

Key Qualifications

- Eight years in a **Senior Marketing Research** role
- Thirteen years of Television and Broadcasting experience
- Five years experience in the Youth Market
- Thirteen plus years media industry experience
- In-depth knowledge of research practices and principles
- Creative problem solver, focused on results and corporation's overall business goals
- Analytical data interpretation
- Effective presenter with the ability to communicate complex data and tailor it appropriately to various audience levels
- Multitask oriented, capable of managing priorities in a constantly changing environment.
- Advanced computer skills including all Microsoft Office tools, Database Programs, Desktop Publishing Software, Internet/web tools and various custom media software such as PMB, Media Adviser, Micro BBM

Achievements

- Designed and produced a research intranet at ABC Media Company
- Designed, produced, and launched first syndicated research study on kids age 9–14 yrs old.
- Designed and began a national study profiling young business owners
- Designed and created a quick facts on Internet use in order to champion new media as an effective advertising tool
- Set up a resource center for up to date information on key advertising developments in the new media environment
- Led a team of programmers to design and create a research software used to disseminate national broadcast data. System is now used across the country and in the U.S.
- Generated new revenue to YCP at the same time as positioning the station as the source of social and consumer behavior of American youth (brought in ↑ $300,000)
- Championed YCP's position as a leader in youth marketing
- Set up centralized Research Department at YCP
- Developed Sales presentations to position YCP television as a viable media choice
- Assessed program performance and evaluated against client's goals and strategies
- Championed YCP's position as a leader in youth marketing
- Assessed program performance and evaluated against client's goals and strategies

Alice J. Johnston ♦ 123 Learning St. ♦ Anytown, USA 10101 ♦
Tel: 999.555.1212. ♦ Fax: 999.555.1313 ♦ email: alicej@yourname.com

TELEVISION: TV Producer

alicej@yourname.com   (p) 999-555-1212

Alice J. Johnston

Television Manager and Producer – excels at launches shows, brands, and networks that attract viewers.

EXPERIENCE:

Managing Producer/Writer - Movies INC - TV Networks Inc.   Aug. 99–present
I researched, wrote, produced, and directed a weekly half-hour entertainment news show and spent 2 months determining the design, format, and content. In addition I:
- Liaised with publicists, talent, studio contacts, and external vendors
- Secured and coordinated celebrity interviews and shoots
- Managed the show's budget, staff, and freelancers
- Marketed the show internally and externally
- Initiated and executed new ideas and programming avenues to strengthen brand
Results: Top New Show on the Network; increased market share 2%

Manager, On Air Promotions & Production - Movieworks Inc.   Jan. 98–Aug. 99
For this company I managed and directed a creative team of 12 employees plus freelancers in these two roles:
Creative Director overseeing all on air products including promotions, TV Marketing campaigns, special projects, and animation packages
- Serviced the production and on air needs of the Marketing, Communications, and Programming Departments
- Negotiated external vendor contracts
- Managed HR issues of the On Air team (hiring, job reviews, etc.)
- Allocated and managed departmental budget
- Developed strategic plans as part of the Senior Management team
- Assisted in the construction and content maintenance of the company website
Supervising Producer of original programming - conceived & developed a half-hour news show which is still on air

TV Producer - Movieworks   March 96–Jan. 98
- Wrote and produced promos and marketing spots
- Produced Sales presentation tapes, and corporate spots including industry spot that opened the 1997 Anycity International Film Festival Gala screenings
- Directed voice talent and camera people

TV Producer; Production Coordinator, Showme Television   Nov. 94–March 96
- Assisted in launching the network; now one of the most highly regarded amongst cable networks for quality programming and market share
- Wrote on-air copy, produced promos, directed talent
- Coordinated and assisted with all on-air production including " Showme Revue", a weekly movie show

TV Production Assistant - TVTV Communications   May 94–Nov. 94
INTERNSHIPS: BIG CITY TV, Researcher & Production Assistant, National NEWS PA
EDUCATION: State Tech University – Post-Graduate Journalism Program - Bachelor of Arts 1994   Major: Broadcast Journalism - Television & Radio
State University – Bachelor of Arts 1992   Double Major: Mass Communications & English
INTERESTS & SKILLS: Cooking, mountain biking, photography, new media, basic HTML, CMC Management courses

RÉSUMÉ

John J. Johnston
123 Learning St.
Anytown, USA 10101

EDUCATION
1988 State University, Anytown
Bachelor of Fine Arts
Specialized in Film Production

1984 Anytown Secondary High School

COMPUTER SKILLS
Word, Word Perfect, Excel

STRENGTHS
Responsible and organized individual who learns quickly and takes initiative. Developer of efficient systems and procedures. Skilled in marketing, communications, and production coordination and administration. Experienced in film, video, and multimedia production.

CAREER GOAL
To become a professional television production manager.

WORK EXPERIENCE
View 2 (Corporate Video)
Production Manager   **November 1996–present**
-work with video producers to produce corporate videos costing from $5,000 to $165,000;
-create budgets & production and shooting schedules;
-secure locations, booked crew, cast talent;
-arrange prop, costume, vehicle & equipment rental and all necessary transportation, meals, and accommodation for cast & crew;
-assist Producer to stay on budget and on schedule (including negotiating rates and terms with suppliers), liaise with clients to set up shoots;
-secure rights for stock footage & stock music;
-arrange union contracts for talent;
-prepare monthly sales reports for Accounting department;
-invoice clients and reconcile budgets after projects are completed;
-maintain video library;

VTC Television (Creative Services Department)
Creative Services Coordinator   **February 1995–September 1996**
-worked with Creative Director of 'in-house advertising agency' ensuring that print ads and on-air promos for television and radio programming were produced on-budget and on-schedule.
-trafficked Creative Director's time, arranged Creative meetings and approval schedules;
-developed and wrote procedures documents;
-assisted Creative Director with implementation and streamlining of practices and procedures;
-liaised between freelance art directors & copywriters and department staff;
-debriefed executive management regarding recently produced print ads and promos;
-coordinated regular department meetings, coordinated outside requests for department

What's Wrong?
- Too many bullet points
- Too much information about out-of-date or inapplicable jobs
- No declared job role
- No accomplishments or specific and measurable results
- Name is too small or address is too large or both

TELEVISION: BAD—TV (cont.)

State Liquor Control Board (Marketing Communications Department)

Project Coordinator (video & print)   **March 1994–February 1995**

-compiled, edited and codesigned monthly SLCB marketing publication used by 600 outlets to plan and install monthly marketing initiatives;

-liaised between Marketing and A/V department for Marketing video projects;

-sourced and hired photographers to record all aspects of Marketing initiatives;

Yack Inc. (Advertising, Corporate Video & Multimedia)

Video Producer   **October 1992–February 1994**

-created motivational and informational videos in English and/or Spanish

-worked with writers, creative directors, account managers, and clients during each stage of production to deliver videos on budget and on schedule;

-production duties included directing crew and talent;

-post production duties included directing video edits and post audio sessions;

Multimedia Producer   **April 1992–February 1994**

-co-ordinated input between client, account manager, art department, and multimedia artist;

-created budgets and critical paths;

-hired multimedia artists, source & book other related suppliers.

Production Manager   **January 1993–February 1994**

-carried out most functions noted under VTC Video – Production Manager

-specialized in Federal Government contracts

Associate Producer   **February 1991–October 1992**

-worked with video producers as a Production Manager during pre-production and as an Assistant Director during production

Researcher, Senior Researcher   **May 1989–February 1991**

-sourced props, costumes, flatcopy, stock footage, film locations & permits;

-made video dubs & compilations; sourced talent for live events;

-beginning March 1990 position involved overseeing Research & Resource department;

Zack Productions Inc. (*Bannished* TV series)

Third Assistant Director   **July–November 1988**

-worked on set with 1st AD to ensure all props, talent, vehicles, animals, and crew were in the right place at the right time

THEATER: Production and Management

JOHN J. JOHNSTON

123 Learning St., Anytown, USA 10101   johnj@yourname.com   (999) 555-1212

Theater Production and Management

EDUCATION

2002–present   **SCHOOL OF MANAGEMENT, STATE UNIVERSITY**
Candidate for Master of Business Administration degree, June 2004.
(Dean's Honor List)
- Intended majors in management & strategy, finance, media management
- Member, Consulting Club, Entertainment and Media Business Network
- Adopt-A-Class Program, Golf Club, Social Impact
- Selected Arts/Entertainment Editor for the student paper

1994–1998   **STATE UNIVERSITY**
Bachelor of Arts (Honors), 1998, First-Class standing
- Received "Robertson" Award for top standing in dramatic theory & history
- Selected as Teaching Assistant for Introductory Drama course
- Managed campus pub during senior year, 35 hours per week, staff of 20

EXPERIENCE

2000–2002   **THEATERROUND,** *General Manager/Founder*
- Developed & implemented business plan for not-for-profit theater company & grew operating budget from $15,000/year to $100,000/year.
- Defined artistic, administrative, & governance structures.
- As producer, headed four theatrical productions employing 20 each.
- Quintupled revenues over 18-month period through public and private sector fundraising initiatives and increased box office revenue.
- Garnered three consecutive City theater award nominations for Best Independent Theater Production.
- Managed cross-functional teams consisting of artists, technicians, and board members.

1999–2002   **SELF-EMPLOYED,** *Actor*
- Selected from over 1,200 applicants for a place in Best Festival of Conservatory for Classical Theater Training.
- Performed in over 60 professional Film, Television, and Theater productions ranging from 9 different Shakespearean plays to nationally televised fast food commercials.

1998–1999   **BIG BANK,** *Financial Adviser*
- Established strategies to target specific demographic segments in order to grow portfolio $6 million.
- Exceeded a yearlong sales target in first 8 months in position.
- Managed a portfolio of 150 clients valued over $30 million.
- Took Securities, Professional Financial Planning courses.

OTHER DATA   Near fluency in Spanish; International Travel includes: North and South
Asia, China, Middle East, East and West Europe. Juggling for fun.

THEATER: Theater Professional

JOHN J. JOHNSTON
123 Learning Street, Anytown, USA 10101
(999) 555-1212   Email: johnj@yourname.com

CAREER OVERVIEW:

Through my varied career and education, I have developed a unique aptitude that provides me with a vocabulary and understanding to skillfully handle the artistic, economic, and cultural issues surrounding the theater.

BUSINESS EXPERIENCE:

2001–Present   **General Manager,** The Pete Standlish Theatre, New York

2002–Present   **General Manager,** R2D2 Theatre, New York

2004   **General Manager,** MY MOTHER'S PANTS, R2D2 Theatre, New York

2003   **General Manager,** CUT, R2D2 Theatre, New York

2001   **Company Manager,** PASQUALE, La TAZ ETC, New York

2000   **Directing Apprentice,** Susie Poker's FIVE, Philadelphia, PA

2000   **Director/Choreographer/Producer,** TEXAS HOLD 'EM, CoProducers

1999–2000   **Production Intern,** Hubert Rossinol Productions, New York

1999–2000   **Choreographer/Dance Instructor,** Sitting and Laughing, New York

1999   **Lead Performer,** Big Cruise Lines, MS Halifax (Flagship)

1997–8   **Actor,** FEVER (Second Lead), European Tour

1993–4   **Actor,** KICK UP HEELS (Dance Ensemble), Pre-Broadway Production, Passway Inc.

EDUCATION & TRAINING:

1999–2002   **State University**
    M.F.A. in Theater Management, Class of 2002

1994–7   **State University**
    B.F.A. in Musical Theater, Class of 1997, G.P.A.: 3.829, Highest Honors

COMMITTEES & BOARDS:

2002–Present   **Community of Theater People,** Steering Committee, New York, NY

2003–Present   **Expats in New York,** Social Committee, New York, NY

Alice Johnston

·123 Learning St. Anycity, AS 10101 · (555) 999-1212 · AliceJ@yourname.com·

PROFILE

Artistically minded professional who believes that theater need not sacrifice its artistic integrity for financial stability. Communicates well with artists and executives alike. Highly organized, articulate, and resourceful. Proven team leader who thrives in fast-paced, deadline-driven environments. Has a keen ability to balance the demands of artistic expression against the realities of fiscal responsibility.

CORE SKILLS

WORKING WITH ARTISTS
* Guided many new playwrights through entire creative and collaborative process from script development and structuring to full stage production
* Experienced building and managing creative teams
* Fostered long-term relationships with stage, lighting, and costume designers
* Over ten years of directing experience working with all levels of actors
* Experienced and comfortable working with high-level artists and executives

FINANCIAL MANAGEMENT
* Structured production, annual, long-term, and enhancement deals budgets
* Created individual giving programs for not-for-profit theater
* Successfully completed corporate, foundation, and government arts funding applications and interviews (such as Network Inc, ABC Company, and XYZ)
* Comfortable discussing financial matters with both artists and financial executives

CONTRACT NEGOTIATION
* Experience negotiating contracts with individuals, agents, and union representatives
* Well versed in contract language concerning advances, royalties, profit participation, and subsidiary rights
* Knowledgeable in copyright law and requirements for all theatrical unions

PRESS, PUBLICITY, & MERCHANDISING
* Strong supporter of Branding and Brand loyalty for not-for-profit theaters
* Designed press campaigns for Broadway and Off-Broadway
* Coordinated communications with reviewers and editors including press releases, press performance invitations, and seating plans as well as opening night parties
* Worked with advertising agencies on direct mail, print advertisements, & radio buys
* Experience guiding talent through press/photo lines and public appearances

* Developed style conscious merchandise for established products and political causes

STAGE PRODUCTION
* Found creative ways to maintain high-production values for very little money
* Coordinated all elements of technical production including scheduling and staffing
* Familiar with a variety of venues, with capacities ranging from 45-1,300
* Managed productions on behalf of both production teams and theater owners

THEATER: Theater Management (cont.)

EMPLOYMENT HISTORY....ALICE JOHNSTON....cont

Image and Performance Consultation, Fun Productions   January 2004 to Present
My own company that provides creative consultation for the music industry
- o Formed and registered this company with the goal of applying my theatrical skills to live music concerts. Met with music agents at John Thompson and XYZ. Did my own research and created business plan. Learned how to pitch an idea and assess the marketplace. Ultimately made the decision to not move forward because the market couldn't bear the cost.

Freelance Theater Producer, Production Company LLC   July 2001 to April 2004
My own production company
- o Produced new plays at theaters such as The Playhouse and the CDE
- o Coproduced six plays in one month in Anycity, all by new playwrights; one piece was published as part of the annual compilation, *Best of Off-Broadway*

Consultant, Show Designs   September 2003 to Present
Anycity based merchandising company
- o Created new merchandise items for the Broadway show *Cool*; the most stylish and lucrative merchandise on Broadway

Managing Director's Associate, Fun Stage Theater   January to June 2002 & 2003
- o During my internship I negotiated the AEA contract that allowed the uptown theater to reopen for a summer season of new plays. I also supported the Managing Director and the General Manager by working on designer contracts and authors' agreements. In January 2003, when the theater hired a new Production Manager, I was asked to act as interim PM and support the theater through the transition. I was acting PM during their major annual fundraiser and coordinated all the production elements for the event.

General Management Associate, Broadway Productions   May to July 2001
Theater general management firm for both Broadway and Off-Broadway productions
- o Management team for: *Serious Play* (Broadway), *About Love* (Off Broadway), *Talking Play* (Anycity)
- o Supported GM and Company Manager and calculated and distributed royalty payments

Graduate Student, State University   Sept 2000 to May 2004
Took periods of time off work to concentrate on course work and write master's thesis
- o Fulfilled internship's requirements at ABC Theatricals, Fun Stage, and the Musician Organization
- o Master's Thesis: "The Film and Television Tax Credit Program Applied to Commercial Theater."

Production Associate, BigName Television   July 1999 to May 2000
- o Worked closely with Executive Producer to produce the pilot of *TV Show*, while assisting the Director of Development of Reality Series, with hands on supervision of *The Talk Show*.

Freelance Stage Director   October 1999 to Present
Directing resume available upon request

Executive Assistant, Movie Giant   August 1998 to July 1999
Department of television series, miniseries, and movies of the week
- o Maintained centralized production files for over 22 productions while supporting four top executives, including the President and Senior Vice Presidents of Production

EDUCATION
State University   September 2000 to May 2004
MFA with distinction in Theater Management and Producing

University of Anycity   September 1994 to May 1998
BA with honors, Art History, Comparative Literature, and Theater

TRAINING: Sales Trainer Retail

Alice J. Johnston

123 Learning Street
Anytown, USA 10101

Residence: (999) 555-1212
Email: alicej@yourname.com

A high-energy, business/sales Trainer and Manager with a solid record of performance in energy, food, travel, and retail businesses. Key strengths include the ability to consistently meet/exceed goals/targets, a knack for connecting with decision-makers and the ability to transfer the 'secrets of marketing/selling' to others.

CAREER SUMMARY

XYZ STORE Marketing **Program Manager/Trainer (Inside Sales)**   *2003–Present*

- Provide strategy and initiatives to a major marketing campaign wherein weekly communication and market assistance is required. Overall project and employee management on an ongoing basis.
- Train, educate, assist, and motivate staff with secrets of winning techniques within a customer relationship building model.

ZIP ALONG-Commercial **Manager/Trainer/Recruiter**   *2000–2002*

- Developed a strategy to increase sales and improve closure skills when presenting energy protection programs.
- Recruited, trained, developed, and managed reps to increase performance results within a business-to-business model; increased number of weekly program closures amongst team by 100% within 60 days, from 20 to 40.
- Maintained and reported on each team's statistics. Evaluated, motivated, and provided the necessary tools for increased productivity on an ongoing basis.

ZIP ALONG-Commercial Sales **Representative**   *2001*

- Analyzed the market, formulated/implemented a plan to assimilate marketing information needed, trained in the marketing of energy protection programs, resulting in a 100% improvement in niche sales abilities.
- Improved strategies to improve and expedite both the presentation and sales closure to small- and medium-sized businesses.
- Formulated/implemented improvements in sales strategy; achieved and held position as Sales Leader within two months and increased sales by 300% over previous sales.

THE DINER **Business Developer**   *1999–2002*

- Developed/implemented a niche market, upscale coffee service within a grocery chain as an alternative solution to employee-operated coffee bars for store employees and their customers.
- Promoted, implemented, and continued to service coffee throughout groceries and other small businesses with an average 25% yearly increase; sold interest in this successful business for a substantial profit.

BLING BLING **Business Developer**   *1991 – 2000*

- Codeveloped a unique watch/high-fashion jewelry business in the U.S. and secured the rights to a complete line of products; recruited/trained sales reps generating $125K annual sales.
- Successfully promoted product lines via public media (Shop via Seat Channel) which resulted in a 75% increase in sales over the next fiscal period; sold interest in the business for a substantial profit.

EDUCATION   *Diploma, Business Administration*

TRAINING: Corporate Trainer

Alice J. Johnston

123 Learning St. ▪ Anytown, USA 10101
Telephone/Voicemail: (999) 555-1212 ▪ Fax: (999) 555-1313 ▪ Email:alicej@yourname.com

▪ **Corporate Education Analyst** ▪ **Microsoft Certified Trainer** ▪ **Curriculum Developer** ▪
▪ **Distributed Learning Specialist** ▪ **Applications Specialist** ▪ **Skills Development Analyst** ▪

Technically sophisticated professional with 9+ years of experience in Information Technology/Learning & Development Services. Highly experienced Applications Specialist with proven expertise in designing, delivering, and facilitating high quality, high-impact, internal/external educational solutions using innovative technologies. Expert in collaborating with subject matter experts to enhance course content and ensure technical accuracy. Certified hands-on technical knowledge of current industry standard computer hardware and software. Strong Team Leader able to motivate and encourage employees to high levels of productivity and efficiency while maximizing morale and job satisfaction.

AREAS OF EXPERTISE

Microsoft Certified Trainer/Engineer (MCT/MCSE)
Curriculum & Course Materials Development
eLearning Course Development & Facilitation
Instructor-Led & Self-Paced Training Delivery

Extensive experience in Adult Education & Theory
Training Program Evaluation & Quality Standards
Instructional Systems Design (ISD) Methods
Project Management

EXPERIENCE HIGHLIGHTS

IT Skills Development Analyst
Pharma Inc. 2001–Present

Offered full-time permanent employment with Pharma Inc. after six months of full-time contract work in the Information Technology department.

Key Achievements:
- Created a measurement tool that accurately evaluated the computer skill levels of over 120 Home Office Employees and 85 Medical Sales Representatives.
- Designed and implemented a tracking database that recorded employees current skill set, updated recommendations and future goals, and aligned company skill development initiatives with performance incentive programs.
- Designed and implemented Pharma's first national corporate Intranet.
- Partnered with ABC to introduce e-ning to the Pharma community.
- Created an eLearning website to compliment technology training for internal and external employees.
- Introduced distributed learning technologies to Pharma's leadership team and home office employees.
- Designed and taught biweekly "Techno Tuesdays" 3-hour topic-specific training sessions to educate Home Office Employees on how to utilize advances in technology specifically in their job function.
- Created and launched "Coaching Corners"—topic specific email-based tips that were sent across the country to Medical representatives.
- Created Documentation Manuals and Quick Reference Guides for all hardware and software at Pharma.
- Designed and created a CD-ROM training library for Home Office Employees and Sales Force—material could be signed out via the Intranet and then picked up or shipped out to the employee's home.
- Provided documentation and support for all IT technology rollouts and initiatives.
- Utilized as a "senior" expert hardware and software troubleshooter for the IT Support Center when required for resolution of escalated calls by the IT support staff.
- **Awarded the "Best of the Best" Award for outstanding achievement.**

Learning & Development Analyst/Corporate Trainer
XYZ Inc., 2000–2001

Joined this newly established pharmaceutical firm as a full-time contractor after working for XYZ Inc. as a self-employed Consultant/Corporate Trainer (Computers & Training by Design) for approximately four years.

Key Achievements:
- Designed and delivered all hardware and software computer-training programs for Home Office Employees and nation-wide Medical Sales Representatives.
- Introduced and developed the first New Hire Computer Training program at XYZ.
- Created customized Manuals and Quick Reference Guides for all standard software and hardware.
- Designed and launched "Techno Tuesdays"—an innovation approach to delivering new technology to home office employees in 3-hour topic-specific training sessions.
- Created and designed the companies semi-monthly newsletter
- Worked closely with the Sales, Marketing, and Information Technology departments to design promotional presentations and materials for new product launches, sales meetings, incentive programs, and rollouts.

IT Consultant/Corporate Trainer
Designers LLC, 1997–Present

Entrepreneur – established a full-time computer consulting and training business that served small to medium-sized companies in various industries.

Key Achievements:
- Worked all over United States delivering computer-training workshops and hardware/software solutions to various companies.

o Plasko	o Small University	o Waters Group
o Local Hospital	o State College	o Anytown General
o Capistrano College	o XYZ Corp	o Small Town General
o Blackball Corporation	o Financial Capital Corp	o Welding Zone

- Attained an ongoing contract with XYZ for computer training services.
- Worked closely with the Human Resources department at XYZ in the design and implementation of the first Employee Performance Incentive Program.

EDUCATION/PROFESSIONAL DEVELOPMENT

Certifications
- Microsoft Certified Engineer (MCSE – NT4)
- Microsoft Certified Trainer (MCT)
- Microsoft Certified Professional (MCP – Windows 2000)
- MOUS – Microsoft Office User Specialist
- CompTIA – A+ Certified Technician
- Train-the-Trainer Certification
- DDI – Development Dimensions International
- Dale Carnegie – Effective Speaking and Human Relations

Diplomas
- Computer Sciences Diploma – State College
- Adult Education Certificate – State College

Professional Associations
- CCE – Community of Computer Educators
- Monkey Institute of Learning
- Training Magazine

TRAINING: Training Professional, Sr.

Alice J. Johnston

123 Learning St.
Anytown, ST USA
10101

Phone: (999) 555-1212
Cell: (999) 555-1313
Email: Alicej@yourname.com

A Training and HR professional with international experience, strong project management skills, communication & facilitation skills, and a collaborative approach with sr. executives, internal, & external customers. Achieved highest performance ratings with "Top Talent" designation.

Ongoing Training, Coaching, and Facilitation at BIG TELE Networks

Training and Facilitation Roles in Human Resources - 2000–2002

- Acted as Account Manager for two State Universities, strengthening the relationship for future hiring. Provided on-site job skills training for career management, and participated in numerous panel discussions and speaking engagements to 100–300 students.
- Appointed coach and mentor for HR team of fifty in communications skills, meeting management, and email etiquette.
- Provided training and one-on-one coaching for twenty-five student recruiters in Communication/Trade Show Skills, and participated in communicating INROADS strengths for diversity in hiring.

Training and Facilitation Roles in Marketing - 1990–2000

- Provided presentation-skills coaching for senior executives and all presenters at Sales Conferences and Senior Management Conferences as part of overall role as project prime for all events.
- Trained all trade show personnel, Customer Center presenters, and sales engineers, plus staff of twenty-five, in communication and sales skills.
- Developed and delivered Managing Relationships and Cultural Sensitivity training for fifty Customer Visit Coordinators from around the world.

Global Education and Training Role - 1987–1990

- Managed Communications and Sales Skills curriculum utilizing outside consultants to complement internal resources. Developed & delivered excellent-rated sales and marketing courses to employees & executives.
- Managed highly successful international training projects focused on communication skills in North America, England, France, Switzerland, and Japan.
- Project lead on all presentation skills training for "Witness This"—a global telecom Olympics held every four years—pre-event at seven global locations and on-site for 110 booth participants. Provided additional one-on-one coaching for senior executives, achieving outstanding project results.

Training Certification

- Communication Skills for the Presenter, Power on the Podium, Negotiating to Yes, Introduction to Sales and Marketing, Counselor Selling, Versatile Salesperson, Account Management, Trade Show Presentation Skills, Managing Interpersonal Relationships, Executive Coaching (through Gilmore and Associates, Wilson Learning, Achieve).
- Other workshops include Interviewing Skills, Resume Writing Skills, Negotiating Salary, Dress for Success, and Email Etiquette, focused on helping the student and new grad achieve career success.

Alice Johnston   2

Other Achievements at Big Tele Networks

Human Resources - Global Recruitment - 2000–2002

- Project lead on all student hiring activity, executing new and innovative marketing initiatives in branding, advertising, monthly eNewsletter, web activity, media relations, employee communications, call center activity, INROADS program for hiring diversity, over 300 events and trade shows, collateral, merchandise, training and development, and communications. 6,500 students hired globally in 2000.
- Managed all recruitment communications for consistency and accuracy of message. Worked closely with employee communications, media relations, and corporate communications to fine tune recruitment messaging.

Wireless Networks - Strategic Marketing Communications - 1999–2000

- Centralized all American wireless communication activity in 2000 making it highly relevant, consistent, and cost-effective to the business.

Global Corporate Advertising and Brand Management - 1997–1999

- Managed $10 million budget and facilitated work with global advertising agencies in New York, Toronto, Dallas, UK, and Singapore. Organized first ever Global Advertising Summit.

North American Customer Presentation Centers (CPCs) - 1995–1997

- Managed activities and personnel with staff of twenty-five in CPCs in five major cites with a focus on staffing, training and development, customer applications, international customers, and the redesign of all centers. Project lead on the "World of Networks Center"—a state-of-the-art facility used as a global headquarters showcase for Nortel Networks customers.

Global Conference Planning/Event Management - 1990–1995

- Managed all customer, senior executive, spousal and internal sales, and marketing events—Circle of Excellence sales incentive programs in Paris, Monte Carlo, Spain, Presidents' Conferences in Bermuda, Caribbean, Hawaii, and North America. All events were on time, on budget with outstanding feedback.
- Project lead for three highly successful Americas Sales Conferences with over 2,000 attendees.
- Highly customer-focused in approach, receiving excellent feedback from sales attendees, top executives, and customer Presidents and Vice Presidents.

Previous Work Experience at a Glance

Sales and Marketing - 1980–1986

Various positions held with ABC Communications, The Travel Group, ABC Board of Education.

Education and Travel - 1973–1980

Working traveler for two years in Australia and New Zealand.
High school teacher and coach.

Education and Related Courses

- Honors Bachelor of Arts, State University 1972
- Education Diploma, State College 1973
- Introduction to Marketing, State University 1987
- Advertising and Sales Promotion, State University 1991
- Strategic Marketing in Telecommunications, State University 1995
- Sales and Marketing 2, Leadership Course, Helping your Employees Manage Change
- The Coaches Training Institute (CTI) – currently working towards coaching certification - 2002

Current Interests

- Vice Chair of the Youth Cancer Foundation in Anytown
- Golf, fly fishing, theater, cottaging

TRAINING: Manager of Training

Alice J. Johnston
123 Learning St., Anytown, ST, USA 10101   (999) 555-1212

TRAINING, DEVELOPMENT, AND LEARNING MANAGER

SELECTED ACCOMPLISHMENTS

TRAINING & DEVELOPMENT

- Designed and developed in-house Coaching Program and Call Monitoring Guide.
- Designed and facilitated all soft skill and technical (mainframe) training for the Pre-Collect/Delinquency and Cure Student Loan Programs.
- Developed and implemented the Intranet and Lotus Notes user manual.
- Designed and facilitated a Train the Trainer session for Customer Service courses.
- Implemented initial training sessions for over 500 employees in National Student Center.
- Certified for facilitation of all core soft-skill courses (DDI) such as Service Plus, Preparing Others to Succeed (Coaching), and Team Building.
- Developed and managed a new Continuing Education Program.
- Researched and implemented a Resource Center.

PEOPLE/PROJECT MANAGEMENT

- Recruited and currently manages a National (8) team comprised of consultants, designers, and facilitators serving a population of 500 clients.
- Collection representative for the Contact Center Forum Learning Committee and current Project Lead for the Evaluation initiative.
- Project Leader for the in-house Coaching Program and the Pre-Collect Student Loan Project.
- Manages over thirty Learning & Training projects on a national scope.
- Designed and implemented a Business Partnership Agreement between Learning & Training and four Business centers.
- Recovered $100,000 in telecommunications and mailroom costs.
- Project Team member for the Intranet/Lotus Notes pilot project.
- Conducted and approved the entire user testing for the setup of the mainframe and laptop applications.

WORK EXPERIENCE

MANAGER, LEARNING & TRAINING – Big Bank Collections   02/99–present
- Provide coaching and leadership to all team members through the regular review of pre-established development plans
- Create a supportive team environment and promote continuous improvement
- Build strong relationships with client groups through the design of the Business Partnership Agreement and supporting tools
- Forecast, plan, and manage all resources to ensure alignment with business objectives
- Take initiative by working independently to meet client needs

ALICE J. JOHNSTON - PAGE 2

LEARNING DESIGNER – Big Bank Collections   04/98–02/99
Coaching Program
- Designed a new coaching program
- Developed and implemented a National rollout strategy
- Developed a National team to facilitate continuous improvement
- Conducted pre/post surveys to evaluate the effectiveness of the National Coaching Package
- Coordinated and cofacilitated Resourcing Workshops and Management Development Pilot for the State Collections Managers

HUMAN RESOURCES FACILITATOR – Big Bank Finance Inc.   06/94–04/98
- Conducted Train the Trainer sessions for soft skills and technical training for the Call Center
- Consulted with client groups and conducted a comprehensive needs analysis
- Conducted Intranet and Lotus Notes training sessions to over 700 users
- Identified training requirements for succession planning
- Conducted pre/post evaluation of course material methodologies

INSTRUCTOR – State College (Part-time)   01/91–05/95
- Developed and instructed students in all aspects of Office Procedures
- Designed and submitted marks for all assignments and tests

TRANSIT ANALYST – ABC Tire Company   05/93–06/94

OFFICE SERVICES MANAGER – ABC Tire Company   05/91–04/93
- Contributed leadership, direction, motivation, and coaching to all Office Services staff
- Interviewed, hired, planned, and assigned work to all of Office Services staff
- Developed and conducted performance reviews

EDUCATION

State University	Currently working towards a Bachelor of Arts Degree in Psychology (2/3 complete)
State College	
1992	Supervisory Management - Certificate
1991	Helping Adults Learn - Teaching Certificate
1989	Management Skills in Personnel Selection
	Communication in Supervision
1983–1985	Business Administration Diploma

AWARDS/PROFESSIONAL MEMBERSHIPS
Employee Achievement Award for Consistently Demonstrating **Professionalism and Performance Excellence** during 1999
Achievement Award for Demonstrating Superior **Customer Satisfaction** – March 1997

Member of Society of Training & Development (STD)
Member of International Society of Performance Improvement (ISPI)

ACTIVITIES
President of the Social Club, Treasurer in 1997
Coordinator of Umbrella Charity Association, Blood Donor Clinics, and Diversity Month

TRAINING: Training and Organizational Dev.

Alice J. Johnston
123 Learning Drive, Anycity, Anystate 10101
(555) 999-1212   alicej@yourname.com

ORGANIZATIONAL DEVELOPMENT & TRAINING PROFESSIONAL

Profile	*You Can Count On*
• Ten years experience in organizational development and training. • Experience managing training projects across all organizational levels. • Skilled at targeting needs, problem solving, and facilitation. • Fluent in English, French, and Italian	• Integrity, innovation, and creativity. • Excellent communication and interpersonal skills. • Committed to personal & professional development. • Dedicated to helping individuals, groups, and the organization as a whole achieve success through improved performance.

FANCY APPAREL LTD.   **1998–2000**
Manager of Organizational Development and Training
With over 100 stores across U.S. and 5000 associates, Fancy is the largest off-price retail organization in U.S.

Provided leadership and consultation in the areas of performance management, competency development, succession planning, and associate training and development programs.

Selected Achievments:

- Provided leadership and consultation in the design of competency-based tools to assist in the recruitment, succession planning, associate development, and compensation areas.
- Provided consultation for two divisions in Team Building which resulted in clarity of roles, responsibilities, and an Action Plan for achieving Departmental objectives.
- Conducted "360° Feedback" meetings for direct reports and senior management which resulted in increased corporate bench strength.
- Conducted needs analysis and implemented training solutions for diversity, performance management, union awareness, coaching, and management-development training.
- Developed and coached senior management, direct reports, field training managers, and supervisors in the areas of program design and development, consulting, gap analysis, and project management.

HR SERVICES INC.   **1995–1998**
Human Resources Development Manager, International Division
HR has an international network of over 1,500 branches that are company-owned and operating worldwide (17 countries) In U.S., HR services has over 7,500 clients in all segments of U.S. industry placing over 30,000 temporary workers annually into a variety of client operations.

Analyzed training and organizational development needs and implemented appropriate interventions for subsidiaries in U.S.

Selected Achievements:

- Developed and implemented training policies, procedures, and programs for ISO-9002 certification.
- Customized a four-day strategic sales training and certification program—worked with the Sales/Operation groups, corporate U.S. peers, and vendor.
- Chaired a ten-member task force on New Employee Orientation. The rollout included an Employee Manual, Leader's Guide, and Learning Plan.
- Developed, piloted, and cofacilitated a one-day Behavioral Interview training program.
- Designed and delivered a two-week training program for branch managers. The "start-up" training materials will be used in other countries such as Spain.

Alice J. Johnston

VAST SERVICES LTD. 1994–1995
Manager, Human Resources Development

Vast employs over 15,000 employees across U.S. which makes it one of U.S.'s larger employers. There are eight divisions and three subsidiaries engaged primarily in Food Services Management.

Assessed corporate training needs and implemented change strategies which impacted 15,000 employees across the country.

Selected Achievements:
- Implemented a "learning organization" strategy. This involved benchmarking, strategic planning, and chairing a committee of twelve people to launch a "Center for Excellence".
- Developed a strategy for senior executives with a focus on team building.
- Designed an orientation strategy for employees across the country. This included a handbook for new employees, a Guide Book for managers, and a workshop for managers.
- Designed a customer service workshop for managers which included a Train the Trainer component and materials including video and handbook.

STATE INSURANCE 1990–1993
Training Team Leader (1992–93)

With over 300 employees and a National network, SI provided health, dental, and life insurance to individuals, corporations, and the government.

Assessed corporate training needs, and implemented solutions including design, delivery, and evaluation of results. Responsibilities included coaching and supervising two trainers, as well as managing consultation and support services for over 300 employees.

Selected Achievements:
- Launched a "Distance Learning" concept by producing a self-study program to meet the needs of sixty-five Federal Government employees across U.S.
- Launched and managed a $40,000. Train the Trainer initiative, which included workshops, developing marketing tools, and purchasing materials.

Training Coordinator (1990–92)

Selected Achievements:
- Planned and implemented, as a member of the Corporate Human Resources redeployment team, a strategy for organizational restructuring activities for over 700 employees.
- Designed and delivered technical training programs, which saved the company over $171,000/year through dental product knowledge training.

ACADEMIC ACHIEVEMENTS

2000   City University, Anycity, Anystate- **M.A. Organizational Development**

1990   St. Saint University, Anycity, Anystate- **Diploma, Adult Education**

1986   Prestige University, Anycity, Anystate- B.A. **Industrial Relations**

PROFESSIONAL DEVELOPMENT

2000   Emery (City University) - **Strategic Planning (Search Conference)**

1999   Strategic Consulting - **Strategic Planning (Preferred Futuring)**

1999   Copper and Associates - **Career Architect** (Certification - Competency Development)

1995   State College - **Diversity Certificate**

1992   Management of U.S. Inc. - **Train the Trainer Certification**

PROFESSIONAL AFFILIATIONS: Association for Creative Change in Organizational Renewal & Development (ACCORD); American Society for Training and Development (ASTD)

TRAVEL & TOURISM: Tourism Marketing Specialist

Alice J. Johnston
Email: alicej@yourname.com Tel: 999-555-1212

PROFILE
Business development and marketing specialist with many years of international experience in the tourism and culture industries. Demonstrated strong organizational, research, product development, and presentation and management skills. Resourceful and enthusiastic individual with proven ability to take initiative, analyze situations, and find productive solutions. Languages spoken: English and Spanish

CAREER HISTORY

International Marketing and Development Consultant (self-employed)   (2005)

- Developed and implemented a marketing program for the Costa Rica sustainable tourism project of World Animal Protection Program

- Developed a marketing proposal for an ecotourism partnership between World Animal Protection Program (WAPP), ecotourism, and adventure tour operators

- Researched and delivered lectures on "Ecotourism Opportunities in America"

State Tourism and Recreation   (1998–2004)
International Tourism - Marketing and Product Development Specialist

- Developed and implemented an aggressive travel trade and media marketing strategy, with an operational budget of 2 million, aimed at the European, Asian, and North American markets

- Directed and analyzed research on travel patterns and demographics in order to anticipate future trends and institute new initiatives

- Conducted educational workshops with private entrepreneurs in the tourism, culture, and leisure industry on product development, packaging, sales, and marketing opportunities, to make them export-ready and more competitive in foreign markets

- Organized and participated in international travel trade marketplaces and sales missions in Europe and North America to position the U.S. with key consumer segments in Europe and Asia

- Provided ongoing direction to advertising and public relations agencies—in America and abroad—in the development of creative strategies, video promotions, TV campaigns, and specialty publications

- Initiated marketing programs and partnerships with tour operators, media, governments, and airlines

Smith & Smith LLC   (1995–1998)
International Adventure Travel and Ecotourism - Operations Manager

- Researched, developed, and administered European cycling tours and North American educational tours

- Participated at trade shows in Europe/Asia to enhance company profile and increase revenue potential

EDUCATION

Bachelor of Commerce Honors, 1993
State University - School of Business

XYZ Scholarship, 1992 & 1993 for high academic standing

PROFESSIONAL AND PERSONAL DEVELOPMENT

Hosted and co-produced a 30-minute TV documentary: *Around the World* **for MTN** (2003)
Profiling independent women travelers
Focus on culture and nature in Greenland

Researched and developed a 26-episode television series *Over the Waves* (1999)
Profiling adventure, nature, and cultural tourism in North America and the Caribbean

TRAVEL & TOURISM: BAD—Travel and Tour

123 Learning Street
Anycity, AS 10101

Phone: 555-999-1212
Email: johnj@yourname.com

John J. Johnston

Summary

Fourteen years of experience in the travel industry in both the wholesale and retail sectors. Experience at managing staff in a highly competitive market. Sound decision-making and analytical skills.

Experience

March 2000–present   U.S. Holidays   Anycity, AS
Manager, Operations and Ticketing

- Responsible for all hotel and air inventory control.
- Responsible for all staffing aspects of the Operations and Ticketing departments; staff of eight.
- Created manuals for software application and job descriptions for those departments.

1997–March 2000   Holiday Company   Anycity, AS
Systems Development Analyst

- Assisted in the design of new in-house system application, as well as training for the new system.
- Liaison between programmers and company executives for program changes to existing application.
- Maintenance of existing application as well as training and trouble shooting.
- Production and design of management statistic reports.

1995–1997   ABC Travel Services   Anycity, AS
Air Operations Manager

- Responsible for all airline contracts, fares, rulings, block space, and marketing of same.
- Responsible for international ticketing and BSP reporting.
- Production of air statistics and forecasting reports.

1994–1995   Adventure Travel   Anycity, AS
Travel Consultant

- Responsible for planning, coordinating, and administering special custom group travel plans.

1990–1994   Fun Holidays   Anycity, AS
Operations Manager

- Control all hotel and air inventory.
- Supervise operations, ticketing, airport, destination of 40.
- On call as duty officer with sole responsibility for m and resolving customer conflicts.

What's Wrong?

- Too much wasted space
- No declared job role
- Uninspiring and boring

TRAVEL & TOURISM: BAD—Travel and Tour (cont.)

	1987–1990	Other Employment	Anycity, AS

Travel Industry Positions
- Various other positions held within the travel industry.

Education	1985–1987	Local College	Anycity, AS

- Graduated Travel and Tourism with Honors.

	1984–1985	ABC Polytechnical Institute	Anycity, AS

- Business Administration

	1980–1984	City Secondary School	Anycity, AS

- High school diploma, Business Scholarship

Skills   Microsoft Word, Excel, PowerPoint, Logibro, SABRE, Apollo, ADS Accounting System.

Interests   Squash, reading, music, and traveling.

John J. Johnston

123 Learning St., Anytown, USA 10101 Telephone 999 555 1212 Cellular 999 555 1313

"Strategic Creative Leadership"
Management Expertise in Tourism Industry with Brand, Marketing, and Partnership-building capabilities.

Mustt Tourism., General Manager.   January 2002–February 2004

Management of the day-to-day operations reporting to the board of directors. Development of marketing programs to increase the number of visits, length of stays, and trip expenditures.

- Reorganized staffing structures and physical building structures to provide increased information and marketing service management.
- Managed central 1800 information and reservation service.
- Developed new brand strategy and, more importantly, managed brand launch strategy to gain consensus among Tourism stakeholders.
- Increased external partner relationships.
- Development and supervision of web-based destination marketing system.
- Organized and escorted familiarization tours within the trade and media market segments.
- Managed the development of trade and consumer travel shows.
- Represented Mustt Tourism at International Travel Trade marketplaces.

Key Accomplishments

- Increased the number of visitors to visitor information centers by 25% over two summers.
- Secured unique promotional partnership valued at $2 million with 431 Beer Stores to promote Mustt resorts and golf courses.
- Secured unique promotional partnership with Car Inc. to promote Mustt within the Greater Anytown region.
- Reengineered existing promotional materials into a new format to be more effective for members and better meet the needs of the 21st century traveler.
- Increased the number of marketing programs over previous years.

Espaniola Limited., Publisher.   September 1997–December 2001

Established Espaniola.com as the most visited website for information and travel planning solutions to the Dominican Republic. Provided real estate and hospitality consulting and business services.

- Developed organic linking strategy of over 1,000 third-party links through the development of proprietary interactive applications as the Spanish Talking Phrase book, virtual walks, interactive maps, and a range of unique message forums.
- Adapted outbound travel application into an inbound travel agent reservation management suite of tools to access existing travel package inventories and create custom travel packages.
- Developed strategic alliances with International travel brand to market travel to the Dominican Republic from North American and UK markets.
- Established travel partnerships with major travel tour operators, hotel chains, and local operators.
- Internet and coaching to local operators to manage online reservation programs.

TRAVEL & TOURISM: GM Tourism (cont.)

Global Solutions., Director of Tourism Marketing and Communications.
Contract position.   June 1996–April 1997

Primary contact with Tourism and managed by Travellex as a fee for service Destination Management System. Managed the launch communications of the Travellex service Travel Industry.

- Achieved a 35% acquisition rate.
- Provided coaching and development for marketing team members.
- Developed 5-year tourism marketing strategy for the Tourism Marketing Task Force.

Words Above North America., Creative Director/Managing Partner.   1986–1996

Successfully managed the roll out of the print production resources of ABC Communications into a graphic 24/7 prepress company.

- Established resource strategy for 24-hour production service.
- Developed proprietary typographic house style as part of added value service strategy.
- Provided coaching and development for sales and production teams.
- Negotiated the purchase of leading edge digital graphic production equipment from American and European suppliers.
- Negotiated demo beta site partnership for North American market.
- Developed best practice employee exchange program with leading UK prepress company.
- Negotiated sale of operations to employee-led group.

ABC Communications., Creative Director/Managing Partner.   1977–1986

Successfully reengineered the existing art studio into a creative below-the-line marketing, promotions, and custom publishing company. Advanced from entry-level creative position to President.

- Secured multiyear publishing contracts within the travel, financial, and home-building sectors.
- Managed all marketing communications for Metro Visitor and Convention Bureau.
- Pioneered the use of digital typography and electronic prepress images from the design station.
- Managed the sale and merger into BBB Advertising in 1987.

Education:

- **State College – Bachelor of Administration Degree**   **1977**

- **Local College – Diploma in Marketing, Specialty in Tourism and Hospitality** 1997

Interests: Personal art and multimedia projects; hiking, camping, and cottaging.

TRAVEL & TOURISM: Sr. Marketing Consultant

ALICE J. JOHNSTON

123 Learning St., Anytown, USA 10101 Tel: 999.555.1212 Email:alicej@yourname.com

> **Marketing professional with management and independent consulting experience gained in the travel and tourism sectors**. This background has involved the development and execution of annual marketing plans, as well as advertising, direct response, media/public relations, promotions, publications, market research, and new business initiatives.

Independent Marketing Consultant   2003–Present/1992–2000

Retained on a project basis to provide strategic and tactical marketing services. Performed extensive work for travel industry clients (1992–2000), including Big Cruises, itravel2000, Northern Lights Group (five business divisions), Big Adventure Vacations.

- Consulted with owner operators/senior management in the development of comprehensive business and marketing plans, and supplier proposals, for the Northern Lights Group. Accountable to the President and CEO, Northern Lights Group, for delivering key business initiatives, which included: formalizing procedures for quantifying/analyzing business results, developing sales forecasts, and monitoring performance metrics; preparation of sales statistics, market share estimates, market studies, and industry/competitive reviews; and the development of best practices.

- Project managed the design, layout, content, and production of more than twenty product brochures, as well as consumer advertising and print collateral. Planned and executed all internal/external communications and promotional events to announce the merger of the Northern Lights Travel Group with Holidays LLC, and launch of Big Holiday brand. Developed and wrote the introductory advertiser media kit and weekly customer e-newsletters for itravel2000.

Anystate Tourism Marketing Partnership Corporation (ATMPC)   2000–2002
Senior Marketing Consultant (Contract Position)

The tourism marketing agency for the state, as a public/private sector partnership that collaborates with domestic and international operators to grow the state's tourism industry. Primary responsibilities included overseeing marketing initiatives in North American and overseas markets, many of which involved participation by industry stakeholders, and the management of a partnership development program. Budgets totalled $13 million.

- Directed the planning and execution of marketing programs to build the tourism brand and drive measurable response to specific promotional offers. Launched the first tour operator partnered direct response television and online/offline response campaigns in the U.K. and Germany. Despite the impact of 9/11 on overseas travel to the U.S., positive results were achieved in 2002, including a 73% increase in bookings by a leading tour operator. Negotiated joint marketing agreements to support these campaigns. Led the development of a successful re-launch initiative in Japan.

- Managed external relationships and liaised with global industry organizations including U.K., France, Germany, Italy, Japan, Australia, New Zealand, international tour operators, and contracted advisory services based in London, Munich, and Tokyo.

- Conducted an in-depth program review to assess the Tourism business model in primary international markets, and evaluate consumer and trade marketing activities. Analyzed proposals and recommended funding levels for new marketing initiatives developed by tourism operators to extend domestic market programs.

TRAVEL & TOURISM: Sr. Marketing Consultant (cont.)

Page 2

ALICE J. JOHNSTON

Big Credit Card Company Inc. 1990–1992
Marketing & Business Development Manager, Leisure Travel

Managed the national marketing programs for the $125 million Leisure Travel Services division. Responsible for the annual marketing plan, business case analysis, and project management of new revenue-generating initiatives, and the planning and execution of national direct marketing and in-store promotional campaigns (English and Spanish). Provided consultative support to more than seventy regional and branch managers in the development and implementation of local area marketing programs, liaised with internal and external partners, and managed and developed staff.

- Strategic planning, feasibility assessment, and launch of new customer-driven programs to grow sales of travel and BCCC products. Increased the frequency and scope of national marketing campaigns to build brand awareness and strengthen regional market shares. Collaborated with regional managers and the supplier management function to secure promotional product and supplier financial support. Integrated local marketing tactics into these campaigns.
- Initiated consumer research to support the redevelopment of brand positioning and communication strategies. Recommended a distribution strategy and market planning model to optimize trade area productivity and branch operating efficiencies. Developed the rationale and executional guidelines for a cross-selling program that was presented as one of several business development workshops at the 1992 Worldwide Travel Network Meeting.

Tourism Anytown 1987–1989
Marketing Manager

Reported to the Vice President Marketing. Responsible for overseeing consumer/trade advertising and publications, market research, merchandising, and visitor information services. Managed budgets of $5 million and a staff of twelve.

ABC Corp. 1983–1987
Advertising & Research Manager

Big Resorts LLC 1979–1983
Marketing Coordinator

EDUCATION

HBA, School of Business, State University, 1979

PROFESSIONAL DEVELOPMENT

CAAP Year II, Institute of Communications & Advertising
Courses in Advertising & Promotional Planning, Brand Management, Direct & Database Marketing,
Presentation Skills, Public Relations, Relationship Management
Conversational Spanish, Speak Spanish School

INTERESTS

Photography, Writing, Eating well, Travel to France, Italy, and other places with great food and wine.

John J. Johnston

123 Learning Street
Anytown, USA
10101

Business: (999)555-1212
Residence: (999) 555-1313
Email: johnj@yourname.com

SENIOR MANAGEMENT EXECUTIVE

Advertising/Marketing • Media Relations • Tourism • Construction/Infrastructure
IT Development/Implementation • Retail Sales • Food Services • Educational Management
Fundraising/Sponsorships • Legal • Environmental Protection • Event/Entertainment
Production

A high-energy, goal-driven leader with extensive experience in senior management, customer service, retail, and related business endeavours. Key strengths include exceptional analytical skills, the ability to negotiate from a position of strength, excellent financial design/management skills, superior media/presentation capabilities, and a leadership style that is balanced between motivating, empowering, and leading by example.

PROFESSIONAL EXPERIENCE

Conservation Lockhart   1998–2004
DIRECTOR, CONSERVATION LANDS
Managed areas included the Scope ski resort, parks, retail/food outlets, the Wildlife Center, a reconstructed Native American Village, eighty-one buildings, and over 6,000 acres of land.
Selected Accomplishments
- Doubled profits and revenues at the Scope Ski Resort and increased attendance by over 60% to 170,000 visitors/yr.
- Increased other area revenues by 85% and total visitation to a record 550,000/yr.
- Developed new Capital and Master plans for all attractions.
- Successfully introduced new retail, food, and rental outlets.
- Implemented millions of dollars in buildings, capital improvements, and upgrades.
- Reengineered program and operational services; improved environmental protection features, modernized the equipment fleet, and updated capital equipment and MIS capabilities.

Responsibilities
- Reporting to the CEO, directed all operational, marketing, and planning activities in the organization's outdoor businesses; managed a multimillion dollar operating budget and oversaw service delivery issues at multiple locations.
- Through 11 direct reports, managed over 450 full- and part-time staff; played a key role in the development and implementation of the organization's Strategic Business Plans.
- Acted as the organizational media spokesperson during numerous Master Planning processes and public/political issues.
- Directed the corporation's construction unit, infrastructure maintenance, vehicle, and equipment fleet management, the development of MIS/POS systems and secure wireless communication networks.

Anytown and Region Conservation Authority   1989–1998
CORPORATE REPRESENTATIVE, BUSINESS DEVELOPMENT   1995–1998
- **Selected Accomplishment** – Negotiated numerous profitable long-term leases
- **Responsibilities** – Developed and negotiated new business initiatives, long-term land leases, private sector partnerships, filming locations, and corporate sponsorships; developed for-profit recreational sites, live entertainment venues, and special events both internally and with other partners and organizations.

TRAVEL & TOURISM: Senior Manager (cont.)

John J. Johnston _____*Page 2*

DIRECTOR (SUPERVISOR), RIGHT CENTER FOR CONSERVATION *1989–1995*
- *Selected Accomplishment* – Surpassed all previous attendance and revenue records.
- *Responsibilities* – General Manager responsible for all aspects of the Center's operation, marketing, planning, and development. The Center offered over 100 different programs and events that served every segment of Anytown area market with over 120,000 visitors annually. The Center—the largest of its type—included retail outlets, licensed food services, and hosted numerous special events and private functions.

American Market Images *1987–1989*
DIRECTOR, INFORMATION AND TECHNICAL SERVICES
- *Selected Accomplishment* – Developed/implemented/upgraded the world's fastest survey scanning equipment.
- *Responsibilities* – As a member of the senior management team, was responsible for in-depth consumer database; eventually directed a staff of seven professionals, in this high-tech start-up, with joint responsibility for operations staff. Directed research and development of new technologies and database products, implemented customer marketing strategies, analyzed consumer profiles, directed MIS staff, database management, and support.

Management Dynamics *1987–1987*
MANAGEMENT AND EXECUTIVE SEARCH CONSULTANT
- New business development, HR consulting, recruitment of candidates, and account management.

Delly Hawk & Sails *1983–1986*
SENIOR MANAGEMENT CONSULTANT
- *Selected Accomplishment* – Developed/negotiated the first international database for every phone company using the logo in North America.
- *Responsibilities* – Worked closely with all levels of the client's staff, systems, and businesses to design and implement new approaches to the management of key business information.

Harp-Gray Corporation *1980–1983*
BUSINESS ANALYST/SYSTEMS ANALYST/PROJECT LEADER
- *Selected Accomplishment* – Directed multidisciplinary project to document the organizational data flow for all information in the corporation before developing a company-wide HIS system.
- *Responsibilities* – Developed information management and billing systems on a variety of computer platforms. Participated in the development and start-up of several entrepreneurial subsidiaries.

OTHER EXPERIENCE

CHAIR, TOURISM ADVISORY COMMITTEE, *Anytown Chamber Of Commerce* *1991/93*
LOANED EXECUTIVE – *Umbrella Charity 1999*
LOANED EXECUTIVE – *Auction Drive (Umbrella Charity) 1998*

EDUCATION State University
               B. Sc. Environmental Science 1979
               B. Sc. Social Science - Minor: Business Administration 1979

VOLUNTEER Region Community Organizations Youth Leader

Alice J. Johnston MBA, CTC

123 Learning Street, Anytown, ST, USA 10101 Telephone: (999) 555-1212

> Global Executive trained in the unique business opportunities of Travel and Tourism. Leads tight teams with bright visions, clearly articulated goals, and good strategy. Excellent at the details of travel business, such as tracking sales and campaigns and tweaking strategies to get above quota results.

MANAGEMENT STRENGTHS:
Analytical - Collaborative – Numerical - Project Coordination - Strategic Thinker

WORK EXPERIENCE:

Int'l Vice President – Sales & Marketing – Banana HOLIDAYS

May 1997–Aug 2003

- Initially hired as the Vice President of Sales & Marketing. After winning the **1998 World award for 'Sales Executive of the Year'** received the role of Brand President.
- Responsible for overseeing all business aspects of this international travel company for America. Primary responsibilities were initiating, planning, implementing, and tracking outbound sales results for the niche segment of the 18-35s vacation travel market.
- Consecutively achieved top production levels for all calendar years in this senior management role, receiving the **'Sales Office of the Year Award' in 2001**. Completed this role with all staff coordination and communications of a restructuring plan with sister coach tour companies into the Travel Corporation with associated brand identities and shared operating resource departments.

Director of Marketing – Icelandic Tours/LIMMY AIRWAYS HOLIDAYS

Sept 1995–May 1997

- Ran the day-to-day reservations and internal sales operation of this high-end tour operator. Responsible for purchasing, pricing, and designing brochure programs for both international cruise and packaged European tour products (including the historic 3 Wishes campaign) for the American marketplace.
- Oversaw all aspects of reservations, operations, ticketing, and sales/marketing initiatives from concept to production of outbound passenger sales results.
- Integral team member for involvement of implementing the Limmy Airways Holidays division for agency wholesaler access via Network's airline support system. The lead liaison between the marketing division of Limmy Airways and the representative reservations/operations departments.
- Also responsible for the initial hiring and coordination of airline training programs to be integrated into the tour operating system. Prepared set up of weekly reservations and sales results for communications with the BA International marketing team.

National Cruise Marketing – Dreamwishes Travel

Feb 1990–Sept 1995

- Part of the national management marketing team for America's largest leisure travel agency. Key responsibilities were to negotiate, design, implement, and communicate all cruise-related activities to three hundred plus retail outlets.
- Complete autonomy for purchasing and coordinating concepts with external advertising agencies, merchandising of store concept, and rolling out targeted marketing plans both internally and externally.
- Primary role for training functionality with planned in-branch meetings and many School at Sea programs that established this chain to become the **number-one cruise-producing agency** within the American marketplace.
- Many charter and specialized group departures were successful by communicating and motivating both the clients and the selling agents on specific product offerings. **International Award Winning campaigns** for full ship theme charters.

TRAVEL & TOURISM: International VP Travel (cont.)

Alice J. Johnston, MBA CTC   **(999) 555-1212**

WORK EXPERIENCE continued:

Sales Executive – High Life HOLIDAYS   Sept 1984–Feb 1990

- My first full-time position within the travel business was as a telephone reservations sales agent, and part-time airport check-in agent.
- Within the first 8 months of joining this company I was promoted into the sales area.
- Visited travel agencies in the State region, and also initiated cold calls on corporate companies for incentive group travel business development.
- During the winter months of 1988 and 1989, I was the on board cruise Passenger Destination Representative in a customer-service-focused position.
- The final role was as the Senior Sales Executive where my responsibilities were team training and company product sessions to support colleagues within the sales department across the U.S.

EDUCATION:

State University – MBA Hospitality and Tourism,   Sept 2003–Jul 2005
School of Hospitality and Tourism Management

(Part-Time Teaching Asst. Dr. Drew, Hospitality Marketing)

- Leading industry educational program designed to give a one-year intensive overview of current business concepts and strategies for the new economy. The most comprehensive graduate program within the U.S. providing essential skills in Organizational Theory & Design, Hospitality Marketing, Financial Management, Service Operation Management, Managerial Skills Development, Hospitality Research Methods, Management Communications, Policy & Strategy in Hospitality Industry, and Tourism Development.
- Part time teaching assistant for a Hospitality Marketing Course – 3rd year students, 8-month contract.

Anthony Robbins Specialized Sales Course – Power of Negotiations,   1993
Company Sponsored 10-week intensive program

State College – Tourist Industry Administration,   Sep 1981–Apr 1984
Tourism Management Program
Graduated with high honors

HOBBIES:
Traveling and exploring especially in jungle settings—the Amazon, Costa Rica, Hawaii, Thailand; Downhill skiing and volleyball; Going to the theater, and staying home to read.

WEB DESIGN: BAD—Web Design

John J. Johnston
123 Learning Street Anytown, USA 10101
(999) 555-1212
johnj@yourname.com

Skills:
- Fluent in both Spanish and English.
- Knowledgeable in MS Office, Visual Basic 6, Flash
- Excellent management, leadership, and problem solving skills
- Ambitious and highly motivated, quick and avid learner

Education:
2000–2004   Universidad Mexico
- Graduated with Computer Systems Engineering Degree
- Specialized in administration and trained in Human Resources

Work Experience:
2000–2001   *Co-Founder* - Group Computer Consulting Co.
- Management
- Computer retail maintenance, prevention, and repairs
- Network installation
- Computer systems analysis and design
- Graphic animation, using Flash Software; assisted in web page design and layout

Winter 2001   *Sales Person* –Christmas Bazaar
- Selling toys and Christmas decorations
- Providing excellent customer service and ensuring their satisfaction

1998–1999   *Cook* – Great Food Restaurant
- Served food and beverages
- Cook of various types of food including sandwiches, soups, Mexican dishes (Specialty)

Summer 1997   *Construction Worker* (various companies & locations)
- Electrical Installation
- Painting, plumbing, and responsible for final touches i.e.: installing faucets, hand rails, etc.
- Warehouse manager

Summer 1994   *Packer* – Local Supermarket
- Packing goods at check-out
- Assisting customers with their purchases

Volunteer Experience:
Summer 2001–2002 *Educational Tutor*
- Giving special courses and additional support for youth in the commu[nity]
  for final exams

2000–2004   *Mechanic*
- Providing free car services, maintenance, and repairs in the communit[y]

Interests and activities:
- Recreational interests: swimming, snow boarding, mechanics, campin[g]
- Other interests: traveling, animation, painting, and cooking Mexican f[ood]

What's Wrong?
- Too much information about out-of-date or inapplicable jobs
- Lackluster objective/profile or lack thereof
- No declared job role
- No accomplishments or specific and measurable results
- Too many unnecessary extras and/or irrelevant information and/or repetition
- Leaves a strange or weird impression or doesn't suit the industry
- Sends a mixed message

WEB DESIGN: Web Designer, Beginner

John J. Johnston
123 Learning Street, Anytown, ST USA 10101
999-555-1212 johnj@yourname.com

Web Developer

Profile

An intelligent college-educated person who strives to achieve excellence in all areas of work. Creative, detail-oriented, enthusiastic, articulate, and very sociable. Possesses three years of experience with hands-on web programming and website design. Enjoys working alone and in teams to meet mission-critical deadlines.

Technical Skills

Java Programming	**Dreamweaver MX 2004**
VB.Net, Visual Basics 6	**Fireworks MX 2004, Photoshop 6**
ASP.Net, ASP	**Flash MX 2004 (with action scripting)**
JavaScript	**Cold Fusion MX**
IIS, Apache	**HTML**
PHP 4.0	**Linux**
Java Server Pages	**Windows XP, 2000, ME, 98, 95**
SQL, Oracle, Access Databases	**XML, XSD**
Cisco CCNA Level 1, 2, 3, and 4	**UML Data Modeling**

Accomplishments

Programming Languages
- Programmed an inventory tracking application to dynamically manage stock using VB.NET which allows for a direct connection between shipping and orders
- Built E-store application with "Shopping Cart" utilizing JSP and Beans to manage items selected, user data, and products available
- Wrote server side applications using various languages to handle user profiles and sessions to give a more customized feel to the website
- Used ASP.NET calendar object to add and remove events from a database to allow privileged users to post dynamically to the website's calendar

Web Design Macromedia Suites
- Constructed custom graphics, animations, and website layouts in Fireworks to deliver an original look and feel for clients
- Used Flash coupled with PHP to allow site administrators to edit a simple text file and dynamically update site content
- Utilized engaging features such as search, upload, database connectivity, and directory management in Cold Fusion with Dreamweaver
- Employed action scripting capabilities in Flash to add dynamic control and features to websites while minimizing graphic repetition to allow for smaller file sizes

Databases
- College studies included techniques for advanced database design, development implementation, and management of web-oriented databases
- Utilized advance concepts such as triggers, stored procedures, and indexes to reduce data redundancy and automate data input checking
- Used SQL Server Agent to schedule tasks, administrate operators, and configure alerts
- Scheduled maintenance tasks to run during non-peak hours to help maximize database efficiency

Networking
- Completed Cisco level 1, 2, 3, and 4
- Writing Cisco Certification within the next year
- Programmed routers and switches locally and remotely
- Configured LANs and WANs
- Designed physical and logical topologies of LANs and WANs

Education

State College September 2001–April 2004
- Internet Technologist Diploma, 2004
- Specialized course work included programming languages, networking, graphics, Internet strategies, securities, e-commerce, project management
- Ranked in the top 5% of graduating class
- Nominated for the Award of Distinction

Employment

Johnston Web Consulting, Sole Proprietor   Dec 2004–Present
- Testing and debugging of web applications
- Preformed contract work for various companies
  - Event Gaming Corporation
  - Colors and Cards
  - Personal
    - HotInternationalBand (fan site)
    - Example Clothing Site
    - North Town Gentlemen's Club
    - More projects and examples available upon request

Snob Clothing Corporation, Assistant Manager   Oct 1999–Nov 2003
- Assisted with recruiting and hiring
- Delegated tasks, goals, and responsibilities to sales staff
- Store consistently met or exceeded projected head office plan under my supervision

Personal

- Member of Northern Komodo Martial Arts (Kickboxing/Kung fu)
- Working out at the gym

WEB DESIGN: Web Designer, Midlevel

John J. Johnston
123 Learning St., Anytown, USA 10101
Phone: 999-555-1212 *Email:* johnj@yourname.com

Career Goal

To build creative and interactive websites with an emphasis on interface design, strategic communications, and project management.

Education

1 Postgraduate Certificate in Internet Management, December 2001
   State College   *Graduated with Honors

2 Bachelor of Journalism, May 1993
   State University   *President's List

3 Bachelor of Arts (English), May 1991
   State University   *Dean's List, Achievement Scholarship

Soft Skills

- Fluent in English & French
- Functional in German: received Zertifikat Deutsch from German School, 2001
- Extensive professional writing & editing experience – portfolio available upon request
- Professional photographic, video & audio experience

Computer Skills

Database
Fluent: MS Access 2000, MS SQL 7, SQL 4
Functional: FileMaker Pro, MySQL 3

Graphics Applications
Fluent: Fireworks MX, Flash MX, Illustrator 10, Paintshop Pro 5, Photoshop 7, QuarkXpress 4
Functional: CorelDRAW 10, FreeHand MX, PageMaker 5, Streamline 4

Multimedia
Fluent: CoolEdit Pro 2, Media Cleaner 5, Real Producer Plus 8.5, Win Media Encoder
Functional: After Effects 5, Director 8, Premiere 6, SoundForge XP Studio 6, Vegas Audio LE

Office Applications
Fluent: MS Excel 2000, MS Outlook 2000, MS PowerPoint 2000, MS Word 2000
Functional: MS Outlook Express 6, MS Project 98

Systems
Fluent: Mac OS 9, MS Windows 98 / NT 4 Workstation & Server / 2000 Pro & Advanced Server / XP
Functional: Linux Mandrake 7, SAP R/3 ver. 3.1, UNIX command set

Web Production
Fluent: Analog 5.2, BBEdit 6.5, CSS 1, DHTML, Homesite 5, HTML 4, XHTML 1.0
Functional: CSS 2, Dreamweaver MX, FrontPage 2000, GoLive 5

Web Programming & Servers
Fluent: ASP 3.0, IIS 4 & 5, VBScript 5.5
Functional: Cold Fusion 4.5, JavaScript 1.2, JSP 1.2, PHP 4.0, XML 1.0

Experience

Web Designer, The Cloak Group, Inc.   Feb 2001–Dec 2002

- Website development for examinethis.com, jobjoker.com, & winnerjob.co.uk: site audits & analysis, communications & strategic planning, competitor analysis, content development, and interface design using a variety of graphics software.
- Created, administered, developed, & troubleshot medium-sized MS SQL commercial database. Administered and troubleshot all components of IIS 4 & 5 servers.
- ASP, Flash, JavaScript, SQL, HTML, DHTML, & XHTML coding and troubleshooting.
- Implemented e-commerce and secure transaction solutions.

Web Designer / Consultant, Trans PipeLines   July 1999–Dec 2000

- Website design using HTML, DHTML, JavaScript, and Macromedia Fireworks. Designed GUI, managed quality control, and conducted usability/user surveys.

Internal Communications Coordinator, Southern Center of Technology
Jan 1999–May 1999

- Researched, wrote, edited, designed, & produced a monthly newsletter for staff and faculty, with a distribution of 2000, using Adobe Illustrator & Photoshop and Quark XPress.
- Conducted readership survey for newsletter and presented compiled results to the Center's president.
- Communications for Freedom of Information & Protection of Privacy Act and the Center's strategic planning process, including communications plans, brochures, promotional posters, and promotional email campaign.

Team Leader, ABC Gas Transmission Ltd.   March 1998–Jan 1999

- Managed one stream of a legacy-to-SAP maintenance database migration project.
- Led a diverse team of associates, contractors, planners, and clerks through tight deadlines.
- Responsible for coaching staff and data integrity. Coordinated workflow within team, managed project issues, and prepared regular status reports for leadership.

Web Designer / Communications Consultant, Fuel Trans Ltd.
May 1997–March 1998

- Website design & maintenance using HTML, DHTML, JavaScript, and CorelDRAW.
- Communications for Investment Value Management implementation team, including communications plan, editing of all online & printed training materials, user survey, audit of training delivery, and development of a promotional brochure.

Web Communications, Regional Municipality   May–July 1997
Group Assistant / Writer, Corporate Communications Ltd.   May 1995–Nov 1997
Production Manager, Local Gazette   Nov 1994–May 1995

WEB DESIGN: Layout and Web Design

John J. Johnston
123 Learning Street Anytown, USA 10101
Phone 999-555-1212 • Cell. 999-555-1313 • email: johnj@yourname.com

<u>PROFILE</u>: Outstanding *layout and graphic design services provider* (print and web), *as well as computer consulting services.*

<u>HIGHLIGHTS</u>
- 12+ years experience in desktop publishing, graphic design software, and in digital printing
- 4 years experience in programming, testing, and maintaining Visual Basic Applications
- Extensive theoretical and practical background of prepress and printing processes
- Extensive experience in PC setup, repairing, diagnosing, and solving hardware and software problems
- Organized, accurate, and detail-oriented person with excellent multitasking abilities
- Ability to work well under pressure, to handle high volume of work, and use time efficiently
- Positive attitude and great sense of responsibility
- Multilingual: English, Italian, some French and Albanian

<u>RELEVANT SKILLS</u>
In-depth knowledge of overall field of IT
Hardware: Solid understanding of PC and Mac platforms as well as LAN (setup and maintenance).
Software: Adobe (PageMaker, InDesign, Photoshop, Illustrator, Acrobat, Distiller as well as Enfocus PitStop Plug-in for Acrobat), MS-Office (Excel, PowerPoint, Publisher, Access), Corel (Ventura, DRAW, PhotoPaint, WordPerfect), Macromedia (Dreamweaver, Flash, Fireworks, Freehand, etc), QuarkXPress, FTP.
Operating System: MS-DOS, Windows 3.1 / 95 / 98 / ME / NT / 2000 / XP, Mac OS, Linux, UNIX.
Languages, Databases, and Technologies: Visual Basic, HTML, XTML, ASP, ASP.NET, Crystal Reports, MS-Access, SQL, dBase.

<u>EMPLOYMENT HISTORY</u>
Desktop Publisher, Graphic and Web Designer, and Computer Consultant (U.S.A.)   2003–present
Major accomplishments: As the owner, I provide "worry-free" services, by helping clients to achieve their goals in less time. Providing these services effectively, as contractor or on call basis, to the following companies:
- **Bonds & Trades Institute Inc.:** Helped in the process of launching the new website of the company (April–June 2004), tested the entire website in different scenarios in English and French, created new pages from scratch, tested and fixed problems found in two other websites of the company in a short time period.
- Worked as part of the marketing department of the company on the publications of this dept. creating new publications and working on the existing ones, changing their layout design to marketing dept. director specs. <u>Software and tools used</u>: QuarkXPress, Word, Photoshop, Dreamweaver, HTML, XTML, Flash. <u>Environment</u>: PC and Mac.
- **Sings & Sings – *Personal Injuries and Immigration Law Specialists*:** Provided full technical service as well as hardware equipments (PCs, printers, and fax machines), influencing the company's buying and technical decisions. Maintained the hardware, software, and file system of the company as well as creating the company's initial webpage as well as the assessment page, used to help the applicants to see if they qualify to start the immigration process. <u>Software used</u>: Access, Dreamweaver, Flash, HTML, ASP. <u>Environment</u>: PC.
- **Treman Inc.:** Worked closely with the leading team of the company on the publishing process of the catalogs set of the company in a very professional and timely manner, drastically improving the way the catalogs were produced, delivering the best catalogs the company has ever published according to CEO and Marketing Director. <u>Software used</u>: PageMaker, Excel, Word, Notepad. <u>Environment</u>: PC.
- **WER Architects Inc.:** Prepared and managed to produce high quality publications (Financial & Working Plan) and PowerPoint presentations as part of the New Kuwait City University and Congress Center Master Plans in a limited time frame. Worked very closely with main partner of the company (project Principal in Charge), his assistant (On-Site Project Manager) and one of the project architects. <u>Software used</u>: Excel, PowerPoint, Word, Photoshop, QuarkXPress. <u>Environment</u>: PC.
- **M.T.P.E. Ltd.:** Provided maintenance services for eight existing PCs of the company and two new PCs, and managing the network of the company (network administrator). Working closely with the Operations Manager of the company. <u>Environment</u>: PC.
- **GrafPlus Ltd. (Albania):** Working as web designer subcontractor (telecommuting). Recent job: designed the whole website of Institute Cultural Monuments of Albania.
- **Other clients: United Associates, West Realty Inc., Ibanez Consulting, Soa Buz Center, Med Assessment Center, DTCG (Dedicated To Computer Group), etc.**

John J. Johnston

Phone 999-555-1212 • Cell. 999-555-1313 • email: johnj@yourname.com

---

Desktop Publisher and Graphic Designer, United Associates (U.S.A.)   2001–2003
Major distributor of stamp and coin accessories, albums, and publications.
Major accomplishment: *Successfully converted the United publications into a fully PDF workflow, integrating and converting the legacy pages and images from previous publications and new information with files received from outside sources with different desktop publishing formats into a final PDF format ready for Computer To Plate press.*

- Worked mainly on two complex projects: United Specialized Catalog of Stamps, a fully color, bilingual, annual catalog and Coins of USA: a black and white, bilingual, annual publication.
- Prepared catalogues, books, ads, and other company-related materials for press.
- Developed good understanding of black and white, spot and color printing, as well as color separations.
- Remained up-to-date on new and upgraded desktop publishing software and plug-ins for them.
- Maintained the six PCs of the company in good working condition via troubleshooting.
- Designed the new website of the company: www.unitedst.com.

Computer Consultant and Desktop Publisher, Software Group Ltd (Albania)   1999–2000
Major accomplishment: *Successfully set up, implemented, repaired, and maintained error-free PC systems and networks for different small and medium companies and worked on data recovery, retrieving considerable amount of information from defective and damaged drives.*

- Worked on different complex desktop publishing projects as catalogs, dictionaries, textbooks, magazines, etc., using DTP, graphic design, and photo editor software.
- Developed financial and inventory applications for small and medium business companies, using VB, Access, & Excel applications and created technical documentation for these applications, using various desktop publishing tools, as well as created and maintained websites for the same companies.
- Taught basic and advanced computer skills to a wide range of people.

Visual Basic Developer and Graphic Designer, Data Rage (Milan, Italy)   1998
Italian Development Software Company
Involved in two different Visual Basic projects:

- Designed and coded interactive applications (Graphic User Interface Design and Data Access Object experience) as well as created the database of the illustrations for this project; worked every illustration to get the best image quality
- Experience in coding, debugging, and testing a financial application project, using Visual Basic, MS-SQL, and MS-Access databases in back-end.

PC and Network Technician, Programmer & Tech Writer, Keepa Corp (Albania)   1996–1998
Albanian Development Software Company
Major accomplishment: *Managed with great sense of responsibility to create, implement, and maintain the entire hardware system and the network of the company.*

- Worked as IT Supervisor and Projects Team Leader of the company, managing the work of 15 employees
- Setup, implemented, repaired, and maintained hardware and software error free the 20 PCs and company network.
- Designed and implemented financial and inventory software packages for small and medium business companies, Visual Basic (4.0, 5.0, and 6.0), back-end MS Access databases, and Crystal Reports for designing printing reports.
- Wrote and compiled online help for these software packages and created the user's manuals.
- Taught database programming concepts and techniques as well as programming languages to potential future employees.

Desktop Publisher and Graphic Designer, Crispin Publishing Co (Albania)   1993–2000
Major accomplishment: *Managed the entire prepress process of the biweekly newspaper from initial concept to final product, helping move all the publications of the company to a fully digital workflow.*
Worked in various progressive positions, being actively involved in typesetting and graphic designing processes of the newspaper and other publications as magazines, books, flyers, business cards, etc., working with layouts, scanning, editing, proofreading, printing, etc.

EDUCATION

Self-Employment Assistance Program – YMCA – Award – Anytown, ST, U.S.	**2003**
Computer Studies – Information Technology Institute – Diploma, Albania	**1993**
Mathematics – Albania University (B.Sc. Degree)	**1989**

WEB DEVELOPMENT & PROGRAMMING: Programmer, Beginner

John J. Johnston

123 Learning St., Anytown, ST USA 10101 · 999-555-1212 · johnj@yourname.com

PROFILE

Self-directed **Programmer** with almost five years of experience seeks software development position in structured group environment at a software development organization. I am willing and able to learn new programming languages and development methodologies.

TECHNICAL SUMMARY

SKILL	SKILL LEVEL	LAST USED	EXPERIENCE
C	Expert	Currently used	7 years
C++	Expert	Currently used	5 years
SQL	Intermediate	Currently used	5 years
RDMS	Expert	Currently used	7 years
Win32 API	Intermediate	Currently used	4 years
Java	Beginner	Currently used	1 year
HTML/CSS	Intermediate	Currently used	3 years
JavaScript	Intermediate	Currently used	3 years
PHP	Beginner	Currently used	4 months
Borland C++ Builder	Expert	Currently used	6 years
C for Palm OS	Beginner	2003	6 months
Financial Accounting	Beginner	2001	2 years

CAREER SUMMARY

SOFTWARE DEVELOPER, ABC Ltd.   1999–2004

Designed, created, and maintained in-house software for accounting, shipping, inventory management, and production at a metal fabrication company. I also helped to integrate existing software with an off-the-shelf accounting package. Worked as part of a team which rewrote existing accounting, shipping, and production software for Windows and Y2K compliance.

- Assessed and implemented requests for new software or improvements to existing programs.
- Provided personal and group training and helped create monthly newsletter to keep staff current on in-house and off-the-shelf software.
- Created program manuals and online help documents to assist users in learning to use software.
- Wrote code and APIs for use in team members' projects.
- Designed and created a large program for company's territory managers and salesmen that allowed salesmen to create professional quotes and track their personal inventory levels.
- Created a GUI-intensive Windows program to interface between a PC and ventilation controllers using serial communications, allowing the company to compete with the largest ventilation equipment companies for work on cutting-edge farming operations.
- Specifically wrote IR communications and user interface modules.
- Redesigned company website (www.abcltd.com) to look more professional, be more user friendly, and generate more business.

Achievements

- Part of web marketing team which created content for website. Increased number of sales leads site generated from two per year to over sixty per month over three years.
- Wrote PIC processor assembly language program for a microcontroller board that was attached to a pressure washer. The program shut off the pressure washer after thirty seconds of idling, thus drastically increasing the life of the unit. The anti-idling board gave ABC an edge over competitors, allowing them to sell more pressure washers.

EDUCATION

Computer Programmer / Analyst Program *State College of Applied Arts and Technology* 1997–1999
- I participated in a one-semester project to write a point of sale program for a local retail store

WEB DEVELOPMENT & PROGRAMMING: Web Developer & Manager

ALICE J. JOHNSTON
Web Developer with Project Management experience

Email: alicej@yourname.com
Phone: (999) 555-1212

SUMMARY
Web Developer 2+ years. Using HTML/DHTML, XML/XSL, JavaScript, JSP.
Web Designer 2+ years. Using Photoshop, Flash, HTML/DHTML.

TECHNICAL SKILLS
Languages:
HTML/DHTML, JavaScript, XML/XSL, JAVA/JSP, UNIX Shell Scripting, PL/SQL, VB/ASP
Tools:
Macromedia Flash, Freehand, Dreamweaver, Adobe, Photoshop, Illustrator, 3D Studio Max
Hardware: IBM PC's and Compatibles
Operating Systems: UNIX/AIX, Windows 98, NT

EDUCATION
1999 Applied Information Technology Diploma, State Institute
1991–1996 BA Honors, Art and Art History, State University
1991–1995 Diploma, Art and Art History, State College

PROFESSIONAL EXPERIENCE
Web Designer/Consultant, BLUEJAY Creative Dec.2000–Present
Design, build new websites, refurbish old sites, and create web presences for individual clients,
be it personal or small business sites. Work closely with the clients providing ideas and advice on
their e-business needs and solutions.   www.Bluejay.com

Web Developer, Max Group. Nov. 2000–Feb. 2000
Contracted to Wireless iMedia for work on the revamping of Quicken.ca to a JSP/XML platform.
Worked mainly on front-end issues using JSP, HTML, XML, XSL and Javascript, under a strict
deadline.

Presentations/Internet Engineer, Team Inc. April 2000–Nov. 2000
Responsible for presentation tier of Team/Quicken's 401K Advisor and complementary website.
Developed Flash animations, graphics, overall web design, and client-side functionality using
JavaScript, JSP, HTML/DHTML, and XML.

Web Developer, Big Company Web Group Jan. 2000–April 2000
Maintained graphical and textual content for Intranet site. Involved in an Intensive Domino
migration project, relocating the entire Marketing site onto the Domino server.

Developer, Biz Prac, Decision Consultants Sept. 1999–Feb. 2000
Developed a 'virtual tour' and complementary website for new eBiz practice using Flash,
JavaScript, and HTML.

Support Analyst, RS/6000 Big Computer Inc. Support Center March 1999–Sept. 1999
Provided phone, email, & test case support to business customers using AIX operating system.

OTHER WORK EXPERIENCE
1996–1998 Japan **ESL Teacher English Institute**
Developed the ESL curriculum and instructed Japanese students of all ages in English
conversation, grammar, and Western culture.

ACCOMPLISHMENTS & INTERESTS
Mural Designer/Painter
Active Interests: basketball, soccer, aerobics, swimming, skiing, tennis, rollerblading, surfing.
Creative Pursuits: painting, photography, music, literature, web surfing.

WEB DEVELOPMENT & PROGRAMMING: Web Developer and Design

John J Johnston

123 Learning St, Anytown, ST USA 10101
Phone: (999) 555-1212 **Email:** johnj@yourname.com

OVERVIEW

I am a dedicated and skilled specialist in web design and development, written and oral communications, and team leadership. I am extremely resourceful in doing all possible to bring projects from start to finish. I work very well both in team and solitary situations and can coordinate a group to best results. I am always eager to develop new skills and am willing to travel to realize opportunities.

COMPUTER SKILLS

- *Web Development* - HTML (6 years), DHTML (4 years), JavaScript (5 years), Cascading Style Sheets (4 years), ASP (2 years), Java 2/JSP (1 year), SQL (2 years), XML (1 year), ColdFusion (3 years), ColdFusion Studio/HomeSite (5 years), Macromedia Dreamweaver (4 years), Macromedia Fireworks (4 years), Macromedia Flash (4 years), Microsoft FrontPage (5 years), Macromedia Director (1 year).
- *Design & Graphics Software* - Adobe PhotoShop (6 years), Adobe Illustrator (3 years), Adobe Acrobat (4 years), QuarkXpress (4 years), Microsoft Publisher (4 years).
- *Web Administration* - Microsoft Internet Information Server (4 years), Apache Web Server (3 years), Netscape FastTrack Server (3 years), WebSphere (1 year), WebTrends Professional Suite (4 years).
- *Operating Systems* - MS-DOS, Windows 3.1, Windows 95/98, Windows 2000, Windows NT 4 Workstation and Server, Linux (Red Hat & Debian), UNIX (Sun and HP), and MacOS.
- *Other Software* - Microsoft Office, Microsoft Access, Symantec PCAnywhere, Visio, Microsoft Project.

EMPLOYMENT HISTORY

Web Systems Officer, State Government   October 2002–present

I am currently responsible for bringing MMAH website content into compliance with the People with Disabilities Act, as well as assisting the ministry's web staff to update and modify MMAH sites as needed. Duties include: Web page creation in HTML and Adobe Photoshop. Integrating web content with ministry's content management system. Use of usability tools such as Bobby and WAVE. Extensive use of Adobe Acrobat's accessibility and tagging features.

Web Developer, Smith & Smith   April 2001–present

Designed and administrated multiple intranet sites for Smith & Smith, as well as served as the lead designer/administrator for their public Internet site. Duties included: Web page creation in HTML, JavaScript, ASP, and Macromedia Flash. Code maintenance on existing ColdFusion applications. Created storyboards and information architecture designs for websites. Graphics creation and modification using Adobe PhotoShop and Macromedia Fireworks. Testing websites and applications for usability and multiple-browser compliance. Serve as point-of-contact between corporate staff and public users. Advise staff and senior management in web strategy and usability.

Contract & Consulting Employment   2000–April 2001

• Web Design and Programming for **Computerized Solutions**
Storyboarded, designed, and administrated client websites with Allaire, HomeSite, JavaScript, and Macromedia Flash. Created web graphics using Adobe Photoshop and Macromedia Fireworks. Provided technical support for Web and network clients. Mentored and provided leadership to junior staff.

• JSP Interface Designer for **Abc Insurance**

Part of team constructing web application for insurance offices to connect to legacy mainframe system via web interface. Designed and coded JSP interface templates for application using Allaire HomeSite and Macromedia Dreamweaver. Programmed various application functions with JavaScript. Created graphics using Adobe Photoshop and Macromedia Fireworks.

• Interface Designer

Developed and prototyped interface templates for automated Intranet application using HTML and JavaScript. Storyboarded application flow and performed use case analysis. Reviewed and updated product documentation and online help. Supported clients regarding customizing product interface.

• Web Design for **Dave Cox Pictures**

Designed online portfolio for high-end photography studio. Programmed entire site using Dynamic HTML and JavaScript. Converted all photographic materials for Web use and created custom web graphics using Adobe Photoshop, Adobe Illustrator, and GIF Construction Set.

Assistant Webmaster, State Government   1999–2000

Administrated multiple Intranet and Internet websites for the government, including the central Public Service Intranet. Duties included: Link checking and creating site reports using WebTrends and InContext WebAnalyzer. Web page creation using Allaire HomeSite, Macromedia Dreamweaver, Adobe Photoshop and Macromedia Fireworks. Created storyboards and information architecture designs for websites. Training and mentoring to departmental student interns. Server maintenance for Internet application and Web Server software using PCAnywhere. Advised other government staff and departments in web development and compliance with State government Internet standards. Administrated public and internal email lists. Developed, wrote, and maintained departmental procedures manual.

Contract & Consulting Employment   1997–1999

• Web Design

Redesigned corporate website for cellular phone sales firm. Programmed entire site using Dynamic HTML and JavaScript. Created graphics for website using Adobe Photoshop.

• Technical Consulting for **SIDD Communications Group**

Consulted company in telephone system, Internet, and system software upgrades. Trained company staff in new hardware and software. Redesigned corporate website.

• Web Design and Programming for **Passing Online**

Designed and updated client websites with Allaire HomeSite, JavaScript, and Macromedia Flash.

Project Lead/Staff Writer, YAY New Media Corp.   1995–1997

Designed lead product for role-playing game product line—coordinating the writing team, editors, and desktop publishers. Oversaw all beta-testing sessions. Coordinated promotions and convention appearances. Researched distribution lines and advertising mediums.

Other duties for YAY New Media: Created and managed company's product knowledge base. Managed product development for shareware compilations and OEM CD-ROMs. Acquired software content and licensing permission. Redesigned corporate website and advised senior management on company's long-term Web strategy.

EDUCATION

• *State College*, Computer Diploma
• *State University*, BA
    Majors – History/Philosophy; Minor – English

References & Letters of Recommendation available upon request

WEB DEVELOPMENT & PROGRAMMING: Senior Java Developer

John J. Johnston

123 Learning St. Anytown USA 10101
Res.: (999) 555-1212   Office: (999) 555-1313
Email: johnj@yourname.com

Profile

Senior **Java** Developer

Qualification Highlights

3+ years Java programming experience - **Sun Certified Programmer for Java 2**

6+ years Oracle RDBMS experience - **Oracle Certified Professional**

6+ years Visual Basic experience - **MCSD Courses Trained**

10+ years software development experience - **Computer Software Engineer**

5+ years project leader experience - **Project Quality & Process Control**

Strong Education Background - **Bachelor Degree of Computer Software**

Computer Skills

- **Language:** Java, C++, **XML**, HTML, **UML**, JavaScript, Visual Basic, etc.
- **Database:** Oracle 8i, SQL-Server 7.0, DB2, Sybase, MS-Access, DBASE, etc.
- **Methodology:** OOP, **CORBA**, **JSP**, **EJB**, JNDI, **Servlet**, **JDBC**, **RMI**, RDBMS, etc.
- **Platform:** UNIX/Linux, Windows NT (4.0)/98, n-tier Client/Server, MS-DOS, etc.
- **Network:** TCP/IP, HTTP, HTTPS, SMTP, etc.
- **Tools:** JDK, JBuilder, Visual Age, SQL-Navigator, Developer 2000, etc.

Experience

1999–Present   **Project Managers Inc.**

➤ Project: <u>ImageArchive WebView of Big Bank</u>

Web B2B: Check image retrieval, administration, statistics, analysis, and security.

- Role: Project leader (lead programmer).
- Language and methodology: Java, JavaScript, JSP, Servlet, JavaBean.
- Tools: JBuilder, J2EE, JDK, JSDK, JSWDK
- Environment: Windows 2000/NT, (UNIX)
- Database: Oracle 8i

➤ Project: <u>ImageArchive 2000 of Big Bank</u>

Image Documentation System. Scan original checks and MICR line, save image to different formats, calculation, retrieval, report, and analysis, etc.

- Role: Lead programmer
- Language and methodology: Visual Basic 6, COM, ActiveX, ODBC, ADO, etc.
- Tools: Visual Studio, ImageMan,
- Environment: Windows 2000/NT
- Database: SQL-Server 7.0

John J. Johnston

123 Learning St. Anytown USA 10101
Res.: (999) 555-1212   Office: (999) 555-1313
Email: johnj@yourname.com

1997–1998   **ABC Data Inc. China**   China

➢ Project: Financial & Warehouse Management GMC Joint Ventures

The management program would supply financial and warehouse (transportation) service to several **Big Car Company Inc.** joint ventures in China, located at different provinces and using various platforms.

- Role: Lead programmer
- Language and methodology: Java, C++, ODBC
- Tools: JDK 1.1.x, Borland C++
- Environment: Windows 2000/NT, (UNIX)
- Database: Oracle 8

1991–1996   **ABC Machinery Corp.**   China

➢ Project: EDI: Letter of Credit Computer Management System

Prepare for WTO and improve work quality, designed a computerized management system for some most important documents, such as L/C, contract, and orders, etc.

- Role: Project Leader, Lead Programmer
- Language and methodology: Java, C++
- Tools: JDK 1.1.x, Borland C++
- Environment: Windows NT/98 (UNIX/Solaris)
- Database: Oracle 7.3
➢ Project: Financial Management Program for Jilin Provincial Mobile Phone

Designed program at **San Francisco**, USA.

➢ Project: Auto Engine Manufacturing Line Program for China First Auto Work

Designed program at **Rome**, Italy, and **HongKong**.

Education & Certificates

2000 - Sun Certified Programmer for Java 2, Sun Microsystems
2000 - MCSD Courses Training, Diginet Computer Training School
1999 - Oracle Certified Professional, Oracle Certified Application Developer
1995 - Computer Software Engineer, Senior Computer Programmer,
          China National Computer Qualification Training & Examination Center
1991 - Bachelor Degree of Computer Science, State University, China

References

➢ Will be supplied upon request

APPENDIX – TIPS ON WRITING COVER LETTERS

Because this is *The Complete Book of Resumes* we didn't have a lot of space to focus on cover letters. But we also didn't want to leave you without some guidance in facing the empty page.

Here are some hot tips for writing great cover letters:

1. One of the biggest obstacles to great cover letter writing is in knowing its purpose. Most of us sit down to write one and end up with a mish mash of clichés and little bits and pieces of our skills and experience. Instead, think about the cover letter doing two important things: demonstrating some real knowledge of the role or company (or both) and tying that knowledge or insight to specific skills and/or accomplishments.

2. Demonstrate real knowledge of the company or role by: saying something meaningful about it in the first paragraph. Over and above saying how much you like the company, make some guesses about who they are and how they see themselves in the marketplace.

3. If you don't know much about the company, make some insightful comments about the role. Why is it important? What do you think they are hoping to find in an ideal candidate?

4. Once you've made a short, insightful comment into understanding the employer's point of view, transition your letter into making the connection between that and your added value skills and abilities. Demonstrate that you ARE the ideal. You can do this in several ways.

A – The Rule of Three – Choose three of your skills and personality traits that connect to the ideal candidate and highlight each one with its own paragraph (no more than two or three sentences). After mentioning each one, give a specific accomplishment tied to that skill.

B – Tell One Story – There is a tremendous power in narrative. Telling a tight one or two paragraph "story" of something that happened in a similar role and its positive outcome (because of you!) is both captivating for the reader and proof you can handle the role.

C – Answer a Question – Ask a question right off the top that might pertain to this company or role, or a question that the employer might have about you. For instance: "How does having a great team of programmers affect the whole company?" or "What does a film have to do with working in project management?" Then spend two or three tight paragraphs focused on selling yourself within the parameters of the question.

D – Offer Solutions – If you are contacting someone or a company in which you have some "back story" on why the job is available, you may want to offer directly from your experience some solutions that might help the situation. Come at the employer as their equal, and your interview may turn into an animated discussion rather than a formal interview.

5. The key to an exceptional cover letter is to keep your message focused, clean, and no more than three or four full paragraphs. Pick the skills and accomplishments you want to highlight and don't stray into a meandering tale of your working life and additional skills. The more you can "understand" the employer's position or problem and speak directly to solutions, the more interested the reader will be in meeting you.

INDEX

ABOUT THE AUTHOR

Karen Schaffer has helped thousands of people to trust themselves to discover their direction, passion, and purpose in their careers. She has been a career coach for the last eleven years. She's written two other books—*Hire Power: The Ultimate Job Guide for Young Canadians*, a Canadian bestseller, and *The Job of Your Life: Four Groundbreaking Steps for Getting the Work You Want*. She has also written for the career sections of major newspapers and has spoken widely on the topic.

For three years she was a partner at Career Management with IQ Partners (http://www.iqpartners.com), and was in the unique position viewing the responses of recruiters to hundreds of résumés, thereby gaining valuable insights into what a professional looks for when scanning a résumé for the first time. She used that learning to create "The Résumé Report Card," an online tool for helping candidates improve their résumés.

Karen holds a master's degree in counseling psychology from the Adler School of Professional Psychology and an honors BA in cultural studies from McGill University. She is currently living in Halifax, Nova Scotia, and career coaching via phone. Her website is http://www.karenschaffer.com.